THE TRUE
AND ONLY
HEAVEN

THE TRUE AND ONLY HEAVEN

Progress and Its Critics

Christopher Lasch

■

W · W · Norton & Company

New York · London

The text of this book is composed in Janson,
with the display set in Electra.
Composition and
manufacturing by The Haddon Craftsmen, Inc..

Book design by Guenet Abraham.

First published as a Norton paperback 1991.

Library of Congress Cataloging in Publication Data
Lasch, Christopher.
The true and only heaven : progress and its critics /
Christopher Lasch.
p. cm.
Includes bibliographical references (p. 533).
1. United States—Intellectual life. 2. Progress. 3. Social
sciences—United States—Philosophy—History. I. Title.
E169.1.L376 1991
303.44'0973—dc20 90-33714

ISBN 0-393-30795-6

W.W. Norton & Company, Inc.,
500 Fifth Avenue, New York, N.Y. 10110
W.W. Norton & Company, Ltd.,
10 Coptic Street, London WC1A 1PU

5 6 7 8 9 0

For Robby and Greta
Hope against Hope

"MANY PASSENGERS STOP TO TAKE THEIR PLEASURE OR MAKE THEIR PROFIT IN [VANITY] FAIR, INSTEAD OF GOING ONWARD TO THE CELESTIAL CITY. INDEED, SUCH ARE THE CHARMS OF THE PLACE THAT PEOPLE OFTEN AFFIRM IT TO BE THE TRUE AND ONLY HEAVEN; STOUTLY CONTENDING THAT THERE IS NO OTHER, THAT THOSE WHO SEEK FURTHER ARE MERE DREAMERS, AND THAT, IF THE FABLED BRIGHTNESS OF THE CELESTIAL CITY LAY BUT A BARE MILE BEYOND THE GATES OF VANITY, THEY WOULD NOT BE FOOLS ENOUGH TO GO THITHER.

". . . THE CHRISTIAN READER, IF HE HAVE HAD NO ACCOUNTS OF THE CITY LATER THAN BUNYAN'S TIME, WILL BE SURPRISED TO HEAR THAT ALMOST EVERY STREET HAS ITS CHURCH, AND THAT THE REVEREND CLERGY ARE NOWHERE HELD IN HIGHER RESPECT THAN AT VANITY FAIR. AND WELL DO THEY DESERVE SUCH HONORABLE ESTIMATION; FOR THE MAXIMS OF WISDOM AND VIRTUE, WHICH FALL FROM THEIR LIPS, COME FROM AS DEEP A SPIRITUAL SOURCE, AND TEND TO US AS LOFTY A RELIGIOUS AIM, AS THOSE OF THE SAGEST PHILOSOPHERS OF OLD."

—*Nathaniel Hawthorne, "The Celestial Railroad"*

CONTENTS

Contents

PREFACE

This inquiry began with a deceptively simple question. How does it happen that serious people continue to believe in progress, in the face of massive evidence that might have been expected to refute the idea of progress once and for all? The attempt to explain this anomaly—the persistence of a belief in progress in a century full of calamities—led me back to the eighteenth century, when the founders of modern liberalism began to argue that human wants, being insatiable, required an indefinite expansion of the productive forces necessary to satisfy them. Insatiable desire, formerly condemned as a source of frustration, unhappiness, and spiritual instability, came to be seen as a powerful stimulus to economic development. Instead of disparaging the tendency to want more than we need, liberals like Adam Smith argued that needs varied from one society to another, that civilized men and women needed more than savages to make them comfortable, and that a continual redefinition of their standards of comfort and convenience led to improvements in production and a general increase of wealth. There was no foreseeable end to the transformation of luxuries into necessities. The more comforts people enjoyed, the more they would expect. The elasticity of demand appeared to give the Anglo-American idea of progress a solid foundation that could not be shaken by subsequent events, not even by the global wars that broke out in the twentieth century. Those wars, indeed, gave added energy to economic development.

The assumption that our standard of living (in the broadest meaning of that term) will undergo a steady improvement colors our view of the past as well as our view of the future. It gives rise to a nostalgic yearning for bygone simplicity—the other side of the ideology of progress. Nostalgia, not to be equated simply with the remembrance of things past, is better understood as an abdication of memory. It makes the past a foreign country, as David Lowenthal puts it. It obscures the connections between the past and the present. Deeply embedded both in popular culture and in academic sociology, the nostalgic attitude tends to replace historical analysis with abstract typologies—"traditional" and "modern" society, gemeinschaft and gesellschaft—that interfere with an imaginative reconstruction of our past or a sober assessment of our prospects. Now that we have begun to understand the environmental limits to economic growth, we need to subject the idea of progress to searching criticism; but a nostalgic view of the past does not provide the materials for that criticism. It gives us only a mirror image of progress, a one-dimensional view of history in which a wistful pessimism and a kind of fatalistic optimism are the only points of reference, a criticism of progress that depends on the contrast between complex modern societies and the close-knit communities allegedly typical of the "world we have lost," as Peter Laslett calls it in his study of seventeenth-century England.

The idea of progress and the communitarian counterpoint that accompanies it encourage a type of speculation that seeks to balance the gains of progress against losses and remains understandably ambivalent about the whole business. What is needed is a point of view that cuts through this inconclusive debate, calls the dominant categories into question, and enables us to understand the difference between nostalgia and memory, optimism and hope. A growing dissatisfaction with the prevailing point of view has led historians and social critics to investigate the Atlantic tradition of republicanism or civic humanism, historically an important competitor of the liberal tradition. Scholars have shown that the political economy of liberalism came to prevail only against vigorous opposition, that its eventual triumph was far from a foregone conclusion, and that the republican tradition continued, well into the nineteenth century, to hold up an ideal of the good society radically different from the one held up by liberalism.

My discussion of nineteenth-century populism or proprietary democracy—broadly understood as a body of social thought that condemned the boundless appetite for more and better goods and distrusted "improvements" if they only gave rise to a more and more elaborate division of labor—builds on the work of J. G. A. Pocock, Gordon Wood, and other historians of the republican tradition. It is my contention, however, that the concept of virtue, which played such an important part in the nineteenth-century critique of "improvement," did not derive from republican sources alone. Recent scholarship, much of it inspired by the hope of reviving a sense of civic obligation and of countering the acquisitive individualism fostered by liberalism, has overlooked the more vigorous concept of virtue that was articulated in certain varieties of radical Protestantism. For a Puritan like John Milton, "virtue" referred not to the disinterested service of the public good but to the courage, vitality, and life-giving force emanating, in the last analysis, from the creator of the universe. Milton associated virtue both with the blessings conferred on mankind by God and with the grateful recognition of life as a gift rather than a challenge to our power to shape it to our own purposes. Jonathan Edwards likewise understood that gratitude implied a recognition of man's dependence on a higher power. For Edwards, ingratitude—the refusal to acknowledge limits on human powers, the wish to achieve godlike knowledge and capacities—became the antithesis of virtue and the essence of original sin.

In the nineteenth century, a time when the progress of human ingenuity seemed to promise a decisive victory over fate, Thomas Carlyle and Ralph Waldo Emerson, latter-day Calvinists without a Calvinist theology, reminded their readers that human beings did not control their own fate. They argued, in effect, that fate could be conquered only by "wonder" and virtue—by grateful acceptance of a world that was not made solely for human enjoyment. Their insistence on human limitations, it seems to me, had a good deal in common with the populist critique of "improvement," even though it was couched in a philosophical rather than a political idiom. Emerson's principle of "compensation" can be understood as an exploration of the moral implications of "unearned increment." Defiance of fate, as Emerson saw it, amounted to a form of tax evasion, an attempt to get something for nothing—to escape the duty on desire. The political economists of progress hoped to unleash wealth-creating desire; Emerson and Carlyle reaffirmed the ancient folk wisdom according to which overweening desire invites retribution, the corrective, compensatory force of nemesis.

William James, in his penetrating analysis of the "twice-born" type of religious experience, explained the "admirable congruity of Protestant theology with the structure of the mind." For the twice-born, defeat and despair were only the prelude to the experience of hope and wonder, all the more intense because it rested on an awareness of tragedy. If James was more dubious about the moral wisdom of self-surrender than Emerson or Carlyle, he shared their belief that spiritual "desiccation," as he put it, posed a greater danger to the modern world than religious fanaticism, superstition, and intolerance—the "bogey" of those who believed that progress ought to enable man to outgrow his childish need for religion. By the beginning of the twentieth century, many others had come to be haunted by the misgivings about progress expressed so clearly by Carlyle, Emerson, and James. Thus Georges Sorel, who acknowledged intellectual indebtedness to James, conceived syndicalism not only as the moral equivalent of an earlier form of proprietorship but as the only form of political action that could sustain a heroic conception of life.

A number of recurring themes informed the kind of opposition to progressive ideology that I have tried to recover and to distinguish from a more familiar lament for the decline of "community." The habits of responsibility associated with property ownership; the self-forgetfulness that comes with immersion in some all-absorbing piece of work; the danger that material comforts will extinguish a more demanding ideal of the good life; the dependence of happiness on the recognition that humans are not made for happiness—these preoccupations, separately or in various combinations, reappeared in Sorel's version of syndicalism, in the guild socialism advocated by G. D. H. Cole and others, in Josiah Royce's "philosophy of loyalty," in Reinhold Niebuhr's account of the "spiritual discipline against resentment," and in Martin Luther King's practice of nonviolent resistance. What these thinkers shared with each other and with their predecessors was a sense of limits—the unifying thread in the following narrative. An exploration of the idea of limits in various guises enables us to reconstruct not so much an intellectual tradition as a sensibility, one that runs against the dominant currents in modern life but exerts considerable force, even today.

It is most simply described, perhaps, as the sensibility of the petty bourgeoisie—difficult to recognize as such, in major thinkers, only because we expect major thinkers to participate in the general revulsion against the petty-bourgeois way of life. These particular thinkers, I believe, embodied the conscience of the lower middle class, giving voice to its distinctive concerns and criticizing its characteristic vices of envy, resentment, and servility. Notwithstanding those vices, the moral conservatism of the petty bourgeoisie, its egalitarianism, its respect for workmanship, its understanding of the value of loyalty, and its struggle against the moral temptation of resentment are the materials on which critics of progress have always had to rely if they wanted to put together a coherent challenge to the reigning orthodoxy.

I have no intention of minimizing the narrowness and provincialism of lower-middle-class culture; nor do I deny that it has produced racism, nativism, anti-intellectualism, and all the other evils so often cited by liberal critics. But liberals have lost sight of what is valuable in lower-middle-class culture in their eagerness to condemn what is objectionable. Their attack on "Middle America," which eventually gave rise to a counterattack against liberalism—the main ingredient in the rise of the new right—has blinded them to the positive features of petty-bourgeois culture: its moral realism, its understanding that everything has its price, its respect for limits, its skepticism about progress. Whatever can be said against them, small proprietors, artisans, tradesmen, and farmers—more often victims of "improvement" than beneficiaries—are unlikely to mistake the promised land of progress for the true and only heaven.

THE TRUE
AND ONLY
HEAVEN

1

INTRODUCTION: THE OBSOLESCENCE
OF LEFT AND RIGHT

The Current Mood

The premise underlying this investigation—that old political ideologies have exhausted their capacity either to explain events or to inspire men and women to constructive action—needs an introductory word of explanation.

The unexpected resurgence of the right, not only in the United States but throughout much of the Western world, has thrown the left into confusion and called into question all its old assumptions about the future: that the course of history favored the left; that the right would never recover from the defeats it suffered during the era of liberal and social democratic ascendancy; that some form of socialism, at the very least a more vigorous form of the welfare state, would soon replace free-market capitalism. Who would have predicted, twenty-five years ago, that as the twentieth century approached its end, it would be the left that was everywhere in retreat?

But the characteristic mood of the times, a baffled sense of drift, is by no means confined to people on the left. The unanticipated success of the right has not restored moral order and collective purpose to Western nations, least of all to the United States. The new right came to power with a mandate not just to free the market from bureaucratic interference but to halt the slide into apathy, hedonism, and moral chaos. It has not lived up to expectations. Spiritual disrepair, the perception of which furnished much of the popular animus against liberalism, is just as evident today as it was in the seventies. Contributors to a recent symposium on the state of American conservatism report widespread "discouragement" with the accomplishments of the Reagan revolution, so called. Like liberals, conservatives suffer from "demoralization," "malaise." The "crisis of modernity" remains unresolved, according to George Panichas, by a "sham conservatism" that merely sanctions the unbridled pursuit of worldly success. The "everyday virtues of honesty, loyalty, manners, work, and restraint," Clyde Wilson writes, are more "attenuated" than ever. In the early sixties, it was still "possible to take for granted that the social fabric of the West . . . was relatively intact." Under Reagan, however, it continued to unravel.

Ritual deference to "traditional values" cannot hide the right's commitment to progress, unlimited economic growth, and acquisitive individualism. According to Paul Gottfried and Thomas Fleming, "skepticism about progress," once the hallmark of "intellectuals identified as conservatives," has all but disappeared. "Political differences between right and left have by now been largely reduced to disagreements over policies designed to achieve comparable moral goals." The ideological distinctions between liberalism and conservatism no longer stand for anything or define the lines of political debate.

Limits: The Forbidden Topic

· ■ ·

The uselessness of the old labels and the need for a reorientation of political ideas are beginning to be acknowledged. A few years ago, in a book heralded as the manifesto of a resurgent liberalism, Paul Tsongas, then senator from Massachusetts, called for liberals to become more conservative on economic issues and more radical on "social issues" like gay rights, feminism, and abortion. Bernard Avishai of MIT, writing in *Dissent*, replied that Tsongas "got it backward" and that the left needed to combine economic radicalism with cultural conservatism. Such statements testify to a growing awareness of the need to rethink conventional positions. They still owe too much, however, to the old terms of debate. We need to press the point more vigorously and to ask whether the left and right have not come to share so many of the same underlying convictions, including a belief in the desirability and inevitability of technical and economic development, that the conflict between them, shrill and acrimonious as it is, no longer speaks to the central issues of American politics.

A sign of the times: both left and right, with equal vehemence, repudiate the charge of "pessimism." Neither side has any use for "doomsayers." Neither wants to admit that our society has taken a wrong turn, lost its way, and needs to recover a sense of purpose and direction. Neither addresses the overriding issue of limits, so threatening to those who wish to appear optimistic at all times. The fact remains: the earth's finite resources will not support an indefinite expansion of industrial civilization. The right proposes, in effect, to maintain our riotous standard of living, as it has been maintained in the past, at the expense of the rest of the world (increasingly at the expense of our own minorities as well). This program is self-defeating, not only because it will produce environmental effects from which even the rich cannot escape but because it will widen the gap between rich and poor nations, generate more and more violent movements of insurrection and terrorism against the West, and bring about a deterioration of the world's political climate as threatening as the deterioration of its physical climate.

But the historical program of the left has become equally self-defeating. The attempt to extend Western standards of living to the rest of the world will lead even more quickly to the exhaustion of nonrenewable resources, the irreversible pollution of the earth's atmosphere, and the destruction of the ecological system, in short, on which human life depends. "Let us imagine," writes Rudolf Bahro, a leading spokesman for the West German Greens, "what it would mean if the raw material and energy consumption of our society were extended to the 4.5 billion people living today, or to the 10–15 billion there will probably be tomorrow. It is readily apparent that the planet can only support such volumes of production . . . for a short time to come."

These considerations refute conventional optimism (though the real despair lies in a refusal to confront them at all), and both the right and left therefore prefer to talk about something else—for example, to exchange accusations of fascism and socialism. But the ritual deployment and rhetorical inflation of these familiar slogans provide further evidence of the emptiness of recent political debate. For the left, fascism now embraces everything to the right of liberalism and social democracy, including such disparate configurations as the Ayatollah Khomeini's Iran, the opposition to the Sandinista regime in Nicaragua, and Reaganism itself. For the right, communism (or "creeping socialism," as it used to be called) embraces everything to the left of, and including, the New Deal. Not only have these terms lost their meaning through reckless expansion, but they no longer describe historical alternatives at the end of the twentieth century.

It ought to be clear by now that neither fascism nor socialism represents the wave of the future. Gorbachev's momentous reforms in the Soviet Union, followed by the collapse of the Soviet empire in eastern Europe, indicate that socialism's moment has come and gone. As for fascism, it cannot be regarded as a generic configuration at all, and certainly not as the final stage of capitalist decay. Nor does the looser concept of totalitarianism provide an acceptable substitute. The history of the twentieth century suggests that totalitarian regimes are highly unstable, evolving toward some type of bureaucracy that fits neither the classic fascist nor the socialist model. None of this means that the future will be safe for democracy, only that the danger to democracy comes less from totalitarian or collectivist movements abroad than from the erosion of its psychological, cultural, and spiritual foundations from within.

The Making of a Malcontent

· ■ ·

"MALCONTENTEDNESS MAY BE THE BEGINNING OF PROMISE."
—*Randolph Bourne, "Twilight of Idols"*

My own faith in the explanatory power of the old ideologies began to waver in the mid-seventies, when my study of the family led me to question the left's program of sexual liberation, careers for women, and professional child care. Until then, I had always identified myself with the left. I grew up in the tradition of Middle Western progressivism, overlaid by the liberalism of the New Deal. I believed in the Tennessee Valley Authority, the CIO, and the United Nations. In the bitter debates about foreign policy that began to divide liberals in the late forties and fifties, I sided with those who advocated continued efforts to reach an accommodation with the Soviet Union. I shared my parents' regret that Franklin Roosevelt's overtures to the Russians had been abandoned by his successors—unwisely and prematurely abandoned, as it seemed to us. Harry Truman was no hero in my parents' circle. His policy of containment, his constant warnings against appeasement, and his ill-advised attempt to co-opt the internal security issue (which only whetted the appetite for tougher measures against domestic "subversion") did not appear to have made Americans any safer in the world. On the contrary, the world seemed to become more dangerous every day.

The mass media have tried to idealize the fifties, in retrospect, as an age of innocence. They did not seem that way to me or to most of my contemporaries. A chronic state of international emergency led to the erosion of civil liberties at home and the militarization of American life. Under Joseph McCarthy, anticommunism reached a feverish pitch of intensity; nor did McCarthy's fall widen the boundaries of permissible debate. Critics of containment, like Walter Lippmann and George Kennan (after 1955), found it difficult to get a hearing, and their plea for "disengagement" from the cold war made no impression, so far as my friends and I could see, on American policy. We felt more and more helpless in a world dominated by huge military establishments, both of them girding themselves for some apocalyptic confrontation and seemingly impervious to the promptings of humanity or even to a realistic assessment of their own national interests.

The rapidly unfolding events of the early sixties pushed me farther to the left. Unlike many of my Harvard classmates, I did not welcome John Kennedy's election or the resulting Cambridge–White House connection. Kennedy's foreign policy—and the international scene continued to dominate my political reactions at this time—seemed even more reckless than Truman's. I was not impressed by the "best and brightest," having had some acquaintance with their kind. To me, the migration of Harvard to Washington meant the political ascendancy of Route 128, home of the high-tech industries that were springing up on the periphery of Boston. This vast suburban sprawl, founded on the union of brains and military power, furnished visible evidence of the military-industrial complex, as Eisenhower called it.

Eisenhower's farewell address stirred me far more deeply than Kennedy's inaugural, with its call to get America moving again. Eisenhower's warning became one of my reference points in the politics of the early sixties, along with Dwight Macdonald's article on the 1960 election, explaining why he did not plan to vote for either candidate. That article led me in turn to Macdonald's political memoir of the thirties and forties, a slashing, witty, and moving indictment of the warfare state. I began to read other social critics who spoke to my sense of foreboding, to the feeling that we Americans had somehow entrusted our destiny to an implacable war machine that ground on almost wholly independent of human intervention, mindlessly going about its business of destruction.

The writings that gave shape and direction to my thinking in the early sixties—Randolph Bourne's war essays, C. Wright Mills's *Power Elite*, William Appleman Williams's *Tragedy of American Diplomacy*, John Kenneth Galbraith's *Affluent Society*, Jacques Ellul's *Technological Society*, Paul Goodman's *Growing Up Absurd*, Herbert Marcuse's *Eros and Civilization*, Norman O. Brown's *Life against Death*—contained certain common themes, I now see: the pathology of domination; the growing influence of organizations (economic as well as military) that operate without regard to any rational objectives except their own self-aggrandizement; the powerlessness of individuals in the face of these gigantic agglomerations and the arrogance of those ostensibly in charge of them.

The Vietnam War confirmed this impression of implacable, irresistible power. When the State Department's "truth squad" rolled into Iowa City (where I was teaching at the time), with orders to correct the dangerous errors spread by academic opponents of the war, I got a small taste of our government's sensitivity to public opinion. I stood up to contest the official justification of American policy, only to be told by one of our helpful public servants to "sit down and shut up." I took heart, however, from the growing opposition to the war, from the formation of a new left, and from the student movement's attempt to explain the connection between the war and the bureaucratization of academic life. Industry's growing dependence on the most advanced technology had drawn the "multiversity" into the military-industrial complex; but while this development had undoubtedly had a deplorable effect on scholarship and teaching, it opened a small window of hope, since a campaign against secret military research—so flagrantly at odds with the academic ethic of publication and open discussion—might disrupt the flow of classified information from the corporations to the Pentagon. Such was the rather wistful reasoning—most fully spelled out, I recall, by the historian Gabriel Kolko—that encouraged some of us to see academic reform, eminently desirable in its own right, as something more than a purely academic affair: a strategic move against the military-industrial machine at its most vulnerable point.

This strategy assumed that the university, deeply compromised by its entanglement with the corporations, the military, and the state, nevertheless honored the ideal of a community of scholars and was therefore open to pressure exerted in the name of that ideal. It soon became clear, however, that the student movement took a different view of the university, one that indiscriminately condemned all institutions and equated "liberation" with anarchic personal freedom. As the new left degenerated into revolutionary histrionics, its spokesmen—clownish media freaks like Jerry Rubin and Abbie Hoffman, seekers of "existential" authenticity like Tom Hayden, connoisseurs of confrontation like Mark Rudd—obviously found it more and more difficult to distinguish between power and authority. My own reading and experience had convinced me that American society suffered from the collapse of legitimate authority and that those who ran our institutions, to the degree to which they had lost public confidence, had to rely on bribery, manipulation, intimidation, and secret surveillance. Work had become a disagreeable routine, voting a meaning-less ritual, military service something to be avoided at all cost. The at-tempt to enlist public confidence in government had given way to the search for "credibility." Authorities in almost every realm had forfeited public trust; but the only way to counter the resulting cynicism, it seemed to me, was to reform our institutions so as to make them worthy of trust, not to play on this cynicism by insisting that it was impossible to trust anyone over thirty.

That I was over thirty myself no doubt colored my perception of these matters. My generation—those of us who hadn't sold out to the New Frontier—found itself caught in the middle of a struggle in which genera-tional issues rapidly overshadowed issues of class and race. The young militants denounced us as enemies of the revolution, by virtue of our having jobs, families, and positions of responsibility (however severely circumscribed by the realities of bureaucratic power), while our elders— the old social democratic, anticommunist left, well on its way to neocon-servatism by this time—lectured us on our ingratitude to the society that had favored us with every advantage and given us tenured positions in its universities. We ourselves regarded our criticism of American society, of the university in particular, as an act of loyalty, designed to restore public confidence in authority. The old social democrats saw it, however, as willful and calculated subversion, another instance of the "treason of the intellectuals"—more reprehensible, if anything, than the rebellion of the *enragés,* which could be excused as an excess of youthful idealism.

My growing dissatisfaction with the new left did not imply any break with the historic traditions of the left, which I held in higher regard the more I came to understand them. The trouble with the new left, it seemed to me, lay precisely in its ignorance of the earlier history of the left, as a result of which it proceeded to recapitulate the most unattractive features of that history: rampant sectarianism, an obsession with ideological pu-rity, sentimentalization of outcast groups. By the late sixties, I thought of myself as a socialist, attended meetings of the Socialist Scholars Confer-ence, and took part in several attempts to launch a journal of socialist opinion. Somewhat belatedly, I plowed through the works of Marx and Engels. I read Gramsci and Lukács, the founders of "Western Marxism." I immersed myself in the work of the Frankfurt school—Horkheimer, Adorno, Marcuse. Their synthesis of Marx and Freud—to whom I had been introduced in the first place by Marcuse and Norman O. Brown, who wanted to put psychoanalysis at the service of social theory—struck me as enormously fruitful, providing Marxism for the first time with a serious theory of culture. The tradition of English Marxism, as articulated by Raymond Williams and E. P. Thompson, appealed to me for the same reason. It repudiated economic determinism and the mechanistic distinction between economic "base" and cultural "superstructure." It showed that class consciousness is the product of historical experience, not a simple reflection of economic interest. The work of Williams and Thompson also showed how Marxism could absorb the insights of cultural conservatives and provide a sympathetic account, not just of the economic hardships imposed by capitalism, but of the way in which capitalism thwarted the need for joy in work, stable connections, family life, a sense of place, and a sense of historical continuity.

In the late sixties and early seventies, Marxism seemed indispensable to me—with the many refinements and modifications introduced by those who rejected the positivistic, mechanistic side of Marxism—for a whole variety of reasons. It provided a left-wing corrective to the anti-intellectualism of the new left—its cult of action (preferably violent, "existentially authentic" action), its contempt for the autonomy of thought, its terrible habit of judging ideas only by their immediate contribution to the revolution. Marxists in the West took the long view and preached patience: the gradual preparation of a new culture. Marxism explained a great many things, it seemed, that could not be explained in any other way, including the aggressive foreign policy that had troubled me for so long. In the late fifties, I had listened attentively to Kennan, Lippmann, and other "realists," who argued that the worst features of American policy originated in misplaced moral fervor. Vietnam convinced me, however—as it convinced so many others—that American imperialism grew out of the structural requirements of capitalism itself, which continued to rest on colonial exploitation. Those who rejected the economic determinism often associated with Marxism nevertheless took it as an essential principle of social analysis that a society's institutions had to be understood as expressions of its underlying structure, of the characteristic configuration of its productive forces in particular.

But the attraction of Marxism, in my own case, lay not only in its ability to provide a general explanatory framework but in its more specific insights into the "devastated realm of the spirit," in Gramsci's wonderful phrase. In this connection, I was much taken by the Marxist critique of mass culture. Here the ideas of the Frankfurt school appeared to coincide with ideas advanced by American socialists associated in the thirties with *Partisan Review* and later with *Politics, Commentary,* and *Dissent.* These native critics, notably Dwight Macdonald and Irving Howe, had condemned Stalinism partly on the grounds that it subjected culture (as it subjected everything else) to the requirements of official dogma. Having defended artistic and intellectual independence against *Kulturbolschewismus* in the thirties, they went on, in the forties and fifties, to defend it against the very different but no less insidious distortions imposed by the market. The reduction of art to a commodity, they argued, had the same effect on culture that mass production had on material objects: standardization, the destruction of craftsmanship, and a proliferation of meretricious goods designed for immediate obsolescence. The critics of mass culture, as I read them, were not primarily concerned with the debasement of popular taste; nor were they arguing that mass culture served as the opiate of the people, a source of the "false consciousness" that lulled the masses into acceptance of their miserable condition. They were on the track of something more ominous: the transformation of fame into celebrity; the replacement of events by images and pseudo-events; and the replacement of authoritative moral judgment by "inside-dopesterism," which appealed to the fear of being left behind by changing fashions, the need to know what insiders were saying, the hunger for the latest scandal or the latest medical breakthrough or the latest public opinion polls and market surveys.

The critique of mass culture provided further evidence, it seemed to me, that our society was no longer governed by a moral consensus. What held it together was "credibility"; and the Watergate affair, coming hard on the heels of the war in Vietnam—itself largely motivated by the need to maintain American credibility in the eyes of the world—seemed to indicate not merely that our public officials no longer cared about the truth but that they had lost even the capacity to distinguish it from falsehood. All that mattered was the particular version of unreality the public could be induced to "buy." Buying did not necessarily imply belief: if "disinformation," as it later came to be called, proved eminently marketable, it was because information itself was in pitifully short supply.

Disinformation monopolized the airwaves. It was not that Americans had become stupid or credulous but that they had no institutional alternative to the consumption of lies. Their only available defense was to turn off the television set, cancel subscriptions to newspapers and periodicals, and stay away from the polls on election day. More and more people in fact availed themselves of these options, to judge by declining newspaper sales, lower and lower ratings for political events, and the shrinkage of the electorate. But public opinion polls now made it possible, in effect, to dispense with the electorate by allowing an infinitesimal but allegedly representative sample of the population to determine the outcome of elections in advance.

The Land of Opportunity: A Parent's View

The question I took up in the mid-seventies—the question of whether changing patterns of family life had not brought about long-term changes in personality structure—grew out of a belief that social order no longer required the informed consent of citizens. Every form of authority, including parental authority, seemed to be in serious decline. Children now grew up without effective parental supervision or guidance, under the tutelage of the mass media and the "helping professions." Such a radical shift in the pattern of "socialization," as the sociologists called it, could be expected to have important effects on personality, the most disturbing of which would presumably be a weakening of the capacity for independent judgment, initiative, and self-discipline, on which democracy had always been understood to depend.

Such were the theoretical concerns, if I can dignify them with that name, that informed my studies in culture and personality; but those studies also grew more deeply out of my experience as a husband and father. Like so many of those born in the Depression, my wife and I married early, with the intention of raising a large family. We were part of the postwar "retreat to domesticity," as it is so glibly referred to today. No doubt we hoped to find some kind of shelter in the midst of general insecurity, but this formulation hardly does justice to our hopes and expectations, which included much more than refuge from the never-ending international emergency. In a world dominated by suspicion and mistrust, a renewal of the capacity for loyalty and devotion had to begin, it seemed, at the most elementary level, with families and friends. My generation invested personal relations with an intensity they could hardly support, as it turned out; but our passionate interest in each other's lives cannot very well be described as a form of emotional retreat. We tried to re-create in the circle of our friends the intensity of a common purpose, which could no longer be found in politics or the workplace.

We wanted our children to grow up in a kind of extended family, or at least with an abundance of "significant others." A house full of people; a crowded table ranging across the generations; four-hand music at the piano; nonstop conversation and cooking; baseball games and swimming in the afternoon; long walks after dinner; a poker game or Diplomacy or charades in the evening, all these activities mixing children and adults—that was our idea of a well-ordered household and more specifically of a well-ordered education. We had no great confidence in the schools; we knew that if our children were to acquire any of the things we set store by—joy in learning, eagerness for experience, the capacity for love and friendship—they would have to learn the better part of it at home. For that very reason, however, home was not to be thought of simply as the "nuclear family." Its hospitality would have to extend far and wide, stretching its emotional resources to the limit.

None of this was thought out self-consciously as a pedagogical program, and it would have destroyed trust and spontaneity if it had been; but some such feelings, I believe, helped to shape the way we lived, along with much else that was not only not thought out but purely impulsive. Like all parents, we gave our young less than they deserved. At least we did not set out to raise a generation of perfect children, however, as many middle-aged parents are trying to do today; nor did we undertake to equip them with all the advantages required by the prevailing standards of worldly achievement. Our failure to educate them for success was the one way in which we did not fail them—our one unambiguous success. Not that this was deliberate either; it was only gradually that it became clear to me that none of my own children, having been raised not for upward mobility but for honest work, could reasonably hope for any conventional kind of success. None of them could hope for abundant, ready-made opportunities, in other words, in some honorable line of work that would make the best use of their abilities, provide them the satisfaction that comes with the exercise of responsibility, and bring them some measure of financial security and public appreciation. Success was no longer to be had on such terms. The "best and brightest" were those who knew how to exploit institutions for their own advantage and to make exceptions for themselves instead of playing by the rules. Raw ambition counted more heavily, in the distribution of worldly rewards, than devoted service to a calling—an old story, perhaps, except that now it was complicated by the further consideration that most of the available jobs and careers did not inspire devoted service in the first place.

Politics, law, teaching, medicine, architecture, journalism, the ministry—they were all too deeply compromised by an exaggerated concern with the "bottom line" to attract people who wished simply to practice a craft or, having attracted them by some chance, to retain their ardent loyalty in the face of experiences making for discouragement and cynicism. If this was true of the professions, it was also true—it hardly needs to be said—of factory work and even of the various crafts and trades. At every level of American society, it was becoming harder and harder for people to find work that self-respecting men and women could throw themselves into with enthusiasm. The degradation of work represented the most fundamental sense in which institutions no longer commanded public confidence. It was the most important source of the "crisis of authority," so widely deplored but so little understood. The authority conferred by a calling, with all its moral and spiritual overtones, could hardly flourish in a society in which the practice of a calling had given way to a particularly vicious kind of careerism, symbolized unmistakably, in the eighties, by the rise of the yuppie.

The unexpectedly rigorous business of bringing up children exposed me, as it necessarily exposes almost any parent, to our "child-centered" society's icy indifference to everything that makes it possible for children to flourish and to grow up to be responsible adults. To see the modern world from the point of view of a parent is to see it in the worst possible light. This perspective unmistakably reveals the unwholesomeness, not to put it more strongly, of our way of life: our obsession with sex, violence, and the pornography of "making it"; our addictive dependence on drugs, "entertainment," and the evening news; our impatience with anything that limits our sovereign freedom of choice, especially with the constraints of marital and familial ties; our preference for "nonbinding commitments"; our third-rate educational system; our third-rate morality; our refusal to draw a distinction between right and wrong, lest we "impose" our morality on others and thus invite others to "impose" their morality on us; our reluctance to judge or be judged; our indifference to the needs of future generations, as evidenced by our willingness to saddle them with a huge national debt, an overgrown arsenal of destruction, and a deteriorating environment; our inhospitable attitude to the newcomers born into our midst; our unstated assumption, which underlies so much of the progaganda for unlimited abortion, that only those children born for success ought to be allowed to be born at all.

Having come to see America in this way, I could understand why the family issue had come to play such a large part in the politics of the seventies and eighties and why so many Democrats had drifted away from their party. Liberalism now meant sexual freedom, women's rights, gay rights; denunciation of the family as the seat of all oppression; denunciation of "patriarchy"; denunciation of "working-class authoritarianism." Even when liberals began to understand the depths of disaffection among formerly Democratic voters and belatedly tried to present themselves as friends of the family, they had nothing better to offer than a "national policy on families"—more welfare services, more day-care centers, more social workers and guidance counselors and child development experts. None of these proposals addressed the moral collapse that troubled so many people—troubled even liberals, although they refused to admit it publicly. Liberals and social democrats showed their true colors when they belatedly pronounced the family a "legitimate object of concern," their words dripping with condescension.

The Party of the Future
and Its Quarrel with "Middle America"

— ■ —

It was not just condescension, however, but a remarkably tenacious belief in progress that made it so hard for people on the left to listen to those who told them things were falling apart. That kind of talk had always been the stock-in-trade—hadn't it?—of those who could not bear to face the future, pined for the good old days, and suffered from a "failure of nerve." The controversies in which I found myself embroiled after the publication of *Haven in a Heartless World* and *The Culture of Narcissism* gave me a better understanding of the left's quarrel with America. If people on the left felt themselves estranged from America, it was because most Americans, in their eyes, refused to accept the future. Instead they clung to backward, provincial habits of thought that prevented them from changing with the times. Those in the know understood that what "cultural pessimists" and "doomsayers" mistook for moral collapse represented a merely transitional stage in the unfolding process of "modernization." If only everyone could be made to see things so clearly! The transition to a "postindustrial" society and a "postmodern" culture naturally caused all sorts of readjustments and dislocations, but the inevitable supersession of older ways, however painful in its side effects, had to be accepted as the price of progress.

Nor was it only material progress that lay ahead. To my surprise, I found that my friends on the left—those who had not by this time written me off as "part of the problem," who still regarded me, in spite of all evidence to the contrary, as potentially salvageable—still believed in moral as well as in material progress. They cited the abolition of slavery and the emancipation of women as indisputable evidence that the ideal of universal brotherhood was closer to realization than ever before. Its realization was chiefly impeded, it seemed, by the persistence of tribal loyalties rooted in the patriarchal stage of social development. The ties of kinship, nationality, and ethnic identity had to give way to "more inclusive identities," as Erik Erikson used to say—to an appreciation of the underlying unity of all mankind. Family feeling, clannishness, and patriotism—admirable enough, perhaps, in earlier days—could not be allowed to stand in the way of the global civilization that was arriving just in time, in fact, to save the human race from the self-destructive consequences of its old habits of national rivalry and war.

The left had no quarrel with the future, I discovered, but only with the backward, benighted, or simply misguided opponents of progress whose blind resistance might prevent the future from arriving on schedule. It was the belief in progress—the death of which I had taken for granted until I began to look into the matter—that explained the left's curious mixture of complacency and paranoia. Their confidence in being on the winning side of history made progressive people unbearably smug and superior, but they felt isolated and beleaguered in their own country, since it was so much less progressive than they were. After all, the political culture of the United States remained notoriously backward—no labor party, no socialist tradition, no great capital city like London or Paris, where politicians and civil servants mingled with artists and intellectuals and encountered advanced ideas in cafés and drawing rooms. In America, the divorce between politics and thought had always found geographical expression in the distance between Washington and New York; and the culture of Washington itself, for that matter, seemed light-years ahead of the vast hinterland beyond the Alleghenies—the land of the Yahoo, the John Birch Society, and the Ku Klux Klan.

By the late seventies and early eighties, I no longer had much confidence either in the accuracy of this bird's-eye view of America or in the progressive view of the future with which it was so closely associated. "Middle Americans" had good reason, it seemed to me, to worry about the family and about the future their children were going to inherit. My study of the family suggested a broader conclusion: that the capacity for loyalty is stretched too thin when it tries to attach itself to the hypothetical solidarity of the whole human race. It needs to attach itself to specific people and places, not to an abstract ideal of universal human rights. We love particular men and women, not humanity in general. The dream of universal brotherhood, because it rests on the sentimental fiction that men and women are all the same, cannot survive the discovery that they differ. Love, on the other hand—flesh-and-blood love, as opposed to a vague, watery humanitarianism—is attracted to complementary differences, not to sameness. A feminist, protesting against the excessive attention paid to sexual differences, urges people to enlarge their "narrow views of men and women," adding that whereas "our biological differences are self-evident, our human similarities are exciting." On the contrary, it is our biological differences that excite us. That progressive men and women have lost sight of this obvious point suggests that they are dangerously out of touch not just with "Middle America" but with common sense.

Once you reject the view of historical progress that means so much to people on the left, their sense of themselves as the party of the future, together with their fear of being overwhelmed by America's backward culture, becomes an object of historical curiosity, not the axiomatic premise from which political understanding necessarily proceeds. As I began to study the matter, I found that the left's fear of America went back a long way, at least as far back as the late thirties, when the New Deal suffered a series of setbacks from which it never quite recovered. It persisted, this uneasiness, even during the long period of liberal ascendancy that followed the Second World War. The conviction that most Americans remained politically incorrigible—ultranationalistic in foreign policy, racist in their dealings with blacks and other minorities, authoritarian in their attitudes toward women and children—helps to explain why liberals relied so heavily on the courts and the federal bureaucracy to engineer reforms that might have failed to command popular support if they had been openly debated. The great liberal victories—desegregation, affirmative action, legislative reapportionment, legalized abortion— were won largely in the courts, not in Congress, in the state legislatures, or at the polls. Instead of seeking to create a popular consensus behind these reforms, liberals pursued their objectives by indirect methods, fearing that popular attitudes remained unreconstructed. The trauma of McCarthyism, the long and bitter resistance to desegregation in the South, and the continued resistance to federal spending (unless it could be justified on military grounds) all seemed to confirm liberals in the belief that the ordinary American had never been a liberal and was unlikely to become one.

The Promised Land of the New Right
· ■ ·

The use of legalistic strategies to advance the rights of minorities divided liberals from the working-class constituencies that once made up the heart of the New Deal majority. Advocating ideals of individualism, social mobility, and self-realization that come closest to fulfillment in the professional classes, liberals defended the underdog in an upper-class accent. Their well-meaning efforts to help black people, women, gays, and other victims of legal discrimination smacked of paternalism. Their confidence in the rectitude of their own intentions, in their moral standing as protectors of beleaguered minorities, verged on self-righteousness. Their faith in administrative expertise offended those who put their faith in common sense. The cumulative effect of their highly organized altruism was to generate a "backlash against the theoreticians and bureaucrats in national government," as George Wallace put it. By 1968, when Wallace's strong showing among working-class voters in the North foreshadowed a new political alignment, Americans were "fed up," in his words, "with strutting pseudo-intellectuals lording over them, writing guidelines, . . . telling them they have not got sense enough to know what is best for their children or sense enough to run their own schools and hospitals and local domestic institutions."

Twelve years later, the working-class revolt against liberalism helped to bring the new right to power under Reagan. But Reagan's defense of "traditional values," it turned out, did not amount to much. A self-proclaimed conservative, Reagan had no more use than people on the left for "naysayers" and "prophets of doom," as he called them. When he denounced those who falsely claimed that America suffered from a spiritual "malaise," he echoed the main theme of Ted Kennedy's unsuccessful campaign in the 1980 primaries. If Reagan succeeded where Kennedy failed, perhaps it was because he managed to create the impression that moral regeneration could be achieved painlessly through the power of positive thinking, whereas Kennedy relied on the usual array of federal programs.

The "traditional values" celebrated by Reagan—boosterism, rugged individualism, a willingness to resort to force (against weaker opponents) on the slightest provocation—had very little to do with tradition. They summed up the code of the cowboy, the man in flight from his ancestors, from his immediate family, and from everything that tied him down and limited his freedom of movement. Reagan played on the desire for order, continuity, responsibility, and discipline, but his program contained nothing that would satisfy that desire. On the contrary, his program aimed to promote economic growth and unregulated business enterprise, the very forces that have undermined tradition. A movement calling itself conservative might have been expected to associate itself with the demand for limits not only on economic growth but on the conquest of space, the technological conquest of the environment, and the ungodly ambition to acquire godlike powers over nature. Reaganites, however, condemned the demand for limits as another counsel of doom. "Free enterprisers," according to Burton Pines, an ideologue of the new right, "insist that the economy can indeed expand and as it does so, all society's members can . . . increase their wealth."

These words crudely express the belief in progress that has dominated Anglo-American politics for the last two centuries. The idea of progress, contrary to received opinion, owes its appeal not to its millennial vision of the future but to the seemingly more realistic expectation that the expansion of productive forces can continue indefinitely. The history of liberalism—which includes a great deal that passes for conservatism as well—consists of variations on this underlying theme.

That "optimism" and "pessimism" remain the favorite categories of political debate indicates that the theme of progress is not yet played out. In the impending age of limits, however, it sounds increasingly hollow. We can begin to hear discordant voices, which always accompanied the celebration of progress as a kind of counterpoint but were usually drowned out by the principal voices. A closer study of the score—the history of progressive ideology and its critics—brings to the surface a more complicated texture, a richer and darker mixture of harmonies, not always euphonious by any means, than we have been accustomed to hear. It is the darker voices especially that speak to us now, not because they speak in tones of despair but because they help us to distinguish "optimism" from hope and thus give us the courage to confront the mounting difficulties that threaten to overwhelm us.

2

THE IDEA OF PROGRESS
RECONSIDERED

A Secular Religion?

The idea of progress, according to a widely accepted interpretation, represents a secularized version of the Christian belief in providence. The ancient world, we are told, entertained a cyclical view of history, whereas Christianity gave it a clearly defined direction, from the fall of man to his ultimate redemption. "It is no accident," Carl Becker wrote in 1921, "that the belief in Progress and a concern for 'posterity' waxed in proportion as the belief in Providence and a concern for a future life waned. The former belief—illusion if you prefer—is man's compensation for the loss of the latter."

Thanks to its Christian background, the Western world found it easy to imagine history as a "process generally moving upwards by a series of majestic stages," as Ernest Lee Tuveson explained. For twentieth-century historians, skeptical about the value of religion in any form, an understanding of the Christian origins of progressive ideology reveals the "radical inconsistency" at its core, in Becker's words, the untenable assumption of historical "finality." Almost everyone now agrees that progress—in its utopian form at least—is a "superstition" that is "nearly worn out," as Dean William Ralph Inge put it in 1920; that we can now appreciate its religious roots largely because "the idea has begun to lose its hold on the mind of society," as Christopher Dawson pointed out a few years later; and that the hope of some final state of earthly perfection, in short, is the "deadest of dead ideas," as Lewis Mumford wrote in 1932—"the one notion that has been thoroughly blasted by the facts of twentieth-century experience."

Utopian visions of the future were definitively discredited by their association with the totalitarian movements that came to power in the thirties. Belief in a secular millennium, rooted in the Christian tradition, seemed to have furnished modern barbarism with much of its spiritual energy. "The more carefully one compares the outbreaks of militant social chiliasm during the later Middle Ages with modern totalitarian movements," wrote Norman Cohn, "the more remarkable the similarities appear." Fascists and communists replaced supernatural explanations of history with secular explanations, but they clung to the apocalyptic fantasy that a final, decisive struggle would establish absolute justice and perfect contentment. "What had once been demanded by 'the will of God' was now demanded by 'the purposes of History.' "

Belief in Progress as the Antidote to Despair

· ■ ·

The collapse of utopia made it clear that a belief in progress could be salvaged—and the same calamities that discredited utopian hopes seemed to make it all the more important to salvage some form of hope—only by disavowing its perfectionist overtones.* "The world today believes in

---

*In his influential book *Ideology and Utopia*, published in 1937, Karl Mannheim gave voice to an uneasiness shared by many others. Would the collapse of the utopian

progress," Sidney Pollard flatly declared in 1986, because "the only possible alternative to the belief in progress would be total despair." Faith in progress could no longer rest on a vision of human perfection, but a more modest conception of progress was not only possible but essential to the "survival" of human society, as E. H. Carr put it in 1963. Since "some such conception" alone could "persuade the present generation to make sacrifices for future generations," Carr proposed a more thoroughly secularized doctrine of "unlimited progress." Without postulating an end to history, he argued, men and women could still look forward to improvements "subject to no limits that we can . . . envisage, towards goals which can be defined only as we advance towards them." Only intellectuals questioned the reality of progress. The condition of the masses had undeniably improved. The "mere accumulation of resources," to be sure, was not enough to justify a belief in progress, unless it brought "increased technical and social knowledge, . . . increased mastery of man's environment." But progress in this broader sense, Carr maintained, could still not be ruled out.

His observations exemplify the dominant view of the matter. If "the belief in progress has exhibited remarkable toughness in twentieth-cen-

---

illusion deprive men and women of the incentive to plan for the future? Having traced the idea of progress, in the usual fashion, to the millennarian tradition of Christianity, which encouraged its heirs to envision the "completion of the past in the future," Mannheim traced the growth of a "skeptical," "prosaic," and "matter-of-fact" mentality that undermined the idea of historical completion and thus brought about a "general subsidence of utopian intensity." Unlike those who welcomed this development, Mannheim wondered whether the modern world could get along without faith in a future utopia. "A removal of the chiliastic element from the midst of culture and politics . . . would leave the world without meaning of life." It would lead to a "decay of the human will." Without "ideals," man would become a "mere creature of impulses." Utopia remained a cultural and psychological necessity even if it no longer appeared to have any solid basis in fact.

More recent defenders of the idea of progress tend to reject Mannheim's assumption that millennial expectations are the only grounds on which to base a belief in progress. As I hope to show, the history of progressive ideology provides a good deal of support for their position. Whether a belief in progress provides the only possible source of "ideals" and hope is quite another matter. A central premise of my own argument is that it does not.

tury America," as Clarke Chambers noted in 1958, it is because liberals and socialists have divorced it from the "heavenly city of the eighteenth-century philosophers," tied it to the cause of democracy and abundance, and brought it down to earth. No one claims any more that progress is inevitable or that it will culminate in some state of final perfection. No one denies that moral improvement often fails to keep pace with material improvement. But the general rise in living standards is obviously desirable in itself. The "average length of life has been steadily extended," Charles Frankel wrote some time ago, illiteracy "progressively eliminated," work made less back-breaking, leisure time increased, and the "basic conditions of human life," in short, "changed for the better" and "changed more radically in the last hundred and fifty years than in all history before that time."* The fact of technological progress simply cannot be denied, according to Barrington Moore, and it is "accompanied by changes in social structure" that provide the "prerequisites of freedom." Material comfort does not assure a good life, but a good life is impossible without it. Material improvements, moreover, can be taken as evidence of a refusal to tolerate conditions formerly taken for granted—poverty, hunger, epidemic disease, inequality, racial bigotry. "Despite the difficulty of balancing gains and losses," Morris Ginsberg argued in 1953, humanitarian sentiment "is gaining in strength. . . . In no previous age has so much been done to relieve suffering, and to abolish poverty, disease and ignorance in all parts of the world." A. J. Ayer likewise sees the "average man" as "more humane, more pacific and more concerned with social justice than he was a century ago."

Progress is the "working faith of our civilization," wrote Christopher Dawson in 1929. Later writers agree. "No single idea has been more important in Western civilization," Robert Nisbet argues. ". . . This idea has done more good over a twenty-five-hundred-year period . . . and given more strength to human hope . . . than any other single idea in Western

---

*"The vision behind liberalism," Frankel noted, "is the vision of a world progressively redeemed by human power from its classic ailments of poverty, disease, and ignorance. . . . To hold the liberal view of history [has always] meant to believe in 'progress.' "

history."* J. H. Plumb joins Nisbet in upholding the idea of progress as a "great human truth." Warren Wagar condemns the "neo-Augustinian theologians, the obscurantists, and all the pious and aesthetic and mystical refugees" who question man's ability to prevail. A. J. P. Taylor, along with Wagar and Carr, dismisses cultural pessimism as the vice of disgruntled intellectuals. Talk about the decline of civilization, Taylor says, means "only that university professors used to have domestic servants and now do their own washing-up."

Against the "Secularization Thesis"

Since the idea of progress, in our time, gains a certain plausibility the more it loses the character of a secular religion, the next step in its rehabilitation might be to deny its religious origins altogether. In *The Legitimacy of the Modern Age,* published in Germany in 1966 but only recently translated into English, Hans Blumenberg subjects the "secularization thesis," as he calls it—the notion that progressive ideology represents a secularized version of the Christian millennium—to an all-out assault. According to Blumenberg, the idea of progress originated not in Christian eschatology but in the seventeenth-century revolt against the prestige of classical art and learning and in the scientific revolution, which provided mankind with a new mastery over the conditions of its existence and suggested by its example that the production of knowledge is cumulative and irreversible. Blumenberg admits that nineteenth-century theorists of progress like Hegel, Comte, and Spencer spun out elaborate theories of

---

*Nisbet finds it alarming that the present age is "almost barren of faith in progress," obsessed with "limits to growth" and "limits of scientific inquiry." In fact, however, those who talk about limits on growth and scientific inquiry remain a small minority. Even Barry Commoner, probably the most prominent environmentalist in the United States, rejects the idea that environmentalism depends on "limiting economic development." The " 'limits of growth' approach," Commoner maintains, rests on the "misconception" that the earth is a "closed system, isolated from all outside sources of support and necessarily sustained only by its own limited resources."

historical stages, later discredited; but that was not because they incorporated elements of the Christian worldview into their systems but because they mistakenly assumed that modern scholarship had to compete with Christianity on its own ground. Attempting to work out theories that rivaled Christian cosmology in their comprehensive scope, nineteenth-century thinkers encumbered the idea of progress with an unnecessary load of world-historical significance. Now that this speculative freight has dropped away, Blumenberg thinks, we can see more clearly what distinguishes the modern conception of history from the Christian conception: the assertion that the principle of historical change comes from within history and not from on high and that man can achieve a better life "by the exertion of his own powers" instead of counting on divine grace.

Just why these considerations should establish the "legitimacy of the modern age" is not clear, but at least they help to distinguish it from earlier ages. The "secularization thesis" has too long obscured differences between the idea of providence and the modern idea of progress. The case for the antiquity of a belief in progress reveals its weakness most clearly just when it is pressed most energetically, as in the work of Nisbet, who claims to find a highly developed theory of progress not only in the Christian fathers but even in classical authors like Seneca and Lucretius. Nisbet assumes that Roman and Christian philosophers shared our high opinion of material comforts. But although they admired the ingenuity that produced those comforts, they believed that moral wisdom lay in the limitation rather than in the multiplication of needs and desires. The modern conception of progress depends on a positive assessment of the proliferation of wants. Ancient authors, however, saw no moral or social value in the transformation of luxuries into necessities. In Augustine's *City of God*, to be sure, we find in book 22 eloquent praise of fecundity, plenitude, and invention—Nisbet calls it his own *"pièce de résistance."* But the flavor of the passage is best conveyed by Augustine's observation that human skill and intelligence reveal themselves even in the "brilliant wit shown by philosophers and heretics in defending their very errors and falsehoods." Man's impressive achievements "console" him, Augustine says, for his fallen state—for the "life of misery, [the] kind of hell on earth" described so graphically in the chapter immediately preceding the one Nisbet quotes at length. But these achievements do not assure salvation. Augustine discusses them in a passage that also praises the superabundant generosity of nature and treats man's intelligence and creative capacity as "evidence of the blessings he enjoys," not as evidence of his own godlike powers.

By throwing classical and Christian authors indiscriminately into the progressive camp, Nisbet loses sight even of the one insight that made the "secularization thesis" plausible in the first place—the recognition that Judaism and Christianity encouraged an interest in history in a way that classical and Oriental patterns of thought did not. The Greeks believed that the "eternal or timeless is the sole, ultimate, and complete reality," as A. D. Ritchie points out, while Jews and Christians believed that God reveals himself "through His creation, the material world, and especially through the course of temporal events we call human history." Such is the accepted and no doubt the correct interpretation—to which it is necessary to add, however, that neither the Hebraic nor the Christian attitude, although they rescued history from randomness, implied a belief in progressive improvement, let alone the crude celebrations of racial and national destiny so often associated with progressive ideologies in the modern world. Nor did they necessarily imply a belief in an earthly paradise in the future. Biblical references to the millennium could be interpreted in various ways, and the idea that the end of the world would be preceded by a thousand years of peace and plenty—allegedly the source of the idea of progress—was never the dominant view among Christians. It was not, in any case, a view that encouraged a progressive interpretation of human history. Premillennialists, as they came to be called in the nineteenth century, held that things were deteriorating at a rapid rate. It was precisely the wretched state of the world that portended the return of the Messiah and his imposition of a new order. Insofar as the idea of progress found favor among nineteenth-century Christians, it found favor among so-called postmillennialists—those who took the position that Christ's appearance in the first century already fulfilled the biblical promise of the millennium and provided man with the spiritual resources that would ultimately ensure his triumph over the powers of darkness.

But the heart of Christian hope lay elsewhere—neither in the earthly paradise at the end of time nor in the Christianization of society and the moral improvements it would bring. The essence of hope, for Christians, lay in the "conviction that life is a critical affair," as Richard Niebuhr once put it, "that nothing in it is abiding, that nothing temporal is able to bear the weight of human faith," and yet that life is good and that a conviction of its goodness forbids us "to give up any part of human life as beyond hope of redemption." In the prophetic tradition—the moral center of Christianity, as Niebuhr argued so eloquently—the Kingdom of God was conceived neither as the end of the world nor as an "ideal for future society" but as a community of the faithful living under the judgment inherent in the evanescence of earthly affairs and more particularly in the "doom of threatened societies."

When the Jews referred to themselves as the chosen people, they meant that they had agreed to submit to a uniquely demanding set of ethical standards, not that they were destined to rule the world or to enjoy special favors from heaven. The seventeenth-century Puritan settlers of New England, much indebted to the Old Testament for their conception of a collective identity, understood their mission in the same way. From this point of view, history mattered because it was under divine judgment, not because it led inevitably to the promised land. Whether the chosen people would prove themselves worthy of the blessings arbitrarily bestowed on them was an open question, not a foregone conclusion; and the prophetic tradition, central to Judaism, to Augustinian Catholicism, and to early Protestantism, served to recall them, again and again, to a painful awareness of their own shortcomings. Prophecy made history much more the record of moral failure than a promise of ultimate triumph. It put less emphasis on the millennium to come than on the present duty to live with faith and hope, in a world that often seemed to give no encouragement to either.

What the Idea of Progress Really Means

Once we recognize the profound differences between the Christian view of history, prophetic or millennarian, and the modern conception of progress, we can understand what was so original about the latter: not the promise of a secular utopia that would bring history to a happy ending but the promise of steady improvement with no foreseeable ending at all. The expectation of indefinite, open-ended improvement, even more than the insistence that improvement can come only through human effort, provides the solution to the puzzle that is otherwise so baffling—the resilience of progressive ideology in the face of discouraging events that have shattered the illusion of utopia. The idea of progress never rested mainly on the promise of an ideal society—not at least in its Anglo-American version. Historians have exaggerated the utopian component in progressive ideology. The modern conception of history is utopian only in its assumption that modern history has no foreseeable conclusion. We take our cue from science, at once the source of our material achievements and the model of cumulative, self-perpetuating inquiry, which guarantees its continuation precisely by its willingness to submit every advance to the risk of supersession.

That nothing is certain except the imminent obsolescence of all our certainties—our scientific theories, our technology, our artistic styles and schools, our philosophies, our political ideals, our fashions—naturally gives rise to the sense of impermanence that has been celebrated or deplored as the very essence of the modern outlook, the sense that "all that is solid melts into air," in the often quoted remark by Marx and Engels. What is less often remarked is that impermanence appears to assure a certain continuity in its own right when conceived as an extension of the self-correcting procedures of scientific discovery, which allow the scientific enterprise as a whole to flourish in spite of the constant revision of particular findings. A social order founded on science, with its unnerving but exhilarating expansion of our intellectual horizons, seems to have achieved a kind of immortality undreamed of by earlier civilizations.

Whatever else we can say about the future, it appears that we can safely take for granted its sophisticated contempt for the rudimentary quality of our present ways. We can imagine that our civilization might blow itself up—and the prospect of its suicide has a certain illicit appeal, since at least it satisfies the starved sense of an ending—but we cannot imagine that it might die a natural death, like the great civilizations of the past. That civilizations pass through a life cycle analogous to the biological rhythm of birth, maturity, old age, and death now strikes us as another discredited superstition, like the immortality of the soul. Only science, we suppose, is immortal; and although the unlikelihood of its melting away can be experienced even more intensely, perhaps, as a curse than as a blessing, the apparently irreversible character of its historical development defines the modern sense of time and makes it unnecessary to raise the question that haunted our predecessors: how should nations conduct themselves under sentence of death?

Providence and Fortune, Grace and Virtue

The biblical conception of history, after all, had more in common (though not in the way that Nisbet imagines) with the classical conception, as reformulated during the Renaissance, than with the modern gospel of progress. What they had in common was an awareness of the "doom of threatened societies"—an understanding, that is, that the contingent, provisional, and finite quality of temporal things finds its most vivid demonstration not just in the death of individuals but in the rise and fall of nations. There is a good deal to be said for J. H. Plumb's thesis that the fall of Rome sharpened the historical imagination in the West, posing both for Christians in the fourth century and for neopagans in the fifteenth and sixteenth centuries a question that could be answered only through speculation about the course of past events. Why had that splendid empire collapsed? For the Romans themselves, it was the desertion of the pagan gods, after the introduction of Christianity, that led to the barbarian conquest. Augustine wrote *The City of God* in order to refute this belief but also in order to put the fall of Rome in the cosmic perspective of God's plan for salvation. "As far as I can see, the distinction between victors and vanquished has not the slightest importance for security, for moral standards, or even for human dignity. . . . As far as this mortal life is concerned, which ends after a few days' course, what does it matter under whose rule a man lives, being so soon to die, provided that the rulers do not force him to impious and wicked acts?" For Machiavelli and his readers—for whom ancient Rome, on the other hand, supplied the "standard by which modern times . . . were measured and found wanting," in Hanna Pitkin's words—it was just this indifference to civic affairs, encouraged by Christianity, that fatally weakened Rome. No matter how it was explained, however, the fall of Rome served as a reminder of glory's fleeting career as well as an incentive to rescue something of permanence from the realm of change. "The world of particular events was ill understood," according to John Pocock; "the temporal flux evaded men's conceptual control," and history unfolded "under the dominion of an inscrutable power, which manifested itself as providence to men of faith and as fortune" to the faithless.

Whatever the conceptual deficiencies in this way of understanding history, at least it did not expose the sixteenth and seventeenth centuries to the delusion that man can control history for his own purposes or build a new kind of social order that will withstand the corrosive effects of time. Those historians who find the seeds of progressive ideology in the linear conception of time, advanced by Christians in opposition to the cyclical conception of antiquity, overlook what the idea of providence had in common with the idea of fortune. No doubt Karl Löwith went too far in the other direction when he claimed that "in the reality of that agitated sea which we call 'history,' it makes little difference whether man feels himself in the hands of God's inscrutable will or in the hands of chance or fate." It does make a difference, one that was already implicit in the contrast between Augustine's unconcern with political matters and Machiavelli's insistence that it is political life alone that enables men to achieve lasting glory and thus to outwit fortune. But Machiavelli's view of fortune did not lack respect, even a certain reverence. He confessed that he was "partly inclined to share the opinion" that "there is no remedy whatever" against fortune. Only the reflection that "our freedom" would be "altogether extinguished" by such an attitude led him to think that although "fortune is the ruler of half our actions," she "allows the other half or thereabouts to be governed by us." He was not so impressed by the example of Rome or the prospects for its revival that he fell into the equivalent of our modern mistake in exempting our own civilization, seemingly immortal in its wealth and its command of the accumulated fruits of scientific knowledge, from the cycle of growth and decay.

The concept of virtue stood in something of the same relation to fortune, in the civic tradition descending from Machiavelli and ultimately from classical stoicism, that the Christian concept of grace stood in relation to providence. Virtue, like grace, enabled men to live undespairingly with the knowledge of finitude, the poignant contrast between the absolute and the contingent. Virtue imposed form on the disorderly flux of temporal events by underwriting a civic order the moral example of which would outlive its allotted span of time. Since the civic ideal defined itself in direct opposition to Christianity, accused by republicans of weakening civic loyalty by demanding exclusive loyalty to God, it is easy to miss their underlying affinity. Both encouraged men and women to find order and meaning in submission to a communal standard of conduct. Both associated the good life with a particular form of community and with the memories that constituted it. There was a world of difference, to be sure, between a community of saints and a community of virtuous citizens, but the two concepts, virtue and grace, "found common ground," in Pocock's words, "in an ideal of austerity and self-denial." The belief in progress carried with it a very different ideal of the good life.

Machiavelli's politicization of virtue, leading to the gradual assimilation of the idea of fortune to the newer idea of civic corruption, made historical processes more intelligible than before but no more amenable to a progressive interpretation. Once the "antithesis of virtue ceased to be *fortuna* [and] became corruption instead," the succession of temporal events, as Pocock explains, "could be defined not as sheer disorder" but as the product of social forces: specialization, the division of labor, and the growth of "luxury." The "ancient equation of change with degeneration," however, still "held fast." In the eyes of Machiavelli's successors— Harrington, Montesquieu, Rousseau—the specialization of civic functions, first dramatized by the emergence of mercenary armies, undermined civic virtue by making it possible for citizens to hand over their civic obligations, including the all-important obligation to bear arms, to professionals. According to republican theorists, standing armies not only posed a threat to liberty but contributed indirectly to corruption by enabling citizens to pursue their private advantage at public expense. Specialization generated new standards of comfort and refinement, encouraged the competitive accumulation of private wealth, and relieved citizens of the obligation to serve the commonwealth. It weakened sociability, in short, while the abundance made possible by an increasingly minute division of social labor inflamed men's imaginations with a taste for pleasure and led them to value evanescent pleasures more highly than durable achievements. Even proponents of commerce like Daniel Defoe spoke of the power of Credit, the personification of instability, in much the same language in which Machiavelli had spoken of fortune, as a jealous mistress whose "despotic" rule over men's fantasies testified to the unsettling "power of imagination." It was left to Rousseau, however, to provide the "first specifically modern theory" of man's self-enslavement to an ever-escalating cycle of wants and needs, in the words of Michael Ignatieff, and to link the "ancient stoic account of moral corruption" to the "economic conditions of modern capitalist society—inequality, acquisitive envy, and the division of labor."

Adam Smith's Rehabilitation of Desire

Now we can see what was so novel about the eighteenth-century idea of progress, the distinctive features of which emerge even more clearly against the background of this republican critique of corruption and civic decline than against the background of Judeo-Christian prophecy. It was not the secularization of the Kingdom of God or even the new stress on processes intrinsic to historical development that chiefly distinguished progressive ideology from earlier views of history. Its original appeal and its continuing plausibility derived from the more specific assumption that insatiable appetites, formerly condemned as a source of social instability and personal unhappiness, could drive the economic machine—just as man's insatiable curiosity drove the scientific project—and thus ensure a never-ending expansion of productive forces. The moral rehabilitation of desire, even more than a change in the perception of time as such, generated a new sense of possibility, which announced itself most characteristically not in the vague utopianism of the French Enlightenment but in the hardheaded new science of political economy.

For eighteenth-century moralists like Bernard Mandeville, David Hume, and Adam Smith, it was the self-generating character of rising expectations, newly acquired needs and tastes, new standards of personal comfort—the very changes deplored by republican critics of commerce—that broke the old cycle of social growth and decay and gave rise to a form of society capable of indefinite expansion. The decisive break with older ways of thinking came when human needs began to be seen not as natural but as historical, hence insatiable. As the supply of material comforts increased, standards of comfort increased as well, and the category of necessities came to include many goods formerly regarded as luxuries. A shirt made from the "most ordinary Yorkshire cloth," according to Mandeville, would have been considered a luxury in earlier times, when man "fed on the fruits of the earth . . . and reposed himself naked like the other animals on the lap of the common parent." Envy, pride, and ambition made human beings want more than they needed, but these "private vices" became "public virtues" by stimulating industry and invention. Thrift and self-denial, on the other hand, meant economic stagnation.

Hume and Smith rejected Mandeville's "licentious system of morality," really an inverted asceticism, as Smith astutely pointed out, in which anything "short of the most ascetic abstinence" became "gross luxury and sensuality, . . . so that there is vice even in the use of a clean shirt." But they sided with Mandeville in opposing the "received notion," as Mandeville put it, "that luxury is as destructive to the wealth of the whole body politic, as it is to that of every individual person who is guilty of it." The "pleasures of luxury and the profit of commerce," according to Hume, "roused men from their indolence" and led to "further improvements in every branch of domestic as well as foreign trade." Hume and Smith endorsed the general principle that a growing desire for material comforts, wrongly taken by republicans as a sign of decadence and impending social collapse, generated new employments, new wealth, and a constantly rising level of productivity. They quarreled only with Mandeville's moral condemnation of "luxury." If luxury meant a "great refinement in the gratification of the senses," there was a good deal to be said for it, Hume argued, on moral as well as on economic grounds. "Indulgences are only vices, when they are pursued at the expense of some virtue."

Smith made the more important point that it was not "luxury," after all, that fueled the modern productive machine but the more modest expenditures of ordinary consumers. Mandeville did not see beyond the extravagant self-indulgence of the rich, which had the happy though entirely unintended consequence of employing "all sorts of artificers in iron, wood, marble, brass, pewter, copper, wool, flax, and divers other materials." Smith, on the other hand, insisted that the "uniform, constant, and uninterrupted effort of every man to better his condition"— not the lavish but unproductive spending of kings and nobles—was the "principle from which public and national, as well as private opulence is originally derived." Unlike Mandeville, who shared the mercantilist prejudice in favor of low wages, Smith defended high wages, on the grounds that "a person who can acquire no property can have no other interest but to eat as much, and to labour as little as possible." The hope of improving his condition, on the other hand, would encourage the working man to spend his income on "things more durable" than the "hospitality" and "festivals" preferred by the wealthy, and the accumulated effect of this kind of expenditure, even though it might reflect a "base and selfish disposition," maintained a whole nation of industrious workers, not just a few servants and useless retainers.

A positive appraisal of the social effects of self-gratification made it possible for interpreters of the new order to exempt modern society, in effect, from the judgment of time—the judgment previously believed, by Christians and pagans alike, to hang like a sword over all man's works. Because the new science of political economy appeared to deliver the modern world from the "doom of threatened societies," in Richard Niebuhr's wonderfully resonant phrase, it is to Adam Smith and his immediate predecessors, rather than to those second-rate thinkers more conventionally associated with the idea of progress—Fontenelle, Condorcet, Godwin, Comte, Spencer—that we should look for the inner meaning of progressive ideology. Compared to Smith's incisive analysis of the social implications of desire, vaporous tributes to the power of reason and to the progress of the arts and sciences, speculations about a perfect state of society in the future, and the various schemes of historical stages that traced social development from the simple to the complex contributed very little to a plausible theory of progress. Human ingenuity, as evidenced by the steady improvement of useful arts, had elicited the qualified admiration even of Augustine. The ancient world was fully acquainted with the achievements of reason; nor was the eighteenth-century world so besotted with those achievements that it overlooked reason's limits. As for the idea of historical stages, equally familiar to the ancients, it led to a theory of progress only when social theorists ceased to model those stages on the biological life cycle, in which growth and maturity led inevitably to senescence and death. Smith's work, especially *The Wealth of Nations,* implicitly repudiated this biological conception of history and the self-denying morality with which it had been associated. The stoic critique of appetite lost much of its force in the face of Smith's contention that insatiable appetites led not to corruption and decay but to the indefinite expansion of the productive machinery necessary to satisfy them.

The case for permanence—for the prospect of a social order capable of withstanding the effects of time—no longer had to rest on divine intervention or the perfectibility of reason. It now rested more securely, if unexpectedly and ironically, on ordinary ambition, vanity, greed, and a morally misplaced respect, as Smith put it, for the "vain and empty distinctions of greatness." In the "languor of disease and the weariness of old age," the moral insignificance of worldly goods appeared in its true light, according to Smith, since neither possessions nor even the beauty and utility so universally admired in "any production of art" proved capable, under conditions of adversity, of bringing true happiness. People seldom looked at the matter in this "abstract and philosophical light," however; and "it is well that nature imposes upon us in this manner," Smith wrote in *The Theory of Moral Sentiments,* in a passage that alluded for the first time to the "invisible hand" that leads men and women to accumulate wealth and thus inadvertently to serve as social benefactors in their pursuit of deceptively attractive but ultimately empty possessions. "It is this deception which rouses and keeps in continual motion the industry of mankind."

Smith's Misgivings about "General Security and Happiness"

Smith's work is instructive, in the unfamiliar context of the development of progressive ideology, not only because it enables us to see what was really distinctive about that ideology—the exemption of the modern world from the judgment of time—but because it illustrates the persistence of certain reservations that qualified the optimism produced by the modern discovery of abundance. His occasional musings on the vanity of acquisition betrayed a lingering attachment to the "stoical philosophy," which sought to base "our happiness upon the most solid and secure foundation, a firm confidence in that [divine] wisdom and justice which govern the world." The only objection to stoicism, Smith noted, was that it aimed "at a perfection altogether beyond the reach of human nature." He knew very well that the "soft, gentle, the amiable virtues" were better suited to commercial societies than the "virtues of self-denial"; yet he preferred the latter, on the whole.

He admitted that modern moralists offered better instruction in "private and domestic affections" than Zeno and Epictetus, whose "stoical apathy" was "never agreeable" when it attempted to moderate parental affection. But even though his own system unavoidably encouraged men to pursue private interest at the expense of public service, Smith had a republican contempt for such a life. He believed that politics and war, not commerce, served as the "great school of self-command." "Under the boisterous and stormy sky of war and faction, of public tumult and confusion, the sturdy severity of self-command prospers most." A commercial society needed the "gentle virtue of humanity," to be sure; and "justice and humanity" rested, in turn, on a "sacred regard" for life and property, necessarily weakened by the "violence of faction" and the "hardships and hazards of war." Even so, Smith reserved his highest praise, not only in *The Theory of Moral Sentiments* but in *The Wealth of Nations* itself, for the soldier's life. He regretted that "the general security and happiness which prevail in ages of civility and politeness, afford little exercise to the contempt of danger, to patience in enduring labor, hunger, and pain." The division of labor made possible an unheard-of expansion of productivity, as he explained at length in *The Wealth of Nations,* but it also dulled the mind and sapped the martial spirit.

His unsparing account of these effects drew on the republican identification of virtue with virility and resourcefulness. "A man, incapable either of defending or of revenging himself, evidently wants one of the most essential parts of the character of a man." Similarly "a man without the proper use of the intellectual faculties of a man is . . . more contemptible than even a coward, and seems to be mutilated and deformed in a still more essential part of the character of human nature." Smith could only hope that a comprehensive program of public education would teach the virtues no longer taught by service in the militia—now recognized as "much inferior to a well-disciplined and well-exercised standing army"—and by active participation in political life.

The harshest critics of modern specialization have added little to the indictment drawn up by its great apologist. But such misgivings were destined to be confined to a shadowy half-life on the fringes of debate so long as the economic and technological advantages of specialization—the central assumption in the ensuing controversy about industrialism and the industrial division of labor—went uncontested. If one conceded the "irresistible superiority" of a "well-regulated standing army" over a citizens' militia, the question of whether "justice and humanity" represented a falling-off from self-command, fortitude, contempt of pain, and "independency upon fortune" became entirely academic. One might regret the passing of the "great and awful virtues" appropriate to the "council, the senate, or the field," but the issue was already decided by the inexorable advance of civilization. "In general, the style of manners which takes place in any nation, may . . . be said to be that which is most suitable to its situation. Hardiness is the character most suitable to the circumstances of a savage, sensibility to those of one who lives in a very civilized society."

So saying, Smith effectively banished regrets, including his own, to the category of harmless speculation about a hypothetical golden age in the past. No one could argue very long against abundance, increasingly perceived as the distinguishing characteristic of a "very civilized society." By 1848, when Macaulay published his *History of England,* the party of progress, confident that it had long since carried the day, had mastered the tone of bluff and jocular dismissal, the unapologetically philistine defense of everyday comforts, the pretense of standing out against the prevailing intellectual fashion of sentimental regret, that have remained its trademark down to the present day.

It is now the fashion to place the Golden Age of England in times when noblemen were destitute of comforts the want of which would be intolerable to a modern footman, when farmers and shopkeepers breakfasted on loaves, the very sight of which would raise a riot in a modern workhouse, when to have a clean shirt once a week was a privilege reserved for the higher class of gentry, when men died faster in the purest country air than they now die in the most pestilential lanes of our towns, and when men died faster in the lanes of our towns than they now die on the coast of Guiana. We too, shall, in our turn, be outstripped, and in our turn envied.

Macaulay's complacency was in no way qualified by the conventional reminder that his own age—since the process of accumulation continues without any foreseeable end—would appear to future generations just as primitive in its standard of cleanliness and comfort as earlier ages appeared to him and his contemporaries, hence equally eligible for perversely wistful retrospection.

Desire Domesticated

The more thoughtful among Macaulay's contemporaries, however, could not entirely suppress the disturbing consideration that a social order based on the promise of universal abundance might find it hard to justify even the minimal sacrifices presupposed by Adam Smith's otherwise self-regulating economy. Hume had astutely pointed out, when the philosophy of plenty was still in its infancy, that it might weaken even the residual inclination to defer gratification. Human beings "are always much inclin'd to prefer present interest to distant and remote," he observed; "nor is it easy for them to resist the temptation of any advantage that they may immediately enjoy." As long as "the pleasures of life [were] few," this form of temptation did not pose a great threat to social order. Commercial societies, however, could be expected to intensify the pursuit of "feverish, empty amusements"; and the "avidity . . . of acquiring goods and possessions" was "insatiable, perpetual, universal, and directly destructive of society."

In the nineteenth century, the hope that commerce would make men "easy and sociable," not acquisitive and rapacious, came to rest largely on the institutionalization of deferred gratification supposedly provided by the family—the heart and soul of the middle-class way of life. Nineteenth-century philanthropists, humanitarians, and social reformers argued with one voice that the revolution of rising expectations meant a higher standard of domestic life, not an orgy of self-indulgence activated by fantasies of inordinate personal wealth, of riches painlessly acquired through speculation or fraud, of an abundance of wine and women. That a commercial society fostered such ambitions troubled them no end; and it was to counter this tawdry dream of success, this unbridled urge to strike it rich, that proponents of a more orderly economic development attached so much importance to the family. The obligation to support a wife and children, in their view, would discipline possessive individualism and transform the potential gambler, speculator, dandy, or confidence man into a conscientious provider. Moral and mental development stimulated material development and tempered it at the same time. An enterprising, intelligent, and self-disciplined population would demand an ever-growing supply of goods and services to satisfy its ever-increasing wants. By tying consumption to the family, the guardians of public order hoped not only to stimulate but to civilize it. Their confidence that new standards of comfort would not only promote economic expansion but level class distinctions, bring nations together, and even abolish war is impossible to understand unless we remember that it rested on the domestication of ambition and desire.

A liberal society that reduced the functions of the state to the protection of private property had little room for the concept of civic virtue. Having abandoned the old republican ideal of citizenship along with the republican indictment of "luxury," liberals lacked any grounds on which to appeal to individuals to subordinate private interest to the public good. But at least they could appeal to the higher selfishness of marriage and parenthood. They could ask, if not for the suspension of self-interest, for its elevation and refinement. Rising expectations would lead men and women to invest their ambitions in their offspring. The one appeal that could not be greeted with cynicism or indifference was the appeal later summarized in the twentieth-century slogan, "our children: the future" (a slogan that made its appearance only when its effectiveness could no longer be taken for granted). Without this appeal to the immediate future, the belief in progress could never have served as a unifying social myth, one that kept alive a lingering sense of social obligation and gave self-improvement, carefully distinguished from self-indulgence, the force of a moral imperative.

In one of the notes made early in the course of his American travels, Alexis de Tocqueville spoke of a "sort of refined and intelligent egoism" as the "pivot on which the whole machine turns"; and he went on to ask himself just "how far . . . the two principles of the good of the individual and the good of the whole really coincide." In *Democracy in America*, Tocqueville repeatedly emphasized the importance of religion and family life as a counterweight to acquisitive individualism. In a commercial society, "men cannot be cured of the love of riches," he observed, but religion might persuade them "to enrich themselves by none but honest means," to value the "natural bonds and legitimate pleasures of home," and thus to discover that an "orderly life is the surest path to happiness." These views were not Tocqueville's alone; they were shared by the prison reformers, educators, and humanitarians on whom Tocqueville relied for many of his impressions of America. In describing himself as a "new kind of liberal," Tocqueville described all those who believed that economic individualism could be safely liberated from mercantilist constraints only if it was disciplined by the inner constraints associated with organized "benevolence" and above all by new modes of "family governance."

Horace Mann, frightened by the Chartist agitation in England and by the possibility that European social extremes were re-creating themselves in America, voiced a pervasive concern when he argued that any system of "political economy . . . which busies itself about capital and labor, supply and demand, interest and rents, favorable and unfavorable balances of trade; but leaves out of account the element of a wide-spread mental development, is nought but stupendous folly." Progress and civilization had "increased temptations a thousand-fold" while doing away with the "fiery penal codes" and the "blind reverence for authority" that had formerly kept them in check. The "race for wealth, luxury, ambition, and pride" had been thrown "open to all" and the most depraved impulses given "full liberty and wide compass." Mann predicted that unless "internal and moral restraints" replaced the "external and arbitrary ones" now ineffective, "the people, instead of being conquerors and sovereigns over their passions," would become "their victims and their slaves."

For liberals like Mann, it was the rapid development of "benevolent" institutions, even more than material improvements, that distinguished progressive societies from backward societies like the American South. In the northern United States, in contrast to the South, progress proclaimed itself, according to Theodore Parker, in the spread of "societies for the reform of prisons, the prevention of crime, pauperism, intemperance, licentiousness and ignorance, . . . educational societies, Bible societies, peace societies, societies for teaching Christianity in foreign and barbarous lands, . . . learned and philosophic societies for the study of science, letters and art." The free states alone, Parker insisted, concerned themselves with the "improvement of the humbler and more exposed portions of society, the perishing and dangerous classes thereof." The voluntary associations on which Tocqueville pinned his hopes for democracy served, as Parker's list makes clear, to discipline the acquisitive impulse. In effect, they served as extensions of the family and were often quite explicitly conceived as such, as when Thomas Hopkins Gallaudet, founder and superintendent of the Hartford Asylum for the Deaf and Dumb, argued that the school ought to be "intimately connected with [the] family state" and to model itself on "government . . . of the parental kind." A "well organized family state," Gallaudet explained, was the basis of social order, which rested not on the "dread of human laws" but on "religious and moral principle," on "early associations of thought and feeling," on "habits formed in childhood and youth," on the "power of imitation," and on the "commanding influence of example in those who exercised authority over the mind in the early stages of its existence."

There is no need to belabor the familiar point that reverence for maternal "influence" and the domestic virtues stood at the very center of middle-class morality. What has to be emphasized, in the face of the equally familiar claim that the nineteenth-century "cult of domesticity" served only to enforce the patriarchal subordination of women and to subject the lower classes to "social control," is that it had progressive, not reactionary implications, since a well-ordered family life allegedly generated the demand for improvements that assured the unlimited expansion of capitalist production. The "cult of domesticity" was part of the rationale for reforms designed to alleviate poverty, shorten the hours of labor, and raise the working class out of the brutalizing conditions of mere subsistence. A Massachusetts bookbinder, pleading for the eight-hour day in 1870, pointed out that "a multiplication of happy homes around the city, would stimulate all industry, and greatly increase the exchange of products. . . . As people are elevated and improved in body and mind, the wants of body and mind are multiplied. On this simple fact depend all trade, prosperity and wealth."

Theodore Parker's recital of the expanding effects of home consumption can stand as a definitive statement of these "plain principles of political economy," as the bookbinder called them. Elaborating on the contrast between Southern backwardness and Northern improvement, in his famous "Letter on Slavery," Parker pointed out that

in Connecticut, every farmer and day-laborer, in his family or
person, is a consumer not only of the productions of his own
farm or handiwork, but also of tea, coffee, sugar, rice, molasses,
salt, and spices; of cotton, woolen, and silk goods, ribbons and
bonnets; of shoes and hats; of beds and other furniture; of
hardware, tinware, and cutlery; of crockery and glassware; of
clocks and jewelry; of books, paper and the like. His wants
stimulate the mechanic and the merchant; they stimulate him
in return, all grow up together; each has a market at home, a
market continually enlarging and giving vent to superior
wares.

Machine production, Parker continued, facilitated the distribution of
comforts and conveniences "more widely than ancient benefactors dared
to dream. What were luxuries to our fathers, attainable only by the rich,
now find their way to the humble home." Class distinctions were further
weakened by the progress of "science, letters, religion," while trade broke
down national barriers and fostered peace. "The soldier yields to the
merchant. . . . The hero of force is falling behind the times; the hero of
thought, of love, is felt to deserve the homage of mankind."

Elsewhere Parker endorsed the conventional view that women, "far in
advance of man" in their "moral feeling, affectional feeling, religious
feeling," were the principal source of the refinements in taste and sensibility associated with the democratization of consumption. Arguing for
woman suffrage, Parker attributed to the growing influence of women
the recognition that "government is political economy—national housekeeping." It was the influence of women, again, that undermined the old
authoritarian ideas about children, which embittered family life and encouraged parents, instead of intelligently providing for their needs, to
regard them as little monsters of depravity. No woman, Parker declared,
"would ever have preached the damnation of babies new-born." Only
"celibate priests," ignorant of paternity, could have "invented these
ghastly doctrines." Such statements make it clear the domestic values
were an essential component of progressive ideology, not just a sentimental gesture to man's "better half," offered in lieu of real equality and
respect.

It is true that the domestic ideal could easily be reduced to the sentimental commonplace that "almost every man of extensive influence," in

the words of a popular manual for young women, ". . . became what he was through maternal influence." But it does not seem fanciful to conjecture that the doctrine of maternal influence commended itself, to an enterprising and forward-looking people, largely because it served to assure them that moral and material progress went hand in hand. "Woman is the mother of the race," explained Julia Ward Howe, a prominent feminist. ". . . In all true civilization she wins man out of his natural savagery to share with her the love of offspring, the enjoyment of true and loyal companionship." Faith in the civilizing power of women made it possible for the nineteenth century to believe that enlightened self-interest would find its characteristic expression not in a ruthless pursuit of the main chance, much less in "luxury" and fashionable dissipation, but in family feeling—in the determination of conscientious parents to provide their children with opportunities unavailable to themselves.

Henry George on Progress and Poverty

· ■ ·

In the long run, of course, it was a lost cause, this attempt to build up the family as a counterweight to the acquisitive spirit. The more closely capitalism came to be identified with immediate gratification and planned obsolescence, the more relentlessly it wore away the moral foundations of family life. The rising divorce rate, already a source of alarm in the last quarter of the nineteenth century, seemed to reflect a growing impatience with the constraints imposed by long-term responsibilities and commitments. The passion to get ahead had begun to imply the right to make a fresh start whenever earlier commitments became unduly burdensome. Economic progress also weakened the economic foundations of Gallaudet's "well ordered family state." The family business gave way to the corporation, the family farm—more slowly and painfully—to a collectivized agriculture ultimately controlled by the same banking houses that had engineered the consolidation of industry. The agrarian uprising of the 1870s, 1880s, and 1890s proved to be the first round in a long, losing struggle to save the family farm, enshrined in American mythology, even today, as the sine qua non of a good society but subjected in practice to a ruinous cycle of mechanization, indebtedness, and overproduction.

The same changes that weakened the family threatened to reverse the trend toward economic equality, on which believers in progress had counted so heavily. Farmers, artisans, and craftsmen became wage slaves; more than any other development of the nineteenth century, including even the Civil War, the reconstitution of a degraded proletariat in the land of plenty—a permanent class of men and women without property—cast doubt on the agreeable assumption that limitless and irreversible innovation would annul the old cycle of growth and decline. Yet the republican idiom that might have enabled Americans to make sense of these reversals had begun to decay from disuse, and those who tried to revive it found themselves ridiculed as cranks and visionaries. Henry George's *Progress and Poverty*, a curious mixture of republicanism and "scientific" history, reached thousands of readers, both in the United States and in Europe, but remained suspect among the learned.

Even those who were moved by George's moral passion found him something of an eccentric, and this feeling, I believe, derived not only from his lack of academic training in economics and his commitment to the "new Jerusalem" of the single tax, as John Jay Chapman called it, but from his old-fashioned, seemingly naive and unsophisticated way of thinking about historical time. John L. Thomas, a sympathetic historian, deplores the "fascination with catastrophe" that intruded itself into *Progress and Poverty*. Henry George unfortunately shared the "fin de siècle obsession with cataclysm," according to Thomas; his speculations about what he called the law of human progress were "essentially ahistorical."

George's offense, it appears, lay in his insistence that the theory of continuous progress—the "hopeful fatalism" that "now dominates the world of thought"—was contradicted by the "rise and fall of nations," the "growth and decay of civilizations." George did not deny that "we of modern civilization" stood "far above those who . . . preceded us." What he denied was that the achievements of modern civilization could be attributed to improvements now "permanently fixed in mental organization." History, he thought, did not support the "current view" that "improvement tends to go on unceasingly, to a higher and higher civilization." The modern world owed its wealth and power to the transmission of skills and knowledge from one generation to the next; but the delicate mechanism of cultural transmission had broken down many times in the past and could easily break down in the future. The process could not be likened to heredity; for "even if it be admitted that each wave of progress had made possible a higher wave and each civilization passed the torch to a greater civilization," it was never the old civilization that built in this way on the foundations of its past but a "fresh race coming from a lower level." One advance did not lead smoothly and continuously to the next. "Over and over again, art has declined, learning sunk, power waned, population become sparse, until the people who had built great temples and mighty cities, turned rivers and pierced mountains, cultivated the earth like a garden and introduced the utmost refinement into the minute affairs of life . . . lost even the memory of what their ancestors had done, and regarded the surviving fragments of their grandeur as the work of . . . the mighty race before the flood."

When civilizations died, much "hard won progress" died with them; only a small part of it was transmitted to their conquerors. The earth was "the tomb of the dead empires, no less than of dead men." Growth and decay were not merely the general rule but the *"universal rule."* Any theory of history therefore had to account for "retrogression as well as for progression," and George proceeded to argue that specialization and the accumulation of wealth steadily widened the gap between the rulers and the ruled; that advanced civilizations accordingly had to devote more and more of their resources to the maintenance of an idle ruling class; that they finally collapsed, top-heavy, under their own weight; and that inequality and mass poverty, in short—the inevitable accompaniment of civilization, as George maintained in the famous title of his treatise, which called attention to the organic unity of poverty and progress— furnished the key that unlocked the "law" of advance and decline.

Naive and unsophisticated? *Progress and Poverty* was "ahistorical," it seems to me, only in its last-minute assurance that reforms prompted by an understanding of the "law of human progress," available for the first time now that George himself had explained it, would save modern civilization from the fate of its predecessors. In his analysis of the central issue—whether industrial societies would find a way to arrest the growth of inequality—George showed himself far more astute than his critics, who minimized the difficulties in achieving a more equitable distribution of wealth. He did not subscribe either to the right-wing illusion that prosperity would somehow trickle down to the masses or to the left-wing illusion—common to Marxism, to Edward Bellamy's "Nationalism," and to the several varieties of social democratic reformism—that the concentration of economic power had laid the foundations of a new order in which the masses would simply expropriate the collectivized forces of production and use them for the common good. George understood that collectivization is equally disastrous whether it occurs under capitalism or under socialism. Whatever can be said against his own ideal—a world of small proprietors, based on common ownership of land—at least it did not pretend to reconcile democracy and republican institutions with the social conditions that "compel every worker to seek a master."

George was not alone in his attempt to revive an understanding of the "law of civilization and decay," as Brooks Adams called it. By 1895, when Adams published his own version of the cyclical view of history, Americans had more reason than ever to worry about the future. As the simple market economy of the early nineteenth century gave way to an industrial economy elaborately organized on an international scale, small producers fell victim to corporate monopolists, farmers were forced off the land, and workers struggled without much success against the brutalizing effects of modern mass production. The Populist movement gave a political direction to many of the same apprehensions that troubled Henry George and Brooks Adams, including the fear that a growing concentration of power in the hands of investment bankers would not only impoverish the masses and reduce democratic institutions to empty forms but choke off the sources of creative energy in American culture, inaugurating a vulgar cult of success. *The Law of Civilization and Decay* might have become part of a searching discussion of the choices still open to America at the end of the nineteenth century. Instead, like the Populist movement itself, it was either brushed aside as a cranky, ineffectual protest against a future the country had no choice except to embrace or selectively absorbed (with considerable assistance from Adams himself) into the new imperialist rhetoric that upheld overseas expansion as a means of reviving the martial spirit.

Even those who admitted that Adams's "powerful" and "melancholy" book contained a "very ugly element of truth," as Theodore Roosevelt wrote in a long review, refused to take seriously the possibility that a further development of industrial civilization, along the lines already laid out, might lead in the long run to ruin. Nor could they accept the proposition that industrialism inevitably led to inequality. The idea that yeomen farmers were helpless in the hands of the moneylenders, Roosevelt said, was "really quite unworthy of Mr. Adams, or of anyone above the intellectual level of Mr. Bryan, Mr. Henry George, or Mr. Bellamy."

Still, the transformation of farmers and craftsmen into proletarians, the accumulation of huge private fortunes, the corporate domination of government, and a growing acceptance of the cynical wisdom that politicians were either criminals or fools indicated that apprehensions about the drift toward "imperatorship and anarchy," as Henry George referred to it, were not misplaced. The acquisition of territorial possessions overseas offered another sign, not only to radicals and Populists but in this case to a considerable body of eminently respectable opinion, that the republican phase of American history had come to an end. The debate about the Spanish-American War and the annexation of the Philippines was one of the last occasions on which the old language of republicanism figured prominently in public affairs. Opponents of annexation stressed the choice between "republic and empire," in the words of George S. Boutwell, president of the Anti-Imperialist League. They foresaw a standing army, the age-old "menace and terror of popular government." They reminded the country of the republican truism that a "standing army means a reduction of wages." According to Moorfield Storey, imperialism also meant a "great increase of wealth and fresh fields for corruption," the "spoils system enormously extended," and the "growth of a class little accustomed to respect the rights of their inferiors." Acquisition of the Philippines represented a momentous departure from the country's founding principles, the beginning of an all too familiar decline from republican simplicity into imperial corruption. History was repeating itself, anti-imperialists believed: the American people, like so many people before them, were about to exchange their liberties for the fatal promise of foreign conquest and military grandeur.

Inconspicuous Consumption, the "Superlative Machine"

There were good reasons, then, for the "fin-de-siècle obsession with cataclysm" that has troubled historians. The subsequent development of industrial civilization does not justify the assumption that the modern world is exempt from the "law of civilization and decay." If the nineteenth century's confidence in scientific laws of history now looks quaint and unsophisticated, its apprehensions about the future seem reasonable enough. If we peel away the pseudo-scientific pretensions with the help of which writers like Henry George and Brooks Adams hoped to get a hearing, we find a solid core of historical realism, and the question no longer presents itself as one of puzzling out subjective reasons for an otherwise unaccountable "obsession" with impending doom. The question is not why the new industrial and imperial order inspired premonitory visions of its decline and fall but why those misgivings were so quickly submerged in a renewed celebration of progress.

The reassertion of the old republican myth of historical cycles might have led to a reassertion of republican principles in politics, education, and social thought—a rededication to the ideal of citizenship that had played such an important part in the nation's founding. Instead, the idea of democracy came to be associated more and more closely with the prospect of universal abundance. America came to be seen as a nation not of citizens but of consumers. The association of progress with consumption, however much it compromised a participatory conception of democracy, enabled Americans to rehabilitate progressive ideology and to place it on a new and seemingly solid foundation.

Adam Smith had already pointed the way; and the impulse to return to Smith—his rediscovery by progressive economists and sociologists otherwise critical of laissez-faire economics—sheds a good deal of light on the intentions underlying the progressive movement of the early twentieth century. For the influential sociologist Albion Small, Smith was the founder of modern sociology, a farsighted moralist and social theorist who refused to separate "technical economics" from "social philosophy." If Smith had lived until the end of the nineteenth century, Small thought, his political opinions would have resembled those of a modern social democrat more closely than those of Herbert Spencer. Smith would have welcomed the effect of democracy "in setting free the physical and mental and moral energies of wage-earners," since it increased the demand for goods and led to a general improvement in the standard of living. Smith's followers, especially Spencer, had given liberalism a bad name, and its rehabilitation, accordingly, demanded a return to its eighteenth-century origins.

Small's unexpectedly admiring appraisal of Smith expressed the essence of the progressive strategy: to recapture the democratic potential of capitalism itself and thus to forestall demands for more radical change. Small insisted that if nineteenth-century liberals had "cultivated the whole philosophy of their teacher, instead of an abstracted section of it"—economic theory lifted from its "necessary moorings" in *The Theory of Moral Sentiments*—"much of the occupation of socialistic sectarians would have been gone." Something of the same reasoning could be applied to the idea of progress, so much more vulnerable to criticism, it appeared, in its nineteenth-century Spencerian form than in the form given it by Smith. When Henry George attacked the "prevailing belief" that "natural selection . . . operates to improve and elevate the powers of man," it was Spencer's theory, after all, that he had chiefly in mind—the notion that "the struggle for existence . . . impels men to new efforts and inventions" and that this "capacity for improvement is fixed by hereditary transmission." But progressive theorists like Small and Simon Patten no longer had to depend on Spencer; they scrapped Spencer's social Darwinism and revived the theory of progress, in effect, in its original version.

Patten's widely acclaimed treatise, *The New Basis of Civilization*, argued quite explicitly that the emergence of a "pleasure or surplus economy" effectively nullified the "ancient tragic model" of civilization and decay. "The story of the rise and fall of nations, repeated again and again, seems to justify the familiar conclusion that the decline of a society after an epoch of prosperity is a natural, incontrovertible law." But "those who would predict to-morrow's economic states from a study of the economic states of Rome or Venice" overlooked the unprecedented abundance made possible by the modern productive system, which placed civilization on a "new basis." Their apprehensions belonged to a "vanishing age of deficit." Thus Henry George and his followers maintained that "good lands and advantageous sites are scarce, and that multitudes are degraded by the pressure forcing them downward to poor locations." On the contrary, man's "dominion over nature" put an end to the "reign of want," according to Patten. "The social surplus is the superlative machine brought forth in the machine age for the quickening of progress."*

---

*By the time of the First World War, according to Guy Alchon, it had become a commonplace, especially among those who favored "managed capitalism" as an alter-

Patten's optimism required the corollary assumption, directly opposed to the linkage of poverty and progress insisted on by George and Adams, that the growth of inequality could be reversed. Like Smith (whose work he nowhere acknowledged, probably because he shared the common misperception of Smith as another "philosopher of deficit"), Patten saw inconspicuous consumption—the "broadened consuming power of the poor," not the lavish spending of the privileged classes—as the motor of social improvement. If poverty starved desire, riches led too quickly to satiation. Neither "sumptuary idleness" nor "hunger, disease, and stagnant misery" enlivened the imagination and generated a demand for improvements. The promise of abundance could be realized only by an energetic program of reform designed to reduce social extremes. It was essential, Patten thought, that the "stragglers of industry, the guerrillas of the subsistence line," be "incorporated" into the "steady ranks of disciplined producers." The "extension of civilization downward" demanded the demolition of the "social obstacles which divide men into classes." Workers had to be seen as potential consumers entitled to an "emotional corrective of the barren industrial grind." Consumption would expand their "wants" and create the "possibility of choice"—including the choice of deferred gratification over immediate indulgence. Their "investment in tomorrow's goods" would make it possible for "society to increase its output and to broaden its productive areas."

Both the progressive movement and the New Deal drew heavily on this kind of thinking, which linked progress to the democratization of consumption and held out the promise of a new civilization based on leisure for all. The same machines that admittedly took the meaning out of work would make it possible to "reduce hours of work and days of work to the lowest minimum," in the words of Patten's student and protégé, Rexford Tugwell, a leading theorist of the New Deal. Those who suffered from "historic homesickness," as Tugwell called it, might lament the decline of craftsmanship, but "the gains seem to most people . . . to outbalance the

---

native both to socialism and to laissez-faire, that the "enormous increase in the productive powers" of capitalism had "called into question the entire range of assumptions made under conditions of scarcity."

losses." Mechanization would enable workers to "find relief from otherwise intolerable conditions in higher wages, more leisure, better recreation." Only a "nostalgic" attachment to the work ethic and other obsolete ideals obscured the "prospect of final release from labor." With Patten, Tugwell believed that the coming age of abundance demanded a "new morality"—in Patten's more colorful formulation, one that challenged the cultural prestige of martyrdom and self-sacrifice, the "philosophy of development through pain," and the moral "art of wretchedness."

The second phase of the New Deal brought the political philosophy of consumerism to its fullest public acceptance. The early New Deal, with its "planned scarcity in agriculture" and its "collusive controls in industry," gave "priority to production over consumption," as Horace Kallen, Tugwell, and other consumerists pointed out. After 1935, however, the Roosevelt administration listened more attentively to Keynes and the Keynesians, made serious efforts to improve mass purchasing power, and even took a few halting steps toward the full-blown consumerist community contemplated by enthusiasts like Kallen. All of capitalism's ills, Kallen thought—the whole problem of social justice—could be reduced to the failure to see the worker as a consumer. The glorification of the producer—economic man—had thwarted the eighteenth-century promise of capitalism. The Declaration of Independence had recognized the primacy of consumption when it upheld the right to life, liberty, and the pursuit of happiness. So had Adam Smith, who rightly took the position that "consumption is the sole end and purpose of all production," in Kallen's words. But these eighteenth-century insights had been forgotten, Kallen argued. "The farther [economists] are from Adam Smith, the more dominantly is their theme the producer.... Marx, the revolutionist, is even more deeply absorbed in him than John [Stuart] Mill, the traditionalist." Under the influence of Marx, Ruskin, and other false prophets, the labor movement adopted as its favorite slogans the "dignity of labor" and the "right to work." "Labor was lifted up from a menial necessity into a free man's dignity" and its "inherent indignities" and "servility" mistakenly attributed to the exploitation of one class by another.

Only when men and women came to see work in its true light, Kallen thought—as a necessarily disagreeable means to the "good life"—would they organize it in such a way as to minimize its importance, to relegate it to the periphery of social life, and to install consumption in its place as the chief end of social existence. Instead of disparaging the "consummative appetite," society needed to honor it and to understand that leisure, hitherto confined to the wealthy, could "without conflict be extended to all employees."

The Keynesian Critique of Thrift

· ■ ·

The Keynesian theory of savings and investment provided the intuitions of consumerists like Patten, Tugwell, and Kallen with a fully developed theoretical rationale. Trained by the eminent economist Alfred Marshall, who claimed to have discovered new formulas to explain why capitalist economies were self-regulating, Keynes eventually broke with the neoclassical school and came to side with the "brave army of heretics" led in his own country by liberal publicists like John A. Hobson. As early as 1889, Hobson challenged the orthodox consensus that savings and investment went hand in hand. Too much saving, according to Hobson, led to underconsumption and declining investment. "In appearing to question the virtue of unlimited thrift," he later wrote, "I had committed the unpardonable sin." Like Henry George, he found himself ostracized by academic economists. Keynes alone understood that "flair" and "instinct" had led Hobson "toward the right conclusion." He himself could not be content, however, to rely on instinct. Having been "brought up in the citadel" of orthodox economics, he "recognized its power and might." He refused to "rest satisfied" until he could identify the "flaw in that part of the orthodox reasoning that leads to the conclusions which seem to me unacceptable."

The flaw, in effect, lay in the failure to reckon with the economic consequences of inequality, specifically with the "psychological law that when income increases, the gap between income and consumption will increase." Since the wealthy could spend only a small portion of their vast incomes, their disproportionate share of the national wealth meant that aggregate savings rose disproportionately as national income increased. A higher volume of savings did not generate a higher volume of investment. It led to a decline of aggregate demand, declining investment, and unemployment. A "somewhat comprehensive socialization of investment," Keynes concluded, would "prove the only means of approximation to full employment." Government spending would put people to work, stimulate consumption, and forestall the need for a more radical attack on the problem of inequality. It would provide an alternative to a redistribution of income, in other words, even if many businessmen still found it difficult to distinguish "novel measures for safeguarding capitalism from what they call Bolshevism."

Orthodox economists had exaggerated the value of thrift, according to Keynes. They thought of the "accumulated wealth of the world as having been painfully built up out of [the] voluntary abstinence of individuals from the immediate enjoyment of consumption," when it should have been "obvious that mere abstinence is not enough by itself to build cities or drain fens." The expectation of profits, not abstinence, was the "engine that drives enterprise." Profits in turn presupposed a rising standard of living in the population as a whole and a general desire for a more abundant existence. Thrift was a miserly virtue, as Keynes saw it, appropriate only to conditions of scarcity. Money was meant to be spent, not hoarded. It had no value in itself. The morality of saving and hard work betrayed a lack of faith in the future, whereas "enterprise" required "animal spirits" and optimism. Keynesian theory elaborated the discovery already proclaimed by the advertising industry in the 1920s, that "prosperity lies in spending, not in saving," in the words of Earnest Elmo Calkins, one of the first advertisers to grasp the principle of "artificial obsolescence."*

---

*A Keynesian *avant la lettre,* Calkins distinguished between goods "we *use*" and "those we *use up.*" Whereas Adam Smith had argued that economic expansion would be impelled by a growing demand for "things more durable" than the wasteful pleasures of the wealthy, Calkins interpreted the revolution of rising expectations as a demand for goods designed to be "used up" as quickly as possible. "Artificial obsolescence" meant the continual redesign of products, "entirely apart from any mechanical improvement, to make them markedly new, and encourage new buying, exactly as the fashion designers make skirts longer so you can no longer be happy with your short ones." The taste for "better things," as another advertising executive pointed out, thus demanded an "ideal of beauty . . . which happens to be current." No doubt Keynes had a more exalted ideal of beauty in mind when he welcomed the liberation of aesthetic appreciation from puritanical repression. But it was not always easy to distinguish the

In 1928, seven years before the appearance of his *General Theory of Employment, Interest, and Money,* Keynes predicted, in a lecture on "Economic Possibilities for Our Grandchildren," that abundance would bring the work ethic into discredit. "We shall be able to rid ourselves of many of the pseudo-moral principles which have hag-ridden us for two hundred years, by which we have exalted some of the most distasteful of human qualities into the position of the highest virtues." In the future, the acquisitive impulse—"the love of money as a possession, as distinguished from the love of money as a means to the enjoyments and realities of life"—would be recognized as a "somewhat disgusting morbidity, one of those semicriminal, semipathological propensities which one hands over with a shudder to the specialists in mental disease."

Abundance, Keynes thought, would assure a "decent level of consumption for everyone" and make it possible to devote "our energies" to the "noneconomic interests of our lives." Automation would eliminate drudgery, reduce the hours of work, and provide men and women with plenty of leisure. The economic virtues would be relegated to a subordinate place in the hierarchy of values; art and learning would come into their own. The idea that the state should confine its attention to "utilitarian and economic" questions would be recognized as the "most dreadful heresy, perhaps, which has ever gained the ear of a civilized people." Now that the world was no longer haunted by the specter of scarcity, it was possible to appreciate the importance of the state's patronage of art and education, the role it might play in raising the general level of taste. "The day is not far off," Keynes wrote in 1924, "when the economic problem will take the back seat where it belongs, and . . . the head and the heart will be occupied . . . by the real problems—the problems of life and human relations, of creation and behavior and religion."

The "behavioral" problems Keynes had in mind included "birth control and the use of contraceptives, marriage laws, the treatment of sexual

---

dictum of G. E. Moore, one of Keynes's early mentors—that the "pleasures of human intercourse and the enjoyment of beautiful objects" represented the highest goods—from the gospel of advertisers who vowed to help people "to enjoy life" and "to make living worthwhile."

offenses and abnormalities, the economic position of women, the economic position of the family." As a feminist, a bisexual, a Malthusian, and a champion of the sexual revolution, Keynes repeatedly insisted that "the problem of population," as he put it in 1921, was "going to be not merely an economistic problem, but in the near future the greatest of all political questions." The "principles of pacifism and population or birth control" represented the "prolegomena to any future scheme of social improvement." War and conquest, like the economic virtues of thrift and deferred gratification, belonged to the age of scarcity. So did the patriarchal oppression of women—the most striking instance of the failure of morals to keep pace with economic change. Under conditions of scarcity, women were valued chiefly as breeders, and the work ethic invaded even the most intimate relations, subjecting sexual pleasure to the duty of procreation. Rigidly defined norms of masculinity and femininity discouraged sexual experimentation. In their private lives, people no longer paid much attention to the old prohibitions, so obviously unsuited to conditions of abundance; but the official morality remained harsh and repressive. "In all these matters the existing state of the law and of orthodoxy is still medieval—altogether out of touch with civilized opinion and civilized practice and with what individuals, educated and uneducated, say to one another in private."

Civilized opinion, as Keynes understood it, demanded an expansion of the range of private choice. The notion of duty was outdated; one's highest duty was to oneself. When Keynes applied for exemption from military service, in 1916, he based his appeal on his right of private judgment. He did not argue the justice or injustice of England's war against Germany or the justice of war in general. He argued simply that conscription represented an intolerable infringement of his personal freedom of choice. He objected, he said, to surrendering his "liberty of judgment on so vital a question as undertaking military service." The British government granted Keynes a deferment, no doubt because he was more useful in the Treasury than in the army, without granting the substance of his argument. A government willing to recognize his "right of decision" as a general principle would not have been able to govern even in peacetime.

Whether Keynes considered the broader implications of his position is unclear; if pressed, he would probably have argued that only a handful of gifted individuals would ever force the issue in this way. His views of conscription, like his views of everything else, were colored by his sense of himself as a member of a select circle of supremely enlightened, unconventional men and women whose intelligence and sensitivity exempted them from ordinary standards. "He had no egalitarian sentiment," wrote his first biographer, Roy Harrod. ". . . In morals the first claim upon the national dividend," in his judgment, "was to furnish those few, who were capable of 'passionate perception', with the ingredients of what modern civilization can provide by way of a 'good life.' "

As a student at Cambridge, Keynes found his element in the Apostles, a coterie of "immoralists," as he later described them, who "repudiated entirely customary morals, conventions, and traditional wisdom." The Bloomsbury set, which grew up around this undergraduate nucleus, self-consciously set out "to establish on French lines a society fit for the discerning minority," in the words of another biographer, Charles H. Hession. In a memoir written in the 1940s, Keynes acknowledged Bloomsbury's snobbery and "superficiality, not only of judgment, but also of feeling." He never modified his belief that civilization was a product of the "personality and the will of a very few," but he now took the position, having lived through two world wars and a global economic crisis, that civilization was altogether more "precarious" than he and his companions had been willing to admit in the confident years before World War I. "We were amongst the last of the Utopians, or Meliorists, . . . who believe in a continuing moral progress by virtue of which the human race already consists of reliable, rational, decent people, . . . who can be safely released from the outward restraints of convention and traditional standards and inflexible rules of conduct."

Keynes's memoir was slightly equivocal. Was the vision of men and women released from outward constraints—the essence of liberalism and the core of the belief in progress—wholly misguided or merely premature? When Keynes questioned the assumption that humanity "already" consisted of individuals who could dispense with convention, he left open the possibility that it might consist of such individuals in the long run. He went on to argue, however, that he and his contemporaries had "completely misunderstood human nature, including our own." Their "irreverence" for "traditional wisdom or the restraints of custom" derived from an excessive confidence in reason. "It did not occur to us to respect the extraordinary accomplishment of our predecessors in the ordering of life ... or the elaborate framework which they had devised to protect this order."

Keynes's theory of "abundance through full employment," as Hession notes, gave "new life to the old ideology of progress and national economic growth." At the same time, his belated appreciation of tradition brought to the surface, if only as an afterthought, a persisting undercurrent of uneasiness in progressive ideology. It was as if the idea of progress required as a kind of counterpoint an exaggerated and slightly sentimental "reverence" for the "restraints of custom." Keynes was neither the first nor the last exponent of progress to rediscover the value of "outward restraints" and "traditional standards" that his own work helped to undermine. But no other career exemplified the contradictory implications of progressive ideology quite so clearly: its assault on convention and its retrospective defense of convention; its theoretical commitment to democracy and its emotional aversion to democracy; its eagerness to assure the widest possible distribution of the good things in life and its deepseated suspicion that most people were incapable of appreciating them. Keynes attacked the old ethic of thrift and saving head-on, by attempting to show that it was objectionable on economic as well as moral grounds. Yet he could not suppress the nagging reservation that an ethic of enjoyment might be incapable of eliciting the "religious" enthusiasm that capitalism required in its struggle with communism.

In *A Short View of Russia* (1925), Keynes spoke of his revulsion from a "creed which ... exalts the boorish proletariat above the bourgeoisie and the intelligentsia." But the bourgeoisie and the intelligentsia, even though they embodied the "quality of life" and carried the "seeds of all human advancement," lacked the spirit of self-subordination. "Modern capitalism is absolutely irreligious, without internal union, without much public spirit, ... a mere congeries of possessors and pursuers." Where could it find new sources of spiritual vitality? Keynes had no answer to this question except to say that "if irreligious capitalism is ultimately to defeat religious communism, it is not enough that it should be economically more efficient—it must be many times more efficient." With considerable ingenuity, Keynes proceeded to argue, in his *General Theory*, that capitalism could become "many times more efficient" not by calling on the people for sacrifices, as the communists did, but precisely by rejecting the principle of sacrifice as a drag on "enterprise." The possibility remained, however, that a willingness to make sacrifices on behalf of some higher cause itself served an important human need, one that would be systematically thwarted in the age of abundance.

Optimism or Hope?

The attraction of progressive ideology, at least in its liberal version, thus turns out to be its greatest weakness: its rejection of a heroic conception of life. The concept of progress can be defended against intelligent criticism only by postulating an indefinite expansion of desires, a steady rise in the general standard of comfort, and the incorporation of the masses into the culture of abundance. It is only in this form that the idea of progress has survived the rigors of the twentieth century. More extravagant versions of the progressive faith, premised on the perfectibility of human nature—on the unrealized power of reason or love—collapsed a long time ago; but the liberal version has proved surprisingly resistant to the shocks to easy optimism administered in rapid succession by twentieth-century events.

Liberalism was never utopian, unless the democratization of consumption is itself a utopian ideal. It made no difficult demands on human nature. It presupposed nothing more strenuous in the way of motivation than intelligent self-interest. Horace Kallen spoke for most liberals when he deplored the "stupidity of the lordly men who are moved by self-interest, but not of the enlightened variety," in whose minds the worker therefore "ceases to figure as a consumer at all." He could still assume that a combination of governmental coercion and rational persuasion would either bring these unenlightened employers to their senses or lead to their replacement by a more intelligent class of employers. It was obvious to him, just as it had been obvious to Adam Smith, that almost everyone had a stake in increased productivity, higher wages, shorter hours of work, and a more creative use of leisure. Capitalism had "raised the general standard of living, . . . transformed scarcity into abundance, awakening wants where none had been before, multiplying few into many, bringing more and more varied goods to more people at lower prices, so that what had been formerly, if at all, available only to a few

. . . was now in reach of many of those who had produced much and consumed little." It remained only to complete the capitalist revolution by making the "blessings of leisure" available to all. No improvement in mental capacity was required in order for the desirability of this goal to be generally recognized; nor did its realization require altruism and self-sacrifice—only a willingness to subordinate short-term pleasures to long-term peace and prosperity.

But if humanity thrives on peace and prosperity, it also needs an occasional taste of battle. Men and women need to believe that "life is a critical affair," in Richard Niebuhr's words. They cannot be satisfied merely with the opportunity to choose their goals and "life-styles," in the current jargon; they need to believe that their choices carry serious consequences. In the Christian cosmos, the forces of good and evil waged a mighty struggle for man's soul, and every action had to be weighed in the scales of eternity. Communism endowed everyday actions with the same kind of cosmic significance, as Keynes and many others understood. In 1940, George Orwell made the same point about fascism. The Western democracies, he observed, had come to think that "human beings desire nothing beyond ease, security, and avoidance of pain." Whatever else could be said about it, fascism was "psychologically far sounder than any hedonistic conception of life." Hitler knew that men and women wanted more than "comfort, safety, short working-hours, hygiene, birth control." "Whereas socialism, and even capitalism . . . have said to people, 'I offer you a good time,' Hitler has said to them, 'I offer you struggle, danger, and death,' and as a result a whole nation flings itself at his feet."

In the same year, Lewis Mumford offered an analysis of the "sleek progressive mind" that could easily have been written by Orwell himself. Progressives, according to Mumford, believed that human nature is deflected from its natural goodness only by external conditions beyond the individual's control. Having no sense of sin, they discounted inherent obstacles to moral development and therefore could not grasp the need for a "form-giving discipline of the personality." They scorned the discipline gained through manual labor, the endurance of discomfort, and the nurture of the young. They sought to free mankind from all manner of hardship and adversity, from the boredom of domestic drudgery, and from natural processes in general. Societies based on progressive principles, Mumford wrote, renounced every larger goal in favor of the "private enjoyment of life." They had created a race of men and women who "deny because of their lack of experience that life has any other meanings or values or possibilities." Such people "eat, drink, marry, bear children and go to their grave in a state that is at best hilarious anesthesia, and at its worst is anxiety, fear, and envy, for lack of the necessary means to achieve the fashionable minimum of sensation."

Confronted with this kind of indictment, progressives usually reply that discipline and adversity are all very well for those who can take a certain level of material security for granted but that impoverished masses can hardly be expected to listen to such appeals. Until everyone enjoys a decent standard of living, material improvement will therefore remain the overriding objective of democratic societies. The trouble with this argument is that political pressure for a more equitable distribution of wealth can come only from movements fired with religious purpose and a lofty conception of life. Without popular initiative, even the limited goal of a democratization of comfort cannot be realized. The favored few cannot be expected to consult the needs of the many, even if their own interests may be served, at least in the long run, by raising the general level of consumption. If the many now enjoy some of the comforts formerly restricted to the few, it is because they have won them through their own political efforts, not because the wealthy have freely surrendered their privileges or because the market automatically assures abundance for all.

Popular initiative, however, has been declining for some time—in part because the democratization of consumption is an insufficiently demanding ideal, which fails to call up the moral energy necessary to sustain popular movements in the face of adversity. The history of popular movements, including the civil rights movement of the fifties and sixties—the last such uprising in American history—shows that only an arduous, even a tragic, understanding of life can justify the sacrifices imposed on those who seek to challenge the status quo.

The idea of progress alone, we are told, can move men and women to sacrifice immediate pleasures to some larger purpose. On the contrary, progressive ideology weakens the spirit of sacrifice. Nor does it give us an effective antidote to despair, even though it owes much of its residual appeal to the fear that its collapse would leave us utterly without hope. Hope does not demand a belief in progress. It demands a belief in justice:

a conviction that the wicked will suffer, that wrongs will be made right, that the underlying order of things is not flouted with impunity.* Hope implies a deep-seated trust in life that appears absurd to those who lack it. It rests on confidence not so much in the future as in the past. It derives from early memories—no doubt distorted, overlaid with later memories, and thus not wholly reliable as a guide to any factual reconstruction of past events—in which the experience of order and contentment was so intense that subsequent disillusionments cannot dislodge it. Such experience leaves as its residue the unshakable conviction, not that the past was better than the present, but that trust is never completely misplaced, even though it is never completely justified either and therefore destined inevitably to disappointments.

If we distinguish hopefulness from the more conventional attitude known today as optimism—if we think of it as a character trait, a temperamental predisposition rather than an estimate of the direction of historical change—we can see why it serves us better, in steering troubled waters ahead, than a belief in progress. Not that it prevents us from expecting the worst. The worst is always what the hopeful are prepared for. Their trust in life would not be worth much if it had not survived disappointments in the past, while the knowledge that the future holds further disappointments demonstrates the continuing need for hope. Believers in progress, on the other hand, though they like to think of themselves as the party of hope, actually have little need of hope, since they have history on their side. But their lack of it incapacitates them for intelligent action. Improvidence, a blind faith that things will somehow work out for the best, furnishes a poor substitute for the disposition to see things through even when they don't.

---

*Some such conviction kept alive the hope of emancipation among slaves in the antebellum South, as Eugene D. Genovese and other scholars have made clear. It would be absurd to attribute to the slaves a belief in progress, on the grounds that they hoped for the promised land of freedom. It was Christianity, Genovese argues, that "gave them a firm yardstick with which to measure the behavior of their masters, to judge them," and to articulate a "promise of deliverance as a people in this world as well as the next."

3

NOSTALGIA: THE ABDICATION OF MEMORY

Memory or Nostalgia?

If the idea of progress has the curious effect of weakening the inclination to make intelligent provision for the future, nostalgia, its ideological twin, undermines the ability to make intelligent use of the past. Seemingly at odds, these attitudes have a good deal in common. For those nourished on the gospel of progress, idealization of the past appears to exhaust the alternatives to a tiresome and increasingly unconvincing idealization of the future.

Just as we should reject the thoughtless equation of progress and hope, so we need to distinguish between nostalgia and the reassuring memory of happy times, which serves to link the present to the past and to provide a sense of continuity. The emotional appeal of happy memories does not depend on disparagement of the present, the hallmark of the nostalgic attitude. Nostalgia appeals to the feeling that the past offered delights no longer obtainable. Nostalgic representations of the past evoke a time irretrievably lost and for that reason timeless and unchanging. Strictly speaking, nostalgia does not entail the exercise of memory at all, since the past it idealizes stands outside time, frozen in unchanging perfection. Memory too may idealize the past, but not in order to condemn the present. It draws hope and comfort from the past in order to enrich the present and to face what comes with good cheer. It sees past, present, and future as continuous. It is less concerned with loss than with our continuing indebtedness to a past the formative influence of which lives on in our patterns of speech, our gestures, our standards of honor, our expectations, our basic disposition toward the world around us.

The barrier that divides the past from the present, as it appears to the nostalgic sensibility, is the experience of disillusionment, which makes it impossible to recapture the innocence of earlier days. From this point of view, the relation of past to present is defined above all by the contrast between simplicity and sophistication. Nostalgia finds its purest literary expression in the convention of the pastoral, with its praise of simple country pleasures. The charm of pastoralism lies, of course, not in the accurate observation of country life but in the dream of childlike simplicity and security. Pastoral evokes a world without work, marriage, or political intrigue—the carefree world of childhood, in effect. Since it makes no claim to depict rural life as it is, it can hardly be faulted for its lack of realism. "It would be tedious," C. S. Lewis says, to explain to those who object that "real country people are not more happy or more virtuous than anyone else" the many good reasons "that have led humanity to symbolize by rural scenes and occupations a region in the mind which does exist and which should be visited often." Lewis's defense of pastoralism recalls Karl Mannheim's defense of utopia: without ideal images of a better world, whether it is located in the past or in the future, our own world would no longer contain either "meaning of life," in Mannheim's words.

The Pastoral Sensibility Historicized
and Popularized

· ■ ·

Although the pastoral convention always drew on images of a golden age, it did little to shape perceptions of history, precisely because it did not pretend to locate the Arcadian idyll anywhere else than in the imagination. In "A Discourse on Pastoral Poetry," Alexander Pope urged that it be kept as artificial and fanciful as possible. The contrast between town and country, moreover—even if anyone took it to refer to actual social conditions—was spatial rather than temporal; and it was only when the contrast began to be historicized, in the eighteenth and nineteenth centuries, that nostalgia began to color the way men and women thought about the historical past.

Before that time, historical speculation was dominated, to be sure, by conceptual schemes (classical or Christian) that tended to equate historical change with degeneration, as we have seen; yet it would be a mistake to call them nostalgic. Neither the Christian call to repentance nor the republican appeal to former glory encouraged people to seek refuge from the present in thoughts of the past; nor did the austere ideal of personal conduct shared by both these traditions have much in common with a cult of idyllic simplicity that took for granted the impossibility of its attainment. Christian and republican views of history implied a program of moral renovation. Imaginary visits to Arcadia, on the other hand, left the visitor refreshed but otherwise unchanged, resigned to the weary world as it was and by no means completely dissatisfied, indeed, with a world the sophistication of which alone made it possible to appreciate untutored simplicity. The celebration of rustic felicity was never intended for rustics. It could be savored only by people of refinement who did not seriously propose, after all, to exchange the advantages of breeding and worldly experience for a life close to nature, no matter how lyrically they sang nature's praises. Nostalgia, in its pastoral form at least, was a luxury only the favored could afford to indulge, just as their spiritual descendants indulge a taste for handmade goods in a world dominated by machine production.

The transformation of historical consciousness in the eighteenth and nineteenth centuries not only historicized nostalgia but democratized it as well. The pastoral convention declined with the decline of aristocracy, but the pastoral mood became far more pervasive than before, now that the town-country contrast appeared to define successive stages of historical development.* Urbanization reflected the growth of commerce, more efficient systems of production and distribution, rising standards of comfort, a rapid increase in the circulation of knowledge—progress, in short, the other side of which appeared to lie in the loss of an earlier simplicity. Since progress affected everybody, drawing people to the city in larger and larger numbers, it created a broad new audience for a metropolitan literature more explicitly retrospective than pastoralism, one that concerned itself not with an imaginary rural retreat but with an actual historical process (as people had come to think of it), the eradication of unspoiled nature by the irresistible forces of progressive change.

It is the assumption that those forces were irresistible that links nineteenth-century agrarian nostalgia to the pastoral tradition and explains why a lament for the vanishing countryside could so easily coexist with the celebration of historical progress, just as the praise of pastoral scenes had coexisted with an appreciation of the fashionable refinements of the court. For middle-class metropolitan readers, the charm of the old agrarian order lay principally in the unlikelihood that any part of it would survive the onslaught of industrialism. The pastoral legacy, transferred now to the pseudo-debate between advocates of progress and those who

---

*The pastoral genre played off idyllic images of country life not so much against the city as against the court—a further indication that it was addressed to a sophisticated, aristocratic audience. It was against the artifice, intrigue, affectation, and insincerity of the court that the artless love play of shepherds and milkmaids appeared so engaging by contrast. When the country came to be seen from the point of view of the city as such, nostalgic depictions of country life began to pay more attention to the social conditions said to be characteristic of the village and the countryside—the absence of envy and resentment, the reciprocal solicitude of rich and poor, the organic solidarity of neighbors. "In country towns," wrote an Englishwoman in 1868, "the gentry and the poor are far less separate than in great cities, and the local interest and local work serve to unite class and class. . . . A small sphere throws men of different classes closely together, and creates a bond of fellowship utterly unknown to the inhabitants of a great city."

idealized the rural past, made it impossible for either side to see, as Raymond Williams notes in his study of this debate, that a "rural economy simply had to persist," in one or another form, even in the "developed metropolitan countries." The long literary controversy between town and country was a pseudo-debate because both sides agreed on the central premise, as Williams puts it, that "the rural experience, the working country, had gone; that in Britain it was only a marginal thing, and that as time went by this would be so everywhere." Williams himself accepted this assumption, he says, "for much longer than now seems possible," until he finally came to understand that the "common idea of a lost rural world" not only rested on a hopelessly abstract view of historical processes but implied an equally misleading view of the future, "in which work on the land will have to become more rather than less important and central." But this kind of common sense unfortunately played no part either in the literature of lost country life or in the ostensibly opposing literature of progress and development.*

---

*In *The Country and the City* (1973), Williams rejected both the "retrospective radicalism" that idealized a lost golden age of English agriculture and the socialism of "certain metropolitan intellectuals," with its celebration of capitalism as a progressive force (hence the necessary preparation for socialism), its ridicule of the "idiocy of rural life" (as Marx called it), and its assumption of a unilinear global progress toward a culmination foreshadowed by the megalopolitan civilization of the industrialized nations. "Between the simple backward look and the simple progressive thrust there is room for long argument but none for enlightenment. We must begin differently," Williams argued—with history, which dissolves the notion of "traditional society" common to both the idyllic and the progressive interpretations of the rural past.

Reviewers praised Williams's book but paid no attention to its contention that agriculture would have to become more important in the future and that the split between the country and the city could be overcome only by resisting both of the stereotypes that dominated the old debate. Instead they saw Williams as another uprooted intellectual unsuccessfully attempting to recover his rural past—a "transitional man," according to Allan Goldfein, who knew the "agony of separation from roots, the conflict of values, the hesitant (and certainly guilt-provoking) adoption of urban ways, the sense of loss of the past." Marshall Berman found the book "incisive and luminous," "admirably honest and courageous," "full of insight and beauty." It had "emotional unity and momentum," according to Berman. As this kind of praise indicates, however, Berman judged the book in purely aesthetic terms and lost sight of its argument. He trivialized the issues at stake by reducing them to personal issues. Williams could not

Images of Childhood:
From Gratitude to Pathos

· ■ ·

The Romantic movement, the first outcry of protest against the new age, captured its sense of historical dislocation in images contrasting the countryside and the city, innocence and experience, the vanishing world of "springing pastures" and "feeding kine," in the words of Matthew Arnold's "Scholar Gypsy," and the metropolis with "its sick hurry, its divided aims, its heads o'ertaxed, its palsied hearts"—"this strange disease of modern life." In an "age of change," as John Stuart Mill called it in his 1831 essay "The Spirit of the Age," the "idea of comparing one's own age with former ages" had for the first time become an inescapable mental habit; Mill referred to it as the "dominant idea" of the nineteenth century. For some, the "spirit of the age" was altogether odious; for others, "a subject of exultation"; but the important point, as Mill noted with great insight, was that the issue should be joined in these terms at all. "The 'spirit of the age,' " he added, "is . . . a novel expression, no more than fifty years old."

Once the pastoral vision came to be associated with an actual period of historical time—with the allegedly flourishing or at least familiar and manageable agrarian society that was beginning to be destroyed by indus-

---

claim to have reestablished a connection with the land, Berman insisted, just because he now lived on a farm. "Even if his farm and his work on it are real, there is something unreal about what it means to him. . . . It can never be his life." His allusions to his own experience did not "quite ring true." After all, he had left the north of England by choice—not because he was dispossessed by grasping landlords or capitalists but because he needed to go to the city if he was to get an education and to make a career as a writer. "For a man dispossessed, Williams has done pretty well for himself"—a Cambridge professorship, a series of highly acclaimed books. "The knot that bound him to the land, and to his past, has been cut and he himself has helped to cut it. To believe that he can tie it again now . . . is to create yet another form of pastoral—and another mystification. Like the rest of us, Williams must live with his nostalgic yearning; the green fields of his childhood . . . are forever beyond his reach." Thus Berman forced the discussion back into the very categories from which Williams had tried to rescue it.

trialism—it was probably inevitable that those living in Mill's "age of transition" should discover in their own recollections of childhood the most compelling image of lost innocence. The nineteenth century "shifted onto the child . . . the obscure tradition of pastoral," as William Empson has observed. Rousseau had already "laid down" the "incontrovertible rule that the first impulses of nature are always right; there is no original sin in the human heart." In *Emile*, he struck a note that was to be sounded again and again. "Love childhood, indulge its games, its pleasures, and its lovable nature. Who has not looked back with regret on an age when laughter is always on the lips and when the spirit is always at peace?" Childhood provided Rousseau, Wordsworth, Blake, Charlotte and Emily Brontë, Dickens, Hardy, Lewis Carroll, and innumerable lesser talents with a haunting vocabulary of loss that could be exploited for social criticism as well as for poetry and fiction or, trivialized and sentimentalized, for pious moralizing about the happy fate of those who die young.

Literary exploration of childhood, ranging from Wordsworth's solemn rapture to the sentimentalism of J. M. Barrie, helps to clarify the distinction between nostalgia and a more active type of remembrance that seeks to grasp the past's formative influence on the present. Samuel Taylor Coleridge contrasted the healing power of a "joyful and tender" memory with the dismissive attitude to the past that leads men to "laugh at the falsehoods that were imposed on themselves during their childhood"; but his remarkably astute analysis of the difference between them applies with equal force to the nostalgic attitude, another way of dismissing the past. Those who remember childhood only as a time when they were "imposed on," Coleridge wrote—and also those who remember it, we might add, as a time of blissful innocence untroubled by self-conscious reflection—

are not good and wise enough to contemplate the Past in the Present, and so to produce by a virtuous and thoughtful sensibility that continuity in their self-consciousness, which nature has made the law of their animal life. Ingratitude, sensuality, and hardness of heart all flow from this source. Men are ungrateful to others only when they have ceased to look back on their former selves with joy and tenderness. They exist in fragments, annihilated as to the Past, they are dead to the future, or seek the proofs of it everywhere, only not (where alone they can be found) in themselves.

Writing in 1809, Coleridge singled out Wordsworth as the poet who had "exprest and illustrated this sentiment with equal firmness of thought and feeling." Wordsworth himself spoke of his work as an attempt to explore the "fructifying," "vivifying," or "renovating virtue" of memory.* Especially in *The Prelude*, he treated the immediacy of the child's experience of "fear and love" as the ground and basis of later experience, the source of mature insight; and it does not seem utterly implausible to suppose that rigorous, unsentimental attention to childhood memories served something of the same end in Wordsworth's Romanticism—notwithstanding all the obvious differences between the two traditions—that a celebration of founding fathers served in classical republicanism, opening thought to a sense of the gravity and joy of existence, more specifically to an awareness of its origins and its indebtedness to the past, and thus reawakening the capacity for devotion.†

---

*A demonstration of Wordsworth's fascination with memory would require a book in its own right. For our purposes, it is enough to note that the very structure of *The Prelude*—its plot, if you will—illustrates the triumph of early memories over the political "idolatry" to which Wordsworth succumbed in his enthusiasm for the French revolution as well as their capacity to sustain hope in the midst of the "melancholy waste of hopes o'erthrown" by the revolution's failure. Coleridge had urged Wordsworth to write a narrative poem "addressed to those, who, in consequence of the complete failure of the French Revolution, have thrown up all hopes of the amelioration of mankind, and are sinking into an almost epicurean selfishness, disguising the same under the soft titles of domestic attachment and contempt for visionary *philosophes.*" That Wordsworth's response should have been a work that celebrates the restorative force of memory seems to me to indicate a deepening of political understanding rather than a retreat from it, as so many have argued, or the assertion of an uncritical loyalty to Britain.

†This supposition gains support from Wordsworth's repeated identification of memory with "virtue." Thus he speaks of Sicily, where Coleridge was living at the time Wordsworth composed one of the many drafts of *The Prelude*, as a land strewn "with the wreck of loftier years" but "lost" to the "reanimating influence" of "memory"— "to virtue lost and hope." Here "virtue" retains its explicitly political connotations, as

Even when he spoke of the "paradise where I was reared" and contrasted the "race of real children" brought up close to nature with those brought up in "the perpetual whirl / of trivial objects," the dominant emotion in Wordsworth's early work was gratitude, not regret for innocence no longer accessible. It was an emotion, however—this "grateful acknowledgment" of "what was given me"—that Wordsworth found hard to sustain in verse; and it began to pass over, in the poem that eventually established itself as the popular favorite, *Intimations of Immortality,* into an elegiac mood that most of his admirers found more congenial, as it turned out—more familiar and hence reassuring, notwithstanding its evocation of loss—than the strenuous mood of *The Prelude.*

> *Whither is fled the visionary gleam?*
> *Where is it now, the glory and the dream?*

Though Wordsworth continued to insist,

> *We will grieve not, rather find*
> *Strength in what remains behind,*

the immortality ode conveyed the death of childhood more vividly than it conveyed the consolations available to a mature and "philosophic mind."* It was not altogether surprising, then, that the nineteenth cen-

---

well as its broader connotations (which seldom fail to accompany Wordsworth's use of the word) of vitality, animating force, and even virility. Elsewhere Wordsworth describes the inspiration the child draws from nature—more precisely, the memory of this inspiration—as a "breeze, that gently moved / With quickening virtue, but is now become / A tempest, a redundant energy, / Vexing its own creation." In still another suggestive passage, he characterizes the infant's sense of security, in its mother's arms, as a "virtue which irradiates and exalts" his surroundings and serves to "connect him with the world." It is the buried memory of primeval experiences of this kind that makes of "simple childhood something of the base" on which the "greatness" of man comes to rest.

*As Philip Davis observes, nineteenth-century readers paid more attention to the end of one stanza, in which the poet addresses the little child:

tury chose to idolize Wordsworth as the poet of "rapture now forever flown." Victorian writers, less and less interested in his conception of childhood memories as the "hiding-places of man's power," much less in his "rigorous inquisition" of those memories, turned the child, no longer "the Father of the Man," into a passive, incorruptible victim of adult domination. Wordsworth's subject, in *The Prelude* at least, was the means

> *Whereby this infant sensibility,*
> *Great birthright of our being, was in me*
> *Augmented and sustained.*

For the Romantic poets in general, innocence was "valuable for what it might become," as Peter Coveney aptly puts it. With the Victorians, however, the emphasis shifted "toward the state of innocence itself, not as a resilient expression of man's potential integrity, but as something statically juxtaposed to experience, and not so much static as actually in retreat."

This retreat found its definitive symbol in the deathbed scene, increasingly obligatory in novels aspiring to any sort of popularity, in which a child neglected, oppressed, or shamefully deserted by those who should have served as its protectors expires without a word of reproach—itself the ultimate reproach, this wordless acquiescence, both to adults directly responsible for such tragedies and to those who merely look on in sorrow. In the world of Victorian and post-Victorian melodrama, innocence had only one role: to die as heartrendingly as possible. Mrs. Henry Wood perfected the formula in *East Lynne* (1861), the most widely sold English

---

> *Full soon thy soul shall have her earthly freight,*
> *And custom lie upon thee with a weight*
> *Heavy as frost, and deep almost as life!*

than to the beginning of the next:

> *O Joy! that in our embers*
> *Is something that doth live,*
> *That nature yet remembers*
> *What was so fugitive.*

novel of the century: "Don't cry, papa. I am not afraid to go. Jesus is coming for me." But it was Marie Corelli, in *The Mighty Atom* (1896), who most fully revealed its significance when she asked "whether for many a child it would not have been happiest never to have grown up at all." She advised her readers not to "grieve for the fair legions of beloved children who have passed away in their childhood," since "we know, even without the aid of Gospel comfort, that it is 'far better' with them so." The idea that children are better off dead casts an unexpectedly lurid light on the nineteenth-century cult of childhood, which held children up to adoration but denied them any compellingly imagined possibility of development, in which early experience would continue to inform adult perceptions. An impoverished view of adulthood, this ostensibly sympathetic view of childhood also falsified the very thing it purported to celebrate, attributing to children Peter Pan's wish "always to be a boy and have fun," a wish that only jaded, embittered adults could have conceived.

The American West, Childhood of the Nation

· ■ ·

Jeremy Bentham, that indefatigable advocate of improvement, noted with approval that in his day the "wisdom of our ancestors" had become a "sarcastic jibe of hatred and insult," the world having learned the folly of idolizing the "wisdom of untaught inexperienced generations." A writer in *Household Words*, a magazine edited for a time by Charles Dickens, made the same point in the course of a diatribe against the worship of the past. "The older the world grows the more experience it acquires," and the "genuine good old times" were nineteenth-century times, not the days of yore. But these writers missed the point: a belief that the world had grown wiser did not prevent the modern world from looking back on less enlightened ages with fond regret. Idealization of the past had come to rest not on respect for ancestral wisdom but on the assimilation of the past to images of childlike innocence. The more emphatically the modern age insisted on its own wisdom, experience, and maturity, the more appealing allegedly simple, unsophisticated times appeared in retrospect. Progress implied nostalgia as its mirror image.

In the United States, this curious conjunction of "improvement" and regret gave the national imagination its distinctive flavor and furnished themes to which interpreters of American life returned again and again, with obsessive interest. As the most rapidly developing nation in the world, clearly destined for riches and power, America had the heaviest investment in the ideology of progress. Not only the country's material wealth but its commitment to the democratization of opportunity, required by theories of progress in order to become fully convincing, made it easy not only for Americans themselves but for foreign observers to see America as the wave of the future; yet Americans were notoriously given to recurrent fits of melancholy, evoked by the suggestion that some primal innocence, some "original relation to the universe," in Emerson's phrase, had been lost in the headlong rush for gold. Many observers were struck by a persistent streak of sadness in the American character, immediately recognizable, for example, in Abraham Lincoln, whose saturnine temperament as much as his racy humor, loose-knit frame, and shambling gait seemed to make him a fitting embodiment and symbol of his people.

American nostalgia, like the vision of irresistible and unlimited American expansion, centered on the West, the rapid settlement of which appeared to dramatize the march of civilization. "Westward the course of empire takes its way." According to a widely accepted way of looking at westward expansion, the rapid succession of historical stages, from the most primitive to the most advanced, recapitulated developments that elsewhere took centuries to complete. But the conquest and settlement of the continent made Americans deeply uneasy, even as it made them insufferably boastful and self-satisfied. The legend of Daniel Boone, the first of a series of explorers to be canonized in his own lifetime, illustrates this ambivalence. Timothy Flint, an early biographer, attributed to Boone the recognition that "this great [Ohio] valley must soon become the abode of millions of freemen; and his heart swelled with joy" at the thought, according to Flint. Yet Flint also told how Boone had been driven out of Kentucky "by the restless spirit . . . of civilization and physical improvement" and how, even in Missouri, "American enterprise seemed doomed to follow him, and to thwart all his schemes of backwoods retirement."

Evidently Boone had no great love for the civilization that pursued him so relentlessly, the expansion of which his own efforts had done so much to bring about. "I had not been two years [in Missouri] before a d——d

Yankee came, and settled down *within an hundred miles of me!!*" Other commentators filled in this portrait of Boone as a fugitive from the future. "As civilization advanced," wrote a reporter for the *New York American,* "so he, from time to time, retreated." A writer in the *North American Review* pictured him "happier in his log-cabin . . . than he would have been amid the greatest profusion of modern luxuries." Another biographer, however, implied a more approving view of progress in Boone's conception of himself—as apocryphal, no doubt, as all the other attitudes and sayings attributed to Boone—as a "creature of Providence, ordained by Heaven . . . to advance the civilization . . . of his country."

The novels of James Fenimore Cooper showed how the solitary hunter, unencumbered by social responsibilities, utterly self-sufficient, uncultivated but endowed with a spontaneous appreciation of natural beauty, could become the central figure in the great American romance of the West. As the heir to a landed fortune and baronial status, Cooper believed in the importance of law, order, and refinement; he could glorify Natty Bumppo and his faithful Indian companion Chingachgook (forerunner of Queequeg, Nigger Jim, and Tonto) only because they stood outside the pale of respectable society altogether and posed no threat to the social hierarchy. Cooper's sympathetic treatment of hunters and Indians, as Henry Nash Smith has pointed out, did not extend to yeoman farmers like Ishmael Bush, who stood on the lowest level of civilized society yet refused to defer to their betters. Clothed in the "coarsest vestments of a husbandman," Bush inspired apprehension and contempt. The farmer's hunger for land, as Cooper saw it, jeopardized the gentry's social and political ascendancy and embittered relations with the Indians, precluding peaceful settlement of Indian claims.

In the politics of the Jacksonian era, it was the genteel classes that opposed Jackson's policy of Indian removal and championed the rights of Indians, at the same time that they pressed for a national policy of economic development, promoted the growth of commerce and industry, and ridiculed the austere and to their mind regressive ideal, so dear to the Jacksonians, of a virtuous republic of small farmers. It should not surprise us, in view of the pastoral conventions that continued to inform the nineteenth-century celebration of untutored simplicity, that the nostalgic myth of the West was largely the creation of genteel writers like Cooper, Washington Irving, and Francis Parkman. Like the eighteenth-century myth of the noble savage, the romance of the wilderness appealed most of all to those farthest removed from frontier conditions, who took it for granted that the frontier was "essentially evanescent," in Irving's words, and for that reason would come to "seem like the fictions of chivalry or fairy tale."

Only a safe distance made it possible to idealize Indians or to portray them as philosophical critics of civilization. On his way to Oregon in 1839, Thomas J. Farnham interviewed a Dartmouth-educated Indian who told him that westward extension of agriculture would destroy the "single-minded honesty, the hospitality, honor and the purity of the natural state." This sounds more like the genteel primitivism of the comfortable classes, a primitivism more sophisticated than anything that could have been acquired even at Dartmouth, than the bitter resentment of white encroachment experienced by Indians—a resentment, of course, that periodically drove nature's noblemen to nasty, bloody reprisals. "As soon as you thrust the ploughshare under the earth, it teems with worms and useless weeds. It increases population to an unnatural extent—creates the necessity of penal enactments—spreads over the human face a mask of deception and selfishness—and substitutes villainy, love of wealth and power, and the slaughter of millions" for the Arcadian conditions that formerly prevailed.

Richard Slotkin, a student of the frontier myth, notes that Kit Carson's biographers gave him a "civilized man's sympathy for Indians." In life a brawling adventurer and gold seeker, Carson, like Boone, became a legendary figure with the attributes of a Leatherstocking—"one of the best of those noble and original characters who have sprung up on and beyond our frontier," according to one biographer, "retreating with it to the West, and drawing from association with uncultivated nature, not the rudeness and sensualism of the savage, but genuine simplicity and truthfulness of disposition, and generosity, bravery, and single-heartedness, to a degree rarely found in society." Charles Webber, a prolific author educated at Princeton Theological Seminary, resorted to the same kind of language in describing Texas cattlemen: "With them the primitive virtues of a heroic manhood are all-sufficient, and they care nothing for reverences, forms, duties, &c., as civilization has them, but respect each other's rights, and recognize the awful presence of a benignant God in the still grandeur of mountain, forest, valley, plain, and river."

A writer in the *Democratic Review* compared Webber's *Old Hicks, The Guide,* to Melville's *Typee* and *Omoo,* adding, however, that Webber's novel contained "more of earnestness and poetry." Melville's South Sea stories, with their repeated insistence that "the Polynesian savage, surrounded by all the luxurious provisions of nature, enjoyed an infinitely happier, though certainly a less intellectual existence than the self-complacent European," appealed to the same sophisticated primitivism that found expression in the more lyrical versions of the Western myth. That even such an original writer as Melville—a writer, moreover, temperamentally disposed to stress the darker side of things—found it difficult to write about the South Seas without invoking the conventions of pastoralism shows just how tenacious those conventions were, especially at a time when American authors still found it necessary to employ the ornate, euphemistic, and windy style deemed suitable for the well-bred man of letters.

> In a primitive state of society, the enjoyments of life, though
> few and simple, are spread over a great extent, and are unal
> loyed: but Civilization, for every advantage she imparts, holds
> a hundred evils in reserve;—the heart-burnings, the jealousies,
> the social rivalries, the family dissensions, and the thousand
> self-inflicted discomforts of refined life, which make up in
> units the swelling aggregate of human misery, are unknown
> among these unsophisticated people.*

An unsentimental literary treatment of the West—of the confrontation between savagery and civilization, the progress of "improvement," and its devastating impact on earlier ways of life—demanded an imaginative suspension of the self-consciously cultivated point of view and the development of a vernacular style, the "nervous lofty language" of *Moby Dick*

---

*Melville's list of civilized "discomforts" clearly derived from the pastoral tradition. Snobbery, social climbing, ostentation, backbiting slander, envy, suspicion, vanity, possessiveness, ambition, and the obsession with appearances were the classic targets of pastoral satire—the classic vices of court life, later generalized to urban civilization as a whole.

or the colloquial rhetoric of *Huckleberry Finn*, that would make it possible to understand the frontier not as an "evanescent" stage of social development but as an object of continuing fascination. These two books alone, among nineteenth-century novels, managed to escape the conventions of the wilderness myth by taking the myth itself as in some sense their subject: the energizing vision of escape to a realm of complete freedom, the megalomaniacal fantasy of self-sufficiency underlying it, its inevitable defeat, and the moral havoc released by its attempted realization.

Even *Huckleberry Finn* conceded more to the Western myth than Twain probably intended. As Slotkin says, it implied that the only alternative to a competitive, commercial society lay "in the personalities of young women, children, and childlike nonwhite races." Notwithstanding Twain's scorn for Cooper's "literary offenses" in sentimentalizing the frontier, *Huckleberry Finn* reproduced the central action if not the diction of the Leatherstocking novels: the flight of innocence in the face of civilization. That Twain was not altogether satisfied with Huck's final decision to "light out for the territory" may be indicated by his decision to undertake a sequel, *Among the Indians*, in which a realistic account of the Indian Territory would deflate the image of the noble savage and underline the impossibility of escape. That the sequel was never completed, or even fairly begun, indicates that a fully developed treatment of the Western theme, one that would explore the significance of the West not merely as a place but as a national memory, continued to elude Twain's grasp.

From Solitary Hunter to He-man

Toward the end of the nineteenth century, idyllic images of the West began to give way to a new set of images that reflected the nation's growing preoccupation with overseas expansion. The solitary fugitive from civilization no longer stood at the center of attention. Now it was the gunfighter, too busy with bad Indians and cattle thieves to commune with nature, who served as the hero of Western romance. He still shared with his predecessor the "primitive virtues of a heroic manhood," to recall Charles Webber's phrase, but it was no longer a "compliment," as Washington Irving had said in his account of Rocky Mountain trappers, "to persuade [a Westerner] that you have mistaken him for an Indian brave." For the Western hero in the age of American imperialism, the only good Indian was a dead Indian.*

Theodore Roosevelt's *Winning of the West,* published in the 1880s, illustrates the assimilation of the Western myth to expansionist ideology. True to its title, this bloodcurdling account of expansion in the old Southwest focused entirely on the warfare by means of which the wilderness was wrested from its original inhabitants. The issues that were beginning to enlist the interest of professional historians and cultural critics—the influence of the frontier on American character, its contributions to the growth of democratic institutions, the legacy of the pioneering mentality—interested Roosevelt not at all. Neither was he impressed by the image of the noble red man or the myth of the hunter's symbiotic union with nature. For Roosevelt as for Parkman, Owen Wister, and other exponents of the patrician ideology of martial prowess and overseas expansion, exposure to the hardships of the frontier was meant to provide a corrective to the demoralizing effects of comfort and overrefinement, a salutary taste of danger that would restore the fighting qualities requisite for statesmanship, diplomacy, and war. The fear of racial decadence haunted men like Roosevelt. The "Teutonic" element seemed to be losing its grip on leadership. Its absorption in business, its fastidious retreat from politics, its declining birthrate, above all its disinclination to go to war, as Roosevelt saw it, all betrayed a loss of manhood. Men with "small feet and receding chins" would prove no match for the cruder, more prolific peoples that were pouring into the country. *The Winning of the West* was a call to arms—a reminder that Scotch-Irish settlers had prevailed in fierce struggles against the Indians and could serve as an inspiration to those who faced a similar challenge to the continuing ascendancy of the old stock.

Owen Wister's enormously popular novel *The Virginian* helped to give

---

*There is a sense, of course, in which this phrase, without its brutality, also describes the position of Cooper and others among the early romancers of the West. As Slotkin points out, "Cooper never loves his Indians so much as when he is watching them disappear."

the new type of Western hero his distinctive characteristics—a touchy sensitivity to insult ("When you call me that, *smile!*"), a chivalrous regard for women masked by tongue-tied shyness, a proficiency with the pistol that spoke louder than words, a love of law and order combined with a willingness to fight outlaws by adopting their own methods. The genre of the "Western" dates from this turn-of-the-century transformation of the Boone-Bumppo archetype into the he-man. The formula established at the outset remained essentially unchanged in hundreds of novels, radio serials, movies, and comic strips. More unambiguously than Boone the advance agent of civilization, the gunfighter still rides off into the sunset when his work is done, unable to bear the constraints that come in the wake of his triumphs; but although he remains a loner, for whom marriage and a cottage covered with morning glories would be unthinkable, he serves only the settlers who stay behind, not the higher calling of nature. If he takes on the qualities of an outlaw, it is only to bring outlaws to book.

Transposed to the urban wilderness, this new-model Western hero becomes a tough cop sometimes forced to operate outside the law in order to circumvent the slow-moving machinery of formal justice, even to adopt criminal disguise in order to penetrate the secrets of the underworld. As a defender of freedom in foreign wars, he has to contend not only against the enemy, for whom he learns a grudging respect, but against military and civilian bureaucracies and against misguided peace lovers, ungrateful beneficiaries of his prowess, who weaken America's will to fight. No longer even-tempered by virtue of an intuitive appreciation of natural beauty, he becomes, in his latest incarnation as Rambo, a creature of pure rage, more savage in his righteous strength than the savages he pursues. In politics—for it is hardly to be expected that imagery so deeply embedded in popular culture would fail to shape perceptions of political leaders, even their own perceptions of themselves—some of his characteristics can be discerned in half-mythical figures like Joseph McCarthy, whose supporters excused his rough methods in the struggle against subversion on the grounds that it was dirty work but someone had to do it, and of course in the more genial person of Ronald Reagan, himself a veteran of the screen and therefore an ideal choice for the real-life reenactment of a role that sums up the chauvinistic, self-righteous, expansionist implications of Western mythology.

The close identification of Western themes with expansionism, in the twentieth century, did not completely extinguish the pastoral image of the West, often invoked by anti-imperialists against the glorification of conquest and hyper-masculinity. The legacy of Daniel Boone, Natty Bumppo, and Huck Finn lived on in American politics, in attenuated form, in the environmentalist movement's fixation on the preservation of wilderness (as opposed to a sensible balance, say, between industry and agriculture, or a more flexible technology); in the romantic cult of "third world" peoples, including the American Indian, as a counterweight to industrial technology; in young radicals' identification with Holden Caulfield, James Dean, Bob Dylan, and other self-conceived fugitives from adult repression, modern Huckleberry Finns; and in the continuing belief that women, children, and "people of color" (an old, condescending, and discredited expression oddly revived by the left in recent years) remain uncompromised by the exercise of power and therefore pure in heart. That images derived (however distantly) from a common source can be claimed by anti-expansionists and expansionists alike underscores the ambiguity that was always inherent in the westward movement, alternately conceived as the wave of the future and as a journey into the past.

The Village Idyll: The View from "Pittsburgh"

As a source of fresh images, however, the Western theme had already exhausted itself by the time of World War I, as is indicated by its formulaic repetition. The nostalgic imagination had to seize on other images, notably that of the elm-shaded small town. Mark Twain once said, during a visit to India, "All the *me* in me is in a little Missouri village half-way around the world." Like so many of Twain's sayings, this was ambiguous. Did it mean that he'd left his heart in Hannibal, or that Hannibal was the prelude to the rest of his life, the hiding place of his power as a man and writer, the "background"—as Sherwood Anderson later wrote on the last page of *Winesburg, Ohio*, where his protagonist, Chicago-bound, watches Winesburg recede into the distance—"on which to paint the dreams of his manhood"? Was Hannibal a memory or merely an imaginative refuge from adulthood? Twain's books wavered between these two approaches; but *Tom Sawyer,* the most popular by all odds, was clearly written in the idyllic mode, and its commercial success practically guaranteed that as the unspoiled wilderness began to lose its imaginative resonance, the small town would replace it as the most evocative symbol of lost childhood.

However "poor" and "shabby," the small town of *Tom Sawyer* was "bright and fresh and brimming with life"—"dreamy, reposeful, and inviting." Dreamy the image of small-town childhood remained in all its subsequent evocations, dimly seen through the Indian summer haze of burning leaves, twilit evenings on the front porch, deeply shaded streets on a summer afternoon, or gently falling snow. From the early novels of Booth Tarkington and Zona Gale right down to the latest television commercials, village life retained its timeless appeal, and even its debunkers found it impossible to maintain a consistently satirical tone. The same Anderson whose *Winesburg* helped to set the fashion for unsparing exploration of the small town's seamy underside later wrote *Home Town,* which held up "thinking small" as an alternative to the "false bigness" of 1940— "men speaking at meetings, trying to move masses of other men, getting a big feeling in that way." The small town looked more attractive to Anderson now that the "big world outside" was "so filled with confusion." Sinclair Lewis, the daddy of debunkers, celebrated homespun horse sense in his novel of the mid-thirties, *It Can't Happen Here,* in which a country editor deflates an aspiring dictator.

Even Theodore Dreiser found the small-town myth intermittently appealing, reaffirming it in his attempt to disavow it. Having "seen Pittsburgh," he explained, he could no longer weave village "charms and sentiments" into an "elegy or an epic." A visit to his fiancée's Missouri homestead reawakened memories of his own boyhood in Indiana and "enraptured" him with the "spirit of rural America, its idealism, its dreams," its belief in "love and marriage and duty and other things which the idealistic American still clings to." But a writer who had lived in the larger world, Dreiser argued, could not hope to memorialize the American village.

In fact, of course, it was precisely the disillusioning view from "Pittsburgh" that commended an elegiac treatment of small-town themes to writers less wholeheartedly committed to literary realism (although they too, many of them, could write realistically about small towns, even bitingly, whenever they chose). Dreiser may have rejected the elegiac mode for himself, but he shared the emotions and, more important, the preconceptions underlying it. In their apparent rejection of nostalgia, his observations on this point represent a classic statement of the nostalgic attitude.

> The very soil smacked of American idealism and faith, a fixedness in sentimental and purely imaginative American tradition, in which I, alas! could not share. . . . I had seen Lithuanians and Hungarians in their "courts and hovels," I had seen the girls of [Pittsburgh] walking the streets at night. This profound faith in God, in goodness, in virtue and duty that I saw here [in rural Missouri] in no wise squared with the craft, the cruelty, the brutality and envy that I saw everywhere else. [Small-town people] were gracious and God-fearing, but to me they seemed asleep. They did not know life—could not. . . . They were as if suspended in dreams, lotus eaters.*

---

*Compare Wordsworth's sharply contrasting account of his residence in London, which exposed him to the same depravity and squalor that horrified Dreiser but left his youthful ideals intact. If anything, those ideals shone more brightly, Wordsworth says, when set off "by this portentous gloom."

> *Neither vice nor guilt,*
> *Debasement undergone by body or mind,*
> *Nor all the misery forced upon my sight,*
> *Misery not lightly passed, but sometimes scanned*
> *Most feelingly, could overthrow my trust*
> *In what we may become; induce belief*
> *That I was ignorant, had been falsely taught,*
> *A solitary, who with vain conceits*
> *Had been inspired, and walked about in dreams.*

Dreiser's experience of the city made the world of his boyhood seem like a dream. Wordsworth's account, on the other hand, stressed the continuity of his experience and the moral and imaginative sustenance he continued to draw from "early feelings."

Confronted again with the world he had left, Dreiser endowed it with the dreamlike quality of suspended animation, notwithstanding his awareness that the impression of immobility may have derived not from actual events but from the "fixedness" of a "purely imaginative" tradition. In the American imagination, the small town never changes: it dreams on, in a world where everything else has changed, and for that reason an observer uprooted from those scenes, himself completely and irrevocably changed by acquaintance with the larger world, can no longer take part in its life or share its ideals. Note the crucial assumption that "idealism and faith" flourish only in a state of innocence. It is this assumption, so radically at odds with the view that childhood experience is the basis of mature conviction, that unavoidably gives rise to the nostalgic attitude in the first place. If a belief "in goodness, in virtue and duty" cannot survive exposure to experience, the past can be seen only as a lost Eden, where illusions alone sustain the capacity for belief—a lovely dream that had to die. In the words of Thomas Wolfe, another novelist torn between elegy and satire, equally unable to imagine any escape from this choice, you can't go home again.

The view from "Pittsburgh" precludes an imaginative reconstruction of the spiritual journey that began in Hannibal, Terre Haute, or Clyde, Ohio. The self-exiled son of the Middle Border can no longer recognize himself in memories of boyhood; he revisits them as a total stranger; and the literary convention that requires an outside observer of the village, at once protagonist and interpreter, as the central point of reference in its story, emphasizes the discontinuity between village and city, childhood and maturity. As Anthony Channell Hilfer notes in his study of the village theme, "The village, in order to be appreciated, had to be seen from the outside. After all, one of its virtues was its supposed lack of self-consciousness." Hence the need for a "narrator or spokesman who speaks from outside the village perspective." An apparent exception, the Stage Manager in Thornton Wilder's *Our Town*, proves the rule, according to Hilfer. For all his rustic pose and speech, the Stage Manager is one of us, the knowing urban audience; and his title, indeed, reminds us even more effectively than the device of the outside observer that the American village is an illusion stage-managed for the entertainment of sophisticated city slickers, object of a wistful yearning that can easily edge over into mockery but has little in common with the imaginative reinterpretation of past events.

Wilder's famous play—a triumph of sorts, in its absolute exclusion of any feeling except that of nostalgia—illustrates another convention of the small-town genre, the exclusion of incident. Nothing happens in our town. The play's three acts are entitled "Daily Life," "Love and Marriage," and "Death." Static, timeless, universal, the small town has no history. Accordingly the story of the small town can never become a story in the strict sense (unless it is the story of exile and aborted return). It has no plot, no conflicts, no resolution, no characters, and certainly no character development. Those things are ruled out by the dreamlike atmosphere of nostalgic reminiscence. Even "reminiscence" is too active a term to catch the mood evoked by this genre. Memory calls up actions and events; it seeks to reconstruct what happened. A world where nothing happens—where people are born, fall in love, marry, and die—cannot serve as a source of memories, loving, painful, or otherwise. Anyone who has ever come to a small town as a stranger, even if he has lived in similar towns before, knows that such towns are not interchangeable and that what the outsider finds hardest to penetrate, when he comes to a new place, are not its customs but its memories, its lore, its highly particularized narrative history, its hotly contested accounts of that history, its feuds and factions, its smoldering enmities and apparently irrational alliances. These are what unavoidably exclude the outsider and unite the insiders in spite of the most bitter disagreements. It isn't his alien manners but his lack of access to a common fund of memories that marks him as an outsider.

But the central significance of memory is just what is missing, most of the time, in the romance of the village, which in its insistence on the timeless recurrence of birth, marriage, and death has more in common with sociology than with historical narrative. Wilder's subheadings recall those of *Middletown:* "Getting a Living," "Making a Home," "Training the Young," "Engaging in Religious Practices," and so on. Sociological studies of the small town—an important genre in their own right—provide a kind of counterpoint and critique of the small-town romance, one that inverts its judgments but presents a similarly static view of the subject matter.

The only form of conflict, still unproductive of dramatic incident, that is allowed to enter the small-town story, in the words of a study of magazine fiction in the 1930s, is the "typical conflict . . . between the essential goodness of small-town types as opposed to a metropolitan moneyed elite; unpretentiousness against pretentiousness, and littleness versus power." Conflict within the village itself plays no part in nostalgic romance; the village stands united—"one big family," in words used both by Tarkington and by Anderson and doubtless by many others—against the outside world. Zona Gale, perhaps the first to use the cloying term "togetherness" in speaking of village life, drew on images of solidarity firmly established by the turn of the century. Anderson likened villagers in his first novel, *Poor White*, to the "members of a great family," in a passage that also insisted on the timeless quality of village life that Wilder sought to capture in *Our Town*. A "kind of invisible roof" sheltered the inhabitants, according to Anderson. "Beneath the roof boys and girls were born, grew up, quarreled, fought, and formed friendships with their fellows, were introduced into the mysteries of love, married and became the fathers and mothers of children, grew old, sickened, and died." Sociologists objected to this theme of solidarity and "togetherness" more strenuously than to any other feature of the small-town myth; they uncovered sharp class divisions and showed that small-town politics were usually dominated by a handful of wealthy families. Studies of "social stratification," however, did not alter the impression of immobility. If anything, the static concept of "stratification" and the sociological division of small-town society into upper, middle, and lower classes reinforced this impression and precluded any discussion of the shifting relations among these social groupings. Whether it was perceived as united or as badly divided, the small town remained changeless, its story—alternately imagined as sociological and satirical or as pastoral and elegiac—essentially a record of vital statistics.

Nostalgia Named as Such: The Twenties

Notwithstanding its long career in literature and popular culture, nostalgia was not always known by that name. Until the twentieth century, the term was confined to medical usage and referred strictly to a condition of acute homesickness recognizable as such by well-defined physical symptoms: loss of appetite, irregular breathing and sighing, gastroenteritis.

Johannes Hofer, a German physician, coined the term in 1678 when he found these symptoms highly developed among Swiss mountaineers removed to the lowlands. Well into the nineteenth century, Switzerland "continued to be recognized by all as the classic land of nostalgia," according to a survey of the medical literature; but the list of sufferers was gradually broadened to include students, soldiers, and domestic servants, groups uprooted from home and exposed to a type of suffering often likened to lovesickness. Psychological disorders were added to the list of symptoms; an 1879 treatise spoke of "ennui, eventually giving way to profound melancholia; an unnatural reserve and silence; complete indifference to the immediate surroundings; vague feelings of unrest; . . . tears; . . . an overwhelming desire to return home." Some authorities attributed to the Celts, as well as to the Swiss, an unusual propensity to nostalgia; the English, on the other hand, were judged too cosmopolitan to suffer in this way from residence away from home. In general, nostalgia appeared to be an affliction of naive, unsophisticated, unlettered peoples, and a few doctors argued for universal education as the only effective means of prevention.

Just when "nostalgia" lost its medical associations and came to refer to a sentimental view of the past is difficult to determine, but the new and broader usage was firmly established by the 1920s. The writings of F. Scott Fitzgerald, to cite only one of the more obvious sources, indicate that the feelings formerly associated with pastoralism, the celebration of the American West, and the myth of the small town were now assimilated quite self-consciously to the phenomenon of nostalgia. Fitzgerald refers to the hour of seven o'clock, the "soft and romantic time before supper," as a "nostalgic hour." Several times he mentions his "vast nostalgia," as a boy growing up in St. Paul, for the East, calling it the "country of my nostalgia." These passages, which identify nostalgia with the promise of romantic excitement, might seem to evoke expectation more than regret, except that Fitzgerald clearly believed—and this belief provides a recurrent theme, indeed the central theme in his work—that experience seldom lives up to its promise, that happiness never lasts, and that repeated disillusionments eventually erode the capacity for wonder (most movingly described in the closing pages of *The Great Gatsby*) and lead to "emotional bankruptcy." Fitzgerald's view of nostalgia is far from simple, and I can hardly do justice to it here, but it is enough for our present purposes to note that he employs the term to speak of lost innocence—more precisely, of lost hopes and of the collapse of the very capacity for hope.

For those who lived through the cataclysm of the First World War, disillusionment was a collective experience—not just a function of the passage from youth to adulthood but of historical events that made the prewar world appear innocent and remote. For the first time, a whole period of historical time began to take on the qualities formerly associated with childhood. Since those who experienced the war most directly as soldiers, ambulance drivers, and military prisoners were literally children before the war, it was natural for them to play off postwar disillusionment against idyllic images of prewar childhood. The fortuitous effect of chronology strengthened the tendency to equate personal and collective history and thus to make the historical past an object of what was now called nostalgia. For the generation born around 1900, the century's youth, prematurely cut off by the war, coincided with their own, and it was easy to see the history of the twentieth century as the life history of their own generation.

It is no accident that the concept of the generation first began to influence historical and sociological consciousness in the same decade, the twenties, in which people began to speak so widely of nostalgia. Karl Mannheim published his influential essay, "The Problem of Generations," in 1927. As Robert Wohl shows in *The Generation of 1914*, those who were young at the time of World War I identified themselves self-consciously as a generation marked by history, one formed by the shared experience of this catastrophic event, and many of them projected their experience backward and reinterpreted all of history as a conflict of generations. In the United States, the war helped to crystallize the rebellion of "Young America," which had already begun to emerge in the prewar writings of critics like Randolph Bourne and Van Wyck Brooks. After the war, generational images of revolt became popularized in the so-called revolution in manners and morals led by "flaming youth."

The principal spokesman for this youth movement in the twenties, of course, was Fitzgerald, whose characterizations of the "jazz age" not only gave it a spurious unity but connected the history of his own generation with the twentieth-century history of the whole country. Here again, Brooks had anticipated this kind of thinking in the title of his literary manifesto of 1915, *America's Coming-of-Age*, but it was Fitzgerald, more than any other writer, especially in stories and articles looking back on the jazz age after it was over, who imposed on popular culture his image of America in the twenties as a society undergoing a kind of protracted adolescence and painfully plunged into maturity by the Depression of 1929.

Writers in the twenties, including Fitzgerald himself, looked back on the prewar years as the period of lost youth, but in the Depression decade, the twenties themselves became an object of nostalgia. The decade of the twenties, according to Fitzgerald's valedictory account, was a time characterized by the "pathos of adolescence." It was therefore impossible to look back on the twenties without a mixture of yearning and embarrassment. As he wrote in *Scribner's*, in 1931,

> Now once more the belt is tight, and we summon the proper expression of horror as we look back at our wasted youth. Sometimes, though, there is a ghostly rumble among the drums, an asthmatic whisper in the trombones that swings me back into the early twenties when we drank wood alcohol and every day in every way grew better and better, and there was a first abortive shortening of the skirts, and girls all looked alike in sweater dresses, and people you didn't want to know said "Yes, we have no bananas," and it seemed only a question of a few years before the older people would step aside and let the world be run by those who saw things as they were—and it all seems rosy and romantic to us who were young then, because we will never feel quite so intensely about our surroundings any more.

This idealization of the twenties, even more than the twenties' own idealization of the prewar era as an age of innocence, marks a turning point in the history of nostalgia. For the first time, nostalgic sentiment—only recently named as such—directed itself not to generic images of childhood or to cultural symbols of childhood like the West or the small town but to a specific and carefully particularized period of historical time, a single decade at that. Those who lived during the twenties thought of themselves, at the time, as a bitterly disillusioned and cynical generation: but now, almost overnight, disillusionment and cynicism took on the "rosy romance" formerly directed to far more distant and immobilized images of the past. This instantaneous idealization of the jazz age suggests a shortening of historical attention, an inability to recall events beyond a single lifetime, which may help to explain another curious feature of the twentieth-century historical imagination: the growing inclination, among journalists, commentators on cultural trends, and even professional historians, to think of ten-year periods as the standard unit of historical time.

In the twenties and thirties, works of popular history began to focus on particular decades. Examples of this new genre included Meade Minnigerode's *Fabulous Forties,* Thomas Beer's *Mauve Decade,* Lewis Mumford's *Brown Decades,* and Frederick Lewis Allen's *Only Yesterday,* a history of the postwar decade that appeared in 1931 and contributed to the romance of the twenties. Mumford's study of the post–Civil War era, the best of these books, sheds light on the close connection between the new preoccupation with decades and the concept of generations. It opens with a riot of imagery in which the predominant color of the period is linked to the progression of seasons. "The Civil War shook down the blossoms and blasted the promise of spring. The colors of American civilization abruptly changed. By the time the war was over, browns had spread everywhere: mediocre drabs, dingy chocolate browns, sooty browns that merged into black. Autumn had come." Mumford goes on to draw certain parallels between the "brown decades" and the 1920s. In both cases, a disastrous war had cut off promising movements of cultural renewal and left people cynical and world-weary. After the Civil War, as in the twenties, the "younger generation had aged; and during the decade that followed the war, cynicism and disillusion were uppermost." It is for this reason, Mumford argues, that the "generation which struggled or flourished after the Civil War now has a claim upon our interest."

History as a Progression
of Cultural Styles

■

History had come to be seen as a succession of decades and also as a succession of generations, each replacing the last at approximately ten-year intervals. This way of thinking about the past had the effect of reducing history to fluctuations in public taste, to a progression of cultural fashions in which the daring advances achieved by one generation become the accepted norms of the next, only to be discarded in their turn by a new set of styles. The concept of the decade may have commended itself, as the basic unit of historical time, for the same reason the annual model change commended itself to Detroit: it was guaranteed not to last. Every ten years it had to be traded in for a new model, and this rapid turnover gave employment to scholars and journalists specializing in the detection and analysis of cultural trends.

As the communications industry expanded its influence over both scholarship and popular taste, the closely related concepts of decades and generations came more and more fully under the sway of fashion. Thus in 1950, *Life* magazine—a publication best understood not as a news magazine but as a fashion magazine, one of the first to show how news could be sold as a form of fashion—published a mid-century issue reviewing the entire period since 1900. Two long editorials, one by the historian Allan Nevins, the other by the cartoonist Bill Mauldin, exploited the generational theme. In "The Audacious Americans," Nevins wrote, "Bold experimentalism gave us five decades of dazzling achievement. That was our adolescence; now we have come to responsible maturity." From now on, the country would have to rely less on amateurism and experimentation and more on professionally organized expertise. Mauldin's editorial, which brought the issue to a close, defended the younger generation—the "scared rabbit generation"—against the charge that it was obsessed with security. The editorial ended with a cartoon bearing the caption, "Every generation has its doubts about the 'younger generation.' " The one thing that is certain in a world of flux, in other words, is that today's styles, today's attitudes, today's ideas will be outmoded tomorrow and that the older generation will regret their passing without being able to do anything about it.

The bulk of this special issue was devoted to a series of pictorial essays, executed with the polish for which *Life* was justly renowned. It is interesting to see which aspects of the fifty-year history of the century the editors chose to emphasize and which they chose to ignore. There was almost nothing about politics or diplomacy, except for a reminder that the cold war confronted Americans with a challenge to which only a mature people could rise. Economic history was reduced to the history of technology, itself treated as another branch of fashion in which yesterday's technology (horsepower) was bound to be superseded, like yesterday's fashions. The same went for yesterday's movie idols (Rudolph Valentino, Clara Bow), yesterday's sports heroes (Red Grange, Jack Dempsey, Bobby Jones), and yesterday's musical comedy—though the 1930s remained the "golden age of popular music." Articles on the New York Armory Show of 1913 and on more recent developments in the art world conveyed the same message: paintings that shocked the "smug and stifling calm" of the Edwardian age had now become part of the accepted modernist canon. An article on American women was illustrated by a series of fashion sketches, decade by decade, and by photographs of movie actresses and models. The history of women was thus derived entirely from changing modes of female beauty.

Articles entitled "Small Town Life" alternated with articles entitled "Acceleration of Science" and "Span of Life Grows Longer." An article called "High Society's High Jinks" depicted the activities of the Four Hundred in the "golden years before the war"—further characterized as a bygone age filled with an "adolescent spirit, boiling with the conflict between youthful naivety and mature sophistication that always marks adolescence in a man or a country. Looking back on that faraway and almost forgotten era, it takes on a soft, golden haze. . . ." Another article featured several pages of color photographs of the Vanderbilt mansions built around the turn of the century—"They Recall the Era of Opulence." Throughout the whole issue—and throughout almost every other issue of *Life* that ever reached the newsstands—a celebration of technological progress, in short, alternated with sentimental retrospect: and it is exactly this counterpoint that seems most clearly to characterize the historical imagination of our time. Looking back on the history of the twentieth century from our own vantage point, we see it as a series of decades and generations, each with its own label: the lost generation, the red generation, the silent generation of the forties and early fifties, the beat generation, the Age of Aquarius (or was it merely the Pepsi generation?), the me generation, the generation of the yuppies. Once history comes under the dominion of fashion, the past can be revived only in a "soft, golden haze." Thus outdated styles in popular music or dress periodically reappear as part of carefully contrived shifts in public taste. We know that earlier styles were taken seriously in their time, but we have lost the connecting thread between earlier times and our own. "When this older, more distant world is invoked," writes George Trow in an essay on mass communications fittingly entitled "The Context of No Context," it has no substance or meaning.

> It is made obvious [by the media] that this world is mystifying and too difficult to be comfortable with. One game-show host asked a question about the First World War and then described the First World War as "certainly a military event of considerable importance." He was assuring his audience that the First World War *was popular in its own day.*

Our collective understanding of the past has faltered at the very moment when our technical ability to re-create the past has reached an unprecedented level of development. Photographs and motion pictures and recordings, new techniques of historical research, the computer's total recall assault us with more information about history—and everything else—than we can assimilate. But this useless documentation no longer has any power to illuminate the present age or even to provide a standard of comparison. The only feeling these mummified images of the past evoke is that the things they refer to must have been interesting or useful once but that we no longer understand the source of their forgotten appeal.

Nostalgia Politicized

· ■ ·

Once nostalgia became conscious of itself, the term rapidly entered the vocabulary of political abuse. In societies that clung to the dogma of progress, no other term was more effective in deflating ideological opponents. Even before the term came into general currency, the style of argument to which it was so well suited had already become fairly familiar, even predictable. In 1914, an editorial writer in the *Nation* chided those who took the position that mass production degraded the working man by reminding them that modern industry led to a "steady shortening of the hours of labor" and created "wider opportunities of pleasure, of spiritual excitement and growth." Criticism of the factory rested on the "old fallacy of the Golden Age," a refusal to understand that "for the great mass," life in the Middle Ages—so often invoked as a standard of comparison—consisted of "crushing, brutalizing toil."

Ten years later, a critic of Lewis Mumford's book on American architecture, *Sticks and Stones,* made the same point when he accused Mumford of seeking to "escape from the consequences of modern life." The establishment of an "urban mechanical civilization" made "all talk of the handicraftsman returning" sentimental and "unveracious." By 1931, Mumford himself could fling the charge of nostalgia against Joseph Wood Krutch and other "mournful and slightly Victorian" critics of modern culture, who found the "soul of man under modernism in a state of uneasiness and exacerbation." These writers suffered, Mumford thought, from "nostalgia for tradition." A year later, John Dewey attacked the "idealizing nostalgia" of those who wished to return to the classical curriculum. Nostalgia had attained the status of a political offense of the first order.

After World War II, criticism of nostalgia figured prominently in the attempt to revive the idea of progress by divesting it of utopian overtones. Those who located the golden age in the past, it was argued, suffered from the same kind of ahistorical thinking that led others to locate it in the future. Change was inevitable and irreversible, and there was no more sense in pining for the past than in hoping that some future utopia would bring the process of change to an end. The attack on nostalgia thus served to deflect attention from more serious issues. Could a belief in progress really be sustained? Was the modern order permanently exempt from the fate of its predecessors? Did the two world wars amount to a European civil war that was destroying European civilization? Would Europe ever be the same again? If the light went out in Europe, would the darkness engulf America as well? Those who raised such questions now exposed themselves to the charge of nostalgia. Almost any criticism of modern society, in fact, could be discredited on these grounds.

Those who deplored nostalgia attributed its appeal to a crisis of nerve, an inability to face up to the realities of modern life. In 1948, Richard Hofstadter introduced his *American Political Tradition*—a book that left a deep imprint on postwar political and cultural debate—with a diatribe against Americans' escapist absorption in the past:

> Since Americans have recently found it more comfortable to see where they have been than to think of where they are going, their state of mind has become increasingly passive and spectatorial. Historical novels, fictionalized biographies, collections of pictures and cartoons, books on American regions and rivers, have poured forth to satisfy a ravenous appetite for Americana. This quest for the American past is carried on in a spirit of sentimental appreciation rather than of critical analysis. An awareness of history is always a part of any culturally alert national life; but I believe that what underlies the overpowering nostalgia of the last fifteen years is a keen feeling of insecurity. The two world wars, unstable booms, and the abysmal depression of our time have profoundly shaken national confidence in the future. . . . If the future seems dark, the past by contrast looks rosier than ever; but it is used far less to locate and guide the present than to give reassurance.

Hofstadter had good reason to complain of the "ravenous appetite for Americana." A more discriminating appraisal of the cultural preoccupations of the thirties and early forties, however, might have distinguished between the sentimental Americanism of the Popular Front, say, and the introspective mood of James Agee's *Let Us Now Praise Famous Men;* between Margaret Mitchell's sentimentalized version of the old South and the more critical appreciation by Allen Tate; between the celebration of nineteenth-century literary history in the later writings of Van Wyck Brooks and the more astringent but still respectful treatment of the subject by Mumford, Waldo Frank, and F. O. Matthiessen; between the cloying treatment of regional themes by Carl Sandburg and their more probing treatment by Robert Frost; between the lifeless restorations at Williamsburg and the indigenous architectural style developed by Frank Lloyd Wright or Bernard Maybeck; between *Appalachian Spring* and *Okla-*

homa. An aggressive, undiscriminating modernism that dismissed all these works as retrograde and politically reactionary—and most of them were subjected at one time or another to this kind of attack, if not by Hofstadter then by like-minded literary critics in *Partisan Review*—left no alternative to nostalgia except a cosmopolitanism wholly contemptuous of American popular culture.

Hofstadter's attack on "Americana" was open to the additional objection that it was internally inconsistent—as it had to be, if it was to enable sophisticated observers of the cultural scene to dismiss resistance to change as irrational, to equate loving memory with escapism, and to shore up a faltering faith in the future without explaining why such a faith was justified. Having attributed the "overpowering nostalgia of the last fifteen years" to a crisis of national confidence brought on by two world wars and the Great Depression, Hofstadter reversed himself and explained, "Although the national nostalgia has intensified in the last decade, it is by no means new." The "longing to recapture the past" had a "history of its own," which could be traced all the way back to the Jeffersonian myth of the yeoman farmer, already out of date at the time of its first appearance. A sentimental agrarian myth had distorted political thinking for a hundred and fifty years and prevented Americans from coming to grips with the urban, industrial civilization their country was clearly destined to become. In *The American Political Tradition* as well as in subsequent works, notably *The Age of Reform,* Hofstadter tried to show that American reform movements, far from embracing the future, had invariably tried to restore the conditions of primitive capitalism, clinging to the Jeffersonian vision of a nation of small landholders when in fact the United States, even in the nineteenth century, was rapidly becoming a nation of wage earners. According to Hofstadter and to a whole generation of historians who followed in his footsteps, reform movements were usually led not by men and women confident about the future but by dispossessed patricians suffering from "status anxiety" and eager to recapture their former social standing.

In 1961, Arthur P. Dudden summed up this line of interpretation, now firmly established, in an essay entitled "Nostalgia and the American." Like Hofstadter, Dudden began by linking nostalgia to the declining faith in progress, only to subvert this contention with the quite different contention that Americans had been afflicted with a debilitating nostalgia all along. But if nostalgia reflected the decline of progressive ideology, why had it flourished when the belief in progress was at its height? If it reflected a widespread resistance to change, why had Americans always welcomed and celebrated change? The incoherence of Dudden's position suggests that the critique of nostalgia, like nostalgia itself, served unavowed emotional needs. Beneath the structure of formal argument, here as in *The American Political Tradition*, we can reconstruct the following chain of associations. Americans in the middle of the twentieth century have taken refuge in nostalgia because they have lost faith in the future. But since closer examination shows that Americans have always pined for a lost golden age, we can dismiss fears about the future as an expression of "romantic pessimism," as Dudden called it. We do not have to consider the case for "pessimism" on its merits. While the future is uncertain today, it has always been uncertain. Without reviving the dogma of progress in its utopian form, we can assume that Americans will continue to manage as they have managed in the past, leaving the dead to bury the dead and the future to take care of itself.

Those who believed that hope always has to rest on the prospect of social improvement thus managed to salvage the appearance if not the substance of hope by deploring the nostalgic habit that allegedly made so many Americans afraid to face the future. By the early sixties, denunciation of nostalgia had become a ritual, performed, like all rituals, with a minimum of critical reflection. A collection of essays published by Arthur Schlesinger, Jr., in 1963, *The Politics of Hope*, contained an attack on conservatism (originally published in 1955) bearing the predictable title "The Politics of Nostalgia." In his 1965 study, *The Paranoid Style in American Politics*, Hofstadter referred repeatedly to the "nostalgia" of the American right and of the populist tradition from which it supposedly derived. But these skirmishes provided only a foretaste of the more comprehensive campaign that followed.

The "nostalgia wave of the seventies," so called, released an outpouring of analysis, documentation, and denunciation. *Time, Newsweek, U.S. News & World Report, Saturday Review, Cosmopolitan, Good Housekeeping, Ladies' Home Journal,* and the *New Yorker* all published reports on the "great nostalgia kick." "How much nostalgia can America take?" asked *Time* in 1971. The British journalist Michael Wood, citing the revival of the popular music of the fifties, the commercial appeal of movies about World War II, and the saturation of the airwaves with historical dramas—"Upstairs,

Downstairs," "The Pallisers," "The Forsyte Saga"—declared, "The disease, if it is a disease, has suddenly become universal." The nostalgic "climate," he said, indicated a "general abdication, an actual desertion from the present." Alvin Toffler advanced a similar view in his *Future Shock*. The transition from industrial society to "postindustrial" society, according to Toffler, left people disoriented and confused. Unable to face the future, all too many sought refuge in the past. "Reversionists" like Barry Goldwater and George Wallace "yearned for the simple, ordered society of the small town," while the left developed its own version of the "politics of nostalgia," based on "bucolic romanticism," an "exaggerated veneration of pre-technological societies," and an "exaggerated contempt for science and technology." In Toffler's view, both left and right harbored a "secret passion for the past." A historian, Peter Clecak, claimed in 1983 that the "theme of nostalgia dominated popular culture" in the seventies and early eighties. "Caught in the transition from industrial to postindustrial society, Americans in large numbers felt themselves losing their psychological, social, and moral bearings." They sought solace in a "thoughtless clinging to the social past," even though "such behavior makes adaptation to present realities difficult if not impossible."

The Frozen Past

Even those who took a more sympathetic view of the "nostalgia boom" shared the prevalent confusion of nostalgia with conservatism, the age-old opposition to change. According to Fred Davis, a sociologist at the University of California at San Diego, the "nostalgia wave of the seventies" represented a response to the "massive identity dislocations" of the sixties. "Rarely in history has the common man had his fundamental . . . convictions . . . so challenged, disrupted, and shaken." Nostalgic "reactions" had always followed "periods of severe cultural discontinuity," but they performed a useful purpose by cushioning future shock. "Collective nostalgia acts to restore . . . a sense of sociohistoric continuity," Davis argued. It "allows time for needed change to be assimilated" and provides "meaningful links to the past." "Nostalgic sentiment . . . cultivates a sense of history."

But a sense of history, as we have seen, is exactly what the nostalgic attitude fails to cultivate. It idealizes the past, but not in order to understand the way in which it unavoidably influences the present and the future. Nor does it unambiguously assert the superiority of bygone days. It contains an admixture of self-congratulation. By exaggerating the naive simplicity of earlier times, it implicitly celebrates the worldly wisdom of later generations. It not only misrepresents the past but diminishes the past. It attempts "less to preserve the past," as Anthony Brandt has observed, "than to restore it, to bring it back in its original state, as if nothing had happened in the interim." Henry Ford's Greenfield Village, the restoration of colonial Williamsburg, and Disneyland's "Main Street, U.S.A." exemplify, in Brandt's view, the passion for "historical authenticity" that seeks to recapture everything except the one thing that matters, the influence of the past on the present. Yet "the past cannot be known except in relation to ourselves." For that reason a real knowledge of the past, in Brandt's words, "requires something more than knowing how people used to make candles or what kind of bed they slept in. It requires a sense of the persistence of the past: the manifold ways in which it penetrates our lives." This persistence, of course, is what the nostalgic attitude denies.

Nostalgia evokes the past only to bury it alive. It shares with the belief in progress, to which it is only superficially opposed, an eagerness to proclaim the death of the past and to deny history's hold over the present. Those who mourn the death of the past and those who acclaim it both take for granted that our age has outgrown its childhood. Both find it difficult to believe that history still haunts our enlightened, disillusioned maturity. Both are governed, in their attitude toward the past, by the prevailing disbelief in ghosts.

Seemingly irreconcilable, the nostalgic attitude and the belief in progress have something else in common: a tendency to represent the past as static and unchanging, in contrast to the dynamism of modern life. We have seen how nostalgia freezes the past in images of timeless, childlike innocence. But the idea of progress, although it perceives ignorance and superstition where nostalgia perceives charming simplicity, encourages an equally lifeless and undifferentiated sense of the past. Notwithstanding its insistence on unending change, the idea of progress makes rapid social change appear to be uniquely a feature of modern life. (The resulting dislocations are then cited as an explanation of modern nostalgia.)

This kind of thinking reduces premodern or "traditional" societies to flatness and immobility.

The impression of a premodern past almost entirely devoid of incident is strengthened by a sociological conception of history that seeks the typical, the average, and the normal as opposed to the idiosyncratic and exceptional. Macaulay, whose name is so closely associated with the Whig view of history as the story of never-ending improvement, once said that the life of a modern nation could be understood only by studying "ordinary men as they appear in their ordinary business and in their ordinary pleasures." Those who wished "to understand the condition of mankind in former ages," according to Macaulay, "must proceed on the same principle," instead of confining their attention to "public transactions, to wars, congresses, and debates." Since it is above all the condition of the masses that furnishes the best index of progress, according to this way of thinking, the long ages in which the masses lived in poverty, illiteracy, and the darkness of superstition, bound to an unchanging round of toil, take on the same timeless appearance, in progressive historiography, that we have already noted in nostalgic representations of the past. The historical record boils down to an uneventful succession of births, marriages, and deaths. The only question it seems to invite is whether the monotony of premodern times was experienced as a comfort or a curse. Did the "immemorially old, clod-like existence" of the premodern masses, as Edward Shils has referred to it, offer the compensatory security of clearly defined social status, reciprocal obligations, and the reassuring knowledge that the future would closely resemble the past?

A conviction that such debates are not only interminable but completely uninformative, and yet that they continue to dominate the historical imagination of our time as well as its politics, has prompted this investigation of the idea of progress and its echo, the homesickness of the "homeless mind." A further exploration of the cultural background of contemporary debate requires an analysis of the long-standing controversy about "modernization" and "community," which has flared up again in recent years. The communitarian critique of modern life recapitulates, in a more explicitly political key, many of the same themes that inform the controversy about progress, only to leave them, once again, unresolved.

4

THE SOCIOLOGICAL TRADITION AND
THE IDEA OF COMMUNITY

Cosmopolitanism and Enlightenment

In the eighteenth century, as we have seen, enlightened men and women welcomed the new order—
notwithstanding their misgivings about the acquisitive impulse and the
probability that it would extinguish the virtues of fortitude and self-
sacrifice—on the grounds that economic abundance gave mankind mastery over its own destiny and broke the age-old cycle of growth and
decline, formerly the fate of nations. They had other reasons to celebrate
the growth of commerce. If merchants were the "most useful race of men
in the whole society," as Hume called them, it was because their activities
broke down the "narrow malignity and envy of nations, which can never
bear to see their neighbors thriving, but continually repine at any new

efforts towards industry made by any other nation." International trade promoted international peace, once it was understood that all nations shared in its fruits. Abundance annulled the first law of social life under scarcity, that individuals or nations prosper only at their neighbors' expense. "Ignorant nations," Bentham said, had "treated each other as rivals, who could only rise upon the ruins of one another." Fortunately the work of Adam Smith had now made it clear, according to Bentham, that "commerce is equally advantageous for all nations—each one profiting in a different manner, according to its natural means." *The Wealth of Nations* showed that "nations are associates and not rivals in the grand social enterprise." Smith's argument in favor of free trade offered a special application of the general principle, as Bentham put it, that "the interests of men coincide upon more points than they oppose each other." As men came to understand this principle and its far-reaching implications, they would adjust their actions accordingly, relaxing their habitual attitude of jealousy and suspicion. "The more we become enlightened, the more benevolent shall we become."

The hope that the "interest of mankind at large" would come to prevail over the "spirit of rivalship and ambition which has been common among nations," as Richard Price put it, now appeared to rest on solid facts, not on wishful thinking. Only unenlightened economic policies, together with the lingering effects of popular prejudice, stood in the way of international understanding. "If commerce were permitted to act to the universal extent it is capable," Tom Paine declared in *The Rights of Man*, "it would extirpate the system of war, and produce a revolution in the uncivil state of governments." The eighteenth-century philosophers prided themselves on their superiority to the narrow patriotism that generated so much ill will among nations. "You will always find it strongest and most violent where there is the lowest degree of culture," Goethe said. Lessing held that patriotism was the "prejudice of the people." Samuel Johnson's view of patriotism—"the last refuge of the scoundrel"—is still quoted; but the same view was expressed, if not always so succinctly, by all those whose writings made the eighteenth century synonymous with the Age of Reason. Hume maintained, "The vulgar are apt to carry all *national characters* to extremes: and having once established it as a principle, that many people are knavish or cowardly or ignorant, they will admit of no exception, but comprehend every individual under the same censures."

The claim that trade broke down narrow habits of mind served as one of the most important arguments in its favor. Eighteenth-century exponents of the new order did not argue, as liberals tend to argue in our time, that economic incentives are usually strong enough to encourage men and women to set aside their national, ethnic, racial, and religious prejudices during business hours, indulging them only in the harmless privacy of their homes and clubs. Twentieth-century experience has demonstrated the tenacity of national and ethnic solidarity, even when exposed to the solvent of the modern megalopolis. The eighteenth century believed, on the other hand, that commerce broke down particularism and promoted a cosmopolitan outlook. "In the stock-exchanges of Amsterdam, London, Surat, or Basra," wrote Voltaire, "the Gheber, the Barian, the Jew, the Mohametan, the Chinese Deist, the Brahmin, the Greek Christian, the Roman Christian, the Protestant Christian, the Quaker Christian, trade with one another; they don't raise their dagger against each other to gain the souls for their religions." Addison put the point even more forcefully in describing a visit to the Royal Exchange: "Sometimes I am jostled among a body of Americans; sometimes I am lost in a crowd of Jews, and sometimes in a group of Dutch-men. I am a Dane, a Swede, or Frenchman at different times, or rather fancy myself like the old philosopher, who upon being asked what country-man he was, replied that he was a citizen of the world."

Our twentieth-century experience of imperial rivalries, international competition for markets, and global wars makes it hard for us to share the Enlightenment's conviction that capitalism would promote world peace. The cosmopolitan ideal articulated by the Enlightenment, although it remains an essential ingredient in modern liberalism, strikes many of us today as at once arrogant, in its contempt for the unenlightened masses, and naive. "Benevolence," moreover—the universal love for humanity assumed to follow emancipation from local prejudice—presents itself to us as a singularly bloodless form of goodwill, founded more on indifference than on devotion. We can appreciate Rousseau's mockery of "those pretended cosmopolites, who in justifying their love for the human race, boast of loving all the world in order to enjoy the privilege of loving no one." Paine's self-congratulatory humanitarianism, on the other hand—

"my country is the world, my religion to do good to mankind"—leaves us a little cold.*

It is important to remind ourselves, therefore, that cosmopolitanism and "benevolence" commended themselves, in the eighteenth century, as an alternative to the fierce partisanship now blamed for two hundred years of religious warfare. Religious tolerance may have reflected a growing indifference to religion, but at least it held out the hope of peace.†
When patriotism seemed so often to travel hand in hand with religious fanaticism, it is not surprising that philosophers preferred to think of themselves as citizens of the "cosmopolis, the world city," in the words of Diderot—"strangers nowhere in the world." Pierre Bayle's advice to the historian—to "sacrifice resentment of injuries, memories of favors received, even love of country" to the "interests of truth"—becomes intelligible against a background of bitter religious dissension, in which competing accounts of the past, each claiming to see the hand of God in historical events, served as propaganda in the struggle between Protestantism and Rome. We might object that Bayle's image of the historian as a man "without father, without mother, without genealogy" seemed to enlist history in the service more of oblivion than of remembrance, especially when it was coupled with an appeal to "forget that he belongs to any country, that he has been raised in any particular faith, that he owes his fortune to this or that person, that these are his parents or those are his friends." To forget, however, is also to forgive: at a time when the memory of former wrongs kept alive enmities that otherwise might have been

---

*According to Paine, Americans were the most cosmopolitan people in the world. "In this extensive quarter of the globe, we forget the narrow limits of three hundred and sixty miles and carry our friendship on a larger scale; we claim brotherhood with every European Christian and triumph in the generosity of the sentiment. It is pleasant to observe with what regular gradations we surmount local prejudice as we enlarge our acquaintance with the world."

†Burke attacked "these new teachers continually boasting of their spirit of toleration," just as Rousseau attacked those who professed a love for all mankind, on the grounds that such professions really revealed a certain indifference. "That those persons should tolerate all opinions, who think none to be of estimation, is a matter of small merit. Equal neglect is not impartial kindness. The species of benevolence which arises from contempt is no true charity."

allowed to die, even this curious plea for a historical scholarship afflicted with amnesia made a certain kind of sense.

The Enlightenment's Critique of Particularism

· ■ ·

Since the remembrance of past times had evidently done more to keep people apart than to bring them together, it is not surprising that cosmopolitan philosophers had little use for either of the disciplines formerly held in such high esteem, law and theology—notoriously disputatious professions given to inconclusive wrangling about precedents, about the interpretation of historical documents, and about the meaning of the past. The Enlightenment hoped to model ethical and political theory not on historical understanding but on the method of science, which promised to lay down axiomatic principles resistant to doubt and thus to enable philosophers infallibly to distinguish right from wrong and truth from mere opinion. Beginning with Descartes, philosophers took up a new task: to analyze and make explicit the procedures that governed clear thinking. Once critical analysis had reduced phenomena to their simplest components, they believed, it could reassemble those components in the form of laws having universal validity.

It was a characteristic and revealing fantasy associated with this new conception of knowledge that language could be remodeled on mathematics—a project, according to Descartes, that would lay the basis for a universal language. The historical associations lodged in language, which lawyers, theologians, grammarians, and rhetoricians had attempted to unravel and decipher, appeared to the new philosophers as a source of contamination. Ordinary language, in their view, embodied cultural prejudices from which reason should struggle to free itself. "Almost all our words," Descartes complained, "have confused meanings, and men's minds are so accustomed to them that there is hardly anything which they can perfectly understand." Knowledge consisted of incontrovertible propositions, according to Descartes, which could be arrived at only by discounting the emotions and interests embedded in ordinary language.

It was therefore necessary to invent a new language of pure and simple symbols, each with its own single and unambiguous meaning, or better yet to convert all experience into numerical form. "In our search for the direct road to truth," said Descartes, "we should not occupy ourselves with any object about which we are unable to have a certitude equal to that of arithmetical and geometrical demonstrations." At one time or another, the idea of a universal language was endorsed by Leibniz, Voltaire, d'Alembert, Condorcet, and Franklin, who pointed out that a universal alphabet designed by John Wilkins, secretary of the Royal Society, "could be well learnt in a tenth part of the time required to learn Latin."

The equation of truth with axiomatic and universally applicable principles could lead to skepticism just as well as to certainty. Hume took the position that scientific procedures could never answer questions pertaining to the "end of man" and concluded for that reason that such questions were not worth asking, since they would always give rise to "pretty uncertain and unphilosophical" thoughts. Like Descartes, he took it for granted that philosophy had to rest on intellectual foundations unassailable by doubt—on "principles which are permanent, irresistible, and universal." These principles, which could be gleaned only from the scientific study of nature, represented the "foundation of our thoughts and actions," without which "human nature must immediately perish and go to ruin." Everything else, Hume thought, was "changeable, weak, and irregular."

Proposals for a universal religion, conceived in the same spirit that gave rise to the project for a universal language, appealed to those who found Hume's skepticism repugnant, if not always for themselves at least for the mass of credulous common folk who presumably needed consolation and firm moral guidelines. A number of eighteenth-century intellectuals argued that religion, like language, could be synthetically constructed on scientific principles, as Helvetius put it, "that are eternal and invariable, that are drawn from the nature of men and things, and that, like the propositions of geometry, are capable of the most rigorous demonstration." Kant's search for a universal morality, a less grandiose version of the same project, entailed the same assumption: that incontrovertibility furnished the only test of socially workable beliefs. Kant did not, to be sure, subscribe to the conviction that informed the work of utilitarians like Helvetius and Bentham, that "morality ought to be treated like all other sciences," in the words of Helvetius, "and founded on experiment, as well as natural philosophy." In making universality the essential condition of ethical imperatives, Kant nevertheless detached morality from its ordinary social context in the same way that Descartes hoped to detach communication from common speech. Moral obligation no longer referred to the duties prescribed by a particular office or social role but to the categorical imperative to follow no rule that could not be recommended as a general rule for everyone.

Conceived in part as a reply to Hume's moral and epistemological skepticism, Kant's elaborately reasoned moral philosophy remained oddly silent about the nature of the good life or the ends proper to man. Kant did not challenge Hume's judgment that these "abstruse questions," as Hume put it, were inappropriate objects of philosophical inquiry. "What is the end of man? Is he created for happiness? Or for virtue? For this life or the next? For himself or his maker?" According to Hume, these issues remained "inaccessible to understanding"; and Kant, for all his laborious effort to ground morality in first principles, had no more to say about them than Hume. Like other enlightened philosophers, he was evidently willing to leave them to individual judgment, on the assumption that the individual was the best judge of his own interests or at least that any attempt to give a particular vision of the good life some kind of social sanction would only give rise to bitterly divisive controversies the world could well do without. Ontology's principal contribution to public life, after all, had been to transform every petty squabble into a holy war against heresy. Politics had been "shamefully depraved" by "supernatural ideas," Holbach explained. Since it was in the very nature of disputes concerning ultimate ends that they could never be settled to anyone's satisfaction, they would always divide mankind into hostile communities, each with its own dogma, its own dialect, and its ingrained suspicion of outsiders.

The Reaction against Enlightenment: Burke's Defense of Prejudice

· ■ ·

The political implications of eighteenth-century rationalism were ambiguous and contradictory. On the one hand, the injunction to ground political speculation in universal, incontrovertible principles tended to narrow the range of debate, to relegate divisive conflicts of opinion to private life, and to promote religious tolerance (though at the cost of trivializing public discussion). On the other hand, the same injunction could encourage ambitious programs of social engineering, supposedly founded on principles to which nobody in his right mind could object. Both the cosmopolitan ideal and the hope for a science of politics rested on the assumption that human beings are all alike. "They all have the same vital organs, sensibility, and movement," as Voltaire put it.

The assumption of uniformity sometimes gave rise to sweeping reforms untempered by the slightest doubt about the ability of enlightened legislators to prescribe for all. Armed with a scientific understanding of the requirements for human happiness, philanthropists like Jeremy Bentham did not hesitate to propose a comprehensive reconstruction of political institutions, in which all the errors allowed to accumulate during unenlightened ages past—errors undeservedly dignified as ancestral wisdom—would be ruthlessly swept aside. Bentham's Panopticon, a penitentiary in which every cell could be observed at every moment by custodians stationed in a central tower, embodied in miniature a system of universal surveillance, a union of "benevolence" and rigorous discipline that could serve as a model for the social order as a whole. A state that aimed only to assure the greatest good for the greatest number could not be accused of enforcing uniformity of opinion in the manner of autocratic regimes. Social discipline became an instrument of popular education, teaching people their real interests, freeing them from inherited superstitions and bad habits, and making it possible for them to lead happy, healthy, productive lives.

The French revolution, far more clearly and dramatically than British utilitarianism, showed that the attempt to remodel society according to abstract principles of justice, to uproot established ways of life and overthrow ancient beliefs, could lead more easily to a reign of terror than to a reign of universal love and brotherhood. Not that the revolution represented in any simple or direct way the application of philosophical principles to politics. A fierce conflict of social classes, together with belated and half-hearted efforts to renovate an antiquated system of administration and finance, accounted for much of the turmoil that convulsed the French nation in the 1790s. Revolutionary ideology, moreover, owed as much to the republican tradition, as reformulated by Rousseau, as it owed to the liberalism of the Enlightenment. Robespierre's reign of virtue, the complete subjection of all activity to politics, exposed the fanaticism lurking in the republican ideal of citizenship. By effectively abolishing private life, the terror helped to discredit republicanism in the same way that Stalinism later discredited socialism.

But the French revolution also discredited eighteenth-century liberalism, at least for those who traced it to the folly of ignoring experience and of attempting to create a new order overnight, one based on nothing more secure than airy speculation. For our purposes, the importance of the revolution lies in its contribution to the Romantic reaction against cosmopolitanism, political abstractions, and the search for the universal principles thought to govern politics and morality. The Romantic reaction in turn left as part of its intellectual legacy the basic categories of modern social thought—gemeinschaft and gesellschaft, "community" and "society," categories rich in ramifying meanings that continue to inform (or deform) political speculation even today.

Even before the terror brought the revolution to its grisly climax, Edmund Burke issued his classic defense of inherited wisdom against reckless innovation, "old establishments" against the "merely theoretical system" devised by "sophisters," "declaimers," and "metaphysicians." Burke urged the value of prejudice, which was "ten thousand times" to be preferred to the "evils of inconstancy and versatility." The Enlightenment condemned prejudice as the enemy of reason; but its usefulness as a source of moral restraint, Burke thought, was unmistakably revealed by the revolution—the work of men and women whose freedom from prejudice enabled them to carry out appalling crimes. Burke equated prejudice with common decency and "untaught feelings," spontaneous promptings of the heart. Thus a "wise prejudice" against patricide prompted Englishmen, as they contemplated the folly of their neighbors across the channel, "to look with horror on those children of their country who are prompt rashly to hack" the French state, "that aged parent, in pieces and put him into the kettle of magicians."

Burke's account of the ordeal of Marie Antoinette, torn from her throne and treated by the revolutionaries as a common citizen, clinched his case for the moral value of prejudice—in this case, the prejudice of "chivalry," which demanded respect both for rank and for women. Richard Price and other admirers of the revolution could take satisfaction in the queen's downfall only by ignoring "natural feelings . . . unsophisticated by pedantry and infidelity," according to Burke.

> In this enlightened age I am bold enough to confess that we [English] are generally men of untaught feelings: that, instead of casting away all our old prejudices, we cherish them to a very considerable degree; and, to take more shame to ourselves, we cherish them because they are prejudices; and the longer they have lasted, and the more generally they have prevailed, the more we cherish them. We are afraid to put men to live and trade each on his own private stock of reason; because we suspect that the stock in each man is small, and that the individuals would do better to avail themselves of the general bank and capital of nations and of ages.

Instead of "exploding general prejudices," philosophers would "better employ their sagacity," Burke thought, "to discover the latent wisdom which prevails in them." Prejudices guided conduct more reliably than reason, by making a "man's virtue his habit, and not a series of unconnected acts." Even superstition had its place in a well-ordered scheme of things. "There is no rust of superstition, with which the accumulated absurdity of the human mind might have crusted it over in the courage of ages, that ninety-nine in a hundred of the people of England would not prefer to impiety."

Burke did not question the opposition between reason and tradition. He simply reversed the values usually attached to these concepts, extolling prejudice and superstition against the Enlightenment's preference for "naked reason," as he called it. The case against reason, as he stated it, was not confined to reason's encouragement of rash, ill-considered actions. It also included the opposite charge that reason encouraged irresolution and doubt. Reason paralyzed the capacity for action, whereas prejudice was "of ready application in the emergency" and did "not leave the man hesitating in the moment of decision, skeptical, puzzled, and unresolved." Such remarks indicate how completely Burke identified reason with free-floating, disembodied, irresponsible speculation utterly indifferent to the consequences of a given course of action—indifferent even to the need for action, decision, and moral choice, as opposed to the extrapolation of social policy from theoretical premises.

Burke's emphasis on the importance of decisive action should not be misunderstood as an Aristotelian defense of "practical reason" against theoretical speculation. Aristotle distinguished practical reason or *phronesis* both from theory on the one hand and from technique on the other. Burke made no such distinctions, viewing reason in general—much as the Enlightenment viewed it—as pure speculation, epistemology. According to Aristotle, the aim of practical reason was neither to establish timeless truths nor to calculate the most economical means to a given result but to promote a harmony of means and ends, to train the capacity for judgment, and above all to encourage self-knowledge. Practical reason proceeded by way of argument—the value of which, however, figured no more prominently in Burke's thought than judgment and self-knowledge. Argument, indeed, was the last thing Burke wanted to promote. When he spoke of the "ancient, permanent sense of mankind," he referred to the unspoken agreement bred by habits and "affections," not to the collective judgment that issues from deliberation.

A brilliant debater, Burke nevertheless preferred silence to the noise of debate or, in his favorite image, the decent clothing of custom to the "nakedness" he associated with reason. He praised religion as the "basis of civil society" but deplored theological controversy. Modern Christians, he wrote, took "their religion as an habit, and upon authority, and not by disputation." When he spoke of Christianity as "the one great source of civilization amongst us," he added that "throwing off" Christianity would "uncover our nakedness." In his tribute to Marie Antoinette, he spoke in the same way of "chivalry." Those who took the position that a "queen is but a woman" stripped away the "pleasing illusions which made power gentle and obedience liberal, which harmonized the different shades of life, and which by a bland assimilation incorporated into politics the sentiments which beautify and soften private society." Note that Burke did not deny the truth of the assertion that "a queen is but a woman, a woman is but an animal,—and an animal not of the highest order." He denied only that it was safe to dispense with the "pleasing illusion" that things were otherwise. According to the "mechanical philosophy" of the Enlightenment,

> all the decent drapery of life is to be rudely torn off. All the superadded ideas, furnished from the wardrobe of a moral imagination, which the heart owns and the understanding ratifies, as necessary to cover the defects of our naked, shivering nature, and to raise it to dignity in our own estimation, are to be exploded, as a ridiculous, absurd, and antiquated fashion.

Burke capped his defense of prejudice with the same figure. To "cast away the coat of prejudice," he argued, would "leave nothing but the naked reason."

Burke's defense of prejudice, together with his insistence on the need for "decent drapery," illustrates the distinction between memory and custom and exposes the mistake of associating tradition too closely with the latter. The concept of tradition "stands in need of clarification," writes Bruce James Smith in *Politics and Remembrance,* a study based in part on an analysis of Burke. Smith maintains that tradition owes more to memory than to custom. Custom concerns the ordinary and unexceptional; memory, the extraordinary and unexpected. Custom surrounds itself with silence, a hushed air of veneration; memory, with oratory, disputation, dialectic. Societies that set a high value on custom take little interest in their own origins, whereas societies unified (and divided) by memories cultivate a founding myth that remains a point of moral reference and recalls men and women to an awareness of their civic obligations.

If we accept these distinctions, we should see Burke not as a traditionalist, strictly speaking, but as the sociologist of oblivion. Smith contrasts him with Machiavelli, whose political thought originated precisely in a fear of oblivion, according to Smith. Machiavelli preferred a republic to a hereditary monarchy because it inspired men with a longing to be remembered for their glorious actions. Memory conferred a vicarious immortality on those who achieved "worldly honor," as Machiavelli put it. In Smith's words, "through remembrance, the deed could acquire a permanence denied to the doer.... Without the glorious deed and its foundation in political memory, men would no longer attempt the 'rare and unparalleled thing.' " Machiavelli spoke of "customs" in connection with hereditary regimes, of "recollections" in connection with republics.

Burke, on the other hand, celebrated the principle of heredity and said of the English constitution that its "sole authority is that it has existed time out of mind." Heredity commended itself as the source of political authority, according to Smith, because the ties of blood are "automatic and inescapable."* Faced with the difficulty that heirs sometimes quarrel over a legacy, Burke could only plead with his countrymen not to allow "their sure inheritance to be scrambled for and torn to pieces by every wild, litigious spirit." Though he knew that custom itself is constantly changing, just as the legacy of the past is always open to dispute, Burke took refuge, according to Smith, in the thought that custom "somehow succeeded in hiding change . . . , purging the mind of the memory of dangerous examples of innovation.... The first task of conservatism must be the obliteration of such remembrance."

---

*Smith points out that "the materialism of the hereditary argument," however, invited the egalitarian rebuttal that flesh and blood make all men the same. In his *History of Florence*, "Machiavelli discusses the tendency of relations founded upon blood to submerge the noble deed as a standard by which to judge men." In the speech he puts into the mouth of a plebeian agitator, he shows how the principle of heredity can be turned back against itself: "Do not be frightened by their antiquity of blood which they shame us with, for all men, since they had one and the same beginning, are equally ancient; by nature they are all made in one way. Strip us all naked; you will see us all alike; dress us then in their clothes and they in ours; without doubt we shall seem noble and they ignoble, for only poverty and riches make us unequal."

Action, Behavior, and the Discovery of "Society"

· ■ ·

The distinction between memory and custom can be elaborated by adding a further distinction between action and behavior. Whereas every action is unique and idiosyncratic, behavior falls into patterns that repeat themselves in a predictable fashion. Action, whether it is reckless and impulsive or deliberate and discriminating, is the product of judgment, choice, and free will, whereas behavior is automatic and reflexive. Action is aware of itself; behavior, habitual and unconscious. Thus custom resembles the "air we breathe in," as Burke put it, operating on people "insensibly." Action is the capacity to initiate, as Hannah Arendt has pointed out, to make a new beginning. Behavior sticks to the beaten path. Action has unpredictable consequences, often at odds with those intended. Behavior, on the other hand, obeys measurable laws, analogous to physical laws of motion. If we think of men and women as creatures of circumstance and habit, we will tend to minimize the role of ideas and initiative in history, stressing instead the "secret, unseen, but irrefragable bond of habitual intercourse," in Burke's words—the "customs, manners, and habits of life" that "approximate men to men without their knowledge." If we think of men and women essentially as moral agents, we are more likely to be impressed with the ironic disjunction between intentions and results, with the capacity of the human will to free itself from natural limitations, and at the same time with its inclination to overreach itself and to wreak destruction in the attempt to dominate its surroundings.

In our analysis of nostalgia, we saw that literary representations of small-town life often fall into a kind of sociological style of thought, concerning themselves with the repetitive cycle of births, marriages, and deaths. In other words, they concern themselves with behavior as opposed to action. As Arendt has shown, the concept of behavior is closely linked, in turn, to the concept of society, since the social realm is distinguished from the political by the absence of conscious determination, the tenacity of customs and rituals the original significance of which has been lost to memory, and the accumulated weight of habits highly resistant to change. In the reaction against eighteenth-century liberalism, "society" became a rallying cry for those who condemned revolution on the grounds that deep-seated habits and prejudices could not be altered overnight, at least not without causing irreparable harm. "Manners are of more importance than laws," wrote Burke in 1796. "Upon them, in a great measure, the laws depend." These words summed up a new consensus, shared not only by enemies of the revolution but eventually even by nineteenth-century socialists, for whom the state was merely a "superstructure" resting on obscure routines governing the provision of material sustenance and the biological reproduction of the species. For conservatives and socialists alike, the discovery of society implied a devaluation of politics. Legislation, war, and diplomacy, it now appeared, made little impression on the underlying structure of social relations. Statesmen operated within the narrow constraints, ignoring them at their peril, imposed by the organization of production, the pattern of beliefs, and the existing state of technology.

Not only the French revolution but the enormous acceleration of commercial development, the beginnings of industrialism, and the articulation of an economic theory that justified these developments in the name of progress contributed to the discovery of the social. Society became visible as such only when it began to lose its familiar shape and to change at a rate hitherto inconceivable. A growing belief that fundamental change of this sort was irresistible—a belief, incidentally, that distinguished nineteenth-century criticism of the new order from republican criticism of commerce in the eighteenth century—helped to focus attention on the subterranean forces thought to underlie it, forces often likened to a geological upheaval, hence lawlike in their operation.* Roman-

---

*On the difference between republican and sociological criticism of modern life, see John T. Miller's study of the social thought of Coleridge, *Ideology and Enlightenment.* Republicans, Miller points out, thought that "social modernization could be halted if only society could muster the will to do so, while [nineteenth-century critics] were convinced of . . . the ineluctability of the process." Miller nevertheless considers republicanism and nineteenth-century conservatism as "parts of a single tradition"—a mistake, I think, because it overlooks an even more important difference. Republicans still believed in the primacy of politics. In the strictest sense, they did not yet have a

tic criticism of the new order deplored the weakening of social ties, the decline of craftsmanship, and the replacement of the sense of reciprocal obligation by competitive individualism; but the overwhelming strength of the forces making for change appeared to guarantee the futility of resistance.

Socialists like Karl Marx, William Morris, and Lewis Henry Morgan accepted most of the Romantic indictment of capitalism—summed up in the concept of alienation—as well as the assumption that it was impossible to return to an earlier stage of social development or even to deflect capitalist development from its preordained course. They took the position, however, that capitalism would give way in turn to a further stage, in which the alienating effects of modern life would be overcome and the old sense of solidarity reestablished on a new basis. "Democracy in government, brotherhood in society, equality in rights and privileges, and universal education," Morgan wrote, "foreshadow the next higher plane of society. . . . It will be a revival, in a higher form, of the liberty, equality and fraternity of the ancient *gentes.*" Only the conviction that capitalism contained the seeds of its own destruction, William Morris said, kept him from joining the ranks of those who merely railed against progress.

Culture against Civilization

· ■ ·

Side by side with the idea of society, there grew up an idea of culture that retained but extended its older associations with the cultivation of the soil and the training of human capacities. "Culture" now served to call attention to the organic links between the organized mental life of a society and its folkways, habits, and patterns of work and play.

Raymond Williams and E. P. Thompson, among other historians, have explained the central role played by the concept of culture in English criticism of industrial capitalism. "Culture" referred not just to art and

---

concept of "society," which treats politics purely as a derivative of underlying social forces.

learning but to a people's whole way of life, and it was the wholesale destruction of deeply rooted folkways that troubled opponents of progress. In German social thought, the contrast between "culture" and "civilization" condemned bourgeois society and upheld German philosophy, German poetry and music, German spirituality against the conquering materialism of the French revolution. Thanks to Coleridge, who immersed himself in German Romanticism, the idea of culture entered English social criticism shorn of its Germanic chauvinism but with its anti-industrial, antimodern implications intact. In England as in Germany, bourgeois society was condemned not simply because it seemed to have so little use for art but because it severed the connection between art and the common life. It was a cardinal tenet of Romanticism that "the art of any country is the exponent of its social and political virtues," as Ruskin put it, and that art could not flourish if it isolated itself from the workaday world or served merely to add a veneer of refinement to activities otherwise dominated by the pursuit of wealth. In France, on the other hand, intellectuals who condemned bourgeois society in the name of art inherited the cosmopolitanism of the Enlightenment. They had little enthusiasm for country life, handicraft production, or the art of the folk. Stendhal, Flaubert, and Baudelaire, enemies of bourgeois materialism and stupidity, nevertheless loved Paris and hated the provinces, which Flaubert described as the "home of imbecility" and Baudelaire as the "breeding ground of blockheads." For Parisian intellectuals, "civilization" lacked the negative connotations it had in Germany and England, where "culture" implied a rejection of the cosmopolitan ideal and a glorification of the decentralized, organic, and largely rural environment without which art would allegedly lose its connection with craftsmanship and with the humble pleasures of ordinary life.

It was not enough to argue the case for art, according to Ruskin, or to suppose that art could somehow serve as a privileged realm in which a few sensitive souls found refuge from industrial squalor. The fine arts reflected prevailing standards of workmanship, and a society that subordinated workmanship to profits could not expect to rival the artistic achievements of earlier ages, in which a love of beauty had informed even the humblest tasks. In Ruskin's writings, which dealt with economics as well as with painting and architecture, "culture" furnished the materials for a radical indictment of industrial capitalism and the progressive ideology that helped to sustain it. The division of labor, Ruskin argued, was misnamed. It was not the labour that was divided but the men, who were "divided into mere segments of men—broken into small fragments and crumbs of life." If "the foundations of society were never yet shaken" as they were in the nineteenth century, it was because men were now condemned to forms of labor that made them "less than men" in their own eyes. "It is not that men are ill fed, but that they have no pleasure in the work by which they make their bread, and therefore look to wealth as the only means of pleasure."

The contrast between "culture" and "civilization," first developed by literary intellectuals, soon found its way into social theory. Originally conceived as a description of the contrasting national character of the Germans and the French, it soon came to be seen as the description of a historical sequence: the displacement of social relations founded on status, in Henry Maine's phrase, by those founded on contract. The characteristics associated with "culture" were now read back into the stage of social development preceding the revolutionary upheaval that had brought it to a close. The opposition between the organic and the mechanical, the customary and the contractual, the familial and the individualistic, the intimate and the impersonal now referred to a "law of progress," as Maine put it, with the understanding, of course, that progress, in this context, did not necessarily mean moral and spiritual advance. On the contrary, most of those who found it convenient to give such concepts a historical dimension, even though they sometimes claimed to withhold moral judgment, found the course of recent history deeply troubling.

Even Marx and Engels, whose sympathies lay on the side of progress, spoke in a celebrated passage in the *Communist Manifesto* of the destruction of "feudal, patriarchal, idyllic relations" by "naked self-interest" and "callous 'cash payment.'" In his study of Manchester, Engels wrote that industrialism's disintegrating effects on the working-class family offended every human feeling. Marx used the same language in describing the collapse of the village communities of India under the impact of British colonialism. Like Engels, he believed that the eradication of "patriarchal" arrangements was a necessary stage in the development of a higher civilization, but he made no attempt to minimize the suffering to which this evolution gave rise. It was "sickening . . . to human feeling to witness those myriads of industrious, patriarchal and inoffensive social organizations disorganized and dissolved into their units, thrown into a sea of woes, and their individual members losing at the same time their ancient form of civilizations and their hereditary means of subsistence." The painful spectacle of dislocation made it all the more important to remember, Marx added, that "these idyllic village communities, inoffensive though they may appear, had always . . . restrained the human mind within the smallest possible compass, making it the unresisting tool of superstition, enslaving it beneath traditional rules, depriving it of all grandeur and historical energies, . . . [and] subjugating man to external circumstances instead of elevating man into the sovereign of circumstances."

Conservatives did not share Marx's confidence that progress led to beneficial effects in the long run, but they agreed about the direction of historical change. The concepts of culture and civilization or their equivalents, endlessly elaborated in further sets of contrasts, furnished a vocabulary common to all shades of political opinion. In the conservative reaction following the revolution, the French themselves, originally the target of this kind of speculation, adopted its general framework if not always the same terms of comparison. Bonald's distinction between the agricultural family and the industrial family was taken over, with modifications, both by fellow conservatives like Ferdinand LePlay and by progressives like Saint-Simon and Comte, who acknowledged their indebtedness to the "retrograde school," as Comte referred to them. Everywhere the transformation of the family appeared to provide the indispensable key to an understanding of social change. Formerly the family had served as the model for every other relationship; now even marriage was based on mutual agreement and subject to revocation if the contracting parties defaulted on their legal obligations. "Status," according to Maine, derived from the "powers and privileges anciently residing in the family," and the "movement from status to contract," accordingly, defined the diminishing influence of the familial principle. "Starting, as if from one terminus of history, from a condition of society in which all the relations of persons are summed up in the relations of family, we seem to have steadily moved towards a phase of social order in which all these relations arise from the free agreement of individuals."

Gemeinschaftsschmerz

━━━━━━━━━━━ · ■ · ━━━━━━━━━━━

By the closing decades of the nineteenth century, the historical movement from the village to the metropolis, from the organic solidarity of the preindustrial community to modern individualism and anomie, had established itself as the central preoccupation of social theory and social criticism. The contrasts that evoked this transition now served as the common coin of the social sciences, providing new disciplines with an endlessly suggestive set of categories and defining the problem that, in one way or another, absorbed almost every social theorist of the age: could the old solidarity be revived on a new basis, or would modern society become so deeply fragmented that only a unitary state, armed with frightening powers of coercion and surveillance, could impose order?

The view of history underlying all this was so widely shared and apparently so inescapable, yet so elusive and amorphous, that it was difficult to criticize it effectively. It is difficult today even to reconstruct its own history—to trace its emergence or to explain how it came to be taken for granted. We can best begin with its classic formulation, *Gemeinschaft and Gesellschaft,* published in 1887 by the German sociologist Ferdinand Tönnies. Since Tönnies, a modest and unassuming scholar, in various writings furnished a full account of his intellectual obligations (constantly revised, like his central categories), his work provides us with a genealogy of sorts, against the background of which this deceptively sketchy and unpretentious little book can be seen both as the founding charter of modern sociology and as a gathering up of ideas already familiar. Indeed the book's immediate appeal and subsequent renown probably derived from the feeling that everything it said had been said many times before, though never with quite such a charming mixture of conviction and vagueness. Less an argument than an appeal to common knowledge, *Gemeinschaft and Gesellschaft* (usually translated as *Community and Society*) was relentlessly abstract and schematic, in the style of Germanic scholarship, but for that very reason allusive and evocative, allowing the reader's imagination to play over the dazzling, glinting surface of its shifting typologies, wave after wave, without the check of anything solid or substantial. Like the sea, the book reflected the mood of those who gazed into it. Looked at in one light, it evoked lost innocence; in another, a golden future illuminated by mature understanding. It embodied not so much a theory as a mythology of social change.

Tönnies's list of his predecessors included practically all the major social theorists of the nineteenth century. Maine's *Ancient Law*, he said, provided the immediate inspiration for his own study. Other legal historians, notably Otto von Gierke, helped him to grasp the difference between a "rationalistic and individualistic philosophy of law" and a historical philosophy more interested in customs and institutions than in individual rights. The "rivers and rivulets of economic and legal history" combined with the work of anthropologists like Johann Bachofen and Lewis Henry Morgan to reveal the "indissoluble relationship between law and culture." Hegel and his successors Lorenz von Stein and Rudolf von Gneist clarified the distinction between society and the state, the former based on custom and common interests, the latter on "association," as Tönnies put it.* Jacob Burckhardt contributed the concept of the state as a work of art (in contrast to the community, a spontaneous growth); Tocqueville, that of individualism. Comte and Saint-Simon showed how an appreciation of the "positive and organic order" of the Middle Ages could be attained "without repudiating science, enlightenment, and freedom." Above all, Tönnies acknowledged the influence of

---

*This distinction was firmly established in German sociology by the 1860s, well before Tönnies began to write. Indeed it furnished the intellectual justification for a separate science of sociology. Lorenz von Stein noted that the state regarded men and women as individuals, whereas "society" rested on the "subjection of individuals to other individuals," on their mutual dependence. Robert von Mohl argued that political science was the study of individuals and the state; sociology, the study of groups. Society grew out of a "shared sphere of life, common interests, the same customs, moral standards, and sentiments." As such, it was to be clearly distinguished from the state. According to Mack Walker, "the almost inevitable consequence of separating 'society' from both state politics and from individual life was to conceive 'society' in the image of the home town," so closely identified (now that German towns were fast losing their corporate powers) with the "ubiquitous yearning for organic wholeness." The separation of sociology from the science of politics had the consequence, in other words, that "society" was conceived in the image of gemeinschaft.

Marx, the "most remarkable and profound of the social philosophers." Unfairly attacked as a utopian, Marx provided him, Tönnies said, with one of his key ideas, "that the natural and, for us, past and gone, yet always basic constitution of culture is communistic, the actual and the coming one socialistic." Under socialism, which Marx showed to be the product not of a utopian pipe dream but of the necessary development of capitalism itself, primitive communism would achieve the higher form of functional interdependence—the dependence of all on all that was inherent in the very process of specialization and differentiation, which severed the patriarchal bonds of kinship but would eventually create new modes of integration, overcoming the "temporary limitation" of nationalism.

Whether Tönnies saw the course of history as benign or malignant remains curiously unclear and, he would have argued, irrelevant, since the course of history, in his view, was irreversible. He passed no judgment: such was his consistent claim. His contribution to social understanding, he said in 1925, was "for the first time" to have given a "theoretical foundation" to a "contrast . . . hitherto . . . utilized unsystematically in . . . poetry, biography, and history" and to have stripped it of "normative overtones," disregarding "ethical implications." In the preface to the first edition of *Gemeinschaft and Gesellschaft,* Tönnies insisted that "moral sentiments and subjective inclinations . . . must not be permitted to disturb the objective evaluation of facts as they are." The student of society had to take his stand "outside the phenomena and, as with telescope and microscope, observe structure and processes" in "the same way" that scientists observed the "course of heavenly bodies and the life processes of elementary organisms."

So stationed, Tönnies thought he could see a future in which the world would become "one large city," a "single world republic, coextensive with the world market, which would be ruled by thinkers, scholars, and writers and could dispense with means of coercion other than those of a psychological nature." Was this vision a reassertion of the utopian speculation Tönnies elsewhere disavowed or an eerie anticipation of the totalitarian state? The ostensibly reassuring remark (in the 1925 essay "A Prelude to Sociology") that his "pessimism" referred to the "future of the present civilization, not to the future of civilization itself," did not shed much light on the question. Again, the question of whether progress was good or bad was pointless, according to Tönnies, who saw "in all this an interconnectedness of facts which is as natural as life and death." Yet the question was also inescapable, since his categories, in spite of his protestations, were unavoidably overlaid with all sorts of "normative overtones" and "ethical implications" that could hardly be "resolved," as Tönnies insisted they ought to be resolved, in the "contemplation of divine fate."

Consider some of the many contrasting typologies that Tönnies piled on the basic contrast between community and "society" or contractual "association." Community rested on feeling, association on intellect. Community appealed to the imagination and the emotions, association to calculating self-interest. Community encouraged belief; association, skepticism. The community was an extension of the family, whereas "family life was decaying" under the principle of association. People now confronted each other as "strangers." "Custom, habit, and faith" governed community life, "cold reasoning" the life of the modern metropolis. The community was feminine, the metropolis masculine. The contrast also corresponded to the contrast between youth and old age or, again, between the common people and the educated classes. Metropolitan life gave rise to a type of thinking and action characterized by the separation of means and ends and exemplified, in its prototypical form, by commercial exchange. Under community, on the other hand, means and ends were inseparable.

"Contrasting dichotomies," as Tönnies called them, cheerfully oblivious to their uselessness either as instruments of sociological analysis or as categories of moral judgment, could be extended ad infinitum, always to the same ethically ambiguous effect. Thus the merchant was the "first thinking and free human being," but he was also the first to make a career of treating other people as means to his own purpose. Gesellschaft transformed "culture" into "civilization" and replaced the "higher and nobler forms of human relations" typical of gemeinschaft into the exploitive relations typical of capitalism. But it also encouraged science in its "battle . . . against ignorance, superstition, and delusion." Gemeinschaft meant intimacy and warmth, gesellschaft loneliness and alienation; but anyone who described "the former, as a period of youth, . . . as 'good' [and] the latter, as a period of senescence, as 'bad' " had "certainly not been my pupil," Tönnies flatly declared, "for the simple reason that I consider such a way of putting it to be thoroughly erroneous." Often his contrasts seemed to leave no other way of putting it, however. The communal principle, he noted, was cooperative, whereas "trade"—the central agency of social change—promoted cutthroat competition, a "concealed war of all against all." As community gave way to "society," production for use gave way to production for exchange, with the result that commodities were now valued purely for the profits they would yield, without reference to their intrinsic merits. A commercial society made even women "enlightened, coldhearted, conscious." Yet it freed them from male domination. In general, trade made for equality, at least insofar as individuals were "capable of engaging in exchange or entering into contracts." But it also made for selfishness and for a callous indifference to human suffering. It extinguished the impulse of pity; charity gave way to bureaucratically administered welfare programs.

The Moral Ambivalence
of the Sociological Tradition

Nothing could be clearer, I think, than the inability of Tönnies's "comparative method" to yield a consistent set of ethical judgments, unless it is the insistence with which his categories nevertheless invite such judgments. It will not do to claim neutrality on their behalf or to pretend that the historical facts they seem to allude to have the same status as the movement of the stars. History is not "fate," at least not as Tönnies understood it. It limits human freedom, to be sure, but it is also the product of human freedom. Tönnies himself never tired of pointing out that even community, notwithstanding its appearance of something organic, originated in acts of will—"essential will," he added, unable to resist another dichotomy, in contrast to the "rational will" that drives metropolitan civilization. For that very reason, however, history elicits moral judgments; and Tönnies's analysis abounds in them. The trouble is that his judgments endlessly circle their object without coming to any resolution.

Uneasily aware that his readers might wonder about the moral of the story or look for some sort of political application, Tönnies could only disavow responsibility for "erroneous explications and for presumably clever applications." Even here he wavered, however. The preface to *Gemeinschaft and Gesellschaft* carried the forbidding warning that the book was intended purely as a contribution to science and that "people who are not trained in conceptual thinking better abstain from passing judgment." But the same preface contained the cryptic admission that "such abstention" was "not to be expected in this time and age." Tönnies himself was hardly indifferent to politics. He was "fervently devoted to socialism in [those] years," he wrote later; nor does he ever seem to have given up the hope that socialism would somehow reestablish gemeinschaft on a new basis. He had no more to say than Marx, however, about the way in which this happy result would come to pass. The main impression left by his work was one of painful ambivalence, as he sought to balance the gains of progress against losses, the emancipation of intellect against the loss of emotional security, equality against the intimacy of the primary group—only to come round again and again to the irreversibility of social processes that rolled on without regard to human preference.

The same ambivalence ran through the work of Tönnies's heirs and successors. Emile Durkheim formulated the classic diagnosis of modern rootlessness, complete with clinical terminology *(anomie)* and statistical correlations between suicide and social disorganization; but Durkheim also observed that a man was "far more free in the midst of a throng than in a small coterie" and that modern society encouraged "individual diversities" and put an end to the "collective tyranny" likely to prevail in small, close-knit groups. Max Weber compared modern rationality to an "iron cage" but celebrated the liberating effects of science and made no secret of his contempt for intellectuals who retreated from the scientific vocation into religion, seeking "to furnish their souls with guaranteed genuine antiques." Sigmund Freud took much the same position: civilization exacted a mounting toll of repression but repaid mankind with a better understanding of itself. The gradual assertion of reason over appetite could be likened to the individual's growth from infancy to maturity. Both individuals and society paid an emotional price for maturity, but it was foolish to pine for the lost innocence of childhood. If the "disenchantment of the world" (in Weber's phrase) had deprived men and women of the childlike security of dependence, it had given them science, which had "taught [men] much since the days of the Deluge and . . . will increase their powers still further." Religion, after all, was "comparable to a childhood neurosis," and society could expect to "surmount this neurotic phase." Freud's tone, like Weber's, was wistful but firm: let us put away childish things. "Men cannot remain children for ever. . . . It is something, at any rate, to know that one is thrown upon one's own resources."*

Georg Simmel's widely admired essay "The Metropolis and Mental Life"—"perhaps the most evocative and stimulating consideration of the culture of cities ever written," in the words of Thomas Bender—provides a particularly striking illustration of the ambivalence that seems inescapably to surround the subject of "community." A reading of this celebrated set piece confirms the impression that speculation of this kind originated among intellectuals recently uprooted from provincial surroundings and therefore exposed to the city-country contrast in their own lives. The "deep contrast" between the city and "small-town and rural life," according to Simmel, could be seen most clearly in the city's effects on "psychic life." In the provinces, life rested on "deeply felt and emotional relations" that grew "in the steady rhythm of uninterrupted habituations," while the city produced an "intensification of nervous stimulation." The urbanite lived "with his head instead of his heart." A money economy encouraged a "matter-of-fact attitude in dealing with men and with things." It transformed attitudes toward time, making a virtue of punctuality and, by extension, exactness in all things. "The passionate hatred of men like Ruskin and Nietzsche for the metropolis," Simmel thought, "is understandable in these terms." Money became the

---

*The anthropologist Robert Redfield, who shared Freud's appreciation of the attraction of the primitive, resorted to the same rhetoric: "I find it impossible to regret that the human race has tended to grow up." In *The Future of an Illusion,* incidentally—one of the two books by Freud that contributed most directly to the debate about progress (the other being *Civilization and Its Discontents*)—Freud stated the problem of progress in its classic form. "While mankind has made continual advances in its control over nature and may expect to make still greater ones, it is not possible to establish with certainty that a similar advance has been made in the management of human affairs." The second part of this sentence contains the usual case for modern "pessimism." But it is Freud's statement of the problem, not his apprehension that human self-control has not kept pace with control over nature, that betrays the influence of the nineteenth-century sociological tradition.

measure of all things, the "common denominator of all values," and thus destroyed the sense of particularity, of the "incomparability" of discrete places or people or events. It "hollowed out the core of things." A money economy made for "formal justice," since it undermined distinctions of rank and made everyone equal before the law; but abstract equality was "often coupled with an inconsiderate hardness."

The city overwhelmed the individual and at the same time freed him from prying neighbors, gossip, and the prejudice against anything distinctive or new. The urbanite cultivated an exaggerated individuality, even a certain eccentricity, as a defense against anonymity. Faced with conditions that made him a "mere cog in an enormous organization of things and powers," he found it necessary to exaggerate the "personal element" in order to "remain audible even to himself." By means of "mannerism, caprice, and preciousness," he sought more and more extravagant ways of calling attention to himself. He flung himself into the pleasures around him but soon became jaded with pleasure. "A life in boundless pursuit of pleasure makes one blasé," Simmel observed; "it agitates the nerves to their strongest reactivity for such a long time that they finally cease to react at all." A "blasé attitude" set the tone of city life.

In moments of boredom or loneliness, the city dweller might long for the remembered warmth of his ancestral home. Having left it, however, he could never find his way back, any more than the modern world could find its way back to the "ancient *polis.*" Nor would he like what he found: "pettiness and prejudices," "jealousy of the whole against the individual," "barriers against individual independence and differentiation" under which "modern man could not have breathed." Athens itself was only a glorified village, "self-contained and autarchic." "The earliest phase of social formations found in history as well as in contemporary social structure is this: a relatively small circle firmly closed against neighboring, strange, or in some way antagonistic circles," "closely coherent," but unwilling to allow individuals more than a "narrow field for the development of unique qualities." The vigor of Athenian culture, Simmel argued, derived not from its narrow tribalism but from the struggle of individualism against it. "Weaker individuals were suppressed," while stronger ones tried "to prove themselves in the most passionate manner."

The modern metropolis, then, not the city-state, much less the average country town, was the "locale of freedom." Modern men guarded their freedom, to be sure, by means of a studied "reserve, with its overtone of hidden aversion." This reserve made city people seem "cold and heartless" to small-town people. The city could not match the intimacy of the "small circle," where "the inevitable knowledge of individuality as inevitably produces a warmer tone of behavior." Urban sociability was predicated on a "mere objective balancing of service and return." At the same time, however, the metropolis offered "heightened awareness, a predominance of intelligence."*

---

*Louis Wirth's "Urbanism as a Way of Life" (1938), an essay extravagantly praised by American sociologists, drew heavily on Simmel's essay, right down to key phrases like the "blasé outlook." In an interesting discussion of this essay, Thomas Bender argues that the classical sociologists intended gemeinschaft and gesellschaft to refer not to historical stages but to contrasting tendencies always present in any given society. It was only after World War II, according to Bender, that American sociologists began to use these concepts in a sequential fashion, thanks largely to the example of Wirth's influential essay. "With the dualistic perspective of Tönnies largely submerged in Wirth's evolutionary formulation, a complex theory with rich possibilities for historical research was transformed into a simplistic typology of social change." The "evolutionary" interpretation, however, did not originate with Louis Wirth. There is no indication in Simmel's essay that "communalism survives, and even thrives, in the heart of the modern metropolis," as Bender puts it. Nor does it give an accurate impression of Tönnies's work to say that he "anticipated that both these forms of interaction were likely to be permanent aspects of all social life." To argue that gemeinschaft would return in the form of socialism was quite different from arguing that "folk and urban ways coexist in the same society," unless we could agree to regard labor unions (on which socialism would be based, according to Tönnies), as quaint expressions of rural folkways. Naturally residual folkways take a long time to die out, but this does not mean that Tönnies advanced a "dualistic" thesis or that his typologies referred to the "character of a whole society in a particular historical period" as well as to contrasting "patterns of human relationships within that society." It is not clear, in any case, how his typology could carry such radically conflicting meanings at the same time, and it does no credit to Tönnies to suppose that he held such an incoherent view of the matter.

Marxism, the Party of the Future

· ■ ·

Simmel ended his essay with the usual disclaimer: "It is not our task either to accuse or pardon, but only to understand." Here again, the pretense of objectivity could not quite conceal emotional ambivalence and moral indecision. Still, ambivalence was a more appropriate response to progress than unyielding opposition or wholehearted approval. Indeed it was the only appropriate response, when progress was identified so closely with fate; and there is a certain heroism in the classical sociologists' determination to face unflinchingly facts that could not be altered, in their view, and to "bear the fate of the times like a man," as Weber put it. Weber's conception of the scientific vocation may have conceded too much to the view that science demands a rigorous abstention from moral judgment, but his warning against "academic prophecy" remains indispensable. "In the lecture rooms of the university," Weber insisted, "no other virtue holds but plain intellectual integrity." It is impossible not to acknowledge the force of this, even for those who have seen Weber's ideal of heroic detachment degenerate into the familiar academic accommodation with political power that sides with the status quo, in effect, while disclaiming any intention of taking sides. "Science as a Vocation" and its companion, "Politics as a Vocation," have been put to purposes Weber himself would have disavowed, serving to excuse moral and political complacency, to rid scholarship of "value judgments," to reinforce the notion that ethical judgments are completely subjective and arbitrary, and finally to banish them even from politics itself, leaving politics to the managers and technocrats. Far from encouraging "intellectual integrity" or protecting the university from political interference, a misconceived ideal of scientific objectivity has brought about a rapprochement between the university and the state, in which academic expertise serves to lubricate the machinery of power; and it is important to remind ourselves that Weber, often invoked by those who wish to limit both scholarship and politics to purely technical matters, never endorsed such a trivial conception of either.

In politics, he condemned the pursuit of ethical absolutes, not the pursuit of ethical ends as such. Ethical absolutes had no place in politics, according to Weber, because they took no account either of the "average deficiencies of people" or the consequences to which a given course of action was likely to lead. Obedience to the absolute injunction against the use of violence—"resist not him that is evil with force"—would have had the political consequence that good people became "responsible for the evil winning out." Politics required an "ethic of responsibility," Weber argued. Since the "decisive means for politics is violence," those who accepted the burden of political action had to weigh the gains promised by any course of action against the "diabolic forces lurking in all violence." They had to weigh the possibility that coercive means, while unavoidable, might nevertheless corrupt even the most unimpeachable ends.

A critique of political irresponsibility began, then, with the salutary reminder that a failure to oppose evil, even if opposition had to avail itself of morally ambiguous means, might lead to a greater evil; but it became irresponsible in its own right, according to Weber—and not only irresponsible but intolerant and fanatical—if it claimed that absolute ethical ends could redeem ambiguous means. Writing immediately after the First World War, Weber was troubled by the ease with which former pacifists and conscientious objectors had suddenly turned into "chiliastic prophets," calling for the forcible abolition of injustice, for wars to end war, or for revolutionary violence that would put an end once and for all to the need for revolutionary violence. He thought the pacifist's refusal to resist evil with force, though it led logically to the triumph of evil, did less practical harm (since common sense usually prevailed over pacifism) than the ex-pacifist's claim that force became ethical in the service of a righteous cause. Weber reserved his greatest scorn for those who preached revolution in the name of love. "He who wishes to follow the ethic of the gospel . . . should not talk of 'revolution.' "

Weber's strictures against "academic prophecy" were directed principally against Christian socialists, many of whom renounced nonviolence in the twenties (in the United States as well as in Germany) and began to advocate a forcible overthrow of capitalism. But the general import of this indictment applied to all those who refused to acknowledge the contingent, provisional, and morally ambiguous nature of political action. It applied equally to Christian socialists and to Marxists, except that the latter justified revolution not in the name of love but in the name of historical necessity. In the debate about progress, Marxists sided with the future. They accepted the sociological tradition according to which the demise of the old agrarian order was preordained and therefore irresistible, but they wasted no time in mourning the past.* Nor did they seek to balance the gains of progress against losses, in the manner of the sociological critics of modern life. They did not minimize the wretchedness brought into the world by capitalism and industrial production. If anything, they had a stake in exaggerating it. Since capitalism laid the material foundations for socialism, however, this suffering could not be avoided. "We say to the workers and the petty bourgeois," Marx wrote in 1849: "It is better to suffer in modern bourgeois society, which by its industry creates the material means for the foundation of a new society that will liberate you, than to revert to a bygone form of society which, on the pretext of saving your classes, thrusts the entire nation back into medieval barbarism."

Throughout his career as a revolutionary, Marx had to contend with backward-looking socialists, as he saw them, who conceived of socialism more as the restoration of precapitalist solidarity than as the completion of the bourgeois revolution. His contempt for this kind of thinking knew no bounds. Christian socialism, with its "religion of love," encouraged "slavish self-abasement," the "voluptuous pleasure of cringing and self-contempt." Those who appealed to the "social principles of Christianity"

---

*It is the assumption that the development of large-scale production is inevitable, with all the other social changes that go along with it, that justifies the consideration of Marxism as an offshoot of the sociological tradition. Large-scale production develops out of the inner logic of historical change, according to this way of thinking, which is shared by Marxists and conservative sociologists alike and increasingly by liberals as well, for that matter. Centralization is inherent in the underlying structure of technological development. The superior productivity it allegedly makes possible guarantees its triumph. Form (in this case, the centralization of productive forces, the rise of the metropolis, the movement "from status to contract," and so on) follows function.

Marxism shares another feature with the sociological tradition. It too is based on the distinction between state and society. As we have seen, this makes society apolitical by definition. Like sociology, Marxism conceives of the good society—in the case of Marxism, that higher form of gemeinschaft known as socialism—as a society without politics.

were deluding themselves. "The social principles of Christianity preach the necessity of a ruling and an oppressed class, and all they have to offer is the pious wish that the former may be charitable. . . . The social principles of Christianity preach cowardice, self-contempt, abasement, submissiveness and humbleness, in short, all the qualities of the rabble."

As for the radicalism advocated by artisans, peasants, and small shopkeepers, even when it was free of religious influences, it was equally misguided, in Marx's view. A regime of "petty industry" and "simple commodity production" was "compatible only with . . . a society moving within narrow and more or less primitive bounds." A system of production in which "the labourer is the private owner of his own means of labour, . . . the peasant of the land which he cultivates, and the artisan of the tool which he handles as a virtuoso" precluded the "concentration of the means of production," a "cooperative division of labour," "control over . . . the forces of Nature by society," and the "free development of the social productive powers." The simple market society to which artisans and farmers wanted to return would have assured the reign of "universal mediocrity."

Marx did not argue simply that capitalist production created preconditions favorable to the development of socialism. His theory of history required him to see "earlier stages as tending irresistibly" toward later ones, as Jon Elster points out. History had a hidden purpose. Thus the capitalist "stage cannot be avoided," in Marx's words, "any more than it is possible for man to avoid the [earlier] stage in which his spiritual energies are given a religious definition as powers independent of himself." Christian socialists could not see that history had moved beyond the stage in which a religious worldview was appropriate, nor could artisans see that small-scale production was doomed to extinction. "At a certain stage of development it brings forth the material agencies for its own dissolution. . . . It must be annihilated; it is annihilated."

The considerations making for an ambivalent assessment of progress in other writers—the decline of craftsmanship, the fragmentation of the community, the loneliness of the modern metropolis, the subordination of spiritual life to the demands of the market—were thus dismissed by Marx and his followers as sheer sentimentality, on the whole. Sociological critics of progress agreed with Marx that the transformation of society was irresistible, but they had deep reservations about it. They may have idealized the old order, but at least they did not idealize the new. Marx, however, sang the praises of the great capitalists—their energy, their rigorous subordination of means to ends, their very ruthlessness. He had no quarrel with modern technology or modern individualism, once the "limited bourgeois form is stripped away." The breakdown of community life might be "sickening," but it was the price that had to be paid for progress.

It is significant that Marx was not greatly disturbed by the sexual individualism that disturbed so many nineteenth-century social critics. The Marxist view of marriage stood in sharp contrast to that of communitarians, who deplored the reduction of marriage to a purely contractual relationship. Marx and Engels had no objection to such an arrangement. They wanted to push it to its logical conclusion, as they saw it. Under socialism, marriage would give way to free unions based solely on personal preference. The social stake in family life, they believed, was confined to reproduction and child rearing and did not extend to the living arrangements into which consenting adults might choose to enter. The goal of socialism was the fullest development of the individual. Capitalism, in spite of its individualizing effects, still encouraged the "greatest waste of individual development," sacrificing the interests of the individual in the process of enlarging the productive capacities of mankind as a whole. Socialism would reconcile the individual and society. It represented a "higher synthesis" between individualism and "organic unity."

Elster, a sympathetic critic, finds the "indiscriminate solidarity" envisioned by Marx and Engels both unconvincing and a little ominous. People need a "narrower focus of loyalty and solidarity than the international community of workers," according to Elster. Altruism flourishes in "small, stable groups" and "declines as the circle of individuals expands." "Free-floating benevolence" is incompatible with "personal integrity and strength of character." The most valuable and persuasive element in Marxism, for Elster, is the way it makes "self-realization" the "central value in society." But this is another way of saying that Marxism owes much of its appeal, at least in the West, to its identification with the central values of capitalism itself—which can allegedly be achieved, in their fully developed form, only after the socialist revolution.

The Structure of Historical Necessity

· ■ ·

Confident that history worked on the side of enlightenment, equality, and individual freedom, Marx and Engels did not have to give much thought to the morality of means and ends, the issue that troubled those who believed, with Weber, that progress was a mixed blessing at best. For Marxists, the choice of means was simple: whatever hastened the proletarian revolution. Whether violence had to be used depended solely on local conditions. The choice of means was a question of revolutionary tactics; morality had nothing to do with it. Conventional morality was a bourgeois swindle: the bourgeoisie had not scrupled to use violence against the feudal nobility, but now they preached nonviolence and parliamentary methods to the workers as a way of keeping them in their place. Exploiting classes could be expected to seize on every moral advantage; revolutionary militancy based on historical understanding, however, was the proper answer to ruling-class hypocrisy, not moral indignation. Hypocrisy aside, the bourgeoisie had done the world a service, with the worst of motives, by destroying the old patriarchal regime, seizing the common lands, consolidating production, introducing modern machinery, and subordinating sentimental considerations to the overriding goal of greater productivity. Thanks to the bourgeois revolution, the workers now had only to take over the existing system of production, at least in countries already industrialized, and to operate it in the interest of mankind as a whole.

The "natural laws of capitalism," Marx said, worked "with iron necessity towards inevitable results." This did not mean that every nation had to go through a bourgeois phase on the way to socialism. When the Bolsheviks seized power in Russia, they could cite Marx's statement that Russia might be able to "obtain the fruits with which capitalist production has enriched humanity without passing through the capitalist regime." Without a bourgeois revolution, however, the socialist regime would itself have to do the work of capitalism, beginning with the expropriation of the peasantry; eventually this became the rationale for Stalinism in the Soviet Union. The upshot of the Marxian scheme of history was that certain things had to happen in sequence, whether they happened under bourgeois or "proletarian" auspices: the destruction of the old landed aristocracy; the rise of a new ruling class in its place; the "annihilation" of small-scale production; the transformation of peasants and artisans into wage workers; the replacement of communal, patriarchal, and "idyllic" arrangements by contractual arrangements; a new individualism in personal life; the collapse of religion and the spread of scientific habits of thought; the demystification of authority. Some such series of developments had to take place whether anyone wanted it or not and no matter what groups happened to be in charge of the state at any given time. Marx's theory of history, Elster writes, was "strangely disembodied." By "working backward from end result to preconditions," it "could dispense with actors and their intentions." Because it dispensed with actors, we should add, it could also reduce questions of morality to the justification of means by the end decreed by "history."

The neglect of human agency not only made for moral obtuseness; it also made for historical miscalculation on a large scale. By denying any capacity for historical understanding or autonomous action on the part of his opponents, Marx assumed that capitalists and workers would carry out their prescribed assignments to the bitter end, the capitalists resisting demands for reform, the workers forced into more and more desperate and revolutionary measures of self-defense. Even in Marx's lifetime, however, it was clear that history had already deviated from "iron necessity" in important ways. The English government had begun to institute reforms that would eventually give the working class a share in political power. The fact that most of these reforms were pushed through by Tory regimes was one indication, moreover, that the "bourgeois revolution" had not brought the bourgeoisie to power either in France or even in England; and while Marx advanced ingenious explanations to show why it was not always in the best interest of capitalists to govern outright, these explanations represented an implicit admission that the course of history is governed not by some overarching set of "natural laws" but by particular events, by specific conflicts over the distribution of wealth and power, and by decisions made in the heat of the moment, often with inadequate information, that often turn out to have quite unexpected results.

The more the grand structure of Marx's theory has to be modified to allow for "exceptions," the less it explains. The entire history of capitalism in the West now has to be seen not as a stage in a rigid sequence of developmental stages—as it was seen not only by Marx but by the nineteenth-century sociologists as well—but as the product of a particular history, a unique conjunction of circumstances unprecedented elsewhere in the world and not likely to be repeated. A growing awareness that modern capitalism rests on a "particular history of political victories and defeats," in the words of Roberto Unger, and that these victories and defeats can no longer be "dismissed as the mere enactment of a preestablished design," has generated growing dissatisfaction with "deep-structure social theories" in general, as Unger calls them, including not only Marxism but classical sociology and its twentieth-century offshoots. The "deeply entrenched necessitarian habits of thought" associated with the sociological tradition have by no means disappeared, as Charles Sabel reminds us; but they have become increasingly hard to defend.

One of the many difficulties that confront structural theories of history is the achievement of "modernization" under conservative direction—for example, in twentieth-century Japan, in late-nineteenth-century Germany under Bismarck, even to some extent in nineteenth-century England under Disraeli. Industrialism, it appears, can take place without a revolutionary redistribution of wealth and political power. Social theorists in the nineteenth century almost all shared the belief, stated in its classic form in Tocqueville's study of American democracy, that the "irresistible" growth of equality had "all the chief characteristics" of a "providential fact," since it was "universal" and "durable" and "eluded all human interference." They argued about whether equality was consistent with order and freedom, but most of them agreed with Tocqueville that "the revolution . . . in the social condition, the laws, the opinions, and the feelings of men" was giving rise to a new order in which "great wealth tends to disappear, the number of small fortunes to increase; desires and gratifications are multiplied, but extraordinary prosperity and irremediable penury are alike unknown"—in short, to a condition of "universal uniformity."*

---

*Having established the "providential" character of the nineteenth-century social revolution, Tocqueville proceeded, in the usual fashion, to draw up a balance sheet of

Here again, history has not lived up to expectations. Even if we ignore the persistence of inequality in the United States and western Europe, the coexistence of industrial development with many features of "traditional" social organization, in a fully developed country like Japan or in many of the developing countries elsewhere in the world, tends to undermine the assumption that industrialization and democracy go hand in hand. Forced to admit that economic development can take place under reactionary regimes, "without a popular revolutionary upheaval," Barrington Moore and other neo-Marxists have argued that a unilinear model of development has to give way to a more complex and flexible model. In opposition to "simplified versions of Marxism," they have called attention to the "Prussian road" as an alternative to the road followed by England, France, and the United States. "Conservative modernization" nevertheless remains an aberrant pattern, in their view. The lingering influence of structuralist habits of thought betrays itself in this formulation, since a deviant pattern of development implies a normal pattern—a revolutionary seizure of power by groups formerly dispossessed, as opposed to a "revolution from above." It was because Germany and Japan never enjoyed the advantages of a bourgeois revolution, according to Moore, that they had to modernize under autocratic regimes and eventually developed into full-blown military dictatorships. The moral is clear: instead of deploring revolutions in developing nations, instead of siding with the forces of order, Americans should support revolutionary movements as the only alternative to the repressive pattern of development sponsored by right-wing regimes. "For a western scholar to say a good word on behalf of revolutionary radicalism," Moore writes

---

progress, painstakingly weighing gains against losses. "There is little energy of character, but customs are mild and laws humane. . . . Life is not adorned with brilliant trophies, but it is extremely easy and tranquil. . . . Genius becomes more rare, information more diffused. . . . There is less perfection, but more abundance, in all the productions of the arts." Confessing that the "sight of such universal uniformity saddens and chills me," Tocqueville quickly added that in all likelihood it is "not the singular prosperity of the few, but the greater well-being of all that is most pleasing in the sight of the Creator and Preserver of men." Democracy may be "less elevated," but it is "more just." The specific content of these judgments concerns us less than the assumption behind them, that of an inescapable necessity.

with a good deal of exaggeration, ". . . runs counter to deeply grooved mental reflexes"; but an understanding of the "characteristic patterns of modernization" forces us to conclude that revolution is the better way.

That this conclusion rests on a tortured reading of history should be obvious at a glance. Early modern revolutions encouraged the growth of democracy, but the same cannot be said of the twentieth-century revolutions in Russia, China, Cuba, and other developing nations. The more we learn about these matters, the less we are likely to believe in "characteristic patterns of modernization." If there is such a pattern, it is surely western Europe whose history deviates from the norm. The Bolsheviks thought of themselves as modern-day Jacobins, but their revolution did not reenact the revolution in France. It was no more democratic than the autocratic programs of development instituted in Germany and Japan. Theirs too was a "revolution from above," as was Mao's revolution in China and Castro's in Cuba. If we consider the history of economic development as a whole, we might well conclude that it has everywhere been imposed from above. Even in nineteenth-century Europe and the United States, it was seldom greeted with enormous popular acclaim. On the contrary, it was greeted (as we shall see) with popular suspicion and often with open resistance.

Nor was this resistance—usually dismissed as mindless opposition to progress—necessarily misconceived. The subsequent history of industrial societies does not justify complacency about their capacity to assure an equitable distribution of the fruits of increased productivity. The relationship between industrialism and democracy looks more and more tenuous and problematical. If we insist on a law of historical development, we might be justified in concluding that "societies based on large-unit production have a verifiable historical tendency to become increasingly . . . hierarchical over time," in the words of Lawrence Goodwyn. "Supporting evidence is so pervasive," Goodwyn adds, "that this may now be taken as law"—a "direct counter-premise to the idea of progress."

"Modernization" as an Answer to Marxism

· ■ ·

Among theorists of development, of every political persuasion, it is almost universally assumed that democracy and development go together, in the normal course of things. The issue is seldom debated; debate turns instead on the question prompted by the rise of Marxism in developing nations and by the neo-Marxist theory of development—the question, that is, of whether developing nations have any choice between the deviant, "Prussian" road and the revolutionary norm. According to the neo-Marxian view, a revolutionary transfer of wealth and power to the masses releases the energies required for development. In the absence of this democratization of social relations, the only alternative (aside from continued stagnation) is the reactionary pattern of development imposed from above.

The theory of "modernization," which enjoyed a great vogue in the two decades following World War II, is best understood as a reply to this argument. Walt Rostow explicitly presented his 1961 treatise, *The Stages of Economic Development,* as a "non-communist manifesto." Modernization theorists attempted, in effect, to refute the contention that revolution is the one true road to the promised land. They stressed the importance of impersonal forces—urbanization, literacy, mass communications or "media growth." Their account of development allowed even less room for human initiative than the Marxist account. The process was directed, insofar as it was directed at all, by "tutelary elites," but these elites acted within narrow constraints. Once information about the modern world had begun to circulate among newly urbanized populations, it was impossible to deny the masses a place in the sun. "Exposure to modernizing influences," as Alex Inkeles put it, generated an irresistible demand for the better things of life. It led to an "openness to new experience," "increasing independence from the authority of traditional figures like parents and priests," a "belief in the efficacy of science and medicine," "ambition for oneself and one's children," and a strong interest in politics—the whole "syndrome of modernity."

Elites could neither resist the popular demand for political representation nor introduce democratic institutions and other "symbols of modernity" where such a demand did not yet exist. According to Daniel Lerner, "the effort of new governments . . . to induce certain symbols of modernity by policy decisions, in a sequence which disregards the basic arrangement of lifeways out of which slowly evolved those modern institutions now so hastily symbolized," would always come to grief. With some irritation, Lerner noted that ill-conceived innovations, "taken in ignorance of the model," introduced a "stochastic factor" into an otherwise predictable sequence of events. In other words, they forced social scientists to rely on guesswork. One of the practical goals of modernization theory, it appears, was to encourage political leaders to stick to the script.

In its unilinear conception of history, its insistence that developing societies had to pass through a prescribed sequence of stages, and its confidence that eventually they would all arrive at the same destination, modernization theory resembled the cruder versions of the Marxism it was intended to refute. In an essay pleading for a "more differentiated and balanced analysis," Reinhard Bendix noted that Lerner, Rostow, Clark Kerr, and other students of development tended to "predict one system of industrialism for all societies in much the same way as Marx predicted the end of class struggles and of history for the socialist society of the future." Bendix pointed out that modernization theory also drew on the whole sociological tradition. It was deeply "beholden," he said, "to the conventional contrast between tradition and modernity." Other critics have made the same observation, calling attention to its dependence on "familiar paired differences." According to Dean Tipps, "modernization theorists have done little more than to summarize" the work of Maine, Tönnies, and Durkheim.

A close reading of the literature bears out this contention. To cite a typical example, C. E. Black, in his *Dynamics of Modernization*, characterized modern society as one in which "the individual is atomized—torn from his community moorings, isolated from all except his immediate family," and deprived "not only of the support and consolation offered by membership in a more autonomous community, but also of the relative stability of employment and social rules that agrarian life provides in normal times." At the same time, modernization brought about a general improvement in the standard of living, according to Black. The "comparative method" showed that as "societies become more productive, wealth tends to be more evenly distributed." The rate of social mobility accelerated; the middle class became larger and larger. "This tendency toward the equalization of income and status . . . is the inevitable result of economic development."

Modernization theory recycled all the assumptions underlying nineteenth-century sociology: that the transition from the old order to the new was a comprehensive process in which everything was related to everything else; that it originated in the internal dynamics of developing societies, not in cultural diffusion or conquest; that new patterns replaced the old ones because they worked better (in spite of some of their undesirable by-products); that the process unfolded in a sequential order, one stage giving rise to the next; and that it culminated in general affluence and equality, however "atomized." Modernization was a "multifaceted process involving changes in all areas of human thought and activity," according to Samuel P. Huntington. According to Lerner, it was a "systemic" process that repeated itself "in virtually all modernizing societies, on all continents of the world, regardless of variations in race, color, creed." It was best understood not as the Westernization of the world but as the recapitulation, in Asia, Africa, and Latin America, of a series of events first played out in Europe. The example of the West might serve to stimulate a desire for change, but change came chiefly from within. Changes in one part of the social organism were functionally interconnected to changes in other parts: thus the growth of trade, the development of a labor market, and the advent of factory production coincided with changes in family structure, the extended family giving way to the nuclear or "conjugal" family. "If the family has to move about through the labor market," Neil Smelser wrote, "it cannot afford to carry all its relatives with it. . . . Connections with collateral kinsmen begin to erode; . . . newly married couples set up homes of their own and leave the others behind. . . . Apprenticeship systems which require the continuous presence of father and son decline as specialized factory production arises." Large extended families, Marion J. Levy explained, are not "consistent with the development of relatively high levels of modernization." "The traditional society tends to be a familistic one," as S. N. Eisenstadt put it, "while the modern one tends to divert the family unit from most of its functions, and the family itself develops more into the direction of the small nuclear family."

Changes in family structure, together with attendant changes in the very structure of personality—including a new "empathy," a "cosmopolitan outlook," and a desire for "achievement"—made it possible for "newly mobile persons to operate efficiently in a changing world," in Lerner's words. For Lerner, the functional interdependence of economic life, family and personality structure, ideology, and politics meant that "the model of modernization follows an autonomous historical logic— that each phase tends to generate the next phase by some mechanism which operates independently of cultural or doctrinal variations." The process reached its "highest phase," the "end of the road," when everyone was "well fed, well educated, and well provided with consumer goods, medical care, and social security," as Black put it. Black warned that "it will be well into the twenty-first century before a majority of the world's societies will have completed the main tasks of economic and social transformation" and entered that happy state in which "there will be nothing more to be done." Like other modernization theorists, however, he entertained no doubt about the eventual outcome. "The problem of poverty is only acute in the short run," according to Ernest Gellner: ". . . in the long run, . . . we shall all be affluent." Heavily indebted to nineteenth-century sociology for its categories and concepts, modernization theory retained nothing of the nineteenth century's ambivalence about progress. Bendix attributed the "invidious personification of modernity and tradition" to the intellectual's snobbish disdain for democracy and his "romantic utopia" of a lost golden age of unalienated labor and artistic creativity. Alex Inkeles ridiculed the idea, propagated by "social philosophers," that "industrialization was a kind of plague which disrupts social organization, destroys cultural cohesion, and uniformly produces personal demoralization and even disintegration." On the contrary, "modernizing institutions, per se, do not lead to greater psychic stress."

It is easy to see why the study of broad social changes appeared to require such a concept as modernization, one that took account of the interrelationship of social, political, and cultural developments without giving causal priority to any one set of determinants. To treat modern society merely as the triumph of capitalism appeared to address only one aspect of a more general change; even "industrialism" seemed to give undue weight to the economic side of the equation. But the "constant search for more inclusive conceptualizations," as Tipps called it, sacrificed analytical precision to a comprehensive typology that abstracted certain contrasts from their historical context, attached new labels to them, but counted on the familiarity of the old images to provide the illusion of explanation. Modernization theorists confused classification with analysis.

They disregarded the admonition, regularly issued by the founders of sociology, against the substitution of disembodied concepts for historical facts. "Ideas or concepts, whatever name one gives them, are not legitimate substitutes for things," Durkheim wrote. ". . . They are like a veil drawn between the thing and ourselves, concealing them from us the more successfully as we think them most transparent." Weber pointed out that when "developmental sequences" are twisted into ideal types, the resulting constructs take on the appearance of a "historical sequence unrolling with the necessity of a law." The " 'before-and-after' model," as Bendix called it, nevertheless continued to dominate the study of modernization; Bendix himself, even though his discussion of modernization theory was quite critical, on the whole, maintained that the "distinction between tradition and modernity" could not be dispensed with "entirely."

The Last Refuge of Modernization Theory

· ■ ·

The concept of modernization no longer dominates the study of economic development in the non-Western world; but the conceptually seductive images with which it is associated still color the West's view of its own history. It was the transformation of Western society by the industrial revolution that first gave rise to the concepts of tradition and modernity, and the habit of charting our course by these familiar landmarks lingers on. Critics have again and again exposed the inadequacies of the modernization model, even for an understanding of the West. It still stands, however—a deserted mansion, its paint peeling, its windows broken, its chimneys falling down, its sills rotting; a house fit only for spectral habitation but also occupied, from time to time, by squatters, transients, and fugitives.

Modernization theory, the critics say, ignores the independent role of the state in social change. It treats the state merely as a product of under-lying social forces, ignoring its capacity for autonomous initiative. The theory underestimates the importance of political conflicts in determin-ing the course of historical events. It puts too much emphasis on internal forces in developing countries and overlooks the extent to which the early advantages seized by the West rested on the exploitation of colonial possessions. Military conquest underlay economic expansion in the six-teenth century, and the discipline required by large-scale industrial orga-nizations was first worked out in military establishments and only later applied to the factory. The modern state's dependence on military power may help to explain the continuing influence exercised by the nobility, allegedly displaced by the rise of commerce and industry. Those who adhere to the modernization model have no way of accounting either for the persistence of traditional elites or for the resilience of traditional institutions like the extended family. The coexistence of traditional and modern elements undermines the claim that modernization is a "sys-temic" process. It now appears to be a highly selective process; and this discovery parallels the growing recognition that progress in technology, say, does not necessarily entail progress in morals or politics.

It should be clear by now that the concept of modernization tells us no more about the history of the West than about the rest of the world. The more we learn about that history, the more the rise of industrial capital-ism in the West appears to have been the product of a unique conjunction of circumstances, the outcome of a particular history that gives the im-pression of inevitability only in retrospect, having been determined largely by the defeat of social groups opposed to large-scale production and by the elimination of competing programs of economic development. Modern mass production was by no means the only system under which industrialization might have been achieved. In the words of Charles Sabel and Jonathan Zeitlin, it did not grow out of the "imminent logic of tech-nological change." It was the product of an "implicit collective choice, arrived at in the obscurity of uncountable small conflicts."

The contrast between "traditional society" and modernity cannot pos-sibly give us an understanding of those conflicts. Instead of discarding the old categories, however, critics of modernization theory merely deploy them, for the most part, in new ways. The truism that every society contains both traditional and modern elements sums up the revisionist consensus. Thomas Bender's lively, intelligent little book *Community and Social Change in America* illustrates the difficulty of breaking with firmly established patterns of thought. It also illustrates the moral ambivalence that has always been associated with the concepts of gemeinschaft and gesellschaft, together with the hope that "community" can somehow be combined with industrial "progress." Bender points out that historians have taken over the old dichotomies without attempting to "test" them with "historical materials"; instead they have "mechanically inserted historical data into the framework supplied by the essentially ahistorical logic of change offered by modernization theory." Like other revisionists, he rejects the assumption that modernization "involves the same sequence of events in different countries" and "produces a progressive convergence of forms." His book attempts to lay out a "more useful narrative structure," one that "assumes the coexistence of communal and noncommunal ways."

After exposing the inadequacies of modernization theory, Bender nevertheless proceeds to tell the same old story. In seventeenth-century New England, "the 'whole of life' was framed by a 'circle of loved, familiar faces, known and fondled objects.'" The quotation comes from Peter Laslett's study of English village life, *The World We Have Lost*—a nostalgic treatment of "traditional society," as its title indicates. "Men and women did not have the compartmentalized lives that characterize modern society," Bender writes. They experienced a "convergence of roles," whereas "modern society multiplies and separates social roles." The New England village was "undifferentiated" and "essentially homogeneous." Bender endorses Kenneth Lockridge's description of the seventeenth-century village as a "self-contained social unit, almost hermetically sealed off from the rest of the world."

The political and religious history of New England, which made this community so intensely aware of its special place in a larger scheme of things, thus recedes into the fog of historical sociology. New England saw itself—no doubt with an absurdly inflated sense of its own importance—as the decisive battleground in the global struggle between Protestantism and the papal Antichrist. For this reason, differences of opinion that might have seemed trivial to outsiders took on world-historical importance. Religious controversy repeatedly shook the colony to its foundations. Roger Williams and Anne Hutchinson were only the first in a long line of dissenters whose expulsion, far from stifling dissent, if anything strengthened the habit of bitter religious debate. Only a misty image of "traditional society" makes it possible to forget such well-known facts and to paint a fantastic picture of colonial New England as a happy little island of ideological peace and quiet undisturbed by dissension and "hermetically" isolated from the outside world.

Bender objects to a historical narrative "shaped by the notion of unrelenting community decline," but his sketch of New England gets thing off to a bad start, and the contrasting picture of the "segmented," "compartmentalized" society that grew up in the nineteenth century barely qualifies the standard view. He wants to argue that "community" and "society" can coexist and that we should think of them not as stages in a historical sequence but as contrasting "forms of interaction." Since "community" no longer has any territorial basis, however, it now has to rest on voluntary association. In the seventeenth century, "community as a place and community as an experience were one." In the nineteenth century, this linkage was shattered. Today the "experience" of community has to be found in the company of "family and friends," which satisfies the need for intimacy in a world governed by the impersonal dynamics of the market. The "coexistence of communal and noncommunal ways" requires "multiple loyalties"; people have to "learn to live in two distinct worlds, each with its own rules and expectations."

The "coexistence" thesis is not new; in one form or another, it has figured in discussions of community from the beginning. It was the hope of sealing off private life as a protected sanctuary from the market that led nineteenth-century moralists to sentimentalize the domestic circle. The same desire to prevent the market from contaminating the "culture of the feelings," as John Stuart Mill called it, underlay the modern cult of art and artistic freedom. But the doctrine of segmented "spheres," whether it is conceived as a program of social reform or simply as a description of modern society, has always been open to insurmountable objections. The principle of "contract" has a tendency to invade the sphere of private life and to corrupt relationships based on "status."

In *The Homeless Mind*, a study of "modernization and consciousness," Peter Berger, Brigitte Berger, and Hansfried Kellner argue that it is "possible to concede the irrevocability and irresistibility of modernization . . . and to look upon the private sphere as a refuge or 'reservation' for other structures of consciousness." They take the same position taken by Bender, in other words; but they do not deny the difficulty of segregating private life from its surroundings. "It would be an overstatement to say that the 'solution' of the private sphere is a failure; . . . but it is always very precarious." The history of the modern family, we might add, shows the difficulty of making domestic life a haven in a heartless world. Not only has marriage become a contractual arrangement, revocable at will, but the pervasive influence of the market—the most obvious example of which is the inescapability of commercial television—makes it more and more difficult for parents to shelter their children from the world of glamour, money, and power.

Quite apart from the impossibility of isolating private life from the commercial, bureaucratic, and technological structures that surround it, the "private solution" trivializes the communal ideal it seeks to protect. Bender recognizes the force of this objection. He raises it himself against the "human relations" school of industrial management, which tries to "engraft elements of community onto the main stem of organization." The business corporation will never become a community, Bender argues, any more than the nation as a whole will become a "family." This kind of talk "trivializes community," "markets the illusion of community," and gives rise to an "unspecified feeling of loss and emptiness that in turn makes Americans vulnerable to the manipulation of symbols of community."

At the end of his book, Bender suggests that the idea of a commonwealth, "rather than community, provides the essential foundation for a vigorous and effective political life." A commonwealth, he notes, "is based upon shared public ideals, rather than upon acquaintance or affection." But this afterthought comes too late to save the rest of his argument. The trivialization of the commonwealth is inherent in the very concept of "community," which has always been associated much more closely with intimacy and "togetherness" than with the search for a "vigorous and effective political life." Political life thrives on controversy, remembrance, and a periodic return to first principles, all of which the communitarian ideal condemns. Bender's own book begins with the classic definition of a community: "shared understandings and a sense of obligation"; "intimate, and usually face to face relationships"; an emphasis on "affective or emotional ties" as opposed to self-interest. A serious attempt to bring about a renewal of our political life will have to start from a different premise. It will have to abandon the whole concept of "community," along with the discourse in which it has historically grown up—the discourse of gemeinschaft and gesellschaft, "tradition" and modernity—and strike out in a new direction.

5

THE POPULIST CAMPAIGN AGAINST "IMPROVEMENT"

The Current Prospect:
Progress or Catastrophe?

Speculation about progress, if the forego-
ing argument is correct, has reached something of a dead
end. As the twentieth century draws to a close, we find it more and more
difficult to mount a compelling defense of the idea of progress; but we
find it equally difficult to imagine life without it.

The best line of defense, as we have seen, links progress to an indefinite
expansion of the demand for consumer goods. The expansion of demand,
however, presupposes conditions that no longer obtain. It presupposes a
constant revision of material expectations, a never-ending redefinition of
luxuries as necessities, continual incorporation of new groups into the

culture of consumption, and ultimately the creation of a global market that embraces populations formerly excluded from any reasonable expectation of affluence. But the prediction that "sooner or later we will all be affluent," uttered so confidently only a few years ago, no longer carries much conviction. In view of the present rate of population growth, the attempt to export a Western standard of living to the rest of the world, even if it was economically or politically feasible in the first place, would amount to a recipe for environmental disaster. In any case, the advanced countries no longer have the will or the resources to undertake such a monumental program of development. They cannot even solve the problem of poverty within their own borders. In the United States, the richest country in the world, a growing proletariat faces a grim future, and even the middle class has seen its standard of living begin to decline.

The global circulation of commodities, information, and populations, far from making everyone affluent, has widened the gap between rich and poor nations and generated a massive migration to the West, where the newcomers swell the vast army of the homeless, unemployed, illiterate, drug ridden, derelict, and effectively disfranchised. Their presence strains existing resources to the breaking point. Medical and educational facilities, law enforcement agencies, and the available supply of jobs—not to mention the supply of racial tolerance and goodwill, never abundant to begin with—all appear inadequate to the enormous task of assimilating what is essentially a surplus or "redundant" population, in the cruelly expressive British phrase. The poisonous effects of poverty and racial discrimination cannot be ghettoized; they too circulate on a global scale. "Like the effects of industrial pollution and the new system of global financial markets," Susan Sontag writes, "the AIDS crisis is evidence of a world . . . in which everything that can circulate does"—goods, images, garbage, disease. It is no wonder that "the look into the future, which was once tied to a vision of linear progress," has turned into a "vision of disaster," in Sontag's words, and that "anything . . . that can be described as changing steadily can be seen as heading toward catastrophe."

As a corrective to the idea of progress, the "imagination of disaster," as Sontag refers to it elsewhere, leaves a good deal to be desired. All too obviously, it simply inverts the idea of progress, substituting irresistible disintegration for irresistible advance. The dystopian view of the world to come, now so firmly established in the Western imagination, holds out such an abundance of unavoidable calamities that it becomes all the more necessary for people to cling to the idea of progress for emotional support, in spite of the mounting evidence against it. Horrifying images of the future, even when they are invoked not just to titillate a perverse and jaded taste but to shock people into constructive action, foster a curious state of mind that simultaneously believes and refuses to believe in the likelihood of some terminal catastrophe for the human race. A sober assessment of our predicament, one that would lead to action instead of paralyzing despair, has to begin by calling into question the fatalism that informs this whole discourse of progress and disaster. It is the assumption that our future is predetermined by the continuing development of large-scale production, colossal technologies, and political centralization that inhibits creative thought and makes it so difficult to avoid the choice between fatuous optimism and debilitating nostalgia.

The Discovery of Civic Humanism

Some such set of considerations, I think—as Michael Sandel puts it, "a growing fear that, individually and collectively, we are less and less in control of the forces that govern our lives"—helps to account for the recent fascination with submerged traditions of social criticism that have been overshadowed by the dominant tradition deriving from the Enlightenment. In the last twenty-five years, historians and political theorists have rediscovered "civic humanism" and "republican virtue," and the heated debates about these ideas, spilling over from scholarly publications into the journals of opinion, indicate that they have more than academic interest. "Republicanism"—which refers, of course, not to the Republican party but to a much older body of ideas stretching back to the Renaissance and, beyond that, to classical antiquity—has become the slogan of those who criticize liberalism, whether from the right or from the left, as a political philosophy increasingly incapable of commanding unselfish devotion to the common good. Only a revival of civic spirit, these critics maintain, will enable us to attack the problems that threaten to overwhelm us; and the republican emphasis on active citizenship speaks more directly to contemporary needs, they claim, than does the liberal philosophy of acquisitive individualism.

Everywhere we see signs of this growing disaffection with liberalism, most clearly perhaps in the widespread complaint that liberalism allows special interests to dominate party politics. Indeed the revulsion against party politics in itself implies dissatisfaction with liberalism. Both Democrats and Republicans now deplore excessive partisanship, the erosion of "community" and "citizenship." In Britain, even Margaret Thatcher, champion of the free market, promises to make "community" the central theme of her campaign for a fourth term as prime minister, drawing criticism from some of her former supporters, who advise her to stick to entrepreneurial individualism. "The notions of citizenship and community are based on a sentimental view of what rural life was like," the *Economist* says reproachfully. ". . . Real Britain is mostly quite different. Its cities are a kaleidoscope of races. . . . One-third of all marriages end in divorce. . . . Young Scots leave their small towns to work on London's building sites, and sleep in barges and caravans. Even homeowners . . . move on average once every seven years. . . . In that kind of Britain, 'community' has little meaning." But these are the very conditions that make so many people regard a revival of community as an urgent necessity. The social fabric seems to be unraveling; the welfare state has not been able to repair it; and the time has come, we are told, for a new set of solutions. Liberalism does not address the "anxieties of the age," according to Sandel—"the erosion of those communities intermediate between the individual and the nation, from families and neighborhoods to cities and towns to communities defined by religious or ethnic or cultural traditions."

The meaning of citizenship varies considerably from one end of the political spectrum to the other. On the right, it means the pledge of allegiance, respect for authority and religion, and the replacement of the welfare state by private agencies that would appeal to the spirit of voluntary cooperation instead of making everyone dependent on the state. For people on the left, a revival of citizenship seems to require not merely political but economic decentralization. After criticizing liberalism, Sandel goes on to criticize contemporary conservatism as well. "Conservative policies cannot answer the aspiration for community," because they ignore the "corrosive" effects of capitalism itself: "the unrestrained mobility of capital, with its disruptive effects on neighborhoods, cities, and towns; the concentration of power in large corporations unaccountable to the communities they serve: and an inflexible workplace that forces working men and women to choose between advancing their careers and caring for their children."

The appeal to citizenship and community can serve to cut across conventional classifications, in which case it has a salutary effect on political debate; but it can also serve to shore them up and to conceal their inadequacies. The language of citizenship, as it is used today, simultaneously clarifies and obscures political issues. There can be no question of its current popularity, however. Books like Sandel's *Liberalism and the Limits of Justice*, Alasdair MacIntyre's *After Virtue*, and Robert Bellah's *Habits of the Heart* have made the civic tradition one of the main topics of political conversation. "Civic virtue" lends itself all to easily, in fact, to the purposes of public exhortation. Thus the president of Yale, Benno C. Schmidt, urges graduating seniors to "rebel" against the "corruption and selfishness that have been such a feature of our public life" in recent years. The "republic of virtue," according to Schmidt, remains a viable ideal, the most important legacy of the "Renaissance tradition of civic humanism." The founding fathers "saw the maintenance of a republic of virtue as the overriding goal of statecraft," and the ideal still informs the "public commitments of many good people," even though it is "beset by doubt and difficulty." Such statements tell us less about the concept of virtue than about the fear of social fragmentation, competitive individualism, and self-seeking that underlies attempts to revive it.

The Civic Tradition
in Recent Historical Writing

· ■ ·

If "republicanism" is to serve as something more than a catchword, the term will have to be used with precision and with an understanding of its historical context. Recent scholarship makes it possible to trace a tenuous line of intellectual descent that began with the Athenian polis and the Roman republic, faded out during the Middle Ages, reappeared in the Florentine Renaissance, was picked up again by James Harrington and his followers in England and by Montesquieu and Rousseau in France, and came down to the founders of the American republic largely by way of the English variant. The republican tradition varied from place to place and underwent many changes over time, the most important of which was Harrington's substitution of land for military service as the social foundation of citizenship. Rousseau's republicanism, with its stress on a unitary state and an all-encompassing "general will," bore little resemblance to the kind of republicanism that sought to limit the power of the state and to balance one kind of power against another—preoccupations that eventually gave rise to the modern theory of the separation of powers.

If there is any justification for speaking of a continuous tradition at all, and of a single tradition rather than several, it lies in the persistence of two characteristic concerns, the combination of which distinguished republicanism from other varieties of political thought. The first, originating in Aristotle's classification of regimes according to their domination by the one, the few, and the many (tyranny, oligarchy, and democracy, respectively), led to efforts to analyze the sources of political instability—which caused regimes to degenerate into one or another of these extremes—and to work out some principle of balance that would combine the advantages of each while nullifying the features that made them oppressive. The second set of concerns arose out of the belief that "virtue" was the object (not the precondition) of citizenship and that any political system should therefore be judged by the qualities of mind and character that it tended to elicit. On this point, there was a considerable range of opinion, from the Aristotelian emphasis on a unified human life to the Machiavellian emphasis on military prowess. For all republicans, however, virtue was associated with self-assertion and self-realization, not with self-abnegation.* Republicans had little use for Christianity, not

---

*It may be true, as Stephen Holmes asserts in a recent polemic against "antiliberal thought," that communitarian critics of liberalism now "assume that when a person transcends self-interest, he is necessarily behaving in a morally admirable way." But this assumption played no part in the republican tradition, even though communitarians appeal to that tradition, without much understanding of it, as an important source of their own ideas. A number of the historians whose work has contributed to the emergence of a "republican synthesis," as Robert Shalhope referred to it some years ago, have inadvertently encouraged the misunderstanding that republicanism was

only because it allegedly undermined civic loyalty but because it held up self-abnegation as an ethical ideal. As Machiavelli put it, Christianity gave men "strength to suffer rather than strength to do bold things." "True Christians," said Rousseau, anticipating Nietzsche, "are made to be slaves."

For republicans, virtue implied the fullest development of human capacities and powers. They condemned a life devoted to the pursuit of wealth and private comforts not because it was selfish but because it provided insufficient scope for the ambition to excel. The contrast between selfishness and altruism, so prominent in recent communitarianism, played little part in the civic tradition. Even a "selfless" devotion to politics, warfare, or some other practice was seen to bring glory and renown—not, to be sure, as its reward, since excellence was its own reward, but as its necessary and appropriate accompaniment and validation. Republicanism condemned self-seeking when it tempted men to value the external rewards of excellence more highly than the thing itself or to bend the rules governing a given practice to their own immediate advantage. Self-seeking was objectionable because it led men to demand less of themselves than they were capable of achieving, and only incidentally because in measuring themselves against false standards they also injured others.

---

preeminently the political philosophy of self-abnegation. Even Gordon Wood, whose meticulous craftsmanship is unrivaled among the republican revisionists, sometimes uses the term "virtue" as if it referred merely to the "sacrifice of individual interests to the greater good," in his words. Lance Banning argues, in a recent paper, that Wood underemphasized eighteenth-century recognition of the self-interested basis of conduct and thus misread as a "call for selflessness" what was really a call for "vigorous assertions of the self within a context of communal consciousness." Republicans associated virtue with virility, Banning points out, not with self-surrender. True, they valued a "self-denying spirit" that would "resist immersion in the private life of acquisition and enjoyment"; but "there was little in this talk that clearly called for self-effacing, totally disinterested regard for an abstracted general good, [and] little to suggest that citizens' decisions would or should be made without consideration of their interests."

"Virtue" had far wider implications even than this, as literary historians have made clear. The division of labor that walls off literary history from political and intellectual history contributes to the confusion surrounding this issue.

"Altruism," "public service," "selfless devotion to the common good"—these terms provide a pallid translation of what republicans meant by virtue. Those who today invoke republicanism in support of those ideals or, again, in the hope of encouraging the spirit of cooperation in what is perceived as an excessively competitive society, would be well advised to rest their case on other grounds. The republican ethic was nothing if not competitive. It was the ethic of the arena, the battlefield, and the forum—strenuous, combative, agonistic. In urging men to pit themselves against the most demanding standards of achievement, it also pitted them against each other. In politics, it set a higher value on eloquence, disputation, and verbal combat than on compromise and conciliation. Political life, for republicans, provided another outlet for ambition, another form of contest—not primarily a means of reconciling opposing interests or assuring an equitable distribution of goods. Economic issues, as the Greek word indicates, belonged to the household *(oikos):* in politics, men chased bigger game.

Because some types of republicans wanted to limit the powers of the state, they have sometimes been confused with modern liberals; because others spoke of civic "virtue," they have been confused with modern communitarians. The first of these misunderstandings describes the state of historical scholarship before the rediscovery of the civic tradition in the 1960s; the second, the confusion inadvertently encouraged by revisionist scholarship. The republican revival began when Bernard Bailyn and Gordon Wood showed that the ideology of the American revolution derived not so much from the liberalism of John Locke as from the "commonwealth" or country-party tradition in seventeenth- and eighteenth-century England. Especially in Wood's version, the revolution had less to do with property rights than with citizenship. Eighteenth-century political debate, according to Wood, turned on the attempt to work out a plan of government that would assure the active participation of citizens in a country where the qualifications for citizenship were much less restrictive than elsewhere—to democratize the republican ideal of political life.

This interpretation of the revolution was advanced in opposition to historians who saw the War for Independence as a bourgeois revolution and argued, moreover, that it was a mild and moderate revolution (unlike the one in France) because America, lacking a feudal past, had been a bourgeois society from the beginning. Louis Hartz took this position in his *Liberal Tradition in America,* but many others subscribed to his thesis that liberalism had never had to contend with serious opposition either in the colonial period or in any subsequent period of American history. The story of American politics, as seen by Hartz, Richard Hofstadter, and others—not necessarily a success story, in their eyes—was the unchallenged ascendancy of liberalism, the triumph of capitalism, and the failure of conservatism and socialism alike. Thus Andrew Jackson, once deified as the tribune of the people, emerged in Hofstadter's *American Political Tradition* as an exponent of "liberal capitalism" and Abraham Lincoln, the Great Emancipator, as the foremost ideologist of the "self-made myth." Whether the intention behind such interpretations was to deplore the absence of a social democratic tradition (as it seemed to be, initially at least, in the case of Hofstadter and Hartz) or to celebrate the absence of ideological division (as in the case of Daniel Boorstin), the assumption of a broad liberal "consensus"—stifling or comforting, as the case might be—dominated historical scholarship in the forties and fifties.

Bailyn and Wood challenged this view by showing that Lockean liberalism was not the only source of revolutionary ideology. But this accomplishment was not enough for a legion of revisionists who followed in their footsteps. The revisionists wanted to make republicanism the dominant theme of American history. If the older historians saw nothing but liberalism, the revisionists saw nothing but civic humanism. When they found liberals who expressed misgivings about acquisitive individualism, they proceeded to call them republicans instead. The American Whigs, enthusiastic promoters of economic development, became republicans because they advocated a regulated pattern of development and a balance between industry and agriculture. The Jacksonians' opposition to monopolies and corruption made them republicans too. But if both parties came out of the same political tradition and held the same views of government, how did they find so much to fight about? Louis Hartz found it necessary to dismiss the rivalry between Whigs and Jacksonian Democrats as a sham battle—an important indication that something was wrong with his hypothesis of liberal consensus. The "republican synthesis" appeared to generate the same difficulty. When all shades of political opinion were forced into the same category, it became more and more difficult to understand what people in the past thought they were arguing about. A republican synthesis was no better than a liberal synthesis when such terms expanded to cover every political persuasion.

Tom Paine: Liberal or Republican?

· ■ ·

One of the circumstances that make it tempting to exaggerate the ubiquity of the republican impulse in eighteenth- and nineteenth-century politics is that anyone opposed to the institution of monarchy became a republican by definition. In Europe, monarchy itself remained a divisive issue, but it was a dead issue in the United States after 1783. In that limited sense, republicanism really was a universal creed, at least for Americans. But we knew that long ago. If the "republican synthesis" can claim to advance our understanding of the past, it is only because it distinguishes republicanism from liberalism, demonstrates its continuing appeal, and thus refutes the hypothesis of liberal consensus. Unfortunately many of the most celebrated republicans in Anglo-American history, so called because of their hatred of monarchy, cannot be seen as republicans in any other sense of the term.

Take the case of Tom Paine, a "republican" if there ever was one in his vigorous attack on the "baleful institution" of monarchy. Apart from this, however, there is very little in Paine's thought that would tie him to the civic tradition. He was untroubled by the question of representation that troubled so many Antifederalists in the 1780s. Opponents of the new Constitution argued that republican government could not flourish in a large nation in which citizens, instead of directly governing themselves, would have to settle for vicarious participation through their representatives. The specialization of political functions was no more acceptable to republicans than the specialization of military functions. Both illustrated the dangers of the division of labor, which undermined self-sufficiency and made men passive and dependent. These concerns in turn underlay the fear that geographical expansion would destroy republican virtue.

Paine did not bother to answer these objections. He simply asserted, without argument, that "by ingrafting representation upon democracy, we arrive at a system of government capable of embracing and confederating all the various interests and every extent of territory and population." He objected neither to the replacement of direct participation by representation nor to men's increasing absorption in commercial pursuits, which drew them away from their civic duties, according to republican theory, and made them too eager to hand over those duties to a new class of professional politicians. Paine had little use for politicians—for government in general—but he did not draw the connection between their growing importance and the growth of commerce.* On the contrary, he proclaimed himself a "friend of commerce," which he referred to as a "pacific system, operating to cordialize mankind, by rendering nations, as well as individuals, useful to each other." Republicans took no such benign view of commerce, nor did they share Paine's enthusiasm for cosmopolitan citizenship. Civic humanism implied citizenship in a particular city or state, whereas Paine called himself a citizen of the world and defended commerce on the grounds, reminiscent of Hume and Adam Smith, that it would "extirpate the system of war" and produce a "universal civilization."

These opinions set Paine at odds with classical republicans, but they did not necessarily make him an exponent of "bourgeois liberalism," as Isaac Kramnick calls him. The commercial society he favored was a democracy of small shopkeepers and artisans, and it was shopkeepers and artisans who kept Paine's memory alive in the nineteenth century, idolizing him as the champion of the "producing classes" in their struggle against the parasites. This distinction, the very essence of popular radicalism in the nineteenth century, appealed to those who condemned the machinery of modern credit as exploitive and unproductive. Paine may have defended the Bank of North America against its critics in the 1780s, but he seems to have thought of banks essentially as repositories for shop-

---

*In *Common Sense*, however, he did observe that commerce sapped the "spirit both of patriotism and military defence." The American colonists, he argued, should not be deterred from declaring their independence by their sparse population and undeveloped economy. "The more a country is peopled, the smaller their armies are. In military numbers, the ancients far exceeded the moderns: and the reason is evident, for trade being the consequence of population, men become too much absorbed thereby to attend to anything else.... The bravest achievements were always accomplished in the nonage of a nation. With the increase of commerce, England hath lost its spirit. The city of London, notwithstanding its numbers, submits to continued insults with the patience of a coward. The more men have to lose, the less willing are they to venture." This is pure republicanism—one of the few unadulterated expressions of republican ideology in Paine's writings.

keepers' savings or "remnant money" and not as sources of large-scale commercial credit. He denounced paper money as an evil second only to taxation. Paper money had "no real value in itself"; its value depended only on "accident, caprice and party." Gold and silver alone—solid, substantial, "sacred"—could be trusted.

> Money, when considered as the fruit of many years' industry, as the reward of labour, sweat and toil, as the widow's dowry and children's portion, and as the means of procuring the necessaries and alleviating the afflictions of life, and making old age a scene of rest, has something in it sacred that is not to be sported with, or trusted to the airy bubble of paper currency.

Andrew Jackson, another hard-money man, later praised *The Rights of Man* as a book "more enduring than all the piles of marble and granite man can erect"—a phrase highly expressive of the preoccupation with solid, durable objects that was so characteristic of the hard-money ideology.

That ideology can be described as "vintage liberalism" only if it is judged against the standards of modern social democracy, according to which a belief in equality implies opposition to private property and support for governmental regulation of the market. It is true that Paine took the position, in *The Rights of Man* (1792), that "commerce is capable of taking care of itself." But he favored price controls during the revolutionary war, advocated a progressive system of taxation, and condemned "all accumulation . . . of personal property, beyond what a man's own hands produce." These opinions lead Eric Foner to characterize Paine's economic program as an early version of the welfare state; but this label seems almost as inappropriate as laissez-faire liberalism. In *Agrarian Justice* (1795), Paine urged that the fund accumulated by taxes on unearned increment be used to "relieve misery," to support the "aged poor," and "to furnish the rising generation with the means to prevent their becoming poor."

> When a young couple begin the world [he explained], the difference is exceedingly great whether they begin with nothing

or with fifteen pounds apiece. With this aid they could buy a cow, and implements to cultivate a few acres of land; and instead of becoming burdens upon society, which is always the case where children are produced faster than they can be fed, would be put in the way of becoming useful and profitable citizens.

Paine's democracy of small property owners had little room for a permanent class of wage earners, much less for a dependent class of paupers maintained at public expense.

Paine can be called a liberal only in the same way that he can be called a republican—by stretching the terms completely out of shape. Eighteenth- and nineteenth-century liberals worked out an elaborate ideology of progress based on the division of labor, unprecedented gains in productivity, the upgrading of tastes, and the expansion of consumer demand. Paine took a far more limited view of the good life. "Every man wishes to pursue his occupation, and to enjoy the fruits of his labours and the produce of his property in peace and safety, and with the least possible expense." In spite of his enthusiasm for commerce, he had serious doubts about the reality of progress. "Whether that state that is proudly, perhaps erroneously, called civilization, has most promoted or most injured the general happiness of man, is a question that may be strongly contested." The contrast between affluence and misery, "splendid appearances" and shocking "extremes of wretchedness," made it impossible for Paine to side wholeheartedly with the advocates of improvement. The "great mass of the poor" had become a "hereditary race," and "this mass increases in all countries that are called civilized."

Paine is best understood, it would appear, neither as a republican nor as a "vintage liberal" but as one of the founders of a populist tradition that drew on republicanism and liberalism alike but mixed these ingredients into something new. The portions varied from one writer to another. In Paine's recipe, liberal ingredients predominated; but this should suggest not that his bourgeois sympathies prevented him from becoming a modern social democrat but that liberalism, in the mind of Paine and his followers, did not yet stand for progress, large-scale production, and the proliferation of consumer goods. Only when it did come to stand unambiguously for these things did the underlying opposition between populism and liberalism become unmistakable.

William Cobbett and the "Paper System"

· ■ ·

The political career of William Cobbett, a fierce antagonist of Paine in his youth but a great admirer in his later years, illustrates the difficulty of forcing eighteenth- and nineteenth-century debate into airtight compartments like "Lockean liberalism" and "civic humanism." Cobbett spoke the language of republicanism, yet he wrote a eulogistic life of Paine and dug up his bones on Long Island for transportation back to England. This belated act of homage appears all the more bizarre in view of the obvious differences between the two men. Paine extolled cosmopolitanism, whereas Cobbett was a fervent patriot who assured his countrymen, on the eve of his flight to the United States in 1817, that he would "always be a foreigner in every country but England." With characteristic exaggeration, he once called Ben Franklin's maxim, "Where *liberty* is, there is *my* country"—a saying eminently worthy of Paine as well—"as immoral and vile a sentiment as ever disgraced the mind of man." Paine spent most of his life in cities; Cobbett celebrated country pleasures and despised the "effeminating luxuries" of the metropolis. Paine advocated commercial development; Cobbett opposed it, partly on the very grounds that appealed to Paine—that it would bring nations closer together. That commerce promoted "intimate connection and almost intermixture with foreign nations" did not recommend it in Cobbett's eyes. On the contrary, he thought of foreign trade as another source of "contagious effeminacy."

Paine, raised as a Quaker, hated war (although he urged Quakers to support the war for American independence), whereas Cobbett never lost his enthusiasm for the manly arts, "which string the nerves and strengthen the frame, which excite an emulation in deeds of hardihood and valour, and which imperceptibly instill honour, generosity, and a love of glory, into the mind of the clown." Paine thought of himself as a humanitarian; Cobbett relished blood sports, dueling, and armed combat. He regarded the humanitarianism of William Wilberforce, his lifelong bête noire, as one more evidence of civic decline. Denouncing a bill to outlaw boxing and bearbaiting, he resorted to the republican idiom in order to trace six stages of national decline: "Commerce, Opulence, Luxury, Effeminacy, Cowardice, and Slavery." Wilberforce and his Society for the Suppression of Vice sought to abolish, Cobbett said, "every exercise of the common people . . . that tends to prepare them for deeds of bravery of a higher order" and "to preserve the independence and the liberties of their country."

To link Cobbett to the country-party tradition requires no historiographical sleight of hand. He drew the link himself, noting that in the old days England had been divided into "a *Court Party* and a *Country Party*, the latter of which was always ready to defend the rights of the people." In his own day, Cobbett said, the country party had tied its fortunes to the Prince of Wales and thus become a court party in its own right, with the result that "the people had no party at all." His standard remained the rural England of his youth—a prosperous society, as he remembered it in the days before "the system" had deprived Englishmen of their beef, their rough sports, and their manly independence. Paine's doubts about progress rested on the conventional contrast between civilization and a state of nature. "A great portion of mankind, in what are called civilized countries, are in a state of poverty and wretchedness, far below the condition of an Indian." (Similar statements can be found in the writings of Adam Smith.) When Cobbett talked of decline, however, he referred to a decline that had taken place in his own lifetime.

> Well do I remember, when old men, common labourers, used to wear to church good broad-cloth coats which they had worn at their weddings. They were frugal and careful, but they had encouragement to practise those virtues. The household goods of a labouring man, his clock, his trenchers and his pewter plates, his utensils of brass and copper, his chairs, his joint-stools, his substantial oaken tables, his bedding and all that belonged to him, form a contrast with his present miserable and worthless stuff that makes one's heart ache but to think of.

As Kramnick and Michael Foot observe, "Cobbett looked back to a medieval golden age; Paine looked forward to a Utopia, to the perfectibility of man." Yet Cobbett came to see Paine as a comrade in arms, and not without reason. They both despised monopolists, speculators, and middlemen—"plunderers" and "bloodsuckers," as Cobbett referred to them, who live in "riot and luxury" on the "plunder of the ignorant, the innocent, the helpless." Both exempted from their attack on the "monied interest" the "fair merchant" and the "honest industrious tradesmen, who holds the middle rank, and has given repeated proofs, that he prefers law and liberty to gold."

For Cobbett, it was above all government borrowing that gave rise to a new breed of "jobbers, brokers, and peculators." Under the "paper system," government was no longer financed by current revenue but by loans from wealthy subjects, who thus gained a decisive influence over the state. A national debt and a standing army—itself a drain on the public treasury, necessitating further loans—led to the emergence of a society "in which there are but two classes of men," as Cobbett put it, "masters and abject dependents."* Paine attributed the same result to the rise of a "landed monopoly" that had "dispossessed more than half the inhabitants of every nation of their natural inheritance" and thus "created a species of poverty and wretchedness that did not exist before." Both he and Cobbett deplored the "enslaving reverence" for "affluence," in Paine's words, and believed that "wealth and splendor, instead of fascinating the multitude," ought to "excite emotions of disgust." Both men allowed their politics, in other words, to be governed in large part by their instinctive revulsion against wealth, whereas Adam Smith, it will be recalled, agreed that respect for the "vain and empty distinctions of greatness" was misplaced but welcomed this "deception" as the source of industry and economic progress.

This comparison of Paine and Cobbett suggests that republican ideology had lost most of its larger resonance by this time and survived mainly in the form of an egalitarian dislike of social extremes, a preference for plain living, and an unmitigated disgust with the growing pretensions of

---

*Here again, his analysis of the source of "corruption," as well as his rhetoric, derived straight from the country-party tradition. In *Cato's Letters,* the classic exposition of eighteenth-century republicanism, John Trenchard and Thomas Gordon attacked the moneylenders in the same language later used by Cobbett: "What Briton, blessed with any sense of virtue, or with common sense: what Englishmen, animated with a public spirit, or with any spirit, but must burn with rage and shame, to behold the nobles and gentry of a great Kingdom . . . bowing down . . . before the face of a dirty stock-jobber, and receiving laws from men bred behind counters, and the decision of their fortunes from hands, still dirty with sweeping shops!"

the fashionable classes. Republicanism, earlier associated with manly prowess and military glory, with the pursuit of excellence through civic participation, a respect for the past, and a tendency to equate social change with degeneration, survived far more vigorously in Cobbett than in Paine. Even Cobbett, however, can be called a civic humanist only in a very general sense. His social thought rested on an appeal to memory, but he invoked the memory of old England, not the memory of classical antiquity or the Renaissance. After Cobbett, the Anglo-American critique of progress drew more heavily on religious than on republican themes, and it came to be associated with a growing admiration for the Middle Ages quite inconsistent with the classical imagery favored by republicans. Social critics like Thomas Carlyle, Orestes Brownson, John Ruskin, and William Morris loved the Middle Ages but found little merit in the Renaissance. Only their assault on the "paper system," together with an occasional reference to Harrington and his followers (hardly ever to Machiavelli), links them to the civic tradition, and even that aspect of their thought is better understood not as a residual republicanism but as a blend of several traditions in which republicanism became a more and more insignificant ingredient. These ingredients came together in a new kind of social criticism that could not be adequately characterized in the old terms. Its distinguishing features—best exemplified, for our purposes, in the American variant—included a defense of small farmers, artisans, and other "producers"; opposition to public creditors, speculators, bankers, and middlemen; opposition to the whole culture of uplift and "improvement"; and an increasingly detailed and eloquent indictment of humanitarianism, philanthropy, moral reformation, and universal benevolence—the "comforting system," as Cobbett scornfully called it.

Orestes Brownson and the Divorce between Politics and Religion

Orestes Brownson's search for a satisfactory synthesis of politics and religion took him down so many twists and turns, so many false starts and blind alleys, that it almost defies attempts to find a thread of consistency or even to find any pattern at all. Once described by Emerson as a "Cobbett of a scribe" (thanks to his rousing essay "The Laboring Classes"), Brownson ran through practically the whole range of Protestant sects—Presbyterianism, Universalism, free thought, Unitarianism—before converting to Catholicism in 1844, and his political views followed a similarly erratic path. An Owenite socialist in his twenties, he later embraced the cause of working-class radicalism, briefly called himself a Jacksonian Democrat, soured on democracy after the log-cabin, hard-cider campaign of 1840, allied himself for a time with John C. Calhoun, and finally settled down as a Catholic conservative in the last twenty-five years of his life.

Since Brownson never kept his opinions to himself or thought them over in private before committing them to print, he "gained a sneer," as he himself noted, for his "versatility and frequent changes of opinions."* He conducted his self-education in public, in the pages of magazines written entirely by himself. "The debate in my mind," he wrote in 1842, "has been going on for the last ten years." In fact it had been going on a good deal longer than that; nor did it stop with his conversion. As a Catholic, he continued to fill *Brownson's Quarterly Review* with dense, erudite, prickly, opinionated articles on theology, ethics, epistemology, law, and politics. More Catholic than the pope, he sometimes had to be disciplined by his clerical superiors, especially when his frequent pleas for the reunification of politics and religion threatened the precarious truce between the Catholic church and the state. The Catholic hierarchy understood its acceptance of the church-state separation as the essential condition of the church's existence in America, and Brownson's zeal for a public religion proved not a little embarrassing.

His inability to accept the separation of politics and religion provides the key, I think, to Brownson's otherwise baffling career—the one element of stability and continuity running through all his inconsistencies and contradictions. From the beginning, he took the position that reli-

---

*Theodore Parker called Brownson "a man of unbalanced mind, intellectual always, but spiritual never: heady, but not hearty; roving from church to church; now Trinitarian, then unbeliever, then Universalist, Unitarian, Catholic—everything by turns but nothing long." Brownson, Parker said, was "not a Christian, but only a verbal index of Christianity—a commonplace book of theology."

gion was far too important to remain a purely private concern; no doubt it was this conviction, in part, that led him to make such a public issue of his own religion, doubts and all. Even during his free-thought phase, he insisted that society needed religion more than ever—the religion of humanity, as he then hoped, that would take the place of Christianity. By the mid-thirties, he had repudiated the man-made religion advocated by the Saint-Simonians.* He wrote his *New Views of Christianity, Society, and the Church* (1836) expressly to refute the contention that society needed a new religion in place of the old one. In the same work, however, he continued to attack the separation of church and state, which rested, he now argued, on a philosophical separation of spirit and matter, mind and body, that ran counter to the doctrine of the Incarnation and to the whole Christian tradition. Three years later, he criticized the idea that clergymen should not "meddle in politics" on the grounds that "all man's duties are intimately connected," that "religion and politics run perpetually into one another," and that "a religion which neglects man's social weal, is defective in the extreme," while a politics set apart from religion

---

*In his autobiography, published in 1857, Brownson explained that he was attracted to the Saint-Simonians because, unlike other radical sects, they foresaw a "religious future for the human race" and held that religious feeling, moreover, had to be embodied in a "hierarchical organization." He found the same ideas in Benjamin Constant, the French liberal whose writings, he said, helped to bring into clearer focus his misgivings about Protestantism—though not yet, of course, to push him toward Catholicism. "The work of destruction, commenced by the Reformation, which had introduced an era of criticism and revolution, had, I thought, been carried far enough. All that was dissoluble had been dissolved. All that was destructible had been destroyed, and it was time to begin the work of reconstruction,—a work of reconciliation and love."

Since "no doubt had as yet risen in my mind as to the truth of the doctrine of progress," Brownson assumed, in the early 1830s, that the religious institution humanity required would take the form of a "church of the future." He took the position that although "Catholicity was good in its day," the mere fact of the Reformation "proved that there were wants and lights which Catholicity did not meet." It was equally obvious to Brownson at this time—or at least in retrospect—that Protestantism had completed its own historical assignment and that the world now cried out for "union." He interpreted the work of Carlyle, among others, as such a cry. "Carlyle, in his *Sartor Resartus*, seemed to lay his finger on the plague-spot of the age. Men had reached the centre of indifference, . . . had pronounced the everlasting 'No.' Were they never to be able to pronounce the everlasting 'Yes'?"

degenerated "of necessity into Machiavelism." In 1842, he said that it was "wrong, wrong," to cite medieval history on the dangers of clerical oppression, as if it were improper for secular authorities to submit to spiritual authority. On the contrary, "it was well for man that there was a power above the brutal tyrants called emperors, kings, and barons, who rode roughshod over the humble peasant and artisan."

The inseparability of politics and religion, as Brownson conceived it, by no means implied the desirability of an official consensus or civic religion. He wanted a "powerful and living synthesis," not an "imbecile eclecticism." In the 1830s and 1840s, liberal Protestants, most of them Whigs, urged the churches to abandon sectarian squabbles and to unite around a few ethical precepts common to all of them, which could serve as a national creed. They feared that without moral discipline, competitive individualism would tear society apart. The separation of church and state was a highly desirable arrangement, in their eyes, because it kept divisive and inconsequential controversies about doctrine out of politics and allowed the churches to devote themselves to the more important work of moral reform. Temperance, thrift, honesty in business, proper work habits, provision for the poor, prompt payment of debts, respect for women, protection of Indian rights: these were the crying needs of the day, as the Whigs saw them—to which the "conscience Whigs" would have added the gradual emancipation of slaves, followed by their resettlement in Africa. This ambitious program of "improvement" presupposed a basic moral consensus, which Whigs hoped to propagate through charitable organizations and other interdenominational agencies—the "voluntary associations" so highly praised by Tocqueville—and through the common schools. The school system envisioned by Horace Mann and other reformers was meant to serve as the main source of social morality.

In his blistering attacks on Mann's educational reforms, Brownson made very explicit the difference between his own view of the proper relation between politics and religion and the Whigs' conception of a civil religion based on the suppression of doctrinal issues. A state-supported system of education, operated on the principles envisioned by Mann, would enshrine the "opinions now dominant" and reinforce the political status quo. It would amount to a "branch of general police." Mann and his friends promoted education as the "most effectual means possible of checking pauperism and crime, and making the rich secure in their possessions." Having failed to perpetuate the establishment of religion, they now sought to reimpose it through a state-supported educational establishment. Their plans were objectionable on religious as well as on political grounds. By suppressing everything divisive in religion, they would leave only a bland residue. "A faith, which embraces generalities only, is little better than no faith at all." Children brought up in a mild, nondenominational "Christianity ending in nothingness," in schools where much was "taught in general, but nothing in particular," would be deprived of their birthright. They would be taught "to respect and pre-serve what is"; they would be cautioned against the "licentiousness of the people, the turbulence and brutality of the mob"; but they would never learn a "love of liberty" under such a system.

Here was the nub of the issue, as Brownson saw it: the impossibility of teaching people "to stand fast in their freedom" unless they were first brought up in a particular religious tradition. "An education which is not religious is a solemn mockery"; but "no Calvinist can teach Christianity, if he be honest, so as to satisfy a conscientious and earnest Unitarian." Before they could respect themselves and others, men and women needed to be taught to respect some body of "important truth." For these rea-sons, education ought to remain under local and as nearly as possible under parental control.* But that was not the end of it; it was only the beginning, according to Brownson. The real work of education did not take place in the schools at all. Anticipating John Dewey, Brownson pointed out that

> our children are educated in the streets, by the influence of their associates, in the fields and on the hill sides, by the influ-

---

*By this time (1839), Brownson had long since repudiated the views of Fanny Wright, which also assigned a central role in social reform to the schools, though for reasons different from Mann's. "It was assumed [by Fanny Wright and her school] that parents were in general incompetent to train up their children in the way they should go." In 1857, Brownson traced the source of "our illusion," the "undue estimate we placed on education," to Lockean psychology, which taught that "the child is passive in the hands of the educator." "Most of the generation to which I belong have been brought up to believe that the mind has no inherent character, and is in the beginning a mere *tabula rasa,* a blank sheet, with simply the capacity of receiving the characters which may be written on it."

ences of surrounding scenery and overshadowing skies, in the bosom of the family, by the love and gentleness, or wrath and fretfulness of parents, by the passions or affections they see manifested, the conversations to which they listen, and above all by the general pursuits, habits, and moral tone of the community.

These considerations, together with Brownson's extensive discussion of the press and the lyceum, seemed to point to the conclusion that people were most likely to develop a love of liberty through exposure to wide-ranging public controversy, the "free action of mind on mind." Strong convictions would not amount to much unless those who held them proved both able and willing to defend them. Public controversy, accordingly, ought to address itself not only to politics but to religion—the "two great concernments of human beings." When he criticized the separation of religion and politics, Brownson meant that questions concerning the "destiny of man" ought to become questions for public debate, not that a new religious establishment should provide authoritative answers. "The day for authoritative teaching is gone by." Efforts to reimpose it would only lead to that "calm, respectable state, which our respectable clergy contend for"; and anything was preferable to the "present deadness of our churches." "Peace is a good thing, but justice is better.... Give us the noise and contention of life, rather than the peace and silence of the charnel-house."

Brownson's Attack on Philanthropy

To call Brownson a republican would be stretching a point. He considered it an argument in favor of democracy that "it takes care not to lose the man in the citizen"—not exactly a republican sentiment. In the free cities of antiquity, Brownson pointed out, "there were rights of the citizen, but no rights of man." Thus Socrates, condemned to death, submitted to the polis instead of heeding his friends' advice to flee. "He had no rights as a man, that he might plead." In Greece and Rome, "there was no personal liberty"; the "individual ... counted for nothing." This subordination of the man to the citizen found its modern application in the dogma of the people as an absolute sovereign, which Brownson consistently opposed. He believed that the "inalienable rights of man" limited the powers of the state, whether it was controlled by "monarchs or mobs." This idea played no part in the civic tradition; those who wanted to find its antecedents, Brownson said, would have to look to the "feudal system, and still more to Christianity," which introduced the "element of individuality."

In his later phase, Brownson sometimes referred to himself as a republican, but only to remind his readers (just as Paine had reminded his) that the term's literal meaning referred to the public good, or else to argue that "the American people committed a serious mistake in translating republicanism into democracy" and should now "restore the government to the true principles of the Constitution." When Brownson invoked Harrington, it was only to disavow the impact of Harrington's work on his own views concerning the "influence of property on politics and legislation." We may dismiss his claim that these views were "original with me"; but wherever he got them, his general point of view clearly owed more to Christian influences, overlaid at times with influences deriving from the Enlightenment, than to the tradition of civic humanism.

His Christian radicalism nevertheless had certain points of contact with the republican tradition: a taste for verbal combat; a confidence in the educative, character-forming discipline of political life and the clash of opinions; a belief that "man has an end," namely to develop his capacities to the utmost; a suspicion that life was not worth living unless it was lived with ardor, energy, and devotion. "Nothing is . . . more nauseating than to be lukewarm," he held. "Give us, we say, open, energetic, uncompromising enemies, or firm, staunch friends, who will take their stand for the truth, . . . to live with it or die with it; and not your half and half men." To live or die for truth was not the same thing, to be sure, as living for glory; but these ideals had more in common than either had, say, with Paine's ideal of "peace and safety," let alone a more fully developed liberalism of the kind articulated by Adam Smith. Brownson thought politics ought to address moral issues of transcendent importance, even at the risk of disturbing the peace; for this reason, he dissociated himself, more than once, from Paine's dictum that government was at best a necessary evil.

His opposition to an educational establishment likewise sprang from considerations not unlike those that underlay republican opposition to a standing army. Brownson argued, in effect, that the people would lose the capacity to educate themselves and their children if they turned education over to a class of professional custodians. Like republicans, he opposed the whole trend toward a more and more highly specialized division of labor; this was his basic quarrel with the political economy of liberalism, as it was theirs. In 1841, still contending that the "mission of this country" was to "raise up the laboring classes, and make every man really free and independent," he regretted the "division of society into workingmen and idlers, employers and operatives," a "learned class and an unlearned, a cultivated class and an uncultivated, a refined class and a vulgar." The only way to reverse this trend, in his view, was to make every man a proprietor. This was the upshot of his famous essay of 1840, "The Laboring Classes"—a piece so radical that it was received, as Brownson later recalled, with "one universal scream of horror."*

With good reason, commentators have seen in "The Laboring Classes" anticipations of *The Communist Manifesto*, launched upon the world eight years later. "All over the world this fact stares us in the face, the working-

---

*"The gravamen of my offence was my condemnation of the modern industrial system, especially the system of labor at wages, which I held to be worse, except in regard to the feelings, than the slave system at the South. . . . I contended that the great, the mother-evil of modern society was the separation of capital and labor; or the fact that one class of the community owns the funds, and another and a distinct class is compelled to perform the labor of production." Brownson conceded that his remedy—to make "every man an owner of the funds as well as the labor of production"—"would have broken up the whole modern commercial system, prostrated all the great industries, or what I called the factory system, and thrown the mass of the people back on the land to get their living by agricultural and mechanical pursuits." But that was precisely "one of the results I aimed at," even though it "went directly against the dominant sentiment of the British and American world" by calling into question "its crowning glory."

Note that Brownson never retracted these opinions. "I am unable even to-day to detect any unsoundness," he wrote in 1857, "in my views of the relation of capital and labor, or of the modern system of money wages." The "practicability" of his reforms was the point on which he later changed his mind, the campaign of 1840 having "disgusted" him with democracy and made him "distrust both the intelligence and the instincts of 'the masses.'"

man is poor and depressed, while a large portion of the non-workingmen . . . are wealthy." The evil, according to Brownson, did not lie in an excess of government, as Adam Smith's disciples believed, but in the "present system of trade," specifically in wage labor—"a cunning device of the devil." The real enemy of the working class was the "middle class, always a firm champion of equality, when it concerns humbling a class above it; but . . . its inveterate foe, when it concerns elevating a class below it." Having defeated the aristocracy, the middle class had turned "conservative, . . . whether it call itself Whig or Radical." The "coming contest," already taking shape in England with the rise of the Chartist movement, would pit the working man against his employer, his "only real enemy." It would not be resolved "without war and bloodshed." Education would do little to improve the lot of the poor. Neither did the answer lie in "self-culture"—the favorite remedy of those who sought reform "without disturbing the social arrangements which render reform necessary." Since the evil was "inherent in all our social arrangements," it could not be cured "without a radical change of those arrangements."

The cure Brownson had in mind, of course, was proprietorship, not communism.

> There must be no class of our fellow men doomed to toil through life as mere workmen at wages. If wages are tolerated it must be, in the case of the individual operative, only under such conditions that by the time he is of a proper age to settle in life, he shall have accumulated enough to be an independent laborer on his own capital,—on his own farm or in his own shop. Here is our work.

Elsewhere Brownson made himself even plainer. In *The Convert,* an autobiography published seventeen years later, he explained that he had intended to abolish the "distinction between capitalists and laborers," the "factory system," the "banking and credit system"—the whole structure of modern progress, in short. "I wished to check commerce, to destroy speculation, and for the factory system, which we were enacting tariffs to protect and build up, to restore the old system of real home industry."

This was the political economy of republicanism, whether or not Brownson drew it from republican sources. It had very little in common

either with liberalism or with socialism. Democracy, as Brownson understood it, was incompatible with forward-looking programs of this kind; it left little room for "improvement." It presupposed a simple market society, the "simple kind of liberty of which Carlyle speaks, to buy where we can cheapest, to sell where dearest." It presupposed the abolition of the "paper money system," although "men on [the stock exchange] will no doubt smile at our simplicity," Brownson admitted, "in demanding a purely metallic currency." It presupposed economic independence; any type of collectivism threatened it at its source.

Independence did not imply solitude. If Brownson resisted a fuller development of the market, it was not because he feared that it would compromise his self-sufficiency. He was no Thoreau, opposed to improvement on the grounds that an elaboration of his wants, beyond the level of subsistence, would entangle him in a web of sociability. On the contrary, he valued sociability far more highly than most individualists, and he rejected the culture of philanthropy and "improvement" precisely on the grounds that it would replace the fellowship of friends and neighbors with the vague and watery fellowship of humanity in general. "Your men from whom all traces of their native land are obliterated, who have that enlarged philanthropy which overlaps all geographical distinctions, and grasps with equal affection all lands, races, and individuals, are quite too refined and transcendental for daily use." Cosmopolitanism represented a higher form of solitude, as Brownson saw it. In developing this argument, he rested his case, as always, on assertions about the nature and destiny of man—that is, about the ends proper to his existence:

> The *nature* of man is to live by means of an uninterrupted communion, with other men and with nature, under the three precise and definite forms of family, country and property. His *destiny*, that is, the design of his Creator in his constitution, is not, then, to place himself physically, sentimentally, and intellectually in communion with all men, and with all the beings of the universe. This were to annihilate him by the vast solitude of Sahara.

Brownson made these observations in the course of one of his many attacks on the "no-government" philosophy advocated by so many in-

dividualists. Paine's cosmopolitan humanitarianism and Thoreau's misanthropy both sprang from the fallacy that man could outgrow the need for government—that is, for active intercourse with those to whom he was bound by "local attachments," a "preference for his own natal soil," and the "peculiar circumstances" in which he was raised. Ideologies of self-sufficiency and ideologies of self-annihilation (in which the man was lost in the citizen, in Paine's case in the citizen of the world) came to the same thing. Both undermined the "condensed" form of solidarity—the "love of family and fatherland"—that human nature required if it was to flourish. Both made excessive demands on human nature, overlooking the crucial fact that "the finite seeks in vain to master the infinite."

The idea conveyed by this last phrase ties together the several themes in Brownson's social thought: the inseparability of matter and spirit, politics and religion; the formative discipline of "peculiar circumstances" as the necessary background of mature personality; the need for any vivid apprehension of reality to be embodied in a particular (and inevitably divisive) set of loyalties rather than a watery eclecticism. Brownson never forgot that human beings have bodies and that "man disembodied," divested of the weight of circumstances and associations, "would be no more man, than the body is man when deprived of the spirit."* Man grasps the universal only through the particular: this was the core of Brownson's Christian radicalism.

---

*For this reason, Brownson opposed any theory of progress that implied a rejection of the past. Having sided in his early writings with "efforts for progress," he proceeded to take his readers "aback by telling them they must not run away from the past." The future could no more be dissociated from the past than the spirit could be dissociated from the body. "There is no foundation for the distinction between the movement party and the stationary party," he argued, "when one looks a little below the surface." Thus the point of his important essay "Reform and Conservatism" (1842) was to dissolve the distinction invoked by the title. "It is idle to war against the past. No man can be a reformer who has no tradition. Divest us of all tradition, of all that we have derived from the past . . . and we were mere naked savages." Brownson's unwillingness to choose between reform and conservatism or to equate political radicalism with a repudiation of the past was typical of the populist tradition.

Lockean Liberalism:
A "Bourgeois" Ideology?
· ■ ·

Without denying the differences that divided them, we can consider Brownson, Cobbett, and even Paine as representatives of a tradition of sorts, defined by its skepticism about the benefits of commercial progress and more specifically by the fear that specialization would undermine the social foundations of moral independence. Brownson achieved a more comprehensive grasp of the implications of "improvement," but he shared Cobbett's hatred of the "paper system" by means of which statesmen like Horace Walpole and Alexander Hamilton sought to attach the propertied classes to new states by appealing not to their "virtue" but to their self-interest as public creditors. Like Cobbett, he detested the "comforting system" as well.* The bureaucratization of benevolence, in his

---

*The new order, he saw, would have to include not only a financial and a military establishment—and it was the expense of standing armies that necessitated the reform of public finance in the first place—but an educational and philanthropic establishment as well. The "comforting system," as Cobbett called it, represented in many ways the most dangerous form of specialization of all, as a result of which the ordinary citizen, already relieved of his military obligations, would hand over to the state even the residual obligations of neighborliness and Christian charity.

Would it be going too far to say that these ideas provide us with the elements of a highly sophisticated theory of the modern state? I cannot claim that Brownson developed them in that direction; after 1840, his "disgust with democracy" prevented him from elaborating his political ideas in a systematic way, and he was never a systematic thinker to begin with. Still, the insights he shared with other populists should not be lost sight of. The usual criticism of populism, which has been revived in recent controversies about republicanism, accuses populists of an excessive interest in problems of finance, credit, and money—in other words, of an undue emphasis on the circulation of commodities as opposed to their production. There is some justice in this charge, though it has to be modified in view of the populist critique of wage labor, which paralleled the Marxist critique even if it did not lead to a condemnation of private property. The failure to recognize private property as the root of the difficulty, according to Marxists and social democrats, doomed populism to analytical and practical futility. Objecting to monopoly, the concentration of economic power in the hands of a smaller and smaller class of capitalists, populists erroneously attributed it to the

view, at once diminished individuals, by exempting them from religious and civic duties, and built up imposing tutelary powers in the state. Having undermined citizens' capacities for self-defense, self-education, and mutual aid, the state would have to assume these functions itself. In order to counter the effects of acquisitive individualism, the state would have to promote a quasi-official religion in the hope of assuring uniformity of opinion. The emergence of interdenominational philanthropies, together with a uniform system of public education based on the same ideology of bland benevolence, suggested to Brownson that the attempt to press religion into the service of the state drained it of substance and weakened religion's capacity to offer effective resistance to the wealthy and powerful. The attempt to base public order on religion required the suppression of just those elements in religion—the doctrines that divided one sect from another but at the same time commanded intense loyalty—that would have given a certain gravity and moral weight to public discussion.

It should be obvious that Brownson's indictment of specialization owed more to Christian than to republican influences, though his analysis of the way specialization tends to erode moral capacities in individuals complemented certain features of the republican tradition. The important point that emerges from a comparison of Brownson, Cobbett, and Paine is that republicanism was not the only source from which opposition to "improvement" could be derived. Christianity provided an

---

"special privileges" bestowed by the state. But if this explanation overlooked the way in which monopoly grew out of the inherent logic of economic competition, it nevertheless captured something overlooked by Marxists: the state's growing dependence on a wealthy class of private creditors (and, in our own time, on a growing class of corporate contractors for military supplies). The founders of modern states, eager to establish their legitimacy and to counter the unsettling effects of these states' revolutionary origins, made no secret of their intention to secure the loyalty of the rich by implicating them in the fortunes of the state. Populists understood the probable consequences of this policy more clearly than those who saw the state merely as the "executive committee of the ruling class." The new ruling class, as populists saw it, was itself the creation of the state—the product of the state's need for a more and more elaborate system of public finance, which grew in turn largely out of the requirements of modern warfare. It is by no means clear that republicans and populists had the worst of the argument about circulation, private property, and political economy in general.

equally important source; but liberalism itself mingled with these other currents in the stream of popular radicalism. Henry George, who stood in the line of Paine, Cobbett, and Brownson, took much of his inspiration (as did Paine himself) from Adam Smith.

In their enthusiasm for a rediscovered republicanism, revisionist historians have played it off against a caricature of liberalism, one that treats liberalism unambiguously as the philosophy of "possessive individualism." Here again, the revisionists have taken over elements of the very synthesis—that of Louis Hartz and C. B. Macpherson—they set out to revise; and it is the belated discovery that even liberals, after all, had reservations about acquisitive individualism that leads so many recent scholars into the further mistake of reading liberalism out of the historical record and of replacing it with a single, all-encompassing, "paradigmatic" tradition of civic humanism. Excessive attention to the republican critique of liberalism has had the effect of obscuring the larger point, stated very clearly by Pocock himself, that "bourgeois ideology, which old-fashioned Marxism depicted as appearing with historic inevitability, . . . had to wage a struggle for existence and may never have fully won it."* The same conclusion emerges from the work of scholars opposed to

---

*Pocock seems to advance two distinct theses, which often work at cross-purposes. The eminently defensible contention that bourgeois liberalism did not "reign undisturbed" does not require the additional contention that everyone in the eighteenth century had to use the language of republicanism, in the absence of clearly defined alternatives. The latter claim is insupportable; yet it is this sweeping though dubious claim that Pocock seems especially eager to assert, even at the expense of the more important point that capitalism had many critics and that serious reservations crept into the writings even of its defenders. The republican "paradigm," he would have us believe, was the dominant, indeed the exclusive frame of eighteenth-century reference. Thus "both factions" in the debate about commerce and public credit shared the "same underlying value system, in which the only material foundation for civic virtue and moral personality is taken to be independence and real property." A more important question, however, was whether government had to rest on "civic virtue" at all. On that point, opinion was sharply divided, as Gordon Wood shows in his study of the American revolution. In opposition to the older view that "public virtue is the only foundation of republics," as John Adams put it, a number of publicists began to argue, in language reminiscent of Mandeville, that a proper system of constitutional checks and balances would "make it advantageous even for bad men to act for the public

a single-minded emphasis on republicanism—for example, from those who insist once again on the central importance of John Locke, in the face of Pocock's attempt to relegate Locke to the sidelines of early modern political debate. Thanks to John Dunn, Richard Ashcraft, Neal Wood, James Tully, and John Marshall, among others, Locke can no longer be understood as a "Lockean"—that is, as a theorist of "possessive individualism." According to Dunn, Locke's praise of enterprise should be read in a Protestant, not a capitalist context. Anticipating the rejoinder that the Protestant doctrine of the calling was itself inspired by the "spirit of capitalism," Dunn maintains that Protestants were more interested in the eradication of the monastic tradition than in the promotion of capitalism or the imposition of modern work discipline on vagrants and idlers. The idea that men and women served God best by devoted service to the worldly tasks to which they were divinely summoned grew up in opposition to the monastic ideal of spirituality and more specifically to the proposition that "salvation could be attained by the observance of a set of rigid rules of behavior." The Calvinist emphasis on the spiritual value of work may have given a certain moral sanction to capitalist enterprise, but "capitalist appropriation and intensive agricultural labor," as Dunn points out, "were equally apt vessels" for the "endless aspiration" to godliness

---

good," in the words of James Wilson. According to John Taylor, "an avaricious society can form a government able to defend itself against the avarice of its members" by enlisting "the interest of vice . . . on the side of virtue." Virtue lay in the "principles of government," Taylor argued, not in the "evanescent qualities of individuals."

An equally important point of contention, as Wood shows, concerned the relation of government to individuals. Republican theory presupposed a society made up of "orders of men, watching and balancing each other," in the words of John Adams. But the theory underlying the state constitutions drawn up during the American revolution, as Taylor pointed out, was that government was "made of individuals." What was distinctive in the republican tradition emerges only in contrast to these liberal views of government and to the liberal view of history, as I have argued in chapter 2. The sharp disagreements between liberals and republicans, however, do not mean that liberals had no reservations about the new society that was taking shape around them (thanks in part to their own policies) or that liberalism could not provide some of the materials for a popular radicalism that condemned the new society in no uncertain terms.

enjoined by Calvinist piety. Far from treating riches as the visible sign of salvation, Locke took the position that "the rich are mostly corrupt," in Dunn's words, and the virtuous "likely to stay poor." "Virtue and prosperity," Locke declared, "do not often accompany one another"—hardly an aphorism likely to justify "unlimited appropriation," as Macpherson calls it.*

In his eagerness to identify Locke with the "political theory of appropriation," Macpherson dismisses his religion as a disposable wrapping that can be discarded without doing violence to the texture of his thought. Not only does he underestimate the strength of Locke's religious convictions; he misunderstands their political import. When Locke extolled enterprise and productivity, "he seems to have had in mind not large manufacturers," as Neal Wood puts it, "but petty producers, small and middling craftsmen-merchants." According to Wood, Locke should be seen as an advocate of "agrarian capitalism" as opposed to mercantile or industrial capitalism. "His fondness for the petty craftsman, the producer who sold his own wares," together with "his objections to the unproductive role of the broker," makes it impossible to consider his theory of property a bourgeois theory in Macpherson's sense.

Macpherson claims that Locke regarded the laboring classes as subhuman and proposed to exclude them from political life. It is by no means clear, however, that Locke's strictures against idleness were directed chiefly against the poor. In the seventeenth century, the "industrious" part of the British nation—against which Locke played off his criticism of the unproductive aristocracy—could still be viewed as a majority or at least as a sizable minority of the population, and the suffrage require-

---

*John Marshall's doctoral thesis on Locke, parts of which have already been published, makes it clear that although Locke was raised as a Calvinist, his mature views were those of an Arminian and eventually those of a closet Unitarian. This does not mean, however, that when Locke spoke of "callings," he used the term purely to refer to occupations, as Marshall contends. Even those who came to reject Calvinist theology continued to believe in the spiritual value of work. For those who had imbibed the atmosphere of the Calvinist Reformation, the concept of a "calling" could not easily be divested of its moral overtones. It referred not merely to occupations but to the moral duty to find work that was suited to one's abilities, useful to one's neighbors, and pleasing to God.

ments, moreover, were much less restrictive than they subsequently became.* Ashcraft points out that the main threat to property rights came not from a mass movement of disfranchised, impoverished proletarians but from the Stuart monarchy, with its attempt to impose taxes without parliamentary authority and to consolidate its claims to absolute power. Macpherson and other historians of "possessive individualism" tend to read the record of nineteenth-century class struggles back into the seventeenth century. They see Locke's defense of property rights as part of a larger strategy of "social control," designed to keep the laboring classes in their place. Locke valued religion, according to this interpretation, only because heavenly rewards and punishments would discourage the poor from demanding justice in this life. As Macpherson's critics point out, however, Locke's proposal that manual laborers be allowed to spend several hours a day in study (while the educated classes spent several hours in manual labor) does not sound like the opinion of a man who relied on ignorance and superstition to keep the lower orders quiet.

It is true that Locke recommended harsh treatment for the idle poor. But he also thought that the laws should make it a crime for any parish to deny relief to those in need of it. He defined the "common rule of charity" so broadly that it would have prevented anyone from enriching himself at another's expense or from exploiting another's "necessity" in order to "force him to become his vassal." James Tully goes so far as to construe these words as a prohibition of wage labor. Tully has been accused of exaggerating Locke's reluctance to endorse the alienability either of property rights or of labor power. But if Locke cannot be seen as a critic

---

*According to a recent study by Derek Hirst, 40 percent of adult males were eligible to vote in the middle of the seventeenth century. Ashcraft, citing this and another study, by Keith Thomas, notes that "not only did wage earners, copyholders, and male inhabitants vote in elections, there are a number of instances in which almsmen were assumed by contemporaries to be included within the common right of suffrage." The suffrage began to shrink only in the eighteenth century. If the Whigs in Locke's day failed to demand an extension of the suffrage, that was because it was "already exercised," according to Ashcraft, "by hundreds of thousands of artisans, tradesmen, shopkeepers, merchants, and small farmers. . . . The late seventeenth century was a high-water mark of democratic participation, not achieved again in England until the mid-nineteenth century."

of wage labor, neither can he be seen as its ardent exponent. He had little to say about wages, pro or con. He lived in a world in which capitalist relations of production had not yet established themselves on a wide scale. When he sang the praises of honest labor, both the wage earner and the capitalist were missing from his field of vision, as Tully notes, "along with the landowner and master," none of whom contributed anything substantial, in Locke's opinion, to the wealth of society. From Locke's point of view, as Tully makes clear, "the ploughman, reaper, thresher, baker, oven-breaker, planter, tiller, logger, miller, shipbuilder, cloth-maker and tanner alone make things useful to the life of man and create value."

Recent scholarship pictures Locke as a thinker who appreciated the effects of trade and commerce in raising the standard of living but distrusted "luxury" and "covetousness." The same thing can be said of other seventeenth- and eighteenth-century liberals. The point is not that early liberals were republicans at heart or that republicanism furnished the only coherent frame of political discourse. The point is that the friends of commerce, at this early point in its development, perceived many of its undesirable effects as well as its benefits. Liberals thought they could dispense with civic virtue, but they could not dispense with enlightened self-interest; and the pursuit of wealth, they knew, could easily lead people to sacrifice long-term interests to the pleasures of the moment. Even those who believed, in opposition to the republican tradition, that "the end of every individual is its own private good," as Richard Jackson wrote to Benjamin Franklin in 1755, could not fail to notice that "luxury and corruption . . . seem the inseparable companions of commerce and the arts." Jackson admitted that "commerce is at this day almost the only *stimulus* that forces every one to contribute a share of labour for the public benefit." He regarded commerce as a mixed blessing, however; if it encouraged enterprise, it also released uncontrollable forces and led men to think that "every thing should have its price." That commerce "softens and enervates the manners" was not a point in its favor, in Jackson's eyes. "Steady virtue, and unbending integrity, are seldom to be found where a spirit of commerce pervades every thing." Like Adam Smith, Jackson believed that only education could "stem the torrent" and bring about a "reconciliation between disinterestedness and commerce."

In America, the economics of an emergent nationalism reinforced misgivings about "luxury." Since Americans exported agricultural staples and other raw materials while importing finished goods, the best way to assure a favorable balance of trade, it appeared, was to discourage expensive tastes. This way of thinking became official policy in the nonimportation agreements of the revolutionary war and later in Jefferson's embargo—experiments in which Americans called on the familiar critique of luxury to support the patriotic cause. When Spartan self-denial was tied to the defense of American liberties in the most direct and compelling fashion, political experience thus joined mercantilist doctrine in retarding the development of a capitalist ideology in which the multiplication of wants became something to be celebrated, not deplored, as the foundation of progress and general prosperity. At the same time, of course, these recurring boycotts of foreign trade, especially the embargo, had the unforeseen effect of encouraging the growth of domestic manufactures by cutting off the supply of foreign goods.

The capitalist economy developed more rapidly than capitalist ideology, however. Well into the nineteenth century, Americans remained deeply suspicious of credit, corporations, and wage labor. Limited-liability corporations were not "restrained by those prudential considerations which prevent individuals from embarking their capital rashly," a Jacksonian Democrat explained, "in the desperate hope of gain." Another Jacksonian, identifying himself as an "anti-corporationist in the broadest sense of the term," urged a law holding stockholders individually accountable for their debts, his object being "to prevent the establishment of the same kind of society here which had been described as existing in other countries." "What primogeniture did on the other side of the Atlantic," he feared, "corporations would do here." The expansion of credit, according to this line of argument, made it possible for men and women to live beyond their means—which for enthusiastic exponents of commercial progress was precisely the point. For old-fashioned liberals, the expansion of credit encouraged envy and emulation, the dictatorship of fashion, and a contempt for honest labor.

Early Opposition to Wage Labor

· ■ ·

The recent preoccupation with republicanism has muddled the history of opposition to "improvement" in two ways: by identifying republicanism as the only source of that opposition, thereby obscuring the contribution of other traditions, including liberalism itself; and by identifying "corruption" and the credit system as the only object of criticism. Recent historical scholarship is curiously silent about the widespread opposition to wage labor in the eighteenth and nineteenth centuries, perhaps because it was influenced more directly by Lockean liberalism (though not by "Lockean liberalism" as conceived by Hartz and Macpherson) than by the ideology of civic humanism. Yet the general uneasiness about the new economic order found its most striking expression in the nearly universal condemnation of wage labor.

Langton Byllesby, a Philadelphia printer, argued in 1826 that wage labor, which destroyed the "option whether to labour or not," was the "very essence of slavery." The division of labor impoverished artisans, Byllesby said, "for every improvement in the arts tending to reduce the value of the labour necessary to produce them, must inevitably have the effect of increasing the value and power of wealth in the hands of those who may be fortuitously possessed of it." In 1834, the General Trades' Union of New York declared, "In proportion as the line of *distinction* between the employer and the employed is widened, the condition of the latter inevitably verges toward a system of vassalage." Such statements recall Locke's argument that anyone forced by necessity to sell his labor lacked one of the essential attributes of freedom. As Mike Walsh put it, "No man devoid of all other means of support but that which his labor affords him can be a freeman, under the present state of society. He must be a humble slave of capital."

Walsh, a Democratic party politician, spoke in the 1840s for New York's artisans; but those who spoke for the manufacturing interest in America took the same position. They could stomach credit and corporations, but they gagged on wage labor. Both Henry Carey and Daniel Raymond, prominent Whig economists, criticized the "English school" of political economy, associated with Adam Smith, on the grounds that it accepted the need for a permanent class of wage earners. "Can it be," Carey asked, "that a beneficent Providence has so adjusted the laws under which we live that laborers *must* be at the mercy of those who hoard food and clothing with which to purchase labor?" Raymond, appealing to Locke's contention that "individual right to property is never absolute," advocated a protective tariff and other measures designed to promote manufactures, but he rejected Adam Smith's argument in favor of human acquisitiveness as the motor of social progress. Acquisitiveness led to an increasingly complex division of labor, as Raymond pointed out, and thus widened the gulf between the propertied and the laboring classes. "Labor's independence," as Allen Kaufman summarizes Raymond's thinking, rested on labor's "technical know-how" and its "ownership of the means of production."

Those who opposed the more and more militant demands made by artisans in the 1830s and 1840s did not quarrel with the claim that wage labor was a form of slavery. They merely denied that a permanent wage-earning class was taking shape in the United States. "In this favoured land of law and liberty, the road to advancement is open to all," as one of them put it, "and the journeymen may by their skill and industry, and moral worth, soon become flourishing master mechanics." Americans took it as axiomatic, a cherished article of political faith, that freedom had to rest on the broad distribution of property ownership. In debates about universal suffrage, opponents of a restricted suffrage conceded the dangers of universal suffrage in societies marked by extremes of wealth and poverty. In the New York constitutional convention of 1821, in which the suffrage question was extensively debated, one speaker after another made this point. David Buel, a delegate from Rensselaer County, pointed out that in England, land was monopolized by the rich, while the "great bulk of the population" was poor. "Did I believe that our population would degenerate into such a state, I should . . . hesitate in extending the right of suffrage; but I confess I have no such fears." Property qualifications were necessary, according to John Ross of Genesee County, only where property was concentrated in the hands of the few and therefore threatened by the many. In the United States, where property was "infinitely divided," the danger had "ceased to exist." Even laborers, Ross said, "expect the most of them soon to become freeholders." According to Martin Van Buren, those excluded under the existing restrictions were themselves freeholders or householders, at the very least—"men who have wives and children to protect and support ... and ... every thing but the mere dust on which they trod to bind them to the country."

Both sides in early-nineteenth-century debates about suffrage and the labor question, in short, linked political freedom to the supremacy of the "middling interest" or "substantial yeomanry," as the Jacksonian Robert Rantoul called them. Both sides took the position that freedom could not flourish in a nation of hirelings. It is anachronistic to see in such views, merely because they did not include a condemnation of private property, the ideology of a "rising middle class," the advance guard of capitalism. They were the views of small producers and of publicists attuned to the needs of small producers—farmers, artisans, master craftsmen, journeymen—who believed that "small but universal ownership," in the words of Robert MacFarlane, a mid-century labor leader, was the "true foundation of a stable and firm republic."

Sometimes the same historians whose work enables us to recognize this characteristic style of thought, neither capitalist nor socialist, fall back into the older ways of thinking when they seek to explain its significance. In his study of the Republican party in its formative years—the last of the major parties to give voice to this producerist ideology—Eric Foner refers to the Republicans as spokesmen for a "dynamic, expanding capitalist society." Their Protestant work ethic, Foner believes, provided a "psychological underpinning for capitalist values." The evidence in his book clearly shows, on the contrary—as does the study of New York artisans by Sean Wilentz, together with many other recent studies—that the producer ethic, as Wilentz puts it, was "not 'liberal' or 'petit-bourgeois,' as the twentieth century understands the terms." It was anticapitalist but not socialist or social democratic, at once radical, even revolutionary, and deeply conservative; and it deserves a more attentive hearing, on its own terms, than it has usually received.

Acceptance of Wage Labor
and Its Implications

=========== · ■ · ===========

By the middle of the nineteenth century, it had become increasingly difficult to deny the existence of a wage-earning class, even in the United States, or to pretend that every wage earner was a potential artisan, shopkeeper, or capitalist. The glaring contradiction between the prevailing ideology and the emergence of a proletarian class nevertheless required the fiction that wage labor was merely a temporary condition, a single step on the ladder of advancement most individuals could expect to climb, as Horatio Alger explained, with a little luck and plenty of pluck. In the Gilded Age, Algerism, with an overlay of social Darwinism, established itself as the dominant ideology of American politics, and many Americans cling to it even today. Failure to advance, according to the mythology of opportunity, argues moral incapacity on the part of individuals or, in a version even more implausible, on the part of disadvantaged ethnic and racial minorities.

Even when Americans finally came to accept the wage system as an indispensable feature of capitalism, they continued to comfort themselves with the thought that no one had to occupy the condition of a wage earner indefinitely—that each successive wave of immigrants, starting at the bottom, would eventually climb the ladder of success into the proprietary class. When the "new immigration" of the 1880s and 1890s cast doubt on this agreeable assumption, that became an argument for imposing severe restrictions on immigration from the Orient and from southern and eastern Europe. Permanent status as wage workers—the newcomers' probable fate—could simply not be reconciled with the American dream as conventionally understood.*

Those who for this very reason urged a reinterpretation of the "prom-

---

*Racial arguments, of course, also figured prominently in the movement to restrict immigration. But the appeal of these arguments cannot be understood without their supporting context. The new immigrants, according to advocates of exclusion, lacked the qualities that would enable them to become property owners.

ise of American life," in Herbert Croly's phrase, recognized the emergence of a permanent class of wage workers as the heart of the matter. The founding editor of the *New Republic*, Croly stated the issue with unusual clarity in *Progressive Democracy*, published in 1914. In an earlier America, "pioneer or territorial democrats," as he called them, "had every promise of ultimate economic independence, possessed as they were of their freeholds." But the private "appropriation of the public domain rapidly converted the American people from a freeholding into a wage-earning democracy" and raised the central question to which modern societies had not yet found the answer: "How can the wage-earners obtain an amount or a degree of economic independence analogous to that upon which the pioneer democrat could count?" Welfare programs, Croly argued—insurance against unemployment, sickness, and old age; measures enforcing safe and healthy conditions of work; a minimum wage—represented a very partial answer at best. Conservatives objected that such reforms would simply promote a "sense of dependence," and this criticism, Croly admitted, had a "great deal of force." The conservatives' own solution, however—"that the wage-earner's only hope is to become a property owner"—was so deeply inconsistent with the whole trend of modern industrialism that it was difficult to treat it "with patience and courtesy." The claim that saving and self-denial would enable workers to become proprietors was utterly unconvincing. "If wage earners are to become free men"—and "the most important single task of modern democratic social organization" was to make them free men—something more than exhortations to work harder and spend less was going to be required.

The syndicalist solution advocated by Croly at this time (to which we shall return in chapter 8) never commanded much support among social reformers and radicals. By 1914, social democracy had already established itself, at least among people with advanced opinions, as the principal alternative to a proprietary conception of opportunity. According to this way of thinking, a proper understanding of the "social question" had to begin with an acknowledgment of the irreversibility of the industrial revolution. Huge corporations, the wage system, a more and more intricate subdivision of labor—these were permanent features of modern society, and it was pointless to seek a restoration of proprietorship or some "analogous" form of independence, just as it was pointless to break up the trusts in the hope of restoring competition among small family-owned firms or partnerships. The wage earner would remain a wage earner; instead of trying to convert him into a property owner or partner, enlightened social policy would see to it that his job was secure, his working conditions tolerable, his wages equitable, and his opportunity to organize unions unimpeded by archaic legal obstacles.

Debate on the left now confined itself to such questions as whether these goals could be achieved without socializing the means of production or at least subjecting industry to sweeping public controls, whether the labor movement should devote itself to pure and simple unionism or press for a broad program of political reforms, and whether unions should be organized on craft or industrial lines. But almost everyone on the left agreed, even those who looked forward to the day when the workers would control the state and thereby own the means of production (in theory), that workers would continue to sell their labor as if it were a commodity, if not to private employers then to the state itself. To think otherwise, it was now agreed—to postulate a return to handicraft production or a restoration of proprietorship in some new form—betrayed a failure of nerve, an inability to come to terms with modern life, a sentimental fixation on the past, a "petty bourgeois" sensibility, an outlook hopelessly clouded by "romantic," "populistic," "individualistic," "nostalgic," and otherwise contemptibly retrograde illusions of self-sufficiency. Samuel Gompers, the conservative exponent of bread-and-butter unionism, resorted to the same terms of abuse, in denouncing the "petty bourgeois" heresy, as the most doctrinaire socialists. The one element in his early exposure to Marxism that Gompers never renounced was the certainty that history advances in a single direction, that no one escapes the iron laws of historical motion, and that opposition to historical necessity represents the worst kind of escapism.*

---

*The growing acceptance of wage labor is only one indication of the narrowing of political debate in the twentieth century. Another indication is the narrowing of the kind of questions asked about work. In the nineteenth century, people asked whether the work was good for the worker. Today we ask whether workers are satisfied with their jobs. A high level of "job satisfaction" then serves to refute those who deplore the division of labor, the decline of craftsmanship, and the difficulty of finding work that

The New Labor History
and the Rediscovery of the Artisan

· ■ ·

These assumptions naturally colored not only the practice of the twentieth-century labor movement but efforts to understand its earlier history. Historians who took a socialist or social democratic point of view could appreciate the labor movement of the nineteenth century only when it seemed to anticipate the enlightened unionism of their own day. Marxist historians and those who belonged to the anti-Marxist school of John R. Commons were equally baffled by the Knights of Labor, with its old-fashioned enthusiasm for "cooperation" and its notorious lack of enthusiasm for strikes. They were equally unable to account for the nineteenth-century labor movement's interest in currency reform, land reform, religion, and temperance, except as evidence of workers' unfortunate susceptibility to middle-class ideologies. Everywhere they looked, they found signs of a backward-looking mentality, confusingly mixed with revolutionary militancy. The Commons school wondered why the development of trade unionism had been so tardy; Marxists, why trade unionism, once achieved, had not given way in turn to a proper class consciousness in the form of socialism. Both schools spent so much time explaining why the labor movement had failed to develop in the proper direction that they barely noticed the developments that had actually taken place. Since history so often failed to conform to their expectations, most of it had to be passed over in silence.

Only in the 1960s did historians begin to throw off these confining preconceptions. The growing conservatism of the AFL-CIO discredited the assumption underlying the work of the Commons school, that trade unionism was somehow more advanced than the broad-gauged workers'

---

might leave workers with a sense of accomplishment. The liberal principle that everyone is the best judge of his own interests makes it impossible to ask what people need, as opposed to what they say they want. Even so, investigations of "job satisfaction" and worker "morale" are hardly encouraging. The dream of setting up in business for yourself, even if it means long hours and uncertain returns, remains almost universally appealing.

movements of the nineteenth century. But recent events also cast doubt on the Marxist alternative to orthodox labor history. Not only in the United States but in all the highly industrialized countries of the world, working-class movements had renounced revolution, while Marxist parties had come to power in preindustrial countries like Russia, China, and Cuba. The course of history seemed to suggest, as Barrington Moore put it in his *Social Origins of Dictatorship and Democracy,* that revolutions are made not by rising classes but by classes "over whom the wave of progress is about to roll."

In one form or another, this intuition informed the new labor history that emerged in the sixties and seventies, much of it inspired by E. P. Thompson's classic, *The Making of the English Working Class* (1963). As Thompson's title indicates, the new generation of labor historians still struggled to reconcile their findings with Marxism, just as Moore struggled to reconcile his analysis of the "Prussian road" to modernization with the Marxist theory of historical development. Thompson argued that the significance of Paine, Cobbett, and other such populists lay in their contribution to the more fully developed working-class consciousness that took shape later on. The work of Thompson's followers, however, made it more and more difficult to escape the conclusion that popular radicalism had lost both its comprehensive scope and much of its intensity the more it identified itself with the particular class interests of industrial workers. The "making of the working class" looked more and more like the solidification of an interest group fighting for "improvements in the capitalist industrial system," in the words of Craig Calhoun, and winning an admittedly important "series of reforms" that were nevertheless granted "without sacrificing the capitalist industrial society, or even most of the cultural hegemony and material power of the elite strata." On the other hand, "primitive" or "premature" rebellions against industrialism, as orthodox Marxists contemptuously referred to them—movements led by artisans and yeoman farmers in the eighteenth and early nineteenth centuries—began to look radical by comparison with what had followed. "The most potentially revolutionary claims," says Calhoun, "were those which demanded that industrial capitalism be resisted in order to protect craft communities and traditional values."

Historians of nineteenth-century labor movements and working-class culture continue to disagree about a number of issues, and it would be misleading to summarize this work in a way that implies unanimity. One finding, however, commands "almost universal agreement," in the words of William Sewell, namely that "skilled artisans, not workers in the new factory industries, dominated labor movements during the first decades of industrialization." One study after another announces the dominant influence of artisans—in France, England, and America alike—as its organizing theme. "This book is about a community of artisans," writes Robert J. Bezucha in his study of silk workers in Lyons, "who organized in order to resist proletarianization and consequently found themselves at the barricades." Joan Scott launches her study of French glassworkers in the same way: "This book . . . analyzes the experiences of artisan glassblowers as their trade was transformed by mechanization from a highly skilled art to a semiskilled operation." Nineteenth-century radicals in England were "artisans, skilled craftsmen, privileged outworkers, and, less often, small tradespeople," according to Calhoun.

Nor did the establishment of the factory system immediately alter this pattern. In New England, "artisan protest inspired factory protest," according to Alan Dawley; in industries where this artisanal background was lacking, militant unions failed to appear. In Cincinnati, according to Steven J. Ross, the working-class movement continued to be led by artisans, even in the 1870s and 1880s. These artisans claimed to represent the "middle classes," as one of them put it, and hoped "to prevent the encroachments of both . . . the extremely rich and the extremely poor." "Despite the profound economic changes that followed the American Civil War," Herbert Gutman writes, "Gilded Age artisans did not easily shed stubborn and time-honored work habits." Even in the factory, artisans often retained control of the rhythm and design of production; and it was their resistance to employers' attempts to introduce a more complicated division of labor and to replace skilled craftsmen with operatives, as much as the fight for higher wages and shorter hours, that shaped working-class radicalism right down to the end of the nineteenth century.

Artisans against Innovation

·■·

The discovery that artisans dominated working-class movements in the nineteenth century leads almost irresistibly to several other conclusions, although these are not always stated explicitly and might be disowned by scholars who still hope to square the new labor history with Marxism. Since artisans struggled above all "to save their craft," as Scott puts it, working-class radicalism should be understood as an "attempt to halt the process of proletarianization rather than an indication that the process was complete." This helps to explain why workers, not only in the United States but in England and even in France, did not more readily embrace ideologies of class struggle, why they often identified themselves as middle-class "producers," and why they directed so much of their indignation not against their employers (who could be regarded as fellow producers) but against bankers, speculators, monopolists, and middlemen. In Philadelphia, many radical artisans believed that it was "futile," according to Bruce Laurie, "to assail bosses . . . if avaricious financiers . . . lurked behind the degradation of craftmanship and the erosion of earnings." Although the growing rift between masters and journeymen made it less and less likely that journeymen would become masters in their own right, journeymen refused to accept the legitimacy or permanence of the new order. They could see that their masters had begun to act more and more like capitalists and that many industries were now controlled not by masters at all but by men without any knowledge of a craft. Their first impulse, however, was to eliminate the distinction between capital and labor, not to accept their position as laborers and attempt to improve it.

A convention of New England mechanics resolved in 1844, "Labor now becomes a commodity, wealth capital, and the natural order of things is entirely reversed." Socialists urged workers to forget about the "natural order of things" and to accept the new conditions as a fact of life. A Cincinnati socialist declared in 1875, "Sons and daughters of the laboring classes . . . have no other choice than to become factory employees for lifetime, . . . without the least hope . . . to become their own masters." Gompers offered exactly the same advice. In 1888, in one of his frequent attacks on the Knights of Labor, he supported a plea for "pure and sim-ple" unionism with the contention that "the wage-workers of this conti-nent . . . are a distinct and particularly permanent class of modern society; and, consequently, have distinct and permanent common interests."

Artisans could not bring themselves, however, to renounce the hope of becoming "their own masters"—not necessarily by accumulating capital as individuals but by cooperatively owning the means of production. Socialists and trade unionists alike ridiculed workers' enthusiasm for co-operative schemes, but the prominent role of artisans in working-class movements makes this enthusiasm quite intelligible. For those who re-jected the whole system of wage labor as a frontal assault on their crafts, cooperation was a perfectly rational alternative, as the shoemakers' union, the Knights of St. Crispin, explained in 1870.

> If labor produces all the wealth of a country, why should it not claim ownership? . . . We claim, that although the masses have advanced towards independence, they will never be com-pletely free from vassalage until they have thrown off the sys-tem of working for hire. Men working for wages are, in a greater or less degree, in the bonds of serfdom. The demand and supply of labor makes them the football of circumstances. . . . We cannot expect to overcome this law of demand and supply; yet we believe, that in proportion as a man becomes his own capitalist, in the same degree does he become indepen-dent of this law. How all men can become their own capitalist, is a question already decided by political economists. The an-swer is—*cooperation.*

The conventional identification of democracy with progress makes it hard to see that democratic movements in the nineteenth century took shape in opposition to innovation. The new breed of capitalists were the real progressives: working-class radicals, on the other hand, struggled to preserve a way of life that was under attack. Students of working-class movements have called attention again and again to their curious mixture of militancy and conservatism. "Workers were not fighting for control of the industrial revolution as much as against that revolution itself," writes Calhoun.

Their appeal to the past took different forms in different countries. In France, it took the form of a defense of the corporate organization of crafts, abolished by the revolution of 1789 but illegally revived by artisans seeking to defend themselves against the competitive market in labor. The laws abolishing corporations exemplified liberal ideology in its purest form: "There are no longer corporations in the State; there is no longer anything but the particular interest of each individual, and the general interest. It is permitted to no one to inspire an intermediary interest in citizens, to separate them from the public interest by a spirit of corporation." Faced with an all-out assault on organizations that regulated the price of labor, arranged funerals, and helped out members in hard times, artisans "found the corporate idiom ... entirely appropriate," Sewell explains, "as a framework for organizing practical resistance to the atomistic tendencies of the new system." The "new socialist vision" advanced by workers in 1848 "was founded on a very old sense of craft community."

In England and America, the appeal to earlier forms of solidarity rested less on an explicitly corporate idiom than on the ancient rights of Englishmen, on Saxon resistance to the "Norman yoke," on images of a formerly "merry England," or, in the American case, on the "spirit of '76," the special promise of American life, and the nation's providential mission to abolish inequality. William B. Sylvis, whose National Labor Union of the 1860s sought to "strike down the whole system of wages for labor" and thus to "do away with the necessity of trades-unions entirely," invoked the "laws and institutions of our country," which embodied "God's ordained equality of man." Again and again, working-class radicals called up the memory of America's original promise of equal rights and fraternity, only to argue that "this most valued jewel" had been stolen from the people's "crown of sovereignty," in the words of Eugene Debs. "America used to be the land of promise to the poor," observed the *Labor Leaf* of Detroit in 1885; but "the Golden Age is indeed over—the Age of Iron has taken its place. The iron law of necessity has taken the place of the golden rule."

American workers also appealed to the social conditions believed to have prevailed in the country's earlier history. In the Terre Haute of his youth, Debs said, "the laborer had no concern about his position. The boss depended upon him, and ... the laborer's ambition was to run a little shop of his own." Shoemakers in Lynn "remembered the self-reliance of the artisan," according to Dawley, "and recalled the time when the tasks of shoemaking intimately intermingled with the tasks of family and community life [and] . . . the journeyman was both shoemaker and householder, whose daily activity followed the intertwining rhythms of both roles." It was this background of "household independence" and "prefactory customs," Dawley argues, that underlay the solidarity of factory workers during the early stages of industrialization. "The militancy of the factory worker is hard to imagine without the legacy of artisan protest against the encroachments of capitalism into the sphere of production."

Most of the new labor historians would probably disown Calhoun's emphatic statement that workers acknowledged the "priority of community over class"; but their work leaves no doubt that the working-class movement drew both moral and material support from local communities in which industrialization threatened an older way of life. Small businessmen, shopkeepers, and even professional people sometimes sided with the workers in their struggle against outside capital. In Braidwood, Illinois, a sheriff disarmed Pinkerton detectives sent in to put down a strike of miners, declaring that he feared the miners "a good deal less" than "a lot of strangers dragooning a quiet town with deadly weapons in their hands." The support workers received from local editors, lawyers, and law enforcement officers helps to explain why their ideology stressed the solidarity of the "producing classes" and identified "parasitic" bankers and speculators, not employers, as the real enemy.

By shifting attention from unionization to the study of working-class culture, the new labor historians have shown that a whole way of life was at stake in the struggle against industrialism. Workers were defending not just their economic interests but their crafts, families, and neighborhoods. The recognition that economic interests are not enough to inspire radical or revolutionary agitation or to make people accept its risks suggests a more sweeping conclusion. Resistance to innovation, it appears, is an important, perhaps indispensable ingredient in revolutionary action, along with a tendency to identify innovation with the disruption of older communities by invasive forces from outside. In the twentieth century, revolutions have typically taken the form of wars of national liberation, and something of the same impulse, it can be argued, underlay working-class radicalism in the nineteenth century. Workers saw their oppressors, the "capitalists" and moneylenders, as outsiders more often than they saw them as members of their own communities—agents of a foreign power, in effect, of a "paper system" or an international "money trust" that robbed Englishmen or Americans of their inherited rights and threatened to reduce them to slavery.

The appeal to the past, in other words, also implied an appeal to local, regional, or national solidarity in the face of outside invasion—something far more substantial than the hypothetical solidarity of the international proletariat. For historians who inherit from the Enlightenment (in the form of Marxism) a belief that moral progress requires the replacement of local attachments and a parochial outlook by successively wider and more inclusive identities, culminating in the Workers' International, the intensely localistic element in nineteenth-century radicalism (not to mention the religious spirit that often informed it) comes as a disconcerting discovery. The new labor history represents the triumph of historical craftsmanship—a stubborn respect for the evidence—over ideology. It is not surprising that some historians seek to soften the blow to their old beliefs by insisting on the "transitional" character of nineteenth-century working-class radicalism. The last remnant of the Marxist assumptions that originally guided so much of this work, the telltale adjective "transitional" seems to imply that acceptance of the wage system should have led to a more accurate perception of workers' interests, a recognition of the "brotherhood of all workers" (as Sewell puts it), and an understanding that a socialist revolution would have to rest on the demonstrable accomplishments of industrial capitalism, not on blind resistance to them.

The steady decline of revolutionary fervor in the industrial working class, however, undermines our confidence in "transitions" of this sort. The "mature" and "progressive" solution usually turned out to be some version of Gompers's oxymoronic dictum that "the way out of the wage system is through higher wages." Alan Trachtenberg notes that Gompers was willing "to accept the wage system in exchange for a secure place within the social order." The same statement, however, applies to the twentieth-century labor movement as a whole, not just to Gompers's "pure and simple unionism."

Agrarian Populism:
The Producer's Last Stand

· ■ ·

The new evidence concerning the artisanal origins of working-class radicalism, its "producerist" ideology, its defense of an earlier way of life against an innovating industrialism, and its strong sense of local, regional, and national identity suggests that working-class radicalism in the nineteenth century should be seen as a form of populism, not as the first, halting step toward "mature" trade unionism and socialism. E. P. Thompson began his work on the assumption that nineteenth-century radicalism reflected the interests and outlook of a rising class. The historical scholarship his work inspired now makes it clear that the "making of the working class" can better be described as the unmaking of a class of small proprietors having more in common with hard-pressed yeoman farmers than with industrial workers. Instead of regarding populism itself as a purely agrarian impulse, we now have to regard the agrarian version of populism as part of a broader movement that appealed to small producers of all kinds. Artisans and even many shopkeepers shared with farmers the fear that the new order threatened their working conditions, their communities, and their ability to pass on both their technical skills and their moral economy to their offspring. In the nineteenth century, "agrarianism" served as a generic term for popular radicalism, and this usage reminds us that opposition to monopolists, middlemen, public creditors, mechanization, and the erosion of craftsmanship by the division of labor was by no means confined to those who worked on the soil.

To speak of populism in such general terms admittedly carries the risk of imprecision. In recent years, journalists and politicians have used the term so loosely that "populism," like every other term in the political vocabulary, seems compromised almost beyond hope of redemption. At one time or another, it has been applied to Joseph McCarthy, George Wallace, George McGovern, Jimmy Carter, Ronald Reagan, and Jesse Jackson, among others. It has been applied both to the new left and to the new right.

Historians too have used the label carelessly; and revisionist scholarship therefore had to begin, a few years ago, by distinguishing the free-silver movement of the 1890s, which culminated in William Jennings Bryan's "cross of gold" speech and the memorable campaign of 1896, from the more radical movement that grew out of farmers' experiments with cooperative finance and marketing. For Richard Hofstadter, Coin Harvey, theorist of free silver, was the quintessential populist, with his harebrained fixation on currency panaceas, his suspicion of foreigners, and his "paranoid" fears of a secret conspiracy to defraud the people of their birthright. For Lawrence Goodwyn, on the other hand, the quintessential populist was C. W. Macune, organizer of the Farmers' Alliance and author of the subtreasury plan, which would have made federal credit available to farmers and thus freed them from dependence on private bankers and supply merchants. The People's party of the early nineties was the product of a specific series of experiences, according to Goodwyn, and those who came late to the movement, without the benefit of that experience, never mastered its lessons.

These "shadow Populists," as Goodwyn calls them, diverted the movement from reforms designed to encourage cooperatives into the free-silver crusade. Seduced by the expectation of overnight electoral success, they maneuvered the party into an ill-considered endorsement of Bryan. Fusion with the Democrats diluted the Populist program, put an end to the Populists' efforts to break the Democratic monopoly in the South, where Populists had achieved considerable success, and destroyed the possibility of a new party that would unite black and white farmers behind a program of far-reaching reforms. In opposition to the conventional view that reforms first advocated by the Populists eventually found their way into the political mainstream, to be enacted during the progressive era by the major parties, Goodwyn argues that the agrarian cause—and the cause of harmonious race relations as well—suffered a crushing and conclusive defeat from which they never recovered.

In *The Age of Reform, The Paranoid Style in American Politics,* and other writings, Hofstadter took the position that the populist "spirit" continued "to play an important part in the politics of the progressive era," went "sour" in the twenties and thirties, when cultural conflicts between city and country nourished "provincial resentments, popular and 'democratic' rebelliousness and suspiciousness, and nativism," and found a more and more reactionary voice in the movements led by Huey Long, Charles Coughlin, and Joseph McCarthy. Even in its prime, populism embodied the baffled response of farmers and small businessmen to the modern world, the complexity of which their simpleminded "yeoman myth" could not explain. Jacksonian democracy, the Grange and greenback movements, and Bryanism all drew on a "popular impulse that is endemic in American political culture," one that Hofstadter also associated with a long tradition of "anti-intellectualism." The People's party was "merely a heightened expression" of this backward-looking, "nostalgic" view of the world, which had consistently thwarted the growth of political realism in America.

Goodwyn's Populists, on the other hand—the genuine as opposed to the shadow Populists—achieved a clear understanding of their situation, an understanding based not on slogans but on practical experience. Finding themselves driven more and more deeply into debt by falling prices, rising railroad rates, and a shortage of credit, they began to see that their only hope lay in the organization of cooperatives. The Farmers' Alliance sent lecturers far and wide to urge farmers to solve the credit problem by pooling their resources and thereby destroying the bankers' monopoly. But the "implacable hostility" of bankers and furnishing merchants soon taught farmers that cooperation could not succeed without federal support. "Those who controlled the moneyed institutions," Macune said, ". . . did not choose to do business with us." In order to enlist the help of the federal government, the Alliance organized the People's party, with Macune's subtreasury at the heart of a comprehensive program of reforms—only to see the subtreasury plan and the party itself swallowed up by the agitation on behalf of free silver.

The essence of Populism, Goodwyn argues, was the political education provided by economic cooperation and their enemies' efforts to crush it. Lecture bureaus and newspapers gave them a "democratic communications network," by means of which the Populists began to break through the "conforming modes of thought" and the "intimidating rules of conduct" that usually discourage popular initiative. The "Populist moment," as Goodwyn sees it, was defined by the promise of a political culture based on popular self-education (the kind of political culture earlier envisioned by Orestes Brownson). When the "the moment passed," it was more than agrarian radicalism that went down to defeat. The decline of Populism was followed by a "corresponding decline in the vitality of public life."

Before Goodwyn, historians sympathetic to Populism stressed the connections between Populism, progressivism, and social democracy, as if the Populists could be redeemed from the charge of benighted rural reaction only by assimilating them to later movements more acceptable to liberal intellectuals. John Hicks and Chester MacArthur Destler saw the Populists as proto-progressives, while Norman Pollack tried to pass them off as socialists in all but name. Goodwyn sees their program of self-education, on the other hand, as more democratic and hence more radical than anything coming out of subsequent movements. It is no part of his defense of the Populists to conscript them into the advancing march of progress. "They saw the coming society and they did not like it." For those who still believe that "modernization" is destined to carry the day, such a judgment will consign the Populists to the garbage dump of history. As Goodwyn notes, "the idea that workable small-unit democracy is possible within large-unit systems of economic production is alien to the shared presumptions of 'progress' that unite capitalists and communists in a religious brotherhood." The obsolescence of small-scale production, a closely related dogma, needs reexamination in its own right, and Goodwyn calls for a new look at the "entire subject of large-scale agriculture in the modern state, both under capitalist and communist systems of organization."

The originality of Goodwyn's interpretation lies in his rejection of the usual assumption that progress brings democracy. He thinks, on the contrary, that a belief in the inexorable laws of development usually goes along with a certain contempt for ordinary people and their antiquated customs and ideas. In the 1890s, the "people" and "progressive society," he argues, represented contrasting and competing, not complementary, symbols. The "contest between 'the people' and 'the progressive society'" ended in the defeat of the former and the rise of the "progressive movement," a more cautious and limited movement than Populism, founded on the ruins of participatory democracy.

The denunciation of Goodwyn's work by Marxist historians confirms his contention that socialists share with liberals a dogmatic commitment to progressive views of history, which makes it impossible for them to see any value in the radical movements once mounted by small proprietors. David Montgomery chides Goodwyn for neglecting a "class analysis of rural America" and for ignoring the distinction between landowners, tenants, and agricultural laborers. "His theoretical categories take no account of the wage-labor relationship and comprehend no exploitation except that which arises in the realms of credit and commodity exchange." Like the Populists themselves, Goodwyn fails to understand the importance of "public ownership of the whole industrial sector as the necessary precondition" of farmers' independence. James Green, after denying that Marxist historians and "capitalist historians" subscribe to the same model of progress, unwittingly proceeds to bear out the justice of this charge. Small forms are "inefficient," Green declares; and Populism, a defense of small farms and "traditional ways of life," was a "rudimentary," "petty-bourgeois" form of social protest. Like Hofstadter, Green dismisses Populism as retrospective and nostalgic; this convergence of liberal and Marxist interpretations, as Goodwyn notes, raises the "intellectual inheritance" behind it to a "new level of visibility." The "condescension" that runs through these interpretations, according to Goodwyn, grows out of the "American historical tradition of conveying the national experience as a purposeful and generally progressive saga, almost divinely exonerated ... from the vicissitudes elsewhere afflicting the human condition." Their acceptance of this tradition, he thinks, may help to explain why American historians, unlike American novelists, have made so little impression on readers outside the United States.

The Essence of
Nineteenth-Century Populism

·■·

American historical writing, to put it another way, takes little account of the possibility of tragedy—missed opportunities, fatal choices, conclusive and irrevocable defeats.* History has to have a happy ending. Thus

---

*"Are there no calamities in history?" Brownson asked in 1843. "Nothing tragic? May we never weep over the defeated? . . . Must we always desert the cause as soon as fortune forsakes it, and bind ourselves to the cause which is in the ascendant, and hurrah in the crowd that throw up their caps in honor of the conqueror?" In our day as

Montgomery denies that the history of radical movements presents us with a "past moment of democratic promise that was irretrievably snuffed out by the consolidation of modern capitalism." Instead, the history of Populism leaves us with the useful lesson that "no successful socialist design for agriculture can be drawn up except by the people who work the land themselves" and that "popular initiatives," accordingly, "will be needed once again to create the agricultural component of a socialist America."

If the democratic movements of the Gilded Age ended in defeat, contrary to these heartwarming assurances from those who still believe against all evidence that history marches steadily onward and upward, it was a defeat not just for farmers but for workers as well. As Montgomery himself points out, workers took part in the Populist movement in considerable numbers, and Goodwyn's neglect of their participation conveys the misleading impression that Populism had no appeal outside the farm belt. Not only did workers in some areas support Populist candidates, but their own organizations, in the days before the AFL established its supremacy, had a strong flavor of populism. As we have seen, the nineteenth-century labor movement envisioned a union of the "producing classes," took a lively interest in the banking and currency questions, and advocated cooperation as the best hope of reasserting workers' control over production. In his history of the Knights of Labor, Leon Fink notes that the members of the Knights, "as independent artisans, small merchants, or skilled wage-earners," took "seriously the 'Lincoln ideal' of a republic of producers." It is precisely these features of working-class radicalism in the Gilded Age, in the eyes of progress-minded historians like Montgomery—its "fixation on currency reform," its capacious definition of "producers," its quixotic opposition to the wage system, its "fantasy" of "imposing moral order on the market economy"—that stigmatize it as sentimental, backward, nostalgic, and naive, the product of "flights of fancy," of the "illusion of a harmonious society," of an "imaginary arcadia of days gone by."

---

in Brownson's, "historical optimism," as he called it, prevails. We love to side with the winning side.

Having learned from Goodwyn that Populism has to be carefully distinguished from the free-silver movement and from a merely rhetorical championship of the redneck, so often confused with populism in American politics, we must nevertheless recognize that nineteenth-century populism found other outlets besides the People's party. We can agree with Goodwyn that neither Bryan nor Pitchfork Ben Tillman of South Carolina nor James K. Vardaman of Mississippi was a populist, although they posed as sons of the soil, and we can agree that William V. Allen, the Nebraska senator who engineered the Populists' fusion with the Democrats in 1896, was a "Populist in name only." But what about Terence V. Powderley, grand master of the Knights of Labor, who favored cooperatives and took a dim view of strikes? What about William B. Sylvis, who condemned the "whole system of wages for labor"? What about the *Boston Voice*, a labor paper that urged the National Labor Union in 1867 to broaden its program so as to attract the "intelligent 'middle classes'—speaking, to be understood, after the fashion of the day—who are not capitalists or otherwise selfishly involved in the present order of things"? What about the Pennsylvania greenbacker who declared in the 1870s that "every producer and laborer who works in a factory, mine, or on a farm, or in any branch of business that creates wealth [is] in the same boat"? Unless we are prepared to write these people off as "sentimental labor reformers" or petty-bourgeois proto-fascists, we should probably agree to call them populists too, along with leaders of the People's party like Ignatius Donnelly, Leonidas Polk, and Tom Watson.

We can extend the term in this way without diluting its meaning or endorsing the current confusion in which a populist is anyone who cultivates a folksy style. Nineteenth-century populism meant something quite specific: producerism; a defense of endangered crafts (including the craft of farming); opposition to the new class of public creditors and to the whole machinery of modern finance; opposition to wage labor. Populists inherited from earlier political traditions, liberal as well as republican, the principle that property ownership and the personal independence it confers are absolutely essential preconditions of citizenship. In the nineteenth century, the validity of this principle was still widely acknowledged, both in England and in the United States. What was not widely acknowledged was that it no longer corresponded to social practice. Most people—including, regrettably, most members of the "producing classes"—"clung to the idea that wage labor functioned as a temporary incubator," as Fink puts it, "conditioning the hard-working young man to the qualities necessary to rise to independent status." Those whom it is appropriate to call populists, on the other hand, looked the facts in the face and decided that the substance of proprietorship could be restored only through the agency of farmers' and artisans' cooperatives.

Unfortunately the discovery that cooperatives could not succeed without state support came too late to enable workers and farmers to make common cause. By the 1890s, the Knights of Labor had fallen into disarray, the AFL was in the saddle, and the subject of cooperatives had been relegated to the labor movement's eccentric fringe. The struggle for "workers' control" continued, but it was now carried on within the narrow limits imposed by a more and more elaborate division of labor. Skilled workers attempted with little success to enforce union work rules, to retain control over apprenticeship, and to prevent their displacement by unskilled operatives. They read Frederick Winslow Taylor and knew that Taylor and his followers would not rest "until almost all the machines in the shop," as Taylor explained, were run by men "of smaller calibre and attainments" than the old craftsmen—men "therefore cheaper than those required under the old system." But the influx of unskilled workers diverted attention from the defense of craftsmanship to the seemingly more urgent need for more inclusive forms of unionization. By the time of the First World War, radicalism in the labor movement had come to be identified not with opposition to the functional differentiation between capital and labor but with industrial unionism. This kind of radicalism, however, posed no challenge to Taylorism or to the new interpretation of the American dream proposed by Taylor, among others, according to which the promise of American life rested not on "manly independence" but on the abundance generated by never-ending improvements in productivity.

Hardly anyone asked any more whether freedom was consistent with hired labor. People groped instead, in effect, for a moral and social equivalent of the widespread property ownership once considered indispensable to the success of democracy. Attempts to achieve a redistribution of income, to equalize opportunity in various ways, to incorporate the working classes into a society of consumers, or to foster economic growth and overseas expansion as a substitute for social reform can all be considered as twentieth-century substitutes for property ownership; but none of these policies created the kind of active, enterprising citizenry envisioned by nineteenth-century democrats. Neither did the seemingly more daring solution adopted in the Soviet Union and eastern Europe, which claimed to abolish "wage slavery" but actually carried it on in a new and even more insidious form, substituting the state for the private employer and thereby depriving workers even of the right to strike.

The condescension and contempt with which so many historians look back on nineteenth-century populism imply that the twentieth century has somehow learned how to reconcile freedom and equality with the wage system, modern finance, and the corporate organization of economic life. Nothing in the history of our times, however, justifies such complacency. The "petty bourgeois" critique of progress deserves an attentive hearing. It may teach us something; and even if its history of defeat does not strike us as wildly encouraging at first, it may help us, in the long run, to come to grips with our contemporary situation and our darkening prospects.

6

"NO ANSWER BUT AN ECHO":
THE WORLD WITHOUT WONDER

· ■ ·

Carlyle's Clothes Philosophy

R esistance to the ideology of progress and its "hopeful fatalism" did not always take a conservative direction, contrary to earlier studies of the subject. A radical critique of "improvement," as we have seen, could be derived from an analysis of proprietorship and the civic virtues associated with it—enterprise, initiative, responsibility. Nineteenth-century populism took far more from the republican tradition and even from early liberal theorists like John Locke than from the conservatism of Edmund Burke. Populists condemned innovation because it undermined proprietary independence and gave rise to "wage slavery," not because it tore apart the delicate fabric of custom. They had little use for custom as such, nor did they cultivate a reverence for the past. But neither were they seduced by the rosy visions of the future that circulated so widely in the Age of Reason and its aftermath.

Criticism of progress drew on a variety of sources, but the most fruitful of all was the tradition of Christian prophecy, as reformulated by Calvin and his followers and, in the nineteenth century, by moral philosophers and social critics—notably Thomas Carlyle and Ralph Waldo Emerson—in whom Calvinism remained a powerful background presence. No longer Calvinists or even Christians in any formal sense, Emerson and Carlyle nevertheless reasserted a prophetic understanding of history and human nature in opposition not only to the reigning celebration of progress but to the Burkean alternative. The contrast between Burke's veneration of human custom and prophetic faith is immediately evident in the very different ways in which Burke and Carlyle deployed the metaphor of clothes. Burke, it will be recalled, liked to compare custom to clothing, which covers the "defects of our naked, shivering nature" with "decent drapery." When the French revolutionaries tore Marie Antoinette from her throne and exposed her as an ordinary woman, they stripped away the "pleasing illusions" without which life becomes brutish and mean. To "cast away the coat of prejudice," Burke said, left men with nothing but their "naked reason"—pathetically inadequate protection against life's rigors.

In *Sartor Resartus (The Tailor Retailored)*, Carlyle elaborated the metaphor of clothes but carried it to conclusions Burke could not have anticipated, much less endorsed. No more than Burke a friend of the Enlightenment, Carlyle nevertheless sided, in retrospect, with the sansculottes, savoring the metaphorical implications of the French label. He saw the French revolution not as a hideous mistake but as a missed opportunity to get to the bottom of things. He had no Benthamite illusions about the dream of "universal Benevolence" that inspired the great divestiture of 1789, but his history of the revolution, the book that made him famous, did not acclaim the restoration of order, as Burke and his friends had acclaimed it at the time. The return of order, as Carlyle understood, meant the return of Mammon, "basest of known Gods, even of known devils."

Like Burke, Carlyle had no faith in "naked reason," but he did not therefore wish to see it clothed in custom. He understood the uses of "clothes," but he also understood that it was sometimes necessary for mankind, as the snake sheds his skin, to shed the "solemnities and paraphernalia of civilised Life, which we make so much of." Clothes made Marie Antoinette a queen, as Burke had pointed out. Carlyle pursued the point only to invert it. "Clothes gave us individuality, distinctions, social polity; Clothes have made Men of us; they are threatening to make Clothes-screens of us"—fashion plates, ambulatory mannequins.

"Custom is the greatest of Weavers," Carlyle wrote. Among her many tricks and artful illusions,

> perhaps the cleverest is her knack of persuading us that the Miraculous, by simple repetition, ceases to be Miraculous. True, it is by this means we live: for man must work as well as wonder: and herein is Custom so far a kind nurse, guiding him to his true benefit. But she is a fond foolish nurse, or rather we are false foolish nurselings, when, in our resting and reflecting hours, we prolong the same deception. Am I to view the Stupendous with stupid indifference, because I have seen it twice, or two-hundred, or two-million times?

The reassuring effect of custom in hiding the terrors of existence behind familiar associations and routines, so highly prized by Burkean conservatives, at the same time deprives us of fresh experience—of an "original relation to the universe," as Emerson would have put it. Perhaps that explains why, living in a world too heavily costumed, we become more and more avid in our search for novelty—which wears thin all too quickly, when we find that new clothes fail to deliver the promised excitement.

Carlyle's unsympathetic account of custom might seem to align him with the party of progress, just as Emerson appeared at times to align himself with the party of hope, as he called it, against the party of memory. But the relevant contrast to custom, as Carlyle saw it, was not innovation but "wonder." He objected to the tyranny of custom because it discouraged men and women from looking beneath the surface of things, not because it discouraged them from experimentation. "Clothing," in his expansive treatment of the image, covered what was usually meant by civilization and progress. It referred among other things to the arts and sciences, to all the products of human ingenuity by means of which men and women seek to make themselves comfortable and secure but also to divert themselves, to beguile the time, and to satisfy the taste not just for conveniences but for beauty. "The first purpose of Clothes," Carlyle thought, ". . . was not warmth or decency, but ornament." Custom, in the strict sense of usage and habit, had to be considered as only one of several types of clothing. Custom itself alluded both to mindless routine and to the false stimulation provided by fashionable glitter. But the technological subjugation of nature could also be considered under the heading of clothes. Technology sheltered mankind from the forces of nature, as clothes protected the body against the cold, but interposed a barrier behind which the inner meaning of the natural world was lost to sight. Art too intruded itself between humanity and a deeper understanding of things. If science destroyed "reverence" for nature, art provided no corrective. Like science, it easily became the object of a cult.

Carlyle shared with Kierkegaard the belief that the aesthetic and the ethical approaches to life are antagonistic. *Sartor Resartus,* a spiritual autobiography several times removed from the actual events of Carlyle's early life and elaborately disguised as the treatise of an obscure German pedant, is a work of great artistry; but it was clearly conceived as a confession, and it gives essentially the same account of unbelief, despair, and the subsequent rebirth of hope that is found in earlier Christian confessions.

> What Stoicism soever our Wanderer . . . may affect, it is clear that there is a hot fever of anarchy and misery raging within. . . . For, as he wanders wearisomely through this world, he has now lost all tidings of another and higher. . . . Thus has the bewildered Wanderer to stand, as so many have done, shouting question after question into the Sibyl-cave of Destiny, and receive no Answer but an Echo. It is all a grim Desert, this once-fair world of his: wherein is heard only the howling of wild-beasts, or the shrieks of despairing, hate-filled men; and no Pillar of Cloud by day, and no Pillar of Fire by night, any longer guides the Pilgrim.

Only those who have lost hope in this way, Carlyle argues, can really expect to regain it. Even the "everlasting No" is better than the conventional religiosity of "cultivated" Christians who know God "only by tradition," if negation leads to an understanding that happiness comes only to those who give up hope of happiness.

To renounce our claims on the world is the "first preliminary moral

Act," because it enables us to value life for itself and not because it smiles on our ambition to enjoy the best of everything, to prosper in all our undertakings, and to remain the center of cosmic attention. When we learn to reduce our claim of cosmic "wages" to a "zero," we will find the world under our feet again. "What Act of Legislation was there that *thou* shouldst be Happy? A little while ago, thou hadst no right to *be* at all." Carlyle's analysis of religious experience, if not conventionally Christian, is nevertheless consistent with the reports issued over the centuries by Christian saints and prophets. Carlyle agrees with them, in particular, in his account of the preconditions for spiritual health. "Love not pleasure; love God." Demand less of life, more of yourself. Learn to recognize the problem of evil—the eternal question of whether a loving God could have admitted human suffering into the world—as the "vain interminable controversy" it is.

Calvinism as Social Criticism

What distinguishes *Sartor Resartus* as the product of the nineteenth century and not of the fifth is that Carlyle's spiritual confession took the form of social criticism, a genre Carlyle helped to invent. A full account of spiritual disintegration and renewal appeared to demand an account of their social effects, as well as an account of the social conditions that contributed to unbelief in the first place and made it more than usually difficult to overcome. It was not just a few individuals, Carlyle could see, who were going through the old experience of alienation and reaffirmation. The experience of unbelief had now become pervasive, thanks precisely to the forward-looking philosophies that assured mankind of health, wealth, and happiness. The celebrated "progress of the age," even with all its glaring inequities, made it much more difficult than before to grasp the fraudulence of this assurance or the inadequacy of a morality that identified good with pleasure and evil with pain.

"Pain is itself an evil," said Bentham, "and indeed, without exception, the only evil." This might have been shallow, but many people clearly found it persuasive. Blinded to the "wonder everywhere lying close on us" by the sheer profusion of human inventions, the triumph of human ingenuity over nature, the men and women of the nineteenth century lived in a mechanical world "void of Life, of Purpose, of Volition, even of Hostility." Formerly a "region of the Wonderful," the world had become "one huge, dead, immeasurable Steam-engine, rolling on, in its dead indifference to grind [man] limb from limb."

Not the collapse of custom but the collapse of faith summed up Carlyle's indictment of the modern world. Note, however, that his was not another lament for the decay of organized religion. "All inferior worships," including the institutionalized church as well as the law, the state, and the economy, fell into the category of "wearing-apparel." The old faith could no longer find embodiment in the old ceremonies, the old incantations, the old dogmas. "It is man's nature to change his Dialect from century to century," and the dialect of predestination, double predestination, prevenient grace, baptism, and atonement, even the dialect of original sin, no longer served to point the way. Because Carlyle spoke a new and often rather exotic idiom—spoke it, moreover, with a German accent acquired from Goethe, Schiller, and other Romantics—many commentators have missed his Calvinism altogether, explaining him either as a forerunner of the fascist cult of leadership or merely as a farsighted critic of industrial capitalism. Neither his interest in great men nor his early championship of the working classes, however, can be understood outside the context of religious beliefs that remained, in their essentials, surprisingly conventional if not exactly orthodox.

Not that Carlyle was indifferent to social issues in their concreteness and immediacy. The widening gulf between wealth and poverty, "dandyism" and "drudgery," horrified him, as it horrified so many of his contemporaries, thanks in part to his own early writings. His social criticism— "Signs of the Times" (1829), "Characteristics" (1831), *Chartism* (1839), *Past and Present* (1843)—named the "condition of England question" and made it the subject of excited debate. But Carlyle advocated neither a working-class revolution (though his criticism of the "cash nexus" appealed to Marx) nor a revival of custom, organic solidarity, and paternalism (though his contrast between medieval unity and modern disorganization appealed to paternalists like John Ruskin, George Fitzhugh, and Henry Adams). If he had a program at all, it consisted of "heroes and hero-worship." But even that was religious in conception, not the expression of a blind cult of power. Hero worship was an act of "true religious loyalty," the hero an embodiment of the spiritual exuberance and vitality that in Carlyle's idiom went by the name of wonder. The prototype of the hero was the prophet.

Carlyle's admiration for great men—Mohammed, Shakespeare, Cromwell, Frederick the Great—divided him further from those who counted on the weight of institutions, traditions, and social habits to provide continuity and discourage rash social experimentation. Heroism was disruptive, in Carlyle's view. Its value lay precisely in its unsettling effect on habits and routine. It divided men and women more often than it brought them together. Carlyle's conception of the man of action had something in common with republican conceptions, and his objection to a political order founded on self-interest occasionally recalled the republican tradition. In the age of machinery, as he called it in "Signs of the Times," men were mistakenly assumed "to be guided only by their self-interests." Government became a "good balancing of these; and, except a keen eye and appetite for self-interest, requires no virtue in any quarter." In "Characteristics" as well as in *Sartor Resartus,* Carlyle spoke of "virtue" with an awareness of the word's resonant overtones, associating it with "Chivalrous Valour," "Nobleness of Mind," and "heroic inspiration" and with a type of bold, impulsive action that sickened and declined when it began to be "philosophised of."*

---

*In a letter describing his arduous method of literary composition, Carlyle repeatedly spoke of the "virtue" it required: "I go into the business with all the intelligence, patience, silence, and other gifts and virtues that I have; find that ten or a hundred times as many could be profitably expended there, and still prove insufficient; and as for plan, I find that every new business requires as it were a new scheme of operations, which amid infinite bungling and plunging unfolds itself as intervals (very scantily after all) as I get along. The great thing is, Not to stop and break down; to know that virtue is very indispensable, that one must not stop because new and ever new drafts upon one's virtue must be honoured!"

Puritan Virtue

· ■ ·

But Carlyle's interest in "virtue" did not make him a republican. He could have learned from his Puritan forebears, just as well as from Machiavelli and Harrington, that virtue had always been associated with courage and manly vigor, with vitality in general, and more broadly still with life-giving creative force. A close reading of *Paradise Lost,* for example—reading more to Carlyle's taste than *Oceana* or *The Discourses*—would have introduced him to a rich conception of virtue that often came close to his own conception of heroism. In the mouth of Milton's Satan, the term retains its republican associations with glory, overarching ambition, and dauntless courage. Exhorting his host of fallen angels to storm the gates of heaven, Satan repeatedly addresses them as "Thrones, Dominations, Princedoms, Virtues, Powers." He tempts Eve by dwelling on the godlike powers conferred by the "virtue" inherent in the apple and falsely predicts that God will praise her "dauntless virtue" if she dares to eat it. Since the "power that dwelt therein," as Eve in turn tells Adam in her tribute to the apple's "virtues," includes not only the "virtue to make wise" but to confer speech on a snake, it is more than merely human vitality that Adam and Eve hope to acquire from the tree of the knowledge of good and evil. The fruit of this "sovereign, virtuous, precious" tree, as Eve calls it, will "make them Gods who taste."

Milton's description of God's own "virtue," which reveals itself in the creation of the world, strengthens the association of virtue with superhuman powers. "Darkness profound / Covered the abyss but on the watery calm / His brooding wings the spirit of God outspread, / And vital virtue infused, and vital warmth. . . ." When God sends his son to disperse Satan's rebel horde, he counts on Christ's "virtue" to carry the day. "Into thee such virtue and grace / Immense I have transfused, that all may know / In Heaven and Hell thy power above compare. . . ." Something of the same force, with its implications of life-giving warmth, resides in the sun's "virtue," according to Milton. The sun's warmth as well as its gravity, its "attractive virtue," testifies to the way in which superabundant vitality sheds its glory on anything that comes into its orbit. Milton assigns to Eve the same "virtue" he assigns to the sun; his description of the marriage of Adam and Eve suggests that Adam is attracted as much by her natural force as by Eve's "innocence and virgin modesty."

The association of virtue with life-giving force and vitality persists in the memorable scene in which Adam and Eve, having fallen into a lustful embrace after eating the forbidden fruit, awake from their exhausted sleep to find themselves, like Samson, "destitute and bare of all their virtue."* When Adam speaks of himself and Eve as "despoiled of all our good," goodness itself is endowed with qualities similar to those elsewhere associated with virtue. Milton conceives of goodness as a grateful and obedient disposition of the human will but also as abundance, plenitude, and fullness of being, gifts bestowed by a beneficent creator—the loss of which, accordingly, awaits those who refuse to acknowledge them as such (and thereby to acknowledge their dependence on a higher power) and who aspire instead to godlike powers and knowledge of their own.

In the republican tradition, virtue and grace stood sharply opposed: virtue enabled men to challenge fate in the absence of faith. In Milton's version of Puritanism, virtue and grace became closely entangled, since it was in the fullness of God's being—in consequence of his virtue, in the richest of the word's many overlapping meanings—that men and women were graciously endowed with all the goods that were theirs to enjoy, including the supreme gift of life itself. The same entangling association of "virtues," "gifts," and "graces" informed Carlyle's concept of hero worship, so easily misunderstood, if its Puritan background is overlooked, as a crude cult of authoritarian leadership.

In *Heroes and Hero-Woship*, Carlyle distinguished several types of heroism, only one of them political—the common denominator consisting of a certain "vital Force" and vigor of insight found only in extraordinary individuals and properly regarded not as attainments of their own but as

---

*The comparison with Samson, shorn of his "virtue" by Delilah, makes Milton's meaning clear. In *Samson Agonistes*, Milton uses the same language in describing the return of Samson's power, by means of which he pulls down the temple of the Philistines. He compares Samson's "virtue, given for lost," to a phoenix, whose "fame survives" during "ages of lives," "though her body die." This passage not only identifies virtue with strength, resolution, and courage but preserves the word's republican associations with fame and glory.

the "gift of Nature herself." The hero's own understanding of them as gifts was an important constituent of heroism. The sense of having been called to a given task, of having been "sent hither" to make the "sacred mystery" of things "more impressively known to us," underlay the hero's actions. The "Heroic Gift"—"sincerity and depth of vision," "Power of Insight," the "vital Force" that "enables him to discern the inner heart of things"—derived from the same creative force that revealed itself in nature. It was virtuous in the fullest sense; wherefore Carlyle could insist that "to know a thing, what we can call knowing, a man must first *love* the thing, sympathise with it: that is, be *virtuously* related to it." The virtue of loving insight overrode "selfishness"; that is, it gave those endowed with it the "courage to stand by the dangerous-true at every turn."*

Carlyle's tribute to the fox—an animal that provided Machiavelli with the prototype of crafty political leadership—unexpectedly emphasized the animal's moral superiority to his human counterpart. Both knew where to find their prey, but what the human predator, bent only on his own advantage, knew by craft and cunning, the fox knew by virtue of the kind of gratuitous, unreflective, and uncalculating understanding that Carlyle associated with heroism.† Machiavelli's fox, in contrast to Carlyle's, lacked "vulpine gifts and graces," just as his lion lacked the unconscious delight in its own powers that made it impossible for an animal to misuse them. The Machiavellian hero, like Milton's Satan a rebel against

---

*"Selfishness," in this context, refers to caution and timidity, excessive prudence, or simple cowardice, not to the inclination to favor one's own interests above those of others. The Christian and republican traditions agree in identifying virtue with a kind of dauntless good cheer, not at all with altruism or self-abnegation. That much they share; what divides them is suggested by Carlyle's coupling of "virtues" with "graces."

†"Does not the very Fox know something of Nature? Exactly so: it knows where the geese lodge! The human Reynard, very frequent everywhere in the world, what more does he know but this and the like of this? Nay, it should be considered too, that if the Fox had not a certain vulpine *morality*, he could not even know where the geese were, or get at the geese! If he spent his time in splenetic atrabiliar reflections on his own misery, his ill usage by Nature, Fortune and other Foxes, and so forth; and had not courage, promptitude, practicality, and other suitable vulpine gifts and graces, he would catch no geese. We may say of the Fox too, that his morality and insight are of the same dimensions; different faces of the same internal unity of vulpine life!"

his lot, sought to master Fortune by means of the hard-earned "virtues"—courage or cunning—available to those without faith in providence. Machiavelli's was the heroism of the "everlasting No." Carlyle's version of heroism, on the other hand, rested on the grateful acknowledgment of endowments for which the hero himself could claim no credit. Thus Shakespeare's genius, according to Carlyle, lay in its unawareness of itself. Shakespeare's intellect was "unconscious"; "there is more virtue in it than he himself is aware of." If Shakespeare was a prophet, a "blessed heaven-sent Bringer of Light," he was *conscious* of no Heavenly message"; and it was the modesty of poetic genius, Carlyle thought, that distinguished the poet from the prophet and made him a superior and more trustworthy type.

Carlyle understood the dangers of hero worship more clearly than his critics have given him credit for. He understood that hero worship turned into idolatry when it attached itself not to the hero's insight but to his false claim of supernatural credentials.* At the same time, he praised the "indestructible reverence for heroism" as an important expression of the capacity for wonder and saw the modern disparagement of heroism, accordingly—far more freely expressed in our own day even than in his—as one of the more ominous among many ominous "signs of the times."

"The Healthy Know Not of Their Health"

· ■ ·

The admirable essay "Characteristics" helps to clarify Carlyle's thoughts about the unconsciousness of virtue, which, when it "has become aware of itself, is sickly and beginning to decline." "The healthy know not of their health, but only the sick." Shakespeare "takes no airs for writing

---

*D. H. Lawrence had the same point in mind, I think, when he coined the aphorism that runs through his *Studies in Classic American Literature:* "Never trust the artist. Trust the tale."

Hamlet and *The Tempest,*" but Milton is "more conscious of his faculty, which accordingly is an inferior one." Byron proclaims the critic the equal of the poet; reviewing spreads with such "strange vigour" that it becomes necessary to publish a *Review of Reviews;* and "all Literature has become one boundless self-devouring Review." Not only literature but every form of expression, knowledge, and work has surrounded itself with commentary and criticism; the creative impulse, smothered by "metaphysical" speculation, runs out of breath. "Never since the beginning of Time was there . . . so intensely self-conscious a society." Everything is "probed into"—"anatomically studied, that it may be medically aided."

The trouble lies in the very developments usually taken as evidence of progress. The advance of intellect is highly desirable, but it will not go very far if it looks constantly backward to admire the distance already traveled. "What . . . is all this that we hear, for the last generation or two, about the Improvement of the Age, the Spirit of the Age, Destruction of Prejudice, Progress of the Species, and the March of Intellect, but an unhealthy state of self-sentience, self-survey; the precursor and prognostic of still worse health?" The more loudly the nineteenth century congratulates itself on its superiority to earlier ages, the more it invites the suspicion of moral and intellectual decay.

In "Signs of the Times," Carlyle called the nineteenth century a "Mechanical Age." In "Characteristics," he adds the seemingly contradictory observation that it also deserves to be called the "Age of Metaphysics." But mechanism and metaphysics are two symptoms of the same malady. When thought becomes too conscious of itself, it loses contact with "vital action" and drifts off into airy, increasingly self-referential abstractions. German idealism and British utilitarianism, the latter with its "cunning mechanising of self-interests, and all conceivable adjustments of checking and balancing," exemplify the split between action and inquiry. The "whole man, heaven-inspired," recedes from view, and partial men stand in his place, incapacitated alike for intelligent action and for original thought. "Virtue, properly so called, has ceased to be practised" and gives way to "benevolence." Only the "outward Mechanism" of man's "self-impulse . . . remains acknowledged: of Volition, except as the synonym of Desire, we hear nothing; of 'Motives,' without any Mover, more than enough."

Carlyle's appreciation of the demoralizing effects of an excessively critical self-consciousness does not imply a lament for lost innocence. "In no
time was man's life what he calls a happy one; in no time can it be so."
Carlyle's Puritanism discloses itself in the reminder that labor is the
human lot; that the age-old dream of paradise, "where the the brooks
should run wine, and the trees bend with ready-baked viands," is an
"impossible dream"; that labor alone, necessarily the "interruption of
that ease, which man foolishly enough fancies to be his happiness," provides him with such ease as he ever enjoys; and that "what we call Evil"—
the "dark, disordered material out of which man's Freewill has to create
an edifice of order and Good"—will exist as long as humanity exists.
Work is our lot; and our works, indeed, bring order out of chaos—as long
as they are carried out in good faith, with the understanding that the
creative power that makes them possible comes to us as a gift of the gods.*

The record of our works, as Carlyle reads it, provides us not with a
reassuring fabric of customs or with evidence of our material and moral
progress but with evidence of the "inward willingness" without which
labor becomes a disagreeable necessity and nothing more. In works lov-
ingly and loyally conceived and carried out, we triumph over necessity,
though not by surrounding ourselves with technologies that eliminate
the need for labor. (Here again, the ideology of progress reveals its kinship with the nostalgic dream of a lost Eden; modern abundance, according to the myth of progress, will eventually relieve us of the need to
work.) Our triumph lies in our ability to transform labor, a necessity, into
an act of faith and free will. In our works, we triumph over necessity even
in its most grievous form, the inevitable force of ceaseless change. Renewed in memory, our collective works remain a source of hope, since
their memory shows that "nothing that was worthy in the Past departs."
For this reason, "the true venerator of the Past," Carlyle says, ". . . sorrows not over its departure, as one utterly bereaved."

---

*If evil is the absence of life, vitality, coherence, order, and creative purpose, then evil,
not vice, is the proper antithesis of virtue. The familiar opposition between virtue and
vice refers to a secondary and much weaker sense of virtue (not to mention a weaker
sense of sin, which should be thought of rather as the antithesis of affirmation, obedience, and submission; in short, as an everlasting no). Vice is a pallid concept, which
sheds its pallor on virtue as well when the two are conventionally paired.

Carlyle and the Prophetic Tradition
· ■ ·

Carlyle's insistence that "nothing is lost"—that the "sum-total of the whole Past" lives on in the present—sharply distinguishes his sense of the past from the pastoral tradition, with its wistful evocation of a lost past, and from the sociological tradition that elaborated pastoralism into a contrast between gemeinschaft and gesellschaft—between the organic unity of simpler societies in the past and modern fragmentation. Carlyle exalts memory over custom. History, as he conceives it, represents the triumph of heroism (suitably commemorated and thus continually renewed) over convention. For this reason, it is misleading to interpret Carlyle, as Raymond Williams interprets him, as Burke's successor in an intellectual tradition that criticized modern society by playing it off against the contrasting concept of culture. For Carlyle, culture is the cloak of custom that makes the world seem familiar and thus stifles the capacity for wonder. His understanding of history as the record of glory and "virtue" is closer to republicanism than to the tradition of Burke, Ruskin, and Continental sociology. It is even closer to a Protestant tradition in which "virtue" referred preeminently to the life-giving powers of the creator, which humans approximate only to the extent that they recognize their source. Carlyle's affirmation of human freedom is balanced by an acknowledgment of our dependence on higher powers. The acknowledgment of this dependence—the fullest meaning of what Carlyle means by "wonder"— becomes for this heir of Calvin and John Knox precisely the condition of man's freedom. The illusion of self-sufficiency, on the other hand, stands in the way of genuine insight and the heroic actions that issue from it. In the modern world, this illusion finds its characteristic expression in the machines by means of which mankind seeks to liberate itself from toil— that is, from the inescapable constraints of human existence.

Carlyle is a "prophet," as many commentators have noted; but the usefulness of this description does not lie in its reference to his oracular manner, to the more portentous features of his literary style, or even to his self-conscious conception of himself as a prophet. He was at his least persuasive when he self-consciously adopted the prophetic stance, for reasons he himself explained when he contrasted the poet's unconscious power of expression with the prophet's delusion of divine inspiration. Not that Carlyle should therefore be seen as a poet. To interpret his writings as "literature" ignores his Puritan reservations about art and literature, not to mention his explicit statement that "for us in these days *Prophecy* (well understood) not *Poetry* is the thing wanted; how can we *sing* and *paint* when we do not yet *believe* and *see?*" But Carlyle's works can be appropriately described as "prophetic"—rather than "poetic"—only if this term refers quite directly and literally to a tradition of religious thought that began with the Old Testament prophets, rose to the surface again in the Reformation, and came down to Carlyle by way of his Calvinist forebears. James Anthony Froude's oft-quoted remark that Carlyle remained a Puritan without the Puritan theology fails to capture the full extent of his indebtedness to the tradition of Judeo-Christian prophecy. Carlyle retained much of the old theology, even though he expressed it in a new and highly idiosyncratic idiom. The power and majesty of the sovereign creator of life; the inescapability of evil in the form of natural limits on human freedom; the sinfulness of man's rebellion against those limits; the moral value of work, which at once signifies man's submission to necessity and enables him to transcend it—these insights represented the heart of Calvinist theology, along with its analysis of religious experience, the psychology of despair and conversion; and they represented the heart of Carlyle's work as well, or at least of the work that continues to matter.

Political and Literary Misreadings of Carlyle

· ■ ·

To present Carlyle in this way admittedly ignores much of his output and skips too lightly over his unpalatable opinions—his increasingly shrill and indiscriminate condemnation of democracy, his defense of slavery as a lesser evil than wage labor, his support of the South in the American Civil War, and the authoritarian implications that lurked in his doctrine of hero worship and became quite explicit in his later works. But a recital of Carlyle's political errors serves no purpose, as Raymond Williams once pointed out, except to deprive twentieth-century radicals of his insight into the "redefinition of what politics should be"—the lesson radicals most need to master. Taken to task by the editors of the *New Left Review*, who complained that "Carlyle was an unbridled racist and imperialist" and that the sympathetic portrait of Carlyle in *Culture and Society* was "incomprehensible," Williams objected to "this marshalling of who were the progressive thinkers and who were the reactionary thinkers in the nineteenth century." He too had written his undergraduate "essay on Carlyle as a fascist." By the 1950s, however, he had "discovered themes profoundly related" to his "sense of the social crisis" of his time "not in the approved list of progressive thinkers" but in "paradoxical figures" like Burke, Carlyle, and Ruskin, who defied left-wing canonization but usually had more interesting things to say about modern life than those who marched under the banner of progress.

In retrospect, Williams conceded that his attempt to reconstruct a tradition of social criticism resistant to conventional political classifications did not do justice to the full range of his subjects' opinions. "The right thing to do would have been to argue the case of each thinker fully and explicitly through and say what was wrong with them." Williams's concession was misplaced. There is no reason a book like *Culture and Society*, the purpose of which is to trace the history of an intellectual tradition, ought to stop at every point to consider writers' works in their totality, to argue the case for and against them, and thus to arrive at a comprehensive set of carefully balanced judgments. Such a procedure is not only unworkable, requiring a full-length treatment of all the important writers under consideration, but irrelevant to the purposes of such a work. The important objection to Williams's treatment of Carlyle is not that he failed to call attention to Carlyle's reactionary views (which he explicitly condemned) but that he placed Carlyle in the wrong tradition—that of Burkean communitarianism rather than Christian prophecy.

At least Williams did not take refuge, however, in the usual academic evasion that Carlyle was a purely literary figure who should not be held accountable for his opinions at all. Political criticism is a risky business, especially in the case of a writer who combined the most penetrating judgments with a good deal of nonsense; and it is always tempting, therefore, to retreat into literary criticism. Thus Harold Bloom calls Carlyle a "prophet of sensibility," who saw that "authority could be established again only upon an aesthetic basis." Like Ruskin, Walter Pater, and other "Victorian prophets," Carlyle "mixed perception and sensation into a new kind of sensibility," according to Bloom—one that depended on an "increasing internalization of the self." Albert J. LaValley likewise treats Carlyle as an early exponent of the "idea of the modern" and identifies the "quest for the self" as the unifying theme of his work. Carlyle was most effective, LaValley thinks, when he "abandoned the chimera of messages" and concerned himself with the "aesthetic bases" of thought. *The French Revolution* should be read as an "epic," *Past and Present* as a "poem" in praise of the "aesthetic fulfillment of continuous creation," and *Sartor Resartus* as an "aesthetic act of self-discovery," a book that offered a "solution . . . almost entirely aesthetic."

By replacing political, ethical, and religious categories with aesthetic categories, literary historians have attempted to modernize Carlyle, to divert attention from his embarrassing "messages," and to make him acceptable to an audience that believes only in "myths" and "metaphors." Carlyle's "new religious myth," LaValley argues, has to be understood "simply" as a form of self-expression, not as an account of the nature of things accompanied by the ethical injunction that submission to the nature of things is the only course of action that brings peace of mind. "Myth for Carlyle and the modern mind becomes a pattern that one creates out of the depths of the self rather than a pattern to which one submits oneself." Carlyle may have clung to the curious notion that "God" refers to "something outside the self," just as he clung to his Puritan prejudice against art, but it was just "this distrust of the aesthetic activity of his own writing and vision," according to LaValley, that drove him into "extremes and confusion."

A. Abbott Ikeler comes to a similar conclusion in his study of Carlyle's "literary vision." Puritan "gloom and pessimism" kept Carlyle from fully accepting the new religion of art. "The whole weight of the Calvinist tradition came down against the artist." Even Eric Bentley, who finds some value in Carlyle's ideas (as opposed to his literary "sensibility"), rebukes him for pouring the "new wine of historical imagination" into "old Calvinist bottles." The real value of Carlyle's "doctrine of hero-worship," Bentley maintains, was aesthetic. It encouraged men and women "to seek the excellent in an age of the average." But Carlyle's ideas cannot be torn out of their moral and religious context, it seems to me, without distortion. His heroes are messengers "from the Infinite Unknown," not just models of "excellence." They bring "a kind of 'revelation.' " Their creative power does not derive from the "self." It is a gift in the fullest sense of the word, entrusted to them for safekeeping, and their intuitive, unself-conscious understanding of this fact is what makes them heroes in the first place. Their heroism lies in their acceptance of their fate, their willingness to be used for purposes not their own. Heroism is thus the reverse of "self-expression"—voluntary, hence triumphant, submission.*

Emerson in His Contemporaries' Eyes: Stoic and "Seer"

Ralph Waldo Emerson introduced *Sartor Resartus* to the American public and made no secret of his lifelong admiration for its author. Carlyle returned the compliment. " 'In the wide Earth,' I say sometimes with a sigh, 'there is none but Emerson that responds to me with a voice wholly human!' " At first, Emerson's association with Carlyle heightened popular misgivings about the fatalistic overtones in his philosophy. George Gilfillan of Edinburgh, one of his most persistent detractors, accused him of promoting "mere negation," of denying the possibility of "steady progress in humanity," and of preaching a "gospel . . . of the deepest and the most fixed despair." George W. Bungay, in a book published in Boston in 1852, called Emerson "one of the most erratic and capricious men in America," a "better and a greater man than Carlyle" perhaps, but still a

---

*This line of thought makes Jesus one among many heaven-sent heroes and thus deprives his revelation of unique significance. At this point, Carlyle obviously parts company with Christians. It would be a mistake, however, to conclude that his doctrine of hero worship therefore represents a secularized form of Christianity in which Jesus is reduced merely to a moral example. One of the many features of Carlyle's position that distinguishes it from religious liberalism of this type (and at the same time links it to an earlier Calvinism) is that he does not associate heroism with morality at all but with reverence and "wonder."

"strange compound of contradictions." Like Gilfillan, Bungay noted that Emerson did not seem terribly "sanguine in his hopes of progress." Noah Porter, another persistent critic, wrote in the *New Englander*, in 1856, that "he is so *naif*, so innocent in his manner, that we scarcely know whether to class him with those innocent souls that have not yet attained to the knowledge of good or evil, or with those subtle souls that know so much of both as to be indifferent to either." Returning to the charge a few years later in a review of *The Conduct of Life*, Porter wrote that the "shallowness and flippancy" of Emerson's views on Christianity revealed his moral and intellectual "incompetence." Porter found the essay on "Fate" particularly "appalling"—the "most horrible" imaginable account of the "merciless and remorseless absolutism of a universe of impersonal law, . . . bereft of its God."*

It was only gradually that a more genial Emerson emerged in the public mind, the familiar "sage of Concord." Early reviewers, even in their outrage, correctly sensed something troubling and difficult in Emerson's work, something not easily reconciled with the prevailing patterns of religious and political belief. In time, however, those who governed public taste agreed to ignore the substance of his thought and to install him in the pantheon of literary worthies as a "seer," an inspiring personality, a

---

*Emerson, Porter thought, was a "stoic in his proud defiance of a Personal Divinity, in his quiet acquiescence in an all-powerful Fate and in the sovereign self-reliance with which he confronts the movements of destiny." Emerson worshiped necessity, instead of seeking to "overcome Fate by substituting in its place a Providence that cares for the best ends of the whole by means of wide-reaching and sternly working laws, while yet it loves, and pities, and comforts the humblest individual that suffers by their action." Whether or not this was an accurate description of Emerson's position, Porter's opposition of "fate" and "providence"—key terms that so long served to distinguish the classical, republican tradition from the Christian tradition (or at least from the dominant tradition in Christian thought)—shows that this vocabulary was still in general use even as late as the mid-nineteenth century.

Emerson was also a "stoic," Porter added, "in his contempt of the unenlightened masses, in his deification of intelligence, and in the arrogance with which he claims to humanity the prerogatives that belong to God alone." These are hardly the qualities usually associated with Emerson today, but they were often attributed to him in the nineteenth century.

representative of the "kindliness of the highest New England culture." His enthusiastic and rather uncritical support of the Union in the Civil War, together with his endorsement of the antislavery cause, now sanctioned by success, made it possible for the literary establishment to assure itself that he had "always" stood on the "right side of great public questions"—William Dean Howells's obituary verdict in 1882. Commentators now spoke of the "triumphant optimism in his view of human nature." James Russell Lowell, among many others, decided that he was "essentially a poet." Another admirer held that he was something even "better, perhaps, than either a poet or a philosopher—a man, . . . a personality so pure, so lofty, and so brave that we may unhesitatingly pronounce it great." In the gently "receding light" of transcendentalism, George William Curtis could see Emerson as the "founder" of American literature, "a poet instead of a philosopher." The comparison with Carlyle now worked in Emerson's favor: whereas Carlyle "seems never to have been reconciled with life," as George S. Merriam complained in 1888, Emerson gave off a "sense of serene and radiant joy." Praising Emerson's "optimism," Joel Benton declared his "way of looking at things . . . just the opposite of Carlyle's." It was to Emerson's credit that Carlyle failed to make him believe in the devil by showing him London's East End. Emerson's "diagnosis was always made on affirmative lines and justified the highest hopes."

Emerson's deceptively conciliatory manner made it easy to miss the abrasiveness of his ideas. Unlike Brownson or Carlyle, he had little taste for public controversy. "The least people," he once said, ". . . most entirely demolish me. I always find some quarter, some sorts of respect from the mediocre. But a snipper-snapper eats me whole." Unsure of his ability to hold his own in arguments, he tended to avoid them.* Disagreement always seemed to take him by surprise. He did not anticipate the furious denunciation that greeted his Divinity School Address, evidently

---

*It is something of a shock, therefore, to find this man of fabled mildness referring to argument as a form of mortal combat—regicide, at that. When a young man showed him an essay taking issue with Plato, Emerson said "pleasantly," according to Howells, "My boy, when you strike at the king, you must kill him." An awareness that the stakes are high may have contributed to Emerson's own reluctance to enter the lists.

assuming that his audience would recognize it as a restatement of positions once widely accepted. He called for bold, fresh ideas, but he did not consider himself, I think, principally an original thinker, whose views would necessarily give offense. Certainly he did not think of himself as a prophet. When he found it impossible to remain in the ministry, the Unitarian church having proved too narrow to contain him, he took to calling himself a scholar, as if to announce that he would continue to work within the conventions of an established calling. He did not set out to invent a new calling or a new way of speaking. He once said of Carlyle that it was only the "despair of finding a contemporary audience" that made it necessary for Carlyle's alter ego, Professor Teufelsdröckh, "to utter his message in droll sounds."* He himself faced the same difficulty. Now that Reformation theology had become unrecognizable as such to the sons and daughters of the Reformation, he could no longer hope to reach them by preaching the old gospel from the pulpit. The good news had to be presented—disguised, even—as "transcendental" philosophy (though Emerson himself never accepted this particular label). Unfortunately, the disguise proved so effective that hardly anyone ever managed to see through it.

The Puritan Background of Emerson's Thought: Jonathan Edwards and the Theology of "Consent"

In order to understand why Emerson found it necessary to adopt an unfamiliar idiom—one that his contemporaries, before they decided to immortalize him in stone, found "extravagant," "perverse," "uncouth,"

---

*Carlyle immediately saw the astuteness of this analysis. He wrote back, "You say well that I take up that attitude because I have no known public, am alone under the Heavens, speaking into friendly or unfriendly space; add only that I will not defend such an attitude, that I call it questionable, tentative, and only the best that I in these mad times could conveniently hit upon."

"barbarous," "grotesque," and "unintelligible"—it is necessary to understand the decay of Calvinism in New England. The Great Awakening of the 1740s had interrupted the steady drift "from piety to moralism," in Joseph Haroutunian's helpful phrase, but advocates of a milder, reasonable religion eventually carried the day. If anything, the Great Awakening itself contributed to the humanitarian reaction against Calvinism, as Haroutunian points out, by popularizing a crude conception of original sin according to which Adam's sin was "imputed" to his descendants. The idea that mankind literally inherited the consequences of Adam's disobedience defied reasonable explanation. Why should upright men and women in the eighteenth century, even spotless infants, share the punishment—eternal damnation—properly inflicted on Adam alone?

Jonathan Edwards tried to explain that sin was not to be thought of as analogous to crime. It lay not in specific transgressions so much as in a rebellious, disbelieving heart. Thus even infants had a "malignant nature, though incapable of doing a malignant action." Such subtleties eluded even Edward's followers. The more they upheld the "vindictive" character of divine justice—as when Joseph Bellamy, his most important successor, defended the seeming paradox that "vindictive justice in the Deity has nothing in its nature inconsistent with his infinite goodness"—the more their religion offended those who equated sin with crime and God's justice with "corrective" discipline and assumed, therefore, that God punished sinners only for their own good, the way a loving parent corrects a child in the interest of its moral development. Infant damnation—and the opponents of Calvinism gladly harped on this issue, sensing their advantage—was inconsistent with the "lovely character of our compassionate heavenly father," as Samuel Webster put it. Reasonable men and women who believed that "sin and guilt are personal matters," in the words of another liberal minister, found increasingly incomprehensible a doctrine that treated them as inherent conditions of human life, universal and inescapable facts of human history. Opponents of Calvinism accused it of undermining rational incentives to good conduct. According to Samuel Johnson, the eighteenth-century Connecticut Anglican, Calvinist determinism destroyed "civil and family government—for what signify all laws and rules of action, all motives taken from praise and blame, hope or fear, reward or punishment, while every thing we do is under a fatal necessity, and we can do no otherwise than we do?"

Edwards replied to this objection, characteristically, not with abstruse speculation about the "imputation" of Adam's sin to his progeny but with observations of ordinary human practice. In one of his sermons, "The Justice of God in the Damnation of Sinners," he pointed out that men commonly speak of a corrupt disposition as something that aggravates an offense instead of mitigating it. "How common is it for persons, when they look on themselves greatly injured by another, to inveigh against him, and aggravate his baseness, by saying, 'He is a man of a most perverse spirit: he is naturally of a selfish, niggardly, or proud and haughty temper: he is one of a base and vile disposition.' " In his treatise on original sin, Edwards elaborated this line of argument. The logical and dialectical but empirically falsifiable objection that "hardheartedness," "obstinacy," and "perverseness"—traits attributed to mankind by the doctrine of original sin—somehow denied man's "moral agency" rested on a confusion of sin with the crimes for which individuals might be held accountable in a court of law. Because no one had ever stood trial for obstinacy and hard-heartedness, people could not see that these qualities defined man's habitual disposition to God and therefore expressed the very essence of what was meant by original sin.

Rebellion against God, Edwards argued, was simply the normal condition of human existence. Men found it galling to be reminded of their dependence on a higher power. They found it difficult, moreover, to acknowledge the justice and goodness of this higher power when the world was so obviously full of evil. To put it another way, they found it impossible (unless their hearts were softened by grace) to reconcile their expectations of worldly success and happiness, so often undone by events, with the idea of a just, loving, and all-powerful creator. Unable to conceive of a God who did not regard human happiness as the be-all and end-all of creation, they could not accept the central paradox of Christian faith, as Edwards saw it: that the secret of happiness lay in renouncing the right to be happy.

Edwards's theology rested on careful observation of what happened to people—himself first of all—who renounced their claims on the universe.

> The appearance of everything was altered; there seemed to be, as it were, a calm, sweet cast, or appearance of divine glory, in almost every thing. God's excellency, his wisdom, his purity

and love, seemed to appear in every thing; in the sun, moon, and stars; in the clouds, and blue sky; in the grass, flowers, trees; in the water, and all nature. . . .

In a "personal narrative" of his own conversion, Edwards recalled how he "used to be uncommonly terrified with thunder, and to be struck with terror" at the approach of a storm. The acknowledgment of God's sovereignty transformed his terror into gratitude and wonderment. "I felt God, so to speak, at the first appearance of a thunder storm; and used to take the opportunity, at such times, to fix myself in order to view the clouds, and see the lightnings play, and hear the majestic and awful voice of God's thunder, . . . leading me to sweet contemplations of my great and glorious God."

These words help to clarify what Edwards meant by "consent and good will to Being in general"—the essence of "true virtue," as he called it in his treatise on that subject. "Consent" implied a love of God's creation in and for itself, without regard to the ways it thwarted or seemed to encourage human designs. When Edwards associated virtue with "benevolence," he did not use the term in the sense of philanthropy. Love of God, not love of mankind, was the "primary" meaning of faith, just as sin, the rebellious antithesis of "consent," was first of all an offense against God, not against humanity or against particular persons. Although it would be fair to say that faith, as Edwards understood it, originated in the emotion of gratitude, he was careful to distinguish a grateful "good will" from the kind of gratitude that depends on the sense of being loved and appreciated. "True virtue primarily consists, not in love of any particular Beings, because of their virtue or beauty, nor in gratitude, because they love us; but in a propensity and union of heart to Being simply considered; exciting absolute benevolence . . . to Being in general."* Man has no

---

*Because Edwards identified virtue with affirmation and consent, sin with an everlasting no, he refused to make a rank order of virtues and vices, each with its appropriate reward or punishment. Consent to being had no degrees, as he conceived it. It was either unconditional or it was nothing. The statement (in "The Justice of God") that "every crime or fault deserves a great or less punishment, in proportion as the crime itself is greater or less," invoked the principles of eighteenth-century penology, pre-

claim to God's favor, and gratitude has to be conceived, accordingly, not as an appropriate acknowledgment of the answer to our prayers, so to speak, but as the acknowledgment of God's sovereign but life-giving power to order things as he pleased, without "giving any account of any of his matters," as Edwards put it in "The Justice of God."

Known today mainly for his famous sermon "Sinners in the Hands of an Angry God"—usually considered the epitome of hellfire preaching, in which God is conceived in grossly personal terms—Edwards in fact stripped God of personal attributes, precisely by insisting on his absolute sovereignty (and also by stressing his revelation of himself in nature). God was simply "being in general." As such, he "was absolutely perfect, and infinitely wise, and the fountain of all wisdom," and it was therefore "meet . . . that he should make himself his end, and that he should make nothing but his own wisdom his rule in pursuing that end, without asking leave or counsel of any." Virtue, then, lay in the joyous affirmation of the beauty and justice of such a God (not, however, in a merely grudging acquiescence to his authority). Like Milton, Edwards associated virtue with a certain "predisposition and will," as he put it, not with the performance of good deeds. The faith that moved mountains, braved the deep, and tamed the thunder, virtue had more to do with courage and resolution—with an exuberance of spirit, a superabundant vitality—than with a scrupulous reckoning of one's obligations to others.*

---

sumably familiar and therefore acceptable to his Northampton congregation, only in order to carry his argument to a conclusion directly at odds with the eighteenth-century idea of God as a moral bookkeeper, carefully adjusting the sentence to the crime. The absolute and unconditional injunction to love God, as Edwards saw it, made the refusal to love God "infinitely heinous, and so deserving of infinite punishment."

Edwards's imagery probably defeated its own purpose. By using the language of crime and punishment, he invited the objection that all crimes are relative and contingent, that none (however reprehensible) deserve an eternity of suffering, and that any God who could inflict such a sentence was nothing more than a petty tyrant. Edwards, his enemies said, equated sin with the crime of lèse majesté—no crime at all, by enlightened eighteenth-century standards of constitutional monarchy.

*In an interesting article in the *Dictionary of the History of Ideas*, "Virtù in and since the Renaissance," Jerrold E. Seigel analyzes the "fundamental division among meanings

Edwards on True Virtue

· ■ ·

Puritan ministers liked to remind their congregations that a good man without grace would still end up in hell. Without grace, the model householder and citizen was hardly better than a hardened sinner. In *The Nature of True Virtue,* one of his last works—the culmination of his career as a theologian, a treatise conceived as a kind of Puritan summa, though never completed—Edwards elaborated this stock theme, in effect, with his customary subtlety and refinement. Beginning with the familiar contrast between self-love and the love of God, he unfolded its implications with a rigor unprecedented in the Puritan tradition.

Self-love, as Edwards understood it, goes well beyond ordinary selfishness and egoism. It is the basis of a mature conscience, the source of man-made morality. Self-love, supplemented by our natural sense of consistency, fitness, and "measure," makes us feel that we should treat others as we would like to be treated by them. Thus it gives rise to a fairly demanding standard of justice—embodied, for example, in the golden rule. "In thinking of others," we tend to "put [ourselves] in their place," and this habitual, unreflective empathy underlies our condemnation of malice, envy, and other vices that "naturally tend to the hurt of mankind." Resenting envy and malice when directed against ourselves, we are led to condemn envy and malice in general. In the same way, self-love prompts the conventional praise of "meekness, peaceableness, benevolence, charity, generosity, and the social virtues in general." It underlies the conscientious performance of "relative duties," in Edwards's phrase:

---

of virtue: on the one hand, a 'moral' sense which focuses on the conformity of actions to approved standards or ends, on the other a 'non-moral' sense concerned with the power of an action (or an actor) to be effective or to achieve a desired end." At first sight, Edwards's *Nature of True Virtue* appears to offer a prime example of the first of these two meanings. Even here, however, the second sense of the term continues to make itself felt. In early modern thought, the two "virtues" often prove very difficult to disentangle. As Seigel notes, "The word 'virtue' . . . is used to attribute some kind of value to conduct or action." Even the "non-moral" meanings of virtue, therefore, carry strong moral connotations.

"duties of children to parents, and of parents to children: duties of husbands and wives: duties of rulers and subjects: duties of friendship and good neighbourhood." Self-love, then, naturally expands to include love of others. Founded on the child's "natural delight in the pleasure of taste and hearing, and its aversion to pain and death," self-love can lead to a love of humanity in general.* Clearly Edwards's distinction between self-love and "consent to being in general" has nothing to do with the conventional contrast between egoism and altruism.

He wavers a little on the question of whether man-made conceptions of justice originate in self-love alone or whether a sense of consistency and proportion should be considered an independent source of "secondary virtue," as he calls it. "There is an agreement in nature and measure, when he that loves has the proper returns of love; when he that from his heart promotes the good of another has his good promoted by the other: for there is a kind of justice in becoming gratitude." At this point, Edwards seems to distinguish "proportion" from empathy and to identify a sense of justice more closely with the former than with the latter. "Indeed, most of the duties incumbent on us, if well considered, will be found to partake of the nature of justice. There is some natural agreement of one thing to another; . . . some answerableness of the act to the occasion; some equality and proportion in things of a similar nature, and of a direct relation one to another." With great insight, Edwards shows the affinity between a sense of justice and an appreciation of beauty and "harmony," only to remind us that a "secondary kind of beauty" can evoke no more than a secondary kind of virtue.† "Who will affirm, that a

---

*Freud's analysis of the ego ideal, which is rooted in the infant's illusion of occupying the center of the universe but later becomes the foundation of man's loftiest ethical ideals, can be read as a twentieth-century restatement of this argument.

†It was some such idea of justice founded on a sense of "proportion" and "measure," I believe, that Edwards's followers had in mind when they defended God's "vindictive" justice on the grounds that punishment is the natural and fitting sequel to crime. The "sense of desert," Edwards explained, consists of a "natural agreement, proportion and harmony, between malevolence or injury, and resentment and punishment; or between loving and being loved, between showing kindness and being rewarded, etc." But Edwards was still speaking of human justice here and probably would have con-

disposition to approve of the harmony of good music, or the beauty of a square or equilateral triangle, is the same with true holiness, or a truly virtuous disposition of mind?" Even so, "approbation of the secondary beauty that lies in uniformity and proportion, which is natural to all," is so important, Edwards seems to suggest at one point, that it should be considered "another ground" on which secondary virtue can rest. Two pages later, however, he says that "there are no particular moral virtues whatsoever"—no secondary virtues, that is—that do not "come to have some kind of approbation from self-love."

Whether or not self-love is the only source of a sense of duty, Edwards clearly dissents from those moral philosophers who postulate an innate moral sense that enables man to distinguish right from wrong.* Our "natural" conscience, he insists—conscience uninformed, that is, by "consent to being in general"—originates in our wish to be loved and cared for, even in the instinct of self-preservation, and in the sense of fitness and "consistency" that makes it so natural for us to assume that this wish to be loved (in others as in ourselves) ought to be gratified, that our need for love ought to evoke an appropriate response not just from other human beings but from "being in general."

---

sidered it inappropriate to extend the same reasoning to the inscrutable ways of providence.

*Edwards follows Locke in rejecting the hypothesis of innate ideas. If the mind is a blank slate at birth, conscience has to be seen as the product of experience, including, of course, the experience of grace, which transforms "natural" conscience into a love of being in general. The distinction between "true virtue" and "secondary virtue" enables Edwards to accept Locke's argument that all natural morality originates in self-love. Only when the theological foundations underlying Locke's own position (and that of liberals like Mandeville, who based a cruder version of this argument on Pascal) began to crumble did liberals find it necessary to stress man's capacity for disinterested public spirit and intelligent sympathy as opposed to empathy (which merely projects the loved self onto others). In his *Inquiry Concerning the Principles of Morals*, Hume took issue with the "selfish system of morals" proposed by Hobbes and Locke. He admitted that "sympathy . . . is much fainter than our concern for ourselves," but for that very reason, he argued, "it is necessary for us, in our calm judgments, . . . to neglect all these differences between ourselves and others and render our sentiments more public and social." Adam Smith took a similar position in *The Theory of Moral Sentiments*.

It is precisely this claim on the universe that Edwards wants us to surrender. Our human concerns, our "private affections," are

> so far from containing the sum of universal being . . . that [they] contain but an infinitely small part of it. The reason why men are so ready to take these private affections for true virtue, is the narrowness of their views: and above all, that they are so ready to leave the divine Being out of their view, . . . or to regard him in their thoughts as though he did not properly belong to the system of real existence, but was a kind of shadowy, imaginary being.

Note once again that Edwards's attack is directed not against ordinary selfishness but against our expectation of happiness, our assumption that happiness belongs to us as a God-given right. Selfishness, universally condemned, is hardly worth condemning all over again. Self-love, moreover, is not unambiguously a bad thing, measured on the scale of purely human values. It can flower into family feeling, patriotism, even into an exalted form of universal benevolence. Self-love can inspire people with a "benevolent affection limited to a party, or to the nation in general, . . . or the public community to which they belong, [even to one] as large as the Roman empire was of old." Self-love can extrapolate itself into "benevolence towards the whole world of mankind, or even all created sensible natures throughout the universe."

Edwards's point—a difficult point, to be sure—is not that men lack brotherly love but that "benevolence," if it leaves out God, still falls short of true virtue. A universal love of mankind, indeed, is the most dangerous of all forms of self-love, since it is so easily confused with the love of "being in general." "The larger the number is, to which that private affection extends, the more apt men are, through the narrowness of their sight, to mistake it for true virtue; because then the private system appears to have more of the image of the universal."*

---

*The same reasoning later led Orestes Brownson to condemn philanthropy as the work of the devil. Here is another reason to prefer local attachments to an abstract love of mankind: they are less easily confused with true virtue.

But if the higher expressions of self-love—patriotism, public spirit, philanthropy—are so easily confused with true virtue, what difference does it make whether or not they spring from "consent to being"? The "natural conscience" of mankind, Edwards says, "should approve and condemn the same things that are approved and condemned by a spiritual sense or virtuous taste." Those who take a purely behavioral view of morality will see this as an admission that the distinctions Edwards is so eager to establish—the distinction between "true virtue" and "secondary virtue," between the "gratitude that is truly virtuous" and the gratitude that comes from "loving those which love us," or again between "remorse of conscience" and genuine repentance—have no practical consequences and are therefore completely irrelevant to moral philosophy. If "natural conscience . . . concurs with the law of God," why do we need the law of God at all? Man-made morality appears to be enough for practical purposes. Indeed the man-made morality outlined by Edwards, apparently indistinguishable in its content from the morality that issues from a love of God, itself appears to hold up an impossibly exalted standard of conduct, one that most people will inevitably fall short of. What good does it do to hold up a standard higher still, especially when we cannot show that it will improve the way anyone actually behaves? Edwards seems to prescribe a morality more suited to angels than to human beings, as Dr. Oliver Wendell Holmes once observed.

Perry Miller points out in his biography of Edwards that Edwards would have agreed with this description of his morality, though not with the corollary that his morality was therefore irrelevant to human purposes. Civic order and social peace, we might add, are simply not the human purposes Edwards chiefly has in mind. Important as these are, they do not exhaust the concerns that ought to be addressed by a well-conceived ethical theory. In Edwards's view, the regulation of collective behavior remains a secondary concern. A more important concern is what men have to do in order to achieve a state of grace—the condition described only imperfectly as peace of mind, inner assurance, trust, overflowing vitality, and spiritual health. Curiously enough, the concept of happiness, that eighteenth-century obsession, may explain as well as any other why the virtue that enables us to live in peace with our neighbors matters so much less, in Edwards's scheme of things, than the virtue that "softens and sweetens the mind" and thus enables us to live in peace with

God—who "himself," Edwards reminds us, "is in effect being in general." Secondary virtue cannot make us happy (to put the point in terms intelligible to the modern mind). It cannot overcome our resentment of the world's imperfections. It cannot solve the "problem of evil." It cannot explain why we should be expected to love life when it is full of pain and suffering, heartbreakingly short, and bounded on either side by darkness. Only "repentance" and "consent" can do that: such is Edwards's answer to the eighteenth-century "pursuit of happiness."*

The "Moral Argument" against Calvinism

· ■ ·

It was an answer, of course, that eighteenth-century rationalists were hardly prepared to accept, or even to understand. Equating goodness with church attendance, observance of the laws, and respect for the rights of others, they found it hard to grasp the central point of Edwards's theology—that goodness lay not so much in outward conduct as in proper "affections," a good "temper," a loving and trustful "propensity of the heart." In the sixteenth century, the doctrine of "justification by faith" had appealed to those who rebelled against Catholic formalism and cor-

---

*But if inner peace is the issue, then it will be objected that Edwards's "angelic" morality, though it may not be irrelevant to all human concerns, remains irrelevant to social and political concerns. From a political point of view, we need to know what makes it possible for human beings to live together without cutting each other's throats, not what makes them happy. It was not Edwards, however, but Thomas Jefferson, that exemplar of eighteenth-century enlightenment, who introduced the question of happiness into our founding political charter, the Declaration of Independence. If it can be shown that Edwards had a deeper understanding of happiness than Jefferson did, that judgment has political implications of great importance. Perry Miller presumably had something like this in mind when he compared Edwards to another illustrious contemporary, Benjamin Franklin, and observed that "although our civilization has chosen to wander in the more genial meadows to which Franklin beckoned it, there come periods, either through disaster or through self-knowledge, when applied science and Benjamin Franklin's *The Way to Wealth* seem not a sufficient philosophy of national life." Is it necessary to belabor the point that our own times, the closing decades of the twentieth century, are such a period?

ruption; but the primacy of faith over works had never been easy to explain to sober, upstanding, industrious citizens who led what appeared to be exemplary lives and expected to be rewarded accordingly. By the eighteenth century, the good people of New England, insofar as they remained Calvinists at all, almost invariably preferred the milder version of Calvinism advocated by the Dutch theologian Jacobus Arminius as early as the 1590s. Preachers like Edwards, who dwelled on the absolute sovereignty of God and urged reconciliation to his inscrutable and apparently arbitrary justice as the essence of religious experience, now found themselves in a small minority. Edwards preached reconciliation to a congregation that felt no need of it, one composed of wealthy, ambitious, and respectable folk, moral by their own lights and therefore unburdened with a burning sense of sin.

Arminians took a contractual view of man's relations to God, according to which God rewarded good behavior and punished only those who freely chose a contrary course. As Edwards pointed out, they held God accountable to human standards of fair dealing, thereby compromising his sovereignty. But the idea of God's absolute sovereignty was hard to square with the prevailing political theory of the times, which held that governments themselves had to obey the law. Part of the trouble here— part of Edwards's difficulty in making himself understood—lay in his attempt to defend a thoroughly abstract, impersonal conception of God with an abundance of political imagery, which invited the objection that his God was a tyrant, jealously concerned with his own honor at the expense of his subjects' needs. The more astute among Edwards's heirs would find it necessary to abandon this political description of God, at the risk, however, of losing the distinction between the creator and his creation.

Edwards's formulation of Calvinism flew in the face of the whole trend of enlightened thought. It was incompatible not only with eighteenth-century political theory but with the new penology, with new conceptions of the family, and with the commercial morality of an enlightened age. At a time when absolute monarchy was everywhere discredited, Edwards made God the sovereign lord of all creation. At a time when the old penal codes were criticized for their harshness, their failure to make the punishment fit the crime, and their inability either to deter crime or to reform the criminal, Edwards upheld God's arbitrary justice. At a time when patriarchal authority in the family was giving way to a new respect for the rights of women and children, he worshiped a God who looked to his contemporaries more and more like a petty domestic despot, caught in the common mistake of trying to frighten his children into good behavior.

The "new divinity" preached by Edwards and his followers offended old-line Calvinists and liberals alike. Those who still thought of themselves as orthodox Calvinists feared that emphasis on inner experience would undermine church discipline, "increase Deism and infidelity" (in the words of Samuel Moody), and lead to the "introduction of paganism in this land," as Joseph Huntington explained. Such concerns had been present in New England from the very beginning, and the controversy surrounding the "new divinity" revived a persisting conflict between Puritan "tribalism," as Edmund Morgan calls it, and a type of piety that was less interested in the problem of social order—in man's relations with his neighbors—than in his relations to God.

Liberals regarded the individual conscience as a more secure foundation of social order than religious institutions, but they too believed, no less than the orthodox, that the "new divinity" would undermine civil religion, in effect—the only force, in their eyes, that could hold an acquisitive society together. "The New Divinity so prevalent in Connecticut will undo the colony," said Charles Chauncy. " 'Tis as bad, if not worse than paganism." Liberals objected to the Great Awakening on the grounds, among others, that it stirred up the rabble. They disliked the authoritarian implications they found in the new divinity, but they also disliked its underlying egalitarianism. "It is monstrous," they said, "to be told that you have a heart as sinful as the common wretches that crawl the streets." They no longer felt comfortable with the requirement that conversion be followed by a public confession. Such an unseemly display of religious emotion seemed to violate new standards of privacy and decorum. Some of the would-be gentlemen of New England, increasingly attracted to the cultural standards set by the English gentry and often to high-church Anglicanism as well, found fault even with the "independent or congregational form of church government," as Samuel Johnson explained in the course of justifying his adherence to the Church of England. He disliked a system "in which every brother has a hand," Johnson said, because it "tended too much to conceit and self-sufficiency." He was sure that "a way so entirely popular could but very poorly . . . answer any ends of government, . . . as every individual seemed to think himself infallible." It was with good reason that Edwards sarcastically referred to his opponents as "gentlemen possessed of that noble and generous freedom of thought, which happily prevails in this age of light and inquiry." Liberals represented the newly enlightened and cultivated classes, who had come to regard religious revivals with genteel contempt.

Jonathan Mayhew, a liberal both in religion and in politics, one of the early leaders of the movement for American independence, once spoke to the young men of Boston on the "most effectual means of securing a good name amongst men." He advised them to seek the "approbation of the few wise and knowing" instead of trying to please the "vast ignorant multitudes, who had neither skill, taste nor judgment in them." On another occasion, Mayhew took exception to the preaching of George Whitefield, next to Edwards the most important voice in the Great Awakening, on the grounds that a religion of the heart appealed only to the "more illiterate sort." "As Yankees became more prosperous and secure," writes Daniel Walker Howe, "some of their sense of dependence on God evaporated." So did their commitment to plain living, their rustic manners, and their old-fashioned dislike of social distinctions. Edwardsian piety conceded too little to the belief in the superiority of their own culture to retain the allegiance of the comfortable, educated classes. It insulted both their intelligence, now that a more liberal education gave them access to the knowledge that promised to set men free, and their need for the respect their worldly achievements appeared to have earned. The more closely Calvinism came to be identified with religious "enthusiasm," the more it struck the better sort of people not just as excessively harsh and uncompromising but as downright unseemly. Humility might be a virtue in the humble, but it was affected in people of standing; and even the humble deserved a religion that promised to improve them—to make them into prosperous, enterprising citizens in their own right, instead of crushing them under the conviction of their own iniquity.*

---

*"Edwards's inscrutable God," Henry May has observed, "could not be drafted into the task of social control." Not that the forces of respectability necessarily wanted to

The crowning indictment of the old religion, culminating in William Ellery Channing's 1820 essay, "The Moral Argument against Calvinism," was that it undermined incentives to do good and thus stood in the way of social improvement and the "progress of the human mind." By insisting on man's "natural incapacity," preachers who dwelled on original sin effectively absolved sinners of any responsibility for their actions. Yet they painted a lurid picture of the punishments awaiting sinners in the next world, seemingly unaware of the "primary and fundamental principle" that "natural incapacity absolves from guilt." They libeled both man, by denying his free will, and God, by endowing him with qualities that "shock our ideas of rectitude." If parents brought their children into the world totally depraved and then pursued them with "endless punishment," everyone would condemn such cruelty out of hand. "Were a sovereign to incapacitate his subjects . . . for obeying his laws, and then to torture them in dungeons of perpetual woe, we should say, that history records no darker crime." But when challenged to explain how the same injustice became just when attributed to God, Edwards's followers took refuge in obscurantism. Human beings, they said, must not sit in judgment of God.

Why not?—Channing wanted to know. God's attributes were perfectly "intelligible," his justice the same as his creatures'. Human conceptions of right and wrong, though "learned from our nature" (the only source from which they could possibly be learned), were quite adequate to the job of judging God: and the God of Jonathan Edwards, Samuel Hopkins, and Joseph Bellamy stood convicted of high crimes and misdemeanors. The pretense that human beings could form no reliable ideas of this unfathomable tyrant was an "affected humility." Why should we "prostrate ourselves before mere power"?

Since Calvinism assigned "unworthy views" of morality to God, it was

keep the common people in their place. Enlightened liberals—those who were liberal in politics as well as in religion, like Mayhew—wanted to make them moral, to elevate and improve them. But Calvinism allegedly held them back, as the *Christian Examiner* argued in 1829, by stressing "stern and self-denying virtues" at the expense of "amiable and pacific" ones—the "virtues," in other words, required by Adam Smith's new system of political economy.

no wonder, Channing thought, that people were deserting the Calvinist churches in droves. They wanted a "rational religion," not a system that "outraged" reason and conscience alike. They wanted a religion that gave them reason to hope that good behavior would enjoy its proper reward. They wanted "encouragement and consolation," not hellfire and brimstone. Channing found the "silent but real defection from Calvinism" one of the "most encouraging" signs of the times—another indication of the "progress of society." But his own religion of "love, charity, and benevolence" soon came under attack in its own right. Liberals triumphed over Calvinism only to find themselves confronted with a "defection" in their own ranks—one that was far from silent.

Emerson on Fate

· ■ ·

Speaking in 1838 at Harvard, the stronghold of Unitarianism, Emerson told Channing's disciples that they belonged to a "decaying church," that they had lost the "principle of veneration," that their Christianity was "petrified," that their Christ was a hero frozen in stone, and that liberals had nothing of any value to say about the "death of faith" in modern society—were themselves partly responsible for it, in fact. In the Divinity School Address, Emerson said to the Unitarians what Jesus said to the high priests, what Luther and Calvin said to the pope, what Edwards said to those brought up in the accommodating faith of his grandfather Solomon Stoddard: that the spirit had been lost in the letter, the substance of religion in its forms, the "eternal revelation in the heart," as Emerson called it, in the rituals and regulations. No more than his predecessors in the prophetic succession did Emerson call for a new religion. "Rather let the breath of new life be breathed by you through the forms already existing."

These particular words are seldom quoted by historians of New England transcendentalism, most of whom see the movement as a further step in the secularization of religion, a step beyond Unitarianism, one more stage in the progress of the human mind, as Channing would have put it. No doubt this is how some of the transcendentalists—Bronson Alcott, for example—actually saw themselves, but Emerson can be called a transcendentalist only in the loosest sense, himself repudiated the label, and showed little interest, for that matter, in the "progress of society." Not a naysayer, a spokesman for the tragic sense of life like Hawthorne or Melville, he was nevertheless no idiotic "optimist." "No picture of life can have any veracity," he once wrote, "that does not admit the odious facts." His thought did not lack awareness of evil, as so often charged. He knew that "things seem to tend downward," as he wrote in his essay on Montaigne, "to justify despondency, to promote rogues, to defeat the just," and to deliver society "from the hands of one set of criminals into the hands of another set of criminals." If he said yes to life, he understood how easy it is to say no. He preached justice and hope, not optimism. It is time to rescue Emerson from his rescuers, those professional Pollyannas who have tried (beginning in his own lifetime) to counter the early impression of his "fatalism" by making him the patron saint of positive thinking.

Those who would like a glimpse of the tougher side of Emerson's thought might begin with his 1860 essay on fate—a subject more Machiavellian, it would seem, than "Emersonian" in the accepted sense. The "question of the times," he begins, resolves itself into the "conduct of life." How shall I live? Social reform—Americans' answer to every question—is no answer at all, merely another sign of American superficiality. The "terror of life" cannot be "talked or voted away," and freedom is not something that can be guaranteed by a constitution, a "paper preamble." Freedom lies in looking fate in the face; the courage to do this is the sign of greatness in men and nations alike. "Our Calvinists in the last generation," Emerson adds, had something of this "dignity," this "firmness under the wheel."

Emerson's detractors, starting with Melville, have always found his view of nature too benign. In "Fate," however, he speaks of the "ferocity" of nature. "Nature is no sentimentalist." It "will not mind drowning a man or a woman, but swallows your ship like a grain of dust." The cold "freezes a man like an apple"; diseases "respect no persons." Nature gladly sacrifices the individual to the species. "In certain men digestion and sex absorb the vital force, and the stronger these are, the individual is so much weaker. The more of these drones perish, the better for the hive." "Wild, rough, incalculable," nature "tyrannically" imposes inflexible limitations on mankind. If Emerson had ever believed that "positive power was all," he retracted that view in a phrase reminiscent of Machiavelli, who said (it will be recalled) that fortune ruled "half our actions," leaving the other half to be "governed by us." Having evidently changed his own mind about this, Emerson writes, "Now we learn that negative power, or circumstance, is half." The natural world evoked so lyrically in *Nature*, Emerson's first book, presents itself in *The Conduct of Life* as the "book of Fate," to which our counterforce seems ridiculously inadequate.* "What is must be." As a man lives out his appointed time, so it is with nations, perhaps even with the human race as a whole. "When a race has lived its term, it comes no more again."

Subject to the limitations laid down by nature, man also dreams of defying them. His own nature is badly flawed and divided. Man is a "stupendous antagonism," the child but also the would-be master of nature. His destiny is to "use and command, not to cringe" before this "element running through entire nature, which we popularly call Fate" but experience as "limitation." This defiance of limitations, if it is ultimately to be condemned, is not to be lightly condemned. "Great men, great nations, have not been boasters and buffoons, but perceivers of the terror of life, and have manned themselves to face it." In language that once again recalls Machiavelli, Emerson praises the courage and resolution men bring to the struggle against fate. Machiavelli called these qualities "virtue," and Emerson uses the term—one of his favorites—in the same way (though not, as it happens, in the present essay). "Every brave youth is in training to ride and rule this dragon."

Nature, however, will not be ruled; she yields very grudgingly to human command, and then only for a time. "The limitation is impassable

---

*This vigorous passage, worth quoting in full, conveys both the vast power that dwarfs human effort and the inexorability of natural processes, especially in their temporal dimension. "The book of Nature is the book of Fate. She turns the gigantic pages,—leaf after leaf,—never re-turning one. One leaf she lays down, a floor of granite; then a thousand ages, and a bed of slate; a thousand ages, and a measure of coal; a thousand ages, and a layer of marl and mud: vegetable forms appear: her first misshapen animals, zoophyte, trilobium, fish; then, saurians,—rude forms, in which she has only blocked her future statue, concealing under these unwieldy monsters the fine type of her coming king. The face of the planet cools and dries, the races meliorate, and man is born. But when a race has lived its term, it comes no more again."

by any insight of man." Real insight lies in the knowledge that nature will prevail in the long run. Submission, not defiance, is the way of true virtue; but Emerson's idea of submission carries no hint of weakness or passivity. "Loving resignation" has nothing in common with cowardice or timidity or with the complaint that we are helpless, blameless victims of circumstance. Submission, as admirable as it is rare in the "instinctive and heroic races" that believe in destiny, "makes a different impression" in the "weak and vicious people who cast the blame on Fate." Rightly understood, it is a "fatal courage," an "energy of will," an "ecstatic," "heroic" affirmation of life that transforms necessity into freedom precisely by acknowledging its fitness and beauty as well as its inescapability. Submission implies a willingness to accept fate not only as limitation but as justice, "as vindicator, levelling the high, lifting the low, requiring justice in man, and always striking soon or late when justice is not done." Submission comes in the heat of the struggle, in the form of a "revelation"—the "revelation of Thought," which "takes man out of servitude into freedom." This "beatitude," Emerson says—firmly rejecting for once his pet notion of the indwelling divinity in man—"dips from on high down to us and we see. It is not in us so much as we are in it."

This rugged little essay, notwithstanding its Machiavellian view of fate and its Darwinian view of nature, ends in a conclusion worthy of Edwards: freedom lies in the acceptance of necessity. In this context, the more recognizably "Emersonian" elements in the essay take on an appearance quite different from anything we are led to expect by the standard picture of Emerson as a nineteenth-century Pangloss, doggedly trying to convince himself that he lives in the best of all possible worlds. The statement that "evil is good in the making" does not deny the existence of evil; what it denies is the possibility that we can abolish it. It is our refusal to admit limits on our freedom that makes limits evil in the first place, and the "beatitude" that finally enables us to accept those limits dissolves their power to dominate us and thus turns evil into good.* The statement

_____

*This may also be the import of the striking observation in Emerson's 1841 essay "Heroism," which Melville found so outrageous. "A lockjaw that bends a man's head back to his heels; hydrophobia that makes him bark at his wife and babes; insanity that

that fate "is a name for facts not yet passed under the fire of thought" carries much the same meaning. The statement, finally, that "what is" not only "must be" but "ought to be" distinguishes stoical resignation from joyous submission to an order of things that we can recognize, even though it was not designed for our convenience or even for our edification, as "best" in some final sense. Emerson's completion of this pregnant phrase by the addition of "ought" to "is" transforms fate into providence.

As Melville understood, more clearly than most of Emerson's critics, this is "theology," Calvinist theology at that; but what Melville intended as a reproach might better be taken as a compliment. Emerson retains the moral realism of his ancestors, while discarding their anthropomorphic conception of God. If God is pure being, he can no longer be adequately characterized as a "sovereign," much less a "father." But neither can he be dispensed with. Only the acknowledgment that "what is must be and ought to be, or is the best," overcomes the tyranny of fate.

"Compensation":
 The Theology of Producerism

· ■ ·

"Fate" is late Emerson and contains a hint of second thoughts, a modification of what he may have come to regard as an excessively bucolic view of nature. But his mature view had already taken shape as early as 1841, when he announced his theory of "compensation," the principle that ran through all his subsequent writings. "Compensation," the third of his *Essays: First Series,* clarifies Emerson's relation to his Puritan forefathers and also to the producer ideology of Anglo-American populism.

---

makes him eat grass; war, plague, cholera, famine, indicate a certain ferocity in nature, which, as it had its inlet by human crime, must have its outlet by human suffering." Deeply offended by the idea that evil originates in "human crime," Melville correctly identified its source and even acknowledged the "nobility" of Emerson's thought. "Look squarely at this," he wrote beside the offending passage, "and what is it but mere theology—Calvinism? The brook shows the stain of the banks it has passed through. Still, these essays are noble."

Even more clearly than the Divinity School Address, "Compensation" explains why Emerson had to renounce his ministry and cut himself loose from the organized church—at whatever cost to his understanding of the social dimension of religion. The essay begins with a biting analysis of the "ordinary manner" of depicting the Last Judgment, where the wicked are condemned and the lowly finally claim their long-deferred reward. This ostensibly comforting picture of the world to come, Emerson points out, implies a bleak picture of the world as it is. It assumes that "judgment is not executed in this world; that the wicked are successful; that the good are miserable," and that good people can hope to prosper only in the next life. Worse, it equates spiritual prosperity with the enjoyment of the very luxuries conventionally condemned as sinful. It assures the meek and lowly, in effect, that they too will have their chance to sin, when the tables are turned in heaven.

Having recently listened to a preacher expound this curious doctrine, Emerson ponders its implications.

> What did the preacher mean by saying that the good are miserable in the present life? Was it that houses and lands, offices, wine, horses, dress, luxury, are had by unprincipled men, whilst the saints are poor and despised; and that a compensation is to be made to these last hereafter, by giving them the like gratifications another day—bank-stock and doubloons, venison and champagne? This must be the compensation intended; for what else? Is it that they are to have leave to pray and praise? to love and serve men? Why, that they can do now. The legitimate inference the disciple would draw was—"We are to have *such* a good time as the sinners have now"; or, to push it to its extreme import—"You sin now, we shall sin by and by; we would sin now, if we could; not being successful we expect our revenge tomorrow."

The "fallacy" in such preaching, Emerson says, lies in the "immense concession that the bad are successful; that justice is not done now." Divine justice, as conventionally conceived, rests on a false idea of justice and a false idea of success. It defers to the "base estimate of the market of what constitutes a manly success." But the conventional preaching Emerson objects to, we might object in turn, at least conveys a realistic account of the social conditions that prevailed in Emerson's day and still prevail. It is a fact that the wicked succeed, by any accepted standard of success, while the good all too often come to grief.* The real "fallacy" of organized religion, we might argue in opposition to Emerson, lies in its appeal to the poor to postpone their revenge to the next life—a counsel of political submission, transparently designed to divert their sense of injustice into the politically innocuous channel of piety and prayer. Why should they have to wait for their reward? Why should they be discouraged—except that the vision of a heavenly reward, of theologically deferred gratification, serves to shore up the existing structures of social injustice—from taking matters into their own hands? Why should social justice be left up to God? Popular religion, we can agree, concedes too much to conventional ideals of success, but Emerson's criticism of those ideals seems to lead to political consequences even more deplorable than the consequences entailed by an uncritical affirmation of them. Popular preaching at least nourishes a justifiable feeling of resentment. Emerson, on the other hand, assures the dispossessed that justice actually reigns, when common sense tells us that it is everywhere in hiding. Emerson is a Pollyanna after all. What can his wildly optimistic assessment of the situation possibly mean? That virtue is its own reward? Cold comfort!

Emerson himself is well aware of these objections. The distinction between more and less—the inequitable distribution not only of wealth but of intelligence, beauty, and imagination—seems to be a "radical tragedy of nature." "How can Less not feel the pain; how not feel indignation or malevolence towards More?" Evil all too often goes unpunished, as far as we can see. "We feel defrauded of the retribution due to evil acts, because the criminal adheres to his vice and contumacy and does not come to a

---

*Those who still cling to the misconception that early evangelical Protestantism celebrated worldly success as the visible sign of salvation will be surprised to hear that popular preaching, on the contrary, stressed the disparity between the obvious injustice that confronted people in this world and the heavenly justice to come. Only the more liberal churches, in Emerson's time, had dropped this theme in favor of an emphasis on the social "improvements" that would eventually assure comfort, if not prosperity, for all.

crisis or judgment anywhere in visible nature." We long for a "stunning confutation" of evil acts, which never comes.

Emerson nevertheless argues that no one who transgresses the laws of nature escapes retribution. "All infractions of love and equity in our social relations are speedily punished" by fear. Whoever cheats his neighbor forfeits his neighbor's trust, imprisons himself behind a wall of enmity and suspicion, and thus cuts himself off from his fellows. He can no longer meet them on the old ground of simplicity and mutual confidence. Often misunderstood as a radical individualist, Emerson considers the loss of human fellowship a grievous affliction, as did his contemporary Hawthorne. His understanding of the importance of socialbility is one of the many things that mark his superiority to Thoreau, often ranked more highly than Emerson both as a writer and as a tough-minded thinker. Emerson wants men and women to become more "self-reliant" precisely so that they can meet each other as equals, without deference or condescension. In "Society and Solitude," one of his last essays, he condemns solitude as a condition "against nature" and notes that sociability, though it should be "taken in very small doses," confers "immense" benefits. "A man must be clothed with society, or we shall feel a certain bareness and poverty" of spirit. Without "children, events, a social state and history," he writes in "Culture" (1860), we lack "body or basis." Alienation from easy intercourse with the world is no trifling matter, then, especially when it springs from fear, the "obscene bird" that hovers over "government and property," feasting on "rottenness" and calling attention by its presence to "great wrongs which must be revised." This gnawing uneasiness never leaves those who prey on their neighbors or rise to power at others' expense. Vultures themselves, they find their peace of mind devoured by the knowledge of their neighbors' envy and resentment.*

Everything exacts its price: "this is that ancient doctrine of Nemesis,

---

*Nietzsche, a writer seldom accused of sentimentality, took a very similar view of the punishment visited on the high and mighty in the form of envy, hate, and fear. An "armed peace," he observed—the only peace possible among predators—conferred no "peace of mind." "One trusts neither oneself nor one's neighbor and, half from hatred, half from fear, does not lay down arms. Rather perish than hate and fear, and twice rather perish than make oneself hated and feared—this must someday become the highest maxim for every single commonwealth too."

who keeps watch in the universe and lets no offence go unchastised."
Injustice defies fate and thus invites retaliation. Sooner or later, in one
way or another, the hollow triumphs it makes possible turn to dust. The
inexorable force of fate, as Emerson sees it, nowhere shows itself more
clearly than in the principle of compensation, the "vindictive circumstance" or "deep remedial force" in nature that overrides our designs and
imposes a heavy tax on every attempt to surmount or circumvent it.
Compensation is the "law of laws," and it is "fatal." Punishment "ripens
within the flower of pleasure"; it grows out of the same stem as the crime.
"Men seek to be great; they would have offices, wealth, power and fame.
They think that to be great is to possess one side of nature—the sweet,
without the other side, the bitter." But sooner or later they find that
"pleasure is taken out of pleasant things, profit out of profitable things,
power out of strong things, as soon as we seek to separate them from the
whole." No amount of unscrupulous boldness or ingenuity can detach
the part from the whole, the cause from the effect, the end from the
means.

Calvinist theologians spoke of God's "vindictive" justice, thereby offending liberal ministers who pleaded for a softer, more amiable conception of justice. Emerson restores the older conception in all its uncompromising severity. He shows that it was not only old-line Calvinists who
recognized the law of retribution; it is universally recognized, according
to Emerson, in the world's mythology and folklore. Like Edwards, he
rests his case on observation of "daily life," which indicates that men and
women intuitively understand the principle of compensation. Preachers
may deny it, but the people affirm it in their proverbs: "Tit for tat; an eye
for an eye; a tooth for a tooth; blood for blood; measure for measure; love
for love." The people see more deeply into things than the official guardians of morality.

> Men are better than their theology. . . . That which the dron-
> ing world, chained to appearances, will not allow the realist to
> say in his own words, it will suffer him to say in proverbs
> without contradiction. And this law of laws, which the pulpit,
> the senate and the college deny, is hourly preached in all mar-
> kets and workshops by flights of proverbs, whose teaching is as
> true and as omnipresent as that of birds and flies.

The political morality of producerism, it might be argued, is still another expression of the folk wisdom that condemns every attempt to get something for nothing. "Unearned increment" is the producer's version of hubris, or pride, which defies limits, overrides natural boundaries, challenges fate, and thus provokes the retaliation of the gods. Emerson repeatedly draws on the proverbial "petty-bourgeois" wisdom about money and credit, thus recognizing its affinity with the principle of "compensation"—itself a resonant term in the realm of exchange. "Always pay; for first or last you must pay your entire debt." Those who live on moral credit will have to pay their debts with interest—with a vengeance, as it were.

A "third silent party," Emerson notes, attends "all our bargains"—nemesis or fate. He translates the old Puritan idea of an honorable calling into the idiom of nineteenth-century populism, thereby achieving, among other things, a new understanding of sin, the old doctrine of the fall of man. Sin is tax evasion—the attempt to escape the duty on desire. Our misplaced confidence in our ability to defraud destiny springs from a "disease" of the will, the disease of "rebellion and separation." Here again, Emerson follows his Calvinist forebears. He regards rebellion and separation as inherent facts of human nature, the natural disposition of human desire. Our fallen nature, "our lapsed estate," discloses itself precisely in our blindness to the "deep remedial force" in nature that pursues us relentlessly. Each man thinks he can avoid the clutches of the revenue collector, even though experience ought to show that no one (not even the high and mighty man with his consultants, accountants, and highly paid tax lawyers) escapes without payment. Each thinks the tax laws apply to everyone but himself—an oversight almost comical in its conceit, if it did not lead to such tragic consequences.

Emerson as a Populist

The justification for reading Emerson's work as a kind of theology of producerism does not lie in "Compensation" alone. In that seminal essay, and in many others besides, Emerson addresses himself to concerns shared by the Calvinist, republican, and even some early liberal traditions—fate, moral corruption, and virtue. In effect, he transposes the political economy of populism (which derived, as we have seen, both from liberal and from republican antecedents) into the higher register of moral and ontological speculation. But he does not always live on these heights. He also talks about more mundane affairs; his consistent preoccupation is to show how ordinary concerns intersect with ultimate concerns—to consider the everyday in the light of the eternal, but also to draw on everyday experience in order to enrich our understanding of last things.

Emerson's works often address the topics of the day quite directly, and his social views can easily be recognized, I think, as the views of a nineteenth-century populist. He has a populist's disdain for the fashionable life of cities, which he repeatedly dismisses as a life fit only for "fops." In *Nature,* he speaks of the "advantage which the country-life possesses, for a powerful mind, over the artificial and curtailed life of cities." He returns to the attack in "Self-Reliance." "A sturdy lad from New Hampshire or Vermont, who in turn tries all the professions, who *teams it, farms it, peddles,* keeps a school, preaches, edits a newspaper, goes to Congress, buys a township, and so forth, in successive years, and always like a cat falls on his feet, is worth a hundred of these city dolls." City society is "babyish," Emerson writes in a much later essay, "Wealth." It fosters vanity, luxury, and frivolous display. Though it sometimes puts wealth to good use in the form of libraries, galleries, and other "civilizing benefits," for the most part it subordinates the public uses of wealth to private amusement and thus makes wealth a "toy." We need cities as "centers where the best things are found," as Emerson calls them in "Culture," but they "degrade us by magnifying trifles." A countryman in the city finds himself "among a supple, glib-tongued tribe, who live for show, servile to public opinion." He misses the "lines of grandeur of the horizon, hills and plains, and with them sobriety and elevation."

Emerson believes in the moral value of manual labor. In "The American Scholar" (1837), he endorses the belief in the "dignity and necessity of labor to every citizen." In "Man the Reformer" (1841), he adds that although fairness clearly requires that a society's manual labor "be shared among all the members," the argument rests not on fairness alone but on the benefits conferred by such work. "A man should have a farm or a mechanical craft for his culture. . . . Not only health, but education is in the work." To the objection that the populist program would forgo the "immense advantages reaped by the division of labor" and "put men back into barbarism," Emerson replies that although he sees "no instant prospect of a virtuous revolution," he would gladly sacrifice some of the "conveniences" of civilization to the moral culture conferred by farming or a craft. "I should not be pained at a change which threatened a loss of some of the luxuries or conveniences of society, if it proceeded from a preference of the agricultural life out of the belief that our primary duties as men could be better discharged in that calling." In "Wealth," he extols subsistence farming in language reminiscent of Brownson or Cobbett.

> When men now alive were born, the farm yielded everything that was consumed on it. The farm yielded no money, and the farmer got on without. If he fell sick, his neighbors came in to his aid; each gave a day's work, or a half day; or lent his yoke of oxen, or his horse, and kept his work even; hoed his potatoes, mowed his hay, reaped his rye; well knowing that no man could afford to hire labor without selling his land. In autumn a farmer could sell an ox or a hog and get a little money to pay taxes withal. Now, the farmer buys almost all he consumes— tinware, cloth, sugar, tea, coffee, fish, coal, railroad tickets and newspapers.

It was precisely the farmer's growing dependence on the market, according to liberals like Theodore Parker, that not only expanded the demand for commodities of every kind but expanded the farmer's intellectual horizons, giving him access—as Emerson's examples remind us—to the news of the day, travel to distant places, and all the other advantages of modern life. Emerson's skepticism about all this puts him directly at odds with the prevailing political economy. So does his conviction that the cultivation of citizens, not the protection of property, is the proper object of political action. In "Politics" (1844), he argues that the prevailing social arrangements allow "the rich to encroach on the poor" and that "the whole constitution of property," moreover, "is injurious, . . . its influence on persons deteriorating and degrading." But the same considerations that lead Emerson to condemn the political economy of Adam Smith and Theodore Parker, "Malthus and Ricardo," also lead him to abstain from an unqualified endorsement of the principal alternatives to it. In

"Wealth," he praises the "socialism of our day" for raising the question of "how certain civilizing benefits, now only enjoyed by the opulent, can be enjoyed by all." He goes on to argue, however, that a more equitable distribution of goods is not enough. A manly, self-reliant, independent "character" is the goal, a fuller access to "civilizing benefits" only a means to that end. "Society can never prosper . . . until every man does that which he was created to do."

Emerson's consistently skeptical attitude toward social reform has to be seen in the same light. He sympathized with many of the social movements of his day, and one of them, abolition, eventually enlisted his almost unqualified support: but for the most part he remained deplorably aloof, from the reformers' point of view. He holds that modern society needs "faith," not reform. In "New England Reformers" (1844), he urges reformers to "look beyond surfaces" and partial remedies. Society needs self-respecting men and women, not a perfect set of institutions. "The disease with which the human mind now labors is want of faith." In effect, Emerson takes the position that the state cannot dispense with virtue, that virtue lies in the citizen, not in the institutions.* He wonders too whether reformers, too eager to level mankind to a common type, will not destroy respect for "genius," which inspires people by its example to live on a "higher plane." "We are weary of gliding ghostlike through the world. . . . We desire . . . to be touched by that fire which shall command this ice to stream, and make our existence a benefit."

---

*It is worth calling attention once again to the contrary view—the cardinal tenet of liberalism—expressed by John Taylor, the Virginia theorist of politics. In opposition to John Adams and other classical republicans, Taylor took the position that "an avaricious society can form a government able to defend itself against the avarice of its members" by enlisting the "interest of vice . . . on the side of virtue." Men needed no other motive than self-interest to see the need for a just and limited government that would keep order, restraining individuals from injuring one another while itself submitting to the restraints imposed by the laws of the land. "If . . . the individuals composing the nation must be virtuous, . . . republics would be founded in . . . the evanescent qualities of individuals." Fortunately, the institutions and "principles of a society may be virtuous, though the individuals composing it are vicious."

Virtue, the "True Fire"

· ■ ·

Emerson's interest in "virtue" and "character" as the proper ends of political life, though seldom couched in the rhetoric of citizenship, links him to the republican and populist traditions. "It is a peremptory point of virtue that a man's independence be secured," he writes in "Wealth." A debtor is a "slave." "When one observes in the hotels and palaces of our Atlantic capitals the habit of expense, the riot of the senses, the absence of bonds, clanship, fellow-feeling of any kind—he feels that when a man or a woman is driven to the wall, the chances of integrity are frightfully diminished." Poverty and luxury alike erode independence. The "manly part" is to find an honorable line of work and to pursue it "with might and main." The "brave workman" forfeits "grace" and "elegance" but gains "a certain haughtiness." The "mechanic at his bench," with his "quiet heart and assured manners," deals "on even terms with men of any condition." Those who speak through their "faithful work" can "afford not to conciliate."

By the middle of the nineteenth century, republican "virtue" had lost most of its earlier associations with the pursuit of glory, as we have seen, and now survived, in a residual form, chiefly as a synonym for the independence conferred by property ownership and an honest calling. Emerson shares his contemporaries' concern with the social preconditions of "virtue and self-respect"—qualities explicitly linked together in "Friendship" and in a number of other essays. But he restores all the earlier connotations of virtue as well: "energy of the spirit," "genius," "force," "vigor." The "vigor of wild virtue" equips us for the "rugged battle of fate." It dissolves "cowardly doubts" and "skepticism." It frees man from "condescension to circumstances." It cannot be learned in libraries or drawing rooms, in "tea, essays and catechism." It needs "rougher instruction"—"men, labor, trade, farming, war, hunger, plenty, love, hatred, doubt and terror." Virtue overcomes "natural force," perhaps because it partakes of this same excess in nature—its overflowing vitality and abundance, its fullness and profusion, its willingness to sacrifice the individual to the species. Virtue is heedless of personal safety and comfort. Its antithesis, as Emerson makes clear in "Heroism" (1841), his most extended elaboration of this stoical conception of virtue, is not selfishness, a lack of altruism, or an unwillingness to subordinate self-interest to the common good but caution, timidity, "false prudence," "sensual prosperity"—an inordinate concern for "health and wealth." "Tart cathartic virtue" is the antidote to the "despondency and cowardice of our religious and political theorists." It is the "plenitude of energy and power" that announces itself in "contempt for safety and ease," in "contradiction to the voice of mankind," and in "good humor and hilarity." It is the "military attitude of the soul," in short, to which "we give the name of Heroism."

Emerson not only revives the stoic ideal of virtue but resurrects another way of talking about this elusive concept—as when he refers to the inherent properties or capacity of an object as its "virtue" or "genius"—that was already archaic, or at least increasingly uncommon, in the English usage of his day. Thus he observes that "the virtue of a pipe is to be smooth and hollow." When he speaks of the "virtue of art" or the "virtue" of logic, he uses the word in the same sense, to describe the intrinsic capacity or (by extension) the intrinsic power and force that fit an object, a particular activity or undertaking, or even a human being to its proper end. Applied to human conduct, this atavistic but eminently useful idea of virtue serves to remind us that virtue lies not so much in the act as in the disposition or temper behind it, as Jonathan Edwards would have put it. Virtue has to be distinguished, Emerson says, from "what is commonly called *choice.*" It issues less from a conscious decision than from the "choice of my constitution." It is therefore "impulsive and spontaneous."

Like Carlyle, Emerson believes that heroism is unconscious—the product not of calculation but of "obedience," as Emerson puts it, to a "higher law than that of our will." Virtue is heroic character speaking through actions. It is the unpremeditated acceptance of natural limits on human freedom, which alone overcomes the power of fate and replaces "seeming" with "being." Virtue is "adherence in action to the nature of things."

"Spiritual Laws," the piece in which Emerson most clearly restates this old-fashioned way of thinking, follows "Compensation" in the *First Series* and serves as its companion. Taken together, these two essays (along with other writings) make it clear that Emerson, like Carlyle, draws not only on stoic and Aristotelian conceptions of virtue but on Christian conceptions as well. "There is no merit in the matter," Emerson insists. "Either

God is there or he is not there." So saying, he assimilates virtue to grace, in effect. The gift of the gods, "virtuous emotion" becomes another term for the "obedience" that follows "revelation." "The individual feels himself invaded by it," so that it warms all his "associations" and "makes society possible." The "true fire" shines "through every one of its million disguises" and reflects something of the vitality and creative force from which it derives. Because it derives from the "aboriginal abyss of real Being," "essence, or God"—from the "vast affirmative" that negates negation—it alone escapes the law of compensation.

"There is no tax on the good of virtue, for that is the incoming of God himself, or absolute existence, without any comparative." For this reason, virtue is the only thing that brings something new into the world, instead of redistributing goods and evils already in circulation. "In a virtuous action I properly *am;* in a virtuous act I add to the world." Here and elsewhere, Emerson resorts to the homely imagery of commercial exchange to drive home his point, and it therefore does no violence either to the spirit or the substance of his thought to see in this exalted conception of a life-giving force that "invades" and overpowers the will—the culmination of Emerson's consideration of virtue—another indication of his indebtedness to the political theory of producerism. The power to create new wealth belongs to producers alone, according to populist ideology; banking, credit, and commercial speculation merely recycle goods already in existence. We have seen that Emerson endows the producing classes with virtue in the more conventional senses of the term; but the association persists even at the highest reaches of his philosophy in the idea that virtue alone escapes nemesis, the fatal tax collector. "Material good has its tax, . . . but all the good of nature . . . may be had if paid for in nature's lawful coin, that is, by labor which the heart and head allow." Armed with virtue, "I no longer wish to meet a good I do not earn, for example to find a pot of buried gold, knowing that it brings with it new burdens."

Virtue in Search of a Calling

· ■ ·

The trouble with modern progress, from this point of view, is not just that it tends to extinguish the spirit of reverence, as man's accumulated ingenuity gives him the illusion of control over nature, but more specifically that it devalues honest labor, "nature's lawful coin." "Work and live," Emerson exhorts his reader; but honest work is hard to come by. The more we need it, the more it eludes us. An honorable calling, which Emerson regards, in effect, as the everyday form of heroism, helps to reconcile us not merely to everyday disappointments but to the metaphysical terror and pain of existence. We are oppressed by the disparity between our oceanic desires and our satisfactions, which are measured out in "drops"; between our longing for immortality and the certainty of death; between our need to know what will happen to us after death and the impossibility of finding out. In a faithless age, Emerson seems to suggest, the religious spirit lingers on chiefly in the "low curiosity" that makes us demand definitive answers to everything, or again in the nagging speculation about the "origin of evil" that he compares to mumps, measles, and whooping cough—adolescent diseases to which the "simple mind" is immune. "The only mode of obtaining an answer to these questions of the senses," Emerson says, "is to forego all low curiosity, and, accepting the tide of being which floats us into the secret of nature, work and live, work and live."

The "smooth mediocrity and squalid contentment of the times," however, give little encouragement to "honor" and "ancient virtue" or even to the demand for self-respecting employment. In "Man the Reformer" and "The Transcendentalist," essays that attempt to explain and interpret the reform movements and "new views" of the time, Emerson attributes the growing dissatisfaction with existing institutions to the lack of opportunities for honest work. The "practical impediments" confronting "virtuous young men" appear insurmountable. The "way to lucrative employments" is "blocked with abuses." Trade has become "selfish to the borders of theft." To buy a farm "requires a sort of concentration toward money, which is the selling himself for a number of years," against which "genius and virtue" instinctively rebel. "From the liberal professions to

the coarsest manual labor, . . . there is a spirit of cowardly compromise."
Young men "cannot see much virtue" in the "daily employments" open
to them, and they cry out for something "worthy to do." In "Character,"
Emerson concedes that even commerce can elicit "genius" but adds that
"this virtue draws the mind more when it appears in action to ends not so
mixed." In the nineteenth century, however, unmixed ends are in short
supply—occupations, in other words, commensurate with the capacity
for devotion and wonder.

English Traits, Emerson's most extended venture into social criticism,
can be read as an elaboration of this last thought. Emerson admires the
English—their "thoroughness" and "pluck," their rude strength, veracity, and common sense, their "supreme eye to facts." He thinks these
qualities, however, might have been brought to the service of a better
cause than "magnificence and endless wealth." England is the "best of
actual nations," but an excessive concern with comfort, a "headlong bias
to utility," and a "self-conceited modish life made up of trifles" have
coarsened the English character and led to a loss of "commanding views
in literature, philosophy and science." Emerson does not minimize the
hardiness and wisdom that have "made this small territory great," turning an "ungenial land" into a "paradise of comfort and plenty." Anyone
who still thinks of him as an addled idealist with his head in the clouds
should read *English Traits,* with its carefully observed social details and its
appreciative account of a "fruitful, luxurious and imperial" civilization.
"No want and no waste," as Emerson sees it, is by no means the worst
principle on which to build a nation; nor is it a negligible accomplishment to have "diffused the taste for plain substantial hats, shoes and coats
throughout Europe." The English make things as if they meant it. "They
build of stone: public and private buildings are massive and durable."
The same quality appears in their speech, their "power of saying rude
truth, sometimes in the lion's mouth."

Their respect for workmanship notwithstanding, the English have
nevertheless created a civilization in which a "manly" life becomes more
and more difficult to achieve. Their very success, which strengthens
"base wealth" and "vulgar aims," dampens youthful ardor or else forces it
into the wrong channels.

> Who can propose to youth poverty and wisdom, when mean
> gain has arrived at the conquest of letters and arts; when Eng-

lish success has grown out of the very renunciation of principles, and the dedication to outsides? A civility of trifles, of
money and expense, an erudition of sensation takes place, and
the putting as many impediments as we can between the man
and his objects. Hardly the bravest among them have the man-
liness to resist it successfully. Hence it has come that not the
aims of a manly life, but the means of meeting a certain pon-
derous expense, is that which is to be considered by a youth in
England emerging from his minority.

This could serve as an equally apt description of the United States today,
a country that has inherited England's power and wealth along with the
spiritual torpor that already, in Emerson's day, foreshadowed England's
decline. The vastness of the British empire, Emerson understands, contains "no vast hope." Englishmen enjoy all the requirements of a good life
except appropriate outlets for their energy and ambition, which therefore aim only to become well educated, clever, and comfortable. It says a
great deal about the reduced scale of this ambition, according to Emerson,
that a "large family is reckoned a misfortune" and that even the "death of
the young" presents itself as a blessing in disguise, since a "source of
expense" is thereby closed.* A society that finds so little for young people
to do cannot welcome new members with much enthusiasm—another
sign, as Emerson puts it in another context, that England now "lives on
its capital."

The Eclipse of Idealism in the Gilded Age
· ∎ ·

In 1856, it was still possible to hope that things would turn out otherwise
in the New World. "There, in that great sloven continent, in high Al-
legheny pastures, in the sea-wide sky-skirted prairie, still sleeps and mur-
murs and hides the great mother, long since driven away from the trim

---

*These considerations may help to explain the curious belief, referred to in chapter 3,
that runs through sentimental Victorian fiction, that children are better off dead.

hedge-rows and over-cultivated garden of England." Whether Americans would ever manage to wake this sleeping beauty depended, however, on whether they took up Emerson's challenge to live on a "higher plane," with ardor, intensity, devotion, and imagination. The course of public events, in the closing decades of Emerson's life, was not encouraging. American idealism appeared to have exhausted itself in the war against slavery. Slavery's legacy of racial antagonism confronted the nation with injustices more mountainous even than slavery itself, to the removal of which, however, it almost immediately proved unequal. Instead of accepting the social obligations implicit in emancipation, Northerners turned the freedmen over to their former masters and threw themselves instead, with a single-minded fanaticism unprecedented in the nation's history, into the business of getting rich. The energies released by the Civil War proved almost wholly commercial and rapacious—the old Yankee shrewdness without its Puritan scruples or even the rustic simplicity that once served as a partial check on the appetite for wealth.

More than ever, the cultivated classes looked to Europe not only for their literary standards but for their standard of the scale of expenditure appropriate to genteel pretensions. The man of affairs was now expected to cut a stylish figure, to make annual trips to Europe with his family, to launch his daughters in "society" with the proper ceremony and expense, to equip his sons for learned professions by educating them abroad, to dress his wife in the height of fashion, to maintain several handsome residences, to give lavish dinners and balls, to surround himself with a large staff of servants, to patronize the arts, to endow churches and universities, to pay for elaborate investigations into the plight of the poor (whose numbers seemed to multiply exponentially, far beyond the remedial capacities of "Christian charity"), and to make generous contributions to the political parties that kept a semblance of public order.

The Yankee ideal of plain living and high thinking had no more attraction for Americans in the Gilded Age than the antebellum appeal for an indigenous national literature. The editors of the *Nation* (the voice of disillusioned abolition), commenting in 1868 on the demand for a "literature truly American," confessed, "We do not know just what is meant by these words so often heard." If the words referred to works in praise of provincial "Yankeehood," or again to the sprawling, ungainly poetry of Walt Whitman (which Emerson, incidentally, had been one of the first to commend), the *Nation* was quite willing—"with no intention of being disagreeable, but rather with sympathetic sorrow"—to "wait." The country would have to wait, in other words, until it had accumulated the material resources, the museums and libraries and national institutes of arts and letters that would support higher learning and cultivated tastes. In the meantime, people who were "anxious that our literature be American" could rest assured that it could not be "anything else." Literature had no obligation to concern itself with the genius of American life, in other words, or with the nation's unique opportunity to reconcile democracy with art and devotion, the satisfaction of material needs with the demands of the spirit. On the contrary, the "dominion of numbers in matters political," as the *Nation* saw it, meant that "matters intellectual and aesthetic" would have to become self-consciously exclusive and fastidious.

Whitman's Civil War poems, *Drum Taps*, illustrated the dangers of an art overly aware of itself as American, according to the *Nation's* reviewer. "The effort of an essentially prosaic mind to lift itself, by a prolonged muscular strain, into poetry," these inept verses contained "nothing but flashy imitations of ideas." Their only aim was "to celebrate the greatness of our armies" and secondarily the "greatness of the city of New York." Patriotism was no substitute for art; in this form, indeed, it was an "offense against art," which showed that "plain facts" could become art only if one viewed them "from a height."

The author of these lines, Henry James, later repented of them as an exercise of youthful impertinence.* At the time, however, they offered a pretty fair reflection of the cultivated point of view. America's war of national unification, the vast wealth that began to accumulate in its aftermath, the rising standards of fashionable expenditure and the growing

---

*In his biography of Whitman, Justin Kaplan writes, "Thirty-eight years later, with a sense of 'deep and damning disgrace,' Henry James confessed to having written this 'little atrocity . . . perpetuated . . . in the gross impudence of youth.' He had come since to regard Whitman as the greatest American poet. Edith Wharton, hearing James read 'Lilacs'—'his voice filled the hushed room like an organ adagio'—found 'a new proof of the way in which, above a certain level, the most divergent intelligences walk together like gods.' "

sophistication of taste, along with the new opportunities for venality and corruption, made writers like Emerson and Whitman appear narrow and provincial and at the same time excessively sanguine in their view of human nature. Emerson's "noble conception of good," James said, was not balanced by a "definite conception of evil." Emerson took no account of "the dark, the foul, the base"—aspects of life "to which Emerson's eyes were thickly bandaged." Reviewing the Emerson-Carlyle correspondence in 1883, the year after Emerson's death, James noted that "both were Puritans," by which he meant that they "looked, instinctively, at the world, at life, as a great total, full of far-reaching relations." It was their "interest in the destiny of mankind" and the hopes with which it was associated that now seemed so badly out of date.

William James: The Last Puritan?

· ■ ·

William James, like his brother a member of a generation more deeply troubled than Emerson's—a generation given to "morbid" thoughts, to use a word this philosopher found indispensable—shared the feeling that Emerson's limitations declared themselves in his "optimism." Emerson had "too little understanding," according to William James, "of the morbid side of life." In his copy of Emerson's works, James referred to Emerson's vision as an "anaesthetic revelation," the "tasteless water of souls." In *The Varieties of Religious Experience,* he assigned Emerson to the category of the "once-born," along with Whitman, Theodore Parker, and Mary Baker Eddy. The piety of the "healthy-minded," James thought, contained no awareness of evil, "no element of morbid compunction or crisis." Parker's statement, "I am not conscious of hating God," exemplified this "muscular" attitude. So did Whitman's "inability to feel evil," as James characterized it.

Yet James was of two minds about Emerson. He wrote elsewhere that "Emerson's optimism had nothing in common with that indiscriminate hurrahing for the Universe with which Walt Whitman has made us familiar." He sensed something deeper in Emerson that made him an exemplary figure, one whose career threw a "strong practical light" on his own. His rereading of "the divine Emerson" in 1903 did him a "lot of good," he wrote to Henry.

The incorruptible way in which he followed his own vocation
. . . and . . . kept his limits absolutely, refusing to be entangled
with irrelevances however urging and tempting, knowing
both his strength and its limits, and clinging unchangeably to
the rural environment which he once for all found to be most
propitious, seems to me to be a moral lesson to all men who
have any genius, however small, to foster.

William James's ambivalence about Emerson reflected his ambivalence
about "optimism" in general and his failure to distinguish between optimism and hope. An awareness of evil did not necessarily lead to spiritual
"sickness," as his own account of the religious experience of the "twice-born" should have made amply clear. Yet James could not rid himself of
the suspicion that submission to a higher will—the central feature of that
experience—contained something a little unmanly and "tender-minded,"
especially if it implied a "monistic" view of the universe in which evil
was seen merely as the product of human perversity and pride, not as an
active principle in its own right. James took the distinction between the
once-born and the twice-born from John Henry Newman, but his formulation of the issue between them often seemed to owe more to Nietzsche.
Nietzsche's violent antipathy to Christianity as a religion of the "sick"
and "morbid" was "itself sickly enough," James wrote in *Varieties*, "but
we all know what he means, and he expresses well the clash between the
two ideals." The strong man glorified by Nietzsche could "see nothing
but mouldiness and morbidness in the saint's gentleness and self-severity." The debate between the two ideals—and the debate was "serious,"
James insisted—came down to the choice between "aggressiveness" and
"non-resistance." Which provided the better "means of adaptation" to a
world in which human projects and expectations so often came to nothing?

James's passionate engagement with these issues marked him as a worthy successor to Edwards and Emerson—a thinker, indeed, whose ideas
are easily misunderstood if this earlier background is allowed to fade out
of sight. But the background of early American Protestantism had already become slightly indistinct even for James himself, who missed
Emerson's call for heroism and read him, in effect, as an advocate of
"non-resistance." Nietzsche, who read Emerson and Carlyle more accurately in this respect and valued them precisely because they too admired

heroism, criticized them for trying to reconcile it with religious submission. Though James did not subscribe to Nietzsche's view of Emerson, he accepted his formulation of the general issue—his equation of submission with weakness and "morbidity." His own preoccupation with "optimism" and "pessimism," together with his identification of these qualities with "health" and "sickness," suggests a certain deterioration in the intellectual atmosphere of the times, from the effects of which even those who set themselves against the times could not altogether escape—a coarsening of thought, which would eventually reduce all spiritual questions to questions of "mental health."

The Philosophy of Wonder

At first sight, James's work appears not merely to foreshadow this therapeutic view of religion, the dominant view in our own time, but to present it in a fully developed form. James conducts his investigation of religion, after all, in the psychological mode. In his *Principles of Psychology*, a work that anticipated Freud, he exposed the importance of unconscious mental associations in the "stream of consciousness." His next major work, *The Varieties of Religious Experience*, applied his psychological method to the analysis of religious "symptoms"—the psychology of conversion. Here he endorses the religious insight that only forces outside a person's conscious control can bring about real changes in character and outlook; but he takes the position that these forces enter the self not from above but from below, from the subterranean depths of the mind. He bids a "definitive good-by to dogmatic theology" and to a personal conception of God, which is "incredible," he says, "to our modern imagination." He judges religious ideas, or at least appears to judge them, solely by their effect on mental health, waving aside the question of their truth. Thus he argues that Christian Science and other mind-cure movements should be taken seriously because they sometimes produce a "change of character for the better," whereas liberal Christianity "does absolutely *nothing*" for the believer.

When we add to such statements James's frequent references to the "cash value" of religion, we seem to be justified in regarding him as the "secular theologian" of the "new therapeutic society," in Clarence Karier's words, someone who valued religion only for its therapeutic properties and took the position that "any therapeutic belief is acceptable as long as it works." But things are not so simple. James expressly repudiates the "re-interpretation of religion as perverted sexuality," along with the "medical materialism" that can so easily be used as a means of "discrediting states of mind for which we have an antipathy." He dissociates himself from attempts to write the "story of the mind from the purely natural-history point of view, with no religious interest whatever." A purely scientific view, he says, falls short of "absolute sufficiency as an explanation of all the facts." Scientific rationalism gives a "shallow" and "superficial" account of man's spiritual life. It cannot explain religious belief even when it tries to argue in support of religion instead of arguing against it. A rationalistic God is no more convincing than a universe with no God at all. If God exists, he now has to be conceived as an altogether "more cosmic and tragic personage," whose presence reveals itself in the depths of emotion evoked by religious belief.

The "subconscious incubation" of religious feeling, James argues, does not rule out the possibility that something lies on the *"farther* side" of consciousness as well as on its subterranean or *"hither* side." The psychological realism of Luther, Edwards, and other Protestant theologians—whose analysis of conversion, James thinks, can hardly be surpassed by a modern psychologist—does not mean that religion should be replaced by psychology. It means only that psychological understanding has been part of the appeal of religion all along. The "admirable congruity of Protestant theology with the structure of the mind" indicates that Luther and Edwards knew what they were talking about and should be listened to respectfully. As for the "cash value" of religion, James takes no credit for the originality of this idea. He sees it simply as a restatement of Edwards's doctrine that religion should be judged by its fruits—its capacity to bring about an underlying disposition of acceptance and affirmation or, in James's words, a "new zest," a profound "love of life," and above all an appreciation of its "heroic" and "solemn" character. James's analysis of religious experience, as he conceives it, carries on Edwards's investigation of "religious affections" and rests on the same assumption, that "religion, in the vital sense, . . . must stand or fall by the persuasion that effects of some sort genuinely do occur."

Even if we had no biographical information about James, even if we knew nothing about the emotional crisis he went through in his twenties—about his early fear that a scientific career would foreclose the "privilege of trusting *blindly* [as he wrote in his diary in 1873], which every simple man owns as a right"—or about his lifelong attempt "to unite empiricism with spiritualism," as he put it in his notes for a course on metaphysics in 1905, the evidence of his books alone, together with the general pattern of his intellectual career, would still force us to reject the view that his interest in religion was purely therapeutic. *The Varieties of Religious Experience* occupied a pivotal position in James's intellectual development. It was the hinge between his early work as a psychologist and his later work as the philosopher of pragmatism; and it would not be an exaggeration to say that the pragmatic test of truth first suggested itself to James in the form of the familiar religious principle that the quality of belief makes itself known in its effects on the conduct of life.

The age-old wisdom that "the uses of religion . . . to the individual who has it . . . are the best arguments that truth is in it" led James to the more general principle, formally stated for the first time at the end of *Varieties,* that "the true is what works well." He did not mean, in the case of religion, that it makes us feel pleased with ourselves, confirms our opinion of our own rectitude, or gives us a comforting illusion of intellectual certainty. He meant that it provides the spiritual vitality that comes with insight into the human condition. An understanding of the religious context in which pragmatism first presented itself to James helps to forestall the vulgar misunderstanding of pragmatism as the philosophical glorification of success. Benjamin Paul Blood was much closer to the truth when he called it the philosophy of wonder—"the only method of philosophizing" that was possible for those who had attained the understanding that "wonder and not smirking reason is the final word for all creatures and creators alike."

Art and Science: New Religions

· ■ ·

When James took the position that the truth or falsity of religion had to be judged by its practical results, he was not thinking of its capacity to encourage good behavior, any more than he was thinking of mental health. True to the Protestant tradition, he regarded the conduct of life as an emotional and not primarily as a moral issue. The question to which religion was the answer was not so much how life should be lived, strictly speaking, as whether it was worth living at all (as he put it in the title of one of his essays). The sense of gratitude associated with religious conversion was experienced as a gift for which "no exertion of volition" was required, and it was this gratitude that distinguished "enthusiastic assent" to life from stoical resignation. The "difference of emotional atmosphere" was what counted, James argued, not morality.

The conduct of life was not an abstract issue for James but a very immediate and personal one; nor was it a question of an individual's obligations to his neighbors. It was a question of an individual's obligation to life itself, and it first presented itself to James, as it does to so many others, in the choice of a calling. As a young man, he found himself torn between science and art. He knew that by choosing science, he would forfeit the possibility of "blind trust"; but he had equally important reservations about the aesthetic attitude toward experience. What he longed for, as he wrote in the depths of his youthful crisis of indecision and "neurasthenic" malaise, was the "health, brightness and freshness" he found in the ancient Greeks after reading the *Odyssey*. He contrasted the "bloody old heathens," with "their indifference to evil in the abstract, their want of what we call sympathy, the essentially definite character of their joys, or at any rate of their sorrows (for their joy was perhaps coextensive with life itself)," with the "over-cultivated and vaguely sick complainers" of his own day, himself included. "The Homeric Greeks 'accepted the universe,' their only notion of evil was its perishability. . . . To them existence was its own justification, and the imperturbable tone of delight and admiration with which Homer speaks of every fact, is not in the least abated when the fact becomes to our eyes perfectly atrocious in character."

The naive trust of the Greeks could not be recaptured in the nineteenth century, at least not by the educated; but the educated classes had all the art of the ages at their disposal, and perhaps they could find a sort of sanctuary there—in the worship of poets like Homer, if not in the worship of the world Homer worshiped. It is significant that the aesthetic approach to life presented itself to James as the answer to questions that remained essentially religious. When he said in 1897, "Religion is the great interest of my life," he meant what he said. In 1884, he gave a remarkably penetrating account of the aesthetic solution to the "dilemma of determinism." The doctrine of free will, James argued, exaggerated the degree to which man was his own master, but determinism (in both its religious and its scientific forms) held that things could not be otherwise than they were and thus forced us either to condemn everything or to approve everything indiscriminately—to adopt Schopenhauer's cosmic pessimism or the foolish optimism of Dr. Pangloss. A "dramatic" view of the universe, however, might offer a way out of the difficulty. What if the "final purpose of our creation" was the "greatest possible enrichment of our ethical consciousness, through the intensest play of contrasts and the widest diversity of characters"? In that case, evil could be said to be necessary because without it, we would know nothing of good. Without the play of contrasts, the world would be as suffocatingly one-dimensional as the "white-robed harp-playing heaven of our sabbath-schools" or the "ladylike tea-table elysium" envisioned by Herbert Spencer and other social Darwinists as the "final consummation of progress." Human nature demanded the "shifting struggle of the sunbeam in the gloom," a "Rembrandtesque moral chiaroscuro." It would always find "pictures of light upon light" disappointingly "vacuous and expressionless."*

James presented this "dramatic," "gnostic," "subjectivist," and "romantic" view of the world so attractively that a careless reader might have mistaken it for his own. He went on to argue, however, that an aesthetic orientation to experience led to "ethical indifference." It transformed life "from a tragic reality into an insincere melodramatic exhibition, as foul or as tawdry as any one's diseased curiosity pleases to carry it out." It gave rise to the cult of "sensibility" exemplifed by "contemporary Parisian literature," the cynical complacency that saw the world as an experimental novel. It was therefore with a sense of relief that one

---

*These words provide a reasonably accurate characterization of the theology of the "fortunate fall," to which the elder Henry James, among others, subscribed. Man's attempt to know and do good would not amount to much, according to this theory, without his knowledge of evil. Close acquaintance with such views probably helped James to give such a sympathetic account of them.

awoke from the "feverish dream" of sensibility into a renewed appreciation of the "unsophisticated moral sense," which wanted the world to be better than it was and resolved to act, instead of merely drinking in the spectacle, so as to reduce the sum of evil in the world.

Having rejected the religion of art, James did not propose to adopt the religion of science by default. He adopted the scientist's calling, but he did not forget its limitations. He was one of the first to see, even while the Victorian faith in science was still running high, that science would never be able to offer a worldview to replace discredited religions. In another early essay, misleadingly entitled "The Will to Believe," James explored the shortcomings of science with the same insight he had brought to the shortcomings of art.* The scientific worldview, he argued, seemingly so "healthy" and "robustious," so "rugged and manly" in its respect for facts, actually concealed a childish desire for certainty. The longing for deliverance from doubt, enshrined in the epistemological tradition of modern philosophy as the distinction between certitude and mere "opinion," had to be regarded not as the beginning of wisdom but as the product of a "weakness of our nature from which we must free ourselves, if we can." Science, at least as it was construed by the Cartesian tradition of philosophy, had inherited the attitude of those who longed to live in a risk-free world. It betrayed an "excessive nervousness" in the face of possible error. Verification, that much-vaunted principle of modern science, was a technique merely for avoiding error, not for wresting truth from chaos. "Better risk loss of truth than chance of error,—that is your faith-vetoer's exact position." It was a position that could never serve as a guide to the conduct of life. The "agnostic rules for truth-seeking" laid down by "scientific absolutists" betrayed a timorous state of mind, an unwillingness to act, a suspension of judgment that ignored the whole field of religious experience and its testimony to the power of faith.

> When I look at the religious question as it really puts itself to concrete men, . . . then this command that we shall put a stop-

---

*The title is misleading because belief is the one thing, according to his own account, that cannot be willed.

per on our heart, instincts, and courage, and *wait*—acting of course meanwhile more or less as if religion were *not* true—till doomsday, or until such time as our intellect and senses working together may have raked in evidence enough,—this command, I say, seems to me the queerest idol ever manufactured in the philosophic cave.

Only when he had disposed of the competing ideologies of art and science did James turn to his psychological and philosophical studies of religion, in the hope of resolving the continuing debate in his own mind between health and morbidity, optimism and pessimism, religious "pluralism" and "monism."

The Strenuous Life of Sainthood

The Varieties of Religious Experience turns on the famous distinction between the once-born and the twice-born. It not only offers a sympathetic analysis of each type; it also, characteristically, tries to evaluate them—to decide what difference it makes to hold one view of the universe or another and which view shows a deeper grasp of things. Most of the time, James seems to come down on the side of the twice-born. His envy of the healthy might lead us to expect a preference for the "healthy-minded" type. Having no awareness of evil, however, the once-born type of religious experience cannot stand up to adversity. It offers sustenance only so long as it does not encounter "poisonous humiliations." "A little cooling down of animal excitability and instinct, a little loss of animal toughness, will bring the worm at the core of all our usual springs of delight into full view, and turn us into melancholy metaphysicians." When that happens, we need a more rugged form of faith, one that recognizes that "life and its negation are beaten up inextricably together" and that "all natural happiness thus seems infected with a contradiction." If nothing else, the shadow of death hangs over our pleasures and triumphs, calling them into question. "Back of everything is the great spectre of universal death, the all-encompassing blackness."

Stoicism, the "highest flight" of the purely natural man (the man without faith) confronts pain, loss, and death with a demand for the "damping of desire." The twice-born type of religious experience, on the other hand, asserts the goodness of being in the very teeth of suffering and evil. Black despair and alienation, James notes—the feelings that the world has become "unhomelike"—often become the prelude to conversion. The awareness of "radical evil," fear and trembling, and a bitter alienation from a God who allows evil and suffering to flourish thus underlie the spiritual intoxication that comes with "yielding" and "self-surrender." The experience of the twice-born is more painful but emotionally deeper than that of their counterparts, because it is informed by the "iron of melancholy." For this reason, religions that stress the importance of instantaneous conversion—a piety of "conquest," as Horace Bushnell reproachfully put it in his plea for "Christian nurture"—follow a "profounder spiritual instinct." Conversion confronts despair head-on and shakes those who experience it to the depths of their being, in a way that Bushnell's piety of love and "growth," centering on ritual and religious education, does not.

In the chapters on sainthood that follow his analysis of conversion, James presents sainthood as the highest type of the "strenuous life." The "general optimism and healthy-mindedness of liberal Protestant circles today," he notes, "make mortification for mortification's sake repugnant to us." James admits that great "vitality of soul" often finds "poor employment" in the lives of saints—endless fasting and prayer, exposure of the person to all sorts of unnecessary ordeals, renunciation not only of wealth and sensual gratification but of every conceivable amenity and human interest. Notwithstanding the narrow forms in which it often expresses itself, however, saintly asceticism, James thinks, gives expression to the "belief that there is an element of real wrongness in this world, which is neither to be ignored nor evaded, but which must be squarely met and overcome by an appeal to the soul's heroic resources, and neutralized and cleansed away by suffering." The "ultra-optimistic form of the once-born philosophy" tries to deal with evil by ignoring it, whereas the twice-born philosophy holds the "element of evil in solution" and is therefore "wider and completer." It represents a "higher synthesis into which healthy-mindedness and morbidness both enter and combine."

The inner assurance that comes with conversion, however poorly employed in saints, overrides everyday inertia and "inhibitions," as James calls them. It overcomes laziness, timidity, the craving for comfort, the exaggerated respect for social conventions, the fear of ridicule, and all the other doubts and misgivings that paralyze the capacity for action. It annuls the desire for "guarantee and surety." A conviction of the "importance of man and the omnipotence of God" has the curious effect of releasing energies formerly subdued. It brings with it an "astringent relish" for life. The "abandonment of self-responsibility" makes it possible to "live with energy." It transforms doubters and cowards into men and women capable of exemplary courage and resolution. The "chief wonder" of religious heroism, James finds, "is that it so often comes about, not by doing, but simply by relaxing and throwing the burden down."

Superstition or Desiccation?

If the debate between "two types of religion," as James put it in *Pragmatism,* raised the "deepest and most pregnant question that our minds can frame," we might imagine that the transformation of the "sick soul" into a strenuous lover of life, as described so vividly in *The Varieties of Religious Experience,* should have settled the matter. But James equated submission to a higher will with a "morbid" confession of weakness. As we noted earlier, he accepted Nietzsche's formulation of the choice between defiance and servile submission, even when his own evidence should have led him to question it. Thus in "Pragmatism and Religion," the last chapter of his next important work, *Pragmatism,* James sided with "healthy-minded buoyancy." "There are morbid minds in every human collection," he wrote, and all of us experience "moments of discouragement . . . when we are sick of self and tired of vainly striving." But James now appeared to repudiate the "attitude of the prodigal son" as an expression of the desire for complete security in an uncertain world. In moods of discouragement, "we want a universe where we can just give up, fall on our father's neck, and be absorbed into the absolute life as a drop of water melts into the river or the sea." But self-surrender was the mark of the tender-minded, who sought safety in the illusion of an omnipotent deity instead of meeting life as a "real adventure, with real danger."

James developed this line of thought most fully in his Hibbert Lectures, delivered at Oxford in 1908–9 and published in 1909 as *A Pluralistic Universe*. Like *Pragmatism* itself, this work should be understood as an attempt to provide the philosophical sequel originally intended to follow the psychological investigation of religion in the Gifford Lectures of 1901–2 *(The Varieties of Religious Experience)*. In *A Pluralistic Universe*, the distinction between healthy-minded and morbid religion was overlaid by the philosophical or theological distinction between pluralism and monism. When stated in this way, the issue began to look quite different from the way it looked before. The question that divided the healthy and the sick, it appeared, was whether the world would inevitably be redeemed or whether redemption should be seen as merely one among several possibilities. To put it another way, the question was whether evil was merely the absence of good or an active force that might well overpower goodness in the last analysis. The "sick souls" praised for their saintly heroism in *Varieties* lined up on the wrong side of these issues, as James now saw it. They needed the emotional security of the absolute, whereas the tough-and healthy-minded, with whom James now identified himself, took their chances in a "pluralistic" world the final form of which had not yet been decided.

Still rejecting the "naturalistic self-sufficiency" according to which the "individual, if virtuous enough, could meet all possible requirements," James once again commended the religious view of a "world wider" than naturalism could imagine, in which "all is well, in *spite* of certain forms of death, indeed *because* of certain forms of death—death of hope, death of strength, death of responsibility, of fear and worry, competency and desert, death of everything that paganism, naturalism, and legalism pin their faith on and tie their trust to." Yet the feeling that "all is well" could not be pushed to monistic conclusions, James argued, without sacrificing the essential insight that all is not well, at least in the short run, and that even the long-range outcome remains in doubt. James left his audience with the impression that the absolute sovereignty of God, the monistic fallacy, was a doctrine originating in "dialectical abstraction" and altogether incomprehensible in the "terms in which common men have usually carried on their active commerce with God." The "monistic perfections that make the notion of him so paradoxical practically and morally" could not be gleaned from the "thicker method" of empirical description, with its absorption in the "confused and unwholesome facts of personal biography." Those perfections represented the "cooler addition of remote professorial minds" occupied with "conceptual substitutes" for God in place of direct experience.

The commonsensical postulate of a finite God and a pluralistic universe, James decided, offered the only "escape from the paradoxes and perplexities" of theology. He advocated this solution at once as the tough-minded alternative and as the "line of least resistance." The best available evidence, the evidence of religious experience, suggested the existence of a "superhuman consciousness" that was nevertheless "not all-embracing." Experience indicated, "in other words, that there is a God, but that he is finite, either in power or in knowledge, or in both at once." Such was James's last word on the subject.

His uncertainty about the moral value of submission and self-surrender illustrates the difficulty of carrying on an essentially theological controversy without its theological context. Even more than Emerson and Carlyle, James believed that this context could now be dispensed with. In its absence, however, Emerson's affirmation of the goodness of being would tend to be construed either as fatuous optimism or as the product of an emotional need for absolute security and reassurance, while heroism, on the other hand—notwithstanding James's warning that "mere excitement is an unworthy ideal"—would degenerate into Nietzsche's "will to power."

In our own time, the heroic ideal is so closely associated with the cult of power (and thereby discredited) that it is important to remember what made it seem so attractive to James and his predecessors. When the British liberal L. T. Hobhouse objected that pragmatism—with its confusion of truth and "cash value," its cavalier indifference to principles, and its preference for action over thought, as Hobhouse saw it—could easily encourage collective irrationality and mob rule, James tried to correct this "travesty" of pragmatism ("by believing a thing we make it true," as Hobhouse put it) and then added, in effect, that the quarrel between Hobhouse and himself arose out of differing assessments of the modern predicament. For Hobhouse, the victory of the Enlightenment was precarious and the danger of a relapse into barbarism always imminent. For James, on the other hand, the victory of the Enlightenment was so complete that it had almost eradicated the capacity for ardor, devotion, and joyous action. "We are getting too refined for anything," he wrote elsewhere; "altogether out of touch with genuine life." Accordingly he told Hobhouse, "Your bogey is superstition; my bogey is desiccation."

The whole question of progress comes down to the accuracy of these rival readings of the signs of the times.

7

THE SYNDICALIST MOMENT:
CLASS STRUGGLE AND WORKERS'
CONTROL
AS THE MORAL EQUIVALENT OF
PROPRIETORSHIP AND WAR

The Cult of "Mere Excitement"

William James was not alone in his fear of "desiccation." By the end of the nineteenth century, the decline of heroism had become a common lament. Cut loose from its religious moorings, however, the defense of the strenuous life degenerated into a cult of sheer strength. The call to live "on a higher plane," as Emerson had put it, became a summons to war and imperial conquest, often accompanied by attacks on modern softness and effeminacy, on various forms of "race suicide," and on governments' ill-advised attempts, said to reward mediocrity and weakness, to interfere with the laws of "natural selection." Critics of modern decadence and "over-civilization" conscripted the heroic ideal into the service of militarism, jingoism, imperialism, and racial purification. Under these circumstances, it became increasingly difficult to distinguish what was valuable in the concept of heroism from what was sinister and pernicious or to reconcile heroism with democracy, racial tolerance, and goodwill among nations.

In 1895, Oliver Wendell Holmes, the future justice, delivered a Memorial Day address, "A Soldier's Faith," in which he set forth a particularly stark and uncompromising version of the new military ethic. Deploring modern hedonism, Holmes insisted that man's "destiny is battle." Commercialism and "philanthropy," the latter with its vision of a world "without much trouble or any danger," had sapped the nation's fighting spirit. Patriotism had given way to "cosmopolitanism," a "rootless self-seeking search for a place where the most enjoyment may be had at the least cost." A misguided notion of justice had led humanitarians to the absurd conclusion that it was "unjust . . . that any one should fail." But the stern test of war had always furnished the highest ideals of manhood, just as "those for women [had] been drawn from motherhood," and the world needed war more than ever as an antidote to "individualist negations" and "wallowing ease." The soldier's faith—"honor rather than life"—was "true and adorable," according to Holmes, precisely because it led the soldier to "throw away his life" in "obedience to a blindly accepted duty, in a cause which he little understands, in a plan of campaign of which he has no notion, under tactics of which he does not see the use."

Much of this no doubt needed to be said, especially on an occasion honoring the Civil War dead, in a building—Harvard's Memorial Hall— newly dedicated to their memory. Holmes's condemnation of the "revolt against pain" and failure, his attack on the "belief that money is the main thing," even his indictment of "rootless cosmopolitanism" (language not yet appropriated and compromised by fascism) exposed important symptoms of moral and cultural decay. But Holmes discredited the heroic ideal by identifying it so closely with unthinking obedience and by glorifying war as an end in itself. "Mere excitement," William James said in reply to Holmes, "is an unworthy ideal." Holmes was not content, moreover, merely to commemorate those who had fallen in the Civil War. "A Soldier's Faith," as James noted, became his "one set speech" for "every occasion." "It's all right for once, in the exuberance of youth, to celebrate mere vital excitement, *la joie de vivre* as a protest against humdrum solemnity. But to make it systematic, and oppose it, as an ideal and a duty, to the ordinary religious duties, is to pervert it altogether."

Even so, Holmes's version of the martial ethic was far more persuasive, even moving at times—more retrospective and less bellicose, less concerned to justify America's imperial future—than the version advanced by Theodore Roosevelt and his coterie of imperialist intellectuals. Roosevelt's famous lecture, "The Strenuous Life"—like Holmes's, a set speech for every occasion—contained nothing of Holmes's moral passion. It was pure bombast. "I wish to preach, not the doctrine of ignoble ease, but the doctrine of the strenuous life, the life of toil and effort, of labor and strife." Like Holmes, Roosevelt balanced his tribute to "virile qualities" with praise of motherhood, but without the mitigating suggestion that motherhood provided an important source of ideals for women. He was more interested in the declining birthrate, which threatened the better sort of people, he thought, with diminished influence in a nation swamped by immigrant hordes. He viewed the duties of women purely in the light of the nation's military requirements, and he lost no time in tying both motherhood and the "strenuous life" to the international competition for colonial possessions, from which the United States, he believed, unwisely might elect to abstain. "The wife must be the housewife, . . . the wise and fearless mother of many healthy children." The flight from motherhood, like the American male's flight from the "great fighting, masterful virtues," would indicate, unless these trends could be reversed, that Anglo-Saxon civilization was "rotten to the core." If Americans continued to "sit huddled within our own borders," shrinking from the course of imperial duty, then the "bolder and stronger peoples" would "pass us by, and win for themselves the domination of the world."

Roosevelt did not hesitate to denounce "commercialism" as another influence that undermined the "hardy virtues," and the great capitalists naturally viewed him with distrust until they discovered that his words spoke more loudly than his actions. He urged his countrymen to renounce "that base spirit of gain and greed which recognizes in commercialism the be-all and end-all of national life." Other imperialists took up the cry. Industrialism should be regarded not as the "goal of national greatness" but only as a means to that end, according to Homer Lea: when it became an "end in itself," it degenerated into "commercialism" and became a "source of danger instead of power." National "opulence" led to "national effeminacy and effeteness": "corruption exists in direct ratio to the wealth of a nation." Lea blamed "excessive national wealth" for the spread of "luxury, feminism, theorism, [and] the decay of martial inclination and military capacity."

The fear of decadence haunted all the "over-civilized" industrial nations at this time, especially the patrician classes, who embraced imperialism not so much as a higher stage of capitalism but as the cure for capitalism—for the "purposeless gluttony," as Lea put it, that sapped the fighting spirit. In order to win businessmen to the cause of expansion, imperialists had to argue, somewhat inconsistently, that colonies would enhance national wealth; but they were happier when they could urge war and conquest for their own sake. Rudyard Kipling glorified the imperial "game for its own sake." Like Holmes, he traced the purity of the soldier's faith to its absolute indifference to instrumental considerations. "Theirs not to reason why, theirs but to do and die." In the imaginative writing prompted by the British rule in India, according to Allen J. Greenberger, "the value of empire-building seems to have less to do with the Empire itself than with the development of certain qualities in the empire-builders." Colonization would revitalize the home country, overcoming the "almost oriental luxury," in the words of a minor novelist, that had "gone far to weaken the fibre" of the British middle class. Henry Stanley, the explorer of darkest Africa, drew the usual lesson in his autobiography: "England is losing her great characteristics, she is becoming too effeminate and soft from long inactivity, long enfeeblement of purpose, brought about by indolence and ease, distrust of her own powers and shaken nerves."

The explorer, conqueror, or colonial administrator, as conceived by novelists and propagandists in France and Germany as well as in England and the United States, was a figure larger than life, often modeled on Cecil Rhodes—a titan, a colossus, a man of pure energy and will. Careless of consequences, indifferent to his own safety, more than a little scornful of his compatriots at home, he inspired awe in the natives, unconditional loyalty among his subordinates. Having exchanged the closed little world of Europe for the immense open spaces of India and Africa, he enjoyed an original relation to the universe. Africa, in particular, appealed to European imperialists at the turn of the century for the same reason that images of the Wild West appealed to Americans. "A man's a man here," says the hero of one of the many English novels celebrating the Boer War. "He means something. He can stretch himself. . . . The

Americans call their land God's country. But what would they say to this, where everything is still as it was at the beginning of creation and no human being has put its mark?" Drawing liberally on Carlyle and Nietzsche as well as on the vitalistic philosophy of Henri Bergson, the propagandists of imperialism depicted the colonizer as a superman, the embodiment of vital force. According to Maurice Barrès, Charles Maurras, and Ernest Seillière, Europeans had lived too long in the mind and forgotten the value of tribal solidarity, unthinking loyalty, and violence. In Italy, F. T. Marinetti's *Futurist Manifesto* of 1909 announced a new art that would "sing the love of danger, the habit of energy and rashness," and galvanize a population enfeebled by an overabundance of material comforts. "We want to glorify war—the only cure for the world—militarism, patriotism. . . . We will sing of great crowds agitated by work, pleasure and revolt."

It was in this feverish atmosphere that the young Mussolini began to dream of restoring Italy to her former glory. In an interview in 1924, Mussolini cited among the formative influences on his fascist ideology not only Georges Sorel, the French syndicalist, but William James, who had taught him "to judge actions from their results." James could not have conceived such an heir; but his advent, however illegitimate, disclosed more possibilities than were dreamed of in the philosophy of wonder.

James on Moral Equivalence

· ■ ·

This last statement needs to be qualified. James did not live long enough to see the coming of fascism, but he saw its premonitory expression in the turn-of-the-century ideology of imperialism, and he promptly disowned it. In one of his last writings, "The Moral Equivalent of War," he singled out Homer Lea as a spokesman for the same cult of vital excitement that he had earlier criticized in Holmes. But James was not content merely to condemn the warlike temper of the times—which had reached the point, he said, that " 'peace' and 'war' mean the same thing" in "military mouths"—or to declare himself a member of the "anti-militarist party." It was not enough to condemn the horrors of war, when the very horrors of war made up its "fascination." Nor was it enough to recommend high wages and shorter hours as the "only forces [capable of overcoming] man's distaste for repulsive kinds of labor." Hard work and even danger ceased to be "repulsive" when they served the "innate pugnacity and all the love of glory" that modern man inherited from his ancestors. Peace-loving people overlooked the importance and legitimacy of those needs, treating them as atavistic impulses destined to wither in the wake of modern rationalism and moral enlightenment. On the contrary, James argued, the need to participate in shared communities of risk and high purpose was inextinguishable. "Martial virtues," accordingly, were "absolute and permanent human goods." If they could not be realized in some other way, they would continue to be realized in war itself. James urged pacifists "to enter more deeply into the esthetical and ethical point of view of their opponents." They needed to understand why their humanitarian utopia "tastes mawkish and dishwatery to people who still keep a sense for life's more bitter flavors." Instead of dismissing out of hand the residual opposition to moral uplift and social improvement, they would do better to see it as the expression of an "unwillingness to see the supreme theatre of human strenuousness closed." Simon Patten foresaw a shift from a "pain economy" to a "pleasure economy," but even Patten, James noted, acknowledged the morally "disintegrative influences" of superabundance. "Where is the sharpness and precipitousness," James wanted to know, "the contempt for life, whether one's own, or another? Where is the savage 'yes' and 'no,' the unconditional duty?" Men and women achieved dignity only when asked to submit to an arduous discipline imposed by some "collectivity"; and "no collectivity is like an army for nourishing such pride." The undemanding life of "pacific cosmopolitan industrialism," on the other hand, could only nourish a sense of "shame" in "worthy breasts."

The only alternative to war, as James saw it, was a "moral equivalent of war," which would make the same demands on people in the name of peace, satisfy the same taste for self-sacrifice, and elicit the same qualities of devotion, loyalty, and ardor. His own solution—an army conscripted into the peacetime war "against *Nature*"—anticipated the Civilian Conservation Corps briefly instituted under the New Deal. It drew on the images of the American West that influenced other spokesmen for martial virtues, like Francis Parkman and Theodore Roosevelt. Life in the great outdoors, as James thought of it, would expose "our gilded youths" to rugged conditions in which they would "get the childishness knocked out of them," so that they could "come back into society with healthier sympathies and soberer ideas."

Edward Bellamy conceived his industrial army, in *Looking Backward*, as a mechanism by means of which labor could be collectivized, performed with the consummate efficiency made possible by an elaborate division of tasks, and thereby reduced to a few hours of the day and a few years out of every life, leaving all the rest of the time free for amusement. James thought of an industrial army, on the other hand, as a means of making work as demanding as possible. For Bellamy, an army was a gigantic machine in which every job was reduced to a routine and the need for individual enterprise and imagination effectively eliminated. For James, enterprise and imagination, along with a sense of "civic honor" and a love of glory, were the very qualities that military life tended to promote. From his point of view, societies that failed to nourish these qualities, either through militarism or through its equivalent, were "fit only for contempt" and could expect "dangerous reactions" against themselves. He seems to have foreseen something like fascism after all; whereas Bellamy, convinced that men and women wish only to enjoy life with a minimum of effort, could foresee only a painless progress toward the celestial city of consumerism.

The introduction of wage labor had destroyed the independence of the small producer (itself originally conceived, by Harrington and other republican theorists, as a moral equivalent of the military calling) and created a permanent class of hirelings. For those who refused to indulge the illusion that wage earners could still become property owners if they set their minds to it, the "social question" now seemed to invite two radically conflicting solutions. The first accepted the wage system, with all its undesirable effects, as the price of economic abundance. The advantages of leisure and comfort would outweigh the moral disadvantages complained of by advocates of the "strenuous life," provided of course that consumer goods were distributed as widely as possible—the only conceivable justification of abundance in the first place. The second solution required the reorganization of work itself, with an eye to the restoration of its character-forming discipline. The first line of attack, exemplified to perfection in Bellamy's utopian novels, conceived of the individual mainly as a consumer; the second, exemplified in embryonic form in James's theory of moral equivalence, conceived of the individual mainly as a producer. In its nineteenth-century form, however, the ideology of producerism no longer addressed the conditions of twentieth-century capitalism. A revival of small-scale production seemed unlikely, and some other form of demanding discipline, some other means of instilling a sense of unswerving devotion to an honorable calling, would have to be found. The search defeated many of those who sympathized with its objectives, and who therefore lapsed into a vague and milky communitarianism that avoided the whole problem of modern work and its discontents.

It is interesting that William James, who described himself as a "rabid individualist" and seldom wrote on social questions, contributed so much more to an understanding of the great social questions of the twentieth century, even in this one little essay, than those who worried incessantly about the decline of "community." The heroic ideal, seemingly resistant to any sort of social application, turned out to speak more incisively to social issues, if often very obliquely, than more fully elaborated social philosophies. In order to see how some of its possibilities could be more fully realized, we must turn to the philosopher of syndicalism, Georges Sorel, who acknowledged intellectual indebtedness to James—with far more justification than Mussolini—and whose work can be read as a more highly developed version of the Jamesian theory of moral equivalence.*

---

*Not that Sorel was influenced by the ideal of "moral equivalents" as such. James's essay appeared after Sorel had completed all three of his most important works (all of which came out between 1906 and 1908): *Reflections on Violence, The Illusions of Progress,* and *The Decomposition of Marxism.* What Sorel took from James was the philosophy of pragmatism in general, which complemented what he had also learned from Bergson, and more specifically James's view of the "cash value" of religion as moral heroism. It is interesting to note that his admiration for James did not extend to the concept of a "pluralistic universe."

Writing to Croce in 1910, he astutely observed, "In the mind of William James, pluralism seems to have the function of explaining the existence of evil in the world; the fact of evil poses some difficulties for philosophers with optimistic leanings (as are the English and Americans); they account for it in a crude way by assuming that there are several worlds and several gods. (*Varieties of Religious Experience* has an intimation of

Sorel's Attack on Progress

· ■ ·

Sorel is highly suspect in progressive circles, of course, and a sympathetic account of his work invites censure. Any defense has to begin by acknowledging what is valid in the case against him. His writing was sloppy and disorganized, his thinking often confused, and his political judgment erratic, to say the least. Like Orestes Brownson, he changed his mind too many times and acquired a reputation for inconsistency. By turns a Dreyfusard, an anti-Dreyfusard, a critic of nationalism, an exponent of nationalism, a monarchist of sorts, and a Leninist of sorts, sooner or later he quarreled with everybody and never gained much of a following. Identified in the public mind with syndicalism, he was eventually disowned even by the syndicalists. Some of the leading thinkers among his contemporaries—Henri Bergson, Benedetto Croce, Vilfredo Pareto, Antonio Gramsci, G. D. H. Cole—spoke well of him; but since those who found his work challenging or claimed to have been influenced by it covered the whole political spectrum, their good opinion merely heightens the impression of inconsistency. If Sorel can be claimed at once by the extreme right and by the extreme left, it is tempting to write him off as a "notorious muddlehead," as Lenin put it, or to draw the familiar conclusion that right- and left-wing extremisms converge in their "apocalyptic view of history and politics," in the words of Edward Shils, which "those who place themselves on the side of the free society" ought to shun like the plague.

Sorel's "polyglot mind," as Irving Louis Horowitz aptly calls it, was full of contradictions. He associated with political reactionaries like Paul Bourget, Maurice Barrès, and Charles Péguy, as well as with radical trade unionists like Fernand Pelloutier and Hubert Lagardelle. He dismissed democracy as the reign of mediocrity. He tended to confuse politics and

---

that thesis.) In a general way, the problem of evil is the stumbling stone of modern thought, unwilling as it is to hear of anything derogatory to its optimism." On this point Sorel, though not a practicing Catholic, remained far more orthodox than James.

religion, as if men could find salvation in the class struggle. But if Sorel stands convicted on all these counts, and probably on the count of anti-Semitism as well, the other charges against him have to be thrown out, since they arise either from misunderstanding, sometimes from deliberate misrepresentation of his views, or simply from the enlightened prejudice against "pessimism." His attack on the idea of progress can hardly be taken as evidence of mental instability. Nor can we accept Horowitz's contention that his championship of small-scale production betrays "nostalgia" and "economic provincialism." Even his scorn for parliamentary democracy has to be removed from the indictment against Sorel, unless we can show that democracy embodies a demanding, morally elevating standard of conduct. If democracy means no more than a "reduction of the work day," in Horowitz's formulation, "improved automatic techniques in production," and "abundance of commodities," it is not worth defending. How can such a paltry vision, as William James said, inspire anything but contempt?

As for the crowning charges—Sorel's advocacy of "irrationalism," his "cult" of violence—these arise from a hasty and superficial reading of his work. Modern liberals, with their rather narrow conception of rationality and their visceral reaction against the merest hint of violence and coercion, cannot be expected to do justice to someone like Sorel, who did not share the dominant prejudices of the age. Liberals' obsession with fascism, moreover, leads them to see "fascist tendencies" or "proto-fascism" in all opinions unsympathetic to liberalism, just as the far right detects "creeping socialism" in liberalism itself. If liberals have been victimized by red-baiting, they have perfected their own technique of dismissal by expanding the concept of fascism to embrace everything that falls outside the tradition of the Enlightenment.

Sorel provides an easy target for this kind of abuse, since opposition to the Enlightenment was the one position from which he never deviated. Progress, humanitarianism, the Cartesian ideal of certitude, utilitarianism, positivism, sexual freedom—Sorel rejected them all. He inherited from his intellectual masters—Pascal, Proudhon, Tocqueville, Le Play—a profound suspicion of the modern mind: of its shallowness and complacency, its unmerited sense of superiority to the past, its fascination with the future, its underlying indifference to the future. He took Pascal's part against Descartes, who tried to reduce everything to formu-

las, with consequences equally deplorable, Sorel thought, for a theory of knowledge and a theory of morals. Strictly speaking, "there is no Cartesian morality" at all, he wrote in *The Illusions of Progress,* only a "rule of propriety prescribing respect for the established usages." It was a mark of his Pascalian, "Protestant-like view of life" (as an Italian admirer, Giuseppe Prezzolini, put it) that Sorel criticized Descartes on the grounds that he "never seemed to have been preoccupied with the meaning of life."

The "great preoccupation" of his own life, he told Croce in 1907, was the "historical genesis of morality," which he traced neither to the French nor to the Athenian enlightenment but to the pastoral, "warlike tribes living in the mountains" of ancient Greece, whose sense of the "grandeur and beauty of creation," preserved in the *Iliad* and the *Odyssey,* "provided the republics of antiquity with the ideas which form the ornament of our modern culture." In modern times, peasants and small proprietors most clearly approximated the Homeric virtues, in Sorel's view. He thought Proudhon's incorruptible peasant morality—his respect for "temperance, frugality, the daily bread obtained by daily labor, a poverty quick to punish gluttony and laziness"—underlay his achievements as a social theorist. Like Le Play, he attached great importance to the family and to the continuity between generations. "The world will become more just," he wrote, "to the extent that it becomes more chaste." He deplored the growing acceptance of divorce, the heavy taxes on inherited property, and the contractual theory of the family that animated these reforms, as a result of which the family came to be seen merely as a collection of individuals.

Sorel's highly original attack on the idea of progress owed a good deal to Tocqueville's insight that the old regime, by consolidating the power of the state and weakening intermediate institutions, had laid the groundwork for the revolution and for the identification of the state with the highest form of reason. The whole structure of modern politics and thought, Sorel argued, rested on the dubious innovations of the age of absolutism. The Cartesian spirit in philosophy, the idea of absolute rights in property, and the theory of enlightened despotism had a certain affinity for each other and for the idea of progress—"the adornment of the mind that, free of prejudice, sure of itself, and trusting in the future, . . . created a philosophy assuring the happiness of all who possess the means

of living well." The old dream of abundance seemed to have become a reality in the eighteenth century, at least for the upper classes. "Towards 1780," thanks to the growth of productive forces, "everybody believed in the dogma of the indefinite progress of mankind." This "feeling of absolute confidence" would be "bizarre and inexplicable," Sorel added, except as the product of economic improvements, since it was so obviously at odds with the experience of mankind. Experience and common sense indicated that "movements toward greatness are always forced," as he wrote to Croce in 1911, "whereas the movement toward decadence is always *natural;* our nature is irresistibly carried in the direction considered bad by the philosopher of history."

Sorel believed that the bourgeoisie, having derived its moral ideas from eighteenth-century absolutism and from the decadent aristocracy fostered by absolutism, was now attempting to instill this ethic of irresponsibility into the workers, seducing them with the promise of endless leisure and abundance. He argued, in effect, that the aristocracy of the old regime, with its cultivation of the "art of living," had anticipated the modern cult of consumption. Aristocrats had traded their power for the brilliant, feverish delights of the Sun King's court. Without civic functions, they determined at least "to enjoy their wealth with relish"; they "no longer wanted to hear of the prudence long imposed on their fathers." The assumption that improvement had become automatic and irresistible relieved them of the need to provide for times to come. "Why worry about the fate of new generations, which are destined to have a fate that is automatically superior to ours?" Aristocrats tried to avoid their obligations not only to the future but to the poor; this escape from responsibility, according to Sorel, was the dominant theme in eighteenth-century aristocratic culture. "At the dawn of modern times, anyone who held any authority aspired to liberate himself from the responsibilities that archaic conventions, customs, and Christian morality had, until then, imposed on the masters for the benefit of the weak." The idea of progress furnished the theoretical justification for the abrogation of reciprocal obligations, the foundation of aristocratic morality in its heroic phase, before enlightened aristocrats were corrupted by easy living.

The Case for "Pessimism"

· ■ ·

Just as progressive ideology concealed indifference to the future beneath apparent concern, so its humanitarian horror of violence concealed the "sanguinary frenzies" of disappointed optimism. Hence the revolutionary terror—perhaps the most enduring legacy of the Enlightenment. Heroic pessimism, Sorel argued, had nothing in common with the bitter disillusionment experienced by those who blindly trust in the future only to stumble against unexpected obstacles to the march of progress. The pessimist understood that "our natural weakness" obstructed the path of social justice. The optimist, "maddened by the unexpected resistance that his plans encounter," sought to assure the "happiness of future generations by butchering the egoists of the present." Humanitarians condemned violence on principle but resorted to a particularly brutal and vindictive form of violence when their plans went awry.

Pessimism rested on a love of life and a willingness to part with it. It expressed an awareness of the "grandeur and beauty of the world," including man's own powers of invention, together with a recognition of the limits of those powers. What Sorel called pessimism was close to what Carlyle, Emerson, and James called wonder—an affirmation of life in the teeth of its limits. Sorel understood that the modern mood is one of revolt, born of the growing impatience with limits that stubbornly persist in spite of all the celebrated advances in science, technology, and organized benevolence. This is why he took so much trouble to distinguish his doctrine of class warfare both from the revolutionary terror carried out by intellectuals armed with a blind faith in progress and from popular insurrections animated by envy and resentment of the rich. Envy and resentment were marks of a slavish disposition, and the bloody revolts they inspired left things very much as they were. French politics in the aftermath of the Dreyfus affair, Sorel thought, were dominated by an alliance between progressive intellectuals and the rebellious masses. The intellectuals, themselves envious of the power exercised by the army, the church, and the financial establishment, played on the envy of the masses. The idealism originally associated with the campaign on behalf of Colonel Dreyfus, wrongly accused of treason in the hope of keeping Jews in their place, had turned sour. In the 1890s, Sorel had taken up socialism, but he soon came to see the socialist movement as the principal embodiment of slavish envy and resentment. Now he took the position that a socialist state would only bring about a change of masters. Jean Jaurès, the socialist champion, became Sorel's prime example of political self-righteousness. Jaurès, he said, was "capable of every ferocity against the vanquished," because "in his eyes the vanquished are always in the wrong." Socialists worshiped success; if they came to power, they would "prove to be worthy successors of the Inquisition, of the Old Regime, and of Robespierre." Experience—always the best guide—showed that "revolutionaries plead 'reasons of state' as soon as they get into power."

Socialists, moreover, had no intention of getting rid of the conditions that required a class of supervisors in the workplace. A socialism that deserved to be taken seriously, according to Sorel, would seek to make workmen their own masters. Jaurès and his kind, however, sought merely to become masters in their own right. The "only difference which would exist between this sham socialism and capitalism" would lie in the "employment of more ingenious methods of procuring discipline in the workshop." Sorel's indictment of socialism did not stop with the reformist school; it extended to revolutionary socialism as well. Syndicalism has often been misrepresented as a movement that began and ended with the demand that parliamentary methods give way to revolutionary violence, as if the issue turned solely on tactics. Sorel's emphasis on violence encouraged this misrepresentation; but even causal readers might have been expected to catch his condemnation of revolutionary terror, which in itself showed that his objection to socialism was not primarily tactical at all but substantive. He wanted a social order in which industry was governed by the workers themselves, not by a managerial class that would always oppress workers whether it owed its influence to capitalists or to the state. Revolutionary movements should first of all seek to make the workers independent, fearless, and resourceful, according to Sorel; instead of which socialists exploited their weakness, encouraging extravagant expectations they would never be able to fulfill. Sorel had no illusions about what would happen if an undisciplined class of workers suddenly took power and tried to impose its slave morality on the state. Lacking both the moral independence and the technical knowledge to organize industry on their own, the workers would soon find themselves in the same old predicament. The "dictatorship of the proletariat" would turn out to be the dictatorship of the intellectuals—the worst form of tyranny imaginable, in Sorel's view.

War as Discipline against Resentment

·■·

The only way to avoid this outcome was to provide workers with the moral and technical resources required for a life of freedom—to make them soldiers, in short. Sorel's defense of the military virtues shocked the sensibilities of his age and continues to stand in the way of a sympathetic understanding of his thought. Even if some of his contemporaries, maddened by the injustice and poverty they saw all around them, could swallow the idea of revolutionary violence, they found it impossible to swallow military discipline. Sorel's praise of warfare, however, is easily intelligible as the product of a long tradition of republican thought in which citizenship had once been closely tied to the profession of arms. In the eighteenth and nineteenth centuries, as we have seen, republicans substituted proprietorship for military prowess as the social basis of citizenship, and the republican tradition mingled with others in a broad current of populist ideology that glorified the small producer. Sorel inherited this populism, along with a "peasant morality," from Proudhon; his originality—a response to the difficulty that small producers appeared by his time to be a vanishing breed—lay in his return to the military model of citizenship, which other republicans had long since renounced. The working class would learn to be free, he argued, only by acting like an army. Class warfare would become the school of modern virtue.

Unlike Bellamy, for whom military discipline implied an intricate division of labor and the efficiency provided by complete regimentation, Sorel believed that war nourished a "passionate individualism." In the wars of the French revolution—his favorite example, next to Homeric Greece, of military life at its best—"each soldier considered himself as an individual having something of importance to do in the battle, instead of looking upon himself as simply one part of the military mechanism committed to the supreme direction of the leader." Sorel's conception of warfare did not imply the blind obedience singled out by Oliver Wendell

Holmes as the essence of the "soldier's faith." What might look like blind obedience was a suspension of personal safety and a sublime indifference to personal rewards—the overcoming of everyday "inhibitions," as James would have put it.

> When a column is sent to an assault, the men at the head know they are sent to their death, and that the glory of victory will be for those who, passing over their dead bodies, enter the enemy's position. However, they do not reflect on this injustice, but march forward.*

Sorel criticized Napoleon for introducing a merit system into the army, thereby weakening its revolutionary ardor. Such devices sapped heroism at its source.†

The object of war was glory, not plunder or personal gain, and it appealed to heroism, not to envy and hatred. Almost everything Sorel said about war comes back to these two points, which can be further condensed into the statement that war represented not just aggression but disciplined aggression and that the specific content of this discipline was the discipline against resentment. "Everything in war is carried on without hatred and without the spirit of revenge: in war the vanquished are not killed; non-combatants are not made to bear the consequences of the disappointments which the armies may have experienced on the fields of battle." No doubt this is an idealized view of war, a preindustrial view at that. But Sorel's eagerness to expound the "idea of war conceived heroically" did not blind him to less exalted ways of making war. He knew that warfare, like any other calling, could be corrupted by the superimposi-

---

*Recall Carlyle's praise of the fox, who does not spend his days lamenting the injustice of his lot; if he did, he would never catch the geese.

†Note the religious parallel. Reformation theology, of the kind that influenced Edwards and Pascal (and ultimately Sorel himself, by way of Pascal), insisted that true virtue lay in indifference to rewards, celestial or otherwise. Religious liberals in the eighteenth and nineteenth centuries began to argue that God hands out rewards in strict conformity to merit. Meritocracy appeared to furnish the only rational principle of justice.

tion of external goods (plunder, personal ambition) on the goods internal to its practice. Imperialism had stripped war of its moral value, he thought. The "object of war" was "no longer war itself." "Its object is to allow politicians to satisfy their ambitions"—to exploit subject populations and to pacify their own populations by giving them easy victories to celebrate. "It is hoped that the citizens will be so intoxicated by the spell of victory they will overlook the sacrifices which they are called upon to make." Under these conditions, the internal goods specific to the military calling could no longer provide a source of civic virtue. But that only strengthened the case for a moral alternative in the form of class struggle.*

The Sectarian Dilemma

Sorel's idea of revolutionary violence bore little resemblance to the ideas advanced by later theorists of violence like Franz Fanon and Jean Paul Sartre, who stressed the purifying force of hatred. Sorel understood that although "hate is able to provoke disorder, to ruin a social organization, to cast a country into a period of bloody revolutions, . . . it produces nothing." Like Emerson, a writer he probably never read, he believed that virtue alone makes something new. In the passage castigating Napoleon's ill-conceived army reforms, he added this eminently Emersonian thought: "The striving towards perfection, which manifests itself, in spite of the absence of any personal, immediate, and proportional reward,

---

*Sorel drew an analogy between the mercenaries who fought the battles of imperialism and the proletarian army as conceived by socialist politicians. For the politicians, he said, "the proletariat is their army, which they love in the same way that a colonial administrator loves the troops which enable him to bring large numbers of Negroes under his authority." By means of the same promises—plunder and revenge—they hoped to conscript the workers into their campaign to gain control of the state. The old distinction between mercenary armies and citizen armies, always a staple of republican thought, underlay this analysis. Sorel wanted the workers to become citizen soldiers instead of hirelings, as it were.

constitutes the secret *virtue* which assures the continued progress of the world" (his italics). He found this virtue in soldiers, in inventors, in artists and craftsmen, and also in exemplary religious figures, whom he extolled with a fervor that may seem surprising in the author of *Reflections on Violence.*

If there is any lingering doubt about the spiritual significance he attached to class warfare, it should be dispelled by his frequent comparisons between the working-class movement and the early history of the Christian church. The early Christians thought of themselves as a "holy army" at war with the devil, according to Sorel, and although their dreamed-of "deliverance did not take place," the dream itself (like the "myth" of the general strike in his own time) "produced many heroic acts, engendered a courageous propaganda, and was the cause of considerable moral progress." The analogy between the Christian apocalypse and the general strike clarifies the meaning Sorel attached to social myths. He did not see them simply as convenient fictions, let alone as illusions or outright falsehoods. They were guiding beliefs about the world that combined moral insight and moral aspiration, and their cash value, as James would have said, lay in their capacity to call up unflagging devotion, to discipline resentment, and thus to change the world for the better. Sorel reserved the term "myth" for ideologies that elicited qualities once associated with the concept of virtue. Progress, on the other hand, was an "illusion," because it elicited only complacency, alternating with the "frenzies" of disappointed optimism.

In one of the many allusions to primitive Christianity in *Reflections on Violence,* Sorel pointed out that Roman persecution of the Christians was fairly mild, on the whole, that torture and execution occurred infrequently, that the Romans themselves paid little attention to these incidents, and that the significance of persecution lay in the Christians' belief that it foreshadowed a decisive struggle between good and evil. Persecution acquired its "dread and dramatic character" only in the context of Christian mythology, which meant nothing to the Romans. In the same way, Sorel suggested, the struggle between capital and labor might lead only to a "few short conflicts," inconsequential from capital's point of view. What mattered was that conflicts between capital and labor evoke in the worker's mind the "idea of the general strike," which would discourage accommodation between the opposing forces in the same way the expectation of the end of the world prevented accommodation between Christianity and Rome. Even when Christianity became the official religion of the empire, the church regarded the new arrangement as strictly provisional, and a sense of the radical cleavage between Christians and pagans persisted through all the subsequent ages of compromise and conciliation, to be revived whenever the church sank too completely into the ways of the world.

Clearly Sorel expected the working-class movement, disciplined by the austere rigors of the class struggle, to inherit the rejuvenating role of Christian sectarians. The church in his own day, like the army—that other source of strenuous ideals—had finally lapsed into a terminal state of moral fatigue, in Sorel's view. He endorsed Ernest Renan's judgment—all the more astute, he thought, for having been offered at a time when so many people "were announcing the renascence of idealism and foreseeing progressive tendencies in a Church that was at length reconciled with the modern world"—that "the two things which alone until now have resisted the decay of reverence, the army and the church, will soon be swept away in the torrent." The defection of the army and the church left "only one force" capable of sustaining an "entirely epic state of mind," according to Sorel—the labor movement, organized around demands not for higher wages but for control of production by the producers.

We are now in a better position, I think, to appreciate both the value and the limitations of Sorel's political vision. The limitations do not lie in his "cult of violence." He expected the working-class movement to "refine the conception of violence." Sorelian violence was so broadly imagined, as Jack Roth observes, as to be quite "compatible" with "Christian non-violent resistance." The trouble with Sorel's approach to politics was not that it exalted raw passions and "irrationalism" and thus prepared the way for totalitarianism but that it was much too refined for daily use—too rigidly divorced from any practical objectives the workers could hope to attain.

More sympathetic critics of Sorel made this point. "What attracted him," as G. D. H. Cole correctly observed, "was the struggle, not the victory." It is true that he envisioned workers' control of the means of production; but even this seemed to figure in his scheme of things not so much as a goal but as a by-product of class warfare. Once the workers had begun to think for themselves, it was almost irrelevant whether they institutionalized their achievement. The "epic state of mind," in fact, was inherently resistant to institutionalization. Moral heroism and the restoration of craftsmanship—the two great objectives of the syndicalist movement, as Sorel understood it—were not completely compatible, not at least in the Sorelian view of syndicalism.

"Art," he wrote, "is an anticipation of the kind of work that ought to be carried on in a highly productive state of society." Workers' collective control of their work would make everyone an artist and thereby revive the pride of workmanship formerly associated with small-scale private ownership. According to Sorel, the superiority of syndicalism to socialism consisted, in part, of its appreciation of proprietorship, dismissed by Marxists as the source of "petty-bourgeois" provincialism and cultural backwardness. Unimpressed by Marxist diatribes against the idiocy of rural life, syndicalists, he thought, valued the "feelings of attachment inspired in every truly qualified worker by the productive forces entrusted to him." They respected the "peasant's love of his field, his vineyard, his barn, his cattle, and his bees."

That Sorel spoke of these possessions as things "entrusted" to man shows how radically he differed from Marxists, who shared the liberal view of nature as so much raw material to be turned to the purpose of human convenience. But he differed also from conservatives, who made a fetish of property ownership as such, not seeing that its value lay only in the encouragement it gave to craftsmanship, which could be encouraged in other ways. "All the virtues attributed to property would be meaningless without the virtues engendered by a certain way of working." It was not ownership so much as the opportunity for invention and experimentation that made work interesting, and the same advantages could be re-created in factories once the workers themselves began to exercise responsibility for the design of production.

This was clear enough; the difficulty lay in reconciling the practical demands of workmanship with an "epic state of mind." On the one hand, Sorel argued that "modern technical education should have as its goal to give the industrial worker" the qualities of an artisan or a successful farmer—to make him "an observer, a reasoner," a person who was "curious about new phenomena." On the other hand, he told workers not to be "*reasonable*, as the professional sociologists wish them to be," or to confine their struggle with capital to "disputes about material interests." Material issues, he warned, furnished "no more opportunity for heroism than when agricultural syndicates discuss the subject of the price of guano with manure merchants." If he meant that workers should assert control over industry instead of merely negotiating for a bigger share of the profits, his advice made good syndicalist sense. Nevertheless it remained something of a mystery how workers were to assume control of industry without discussing the price of guano and other prosaic subjects. Too much emphasis on heroism could easily divert the syndicalist movement from the question of workers' control to the pageantry and spectacle of strikes, which left behind a legendary history for later generations to savor—as in the case of the IWW in the United States—but nothing in the way of solid accomplishments.

Without the supporting ideology of workers' control, syndicalism could easily degenerate into a mystique of "struggle" for its own sake. Without its "epic" component, on the other hand, it would degenerate in the opposite direction, producing an abundance of "reasonable" proposals for industrial reorganization that nevertheless failed to generate much enthusiasm. The syndicalist movement had to grapple with the same dilemma that had baffled the Christian church throughout its history, the choice between the equally unsatisfactory alternatives of sectarian withdrawal and institutional rigidification. What good was religion practiced only by a handful of zealots, each claiming his own special revelation and acknowledging obedience only to his inner voice? But what good was a religion of public rituals and empty formulas, held together by hierarchical discipline? If syndicalism remained a sect, united only by vows of revolutionary purity, it would accomplish nothing except to save its own soul. But if it renounced the myth of the general strike and began to concern itself with the practical details of production, it would lose sight of the intuition that made it attractive in the first place—that life can be lived on a higher plane, as Emerson would have said.

The point, of course—in politics as in religion—was to hold these irreconcilable elements in some kind of tension, so that neither obscured the other. Only a theorist as disorganized as Sorel could manage this feat very successfully. His most obvious weakness—his incapacity for systematic thought—enabled him to live with contradictions that more orderly minds would be tempted to resolve.

Wage Slavery and the "Servile State":
G. D. H. Cole and Guild Socialism

In the first decades of the twentieth century, a period of instability and ferment in the British labor movement, syndicalism "took the restless, the discontented and the extremist" by storm, as G. D. H. Cole observed in 1913. Beatrice Webb, the personification of Fabian socialism and therefore the target of syndicalist contempt, admitted in 1912 that syndicalism had "taken the place of old-fashioned Marxism." She noted with disapproval that it appealed equally to the "glib young workman," whose tongue ran away with him as he mouthed the "phrases of French Syndicalism instead of those of German Social Democracy" and to the "inexperienced middle-class idealist," who welcomed the new movement as a "new and exciting Utopia."

Utopian or not, syndicalism exposed the shortcomings of parliamentary socialism. It appeared on the scene at a time when many people were beginning to wonder whether "state socialism," as the Fabian program was called by its enemies, would represent any improvement over the "state capitalism" that was emerging as a result of the corporations' growing dependence on big government. Hilaire Belloc called attention to the dangers of centralization in *The Servile State* (1912), a book that made a deep impression even on those who rejected his demand for the restoration of small-scale ownership. Almost everyone on the left, syndicalist and socialist alike, now took it for granted that small proprietorship was a thing of the past. "The factory has come to stay," said Cole, "and the machine has come to stay. . . . We cannot . . . set back the hands of the clock." But that did not mean that the problems of modern society could be solved by increasing the powers of the state. The Fabian solution, Cole argued, was "altogether wrong," and Belloc had rendered an important service by showing how "the vast extension of the sphere of State action . . . led to the confrontation of the pygmy man by a greater Leviathan, and produced a situation extremely inimical to personal liberty."

No English radicals of any importance agreed with the syndicalists that "direct action" could completely replace political action, but a great many of them agreed that party politics would never accomplish anything all by itself. The Fabians, having captured the Independent Labour party, hoped to gain control of Parliament and achieve socialism through legislative reform. But "if you place the least reliance upon political means to achieve industrial reform," S. G. Hobson bluntly told the Trades Union Congress in 1913, "you are criminal fools." Hobson, a guild socialist, pointed out that more than forty members of the Labour party had been elected to Parliament in 1906 but that working conditions continued to deteriorate. Cole argued in 1913 that the Labour party could never hope to become a majority. His objections to Fabianism, however—many of which applied to Marxian socialism as well—went far beyond tactical considerations. Marx had "infected" socialists with an "economic fatalism," he argued, which made them acquiesce in centralization and top-down control of industry as an unavoidable precondition of economic efficiency. Instead of taking concrete steps to counter hierarchical authority in the workplace, they staked everything on the hope that socialist parties could gain control of the state. Social democrats and revolutionary socialists disagreed merely about the means by which this goal could be accomplished. Neither side appeared to understand that a change of masters would do the workers very little good. The object was to get rid of masters altogether and to make the workers "fit" to operate the industrial plant by themselves.

Cole rightly suspected that most socialists had no interest in this project and no confidence that workers could ever take over the control of production. Beatrice Webb, evidently speaking for the Fabians as a group, wrote in her diary, "We have little faith in the 'average sensual man,' we do not believe that he can do much more than describe his grievances, we do not think he can prescribe his remedies." Even in public, the Fabians did not attempt to conceal their low opinion of the workers they professed to champion. Democracy, the Webbs argued, required only "assent to results," not participation in the deliberations by which they were achieved. This was a much too narrow and grudging idea of democracy to suit Cole and other guild socialists.*

---

*Cole also criticized the cosmopolitan ideal shared by Fabians and Marxists. He believed in the value of national attachments and took the position that socialism would

State socialists, or "collectivists," as Cole and his friends referred to them, regarded social justice simply as a matter of achieving a more equitable distribution of the goods produced in such quantity by modern technology. In their eyes, socialism was a "business proposition," according to Cole; they forgot that it was a " 'human' proposition also." Putting their faith in the state, they "forgot that the State cannot . . . be better than the citizens, and that, unless the citizens are capable of controlling the Government, extension of the powers of the State may be merely a transference of authority from the capitalist to the bureaucrat." Collectivists saw things from the consumer's point of view. They assumed, Cole said, that "production on a large scale" was the "cheapest and most efficient method" and that large-scale production had to be centrally controlled. They assumed that workers would still remain a "cog in the machine" under socialism, as Cole put it, but would gladly submit to factory discipline if their material position could be made tolerably secure. The pleasures of consumption would make up for the monotony of the job.

Guild socialists had learned from William Morris that the case for socialism had to rest on the right to expect pride and pleasure from one's work. Cole had been "converted" to socialism by Morris's utopian novel, *News from Nowhere,* which justified socialism on the grounds of "morals and decency and aesthetic sensibility," as Cole put it. It was a mistake to argue for socialism on the grounds that the workers had a "right to the whole product of his work." Even syndicalists subscribed to the labor theory of value. They could make a "far more reasonable case," according to Cole, if they gave up "abstract economics," left the "theory of value to take care of itself," and embraced "concrete and commonsense ethics." Justice and expediency both suggested that "the producer should have the fullest possible share in the control of the conditions under which he works."

---

have to rest on a respect for particular cultural traditions. The socialist myth of the worker as a man without a country, a "pure class-conscious cosmopolitan," a kind of disembodied essence of exploitation, was just as abstract and "unreal," in Cole's view, as the " 'economic man' of the older economists." Indeed the class-conscious cosmopolitan was the direct descendant of economic man; here again, the socialist movement drew heavily on the liberal ideologies it claimed to reject.

Workers' control of production offered the only cure for apathy and the only solid basis for democratic citizenship. Wage labor amounted to a form of slavery, and it was on these grounds that it had to be resisted.

> It is too little realised, even by Socialists—especially by Marxians—that the whole question of the control of industry is not economic but ethical. The attempt to found "justice" on the theory of value revives the old conception of individual natural right in its least defensible form. The right of Labour to a life of comfort and self-expression is quite independent of whether it creates all wealth or not.

Socialists advocated "a fair day's wage for a fair day's work" instead of attacking the wage system itself, the real source of the worker's suffering. Slavery, not poverty, was the "fundamental evil." Socialists "fixed their eyes upon the material misery of the poor without realizing that it rests upon the spiritual degradation of the slave."

The Attempt to Reconcile Syndicalism with Collectivism

Guild socialists regarded trade unions as embryonic governments, not simply as agencies through which workers could bargain for higher wages and better working conditions. In referring to unions as "guilds," they did not intend to revive a medieval system of production, although some of them, notably A. J. Penty, had absorbed from Ruskin and Morris an abiding admiration for the Middle Ages. Cole reminded his readers that "the twentieth century is not the fourteenth," but he still believed that the term "guilds" served to call attention to a "morality in industry which we have lost and which it is important to restore." Unions had to be conceived far more broadly than they had been conceived in the past. With proper encouragement, they could become educational institutions, the modern equivalent of apprenticeship, in which workers would acquire the technical knowledge without which they could not expect to expropriate the capitalists. As some point, the unions would also take on the welfare functions of the state. They would dispense old-age pensions, sick benefits, accident insurance, and "much else," as S. G. Hobson put it. By submitting a whole range of important issues to the workers' collective judgment, they would make "better citizens"—the ultimate test of any system of government, in Hobson's opinion. They would also promote fellowship and solidarity and thus counter the atomizing effects of industrial capitalism.

According to the editor of the *New Age,* A. R. Orage, the reduction of labor to a commodity—the essence of "wagery"—required the elimination of all the social bonds that prevented the free circulation of labor. The destruction of the medieval guilds, the replacement of local government by a centralized bureaucracy, the weakening of family ties, and the emancipation of women amounted to "successive steps in the . . . cheapening of the raw material of labor," all achieved under the "watchword" of progress. Since wage labor depended on the "progressive shattering to atoms of our social system," those who opposed it would have to make the unions into agencies of social cohesion and civic trust.

Because syndicalists sought to base the new order on the unions, not on the party and the state, guild socialists welcomed them, with some misgivings, as allies in their struggle against collectivism. Syndicalism, they believed, reasserted the producers' point of view. It refused to equate socialism with a more equitable distribution of consumer goods. It recognized the irreconcilable conflict between capital and labor and rejected the possibility of compromise. It condemned parliamentary socialism on the grounds that it merely elevated the most enterprising members of the labor movement into the middle class, where they soon forgot their revolutionary principles. For all these reasons, syndicalism—"from which Guild Socialists learnt much," Cole wrote in 1920, "in the early days of their own movement"—looked like a considerable advance over orthodox socialism.

But syndicalism was open to objection in its own right. It went too far in asserting the interests of producers, overlooking the need for an agency—the state—to protect the interests of consumers. Guild socialism, according to its proponents, would combine the best features of the socialist and syndicalist programs. The guild system assumed the nationalization of industry not as a panacea but as an essential precondition of workers' control. Without nationalization, the transformation of unions into guilds would remain incomplete, since industry would still be governed by the need to show profits. On the other hand, powerful unions would nullify the danger of a "servile state." The state could safely be entrusted with coordinating powers over production and distribution as long as the guilds had a hand in major decisions. For "those who had caught the fever from France," as Cole referred to them, "direct action" and local control had become an obsession in the same way that nationalization had become an obsession for the Fabians. Localism was a "hopeless attitude"; "central control alone" could "meet the needs of modern industrial warfare" and modern industrial planning.

The uncompromising quality of syndicalism, especially in its Sorelian version, offended the British sense of practicality. English radicals did not know what to make of Sorel's "myth of the general strike." Bertrand Russell, during his brief flirtation with guild socialism, warned that if the workers "were brought to believe that the General Strike is a mere myth, their energy would flag, and their whole outlook would become disillusioned." Much as they felt the need of an antidote to the "apathy" and "stupidity" of the British labor movement, guild socialists found syndicalism too exotic for their taste. Some of its shortcomings, Cole thought, derived from the survival of small-scale production in France, which made Sorelians underestimate the need for centralized control. In general, syndicalists paid too little attention to the practical details of organization, urging the workers instead to gird themselves for the final showdown with their masters. Whether the general strike was conceived as a myth or as an actual event, it was "grotesquely unpractical and even without instinctive appeal," in Cole's opinion. "The English worker is far too stably organized, and far too conservative in nature, to take any such leap in the dark."

Sounding a little like Burke, Cole defended British stodginess against Gallic flamboyance, with heavy sarcasm. "In countries like England, painfully afflicted with the art of compromise and 'muddling through,' ideas gain more by being turned into 'business propositions' than by being artistically and dramatically expressed." At the same time, he criticized the Fabians for making socialism a "business proposition." It was a fine line he was trying to walk; instead of "reconciling" syndicalism and collectivism, he was always in danger of falling off his tightrope into the "state socialist" camp.

Syndicalism was "theory-ridden," Cole said; the guild socialists would make it practical. Hobson assured the Trades Union Congress, "We have been at pains to elaborate a constructive programme." Their efforts to bring syndicalism gently down to earth, however—as we can see with the benefit of hindsight—were more likely to end in a fatal plunge into a jungle of proposals and counterproposals, recommendations and revisions, organizational blueprints and paper constitutions, in which the clear light of moral purpose seldom shone. The more the guild socialists struggled to fill in all the details of an ideal scheme of government, the more ground they had to concede to the Fabians' demand for facts and figures, workable reforms, clearly articulated rules and regulations, demonstrable proofs that social justice would not interfere with economic efficiency.

In *Guild Socialism Restated* (1920), Cole tried to spell out procedures under which the workers in each industry would elect their managers, legal safeguards against arbitrary dismissal of managers, mechanisms that would regulate the relations among the various guilds, the coordinating powers of the Congress of Industrial Guilds, the scheme of representation that would protect consumers from exploitation by the guilds, the conditions under which small farmers and independent proprietors would be permitted to exist, and all the difficulties that would have to be considered during the intervening period of "transition" to a fully developed socialist state. No one could have accused him of expressing ideas "artistically and dramatically." If he proved nothing else, he proved that he and his fellow "guildsmen" could make socialism almost as dull as the Fabians made it.

He admitted that a "discussion of the methods of choosing leaders under a democratic industrial system may seem to be somewhat dull and detailed." He remained unshaken, however, in the belief that it was necessary "to state the case" for socialism "in a more practical way." He knew that "any picture . . . of the working of social organization" was far "from being a picture of the real life of the community," since it left out the "unorganized spirit of the people." He knew that "a theorist who sets out to plan a social system for the future cannot call up this spirit, although he knows that his work, because of its absence, runs a big risk of seeming unreal and out of touch with the deepest human needs." As a democrat, Cole could not afford to ignore those needs, as the Fabians did. As long as he accepted the constraints of British political discourse, however—the constraints of "practicality"—he had no way of addressing them very effectively. Instead of making the "deepest human needs" his starting point, he could only bring them in as an afterthought, reminding himself that "unorganized spirit" should not be lost in the rage for organization. He was too honest to conceal his uneasy awareness that such a procedure left something to be desired. "The impression conveyed by this book," he admitted, ". . . may be that of a terrible and bewildering complexity of social organization in which the individual will be lost."*

From Workers' Control to "Community": The Absorption of Guild Socialism by Social Democracy

∙ ■ ∙

His concessions to Fabian socialism went beyond matters of argumentative style. He made substantive concessions too, which nullified much of guild socialism's potential appeal. Having boldly declared, in *The World of Labour,* that when socialism ignored the producer it became a "dead theory incapable of inspiring enthusiasm or bringing about a change of heart," he immediately retreated into the cautious reminder that the producer's interests had to be balanced against the consumer's. If socialism neglected the consumer, he said, it would "fall into sectional egoism and lose the element of community and brotherhood in individualism and self-esteem."

The trouble with this characteristically judicious formulation was that workers were more likely to find "community and brotherhood" in the "sectional egoism" of class warfare than in carefully designed proposals for a new constitution in which everybody's interest would find appropriate mechanisms of representation. "Individualism and self-esteem,"

---

*"I accept my full share of the blame," Cole wrote in *The Next Ten Years* (1929), for the "excesses of Guild Socialist system-making." The movement took the "wrong turning," he said, "when it ceased to be an idea and aimed at being a system. Then the life went out of it."

virtues too long monopolized by capitalists, were just what workers needed, as Sorel pointed out, in order to overcome servile habits of thought. Workers needed to assert themselves in the immediate present, moreover, not in some distant socialist future. What made syndicalism appealing was not just its rejection of compromise but its rejection of delay. Sorel did not worry about the "transition" to a new social order. Indeed he did not think of a new social order as the object of political action. The object of political action was precisely to gain individualism and self-assertion, and the workers could achieve those things, Sorel thought, without waiting for the revolution.

The guild socialists appreciated the importance of immediate actions that would prepare workers for the management of industry. Their insistence that workers' control depended on the nationalization of industry, however, tended to weaken the "nascent demand for the control of industry . . . springing up within trade unionism," notwithstanding Cole's emphasis on the importance of an "unremitting propaganda for control." He warned the labor movement "not to put too much faith in the State and the public," but he still made nationalization the precondition, the "half-way house to producers' control." Although he understood that producers' control would never be effective as long as industry remained highly centralized, he rejected the possibility of an immediate return to handicraft production and local markets. Decentralization remained a distant prospect, with which the workers were to console themselves, it appeared, while they worked for immediate reforms that would inevitably have the opposite effect. Cole could not offer a convincing justification of his belief that decentralization would somehow follow nationalization. Nor could he explain, for that matter, how nationalization would be carried out in the first place, if the Labour party, by his own estimate, could not expect to gain a parliamentary majority. He could only hope, as he put it in *Guild Socialism Restated,* that once labor was in control of the state, "there will come, from producer and consumer alike, a widespread demand for goods of a finer quality . . . and that this will bring about a new standard of craftsmanship and a return, over a considerable sphere, to small-scale production."

Even at the peak of its influence, then, guild socialism had compromised too deeply with social democracy and the ideology of progress to provide effective opposition to the dominant tendencies in the labor movement. Guild socialists saw themselves as part of a "progressive movement"; they did not want to be left behind by history. They absorbed a good deal of Sorel but paid little attention to his attack on progress. Most of them gave up on guild socialism altogether when the course of public events, in the 1920s, drastically narrowed the boundaries of political debate.

The Bolshevik revolution made it more difficult than ever to resist the contention that "wage slavery" could be ended only by the socialist conquest of the state. Lenin and Trotsky appeared to have vindicated that position; the only question that now seemed to matter was whether socialists would come to power through revolutionary or parliamentary means. In the twenties, opposition to parliamentary socialism took the form of communism, not syndicalism. Active, aggressive communist parties in the West preempted the revolutionary militancy formerly associated with syndicalism, while those who regarded a revolutionary seizure of power as a childish delusion, as Cole did, found themselves forced into an alliance with the social democrats.

The economic depression that followed the war threw labor on the defensive. Faced with an immediate threat to their standard of living and the survival of their unions, workers lost interest in control of production. In 1913, Cole predicted that the struggle over scientific management would end either in one of the "greatest steps" toward workers' control or in "Labour's most crushing defeat." By the early twenties, however, the unions had come to terms with scientific management (as had the Bolsheviks, for different reasons), in order to concentrate all their efforts on the maintenance of wartime wage levels.

Both the emergence of communism and the deterioration of working conditions strengthened the Labour party—the only effective counterweight, it seemed, to the combined threat of reactionary employers and irresponsible revolutionaries. By the late twenties, a Labour majority in Parliament no longer appeared impossible, and Cole now devoted himself to formulating a short-range program around which the Labour party could unite.* In 1929, he told the Fabian Society that "in present circum-

---

*In *Socialist Control of Industry* (1933), he argued quite explicitly that workers' control would have to wait until a Labour government had nationalized the means of produc-

stances," socialism needed "sober prose writers" more than it needed "poets." In the same year, he published *The Next Ten Years in British Social and Economic Policy*, a flat-out defense of social democracy. He now argued, just as the Fabians always had, that industrial labor contained an irreducible element of drudgery and that workers would have to find self-expression largely in leisure and consumption. He dismissed the guild socialists' hope of reviving the joy of craftsmanship as "our particular form of cant." He repudiated the "idea of government as a moral discipline." *Guild Socialism Restated*, with its elaborate description of a new form of social organization, now struck him as a "politically minded person's utopia." He decided that there was a "great deal to be said," after all, "for 'the greatest happiness of the greatest number' as the supreme maxim for political conduct." The guild socialists, he said, had exaggerated the average man's capacity for citizenship. They had failed to reckon with the "great strength of conservatism"—its refusal to make the "mistake of supposing man to be continuously an active political animal."

Like many other liberals and social democrats, Cole found himself increasingly attracted to social psychology in the twenties and thirties. He was impressed by psychological evidence that seemed to back up his suspicion that guild socialists had taken too generous a view of human nature. People wanted leisure and security, not the arduous pleasure of doing things for themselves. Irrational fears and anxieties played a larger part in human conduct than he and his friends had imagined. In the thirties, Cole came to see fascism as the clearest evidence of "deep irrationalities in the human mind," which would be exploited by the right if the left could not satisfy the need for security. Without security, man would be "flung back merely on his unreasoning and amoral under-self, which is ruled by appetite and is capable of believing anything that will serve its appetitive ends."

Eventually Cole's preoccupation with "mass society" drove him back to a position vaguely reminiscent of guild socialism, except that he now

---

tion: "When we have got our schemes of socialization into working order, we can begin rapidly to devolve responsibility within them; but we cannot afford to risk failure and confusion by trying to be too 'democratic' at the very start."

saw the antidote to "hugeness" not in the self-governing workshop but in the much more nebulous notion of "community." Since he still accepted centralization as an unavoidable imperative of modern technology and politics, and since the Labour party had long since "abandoned the goal of workers' control," as Robert Dahl observed in 1947, he had to take refuge in the fragile hope that "small groups," if they could be given a "functional place in our society," would counter the "tendency towards bureaucratisation." "We must . . . at once accept hugeness as the environment of the coming society, and find means of not being drowned in it."

In the forties and fifties, Cole criticized the Labour party for advocating a program of "further nationalisation" for which "nobody feels any enthusiasm." The party, he said, had fallen victim to the "tendency towards centralisation and authoritarian control, which it should have been its mission to fight." Yet he endorsed the expansion of the welfare state, even though it took over services formerly provided by families, mutual-aid societies, and neighborhoods and thereby undermined the "small groups" he wanted to preserve.

Cole's rediscovery of "group life" coincided with another period of revulsion, on the British left, against the dominant socialist tradition. It was in the fifties that E. P. Thompson resurrected William Morris, while Raymond Williams found unsuspected insights in the conservative criticism of modern culture. Cole himself turned to historical studies at this time. His *History of Socialist Thought* singled out for special praise the very figures despised or dismissed both by Marxists and by Fabians: Fourier, Proudhon, Bakunin, Kropotkin, Ruskin, and Morris. Cole's work in the last phase of his career thus contributed to a vigorous new school of historical scholarship and more generally to the emergence of the new left, which would once again attempt to combine socialism with localism and "community"—with no more success, in the end, than the guild socialists had enjoyed in their own day. Repeated failures of this sort indicate that it is the basic premise of progressive thought—the assumption that economic abundance comes before everything else, which leads unavoidably to an acceptance of centralized production and administration as the only way to achieve it—that needs to be rejected. Until it is, "community" will remain an empty slogan.

8

WORK AND LOYALTY IN THE SOCIAL
THOUGHT OF THE "PROGRESSIVE" ERA

Progressive and Social Democratic
Criticism of American Syndicalism

Syndicalism and guild socialism, unlike the various "progressive movements" that eventually overshadowed them, mounted an impressive challenge to the wage system—the last such challenge, as it turned out. They rested on a shared belief that "slavery," not poverty, was the overriding issue of modern times. They differed, however, in the degree to which they were prepared to compromise with progress. In England, guild socialism was eventually absorbed by social democracy. In France, the syndicalist movement remained intransigent and unregenerate; after its collapse, around 1910, syndicalists tended to gravitate to the extreme left or to the extreme right.

For the French syndicalists, the servile mentality allegedly fostered by wage labor could be countered only by a movement that upheld discarded ideals of honor, glory, and "pessimism." Guild socialists, more heavily committed to the Enlightenment, had little enthusiasm for austerity and self-denial. They were more concerned with the practical business of showing how workers' control of industry could be reconciled with the technological advantages of large-scale production.

The contrast between the two movements was not simply a matter of national temperament. In England, the factory system was far more deeply entrenched than it was in France, where small workshops still predominated, even on the eve of the First World War. An American observer, the radical socialist William English Walling, pointed out in 1912 that France remained "economically backward in some respects." The middle class of small proprietors was still quite large, the workers constituted a minority of the population, and skilled workers still made up a large section of the "proletariat." It was the "craftsmen and artisans," Walling noted, who spoke the "revolutionary and syndicalist phrases," even though "in actual practice" they were "more conservative" than the unskilled workers. Their radicalism derived in part from their resistance to new machinery. The class composition of the syndicalist movement, Walling thought, helped to explain why the movement represented a dead end. His unsympathetic account caught something of the mixture of radicalism and moral conservatism that distinguished French opposition to "wage slavery" from its British counterpart. Notwithstanding its willingness to embrace such advanced thinkers as Bergson and James, syndicalism is best understood, it would seem, as part of a continuous tradition of popular radicalism in France that drew most of its strength from artisans' long-standing resistance to factory production.

In the United States, on the other hand, the factory system had established itself even more firmly, by the turn of the century, than it had in England. Criticism of wage labor therefore had to contend with an apparently irreversible trend. Even so, the ten years preceding World War I were a time of intense political and intellectual excitement, in the United States as in Europe. The prospects for a radical transformation of the industrial system seemed brighter, on the whole, than they have seemed in any subsequent period.

As in Europe, the rise of syndicalism touched off a bitter controversy on the left. Progressives and social democrats united in their opposition to the Industrial Workers of the World, which was founded in 1905 and achieved national prominence after its victory in the textile strike at Lawrence, Massachusetts, in 1912. John Graham Brooks, a progressive, saw the syndicalist movement as an ominous foretaste of the social convulsions that could be expected if the nation failed to provide a better standard of living for the workers and refused to allow them "some voice in management." Founded on a "convulsive and incendiary appeal to the forgotten masses," syndicalism effectively exploited their misery. It was the "child of disillusionment." Its leaders could point to the failure of political reforms as an argument for "direct action." They had no "constructive" program of their own, according to Brooks, but they would continue to win new recruits as long as American society remained indifferent to the workers' reasonable demand for a better life.

Social democrats, more immediately threatened by the IWW, took a harsher stand against violence, sabotage, and "dual unionism" (the attempt to replace craft unions with industrial unions committed to the strategy of direct action). In 1912, the Socialist party voted to expel anyone who rejected political action or advocated "crime, sabotage, or other methods of violence." Party leaders seemed to regard syndicalism as a greater menace to the working-class movement than capitalism itself. Morris Hillquit, speaking for the resolution to expel the IWW, said that neither the "capitalist class" nor the Catholic church could "check or disrupt the Socialist movement," only "injudicious friends from within."

Progressives deplored working-class violence but pointed out that it was often provoked by the violence of employers. When capitalists themselves openly defied the law, they could hardly expect workers to renounce the use of force. Brooks objected to the "moral poltroonery of forcing a standard upon the weak which the strong will not recognize or obey." Such qualifications seldom appeared in the attacks on the IWW launched by social democrats. John Spargo denounced violence as the "weapon of the slum proletariat." It grew out of a "slave morality," according to W. J. Ghent, not a "working-class morality." The "practical policies" of the IWW were "purely anarchistic and anti-socialist," Spargo declared, and a compromise between syndicalism and socialism was unthinkable. In his *Syndicalism, Industrial Unionism and Socialism* (1913), Spargo tried to show that syndicalists had merely revived the overheated fantasies of Robert Owen and Pierre-Joseph Proudhon, long since discredited by Marx. Their movement was pre-Marxist and prescientific,

utopian rather than "evolutionary." Their mindless opposition to technological progress recalled the Luddites, as did their inability to see beyond
the workers' immediate interests—their "avowed indifference to social
interests, and their avowed readiness to adopt methods to secure the immediate gain of the proletariat which are, from the point of view of society, retrogressive."

Revolutionary Socialism versus Syndicalism: The Case of William English Walling

· ■ ·

Revolutionary socialists found the syndicalist movement even more
threatening to their own position than social democrats did. They had to
find a way to distinguish themselves from the syndicalists on their left
while also distinguishing themselves from the contemptibly mild-man-
nered reformers and social democrats on their right. William English
Walling attempted this feat in two books written at the height of the
uproar over syndicalism, *Socialism as It Is* (1912) and *Progressivism—and
After* (1914). Walling attributed the "ultra-utopian" and "anarchistic" elements in syndicalism to its class origins. The movement reflected the
sensibility of a "decaying class which has no future," namely the artisans
and craftsmen, squeezed out by centralized factory production. "Decaying trades and crafts" hoped to establish socialism by insurrection and
general strike," Walling said, whereas "state capitalists" and "state socialists," equally misguided, hoped to establish it by the "beneficent rule of
. . . the intellectuals."

Walling commended syndicalists for seeing the need for industrial unionism but deplored their indifference to political action. Workers alone
could not achieve socialism. They needed leadership from a socialist party
committed to capturing the state. But the Socialist party would have to
become more militant if it expected to succeed. It could not afford to
forgo the use of violence, either in daily struggles in the workplace or in
the final showdown with the capitalist state. The party had made a mistake in expelling the IWW, especially since a number of syndicalists had
now modified their formerly unconditional opposition to political action.

At first sight, Walling's revolutionary socialism seemed to have more in common with syndicalism than with social democracy. The appearance was deceptive, however. Like many Americans, Walling equated syndicalism with industrial unionism. In fact, hard-line syndicalists opposed the IWW's attempt to force all workers into industrial unions. William Z. Foster, at that time head of the Syndicalist League of North America (later a leading communist theoretician and organizer), pointed out that the IWW was not really a syndicalist organization at all. It aimed to organize all workers into "one big union," whereas syndicalists favored decentralization and local autonomy. IWW president Bill Haywood and his friends proposed to entrust leadership of the labor movement to a "beneficent, omnipotent executive board," which they themselves would presumably dominate. They aimed to replace existing craft unions with industrial unions, even though successful attempts to "propagate revolutionary ideas in the old unions," in Britain and France, showed that craft unions had "marked capacities for evolution." The "ridiculous theory" that "nothing can be accomplished in the old unions" had merely left them in the "undisputed control of conservatives." "Syndicalists by no means put as strong emphasis upon the industrial form of labor union as the industrial unionists do," Foster wrote. They saw that centralization was the issue, not any particular form of organization, and that highly centralized industrial unions were actually "inferior to a number of craft unions covering the same categories of workers."

In supporting the IWW's industrial unionism, revolutionary socialists like Walling thus supported a program that was repudiated by proper syndicalists. Except for its opposition to political action (by no means unqualified in any case, as Walling noted), Haywood's program was indistinguishable from left-wing socialism. Ostensibly the IWW condemned "wage slavery," but in fact, like all Marxian socialists, its leaders merely asserted the worker's right to the "full product of his labor."* "All wealth is produced by labor," Haywood declared. This formula, with its corol-

---

*As G. D. H. Cole pointed out, the implications of this slogan were not very radical (see above, p. 319). Like Foster, Cole noted that although the IWW talked about the "abolition of the wage system," it was far more interested in organizing unskilled workers.

lary that "wealth belongs to the producer thereof," made social justice a matter of distribution. Neither Haywood nor Walling grasped the point made by G. D. H. Cole when he said that slavery, not poverty, was the real issue. "Wage slavery," in their view, was a function of the private ownership of the means of production, which deprived the worker of "his share in the income of society," as Walling put it. Once capitalism was abolished, "wage slavery" would come to an end, even though wage labor, of course, would continue. There was "no authority" in Marx, Walling correctly observed, for the belief that "it would be necessary to abolish wages" in a socialist society. "It is 'wage slavery' or 'the wage system' that is to be abolished"—that is, the system of private ownership that prevented the worker from getting the "total product" of his labor. The capitalist's appropriation of the worker's "share," Walling argued, was the "very essence of social injustice." "The question . . . is not whether from time to time something more falls to the workingman, but what proportion he gets of the total product."

Walling counted on this expansive conception of distributive justice to distinguish revolutionary socialism from progressivism and social democracy. Unlike revolutionaries, reformers aimed, he said, only to "increase the nation's wealth" and thereby "to increase everybody's income to some degree" without achieving a "fairer *distribution* of this increased national wealth and income" (his italics). Unfortunately for this argument, progressives and social democrats also favored a redistribution of wealth. Arthur Brisbane, chief editor of the Hearst newspaper chain, argued, in Walling's own words, that the worker had a right to the "full product of his labor"—a phrase, as Walling pointed out, that "might have been used by Marx himself." John Graham Brooks, noting that the gap between "large incomes and small ones" had grown steadily, declared, "The wage earner's contention that he should have a relatively larger share is justified." Mary Simkhovitch, a well-known leader in the settlement movement, also endorsed the worker's demand for higher wages and more leisure. Like many settlement workers, she criticized reform "from above" just as vigorously as Walling did, and for the same reason: it did not attack the problem of inequality. Paternalistic reforms made the "upper classes feel like benefactors," she wrote, but they did nothing "to redistribute wealth through improved methods of taxation."

What then became of the distinction between reform and revolution, which Walling was at such pains to establish? The "essential or practical difference," Walling thought, was that reformers expected "to work, on the whole, with the capitalists who are to be done away with, while socialists expect to work against them." Piecemeal reforms would never assure the worker of the "total product" of his labor. Maybe not; but it was unclear why the worker would still be "shut off" from "all the possibilities of modern civilization," as Walling claimed, just because his share fell short of the "total product." Nor was it clear exactly what "possibilities" Walling had in mind, except that they did not include the possibility of a return to the kind of small-scale, locally controlled production under which the workers became directly responsible for their work. If the "possibilities of modern civilization" referred simply to a more equitable distribution of wealth, it was hard to explain why the workers could not achieve this goal without a revolution.

Syndicalists and guild socialists, as we have seen, believed that small-scale proprietorship conferred moral independence, self-respect, and responsibility. They did not seek to restore proprietorship as such, but they never lost sight of the virtues associated with it. They envisioned a society of small workshops, in which effective control over production remained at the local level. For those committed to the dogma of progress, the syndicalist sociology of virtue was deplorably regressive and "utopian," and it found most of its adherents, as they never tired of pointing out, in "backward" countries like France and Italy. They could not deny, however, that its adherents displayed an intensity of revolutionary conviction unmatched by any other social movement. Herein lay the scandal of syndicalism: it was retrograde but obviously revolutionary and therefore difficult for people on the left to dismiss. Its existence was particularly embarrassing to revolutionary socialists, because its radicalism made Marxism look tame by comparison and served to reveal the many points of agreement between Marxism and the "new liberalism." Syndicalism (like populism) fell outside the broad consensus in favor of progress, centralization, and distributive democracy. It undercut the Marxist claim to offer a radical alternative to the capitalist regimentation of the workplace. It forced Marxists to justify their program on the grounds of superior efficiency, on the increasingly implausible grounds that only a socialist state could assure prosperity for all, or on vague appeals to the progress of the human race.

The difficulty of distinguishing revolutionary socialism from progressivism or the "new liberalism" was illustrated by an anonymous letter from a "socialist social worker" to the editors of *Survey,* quoted by Walling as an incisive contribution to the debate. The "difference between the near socialist and the true socialist," according to this writer, lay in the latter's concern with the "positive side" of the "social problem." Instead of confining his attention to the "condition of the submerged classes," the true socialist kept in mind the "wonderful development, power and life that would come [about] ... if a wise and social use were to be made of the surplus of industry." The disposition of the "social surplus" furnished the best "criterion of social justice in every civilized community." In the past, the surplus had gone into "pyramids," "wars," and a "sensuous life for ... a privileged class." The writer did not bother to explain the advantages of a more equitable distribution of the surplus. Monuments for the masses? A "sensuous life" for all? Nor did he clarify his uninformative observation that "the main indictment of capitalism is that it selfishly and stupidly blocks the road of orderly and continuous progress for the race." The advantages of socialism, specifically of revolutionary socialism as opposed to "near socialism," remained nebulous and unspecified. Distributive democracy evidently needed no justification. Neither Marxists nor liberal democrats attempted to answer the objection that the most efficient instrument of democratizing the social surplus might turn out to be the "servile state."

The IWW and the Intellectuals: Love at First Sight

The social conditions that generated the syndicalist explosion in Europe—the imposition of industrialism on economies still dominated by small workshops, a highly combustible mixture—had their nearest American equivalent in the West, where the traditions of the mining camp, the logging camp, and the bunkhouse came face to face with corporate capitalism in its most ruthless, predatory form. The IWW was the direct descendant of the Western Federation of Miners, a union that appealed to the same sense of manly independence and the same love of combat to which syndicalism appealed in France and Italy. Here too, workers experienced industrialism and the wage system not only as a decline in their standard of living but above all as a drastic infringement of their control of the workplace, of their very status as free men. The company towns that sprang up in the mining states seemed to make "wage slavery" a literal description of the new order, not just a rhetorical analogy. The company controlled not only the workplace but housing, credit, and all the other necessaries. The worker who could remember life as a prospector or cowboy now found that he owed his soul to the company store. He felt literally sold into slavery, and he embraced the philosophy of "direct action" as the only way out.

While social conditions in the West bore some resemblance to those created by the early stages of industrialism elsewhere, the cultural traditions that workers were trying to defend obviously differed from those that underlay European syndicalism. In the American West, the ideal of independence was associated not with the small proprietor's control over his household, his land or shop, and his tools but with the wandering life of the unattached male. It was not surprising that the IWW glorified the hobo, the drifter, the "nomadic worker of the West," in the words of its newspaper, *Solidarity*. The West was still a "man's country," according to Charles Ashleigh, an English radical who emigrated to the Pacific Northwest and became a "hobo and a Wobbly," like the hero of his novel, *Rambling Kid*. Ashleigh admired the "reckless rambling boys who despised the soft security and comfort of a dull city-paced existence." Ralph Chaplin, the Wobbly poet and songwriter, was attracted to the movement by its "glamorous courage and adventure," which he too associated with the West. Those who admired the Wobblies from a distance likewise emphasized its western origins. The Lawrence strike was a "western strike in the East," Lincoln Steffens wrote; "a strike conducted in New England by western miners, who have brought here the methods and the spirit employed by them in Colorado, Idaho, and Nevada."

European syndicalism was informed by an austere ethic of thrift and self-denial. In America, the syndicalist movement came to be associated with an ethic of self-expression and defiant irresponsibility—the new "paganism" of Greenwich Village. Literary intellectuals saw the Wobblies as cultural outcasts like themselves, free spirits, rebels against respectability. They sensed the affinity between their own ideal of the emancipated individual, unburdened by the cultural baggage of the past, and the hoboes and migratory workers glorified by the IWW. Having absorbed from modern literature an image of the "beauty of the essentially homeless and childless and migratory life," as Floyd Dell put it, they recognized the Wobblies as soul mates. "Anarchism and art," said Margaret Anderson, editor of the *Little Review,* "are in the world for exactly the same kind of reason." Hutchins Hapgood, the personification of the bohemian intellectual, called anarchism the fine art of the proletariat. He compared the Armory Show, which brought modern art to New York in 1913, to a "great fire, an earthquake, or a political revolution."

The Wobblies did not object to this assimilation of art and revolution. They too saw themselves as artists. "I have lived like an artist, and I shall die like an artist," said Joe Hill before his execution for murder. Bill Haywood allowed himself to be lionized by Mabel Dodge and other members of her famous salon. He regarded the Paterson Strike Pageant of 1913—the fruit of this *rapprochement* between the IWW and Greenwich Village—as the high point of his career. Conceived by Mabel Dodge, the pageant was intended to dramatize the workers' exploitation by capitalism, but it exposed them to a more insidious kind of exploitation by turning radical politics into entertainment. "Life passed over insensibly into a certain, simple form of art," said Hapgood. ". . . That is the great thing about it, the almost unprecedented thing." Papers opposed to the IWW gave the pageant enthusiastic reviews: what was condemned as politics could be savored as theater. Both Haywood and Elizabeth Gurley Flynn, the IWW's most flamboyant orator, had earlier turned down invitations to put themselves on the lecture circuit or stage. In her case, the offer came from no less an impresario than David Belasco, who could see the theatrical possibilities of revolutionary activism as clearly as John Reed. At the pageant, Reed led the Paterson strikers in a song he had written for the occasion, "The Haywood Thrill." Haywood thus resisted the lecture agents only to fall into the clutches of the avant-garde, leaving Flynn to wonder whether the distractions of the pageant had not contributed to the defeat of the strike itself.

"I object to responsibility," declared Marcel Duchamp, whose *Nude Descending a Staircase* was the sensation of the Armory Show. These words summed up the cultural program that linked American anarchists with avant-garde intellectuals in a common assault on bourgeois morality. The Wobbly's "cheerful cynicism," as described by *Solidarity*—"his frank and outspoken contempt for most of the conventions of bourgeois society"—made him the natural ally of disaffected intellectuals like Reed. In his editorial announcement for *The Masses,* launched in 1912 as the organ of artistic and political emancipation, Reed urged contributors "to be arrogant, impertinent, in bad taste," and "to everlastingly attack old systems, old morals, old prejudices—the whole weight of outworn thought that dead men have settled on us." In Europe, the syndicalist movement, at least as interpreted by Sorel, combined political radicalism with cultural conservatism. In America, on the other hand, it joined forces with the enemies of the past.

Emma Goldman's *Mother Earth,* no less enthusiastically than *The Masses,* sided with every movement that "boldly tears the veil off . . . forbidden subjects." Goldman endorsed syndicalism as the "economic expression of anarchism," but she also endorsed birth control, sex education, "free love," nudism, feminism, atheism, and modern art. She advocated the abolition of prisons, the abolition of the family, the abolition of national boundaries and national loyalties, the abolition of religion, the abolition of government, and the abolition of anything else that might interfere with personal freedom. Proudly declaring herself a "libertarian," she dismissed as "absurd" the "claim that ours is the era of individualism." It was the era of conformity and the "herd mind," she insisted. The only thing she had in common with Sorel, aside from her belief in the need for a "complete overthrow of the wage system"—itself a highly ambiguous slogan, as we have seen—was a hatred of democracy. But whereas Sorel objected to democracy because it left no room for heroic "pessimism," Goldman saw it as a drag on progress—on the individual's emancipation from tradition, from a misplaced sense of responsibility, and from social conventions that inhibited freedom of expression. Progress was always the work of enlightened minorities; under democracy, these were doomed to be "misunderstood, hounded, imprisoned, tortured, and killed."

Even Foster, whose syndicalism—while it lasted—was closer to the European type, subscribed to all the standard positions that now defined a commitment to cultural progress. "The syndicalist," he wrote, "is a 'race suicider.' He knows that children are a detriment to him in his daily struggles, and that by rearing them he is . . . furnishing a new supply of slaves to capitalism." This was hardly the argument for family planning preferred by Goldman, who was offended by the "indiscriminate breeding of children by unfit parents." Goldman stressed the "right of every child to be well born," whereas Foster saw families merely as *impedimenta* that weighed down the army of revolutionary workers and inhibited its freedom to maneuver. His perfunctory support of the cultural revolution lacked Goldman's zeal. "The syndicalist accepts on principle the anarchist positions on the modern school, neo-Malthusianism, marriage, individualism, religion, art, the drama, etc., that go to make up the intellectual revolution"; but he cared about these issues, Foster added, "only in so far as they contribute to the success of his bread and butter fighting organization." Neither as a syndicalist nor later as a communist did Foster show much interest in the cultural program of the left. He simply went along with enlightened opinion, not caring enough about these issues to challenge the prevailing consensus.

Herbert Croly on *"Industrial Self-Government"*

· ■ ·

If the syndicalist movement in England was absorbed by social democracy, in America it was absorbed by the intellectuals' revolt against "middle-class morality." For a time, however, it posed a radical alternative to the welfare state and to a purely distributive conception of democracy. Even people who thought of themselves as part of the "progressive movement" in politics were attracted to it, as well as to guild socialism, to Hilaire Belloc's critique of the "servile state," and to the political "pluralism" advocated by J. N. Figgis and Harold Laski (before he too became a collectivist). Mary Parker Follett, a communitarian progressive who drew on Figgis, Laski, and Cole, recommended guild socialism, in *The New State* (1918), as a happy blend of "state socialism" and syndicalism. Syndicalism had "gained many adherents," she wrote, because "people do not want the servile state and, therefore, may think they do not want any state" at all. Guild socialists, on the other hand, favored "state ownership of the means of production" as long as "control of each industry or 'guild' " was "vested in the membership of the industry." A strong central government was both necessary and desirable, Follett argued—but only if it was balanced by strong households, strong neighborhoods, and strong workingmen's "guilds."

Herbert Croly, whose *Promise of American Life* (1910) provided the ideological underpinning for Theodore Roosevelt's "New Nationalism," took a position similar to Follett's in his *Progressive Democracy*, a more radical book than the book for which he is better known. As we have seen, Croly conceded the force of conservative objections to a welfare state but took issue with the conservatives' conclusion that "the wage-earner can secure independence only by becoming a property-owner." Responsibility, not property ownership as such, was the real issue.* The "most important single task of modern democratic social organization" was to transfer responsibility for production to the workers. Only in this way could "wage-earners . . . become free men." Croly rejected the syndicalists' "abhorrent" methods but commended them for having introduced a "necessary ferment" into the labor movement. He too believed that workers should have the "opportunity and responsibility of operating the business mechanism of modern life." Although he deplored violence, he agreed with the syndicalists that workers could be trained for "self-government" only in the school of class "warfare." Their "independence . . . would not amount to much," he thought, if it was "handed down to them by the state or by employers' associations."

Like Cole, Croly believed that Frederick Winslow Taylor's scientific management might precipitate a struggle for workers' control of production. The unions could not be expected to welcome appeals for greater efficiency as long as the "elimination of waste" served merely to speed up

---

*In all likelihood, Croly took this idea directly from Cole's *World of Labour*. Cole wrote, "Not the sense of ownership, but the sense of responsibility, is the secret of the success of the small agriculturist. . . . The sense of being owned is deadening; the sense of possession means, not so much that a man desires to have the title-deeds of his estate, as that he desires to work for himself and the community and not for a private master. . . . The new spirit cannot come unless every worker can be made to feel . . . responsible for the work he has to do."

production and to replace skilled workers with machines. No doubt the American worker needed to acquire the "fearless, critical, candid and disinterested scientific spirit." Since a properly organized society would demand a "huge increase in both production and consumption," industrial workers would have to accept "regimentation not dissimilar to that required by an army." But this discipline would become intolerable unless workers imposed it on themselves. Imposed from above, it would lead either to fatalistic resignation or to mutiny. If industrial production had to be organized on a military model, the choice, for Croly, presented itself as a choice between a citizen army and a standing army of mercenaries.

Croly prefaced this analysis of "industrial self-government" with a complementary analysis of "direct democracy" in the political realm. Here too, he tried to show that "direct government is not retrogressive." The political devices favored by so many progressives—the initiative, referendum, and recall—should not be thought of, he argued, "just as a way of improving representative democracy." The development of modern communications had called into question the old assumption that republican government had to give way to representative government "outside of city or tribal states." Civic participation was now possible on a wider scale, if only Americans could agree to subordinate administrative efficiency to the moral and political education of the citizens themselves. Americans attached too much importance to "specific results, and too little to the permanent moral welfare" of the community as a whole. They did not seem to understand that efficiency imposed from above, in politics as in industry, would result in "popular servility or organized popular resistance."

Walter Weyl's Orthodox Progressivism: The Democracy of Consumers

· ■ ·

The radicalism of Croly's position emerges quite clearly in contrast to Walter Weyl's *New Democracy* (1912), usually considered a more militant statement of the progressive creed. Since Weyl and Croly collaborated as coeditors of the *New Republic*, they obviously did not regard their positions as unalterably opposed. The differences between them are striking, however, even though they probably emerge more clearly in retrospect than they did at the time. We can see now that it was absolutely essential for Americans at this time to grasp the debilitating effects of centralized control, both in the workplace and in politics, to reformulate a participatory conception of democracy, and to encourage a revival of active citizenship. We can also see how few of them managed to confront these issues in any sustained way, in spite of all the talk about "civic spirit" in which prewar progressives liked to indulge. Croly was one of the few who did confront them, and the *New Republic*, under his direction, devoted a good deal of attention to syndicalism, guild socialism, and workers' control.

Weyl, however, took the view that distribution, not participation, was the overriding issue. If the country was in a "somber, soul-questioning mood," it was because "plutocracy" could no longer assure equal access to the goods turned out with such marvelous efficiency by modern industry. Weyl took his cue from Simon Patten's "brilliant" analysis of the "transition from a pain economy to a pleasure economy." Henceforth the "hope of a full democracy" would have to rest on abundance, which generated a growing demand for a "full life for all members of society." The old competitive individualism of the frontier, the ethic of scarcity and "conquest," had outlived its usefulness. The age of abundance and large-scale organization required an ethic of cooperation. Even businessmen now condemned cutthroat competition. The trusts had brought order out of commercial chaos; public regulation of industry was the next step.

When guild socialists conceded an important role to the state as the representative of the consumer, they took the precaution of pointing out that consumers were only one group among many and by no means the most important. But Weyl regarded consumers as the only group that embodied the interests of society as a whole. They alone bore the cost of rising prices, adulterated goods, shortages, strikes and shutdowns.* Since

---

*Progressivism was a consumers' movement, according to Weyl. "The consumer . . . appears in the political arena as the 'common man,' the 'plain people,' the 'straphanger,' 'the man on the street.' " It was these people the progressives invoked when-

the state spoke for consumers, and consumers in turn spoke for society as a whole, Weyl had no qualms about a "servile state." He saw it as the institutional expression of the new cooperative spirit. In the clash between the "old poverty ethics of survival and the new wealth ethics of social improvement," the state stood on the side of progress. Its monopoly of physical force put an end to private violence and to the need for violent revolution. The expansion of its protective powers guaranteed the "rights of children" and replaced the "parental tyranny of former days" with "enforced parental responsibility." Its power of taxation socialized consumption, as Weyl put it, by discouraging "fashion, conspicuous waste, [and] absurd extravagance"—for example, by laying heavy duties on tobacco and alcohol. Its powers over education could be used by civic-minded reformers to create a "differentiated, modernized" educational system that would discourage "mere competitive egoisms" and "guide society and individuals in the wise consumption of wealth."

More efficient production, a more equitable distribution of its fruits, and a more discriminating use of leisure summed up Weyl's view of the tasks confronting democracy. Americans had been too busy with the conquest of the continent, Weyl thought, to master the intelligent use of leisure. He reminded those who were "obsessed by the doctrine of the strenuous life" that a more equitable distribution of wealth was more important than feats of moral heroism. Democracy had "put down the mighty 'great man,' who once obsessed history," and exalted the "unnamed multitude." The Carlyles might sneer, but "until the material problems which beset mankind are solved, . . . humanity will not be able to essay the problems of mind."

---

ever they wanted to justify a new regulation or stricter enforcement of the existing ones.

Rival Perspectives on the Democratization of Culture

· ■ ·

Herbert Croly and Mary Parker Follett could have assented to much of this. The evils of competition; the need for a new ethic of cooperation; the priority of material improvement as the necessary precondition of attempts to address "problems of mind"—these were staple themes of progressive thought. There was a considerable difference, however—even if its implications were never explored very systematically—between Weyl's enthusiasm for the state and the much more cautious attitude toward central power expressed by Follett and Croly; between Weyl's emphasis on consumption and Croly's emphasis on production; and between Weyl's equation of democracy with an equitable distribution of goods and Croly's concern for participatory citizenship.

> A democratic nation [Croly said] cannot provide the mass of the people with the needed opportunity of activity and life merely by distributing among them the wealth owned by the minority. Any such distribution would scatter among the poor the germs not of social activity, but of social lethargy. The masses need, of course, a larger share of material welfare, but they need most of all an increased opportunity of wholesome and stimulating social labor. Their work must be made interesting to them not merely because of its compensation, but because its performance calls for the development of more eager and more responsible human beings.

The distinction between a distributive view of democracy and a participatory view, though seldom stated so forcefully, was implicit in the wide-ranging debates about the democratization of culture that took place during the progressive era. Many people believed that democracy was simply incompatible with excellence and that the popularization of culture could lead only to its debasement. Those who rejected this view were left with two alternatives. The first envisioned the democratization of leisure and consumption; the second, the democratization of work. If culture was a function of affluence and leisure, then universal abundance, together with an ambitious program of popular education designed to instill appreciation of the classics, held out the best hope of cultural democracy. Once the masses enjoyed leisure, affluence, and education, they would become discriminating consumers of art, letters, and ideas. Museums, concert halls, circulating libraries, and the new technologies of cultural reproduction—phonograph records, cheap editions of books, photographic copies of famous paintings—would give ordinary people access to the "best that had been thought and done in the world." Matthew Arnold's familiar phrase summed up this particular conception of culture, which many progressives (unlike Arnold, who thought the "best" could be appreciated only by the few) now proposed to universalize in the expectation that this would not require any appreciable alteration of its content.

The second position, advanced by Thorstein Veblen, Frank Lloyd Wright, John Dewey, Randolph Bourne, Lewis Mumford, Van Wyck Brooks, and Waldo Frank, among others, rested on a very different idea of both culture and democracy. These writers distrusted the missionary impulse they detected in the progressives' program of cultural uplift. Instead of popularizing leisure-class values, they advocated a new set of values based on the dignity of labor. Their program derived from William Morris rather than from Arnold. They did not necessarily share Morris's enthusiasm for handicraft production, but they followed him in making a revival of craftsmanship the prerequisite of a democratic culture. In his influential essay "The Art and Craft of the Machine" (1901), Wright tried to show that craftsmanship could be reconciled with machine production. Veblen argued that exposure to machinery fostered an "iconoclastic" state of mind among workers. It taught them to think for themselves, to understand cause and effect, and to question received opinions and established cultural authorities. Modern industry made every man his own scientist, according to Veblen, and gave free play to the "instinct of workmanship."

Dewey thought of his educational reforms—the clearest expression of this prewar speculation about the democratization of culture—as another method of bringing about a rehabilitation of labor. Like Veblen, Dewey deplored the "cultured" contempt for honest labor—a legacy, as he saw it, from the aristocratic past. By emphasizing the connection between the school and the workplace, Dewey hoped to overcome the split between thought and practice and to provide a setting in which the "interest of each in his work is uncoerced and intelligent." He had no use for the notion of culture as a body of unchanging, unchallenged truths to be transmitted intact to each successive generation. Conventional pedagogy, he thought, fostered intellectual passivity, an exaggerated respect for authority, and a prejudice against practical activity. Literary culture could not be separated from daily life without impoverishing both. The divorce between thinking and doing reproduced itself in the social division of labor, which assigned these activities to different social classes, a thinking class and a class of manual workers trained merely to carry out instructions. The school, as Dewey conceived it, served as a model workshop in which the technologies underlying modern production became intelligible through practical application and experimentation. His classroom was the antithesis of Taylorism: instead of discouraging curiosity and initiative, it aimed to foster an awareness of the productive process as a whole, and of social processes as well, by showing how each operation contributed to the final result.

Randolph Bourne, who thought of himself as a disciple of Dewey and William James (until Dewey's support of World War I caused him to have second thoughts), described the practical application of Dewey's educational ideas in the public schools of Gary, Indiana. He was struck by the absence of vandalism, by the students' pride in the appearance of the halls and classrooms. The need for nagging discipline vanished once young people came to see the school not as the embodiment of an alien authority but as an institution for which they themselves shared the responsibility. If the same feeling of proprietorship could be extended to the factory, hierarchical work discipline might yield to voluntary cooperation. Labor might become an end in itself, something that satisfied the individual's need to regard himself as part of a common enterprise. Bourne endorsed James's proposal for a "moral equivalent of universal military service," a national youth service that would restore the joy of labor and promote a sense of common responsibility for the upkeep of public buildings, parks, and playgrounds.

In the articles on education, town planning, and civic culture he contributed to the *New Republic* in 1915 and 1916, Bourne explained his objections to Matthew Arnold's kind of culture, which led to an "emphasis on acquisition"—on the collection and appreciation of masterpieces. Arnold's ideas discouraged "spontaneous taste" and had the "unpleasantly undemocratic" effect of separating "highbrows" from "lowbrows." In America, they perpetuated a slavish dependence on European models. The United States needed arts of its own, civic arts that would surround everyday life with order, beauty, and dignity. Bourne was oppressed by the "dishevelled and barbaric streets" of American towns and by the shabbiness of their "civic clothing." Instead of constructing a pleasant and convivial environment to live in, Americans ransacked Europe for its cultural treasures and enshrined them in museums carefully secluded from ordinary working life.

Lewis Mumford too saw the museum as a symbol of the divorce between art and life. In 1918, he drew on Ruskin, Morris, and Patrick Geddes, the leading advocate of city planning, to support his attack on the leisure-class culture institutionalized in the museum. He too wanted to put art at the disposal of the whole community and to restore "to the artist the opportunity for public service which disappeared with the decline of the Middle Ages." Many years later, Mumford said that this essay, with its plea for the reintegration of art and work, "struck the essential chord of the rest of my intellectual life."

Van Wyck Brooks and the Search for a "Genial Middle Ground"

The most vigorous, witty, and irreverent assault on the ornamental conception of culture came from Van Wyck Brooks, whose bold little book *America's Coming-of-Age* achieved the status of a manifesto for the prewar generation of literary intellectuals. According to Brooks, Americans had always made too sharp a division between business and what they thought of as culture—between "high ideals and catchpenny realities." "Desiccated culture at one end and stark utility at the other have created a deadlock in the American mind, and all our life drifts chaotically between the two extremes." The work of pioneering had absorbed most of the national energy. Business became the great American adventure, and culture, like other luxury goods, had to be imported from Europe. The excessive individualism of the frontier "prevented the formation of a collective spiritual life" and "despoiled us of that instinctive human reverence for those divine reservoirs of collective experience, religion, science, art, philosophy, the self-subordinating service of which is almost the measure of human happiness."

The social division of labor between the "machinery of self-preservation and the mystery of life" coincided with a sexual division of labor that made women the principal custodians of art and religion. "We have in America two publics, the cultivated public and the business public, the public of theory and the public of activity, the public that reads Maeterlinck and the public that accumulates money: the one largely feminine, the other largely masculine." Having made women the arbiters of polite taste, even serious writers like Mark Twain and William Dean Howells submitted to female censorship. Literature became genteel; it confined itself, in Howells's notorious phrase, to the "smiling aspects of American life." The spirit of Tom Sawyer's Aunt Polly presided over American letters.

Laying about him with gusto, Brooks ridiculed the literary worthies—Longfellow, Lowell, Whittier—venerated by those who confused culture with high-minded sentiments unconnected with everyday experience. Even Hawthorne and Poe, who might have flourished in a more congenial atmosphere, retreated into their "diaphanous private worlds," according to Brooks. Emerson too was stunted by his surroundings. A "ventriloquist," an "attenuated voice coming from a great distance," Emerson was "abstract at the wrong times and concrete at the wrong times." He "presided over and gave its tone" to a "world of infinite social fragmentation and unlimited free will." His style, overpraised by undiscriminating admirers, illustrated the difference between "literary English in England," a "living speech" that occupied the "middle of the field" and expressed the "flesh and blood of an evolving race," and literary English in America, which merely reflected the "prestige and precedent and the will and habit of a dominating class."

Of all the nineteenth-century American writers, Whitman alone escaped Brooks's censure. In spite of Whitman's uneasiness "on the plane of ideas" and his inclination to affirm everything indiscriminately, he taught American intellectuals to seek their inspiration in the common life around them, instead of looking to Europe for literary models. The first writer to break decisively with genteel conventions, Whitman became the "precipitant" of a new American culture. His example made it possible for Americans to begin to re-create some of the "happy excitement of European thought" simply by overcoming their obsession with its superiority.

This analysis of the derivative and "colonial" character of American literature no doubt had salutary effects, but the concerns behind it distorted Brooks's view of cultural history. His preoccupation with the "genteel tradition," as George Santayana called it, made it impossible for him to see any value in the tradition of radical Protestantism exemplified by Edwards, Emerson, and William James or to recognize the kinship between his predecessors' concerns and some of his own. They were just as impatient as he was with a metaphysical approach to moral questions that made no contact with practical experience. Yet Brooks could see "puritanism," one of his favorite targets, only as another expression of the genteel tradition, pragmatism as its equally unsatisfactory antithesis—a crude celebration of practical results. The two movements, as Brooks saw them, typified the extremes between which Americans continued to drift. As early as the eighteenth century, they found their respective spokesmen in Edwards—"intellect unchecked"—and Benjamin Franklin, the practical man par excellence. Between them, Edwards and Franklin summed up the "experience of New England," an "experience of two extremes—bare facts and metaphysics." What was missing, Brooks insisted, was "experience of the world, of society, of art, the genial middle ground of human tradition."

Brooks took too much of his indictment of American culture from Santayana and too little from James, with whom he also studied at Harvard. His attempt to find a "genial middle ground" between the "highbrow" and "lowbrow"—Santayana's categories again—led him to ignore James's more incisive analysis of cultural "desiccation." James too wanted to "bring the ideal *into things*"—more specifically, to "restore to philosophy the temper of science and practical life." He too condemned a "Sunday Christianity" that had no effect on everyday conduct. In view of his well-known opposition to the "bitch-goddess, success," it is safe to say that he would have endorsed Brooks's statement that the American writer's failure "to move the soul of America from the accumulation of dollars" provided "some sort of basis for literary criticism." The "use of most of our thinking," James maintained, was "to help us to change the world." The way to do this, however, was to recognize that ideas matter only when they evoke passionate conviction, not when they serve merely to make people reasonable, tolerant, and "genial." James admired the martial virtues and harbored deep misgivings about the "strange moral transformation" that had brought them into discredit. He saw nothing wrong with the love of adventure; the trouble, he thought, was that it often failed to find suitable forms of expression. Neither the obsessive self-mortification of sainthood nor the self-transcendence of warfare provided adequate outlets for "spiritual vitality."

Brooks and Santayana, however, regarded the "militant existence" glorified by James with a mixture of horror and amused condescension. They associated it with intolerance, fanaticism, individualism run riot. The puritan and the pioneer were twins, according to Brooks, in spite of their mutual dislike: prickly, quarrelsome, impatient with opposition. Neither had any talent for ordinary social intercourse. The spiritual life of the pioneer, insofar as he had one, was "spectral and aloof," "impersonal and antisocial." Whether American thought defined itself in "metaphysical" opposition to ordinary life (puritanism) or glorified ordinary life in its crudest form (pragmatism), it suffered from the "want of a social background."

Thanks to Brooks, the alleged affinity between puritanism and pioneering became a staple of cultural criticism. In an essay published in 1917, "The Puritan's Will to Power," Randolph Bourne argued that an obsession with "being good" bore a close resemblance to an obsession with "making good." Seemingly self-abnegating, the puritan found a "positive sense of power" in the "raw material" of "renunciation." "In the compelling of others to abstain, you have the final glut of puritanical power." Waldo Frank elaborated this critique of puritanism and pioneering in *Our America* (1919), assimilating these categories more closely than ever to the aesthetic categories of "highbrow" and "lowbrow." The "frugal and self-denying life" idealized by puritanism, according to Frank, diverted energies that might have gone into art into pioneering. The desire for beauty did not die out altogether, but it fled from "reality" into the thin upper air of transcendentalism. Culture became a "philosophic decoration." Hence the appeal of Emerson, who "supplied the dualism which our material obsession needed to survive." The "sage of Concord ruled supreme in thoughtful circles," to the neglect of Whitman and Thoreau, because his "vague," "remote" idealism justified the "hypocrisy of the American who goes to church on Sunday and bleeds his brother Monday, who leads a sexually vicious life and insists on 'pure' books." As for pragmatism, it represented a "sublimated" form of pioneering. Frank echoed the charges Bourne angrily brought against Dewey, when Dewey's support of the war led Bourne to argue that pragmatism had degenerated into a cult of technique. Pragmatism had contributed to America's "liberation from the genteel," Frank thought, but the pressure of war had revealed its inadequacy for the task of "creating values of our own." The pragmatic philosophy now stood unmistakably revealed as a "mere extension of the pioneering mood."

Mumford repeated this argument in *The Golden Day* (1926), broadened to include James as well as Dewey. Having ignored his own "innermost wishes" and missed his calling as an artist, James became the philosopher of "acquiescence." Pragmatism gave philosophical sanction to the "newspaper platitudes" of the Gilded Age—the "supremacy of cash-values and practical results," the "gospel of smile." Its "compromises and evasions" betrayed the desire for a "comfortable resting place." Compared with Emerson, James was "singularly jejune." By treating Emerson himself as a "great poet," Mumford missed the religious interests that James and Emerson had in common. His contention that the "American mind . . . had begun to find itself" in the "golden day" before the Civil War was unsupported by analysis of the substance of Emerson's thought, let alone that of Thoreau and Melville, whom Mumford rated more highly. Like Brooks, Mumford was concerned to illustrate the "broken rhythm of American life, with its highbrows and lowbrows, its Edwardses and Franklins, its transcendentalists and empiricists," and to show that "the gap between them widened after the Civil War."

The Controversy about Immigration: Assimilation or Cultural Pluralism?

· ■ ·

It is a pity that critics so keenly aware of the importance of tradition should have turned away from the traditions with which they had most in common. In their search for a "usable past," as Brooks called it, they ignored the past that lay close at hand and rummaged in all sorts of out-of-the-way places. They tried to piece together a cultural tradition from the works of neglected or minor writers or, in Frank's case, from the "buried cultures" of the Southwest, where Mexicans and Indians had once lived "in harmony with Nature." In an early work, *The Wine of the Puritans* (1909), Brooks had warned himself that it was impossible "deliberately [to] *establish* an American tradition." By 1918, however, he had decided that since "the past that survives in the common mind of the present is a past without living value," it might be possible, after all, to "discover" or even to "invent" another one.

He was right the first time. He and his friends might have addressed themselves to the important task of rescuing the puritan tradition from its genteel captivity. Because they dismissed it out of hand, the rehabilitation of puritanism had to wait for Perry Miller and other historians of the thirties and forties. By that time, the conditions for such a reappraisal were much less auspicious: the negative stereotype of puritanism had sunk too deeply into the popular mind to be easily dislodged, and Miller's work, academic in conception and execution, made little impression on the general public.

For Brooks and Bourne, Mumford and Frank, "puritanism" meant genteel pretensions, prudery, and censorship. At a time when genteel critics like Barrett Wendell and Stuart Sherman claimed official custodianship of the puritan legacy, the rebellious "young intellectuals," as they called themselves, had good reasons to distrust this particular past. The New England tradition was now identified with the social and political ascendancy of an Anglophile elite led by people like Henry Cabot Lodge and Nicholas Murray Butler. It was identified with movements to restrict immigration, to stifle cultural diversity and political dissent, and to impose "Americanism" as a kind of public religion. The fierce debate about immigration, one of the most important intellectual events of the progressive era, raised many of the same issues raised by debates about the democratization of culture. The same kinds of arguments were advanced in both contexts; the same alignment of opinion emerged; and the "puritans" lined up on the wrong side of the issue, associating themselves either with a narrow view of democracy or with outright opposition to democracy.

In the immigration debate, three distinct positions came to the surface: exclusionist, assimilationist, and pluralist. These positions coincided quite closely with positions taken by those who debated the democratization of culture. The same people who believed that "culture" presupposed wealth and leisure tended, on the whole, to oppose unrestricted immigration, just as they opposed attempts to guarantee universal access to the "best that had been thought and done in the world." The democratization of culture would only bring about its dilution, they argued, in the same way that unrestricted immigration would dilute the Anglo-Saxon stock and make the United States a nation of mongrels.

Democrats naturally found such opinions repugnant, but they did not agree among themselves about the best alternative. Those who wanted, in effect, to democratize the consumption of high culture advocated a similar approach to the immigration problem: unrestricted immigration, coupled with an aggressive program of cultural assimilation. Israel Zangwill's play *The Melting Pot*, first performed in 1908, provided a classic statement of the assimilationist position. Zangwill condemned both anti-Semitism and Jewish nationalism. The action of his play turned on intermarriage, which he treated as the best way to bury old-world animosities. In America, he wrote, "we must look forward" by "forgetting all that nightmare of religions and races." Assimilation implied oblivion. The "heritage from the Old World, hate and vengeance and blood," held back racial reconciliation and progress. "The ideals of the fathers shall not be foisted on the children. Each generation must live and die for its own dreams." The symbolism of the melting pot—"this great new continent that could melt up all racial differences and vendettas"—made quite explicit what had always been implicit in the ideology of progress: the dependence of progress on amnesia.

The anthropologist Franz Boas, a consistent champion of racial tolerance, made the same kind of case for assimilation, calling in social science to provide it with secure foundations. The myth of white racial superiority, Boas pointed out, had no scientific standing. Particularism was atavistic and irrational in any form. Tribalism, ethnocentrism, nationalism, and class consciousness all rested on a primitive fear of the stranger. The "enlargement of political units" in the modern world was an eminently desirable development, since it broke down the "emotional feeling of the solidarity of the group" and led people "to recognize equal rights for all individuals." The mass migrations of modern times, culminating in the latest wave of immigration to the United States, had the same effect. The "masses in our modern city populations," having known nothing of the "conservative influence of a home in which parents and children lived a common life," had escaped the "unconscious control of traditional ideas." Modern social conditions encouraged racial and ethnic intermarriage and a growing acceptance of the idea that people had a "right to be treated as individuals, not as members of a class." Boas did not deny the tenacity of racial prejudice, but he counted on "intermixture" to weaken the "consciousness of race distinction." When the "Negro blood" had been so much diluted" that it could "no longer be recognized as such," the "Negro problem" would "disappear," just as anti-Semitism would dissolve when "the last vestige of the Jew as a Jew" had "disappeared."

Cultural pluralists agreed with Zangwill and Boas in condemning racial and ethnic intolerance, but they objected to a definition of democracy that laid so much stress on uniformity and the eradication of group memory. Bourne's 1915 essay, "Trans-National America," though directed against a cruder version of the assimilationist ideal, implicitly questioned more refined versions as well. Unlike Boas, Bourne did not see the disintegration of "nationalistic cultures" as a positive development. In his view, it produced "hordes of men and women without a spiritual country, cultural outlaws, without taste, without standards but those of the mob." The melting pot brewed a "tasteless, colorless fluid of uniformity." Boas thought that men and women uprooted from tribal loyalties had a chance to become individuals. Bourne thought they became the "flotsam and jetsam of American life, the downward undertow of our civilization with its leering cheapness and falseness of taste and spiritual outlook."

Royce's Philosophy of Loyalty

· ■ ·

Instead of assimilation, Bourne favored a kind of "dual citizenship," an institutionalization of divided loyalties. He wanted tribal minorities to expose themselves to wider currents of thought without acquiring the mental habits of "cultural half-breeds." His position resembled that of Orestes Brownson, although there is no evidence that he was acquainted with Brownson's work. Like Brownson, Bourne maintained that individuality had to rest on early instruction in a definite, particular set of cultural practices. His position also resembled—and in this case was strongly influenced by—Josiah Royce's defense of provincialism, even though Bourne referred to his own "trans-national" ideal as a form of cosmopolitanism. For years, Royce—the third member of Harvard's distinguished triumvirate of philosophers—had been warning against the "levelling tendency of recent civilization," which threatened to "crush the individual." "Frequent changes of dwelling-place" destroyed "community spirit," according to Royce. Newspapers, "read by too vast multitudes," fostered a "monotonously uniform triviality of mind." "Industrial consolidation" and "impersonal social organization" strengthened the "spirit of the crowd or of the mob." Provincialism—loyalty to the "small group"—furnished a necessary counterweight, Royce argued, to the homogenizing effect of modern life, as long as it did not degenerate into "ancient narrowness."

Neither Bourne nor Royce explained what would happen if particular loyalties came into collision. How would the resulting conflicts be resolved? It was the fear that they could not be resolved short of open warfare that made the assimilationist program attractive as the best hope of social peace. Groups, it appeared, were inherently warlike and contentious. They operated according to the principle of exclusion: all that held them together was a common antipathy to outsiders. Social order, accordingly, seemed to depend on the dissolution of groups into their constituent individuals. Individuals had rights that could be recognized and guaranteed by the state, but groups characteristically refused to recognize the rights of competing groups, even to recognize their humanity. "Those who are not members of the tribe are not human beings," Boas noted with disapproval.

If Royce and Bourne failed to give enough attention to the reconciliation of conflicts and the mechanisms of social cohesion, it was because they saw desiccation as a greater danger than social conflict. The debate about cultural pluralism came down to the issue posed by William James in his exchange with Hobhouse. The assimilationists, like Hobhouse, worried about intolerance and fanaticism, whereas the pluralists, like James, saw "insipidity" as a greater danger—the "tame flabbiness," as Bourne put it, that was "accepted as Americanization." In their view, the rootless, emancipated, migratory individuals so highly prized by critics of particularism were cultural renegades who believed in nothing except their own right to a good time. Boas was impressed by the traits shared by all men and women, once the differences imposed by culture were peeled away.* Royce and Bourne, like Brownson, attached more importance to cultural differences and to the loyalty they inspired. They were less concerned with the danger of competing loyalties than with the erosion of the very capacity for loyalty.

Even blind loyalty, Royce thought, was better than a "thoughtless individualism which is loyal to nothing." Modern life gave rise to "social motives that seem to take away from people the true spirit of loyalty, and to leave them distracted, unsettled as to their moral standards, uncertain why or for what they live." Utilitarianism obscured the existence of "something much larger and richer than the mere sum of human happiness." The "spread of sympathy" and the spirit of universal philanthropy made people forget that when philanthropy was "not founded upon a

---

*His exposure to the Eskimo, on the first of his many field trips as an anthropologist, taught him, he said, that "they enjoyed life, as we do; that nature is also beautiful to them; that feelings of friendship also root in the Eskimo heart; that, although the character of their life is so rude as compared to civilized life, the Eskimo is a man as we are; his feelings, his virtues and his shortcomings are based on human nature like ours." It is impossible not to be touched by these sentiments, typical of the liberal mind at its most generous and expansive. The appeal to universal human traits, however, contains an unanticipated pitfall. If all men are alike, they should look, act, and think alike. When the fact of diversity contradicts the fiction of brotherhood, liberals often find it hard to maintain an attitude of exemplary tolerance. Diversity affronts their vision of the unity of all mankind. Thus Boas, staggered by the depth of racial animosities in the United States, argued, as we have seen, that the race problem would disappear only when observable racial differences themselves disappeared.

personal loyalty of the individual to his own family and to his own personal duties," it became "notoriously a worthless abstraction." Those who sought "simply to help mankind as a whole," without first undertaking "to help those nearest to themselves," dissipated their energies. Since "a self is a life insofar as it is unified by a single purpose," moral passion had to be concentrated on particular objects, even at the risk of narrowness.

If these objects came into conflict with each other, Royce suggested, the principle of "loyalty to loyalty" might supply its own corrective. This was no empty phrase. It implied respect for a worthy opponent, not the liberal principle of live-and-let-live. When Royce left "to the individual the . . . choice of the cause," he did not mean that one cause was as good as another or that it was impossible, at any rate, to adjudicate their conflicting claims. Nor did he pretend that people holding conflicting opinions would agree not to push them to the point of open conflict, in view of the difficulty of defending the moral superiority of any one of them. He assumed, on the contrary, that those moved by loyalty to a cause would defend it to the death. They would defend it, however, without hatred or bitterness and without denying their opponents' humanity. Loyalty to a cause, as Royce conceived it, carried with it an appreciation of loyalty for its own sake, without regard to the ends on behalf of which it was enlisted. In his *Philosophy of Loyalty,* he compared its effects to those of "divine grace in an older theology."

Those effects included both undeviating devotion to a cause that "must control you" and a respect for the same devotion in your enemies. Royce argued, in effect, that respect for enemies was more likely to encourage men and women to treat each other as human beings than the denial of enmity or the fiction of universal brotherhood. Those who believed in their own cause were less likely to disparage others. For those animated by loyalty, "cheerful rivalry" prevailed in war as in sports. Loyalty carried with it a refusal to allow the end to justify the means. It might lead to war, "but even then," it refused to "assail" whatever was "sincere and genuine" in the enemy's conduct. Loyalty encouraged "fair play in sport, chivalrous respect for the adversary in war, tolerance of the sincere beliefs of other men." It held the "key to all the familiar mysteries about the right relation of the love of man to the strenuous virtues."

Royce did not explain how conflicts between competing loyalties were to be mediated or prevented, but he did something better: he showed that the important question was not how to prevent conflicts but how to conduct them with dignity. No doubt his concern with fair play will seem quaint to self-proclaimed realists who assume that conflict is inherently brutalizing and who therefore see conflict resolution as the overriding objective of political action. Royce had the good fortune to live in a time when it did not yet seem utterly absurd to speak of honor and warfare in the same breath. In the twentieth century, of course, war has degenerated into cruelty on a grand scale, and peace, accordingly, has come to stand as the highest social good. We are all pacifists now. But the vast and understandable revulsion from war—which has not led to a more peaceful world, incidentally—has had the unfortunate effect, as William James predicted it would, of discrediting the "permanent human goods" formerly associated with the ethic of honor, glory, and self-sacrifice. That would be bad enough, in the absence of a "moral equivalent" of war; but the loss of the virtues associated with loyalty has had the additional effect of making war itself (and by extension, every form of conflict) more bloodthirsty and degrading than it ever was in the past.

The twentieth-century degradation of war, far from discrediting Royce's argument, gives it additional support. Like James, Royce understood that peace and plenty were inadequate social goals and that it was more important to settle the "right relation of the love of man to the strenuous virtues." He did not mean that the "love of man" provided the corrective to the "strenuous virtues." He meant that it depended on them. Loyalty to an abstraction like loyalty itself (with its respect for the principle of fair play) could take root only in loyalty to something quite specific. The misguided attempt to remove the sources of social conflict by discouraging particularism, in the hope that brotherly love would then come into its own, killed the very possibility of brotherly love by cutting off its roots.*

---

*Royce's point was essentially that of Brownson: man grasps the universal only through the particular.

The Postwar Reaction against Progressivism

·■·

In a famous passage in *A Farewell to Arms,* Ernest Hemingway noted that World War I discredited words like "honor," "glory," and "sacrifice." For the American left, it also discredited the concept of loyalty, now associated with nationalistic fanaticism, hatred of the Hun (later displaced onto the Bolsheviks), "100 percent Americanism," and a growing intolerance of political dissent. The left had been suspicious of particularism all along, but the war confirmed these suspicions and foreclosed the possibility of further debate about cultural pluralism and "loyalty to loyalty." Indeed the war put an end to a whole series of interlocking debates about democracy, the intensity of which had made the intellectual climate of the prewar years so invigorating. In the years to come, the assimilationist, consumerist, distributive version of the democratic dogma would seldom be subjected to such searching criticism.

The value of "progressive" social thought, the label notwithstanding, was that much of it worked against the progressive grain. "Progressivism" was not completely compatible with the ideology of progress. It is true that the syndicalist movement in America never mounted a head-on challenge to that ideology, as it did elsewhere, but the wide-ranging discussions of "industrial self-government" launched by Croly and others served to remind people that large-scale production might destroy the worker's sense of responsibility and thus undermine the moral foundations of democracy. The controversy about the democratization of culture, as we have seen, raised some of the same issues in another form. Those who took the position that leisure and abundance would democratize leisure-class standards of beauty had to contend with a much livelier conception of democracy, according to which the rehabilitation of work, not the democratization of consumption, ought to be seen as the principal goal of cultural criticism and political action alike. The controversy about assimilation and cultural pluralism raised these issues even more sharply. Advocates of particularism challenged one of the central tenets of enlightened ideology, the equation of progress with the eradication of tribal loyalties and their replacement by an all-embracing love for the whole human race.

In the postwar climate of discouragement and cynicism, all these issues quickly dropped out of public discussion. Many intellectuals, in fact, began to question the very possibility of public discussion. H. L. Mencken's ridicule of the "booboisie" set the tone of the twenties. "Mr. Mencken has arrived," wrote John Gunther in 1921. ". . . His name, already the war cry of the younger generation, is beginning to penetrate all quarters, even the most holy and reverend. One finds him everywhere." He and Sinclair Lewis had become the "most read and considered interpreters of American life," according to Robert Morss Lovett. Mencken had "assumed such importance as an influence on American thought," Edmund Wilson declared, that "optimism, Puritanism, and democratic ineptitude" had become "stock reproaches among the intelligentsia." F. Scott Fitzgerald said that he valued Mencken's opinion more highly than that of anyone else in America. In 1926, Walter Lippmann described him as the "most powerful influence on this whole generation of Americans." Mencken returned the compliment in a laudatory review of Lippmann's *Phantom Public:* having "started out in life with high hopes for democracy," Lippmann had "come to the conclusion that the masses are ignorant and unteachable." This was high praise from the editor of *Smart Set* and the *American Mercury.* Lippmann's disillusionment with popular government identified him as a member of the "civilized minority," as Mencken liked to call it.

Sometimes mistaken by liberals as one of themselves, Mencken preferred to label himself a "libertarian." Liberty, he insisted, was the "first thing and the last thing." Liberals wanted to reform people, to free them "against their will," often "to their obvious damage, as in the case of the majority of Negroes and women." Mencken wanted only to leave them alone, not just because he believed in free speech but because it was a mistake, in his opinion, to interfere with the laws of natural selection. He took his social views straight from William Graham Sumner, the nineteenth-century social Darwinist. Liberals now repudiated social Darwinism, but many of them had come to share Mencken's belief that the "finest fruits of human progress, like all the nobler virtues of man, are the exclusive possession of small minorities." The democratization of virtue now struck them as a contradiction in terms.

A disillusioned educator, writing anonymously in the *New Republic*, recalled the heyday of "uplift and enlightenment," when people believed in education as a "general religion." As a young man, he was inspired by

Santayana's remark that "if a noble and civilized democracy is to subsist, the common man must be something of a saint and something of a hero." Democracy was a "younger and brighter goddess in those days, worshipped with a pride and confidence of which our present Rotarian oratory is only the echo." His experience in a state university in the Middle West, however, had turned Santayana's "battle-cry" into "bitterest cynicism." He concluded that education was the "wrong road to popular intelligence." Indeed, he "gave up popular intelligence." Later he became head of an educational foundation, a position that required him to "express faith in the coming democracy." But he had "no such faith," he confessed. "It has slowly ebbed away." The only "thing that is really worth doing," he decided, was "to sit on the boulevard" in Paris and "watch the crowds go by," with "an open Montaigne on the little table before me."

Before the war, only conservatives disparaged popular intelligence and public opinion. In 1915, a writer in the *Unpopular Review*, a right-wing magazine, observed that public opinion was another name for mob rule. "The modern public, when hypnotized by a dominant impulse, is quite as capable of manifestations of mob-mind as any Shakespearean multitude." By the mid-twenties, liberals were saying the same thing. They had "lost their former confidence," according to the *New Republic*, "in the ability of progressive agitators to convince popular opinion of the desirability of radical changes." Wartime repression, the postwar red scare, the prohibition amendment, the National Origins Act of 1924, the Sacco-Vanzetti affair, and the Scopes trial had taken their toll. The people, it seemed, responded only to movements that played on their emotions—nativism, fundamentalism, the crusade against the city. "People who think are in a minority in every country," said the *Nation*, approvingly quoting one of Mencken's attacks on fundamentalism—on the "belligerent sense of election cherished by vulgar and ignorant men." The popularity of Calvin Coolidge dealt the final blow to the old progressive faith in public opinion. "The Coolidge myth has been created by amazingly skilful propaganda," the *Nation* complained. "The American people dearly love to be fooled."

The election of Hoover in 1928, following a campaign in which the Republicans appealed to anti-Catholic prejudice against Al Smith, did nothing to revive liberals' confidence in the people. "The characteristic trait of liberals nowadays," Matthew Josephson noted in 1930, "is their disappointment at finding that the people care little for liberty." Josephson did not deny that liberty was "nearly dead," crushed by a "triumphant equality." He denied only that there was anything anyone could do about it. An "immense mechanization" had "visibly shifted the seats of power," raising a class of millionaires who shared the plebeian tastes of the "man of the filling station"—"the same horizons, the same preoccupations." The new rulers of America were men elevated from the crowd and imbued with the crowd mentality. "Their hours of toil are the same; their pleasures are similarly the familiar drives on Sundays, the passive vigil before the universal receiving set." Liberals, Josephson argued, were now obliged "to resist the majority, the vox populi, the great crowd" they had formerly worshiped. But they were also obliged to resist the new "humanists" and other reactionaries who demanded a "return to ancient systems of authority, discipline, culture." As "good determinists," liberals knew that history always marches forward. "The human race never turns back to an old order." The best hope lay in an orderly "transition to that which Dewey and Beard have called a 'technological-rationalist society.'" even if the "more valid equality" it promised meant the "inevitable sacrifice" of individual liberties. "There is something ponderously fatal about such a transition," Josephson mused, "but if it results in order, enthusiasm, harmony, we will be content with our sacrifice."

Lippmann's Farewell to Virtue

The most sobering assessment of the public's incapacity for critical judgment and self-government came from Walter Lippmann, who devoted four separate studies in the twenties, each gloomier than the last, to the problem of public opinion. The first of these, *A Test of the News*, written with Charles Merz and published as a supplementary issue of the *New Republic* in 1920, examined press coverage of the Russian revolution. According to Lippmann and Merz, American papers gave their readers an account of the revolution distorted by anti-Bolshevik prejudices, wishful thinking, and sheer ignorance. *Liberty and the News* (1920) was also prompted by the collapse of journalistic objectivity during the war, when the newspapers had appointed themselves "defenders of the faith." The result, according to Lippmann, was a "breakdown of the means of public knowledge." The difficulty went beyond war or revolution, the "supreme destroyers of realistic thinking." The traffic in sex, violence, and "human interest"—staples of modern mass journalism—raised grave questions about the future of democracy. "All that the sharpest critics of democracy have alleged is true if there is no steady supply of trustworthy and relevant news."

In *Public Opinion* (1922) and *The Phantom Public* (1925), Lippmann broadened his indictment to include not only the press but the public itself. He no longer argued simply that the press ought to keep the public better informed. Instead he proposed to confine the role of public opinion in policy making to strictly procedural questions, reserving substantive decisions to an administrative elite. "The public interest in a problem," Lippmann argued, "is limited to this: that there shall be rules. . . . The public is interested in law, not in the laws; in the method of law, not in the substance." Questions of substance should be left to experts, whose access to scientific knowledge immunized them against the emotional "symbols" and "stereotypes" that dominated public debate.

Lippmann acknowledged the conflict between his recommendations and the principles that usually guided "democratic reformers." Those principles were simply "false," in his view. He rejected the "mystical fallacy of democracy" and the "usual appeal to education as the remedy for the incompetence of democracy." Democratic theory presupposed an "omnicompetent citizen," a "jack of all trades" who could be found only in a "simple self-contained community." In the "wide and unpredictable environment" of the modern world, the old ideal of citizenship was obsolete. Nor could it be revived in the workshop, as guild socialists proposed. Democratic control of the workshop would not eliminate the difficulty that the relations between one shop and another raised issues that "transcend immediate experience." Unless guild socialism was to degenerate into a "chaos of warring shops," the management of their "external relations" would still have to be delegated to elected officials, and the whole problem of representation would arise all over again. "The public opinions of a shop about its rights and duties in the industry and in society, are matters of education and propaganda, not the automatic product of shop-consciousness." The guild socialists could not escape the "problem of the orthodox democrat." In a complex industrial society, government had to be carried on by officials who were expected to "conceive a common interest." In their attempt to stretch their minds "beyond the limits of immediate experience," these officials would be guided either by public opinion or by expert knowledge. There was no escape from this choice.

Public opinion was unreliable, according to Lippmann, because it could be united only by an appeal to slogans and "symbolic pictures." In a society ruled by public opinion, government became the art of "manipulation"—the "manufacture of consent." "Where all news comes at second-hand, where all the testimony is uncertain, men cease to respond to truths, and respond simply to opinions. The environment in which they act is not the realities themselves, but the pseudo-environment of reports, rumors, and guesses. . . . Everything is on the plane of assertion and propaganda." Lippmann's analysis rested on the epistemological distinction between truth and mere opinion, enshrined in the dominant tradition of modern philosophy. The pragmatic philosophers had attempted to demolish this distinction, most recently in Dewey's *Quest for Certainty;* but Lippmann, though professing indebtedness to James and Dewey, paid no attention to their argument that even scientific knowledge is colored by "expectations," as Lippmann put it, and that science cannot be distinguished from opinion on the grounds that it puts an end to doubt. Truth, as Lippmann conceived it, grew out of disinterested scientific inquiry; everything else was ideology (though he did not use that word, not yet in general circulation). The scope of public debate, accordingly, had to be severely restricted. At best, public debate was a disagreeable necessity—not the very essence of democracy, as Brownson or Bourne would have argued, but its "primary defect," which arose only because "exact knowledge," unfortunately, was in limited supply. Ideally public debate would not take place at all; decisions would be based on scientific "standards of measurement" alone. Science cut through "entangling stereotypes and slogans," the "threads of memory and emotion" that kept the "responsible administrator" tied up in knots. Like Edmund Burke, Lippmann distrusted memory as an important source of conflict and disagreement. He proposed to counter its influence, however, not with custom but with "organized intelligence."

Even Lippmann's opponents conceded the force of his argument. If he was right, it was time to bid a definitive farewell to virtue—that is, to the hope that democracy would create a "whole world of heroes," in Carlyle's memorable phrase. "A political theory based on the expectation of self-denial and sacrifice by the run of men in any community," Lippmann said, "would not be worth considering." The best argument for democracy—that the responsibilities of self-government would elicit unsuspected capacities in ordinary men and women—had to be abandoned as another relic of the preindustrial past. An earlier theory of democracy had considered ordinary citizens at least competent to manage their own affairs, if not consistently capable of self-denial and sacrifice. Their opinions were held to command respect, as Lippmann saw it, because the business of government did not greatly exceed their experience. But it was "not possible to assume that a world, carried on by division of labor and distribution of authority, can be governed by universal opinions in the whole population." Under the altered conditions of industrial life, popular participation in government would only lead to anarchy and mob rule. Participatory democracy had to give way to distributive democracy. Instead of "hanging human dignity" on self-government, Lippmann argued, democrats would do better to hang it on universal access to the good things of life. The test of democracy was not whether it produced self-reliant citizens but whether it produced essential goods and services. The question to ask about government was "whether it is producing a certain minimum of health, of decent housing, of material necessities, of education, of freedom, of pleasures, of beauty, not simply whether at the sacrifice of all these things it vibrates to the self-centered opinions that happen to be floating around in men's minds."

Dewey's Reply to Lippmann: Too Little Too Late

By the mid-twenties, hardly anyone cared to question Lippmann's passive conception of democracy or his explanation of the futility of public debate. Dewey was almost alone in attempting to work out a reply, but even Dewey admitted that his objections might have derived simply from a prejudice in favor of democracy—from a "subjectivism about democracy, which even Mr. Lippmann's treatment has not purged." He did not deny the vigor of Lippmann's "relentless and realistic analysis"—"perhaps the most effective indictment of democracy . . . ever penned." He tried to sidestep the indictment, however, by disavowing the notion of the "omnicompetent citizen"—the "man of straw" against which so much of Lippmann's argument was directed.

Lippmann's strictures, Dewey claimed, applied only to a nineteenth-century notion of democracy that had been "nullified by the course of events." The old individualism—the source of the fiction of the "omnicompetent citizen"—rested on a "false psychology" that exaggerated individuals' self-sufficiency and their "intelligent and calculated regard for their own good." The discovery that "crudely intelligized emotion" and "habit" played a larger part in human conduct than rational self-interest invalidated individualism, not democracy. It was not enlightened self-interest, however, that qualified ordinary men and women to manage their own affairs, according to Dewey; it was their access to a common fund of knowledge, the product of "association," "communication," "tradition," and of "tools and methods socially transmitted, developed and sanctioned." In the twentieth century, this socially generated knowledge took a rigorously scientific form, but that did not mean that only experts and "insiders," as Lippmann argued, were in a position to understand or make use of it. Government by experts was not only undesirable but "impossible." "In the degree to which they become a specialized class, they are shut off from knowledge of the needs which they are supposed to serve." An understanding of these needs could be acquired only in the course of "debate, discussion and persuasion"—the "improvement of the methods and conditions" of which therefore became the central challenge confronting twentieth-century democrats.

These arguments, outlined in two long reviews of Lippmann's work and elaborated in *The Public and Its Problems* (1927) and *Individualism Old and New* (1930), did not meet the central issue raised by the rise of mass communications—the same issue that was raised, in another form, by the rise of mass production. Just as the consolidation of industry undermined workers' control of production, so the consolidation of communications deprived the public of an "articulate voice" in public affairs, as Dewey himself appeared to admit. Criticism of individualism, to which Dewey devoted so much of his energy in the twenties and thirties, did not address the deeper questions that had preoccupied theorists of republican virtue all along, the question of whether self-government could work beyond the local level. Not that Dewey failed to recognize the importance of the question. "The significant thing," he wrote in passing, "is that the loyalties which once held individuals, which gave them support, direction, and unity of outlook on life, have well-nigh disappeared." Industrialism, moreover, had "excluded" individuals from the use of thought and emotion in their daily occupations and from the "assumption of responsibility," without which "there can be no stable and balanced development of mind and character." Although he held out the hope that "the Great Society may become the Great Community," Dewey knew that it could "never possess all the qualities which mark a local community." "In its deepest and richest sense a community must always remain a matter of face-to-face intercourse. . . . Vital and thorough attachments are bred only in the intimacy of an intercourse which is of necessity restricted in range."

What Dewey could not explain was just how loyalty and responsibility would thrive in a world dominated by large-scale production and mass communications. He took for granted the "disintegration of the family, church and neighborhood." What was to fill the resulting "void"? Dewey did not say. "It is outside the scope of our discussion," he wrote, "to look into the prospect of the reconstruction of face-to-face communities." His commitment to the idea of progress prevented him from pursuing the point. In a 1916 essay on progress, he argued that although the replacement of a "static" social structure by a "dynamic or readily changing social structure" did not guarantee progress, it created the preconditions of progress—of "constructive intelligence" and "constructive social engineering." In any case, there was "no way to 'restrain' or turn back the industrial revolution and its consequences."

Under these circumstances, it was impossible to defend his belief in the possibility of a "return movement . . . into the local homes of mankind." Since nothing in Dewey's social philosophy justified any such hope, the subjects of work and loyalty had to be relegated to the margins of his work, as, increasingly, they were relegated to the margins of the liberal tradition as a whole.

9

THE SPIRITUAL DISCIPLINE AGAINST
RESENTMENT

Reinhold Niebuhr on Christian Mythology

In the summer of 1919, Reinhold Niebuhr, still an obscure minister in Detroit, wrote a letter to the *New Republic* that foreshadowed much of the left's postwar reaction against liberalism. The Treaty of Versailles had shattered hopes "for a better world," Niebuhr said. But it was pointless to blame Woodrow Wilson, as many liberals were doing, for his willingness to compromise with the Allies' demand for a harsh and punitive settlement. Wilson's defeat revealed the "limitations of liberalism itself." Liberals were "afraid to tear down old houses and build new ones." They refused "to take a chance and accept a challenge." They approached the old order "with friendly mien," hoping to lead it "blindfold" into the future without alerting its defenders. Liberalism was dominated by the "gray spirit of compromise." It lacked "fervency"—the "spirit of enthusiasm, not to say fanaticism, which is so necessary to move the world out of its beaten tracks." It was the "philosophy of the middle aged."

This outburst, dashed off in the impetuous indignation of youth, already announced one of the themes of Niebuhr's mature work, the positive force of "fanaticism." "Liberalism is too intellectual and too little emotional to be an efficient force in history," Niebuhr told the readers of the *New Republic.* Like Sorel, he believed that only "myths" had the power to inspire effective political action. Like James, he saw desiccation, in effect, as a greater menace than superstition and fanaticism. "Contending factions in a social struggle require morale," as he put it in *Moral Man and Immoral Society* (1932); "and morale is created by the right dogmas, symbols and emotionally potent oversimplifications." Industrial workers would never win "freedom" if they followed liberals' advice to rely on "intelligence" alone. Nor would Negroes achieve justice in this manner. Liberals like Dewey mistakenly put their faith in moral suasion, education, and the scientific method. They imagined that "with a little more time, a little more adequate moral and social pedagogy and a generally higher development of human intelligence, our social problems will approach solution." But science could not provide the nerve and will that enabled "disinherited groups" to resist injustice. In order to defeat their oppressors, they had "to believe rather more firmly in the justice and in the probable triumph of their cause, than any impartial science would give them the right to believe."

In 1919, Niebuhr still adhered to the liberal theology of the social gospel, notwithstanding his impatience with liberal politics. His first book, *Does Civilization Need Religion?* (1926), rested on a liberal version of the Protestant tradition. By 1932, however, religious liberalism had been shaken to its foundations by Karl Barth's reassertion of dogmatic theology. Niebuhr had reservations about the political implications of Barth's neo-orthodoxy, which seemed to him to write off the political realm as irredeemably corrupt; but he too came to accept original sin as an "inescapable fact of human existence," to reject the shallow optimism of liberal theology, and to acknowledge the impossibility of justifying religious belief on purely rational grounds. In the face of "nature's ruthlessness"— of the "brevity and mortality of natural life"—feelings of trust and gratitude (in other words, a belief in God) could not be defended by an appeal to reason, as Niebuhr explained in *An Interpretation of Christian Ethics*

(1935). Just as an "impartial science" could not fully justify the "right to believe" in justice or in the possibility that justice would prevail in the political order, so it could not justify a belief in the goodness of God's wicked world. Hope—"the nerve of moral action"—had to be asserted in the face of evidence that could easily justify the conclusion that the world is "meaningless." Hope was the product of emotion, not intelligence. It sprang from "gratitude and contrition"—"gratitude for Creation and contrition before Judgment; or, in other words, confidence that life is good in spite of its evil and that it is evil in spite of its good." Hope had to be distinguished, therefore, from optimism or "sentimentality," which closed their eyes to the dark side of things and attributed evil merely to ignorance or "cultural lag"—the failure of a science of morals and society to keep pace with the scientific understanding of nature. Without hope, the world was seen "either as being meaningless or as revealing unqualifiedly good and simple meanings." Yet hope exceeded strictly reasonable and realistic expectations. For this reason, Christian orthodoxy had always equated hope with a state of grace, which could not be achieved simply by the exertion of will or intelligence.

In his *Interpretation of Christian Ethics,* more fully and explicitly than in his other works, Niebuhr treated Christianity—more specifically, the prophetic tradition in Judaism and Christianity—as a life-giving mythology, in very much the same sense that Sorel spoke of the myth of the general strike. As we have seen, Sorel's use of this concept puzzled his critics, who insisted that workers would never rally to a purely imaginary promise of liberation. Niebuhr's argument invited the same misunderstanding. It is important to emphasize, therefore, that he did not mean to say that Christianity was an illusion, however sustaining in its psychological effects. Mythology, as he understood it, offered a coherent account of human history, in the form of narratives that embodied ethical insight and emotional truth in symbolic form; but the truth of this account, because it rested on intuition and emotion (in the Christian case, on the emotions of trust, loyalty, gratitude, and contrition), could not be established simply by argumentation. Niebuhr did not recommend the prophetic myth—the narrative of creation, the fall, God's judgment and redemption of history—as an object of aesthetic appreciation, a set of agreeable fictions. He maintained that it gave a true account of the human condition, superior to other accounts. Judeo-Christian prophecy, like any other myth, was prescientific, but it was also "supra-scientific." Myths originated in the "childhood of every culture when the human imagination plays freely upon the rich variety of facts and events in life and history, and seeks to discover their relation to basic causes and ultimate meanings without a careful examination of their relation to each other in the realm of natural causation." In this sense, mythical thinking fell short of science in its power to explain the world; but it also transcended science by virtue of its power to illuminate the "end of existence without abstracting it from existence." In the latter sense, myth alone was "capable of picturing the world as a realm of coherence and meaning without defying the facts of incoherence."*

Niebuhr distinguished prophetic religion not only from scientific rationality, which cannot justify hope, but from mystical religion, which cannot justify it either, except by turning its back on the "facts of incoherence." If science dismissed the existence of moral order and coherence in history as an illusion, mysticism dismissed the natural world itself as an illusion, together with the whole course of human history. For the mystic, reality dwelled in the timeless realm of pure essence, the contemplation of which, undistracted by unruly historical facts, became the goal of religious aspiration. Mysticism, according to Niebuhr, was rationalism's mirror image. It carried the "rational passion for unity and coherence to the point where the eye turns from the outward scene, with its recalcitrant facts and stubborn variety, to the inner world of spirit." The prophetic tradition found moral significance in history (since history is under God's judgment) without denying the reality of incoherence and evil. The achievement of the "prophetic movement in Hebraic religion," Niebuhr wrote, lay in its ability "to purge its religion of the parochial and puerile weaknesses of its childhood without rationalizing it and thus destroying the virtue of its myth."

His reference to the "virtue" of the prophetic myth, when we recall the rich associations and multiple meanings of the term, provides the clearest indication of the meaning of mythology, as Niebuhr understood it. In the

---

*"This voice of fable has in it somewhat divine," wrote Emerson in "Compensation," with specific reference to the concept of Nemesis. "It came from thought above the will of the writer."

prophetic tradition, virtue is the truth that breaks the cycle of excessive optimism and disillusionment. It asserts the goodness of life without denying the evidence that would justify despair. Thus "Hebrew spirituality," Niebuhr argued, "was never corrupted by either the optimism which conceived the world as possessing unqualified sanctity and goodness or the pessimism which relegated historic existence to a realm of meaningless cycles."

The Virtue of Particularism

Because the religious tradition founded on Hebraic mythology took history seriously, as mystical religion did not, it was always exposed to the temptation to historicize its central concepts, as Niebuhr pointed out—to read the myth of creation as an "actual history of origins when it is really a description of the quality of existence," to make the myth of the fall into an "account of the origin of evil, when it is really a description of its nature," or "to construct a history of sin out of the concept of its inevitability." It was just this historical misreading of Christian prophecy, as we have seen—of the doctrine of original sin in particular—that had opened the followers of Jonathan Edwards to liberal counterattack. When they argued that mankind inherited Adam's sin, the preachers of the "new divinity" soon found themselves in a conceptual tangle that could have been avoided if they had remembered, as Niebuhr now put it, that original sin was an "inevitable fact of human existence," not an "inherited corruption" that somehow made the sons responsible for the crimes of the fathers. Prophetic mythology threw a powerful light on history, but it was not to be confused with the actual historical record.

Neither was the Christian ethic to be taken as a literal description of the well-ordered society. The ethical teachings of Jesus referred to the relations between man and God. Thus Jesus exhorted his disciples to "hate" their parents, wives, and children and to give their loyalty to God alone. Such commandments, Niebuhr observed, could hardly guide social morality, where the claims of the family had to be weighed against other claims. "One is almost inclined to agree with Karl Barth that this ethic 'is not applicable to the problems of contemporary society nor yet to any conceivable society.' " Political life could not become a realm of moral perfection; but that did not mean, as Barth seemed to imply, that it was therefore exempt from discriminating moral judgments. Prophetic religion, according to Niebuhr, maintained an "intolerable tension" between the absolute and the contingent. Neo-orthodoxy dissolved this tension in its blanket condemnation of political life as a struggle for power unredeemed by any higher purpose. But the social gospel, in its attempt to historicize the Kingdom of God, also dissolved the tension between the universal and the particular. It mistook Christian ethics, with their absolute injunction against violence, as a blueprint for social reform, overlooking the need for violence and coercion in politics and relying on the "pious hope that people might be good and loving, in which case all the nasty business of politics could be dispensed with." Since people were not good and loving—not at least in their dealings with each other as members of "collectives, whether races, classes or nations"—politics and morality would always collide.

In *Moral Man and Immoral Society,* Niebuhr traced the "immorality" of political life to the intractable particularism of groups. The opposition announced in the title attracted so much attention, in the ensuing controversies between Niebuhr and exponents of the social gospel, that most readers missed his contention that particularism remained a source of "virtue" as well as "demonic fervor." In his *Christian Ethics,* he spoke of "those virtuous attitudes of natural man in which natural sympathy is inevitably compounded with natural egoism." Liberals denounced "narrow loyalties" and "circumscribed sympathy," but Niebuhr saw their positive side, just as he saw the positive side of fanaticism. "It is natural enough to love one's own family more than other families and no amount of education will ever eliminate the inverse ratio between the potency of love and the breadth and expansion in which it is applied." The value of mythology consisted, in part, of its "understanding for the organic aspects of life which rationalistic morality frequently fails to appreciate." Liberals and socialists made the mistake of dismissing the "organic unities of family, race, and nation as irrational idiosyncrasies which a more perfect rationality will destroy." Thus John Strachey took the position that "separate national cultures, separate languages, and the like" would have no place in a "fully developed world communism." People would "tire of the inconvenient idiosyncrasies of locality" and "wish to pool the cultural heritage of the human race into a world synthesis." It was difficult, Niebuhr said, "to find a more perfect and naive expression of the modern illusion that human reason will be able to become the complete master of all the contingent, irrational, and illogical forces of the natural world which underlie and condition all human culture."

He did not deny that particularism often took a "frantic and morbid" form, as in the Nazi cult of the Aryan race. But the left's indifference to the value of particularism made it easier for movements like National Socialism to pervert it. The left's blindness to the "perennial force and the qualified virtue of the more organic and less rational human relations" enabled the right to appropriate the symbols of organic solidarity for its own sinister purposes. Particularism was dangerous and needed to be criticized, but it could not be eliminated. "The effort to do so merely results in desperate and demonic affirmations of the imperiled values" that were inextricably associated with it.

Niebuhr found another example of this misguided search for unity— for an "absolute perspective which transcends the conflict" between competing loyalties—in Dewey's little book on religion, *A Common Faith* (1934). Dewey lamented the divisive effects of religion and urged the churches to become more truly catholic. They devoted too much of their attention, he thought, to the attempt to distinguish the saved from the lost, instead of recognizing that "we are ... all in the same boat." Niebuhr considered Dewey's plea for a "religious faith that shall not be confined to sect, class, or race" as an attempt to "eliminate conflict and unite men of good will everywhere by stripping their spiritual life of historic, traditional, and supposedly anachronistic accretions." Dewey's position exemplified the "faith of modern rationalism in the ability of reason to transcend the partial perspectives of the natural world in which reason is rooted." Dewey did not understand that competing loyalties were rooted in "something more vital and immediate than anachronistic religious traditions." The fervor they evoked could not be modified or resolved, as Dewey seemed to think, by a "small group of intellectuals" who enjoyed the "comparative neutrality and security of the intellectual life."

Forgiveness, not tolerance, furnished the proper corrective to the egoism and self-righteousness of groups, Niebuhr argued. "The religious ideal of forgiveness is more profound and more difficult than the rational virtue of tolerance." Niebuhr endorsed G. K. Chesterton's observation that tolerance is the attitude of those who do not believe in anything. Forgiveness, on the other hand, made it possible for contending groups to fight to the death without denying each other's humanity—"to engage in social struggles with a religious reservation." Since the sources of social conflict could not be eradicated, it was "more important to preserve the spirit of forgiveness amidst the struggles than to seek islands of neutrality."*

The "Endless Cycle of Social Conflict" and How to Break It

Most of those who came to regard Niebuhr as a political mentor missed his defense of particularism and paid attention only to his analysis of its dangers. Since they shared his disbelief in the political efficacy of moral suasion and "intelligence," priding themselves on their political realism, they concluded that politics would always remain a matter of "checks and balances and countervailing forces," in the words of Michael Novak. Novak quotes *Moral Man and Immoral Society* on the "power of self-interest and collective egoism in all inter-group relations," which makes "social conflict an inevitability in human history." But this was only the beginning of Niebuhr's argument: one of its premises, not its conclusion. Novak wants to use Niebuhr's thought to justify familiar ideas about the importance of "institutions, habits and associations that will provide checks and balances against the ineradicable evils of the human heart." For Niebuhr, however, the irreducible need for coercion in politics defined the problem, not its solution. If politics consisted of nothing more than "checks and balances," the struggle of force against counterforce, it

---

*This is what Lincoln tried to accomplish, "with malice toward none," in his second inaugural, a striking expression of the "religious reservation" that characterized his conduct of the Civil War. "Both [sides] read the same Bible, and pray to the same God; and each invokes His aid against the other." To invoke God in defense of slavery might seem "strange" to Northerners, Lincoln said; but "let us judge not that we be not judged.... The Almighty has His own purposes." Lincoln's statesmanship exemplifies the distinction between action and behavior, explained in chapter 4. Action issues from the capacity to initiate things, to make a new beginning, and it finds its fullest expression, as Hannah Arendt pointed out, in forgiveness. Action is to behavior what forgiveness is to tolerance.

could never have anything to do with morality. He rejected Barth's argument to that effect as another expression of the historic flaw in Reformation theology, which led to a rigorous separation of religion from politics and thus guaranteed the brutalization of the political order. Niebuhr had no illusions about the political order, but neither did he propose to abdicate it to those whose readiness to use force was unrestrained by conscientious scruples.

His most suggestive formulation of the problem of politics, in *Moral Man,* took the form of a tightly constructed series of questions, each dependent on the others. "If social cohesion is impossible without coercion, and coercion is impossible without the creation of social injustice, and the destruction of injustice is impossible without the use of further coercion, are we not in an endless cycle of social conflict?" Under these conditions, an "uneasy balance of power" appeared to be the "highest goal to which society could aspire." Niebuhr's refusal to stop at that point distinguished him from most of his followers, whose realism begins and ends with an acknowledgement of the inescapable role of force in politics. His search for a way out of the "endless cycle of social conflict" linked him to his political roots in the progressive movement and the social gospel. Even after he had come to reject progressivism's faith in moral suasion—and much of *Moral Man* consisted of a relentless attack on the illusion that the powerful would surrender their power without a struggle—he still refused to regard politics as a struggle for power unredeemed by considerations of justice and morality. When he declared that "social cohesion is impossible without coercion," he parted company with many progressives; but in the next clause in this series, he dissociated himself from Marxists and other revolutionaries, including radicalized adherents of the social gospel, forerunners of liberation theology today, who wished to put religion at the service of the proletarian struggle against capitalism. Unlike progressives, revolutionaries gladly accepted the need for coercion, but they refused to admit that "coercion is impossible without the creation of social injustice." They believed that revolutionary coercion would create conditions of perfect justice, or at least that the new order would represent such an improvement over the old that a few passing injustices, committed on behalf of a good cause, must not be allowed to stand in its way.

The only way to break the "endless cycle" of injustice, Niebuhr argued, was nonviolent coercion, with its "spiritual discipline against resentment," its deflation of the "moral conceit" of entrenched interests, its recognition of the adversary's humanity, and its appeal to "profound and ultimate unities." Note that Niebuhr advocated nonviolent "resistance" or "coercion," not "nonresistance." There was no virtue in passive submission to injustice, in his view; even violence was better than submission. The choice between violence and nonviolence, indeed, presented itself to him as a tactical choice, not one of principle. Gandhi himself, he observed, introduced tactical considerations into the case for nonviolence, arguing that it served the interests of a group that "has more power arrayed against it than it is able to command," as Niebuhr put it. Gandhi thus implied that violence itself "could be used as an instrument of moral goodwill, if there was any possibility of a triumph quick enough to obviate the dangers of incessant wars." What mattered was "moral goodwill," not the choice of nonviolent over violent methods.

What mattered, in other words, was the "spiritual discipline against resentment," which discriminated "between the evils of a social system . . . and the individuals who are involved in it." William Lloyd Garrison, Niebuhr argued, solidified the South against abolition when he condemned slaveholders as sinners. Self-righteousness and resentment, as Niebuhr understood the latter term, went hand in hand. Victims of injustice, whose suffering entitled them to resent it, had all the more reason to renounce resentment, lest it confer the sense of moral superiority that allegedly excused them in retaliating against injustice with injustice of their own. In order to undermine their oppressors' claims to moral superiority, they had to avoid such claims on their own behalf. They had to renounce the privileged status of victims. They needed "repentance" no less than their oppressors. They needed to recognize, in other words, that "the evil in the foe is also in the self." "The discovery of elements of common human frailty in the foe," Niebuhr argued, ". . . creates attitudes which transcend social conflict and thus mitigate its cruelties." The "profound and ultimate unities" Niebuhr hoped to awaken rested on a sense of sin, not on the assumption that all people ultimately had the same interests and that intelligent awareness of this harmony of interests would prevent social conflict. He did not regard the prevention of conflict as possible or even desirable. The most that could be hoped for in politics was to "mitigate its cruelties."

Niebuhr's Challenge to Liberalism Denatured and Deflected

· ■ ·

The standard interpretation of Niebuhr's career, which treats him simply as a critic of the social gospel and of its exaggerated faith in public opinion, overlooks his criticism of the political "realism" that reduces politics to a struggle for power and thus precludes any public life at all. Niebuhr himself, it must be said, was partly responsible for this misunderstanding. In his political writings of the thirties and forties—in his journalistic polemics against Christian pacifism as well as in his books— he devoted far more attention to the illusions of the social gospel than to the dangers of an excessively hard-boiled political realism. He ridiculed liberals for their trust in human nature and the power of good intentions. With considerable relish, he set out to disabuse them of their fantasy of painless social change and to expose the moral insincerity that made it so easy for the rich and powerful to condemn the resort to violence on the part of the poor. The dominant classes, he argued, could easily proscribe violence because they had more effective means of coercion at their disposal.

No doubt the more naive exponents of the social gospel deserved this rebuke, but Niebuhr's invective against pacifism gave undue emphasis to such matters. Eager to make the point that "sentimentality is a poor weapon against cynicism," he said too much about sentimentality and too little about cynicism. In any case, Christian socialists like Walter Rauschenbusch expressly repudiated the views attributed by Niebuhr to the social gospel. "Moral suasion is strangely feeble," Rauschenbusch wrote in 1912, "where the sources of a man's income are concerned." History offered no "precedent for an altruistic self-effacement of a whole class." For this reason, "intellectual persuasion and moral conviction . . . would never by themselves overcome the resistance of selfishness and conservatism." It is true that Rauschenbusch disparaged violence, but he did not close his eyes to the need for pressure and force. "Christian idealists," he said, "must not make the mistake of trying to hold the working class down to the use of moral suasion only"—an eminently Niebuhrian statement. He disavowed the principle that the "use of force against oppression can always be condemned as wrong," adding that the United States owed its national existence to revolutionary warfare. He objected only to the "idea that violence can suddenly establish righteousness," which he thought "just as utopian as the idea that moral suasion can suddenly establish it."*

By ignoring Rauschenbusch, Niebuhr invited the suspicion that his position was developed in opposition to a caricature of the social gospel. This made it possible for his adversaries to shrug off most of his criticism. He forced the liberal party in American Protestantism to admit that "we can no longer speak of a 'Christian' social order," as John C. Bennett put it in 1935, and that politics represented a "compromise" between the "ideal and the possible." In the absence of a more fully developed Niebuhrian critique of the politics of compromise, however, liberals could

---

*As Donald Meyer notes in his study of the social gospel in the twenties and thirties, "Rauschenbusch's conception of political strategy was not an appropriate windmill for Niebuhr's tilting." This helps to explain why, for the most part, Niebuhr left Rauschenbusch alone and singled out weaker opponents like Shailer Mathews and Francis Peabody. His own position would have been clearer, however, if he had forced himself to develop it in opposition to the most rigorous version of the social gospel. Rauschenbusch not only denied the efficacy of political strategies based solely on moral suasion; he tried to revive elements of theological orthodoxy that liberals, he thought, had prematurely surrendered. He "took pleasure," he wrote somewhat provocatively in *A Theology for the Social Gospel,* in defending such seemingly unprogressive doctrines as original sin. He may not have succeeded in restoring the doctrine of original sin in all its "reality and nipping force," as he intended, but his attempt to combine political radicalism with theological conservatism nevertheless anticipated Niebuhr's, and Niebuhr should have confronted it. But even on the occasion of the 1934 Rauschenbusch lectures in Rochester—the lectures later published as *An Interpretation of Christian Ethics*—Niebuhr continued to avoid such a reckoning. His introductory explanation that these "lectures did not offer as large an opportunity as might be desirable to come to grips with the dominant note in Rauschenbusch's theology" was disingenuous. What better opportunity could he have asked for? Perhaps it was his predecessor's ghost, hovering over the precincts of the Colgate-Rochester Divinity School, that wrung from Niebuhr the uncharacteristic concession that the preachers of the social gospel were "usually realistic enough to know that justice in the social order can only be achieved by political means, including the coercion of groups which refuse to accept a common social standard." But if that was the case, why did he spend so much time attacking the social gospel?

concede this point without making the larger concession that an "uneasy balance of power" was no more satisfactory than utopian efforts to eliminate conflict altogether. Liberals took enough Christian realism from Niebuhr to counter the charge of sentimentality but not enough to make them see why a politics of compromise, unredeemed by a "spiritual discipline against resentment," led to a dead end. Bennett foresaw that Niebuhr's impact on American liberalism would be less drastic than some people feared. Liberals needed to cultivate a "more realistic view of human nature," according to Bennett, without falling back "uncritically upon traditional modes of thought." Niebuhr's "contribution" lay in his ability to provide theological realism without pessimism and political retreat. "Through [Niebuhr] more effectively than through any one else the European criticism of liberalism is being mediated to American Christianity, and the dose is mild enough to be taken without too much risk of complications."

Niebuhr's analysis of the "endless cycle of social conflict" challenged the whole ideology of progress, the most dubious legacy of the social gospel; but his failure to press the point allowed liberals to disown an excessively optimistic view of human nature without giving up their belief in progressive moral improvement. "Those who put aside the hope of progress," Bennett said, "are just as wrong as those who believe in inevitable progress." The abolition of slavery, torture, dueling, human sacrifice, religious persecution, and child labor showed "how much real progress there has been in the public conscience." Shailer Mathews agreed that public opinion, thanks to the "educational influence of the Christian group," had achieved important advances—for example, a "more intelligent conception of punishment" that brought with it the understanding that "God is more than a sovereign, and his relations with the universe are not those of a seventeenth-century king." The "most thoroughgoing realist," declared F. Ernest Johnson, was the "most authentic herald of a new day." According to Chester Carlton McCown, "present disillusionment cannot destroy the facts of social evolution." "Progress has been and will be made," McCown maintained, after reviewing the case against it. "Electric light and power, the telegraph, the telephone, and the radio were impossible so long as men knew only the thunderbolt in the hands of Jupiter." Progress could no longer be attributed to a friendly providence, but the collapse of that belief forced humanity to depend on its own resources. Improvements in "economics, ethics, and religion" would catch up with technological improvements as soon as men learned "to discard the superstitions and dogmatisms of the past and give themselves without reserve to the study of the facts of history, psychology, and society." The historical record showed that the "human race moves slowly onward and upward," and a "black fog of pessimism" was no more defensible than "rosy clouds of optimism."

Liberal Realism after Niebuhr: The Critique of Tribalism

· ■ ·

By directing so much of his attention to the "utopianism" of the social gospel, leaving its belief in progress largely uncriticized, Niebuhr made things unnecessarily easy for his opponents and enabled his followers to ignore the deeper implications of his work. In the late thirties and forties, his polemic against "sentimentality" became increasingly one-sided. He gave so much attention to the first of the interlocking propositions announced in *Moral Man and Immoral Society*—the impossibility of politics without coercion—that he effectively authorized his followers to overlook the second, that "coercion is impossible without the creation of social injustice." Thus Arthur Schlesinger, Jr., invoked Niebuhr on behalf of his own distinction between "utopian" liberalism and "pragmatic" liberalism. In *The Vital Center* (1948), Schlesinger argued that Niebuhr's theology exposed the former's "soft and shallow conception of human nature." By calling attention to the "dimension of anxiety, guilt, and corruption," Niebuhr demolished the utopian illusion that "man can be reformed by argument" and that "the good in man will be liberated by a change in economic institutions." Elsewhere, Schlesinger asserted that Niebuhr had made it impossible to believe, as Rauschenbusch had believed, that the "simple moralism of the gospels would resolve the complex issues of industrial society," that the "Kingdom of God could be realized on earth," or that the "commandment of love" was "directly applicable to social and political questions."

In the forties and fifties, "pragmatic" liberals thus came to agree that politics would always remain a contest among opposing interest groups. Political justice and stability would be achieved not by persuading those groups to observe the "commandment of love" but by confronting power with "countervailing power," as John Kenneth Galbraith put it in *American Capitalism* (1950). Neither central planning nor a return to economic competition among small producers, according to Galbraith, represented a viable strategy for industrial societies. The struggle between organized interest groups would continue, and political wisdom lay in the encouragement of counterorganization against groups that threatened to capture too much power—labor against capital, consumers against both. The same considerations applied to the international arena, as George Kennan, Walter Lippmann, and other self-proclaimed realists pointed out in the course of their attack on the kind of idealism typified by Woodrow Wilson, who wished to make the world safe for democracy by waging wars to end wars. Diplomacy had to be based on "national interest," just as domestic politics had to be based on interest groups.

By this time, Niebuhr's warning that such a politics could achieve only an "uneasy balance of power," at best, had long since been forgotten, even by Niebuhr himself. In *The Irony of American History* (1952), he ridiculed the "liberal hope of redeeming history" and commended the politics of countervailing power. Although Kennan's seemingly unqualified defense of "egoism" made him a little uneasy, he could no longer explain why it was no answer to the "sentimentalities and pretensions of yesterday." The "illusions of childlike innocency"—by this time a constant refrain in Niebuhr's political writing—presented a more inviting target for his invective. American national innocence, he maintained, prevented the nation from facing up to the responsibilities of world power and the need to oppose force with force.* He cited Hobbes on the intractability of

---

*These views made Niebuhr an effective apologist for American foreign policy in the age of "containment." In his biography of Niebuhr, Richard Fox claims that Niebuhr should not be seen as a cold warrior, but he provides plenty of evidence for a contrary interpretation. He shows, for example, that Niebuhr had little trouble overcoming his early reservations about John F. Kennedy and establishing cordial relations with the New Frontier. This evidence suggests that his initial reservations largely concerned matters of political style and that on substantive issues Niebuhr came to see eye to eye with those who identified political realism with American world domination.

self-interest. He argued that the egoism of groups originated not only in their determination to advance their economic interests but in the ethnocentrism that converted partial loyalties into absolute loyalties and thus generated utopian movements designed to achieve political "salvation."

Here was another respect in which his position became increasingly one-sided. His earlier works had considered particularism a source of constructive moral energy as well as a source of "demonic fervor." After the mid-thirties, he tended to stress its destructive aspect alone. He forgot that the trouble with the kind of liberalism represented by the social gospel was not just that it underestimated the "egoism" of groups. It also undervalued "natural sympathy," as Niebuhr called it. Liberals could not see that parochial attachments called forth an intensity of conviction unmatched by an abstract attachment to humanity as a whole. If liberalism lacked "fervor" and "fanaticism," as Niebuhr complained in 1919, it was largely because it condemned all forms of tribalism as backward and unprogressive, demanding that they give way to more and more inclusive (and necessarily attenuated) allegiances. With mounting impatience, Niebuhr criticized liberals for thinking that moral suasion and organized "intelligence" could overcome the egoism of groups. But he said too little about the underlying assumption that intensively focused loyalties were unambiguously undesirable.

Political realism thus came to be identified with a grudging acknowledgment of the tenacity of particularism, coupled with the hope that secularization would at least weaken its crusading fervor, if not eliminate it altogether. In the thirties, Niebuhr had cited Strachey's forecast of the coming "world synthesis" as an example of the modern illusion that reason would eventually master all the irrational forces in nature, including the force of natural sympathy, as Niebuhr called it. By the sixties, even a Christian realist like Harvey Cox, described by one of his admirers as a "post-Barthian" thinker who had absorbed neo-orthodox insights and thereby overcome Rauschenbusch's "easy optimism," could argue that the growth of the "secular city" undermined tribal idolatries and made possible a higher form of religious life.* The disenchantment of the

---

*Critics of *The Secular City* argued that Cox had merely restated Rauschenbusch's position, with all the usual objections to which it was open. Neither side in the heated

world, according to Cox, delivered mankind from "dependence on the fates" and "expelled the demons from nature and politics." Tribalism took root in fear and superstition, which would inevitably diminish as man became master of his destiny. *The Secular City* (1965) celebrated society's evolution from tribe to town to city, the progress from the "fishbowl of town life" and all the "cloying bondages of pre-urban society" to urban anonymity, with the new forms of "creativity" it made possible. For the first time, man depended entirely on himself. His "adolescent illusions" shattered, he had "come of age." Remnants of idolatry and superstition remained, to be sure. Thus communism, a powerful force for secularization and progress, was also an "ecstatic sectarian cult complete with saints and a beatific vision." Its "messianic utopianism" suggested the presence of "stubborn deposits of town and tribal pasts." The general trend of history, however, supported the hope that man would outgrow "juvenile" habits of mind. "Dependency, awe, and religiousness"—the "tribal residues" that led men and women to give unconditional allegiance to partial truths—would eventually be "exorcised" by man's growing "mastery over the world." Once people understood that man himself was the "creator of meaning," they would come to acknowledge the cultural relativity of values and give unconditional allegiance to God alone.

Cox's thesis—secularization as the path to true faith—did not lack ingenuity; but it ignored the possibility that ultimate loyalty to the creator of being has to be grounded in loyalty to families and friends, to a particular piece of earth, and to a particular craft or calling. Man's collective mastery of nature, moreover—even if we could ignore the mounting evidence that this too is largely an illusion—can hardly be expected to confer a

---

debate about *The Secular City* questioned the standard caricature of Rauschenbusch himself, formerly exempted from the harsher judgments against the social gospel but now lumped together with Shailer Mathews, Francis Peabody, and the rest as an incurable dreamer. Neither side stopped to consider the difference between Rauschenbusch's belief in progress, which, however exaggerated or misguided, at least measured progress against an absolute ethical ideal, and the more familiar version of progressive ideology that measured it only against the follies and superstitions of the tribal past.

sense of confidence and well-being when it coexists with centralizing forces that have deprived individuals of any mastery over the concrete, immediate conditions of their existence. The collective control allegedly conferred by science is an abstraction that has little resonance in everyday life. Scientific technology has made life more secure in many ways, but its destructive side, most dramatically revealed by the development of nuclear weapons, adds to the feeling of insecurity that derives from the individual's diminishing control over his immediate surroundings. The "shallowness and lostness of modern man" cannot be dismissed as a nightmare dreamed up by intellectuals, as Cox put it, in an "orgy of ritual self-laceration." The structure of modern experience gives little encouragement to the belief that we live in a benign universe. It gives far more encouragement to a sense of helplessness, victimization, cynicism, and despair; and even the myth of progress, which for a long time provided a substitute for religious faith, has now lost much of its plausibility. For millions of people, the expectation of a better world—even if it is only the expectation of a greater supply of material possessions—is no longer experienced as a daily reality.

Martin Luther King's Encounter with Niebuhr

= · ■ · =

Social theories derived from the Enlightenment, which assume that scientific mastery over nature ought to "exorcise" fear and awe and thus to make people feel more secure, cannot explain why so many of them feel more insecure than ever and find it tempting, therefore, to think of themselves as helpless victims of circumstances. Nor can such theories explain why the most effective resistance to the prevailing sense of helplessness, in recent years, has come from the very people having the best reason of all to identify themselves as victims, namely the black people of the South, oppressed first by slavery and then by peonage, political disfranchisement, and a vicious system of racial segregation. Culturally backward by Cox's enlightened standards, Southern blacks lived in a culture full of "tribal residues"; yet they showed more confidence in the goodness of things—in the "existence of some creative force that works for universal wholeness," in the words of Martin Luther King, Jr.—than those who enjoyed fuller access to the fruits of scientific enlightenment. Their experience in the South gave little support to a belief in progress; yet they seemed to have unlimited supplies of hope. They had every reason to sink into cynicism and despair, to accept exploitation passively, or on the other hand to throw themselves into a politics of resentment and revenge. Yet it was in the civil rights movement, launched by Southern blacks in the 1950s, that the "spiritual discipline against resentment" flowered in its purest form. Social theories that equate moral enlightenment with cosmopolitanism and secularization cannot begin to account for these things.

In his analysis of nonviolent coercion, in *Moral Man and Immoral Society*, Niebuhr predicted, with uncanny accuracy, that the "emancipation of the Negro race probably waits upon the adequate development of this kind of social and political strategy." The world waited for "such a campaign with all the more reason and hope," he said, "because the peculiar spiritual gifts of the Negro endow him with the capacity to conduct it successfully." Niebuhr did not stop to analyze the source of those "spiritual gifts." If he had, he might have discovered additional evidence against the enlightened view that "organic unities of family, race, and nation" were "irrational idiosyncrasies" destined to be destroyed by a "more perfect rationality." The history of the civil rights movement indicates that the gifts Niebuhr admired originated in a way of life distinctive to Southern blacks. The movement's discipline against envy and resentment began to weaken when the Southern Christian Leadership Conference tried to mobilize blacks in the North, where that way of life had broken down. It was precisely the "idiosyncrasies" of racial and regional identity, expressed in a highly idiosyncratic form of the Protestant religion (however "irrational" in comparison with more liberal versions), that sustained the spiritual resources—courage, tenacity, forgiveness, and hope—on which the movement drew so heavily. When civil rights agitation moved into the Northern ghettos, it had to address a constituency that was no longer shaped and disciplined by the culture black people had made for themselves in the South. Uprooted from its native soil, the movement withered and died.

As a divinity student at Crozer Theological Seminary and later at Boston University, Martin Luther King read Niebuhr's works with great interest and might have been expected to pay special heed to his analysis of coercive nonviolence as a political strategy well suited to the needs and abilities of American Negroes. It was Niebuhr's criticism of pacifism, however—and his criticism of the social gospel in general—that caught King's attention. By the late forties and early fifties, Niebuhr was so closely identified with "neo-orthodoxy" (in spite of his rejection of the label) that it was increasingly difficult for readers to appreciate the complexity of his thought or to recall his objections to the political implications of Karl Barth's theology. His attack on pacifism, directed with increasing vehemence against Christians who opposed American involvement in the European crisis of 1939–41, had created an uproar in religious circles that drowned out his earlier advocacy of coercive nonviolence as the most effective escape from the "endless cycle of social conflict." Accordingly King, whose political sympathies lay with the social gospel, came to regard Niebuhr not as a political ally but as a formidable adversary whose grimly realistic but intellectually compelling theology made it necessary to restate the case for pacifism in a more rigorous form.

King's intellectual development retraced the recent history of Protestant theology in the United States. Raised in the fundamentalist tradition of Southern Baptism, he studied sociology at Morehouse College, where "the shackles of fundamentalism," he later wrote, "were removed." Exposure to wider currents of thought made him wonder for a time whether religion of any kind was "intellectually respectable."* He went through a "state of skepticism" until a course in the Bible convinced him that biblical "legends and myths" expressed "many profound truths" in symbolic form. At Crozer, he read Rauschenbusch, whose works "left an indelible imprint," providing a "theological basis" for his social concerns. During his senior year at Crozer, a reading of Niebuhr caused him to reconsider his position once again. "The prophetic and realistic elements in Niebuhr's passionate style and profound thought were appealing to me," he recalled, "and I became so enamored of his social ethics that I almost fell

---

*He began to wonder, that is, whether it could stand up in the face of the most rigorous achievements of the modern critical intellect. But he also "revolted against the emotionalism of Negro religion, the shouting and the stomping." "I didn't understand it," he said, "and it embarrassed me."

into the trap of accepting uncritically everything he wrote." Niebuhr's "critique of pacifism," King later wrote, left him at first in a "state of confusion." Later he decided that Niebuhr had misunderstood pacifism as "nonresistance to evil": but he never repudiated Niebuhr's insights into the "illusions of a superficial optimism concerning human nature and the dangers of a false idealism." He still believed in "man's potential for good," but Niebuhr made him "realize his potential for evil as well." Many pacifists, he decided, took too kindly a view of human nature.

> All too many had an unwarranted optimism concerning man and leaned unconsciously toward self-righteousness. It was my revolt against these attitudes under the influence of Niebuhr that accounts for the fact that in spite of my strong leaning toward pacifism, I never joined a pacifist organization. After reading Niebuhr, I tried to arrive at a realistic pacifism. In other words, I came to see the pacifist position not as sinless but as the lesser evil in the circumstances. I felt then, and I feel now, that the pacifist would have a greater appeal if he did not claim to be free from the moral dilemmas that the Christian nonpacifist confronts.

At Boston University, where he completed his preparation for the ministry with a doctorate in divinity, King encountered a post-Niebuhrian version of liberal theology in the "personalism" taught by Edgar S. Brightman and L. Harold DeWolf. He came to the conclusion that Niebuhr had "overemphasized the corruption of human nature." Brightman, DeWolf, George W. Davis of Crozer, and other teachers deplored the neo-orthodox "revolt against reason," as DeWolf called it, and stressed the power of Christian love or *agape*, which later came to play an important part in King's theory of nonviolence. Sounding a little like John Bennett, King later explained that his studies in Boston enabled him to put Niebuhr's work in perspective. "Niebuhr's great contribution to contemporary theology is that he has refuted the false optimism characteristic of a great segment of Protestant liberalism, without falling into the anti-rationalism of the continental theologian Karl Barth." The Boston personalists enabled King, in effect, to reconcile Niebuhr and Rauschenbusch. He came to reject the "pessimism" he found in Niebuhr, but he never ceased to believe in the reality of sin. In a student paper, he objected to the "perilous" liberal doctrine that sin is merely a "lag of nature," to be "progressively eliminated as man climbs the evolutionary ladder." Niebuhr's theology, he noted in another essay written when he was a doctoral student, furnished a "persistent reminder of the reality of sin on every level of man's existence." His own experience with a "vicious race problem" in the South, he added, made it "very difficult . . . to believe in the essential goodness of man."

The Christian injunction to love your enemy did not imply such a belief, as King understood it. The enemy deserved to be loved not because he was good but because he was the object of God's love, like all sinners. The brotherhood of man rested on common weakness and frailty. Pacifism, for King, dictated a constant struggle against the self-righteousness that so often tempted its practitioners. As Niebuhr had shown, man was a "being in need of continuous repentance," and pacifists were not exempt from this generalization. They too needed to cultivate the "habit of perpetual repentance," which "preserves us from the sin of self-righteousness."

Hope without Optimism

· ■ ·

King's student essays at Crozer and Boston University, as quoted in John Ansbro's study of his intellectual development, show a depth and seriousness beyond his years. He did not exaggerate when he later referred to his "fondness for scholarship." After completing his doctorate, he weighed several teaching offers before deciding to return to the South as a minister. His teachers pronounced him a "scholar's scholar," capable of "creative and prominent" work in theology or the history of religion.

One measure of his intellectual independence and maturity was his unwillingness, notwithstanding his efforts to reconcile liberal theology with Christian realism, to accept the extravagant theories of progress advanced by his teachers. According to Brightman, personalism entailed an "affirmation of the possibility of infinite progress." Man's capacity for goodness made it impossible to set "any limit" to the "inexhaustible possibilities of progress." Davis cited the decline of patriarchy, the abolition of slavery, the growing subordination of property rights to human rights, the abolition of child labor, the substitution of medical treatment for persecution of the mentally ill, the protection of the elderly under Social Security, and the growing respect for human personality, in short, as "signposts of true progress." God's "great plan for this world" aimed at universal brotherhood, in which "every man recognizes the dignity and worth of all human personality." When Davis spoke of the "nemesis of all dictatorships," he meant that dictators fell "by the wayside" because they ignored the "directional signs of history," which pointed to a "world where all men will live together as brothers." King invoked the "goddess of Nemesis," on the other hand, not to support a theory of progress but to reaffirm the ancient intuition that "something in the very structure of the cosmos . . . will ultimately bring about the fulfillment and the triumph of that which is right." He knew better than to historicize the concept of nemesis. He traced the conviction of fundamental justice in the order of being to something "deep down within," whereas Davis associated it with the "lessons of history."

Near the end of his life, King told his old Montgomery congregation that he was no longer an optimist, although he still had hope. The distinction between optimism and hope was implicit in many of his earlier statements as well. He had seen too much suffering to embrace the dogma of progress, even though he was always careful to explain that he objected only to theories of "automatic" or "inevitable" progress and to "false," "superficial" optimism. This was standard liberal rhetoric in the post-Niebuhrian age, and Boston University (together with his own political convictions) made King a post-Niebuhrian liberal. But liberalism was superimposed, in his case, on a deeper awareness of life's tragic dimension, rooted in the Baptist fundamentalism of his childhood and therefore antecedent to and not dependent on exposure to "neo-orthodoxy." "The most important source for King's thought," writes James Cone, "was unquestionably the black church tradition from which his faith was derived and to which he returned for strength and courage." He himself attributed his unshakable belief in a "basically friendly" universe to his "childhood experiences."* But his sense of "cosmic companionship" co-

---

*These experiences, it should be noted, included not only the suffering and humiliation inflicted by membership in a persecuted racial minority, together with exposure to a religious tradition that insisted on the redemptive meaning of suffering, but a

existed with a painful awareness of evil, and this too derived, surely, from the black church and more generally from the sufferings of black people in the South. "We are gravely mistaken," he said in 1967, "to think that religion protects us from the pain and agony of mortal existence. Life is not a euphoria of unalloyed comfort and untroubled ease. . . . To be a Christian one must take up his cross."

Niebuhrian realism and the distinctive brand of fundamentalism preached in the black churches of the South thus tempered King's liberalism. By his time, liberalism was the unchallenged lingua franca of American public life, and King had to speak it if he expected to address a national audience. But he also spoke the language of his own people, which incorporated their experience of hardship and exploitation yet affirmed the rightness of a world full of unmerited hardship. Alone among the political leaders of his day, he found it possible to address diverse audiences at the same time, from the simplest to the most sophisticated. When the need arose, he could speak the language of liberal optimism, severely qualified by Niebuhrian realism; but he also knew how to explain the deeper sources of hope to people who had every reason to resign themselves to hopelessness. He became a liberal hero—the last liberal hero?—without pulling up his roots. If his career constantly invites comparison with that of Lincoln, whom he admired, it is not only because both men found themselves caught up in the central American tragedy of Negro slavery and took much of the moral burden of slavery onto their own

---

happy childhood in the home of one of Atlanta's leading ministers and a pillar in the black community. King's inheritance included both suffering and security, as is evidenced by two contrasting formulations of his childhood memories. "Although I came from a home of economic security and relative comfort," he wrote in *Stride toward Freedom* (1958), "I could never get out of my mind the economic insecurity of many of my playmates and the tragic poverty of those living around me." In one of the sermons collected in *Strength to Love* (1963), he gave quite a different account of his early years: "The first twenty-four years of my life were years packed with fulfillment. I had no basic problems or burdens. Because of concerned and loving parents who provided for my every need, I sallied through high school, college, theological school, and graduate school without interruption. It was not until I became a part of the leadership of the Montgomery bus protest that I was actually confronted with the trials of life." Neither of these accounts can be ignored in accounting for King's strength of character.

shoulders but because both mastered the official language of American politics without losing touch with a popular religious tradition whose mixture of hope and fatalism was quite alien to liberalism. This made it possible for them to speak to ordinary people without condescension or false humility and to the learned without a self-important display of their own learning. Far more convincingly than most leaders, they could claim to speak for the whole nation, even though both spent their public lives in the defense of principles that proved enormously divisive.

Indigenous Origins
of the Civil Rights Movement

Like Lincoln, King urged his followers to refuse any compromise with injustice but to combine militancy with moral forbearance and forgiveness. Having grown up under an intolerably oppressive system of race relations, he understood the equally dangerous temptations of acquiescence and revenge. When he first experienced the full impact of segregation, as a boy, he found himself "determined to hate every white person," and "this feeling continued to grow," he later said, even though his parents told him that he "should not hate the white man, but that it was [his] duty, as a Christian, to love him." The only way to overcome hatred of your enemy, however, was to stand up to him: such was the first principle of militant nonviolence, as King came to understand it as an adult. Black people had to overcome their deep feelings of inferiority, to confront their oppressors as equals, and to challenge segregation head on. They could no longer be content, like Daddy King, simply to stake out a subordinate position of relative security in a permanently segregated society. But they had to declare war on segregation—here was the second principle underlying King's position, even more difficult to grasp than the first, let alone put into practice—without appealing to their history of victimization in order to claim a position of moral superiority. That King should have come to see that racial hatred feeds off self-righteousness and acquiescence alike testified to his capacity for spiritual growth. What is even more remarkable is that he was able to implant this understanding in the heart of the civil rights movement and to hold the movement to its difficult course through ten years of frightful tribulations.

Inspired leadership alone, of course, does not explain the movement's notable combination of militancy and moral self-restraint. Its triumphs rested on the more humble achievements of people like King's father, who had managed, over the years, to build a vigorous black community in Southern towns and cities, under the most unpromising conditions. The core of that community was the church, and the civil rights movement was "strong," as Bayard Rustin pointed out, because it was "built upon the most stable institution of the southern Negro community—the Church." The church furnished institutional as well as moral support. In Montgomery, Birmingham, and Selma, it was the organizational structure of the church, as much as its vision of the promised land, that sustained the movement. The clergy provided indigenous leadership, and the churches served both as channels of communication and as sources of funds. During the boycott of segregated buses in Montgomery, the churches raised most of the money that sustained a car pool for twelve months. The success of the boycott also depended, initially at least, on the willingness of black cab companies to charge passengers the standard bus fare—a reminder that the black community in the South had other institutional resources besides the church. It had stable families; businesses, newspapers, radio stations, and colleges; and enough buying power, in some localities, to make boycotts an effective economic weapon. "The Negro has enough buying power in Birmingham," King noted, "to make the difference between profit and loss in a business." He attributed the failure of his campaign in Albany, Georgia, partly to the community's lack of economic leverage.

The movement achieved its greatest success wherever it could build on a solid foundation of indigenous institutions and on the middle-class ethic of thrift and responsibility that made them work. Recognizing the importance of an institutional infrastructure in the struggle to achieve dignity and independence, King urged the black community to organize cooperative credit unions, finance companies, and grocery stores. Boycotts of segregated businesses, he pointed out, not only undermined segregation but encouraged Negro enterprise, bringing "economic self-help and autonomy" to the "local community." He preached the dignity of labor and the need to achieve "painstaking excellence" in the performance even of the humblest tasks. He reminded his followers that too many black people lived beyond their means, spent their money on "frivolities," failed to maintain high standards of personal cleanliness, drank to excess, and made themselves objectionable by "loud and boisterous" behavior. "We must not let the fact that we are the victims of injustice lull us into abrogating responsibility for our own lives."* If he had been accused of upholding petty-bourgeois values, King would probably have taken the accusation as a compliment. He did not hesitate to condemn rock and roll as "totally incompatible" with gospel music, on the grounds that it "often plunges men's minds into degrading and immoral depths." Andrew Young did not misrepresent the civil rights movement when he described it, "up until 1965 anyway," as "really a middle-class movement," with "middle-class aspirations" and a "middle-class membership." "Even though a lot of poor people went to jail," Young said, ". . . it was still essentially a middle-class operation."

The movement drew its strength not only from the lower-middle-class culture of Southern blacks but also from the regional culture of the South itself, to which it bore a complex and ambivalent relationship. Since the dominant view of the Southern way of life included a determination to keep the South a "white man's country," the movement might have been expected to swear eternal enmity to everything Southern. Instead it was informed by an understanding that the history of Southern blacks was intricately intertwined with that of their oppressors. Explaining his decision to return to the South after completing his studies in Boston, King spoke not only of a "moral obligation" but of the positive attractions of the land of his youth. "The South, after all, was our home. Despite its shortcomings we loved it as home and had a real desire to do something about the problems that we had felt so keenly as youngsters." In his

---

*According to David Garrow, Stanley Levison urged King to eliminate this discussion of self-help from the manuscript of *Stride Toward Freedom*, his autobiographical account of the Montgomery bus boycott. "The section on Negro self-improvement is undesirable," Levison said. ". . . The goal should be to activate, and organize people toward the main objective rather than appeal for change of character separated from the pursuit of social goals." The burden of Levison's advice, over the years, was consistently to urge King toward a social democratic position.

famous speech at the Lincoln Memorial in 1963, he declared his intention to "return to the South" with his "dream" of deliverance and racial brotherhood. Among the considerations that led to his decision to involve himself in the strike of garbage workers in Memphis, where he met his death in 1968, the one that weighed most heavily, in all likelihood, was the plea of civil rights workers there that King belonged in the South and that Southern blacks still believed in nonviolence. He always spoke of himself as a Southerner. In his "Letter from Birmingham Jail," he referred to "our beloved Southland." He honored the best in the Southern heritage and insisted that "we Southerners, Negro and white, must no longer permit our nation and our heritage to be dishonored before the world." The diehard segregationists, he claimed, did not represent the real South. "One day," he said in the Birmingham letter, "the South will recognize its real heroes"—the "disinherited children of God" who were "standing up for what was best in the American dream."

By addressing their oppressors not only as fellow sinners but also as fellow Southerners, King and his followers exposed the moral claims of the white supremacist regime in the South to the most damaging scrutiny; and the appeal to a common regional past was probably just as important, in the eventual victory over segregation, as the appeal to "profound and ultimate unities," in Niebuhr's phrase. King always believed, even in the face of what sometimes must have seemed overwhelming evidence to the contrary, that "there are great resources of goodwill in the Southern white man that we must somehow tap." When Lyndon Johnson became president, it was important to King to point out that Johnson was a "fellow Southerner" who was "concerned about civil rights." Sympathetic Southern whites sensed that King spoke not only for black people but for the soul of the entire South. Hence the "admiration," as Lillian Smith told King, of "thousands of white Southerners" for what he was doing.

Leslie Dunbar, a white participant in the civil rights movement, attended a White House reception for civil rights activists, listened to the "Southern accents buzzing hungrily" around a plate of barbecued ribs, and found himself touched by the "fraternity of white and black that for the moment makes every Northern white man and every Northern Negro . . . an outsider." With all her sins, Dunbar wrote, "the South inspired her sons and daughters, even her suffering black ones, to love her." Many white Southerners had come to love her, however, with an uneasy conscience, and King knew how important it was to keep up an unremitting pressure on the "conscience of the community." He did not expect segregationists to give up without a struggle, but neither did he expect the struggle to accomplish anything unless it was based on a "great moral appeal." That this appeal was not lost on those to whom it was immediately addressed—conscience-stricken Southern moderates—is indicated by a minister's remark that white clergymen had become "tortured souls." Very few of them, he said, "aren't troubled and don't have admiration for King." Dunbar described civil rights activists as "strange revolutionaries," who "come as defenders of the land and its values. They come, as one prominent white Southerner once put it to me, to give us back our country." The movement's claims could be interpreted in this way only because it was able to recognize itself as the product of the culture it was seeking to change—the product, specifically, of the "characteristically theological cast of Southern thought," as Dunbar put it, with its habit of "seeing all lives as under the judgment of God and of knowing, therefore, with certainty the transience of all works of men."

The civil rights movement did not direct its moral appeal exclusively to white Southerners, of course. It depended on public opinion in the North, ultimately on federal intervention. Leaders of the movement recognized the importance of "public relations," in King's words. "Without the presence of the press," he wrote in 1961, "there might have been untold massacre in the South." "Little would have been accomplished," according to Coretta King, "without television. . . . When the majority of white Americans saw on television the brutality of segregation in action, . . . they reacted . . . with revulsion and sympathy and with demands that somehow this . . . must stop." A "dramatization to the nation of what segregation was like," in the words of Wyatt Walker, required the presence of national news media. According to Andrew Young, "we were consciously using the mass media to try to get across to the nation" the evils of racial discrimination. When the young radicals in SNCC reproached the Southern Christian Leadership Conference for its preoccupation with national media coverage, they were reminded that the movement could not succeed without it. When they complained that the SCLC never stayed in one place long enough to build up a permanent local organization and thus left behind a "string of embittered cities," Hosea

Williams replied, "We can bring the press in with us and they can't."

But the "dramatization" of injustice proved moving and therefore politically effective only because the SCLC managed to school its members in the discipline of nonviolence, because it could convincingly claim to speak for the best in the regional heritage of the South, and because, finally, it also stood for "what is best in the American dream." King did not disclaim the African elements in black culture, but he ruled out a "mass return to Africa," advocated by some separatists, as an escapist solution of the race problem. "We are American citizens," he argued, "and we deserve our rights in this nation." "Abused and scorned though we may be," he declared in the Birmingham letter, "our destiny is tied up with America's destiny." Even in his harshest indictments of the United States, he invoked the Constitution and the Bible, embodiments of its shared political and religious traditions. "Our beloved nation," he said in 1967, when he finally began to show signs of running out of patience, "is still a racist country"; but it was beloved nevertheless.

The Collapse of the Civil Rights Movement in the North

· ■ ·

After ten years of successful agitation in the South, culminating in the passage of the Civil Rights Act of 1964 and the Voting Rights Act of 1965, the movement rapidly disintegrated when it ventured into the North. The usual explanation of its failure in the North—that the struggle against legal discrimination in the South raised "clear and simple moral issues," in President Johnson's words, whereas de facto discrimination could not so easily be dramatized as a contest between good and evil—misses a good deal of the truth. No doubt the difficulty of staging the kind of confrontations that stirred up public opinion against Bull Connor, Sheriff Clark, and other symbols of Southern racism diminished the chances of attracting favorable attention from the media. The plight of the Northern ghettos, moreover, did not lend itself to simple legislative solutions. But a more important difference between the North and the South lay in the demoralized, impoverished condition of the black community in cities like Chicago, which could not support a movement that relied so heavily on a self-sustaining network of black institutions, a solidly rooted petty-bourgeois culture, and the pervasive influence of the church. The movement sought to give black people a new dignity by making them active participants in the struggle against injustice, but it could not succeed unless the materials of self-respect had already been to some extent achieved.

As he toured the Northern ghettos after the first wave of riots, in 1965, King was staggered by the desperate poverty he found, but he was even more discouraged by the absence of institutions that would sustain the black community's morale. He did not join in the criticism directed by black militants and newly radicalized white liberals against the Moynihan Report, accused of shifting attention from poverty to the collapse of the family and thus of "blaming the victim" for the sins of white oppression. "The shattering blows on the Negro family," he argued, "have made it fragile, deprived and often psychopathic. . . . Nothing is so much needed as a secure family life for a people to pull themselves out of poverty and backwardness." Institutional breakdown was a cause as well as a consequence of poverty, according to King. Whereas some observers tried to picture the ghetto as a workable subculture, he took the position that "jammed up, neurotic, psychotic Negroes" in Northern cities were "forced into violent ways of life." These conditions led him to demand the abolition of the ghetto through open-housing ordinances and massive federal action against poverty. His advocacy of such programs constituted a tacit admission that the North lacked the stable black communities on which the civil rights movement rested in the South. Hosea Williams made the same point more openly. "I have never seen such hopelessness," he said after a month in Chicago. "The Negroes of Chicago have a greater feeling of powerlessness than any I ever saw. They don't participate in the governmental process because they're beaten down psychologically. We're used to working with people who want to be freed." This last remark summed up the contrast between the North and the South.

Even before SCLC made its fateful decision to launch a civil rights campaign in Chicago, King faced mounting criticism from SNCC, still officially committed to nonviolence but increasingly impatient not only with King's moderation but with the cult of his charismatic leadership.

"We don't believe in leadership," said James Forman. "We think the people should lead, but SCLC thinks there should be one leader." It was only when the civil rights movement bogged down in Chicago, however, that Forman, Stokely Carmichael, and other militants successfully challenged King's preeminence in the movement, renounced nonviolence, and took up the cry of "black power." King could easily identify the moral and strategic objections to the new slogan, but he could not persuade the angry young militants to give him a hearing. They disrupted his meetings with boos and heckling, denounced him as an Uncle Tom, and cheered when former supporters like Adam Clayton Powell referred to him as "Martin Loser King." Once the scene of his activities shifted to the North, he no longer addressed a constituency that cared to hear about self-help, the dignity of labor, the importance of strong families, and the healing power of *agape*. According to black militants, honkies would listen only to gunfire and the sound of breaking glass. Faced with the boundless rage of the ghetto and the growing influence of leaders like H. Rap Brown, who urged blacks to arm themselves against a white war of extermination, King became increasingly discouraged and depressed. Toward the end of his life, he told Ralph Abernathy that "those of us who adhere to nonviolence" might have to "step aside and let the violent forces run their course."

Temperamentally incapable of stepping aside, he drove himself more relentlessly than ever. In the last two years of his life, he struggled to keep up his spirits in a sea of troubles. Black desertions from the nonviolent movement were discouraging enough, but he also had to contend with constant threats to his life, harassment from the FBI, denunciations from the Johnson administration to the effect that his stand against the Vietnam War constituted nothing less than treason, growing criticism from white moderates, and dissension within his own organization about his efforts in the North and his plans for a second march on Washington, not to mention a crushing schedule of speaking engagements designed to shore up SCLC's depleted treasury. Exhaustion and near-despair, together with the pressure from black separatists and his own increasingly gloomy assessment of the prospects for racial harmony, pushed King farther to the left. At times he joined the militants in condemning American society as irredeemably racist, even though the catchword of "white racism" had the effect of obscuring his earlier warnings that black people should not fall into the habit of blaming everything on whites. He defended nonviolence more and more narrowly on tactical grounds, suppressing the moral arguments that once made it so compelling. He promised bigger and bigger demonstrations, though he could no longer produce volunteers in large numbers or assure anybody that they would refrain from violence. In the years from 1966 to 1968, when he needed a period of rest and reflection in which to puzzle out where his movement had gone wrong and how it might recover a sense of direction, he forced himself again and again to "go for broke," to draw up plans for "massive dislocation," and to make more and more drastic demands on his own capacity for suffering and self-sacrifice. By the end of 1967, he was planning to occupy Washington until Johnson ended the war in Vietnam and launched a comprehensive attack on poverty. "This is a kind of last, desperate demand for the nation to respond to nonviolence," he told his aides. ". . . We've gone for broke before, but not in the way we're going this time, because if necessary I'm going to stay in jail six months—they aren't going to run me out of Washington."

His exposure to heart-rending poverty in the Northern ghetto forced King to the conclusion that the only hope for American society lay in an immediate redistribution of wealth. He was never indifferent to the importance of economic equality; but the issue presented itself with greater urgency after 1965 and made him increasingly intolerant of halfway measures. As early as 1964, King urged his followers to advance from protest to politics: "We are now facing basic social and economic problems that require political reform." Unfortunately the strategy of nonviolent protest, which had worked so well in the South, was ill-suited to a campaign against poverty in the North. In Chicago, open-housing marches into white neighborhoods had no discernible connection with the political goals King now espoused; their only result was to arouse fierce hostility in the neighborhoods thus invaded. The black militants in Chicago, notwithstanding their infatuation with "guerilla warfare," had a better understanding of the situation than King. They criticized open housing as a delusion. Even if it was desirable to break up the black ghetto by encouraging migration to white neighborhoods, they pointed out, most black people could not afford the price of housing there. The migration of middle-class blacks would only drive out whites in any case, re-creating the conditions from which they hoped to escape. The only thing accomplished by open-housing marches was to encourage "many people who perhaps would at least have been maybe neutral . . . to become anti-Negro."

Not only did King fail to admit the justice in such arguments, he did not seem to understand the source of white hostility to his Chicago campaign. He did not distinguish between die-hard segregationists in the South and hard-pressed working-class and lower-middle-class communities in the North, where the open-housing marches met with a reception more "hostile and hateful," he said, than anything he had seen in Selma or Birmingham. Instead of analyzing the implications of this contrast, he fell more and more into the accusatory posture of moral indignation, charging whites with "psychological and spiritual genocide." From his ill-conceived campaign for open housing in Chicago, he drew only the lame conclusion that "we had not evaluated the depth of resistance in the white community." If he had forced himself to understand the content of this resistance, he might have seen that blacks could not hope to achieve their objectives by demanding the dissolution of white communities whose only crime, as far as anyone could see, was their sense of ethnic solidarity.

From Civil Rights to Social Democracy

· ■ ·

In the South, the civil rights movement built on the integrity of the black community, vigorously opposing the "glib suggestion of those who would urge [Southern blacks] to migrate en masse to other sections of the country," as King put it. "The Negro's problem," he said firmly, "will not be solved by running away." In the campaign for open housing and educational integration in the North, however, King seemed to advise flight from the ghetto as the only hope. A better course, one might have imagined—one more consistent with the movement's original emphasis and aims—would have been to try to transform the ghetto into a real community. The civil rights movement in the North might have identified itself with the tentative, ultimately abortive movement for "community control," which some black radicals were beginning to see as the most promising approach not only to the race problem but to the centralization and bureaucratization of American life. The radicals' critique of open housing foreshadowed a line of analysis that led, shortly after King's death, to various attempts to institutionalize local control of the school system and to shape the schools more closely to the needs of the black community. Nothing came of these experiments in decentralization, notably the one in the Ocean Hill–Brownsville section of Brooklyn. The idea behind them, however, made a good deal of sense. It made more sense, that is, to strengthen the black community than to attempt its dispersal by integrating white neighborhoods and their schools.

Whereas King's "bill of rights for the disadvantaged" included, among other things, a "social-work apparatus on a large scale," Leslie Dunbar asked whether the black community needed "another white social worker as much as it needs, as a small business loan, the money his or her education would cost." "Since community strength is so necessary," he argued, the civil rights movement should be willing to ask "unpleasant questions" of this kind. Should the government build public housing projects in black neighborhoods, "knowing in advance that [they] would [weaken] community cohesiveness"? Should it bus children away from black neighborhoods, "thus weakening the influence of the school as a community center"? "Should there be any white policemen in Negro neighborhoods? (How many Italian policemen ever patrolled the Irish beats?)" This line of speculation seemed to lead to the conclusion that the advantages of community cohesion (necessarily underwritten, of course, by large amounts of federal aid) outweighed the dangers of racial separation that haunted liberals.

King himself conceded, in the last weeks of his life, that it might be necessary to accept "temporary separation as a way-station to a truly integrated society." Reflection on his Chicago campaign, he said, had convinced him that "we must seek to enrich the ghetto immediately in the sense of improving the housing conditions, improving the schools in the ghetto, improving the economic conditions." His attempt to reconcile this approach with a continuing effort to "disperse the ghetto" was not very convincing, but his second thoughts about the possibility of working "on two levels" at least suggested that he had not been altogether inattentive to the implications of the movement's failure in Chicago. Not only his distaste for anything smacking of separatism but a growing interest in social democracy, however, prevented him from developing his ideas more fully in the direction of community control. "Something is wrong with the economic system of our nation," he told the SCLC staff in 1967. ". . . Something is wrong with capitalism. . . . There must be a better distribution of wealth, and maybe America must move toward a democratic socialism." Early in 1968, he told his staff "to turn off the tape recorder" and proceeded to talk "about what he called democratic socialism," as one of his aides recalled. "He didn't believe that capitalism could meet the needs of poor people, and that we might need to look at what was a kind of socialism, but a democratic form of socialism."* More and more deeply convinced that "the main issue is economic," he began to advocate a guaranteed annual income and to argue that "our emphasis should shift from exclusive attention to putting people to work [to] enabling people to consume." "If we directly abolish poverty by guaranteeing an income," he declared in 1967, "we will have dealt with our primary problem." He did not explain how a guaranteed income would restore self-respect or the pride of workmanship, on which he had once placed so much emphasis.

King's growing commitment to social democracy tended to make poverty, not slavery, the central issue, as G. D. H. Cole would have put it. It made distribution rather than participation the test of democracy. In his speech accepting the Nobel Peace Prize in 1965, King had taken a different view of things. The most important feature of the civil rights movement, he said, was the "direct participation of masses in protest, rather than reliance on indirect methods which frequently do not involve masses in action at all." By 1968, however, he was advocating policies that required comprehensive federal intervention. The original goals of the movement,

---

*The Marxist historian C. L. R. James recalled a conversation with King at this time: "[He] wanted me to know that he understood and accepted . . . the ideas that I was putting forward—ideas which were fundamentally Marxist-Leninist." James described King as a man "whose ideas were as advanced as any of us on the Left, but who, as he actually said to me, could not say such things from the pulpit." This report confirms the impression that King was more and more inclined to regard socialism as the only hope for the poor. The statement that he could no longer speak his mind to his own constituents indicates, however—if James's slightly melodramatic and conspiratorial account can be trusted—that his capacity for leadership was now exhausted.

he decided, were too limited. They amounted to little more than enforcement of rights already guaranteed, in theory at least, by the Fourteenth Amendment. Now it was necessary to address the underlying causes of inequality, not just legal discrimination. But the real importance of the civil rights movement, as King should have been the first to remember, lay not in its admittedly conventional goals but in its ability to overcome black people's "corroding sense of inferiority," in his own words. The act of standing up for their rights was far more important than any of the tangible gains his people had won—not that these were insignificant either. This is why King could tell himself that victory had already been achieved at the very outset of the Montgomery bus boycott, long before the movement's demands—themselves so modest that they fell short even of the standards set by the NAACP—had been approved.* After a mass meeting had agreed to launch the boycott, "I said to myself, the victory is already won, ... a victory infinitely larger than the bus situation. The real victory was in the mass meeting, where thousands of black people stood revealed with a new sense of dignity and destiny." As he put it in his 1958 account of the bus boycott, "a once fear-ridden people had been transformed."

As his attention shifted from participation to poverty, King redefined his constituency as an interracial coalition of blacks, Puerto Ricans, Mexi-

---

*The main issue in Montgomery, incredible as it may seem, was simply whether blacks had to stand while there were seats left unoccupied by whites. Under a Montgomery city ordinance, no black person could sit parallel with a white. When all the front rows were filled, black people sitting in the next row were required to vacate all four seats if a single white passenger boarded the bus. They were required to stand even if three of the four seats in that row remained vacant. This was the situation when Rosa Parks, unlike the other three black passengers in her row, refused to stand and went to jail instead. The Montgomery Improvement Association—forerunner of the SCLC—proposed a change in the city law that would "make it possible for Negroes to sit from back toward front, and whites from front toward back until all seats are taken." Such a plan was already in effect in Mobile and other Alabama cities. "We are not asking for an end to segregation," King told reporters in December 1955. "That's a question for the legislature and the courts. We feel that we have a plan within the [existing segregation] law. All we are seeking is justice and fair treatment in riding the buses. We don't like the idea of Negroes having to stand when there are vacant seats."

can-Americans, and American Indians—an early version of Jesse Jackson's rainbow coalition. The poor people's march on Washington, he declared, would consist of people with "nothing to lose." In the early days of the civil rights movement, King had resisted the temptation to define black people simply as victims of white oppression. Instead he tried to encourage initiative, self-reliance, and responsibility. He understood that people who thought of themselves as victims either remained helplessly passive or became vindictive and self-righteous. His later attempt to organize a national alliance of "disadvantaged" groups, however, forced him to rely on just this kind of morally flawed appeal, since a common feeling of marginality was the only thing that could hold such an alliance together. As victims of racism, exploitation, and neglect, King now argued, outcast groups had a right to "compensatory treatment." In his earlier account of direct action in Montgomery, he tried to assure whites that "the Negro, once a helpless child, has now grown up politically, culturally, and economically" and that "all he seeks is justice, for both himself and the white man." The Negro, King said, "understands and forgives and is ready to forget the past." Ten years later, he went out of his way to remind people that blacks had suffered a special history of discrimination that set them apart from white immigrants. "When white immigrants arrived in the United States in the late nineteenth century, a beneficent government gave them free land and credit to build a useful, independent life." Blacks, on the other hand, experienced nothing but prejudice and persecution. Their history of oppression, as King explored its implications, appeared to justify a double standard of political morality. Black rioters, he admitted, had engaged in "incontestable and deplorable" crimes, but those crimes were "derivative," "born of the greater crimes of the white society." Moreover, they were directed "against property rather than against people," implicitly demanding a more equitable distribution of wealth and thus anticipating the goals of the poor people's campaign.

In order to compete with the militants on his left and to rally support for the highly disruptive demonstrations he planned to stage in Washington, King had to falsify the history of his own movement. In retrospect, he represented it as a movement of alienated youth opposed to "middle-class values." "It was precisely when young Negroes threw off their middle-class values," he maintained in 1967, "that they made an historic social contribution" to the cause of racial justice. "When they cheerfully became jailbirds and troublemakers, when they took off their Brooks Brothers attire and put on overalls to work in the isolated rural South, they challenged and inspired white youth to emulate them." By referring to civil rights volunteers as "school dropouts," King sought to counter the sneer that his demonstrations in the South had been peopled by "pious elderly ladies." Those demonstrations, he claimed, had "totally disrupted the system," just as the poor people's march on Washington would paralyze the national government and force it to enact an "economic bill of rights."

The Politics of Resentment and Reparation

King's assassination in April 1968 destroyed any hope that his poor people's coalition would come into being; but his own associates had already raised serious objections to another march on Washington and to the strategy behind it. Marian Logan argued that disruptive demonstrations would "harden congressional resistance" and contribute to the defeat of liberal candidates in the forthcoming elections. Bayard Rustin agreed that "any effort to disrupt transportation, government buildings, etc." could "only lead to further backlash and repression." He doubted the feasibility of an interracial alliance of the poor. The labor movement, he pointed out, had repeatedly failed to organize the kind of people on whom King now pinned his hopes, and there was no reason to think a black civil rights agitator would fare any better. "There is no way for Martin Luther King to bring white poor, Puerto Rican poor, black poor, Irish poor together," Rustin said.

By February 1968, King admitted, "We're in terrible shape with this poor people's campaign. It just isn't working. People aren't responding." The civil rights movement in the North did not transform itself, as he had hoped, into a social democratic alliance, nor did it achieve any lasting gains for the black masses. Its legacy to the North was a bitterly divided Democratic party, officially committed to busing and affirmative action but faced with growing opposition to these policies in its own ranks.* The revolt against "McGovernism," which eventually led to wholesale defections and to the rise of Reagan's new right, had its origins in the events of the late sixties. The ghetto riots, the rise of black power, the collapse of nonviolent agitation for equal enforcement of the laws, and the antiwar movement—in which King came to play a leading part, against the wishes of most of his advisers—polarized the country and generated a "backlash" not only against civil rights but against liberalism in general.

---

*Note again the contrast with the South, where the civil rights movement achieved a notable improvement in race relations, in the face of determined opposition that for a long time seemed almost insurmountable. The combination of militant confrontation and moral self-discipline gave black people courage and self-respect, led many Southern whites to acknowledge the justice of their cause, forced the hand of national politicians like Kennedy and Johnson, and created a public consensus in favor of impartial law enforcement. By the summer of 1963, public opinion polls showed large majorities, according to Harvard Sitkoff, "in favor of laws to guarantee blacks voting rights, job opportunities, good housing, and desegregated schools and public accommodations." Under the weight of federal legislation, backed up by solid public support, segregation gave way, together with the system of disfranchisement that had kept blacks politically powerless ever since the 1890s. By 1970, two-thirds of Southern blacks had registered to vote. By 1980, there were 2,500 elected black officials in the South. Mississippi, the last bastion of resistance to the new order, now had more black officeholders than any other state in the Union. Even George Wallace, as Sitkoff points out, "appointed blacks to high state positions, crowned a black homecoming queen at the very university he had once sworn to deny to black students, and in 1979 sat on the podium applauding the inaugural remarks of Birmingham's first black mayor." Only sixteen years earlier, Wallace had proclaimed the slogan of the unreconstructed South: "Segregation now! Segregation tomorrow! Segregation forever!" David Lewis, who dismissed the gains of the civil rights movement as largely symbolic in his biography of King, published in 1970, recanted his earlier judgment—a "judgment without benefit of perspective"—in a postscript written in 1978. "Exemplary stories about the New South—the South of Martin King and Jimmy Carter—abound. Mine recounts a two-day visit to Orangeburg, South Carolina, in 1974, as guest lecturer at South Carolina State College, site of the 1968 deaths of three black students gunned down by local police during a campus protest. [With] its bi-racial prosperity and absence of racial friction, Orangeburg might have been Xenia, Ohio. Faculty and students are integrated; and where the three students fell, a building stands, constructed with state funds and bearing a plaque commemorating their deaths. My realization of the extraordinary changes wrought by the Civil Rights and Voting Rights Acts, even in communities where fear and violence had ruled six years before, was startling."

There was nothing King could have done to prevent any of this, but his shift from "freedom" to social democracy probably made a bad business even worse. By taking up the charge of "white racism," he antagonized working-class and lower-middle-class whites without appeasing the black militants. When he identified civil rights agitation with a revolt against "middle-class values," he lost any chance to forge a biracial coalition based on the ideals of responsibility, self-help, and the defense of threatened neighborhoods and communities. Instead of appealing to the nation's sense of justice, he now had to appeal to the mixture of pity and fear that came to be known, inappropriately (since it was activated less by conscience than by nerves), as "white liberal guilt."

To the end, King upheld nonviolence both as a tactic and as a principle (though with growing emphasis on the former). But the definition of black people primarily as victims could only encourage a politics of resentment, with or without violence. Whether blacks rioted in the streets or merely demanded compensatory treatment in the courts—and the two strategies proved quite compatible—they now claimed a privileged moral position as the victims of "four hundred years of oppression." Their history of victimization, they argued, entitled them to revenge, although they indicated a willingness to settle for reparations. For obvious reasons, liberals could agree to reparations in order to escape reprisals; but their sponsorship of busing and affirmative action carried no moral weight as gestures of "compassion." Those who supported busing and affirmative action—comfortable members of the professional and managerial classes, for the most part—did not have to live with the consequences of their actions. The burden of busing notoriously fell on ethnic neighborhoods in the cities, not on suburban liberals whose schools remained effectively segregated or on wealthy practitioners of "compassion" whose children did not attend public schools at all.

The suspicion that much of their "caring" was morally fraudulent had a damaging effect, I believe, on liberal morale. But compensatory justice had an equally damaging effect on black morale. Not only did it not solve the problem of black poverty; it did not even address the deeper problem of self-respect. If anything, affirmative action undermined self-respect by creating the impression that black people had to be judged by standards lower than the ones applied to whites. At best, compensatory programs made it possible for talented individuals to escape from the ghetto, widening the gap between the black middle class and the poor. The politics of resentment and reparation also widened the gap between liberals and the American public, which supported laws against segregation and disfranchisement but drew the line at busing and affirmative action. In the absence of a public consensus in favor of reverse discrimination, as it came to be called, liberals had to rely more and more on the courts, which proceeded to create a new category of prescriptive rights and to expand their own authority into the field of social engineering. As Leslie Dunbar pointed out in 1966, "not every valid interest is a right. . . . A right is a defense against social power, not a prescription of the kind of society there must be." Judicial decisions forbidding religious instruction in the schools or requiring the schools "to compensate for all the evils inherent in housing segregation" tended to "usurp the community's instinctive feeling of responsibility for rearing the young" and eventually brought the law itself into contempt. In their eagerness for legal remedies, liberals had forgotten that "we must . . . live as a people bound together by ties of mutual trust, not as a people armored against each other."

Dunbar's warning against excessive reliance on judge-made law has gained cogency with the passage of time. He found it curious that liberals should be the ones to applaud when the Supreme Court overruled a Colorado plan for legislative reapportionment, even though it had been approved by the electorate, on the grounds that it violated the court's interpretation of the Fourteenth Amendment. "Can this be the authentic voice of liberalism?" Dunbar asked. Such decisions encouraged the "sense of estrangement between the superstructure of an institution and its constituent body which is a fearsomely prevalent and growing feature of American social life."

The growing "separation of leadership from its primary constituency," Dunbar thought, was the most ominous development of recent years. Noting that the Protestant clergy had played an active role in the civil rights movement, he commended their courage but wondered why they had invested so little of their energy in an attempt to change the racial attitudes of their own congregations. "Instead of seeking to reform their congregations directly, the Protestant leaders have given their greater energies to going outside them, witnessing in the streets of Selma or Chicago or the cloakrooms of Congress." When this pattern became "prevalent in one social field after another," Dunbar observed, it led to "deep alienation between the power holders of a society and the masses."

Such were the fruits of "compassion." The politics of pity and fear deepened the split between the "civilized minority" and the racist majority, as liberals now thought of it. The civil rights movement, originating in a powerful challenge to self-righteousness and resentment, ended by reinforcing the worst qualities in American liberalism: a sense of superiority to the unenlightened masses, a refusal to credit opponents with honorable intentions, a growing reluctance to submit their policies to public approval. But liberals had begun to lose faith in public opinion, as we have seen, as early as the twenties. Subsequent success had never entirely removed their suspicions. On the contrary, their sense of estrangement from America continued to grow, for reasons we must now attempt to reconstruct in some detail.

10

THE POLITICS OF THE CIVILIZED
MINORITY

*Liberal Perceptions of the Public
after World War I*

Around the turn of the century, social reformers began to refer to themselves as progressives rather
than liberals. "Liberalism" was too closely associated with laissez-faire
economics to serve their purposes. Only in the closing phase of World
War I did the term come back into favor, partly because advocates of
peaceful change now found it necessary to distinguish themselves from
the Bolsheviks and their partisans, but also because wartime repression
gave new importance to the defense of civil liberties. In a polarized
world, political and cultural freedom was endangered both by revolutionary terror and by the counterrevolutionary activities of the capitalist
state.

War and revolution had generated a climate of intolerance and fanaticism, according to Harold Stearns. Neither the right nor the left hand had any faith in "rational persuasion"; they were "interested only in their own propaganda." In his postwar analysis of the "temporary collapse" of liberalism, Stearns identified liberalism with "hatred of compulsion," "respect for the individual," and "tolerance." *Liberalism in America* (1919) gave the impression that people who believed in these things now considered themselves a beleaguered minority. The war had strengthened the "violence-loving tradition" in American life and thereby weakened liberalism. Not just a set of political programs, liberalism was a "whole philosophy of life," according to Stearns—"scientific, curious, experimental." In a world full of the clamor of "political idealists, diplomats, labor leaders, prohibitionists, reformers, revolutionists," liberals remained *"au-dessus de la mêlée,"* convinced that "liberalism's best service can be performed through creating a certain tolerant temper in society at large." Liberalism was "urbane, good-natured, non-partisan, detached." It was not clear, however, that American society had much use for these qualities or that it could "get through the impending social revolution without widespread violence."

Liberalism thus reentered the political vocabulary at a time when liberalism appeared to be in retreat. "The chief distinguishing aspect of the Presidential campaign of 1920," wrote Herbert Croly as the campaign was drawing to a close, "is the eclipse of liberalism or progressivism as an effective force in American politics." "Capitalist domination" of the state had led to the replacement of "good humored toleration" by a "policy of intimidation." Nor was the danger to freedom confined to the state. The public clearly approved the government's suppression of political dissent—the Palmer raids, the Lusk committee's crusade against subversion, the deportation of foreign-born radicals, the imprisonment of Debs. The postwar reaction convinced many liberals that the American people had even less tolerance for unpopular opinions than the state. Led by demagogues like William Jennings Bryan, once a progressive hero but a contemptible figure in the eyes of postwar liberals, the people passed laws forbidding the teaching of evolution in the public schools. They clamored for "100 percent Americanism" and an end to immigration. They revived the Ku Klux Klan and used it to terrorize Jews and Catholics as well as Negroes. They demanded passage of the prohibition amendment, a measure supported by many "progressives" but universally condemned by the new breed of "liberals" as the very essence of intolerance. More than any other single issue, prohibition symbolized the ascendancy of narrow-minded bigotry and popular "puritanism," opposition to which now served as the distinguishing mark of American liberalism.

Liberals agreed that ignorance, superstition, and intolerance posed a grave threat to freedom, but they disagreed about the causes of the post-war reaction and its implications. Some of them took the position that liberals had failed to create a public consensus in favor of liberal programs and would have to redouble their efforts. Others argued, as we have seen, that the public could not be expected to listen to reason. "Public opinion" was shaped almost entirely by emotional appeals, according to this second view. If liberals hoped to win a popular following, they would either have to master the new techniques of advertising and propaganda, used so effectively by their opponents, or seek to minimize the influence of public opinion on policy, to limit popular participation to broad questions of procedure, and to see to it that policy-making was conducted exclusively by experts.

The *New Republic,* under Herbert Croly's editorship, emerged in the twenties as the principal exponent of the first of these positions. According to Croly, liberals had neglected popular education in their eagerness to win elections. Attaching themselves first to Theodore Roosevelt and then to Woodrow Wilson, they had counted on strong leaders to sponsor liberal programs and to give liberals a controlling influence in national affairs. The debacle of Wilsonian liberalism showed the futility of this strategy. Without a solid basis in public support, even liberal administrations would always subordinate liberal purposes to the domestic and international purposes of the capitalist class. By 1920, Croly had come to the conclusion that liberals should side with the labor movement as the best hope of restoring a "wholesome balance of economic and social power in the American commonwealth." Their support of labor, however, had to be tempered by a continuing commitment to the "search for a liberating knowledge of human nature and society." Since this knowledge could emerge only in the process of political discussion and experimentation, public education had to be conceived as an end in itself, not just as a means whereby liberals could hope to acquire political power. Any power liberals managed to acquire would "depend upon a vitality of opinion, upon a translation of opinions into a nearer approximation to truth, which the competition for power undermines."

Croly's point—a Niebuhrian point, though neither he nor Niebuhr recognized it as such—was not that "competition for power" should be somehow proscribed but that it would not, in itself, lead to "truth." Far from disparaging the struggle for power, Croly upheld it as the only way "a nation learns to know its own mind." To those who criticized the *New Republic* in the twenties for its failure to put forward a concrete program for social change, he replied that programs had to come from "political, social or occupational groups" seeking to advance "common interests," not from liberal intellectuals. "One of the ways in which a people exhibits moral initiative and develops its aptitude for self-government is by giving birth to projects of this kind." The "clash," "comparison," and "revision" of "group programs" provided an "indispensable and abundant source of political and social education." Conflicting programs and purposes supplied the "medium in which the customary conduct and ideas of a people are tested, adjusted, modified and transcended." Those who fought for them, however, inevitably took a partial view of things. They regarded their own purposes as "all-sufficient." Embattled groups seldom conceived of political agitation as an "experimental activity which is to be tested by its results."

The job of intellectuals was to call attention to this partiality of collective purposes (this egoism of groups, as Niebuhr would have put it) and to encourage "self-watchfulness on the part of those people whose lives are dedicated to imposing their own ways and ideas upon other people." The labor movement would become self-righteous and "destructively pugnacious" without the critical support of liberal intellectuals. Croly did not mean that intellectuals should try to mediate among contending interests or that they alone, from a position above the battle, could speak for society's common purposes. Common purposes would emerge only from the competition among rival interests. Unless that competition was disciplined by "self-watchfulness," however, ideas would become "merely rationalizations of interests or of activities." Programs were not just instruments by means of which groups sought to achieve their particular ends; they were also instruments societies employed "to make up their minds." The overriding end of political action, moreover, was to "transform political activities" into "schools" of "character, discrimination and judgment" for the "virtuous social actor." "The ultimate value to civilization of any social project such as a proposed war, a new or old party, or some radical reforming agitation depends less upon the desirability of the particular end which the project seeks to achieve than upon the quality of the individual men and women which participation in it tends to bring to the surface."

But this educative dimension of politics would never come to the surface at all, Croly argued, unless the program makers were "kept conscious of the stumblings, the retreats, the misgivings, and the mistakes as well as of the long marches and the glorious victories of their expeditionary forces." Political activists and program makers needed "disinterested chroniclers and historians of their exploits," not propagandists, high-level strategists, or ideological masterminds. In retrospect, we can see that if intellectuals had been willing to settle for this "minor but still indispensable role," the subsequent history of the American left might have been very different.

America the Unbeautiful

Croly's confidence in public opinion and "virtuous social actors" struck most liberals by this time as old-fashioned and unsophisticated. They were more impressed by Walter Lippmann's analysis of the irrationality of public opinion and by H. L. Mencken's ridicule of democracy as the reign of the "booboisie." Mencken taught liberal intellectuals to think of themselves as a "civilized minority" and to wear unpopularity as a badge of honor. A man of intelligence and taste would always find himself "in active revolt against the culture that surrounds him." Praising Sinclair Lewis, Mencken laid it down as a dogma that "the artist is . . . a public enemy; *vox populi*, to him, is the bray of an ass." The best thinking was always carried out in "conscious revolt" against the majority.

The postwar reaction made it easy for liberals to accept Mencken's low opinion of the average American. Not only liberalism but civilization itself, it seemed, had no future in America: such was the conclusion reached by most of the contributors to Harold Stearn's celebrated symposium, *Civilization in the United States* (1922). Another collaborative project, a state-by-state survey conducted by the *Nation* in the early twenties, conveyed the same impression, on the whole; even more than the Stearns collection, "These United States" revealed liberals' deep revulsion from American politics and popular culture.

In launching the series, the editors of the *Nation* expressed the hope that "variety and experiment" in the United States would prevail over the forces making for "centralization and regimentation." The picture of America that emerged from most of the articles, however, looked more like the one made familiar by Mencken and Stearns. Mencken himself contributed the piece on Maryland: "No light, no color, no sound!" Several articles were written by authors well known for savage satires of provincial life: Sinclair Lewis on Minnesota ("Scandinavians Americanize only too quickly"); Sherwood Anderson on Ohio ("Have you a city that smells worse than Akron, that is a worse junk-heap of ugliness than Youngstown, that is more smugly self-satisfied than Cleveland?"); and Theodore Dreiser on Indiana ("dogmatic religion," "political somnolence," "pharisaical restfulness in its assumed enlightenment"). At least two articles ("Michigan: The Fordizing of a Pleasant Peninsula" and "West Virginia: A Mine-Field Melodrama") were written by protégés of Mencken on the *Baltimore Sun;* another ("Arkansas: A Native Proletariat") referred to him repeatedly; and several others, including Ludwig Lewisohn's scatching piece on South Carolina ("appalling and intolerant ignorance and meanness of spirit"), were done in the Mencken manner. Evidently the editors of the *Nation* saw no contradiction between a celebration of regional diversity and a satire of local customs bound to leave the impression that the United States was populated largely by rednecks, fundamentalists, and militant adherents of the Ku Klux Klan. They conceived of the series as a "contribution to the new literature of national self-analysis"; but they did not distinguish between self-analysis founded on a writer's identification with his community and a social criticism that reflected an impregnable sense of superiority to the surrounding culture.

The South in particular—condemned as much for the backwardness of its provincial culture as for its deplorable race relations—elicited this second type of criticism. In Alabama, a state "saturated with provincialism," the ideas of the arch-reactionary G. K. Chesterton "would be considered advanced," according to Clement Wood. The state's "mental and spiritual sterility" had been analyzed "with devastating impertinence" in Mencken's well-known diatribe against the South, "The Sahara of the

Bozart," and Wood found it difficult to add anything to Mencken's indictment. He could only ask, once again, what Alabama had contributed "to music, to drama, to sculpture, to painting, to literature," or to the "absorbing world of science, that handmaiden of man in his progress from beasthood." Only Virginia and North Carolina, among Southern states, came in for mildly favorable comment. According to Douglas Southall Freeman, the "new educational movement" was the "hope of every progressive Virginian." Robert Watson Winston took comfort from the existence of an "active, forward-looking element" in North Carolina, a state that no longer proclaimed herself "provincial and proud of it."

Condemnation of Southern backwardness, in a liberal weekly, might have been expected. More surprising was that a series conceived as an exploration of diversity so often ended by holding up a uniform standard of cultural progress, one measured by great works of art and notable achievements in science and technology. None of the contributors asked whether a new order in the South would not have to rest on traditions indigenous to the region. None showed much interest in the requirements for a vigorous civic life, as opposed to the number of orchestras, art galleries, libraries, and universities. The implication was that "civilization," if it was ever to come to the South, would have to come from outside. The only hope for Mississippi, according to Beulah Amidon Ratliff, was an invasion of "missionaries" from the North. Like the rest of the South, Mississippi needed "educational missionaries, to bring both white and colored schools up to modern standards; medical missionaries, to teach hygiene and sanitation; . . . agricultural missionaries, to teach modern methods of farming." Only in the wake of a second reconstruction would the "light of civilization penetrate the uttermost parts" of Dixie.

The South was evidently not alone in its cultural stagnation. Nevada was the "most backward" state of all, according to Anne Martin; but it had plenty of competition. The West as a whole had known democracy only in its crudest form, as in Walter C. Hawes's Wyoming, where a "community of roistering young bachelors" had set the cultural tone. The history of Colorado, like that of other western states, was a "continuous story of colossal waste," as Easley M. Jones saw it. In Idaho, the "gambling spirit" at least helped to counter the "tendency toward conformity," in the opinion of M. R. Stone, although it also diverted energy from "cultural interests" to "practical problems."

Even Kansas and Iowa, states that prided themselves on their spirit of improvement, remained culturally backward. William Allen White described Kansas as a "Puritan survival." Although he conceded her civic spirit, her elimination of poverty and crime, and her rising standards of health and education, his account stressed the negative side of "Puritanism." The "dour deadly desire to fight what was deemed wrong" had stunted the sense of beauty. Kansas had produced "no great poet, no great painter, no great musician, no great writer or philosopher," only the "dead level of economic and political democracy." Johan J. Smertenko used the same kind of language in his account of Iowa, a "cautious, prosaic, industrious, and mediocre" place in which the prospects for "cultural expression" were "bleak indeed." Lacking any "generous purpose" or "spiritual background," Iowa was a "dull, gray monotone." "Seldom has a people been less interested in spiritual self-expression and more concerned with hog nutrition."

John Macy, the *Nation*'s literary editor, painted an equally unflattering portrait of Massachusetts, where Yankee traditions had been modified by Catholic immigration without producing anything more than a "complaisant and insignificant conformism." If Catholics "mistakenly and stupidly" abused their "new-found strength" by banning works on the Spanish Inquisition or the novels of Zola from public libraries, their attempt to impose intellectual uniformity marked only a "slight transformation of Puritan zealotry." The "more enlightened citizens of Massachusetts" could take pride in Holmes and Brandeis, but mediocre politicians like Henry Cabot Lodge, David Walsh, and the "yokel" Calvin Coolidge more accurately represented the electorate. The people of Massachusetts got the politicians and the newspapers they deserved. Except for the *Christian Science Monitor*—a national rather than a local paper—the press exhibited the "dress and cultivation of a boom mining-town."

That states as different as Iowa and Massachusetts could prompt the same kind of disparagement suggests that the conventions underlying this disparagement had acquired a life of their own. The equation of civic culture with progress and enlightenment made it difficult to see anything but arrested development even in a state like New York, depicted by Charles F. Wood as a benighted region dominated by "fear and suspicion" of the modern world. The "backwoods" element, Wood said, had a "throttle-hold upon the state." "Resistance to change is their most sacred principle. Modern conveniences appear as signs of degeneracy to them; and the boy who leaves home to go to the city is still their most popular theme of tragedy." It did not occur to Wood that a wholehearted celebration of rural depopulation was not the best index of a flourishing civilization or that a reluctance "to accept the automobile," in communities threatened with outward migration, did not necessarily indicate the idiocy of rural life.

Upstate New York (the city having been assigned to a separate contributor, as if to signify its special relation to the rest of the state and to the nation as a whole) "lagged" in prison reform, in health care, in progressive legislation. The guardians of moral order censored movies for fear that "young folks might get some suggestion out of harmony with the permanent and fixed morality of 'back home.' " They were making "strenuous efforts" to extend this censorship to books and periodicals. It was still a crime to disseminate information about birth control. "Laws forbidding this and that are as common in New York as they are in Kansas." The universities took no more interest in new ideas than the state legislature. "Free speech does not exist." But industrialism was transforming the state in spite of herself. "It is a popular sport among intellectuals," Woods observed, "to sneer at mere industrial advance," but the gains outweighed the losses. Sentimental critics of technology lamented the "despoiling of Niagara Falls," but the "discovery by scientists that Niagara can be enslaved is producing a dream of human freedom which is mightily affecting New York State today." Niagara was doomed; "but on the other side of the ledger millions of people are breaking from the past."

Taken as a whole, these reports conveyed an unmistakable impression of liberal intellectuals' sense of alienation from America. It was not that the country had failed to "keep faith," as Croly wrote in 1922, "with its original idea of the United States as a Promised Land." The *Nation*'s contributors seldom invoked the "original idea" of America. Most of them wrote as if the "promise of American life" had been a swindle from the beginning. Croly's brand of social criticism implied that whatever democracy Americans managed to achieve in the future would have to rest on their achievements in the past. The authors of "These United States" assumed, on the other hand, that "breaking from the past" was the precondition of cultural and political advance. That Americans refused to make the break proved the country's backwardness and immaturity, its hatred of intellectual and artistic freedom, its fear of new ideas, its intolerance of anything that called the old ways into question, its puritanical obsession with sexual purity, and worst of all, its suspicion of intellectuals. Since liberals retained at least a formal allegiance to the idea of democracy, they tended to regard its shortcomings with indignation rather than with Mencken's ironic detachment. They shared his contempt for the majority, however. As they understood it, democracy meant progress, intellectual emancipation, and personal freedom, not popular self-government. Self-government, it appeared, was incompatible with progress.

Social Criticism, Disembodied and Connected

· ■ ·

A handful of contributions to "These United States," in contrast with the rest, defended cultural particularism and local self-government. In New Mexico, Elizabeth Shepley Sergeant found a clearly articulated sense of the past that might make it possible to achieve material well-being without "cheapness." She saw the state's mixture of Spanish, Indian, and Anglo-Saxon populations as a model of cultural pluralism. Willa Cather likewise attributed Nebraska's vigor and prosperity to the presence of Bohemian, Scandinavian, and German immigrants. She questioned the "rooted conviction" of "legislators that a boy can be a better American if he speaks only one language than if he speaks two." Like Randolph Bourne, she conceived of cosmopolitanism as a meeting of well-articulated national cultures, not as the subordination of national and ethnic peculiarities to some universal pattern. "It is in that great cosmopolitan country known as the middle West," she wrote, "that we may hope to see the hard molds of American provincialism broken up."

A couple of contributors went so far as to find positive value in provincialism. Maine, according to Robert Herrick, had achieved a "stable condition of comfort, self-reliance, non-parasitic occupation common in the New England of a previous generation, which makes for sturdiness, individualism, and conservatism." Maine lacked the "lighter, the more suave growths of civilization," but it had more substantial accomplishments to its credit: a sound balance of industry and agriculture; town meetings; houses with a "solidity and abidingness about them which makes them part of the rugged landscape." Dorothy Canfield Fisher made a spirited case for backwardness in her essay on Vermont, "Our Rich Little Poor State." Vermont's secret, Fisher thought, lay in her refusal to live beyond her means. She had not yet acquired the fear of poverty that made the "modern world go around."* She refused to exchange an "unenvious satisfaction with plain ways" for the illusory advantages of wealth, power, and status. Outsiders, driven by what they called "strictly business lines of industrial efficiency," might confuse this absence of envy with "bucolic stolidity," but Vermonters knew better and were undisturbed by the world's adverse judgment of their rustic ways. "It makes an ironic quirk come into the corner of their mouths, as at the transparent absurdity of a child."

No doubt the Vermonter paid "for his high-handed scoffing at sacred social distinctions by a rough plainness, not to say abruptness, of speech and manner." But his plain style freed him not only from the fear of poverty but from the paralyzing skepticism about politics that made other Americans feel that they would never be able "to get what they want through political action." Lacking an obsession with money-making, Vermonters had no need for that "lazy substitute for self-government"—representative democracy. Dependent neither on employers nor on a governing class, Vermonters enjoyed the "ability to deal with life at first hand."

The contrast between these four essays and the series as a whole shows how completely most liberals had come to identify liberalism with a cultural critique of backwardness and provincialism. Thinking of themselves as a civilized minority in a nation of Babbitts, Rotarians, and rednecks, liberals fell into a style of social criticism that had the curious effect

---

*This might be taken as an admirably succinct statement of the essence of Adam Smith's political economy. The fear of poverty—the morally suspect but economically invigorating overestimation of wealth and luxury—makes the world turn, according to Smith. But Fortune smiled on Vermont: the idea of progress never took hold there.

of reinforcing complacency instead of disturbing it. The authors of "These United States" implicitly invited their readers to count themselves among the elect. The rest of America might live in darkness, but they themselves—the knowing authors and their readers—had seen the light. A perceptive commentator, Louis Siegel of Cleveland, noted in a letter to the *Nation* that Mencken's criticism of American life, seemingly so sweeping, lost most of its force in its very excess, since readers understood that his spleen was directed not at themselves but against everyone else. Mencken voiced the mockery and contempt for their neighbors, based on a conviction of their own superiority, that his readers also felt but hesitated to express. "Each and every American thinks himself too intelligent to be the target of Mencken's venom, admiringly endorses it as aimed at his neighbor, and takes a vicarious satisfaction in brutality his [own] humaneness inhibits." The only readers who resented Mencken's satire were those who failed to recognize his appeal to exempt themselves from his indictment of the common man.

Mencken's view of social criticism assumed that since we find fault with others more easily than we find fault with ourselves, we need to turn our neighbors into aliens before we can find fault with them. But "such easy fault-finding," as Michael Walzer has recently remarked in another context, quickly becomes self-defeating. It makes social criticism "superfluous," Walzer argues, because it does not "touch the conscience of the people to whom it is addressed"—and the "task of the social critic is precisely to touch the conscience." A proper understanding of the function of social criticism requires us to reject the "standard view of the social critic as someone who breaks loose from his particular loyalties and views his own society from the outside—from an ideal point, as it were, equidistant from all societies." In place of this disembodied or "desocialized" criticism, Walzer advocates "connected" criticism, which tries to steer between the universal and the particular, the abstract and the concrete. Unconditional commitment to the universal tends to create an "ideologically flattened world" in which particular human beings disappear and the critic's "impartiality slides into a cold indifference." Unconditional commitment to the particular, on the other hand, leads to undiscriminating acquiescence in a community's good opinion of itself, to an acceptance of its self-serving illusions at face value. Loyalty to a particular way of life, unless it is attentive to the disparity between profession and practice, undercuts the very possibility of social criticism, while the refusal of loyalty, on the grounds that the intellectual's only allegiance is to truth and justice in the abstract, renders it harmless and irrelevant.

Considered in the light of this contrast between connected social criticism and sociological satire, the *Nation*'s survey of the United States leaves a somewhat ambiguous impression. Though most of the contributors struggled to see America from an outsider's point of view, few of them regarded it with "icy indifference." They could not quite bring themselves to regard democracy, as Mencken did, purely as an endlessly engaging spectacle for the connoisseur of popular stupidity. Their indignation implied a residual belief in the American people's capacity for self-government, even though their disparaging account of American society did not give much support to that belief.

Sociology as Social Criticism: The Apotheosis of the Expert

·■·

The same ambiguity appeared in contemporary reactions to the much-discussed study of Muncie, Indiana, by Robert and Helen Lynd—the first in a long line of community studies in which sociology served as a mode of social criticism. Mencken was delighted with *Middletown*—a book that showed, he said, "how far short of libel Sinclair Lewis fell in 'Main Street' and 'Babbitt.' " He commended the authors for adopting a position of complete detachment from their own culture. They "went to Middletown precisely as W. H. R. Rivers and Bronislaw Malinowski went to Melanesia," without preconceptions or a "thesis to prove." They studied their subjects "as an anthropologist anatomizes a savage tribe." To John Dewey, on the other hand, *Middletown* seemed to accuse Americans of not living up to their own ideals—quite a different indictment from one that merely dismissed their "unbelievable stupidities," as Mencken put it. What the Lynds discovered, according to Dewey, was the contradiction between "institutions" and "creeds," "practice" and "theories." Their most distressing finding concerned the debasement of religion. "The glorification of religion as setting the final seal of approval on pecuniary success, and supplying the active motive to more energetic struggle for such success, and the adoption by the churches of the latest devices of the movies and the advertiser, approach too close to the obscene." In Dewey's reading, the city of Middletown was a "house divided against itself," preaching idealism and practicing materialism—not, as Mencken saw it from his lofty position of satirical disengagement, a "city in Moronia."

Dewey's point about religion implied respect for the ideals Middletown claimed to live by. The disparity between preaching and practice was "obscene" only because those ideals deserved to be taken seriously. Mencken, on the other hand, made a point of taking nothing seriously, least of all religion, and therefore had no standard that would have justified the use of such strong language—all the more telling in this case because Dewey used this kind of language, the language of the American jeremiad, so sparingly.

The Lynds exposed themselves to conflicting readings of their work because they themselves wavered between connected and disembodied criticism of American society. Robert Lynd was a product, after all, of the small-town Middle Western culture he was trying to understand. His descent on Muncie had something of the character of a homecoming. He chose Muncie as the site of his research because he wanted to study the effects of industrialism uncomplicated by ethnicity, but also because he still believed that the old Protestant communities of the Middle West remained a source of "spiritual energy." *Middletown* thus took on some of the characteristics of a "secular jeremiad," as Richard Fox calls it, one that "lashed its readers with a relentless chronicle of their faults while calling them to repentance and conversion."* But it was also a satire of small-town life in the spirit of Mencken and Sinclair Lewis. The satirical note came out even more prominently in the sequel, *Middletown in Transi-*

---

*"My demand in Washington is 'repent, America,' " said Martin Luther King of his poor people's march. Robert Lynd, like King, came out of the social gospel tradition. He studied for the ministry at Union Theological Seminary and abandoned the church only when he decided that social scientists were more likely than preachers to succeed in "helping people to face the facts and think through their problems." He assigned to social science, in other words, the role the social gossip assigned to religion.

tion, with its assault on the "Middletown spirit"—the "intense national-ism," the "united front against radicalism," the refusal to question the "adequacy of the reigning system," and the general fear of the outside world that seemed to have grown even stronger as a result of the Depres-sion. The more the Lynds immersed themselves in Muncie, the more they fell into the point of view of alien intruders. Indignation gave way to a sort of bemused contempt.

Not that they became more conservative in their politics, as Mencken did. On the contrary, they became increasingly outspoken in their con-demnation of capitalism, like many liberals in the thirties. But they saw no reason to revise their low opinion of the political capacities of ordi-nary Americans. In *Knowledge for What?* (1939), Robert Lynd cited a grow-ing body of evidence to the effect that "liberal attitudes are correlated with intelligence." If that was the case, social change would presumably have to be engineered from above. The masses were creatures of habit, and modern society had grown too complex, in any case, to be governed by the rule of the majority. "Many public issues today are of a highly technical character that should not be disposed of by a show of hands." Public opinion could not be ignored, of course, but neither could it be guided by reasonable arguments or even by an appeal to enlightened self-interest. Advertisers and political demagogues understood the im-portance of emotional appeals even if liberals did not. The "stark manipulative rightness of modern advertising" lay in its skillful use of symbols, just as the "tactics of a Hitler" were "profoundly right" in recognizing the "need of human beings for the constant dramatization of the feeling of common purpose." Those who believed that capitalism was "bankrupt" and that "alternatives to capitalism" held out the only hope of social justice would have to master the propaganda techniques used so effectively by their rivals. Elsewhere Lynd dismissed the "high degree of rationality" in "consumer choices" as an unwarranted assumption. The consumer was better understood as a "hard-beset mariner willing to make for almost any likely port in a storm." Public opinion thus became "largely a question of whose signal lights can beckon to him" most "allur-ingly."

Knowledge for What? attacked the intellectual foundations of nine-teenth-century liberalism as well as its laissez-faire economics. As a soci-ologist, Lynd inherited an intellectual tradition that had always given more weight to customs, habits, and emotions than to reason. Psychoanalytic theory, by showing "man to be basically emotional in his motivations and only sporadically able to sustain the tensions involved in taking thought in order to sustain his actions," reinforced the sociological disposition to emphasize the nonrational sources of social cohesion. But most Americans still clung to the political culture of individualism. They exaggerated the "omnicompetence of human beings" and left "everything up to the individual's precarious ability to 'use his head.' " They refused to admit that individuals varied in their capacities and that many of them inevitably lost out in the "individual scramble for wealth." Egalitarian dogma thus led in practice to radically inegalitarian results. Only the state could correct the inequalities generated by competitive capitalism and protect the weak against the strong.

Although the sociological tradition originated in the romantic counter-revolution against the Enlightenment and the idea of progress, it was taken up in the twentieth century by social democrats who objected to capitalism's "extreme emphasis upon competitiveness," as Lynd called it. Like the romantic sociologists, social democrats insisted that individuals had no being apart from society.* They too regretted the decline of "community," but they relied on the state, not on small intermediate groups or voluntary associations, to restore a sense of connection. When Lynd asked whether it was possible to "build urban people into vital communities," the grammatical structure of his sentence revealed more than he may have intended. People were the objects, not the subjects, of "community," as he understood it.

In the conservative sociological tradition, the tenacity of custom was seen as a useful check against innovation. For Lynd, "folkways" meant "cultural lag." Habits and "values" failed to keep pace with economic and technological change.† Americans retained the mental habits of pioneers

---

*"Modern science," wrote Lynd, "has discarded [the] earlier conception of a discrete, autonomous individual. . . . There are no Robinson Crusoes, no 'individuals' apart from other individuals." This discovery (the novelty of which Lynd exaggerated, being ignorant, like most sociologists, of the history of his own discipline) made it necessary, he argued, to discard other "folkways" as well—for example, the quaint idea that man has "soul," "mind," and "will."

†Lynd quoted Carl Becker's *Progress and Power* (1936): "Mankind has entered a new phase of human progress—a time in which the acquisition of new implements of

even though their lives were now governed by elaborate organizations and complicated technologies. Their "adaptation" to modern conditions would have to be guided by social science, with its relentless "revision of implicit assumptions." Many people thoughtlessly blamed technology for the modern malaise; but it was the "intractability of the human factor, and not our technology, that has spoiled the American dream." Social scientists alone understood the "human factor." If democracy was to "function in a population of widely unequal individuals," social science would have to "show the way to restructure the culture so as to care for those inequalities." Scientific research could discover "which differences are so biologically controlled that favorable cultural conditions cannot materially change them." It could show policymakers how to erect "appropriate safeguards" against the exploitation of "specific groups of unequal persons." It could thus lay the basis for a fully developed form of the welfare state that would protect people from the consequences of their own shortsightedness, ignorance, and folly.

> What would our American culture need to do if it were to set itself to see that its citizens from birth to death had as little chance as possible to invest their savings ignorantly, to purchase sub-standard commodities, to marry disastrously, to have unwanted children "accidentally," to postpone needed operations, to go into blind-alley jobs, and so on?

The question, as Lynd framed it, could have only one answer: all power to the experts. In order to make everyone happy and safe, America would have to institutionalize expertise in the form of social insurance, consumer protection, planned parenthood, "manpower selection," vocational guidance, and socialized medicine. It would have to "resolve, in the engineer's favor, the conflict between the engineer and the businessman." Failure to do so would betray the old illusion that autonomous,

---

power too swiftly outruns the necessary adjustment of habits and ideas to the novel conditions created by their use." He could have found this banal concept of "cultural lag" in hundreds of other sources.

omnicompetent individuals could manage everything for themselves. Americans could no longer indulge themselves in that illusion, any more than they could afford to believe in the "mind," "soul," and "will" of humankind.

Experts and Orators: Thurman Arnold's "Anthropological" Satire

· ■ ·

By the time Lynd published *Knowledge for What?*, liberals and social democrats had returned to power under the New Deal; but their doubts about Americans' capacity for self-government, hardened by political adversity in the twenties, did not break up in the Democratic landslide of the thirties. The voters overwhelmingly supported Franklin Roosevelt in 1936, but it was not clear that they endorsed the New Deal, let alone the comprehensive social engineering favored by liberals and social democrats. The New Deal itself represented an alloy of welfare liberalism, old-fashioned laissez-faire liberalism, and sheer opportunism. Led by a man who courted popularity at the expense of programmatic consistency and coherence, it had no sense of purpose or direction. Dedicated New Dealers like Rex Tugwell—those who advocated an all-out assault on the theory and practice of competitive individualism—often despaired of the New Deal. They suspected that Roosevelt owed his victories at the polls to his charm rather than to any widespread enthusiasm for his principles, such as they were. Although some of the New Dealers joined the left-wing celebration of the American people and the American past that reached its climax in the Popular Front culture of the late thirties, most of them remained curiously aloof. They trusted programs, not people, and they found the new mood of affirmation—"the people, yes," in Carl Sandburg's cloying phrase—more than a little embarrassing. They had plenty of compassion; they grieved over the hard lot of the sharecropper, as documented by the photographers made famous by the Farm Security Administration; they learned the workers' protest songs, defended their right to strike, and condemned employers who resorted to violence and intimidation; but although their hearts went out to the victims of injustice, they did not completely trust the American people as a whole. Indeed their feelings about the people more nearly approximated Mencken's than Sandburg's.

Thus it was Thurman Arnold, the quintessential New Dealer, who raised political satire à la Mencken to a new level of urbanity and sophisticated cynicism in *The Symbols of Government* (1935) and *The Folklore of Capitalism* (1937). Mencken read the second of these tracts in manuscript and must have been pleased to find that Arnold shared his contempt for democracy and his belief in the futility of public debate. But Arnold went on to advocate positions that Mencken himself loudly opposed: government regulation of industry, redistribution of income, welfare programs—in short, a more radical version of the New Deal. He went so far as to defend Roosevelt's unpopular plan to pack the Supreme Court. That liberals joined conservatives in denouncing the plan proved the bankruptcy of old-fashioned liberalism, in his view—its infatuation with abstractions and with symbolic or "theological" modes of thought. Like Mencken, Arnold saw cultural history as a long struggle of science against superstition. He tried to view American "folkways" as they would appear to an anthropologist or a "man from Mars." The view from outside led him to question economic superstitions as well as the more obvious fundamentalist superstitions ridiculed by Mencken. This appropriation of Mencken's "anthropological" technique of social satire by an ardent New Dealer marked a new stage in the history of American liberalism.*

A law professor at Yale before entering the Roosevelt administration in the mid-thirties, Arnold had become increasingly critical of the Supreme Court's dogmatic defense of laissez-faire, specifically of its use of the Fourteenth Amendment to protect corporations from regulation. The

---

*"Thurman Arnold," wrote Richard Hofstadter in *The Age of Reform*, "wrote works of great brilliance and wit and considerable permanent significance—better books, I believe, than any of the political criticism of the Progressive era." These books, in Hofstadter's judgment, exemplified the "pragmatic temper" of the New Deal, its attack on the "moralism" of the prewar progressives. They represented the "theoretical equivalent of FDR's opportunistic virtuosity in practical politics."

pretense that corporations were individuals entitled to protection under the due process clause struck him as a triumph of "metaphysical" over "factual" thinking. Corporations were clearly organizations, not individuals, and they wielded powers that could better be understood as governmental than as entrepreneurial. Their ability to set prices amounted to a power of taxation, which should be recognized as such and subjected to public control. The mythology of private enterprise—which Arnold compared to the "medieval myths which impeded medical knowledge for hundreds of years"—had the effect of encouraging the "type of organization known as industry or business" and of discouraging the "type known as government." A more rational approach would have recognized their underlying similarity and judged them by the only appropriate standard, that of efficiency. Arnold did not bother to defend the "standard that it is a good thing to produce and distribute" as many goods as possible. He did not propose to debate "whether medieval civilization is really better than modern civilization." He simply took for granted the "standard . . . of a society which produces and distributes goods to the maximum of its technical capacity." The only question worth discussing, therefore, was whether private or public corporations—or more precisely, what particular mix of public and private control—best served that purpose.

Arnold's analysis of the quasi-governmental powers exercised by allegedly private corporations, though not especially original, was penetrating and important. The point he was making can hardly be made too often, since it is the collectivization of private property that deprives it of the moral virtues formerly associated with it. The refusal to recognize this dooms American conservatism, so called, to complete irrelevance in any serious discussion of the moral implications of modern capitalism. Conservative opponents of the New Deal often used rhetoric vaguely reminiscent of nineteenth-century republicanism or producerism, but they never faced up to the obvious differences between private property as it existed in the nineteenth century and the modern corporation, which cannot possibly confer on its stockholders or employees the independence and resourcefulness classically said to go with proprietorship. Conservatives opposed legislation regulating corporations on the grounds that it penalized "initiative, courage, hardihood, frugality, and aspiration," as if those virtues had any place in corporate life. Such a position could be sustained only by pretending that corporations were really individuals, and as Arnold pointed out, this was more than a reasonable person could be expected to believe. By ignoring the plain facts of modern organization, conservatives discredited the language of civic republicanism and thus contributed to the impoverishment of public debate. But liberals like Arnold trivialized public debate in their own way, not only by directly questioning the need for it but by reducing all political questions to the production and distribution of goods. Any other considerations, according to Arnold, belonged to the realm of "metaphysics," not government. The "practical comfort of the moment" outweighed the "great moral issues of the future." The question of how to provide "practical comfort" was a technical question, not something that could be settled by an appeal to first principles. It was a question for "experts," not for "orators."

As a lawyer, Arnold might have been expected to recognize the intractability of conflicting interests and to doubt the possibility of making politics an exact science. His faith in expertise, however, exceeded even that of many social scientists. He measured intellectual progress precisely by the absence of debate. Doctors, he argued, no longer engaged in pointless controversies about the rival claims of homeopathic and allopathic schools of medicine. The medical profession had been "taken over by men of skill rather than men of principle," with the result that there was "little left in medicine for thinking men to debate." Whereas medical learning had become "technical rather than philosophical," however, economic and legal learning remained "predominantly philosophical"—a sure sign of cultural lag. Arnold's explanation of the pointlessness of debate echoed Lippmann's. Although Lippmann, like Mencken, vehemently opposed the New Deal, Arnold saw nothing incongruous in a defense of the New Deal that drew so heavily on the ideas of those explicitly critical of democracy. He too dismissed as "irrational" the notion that "the cure for the evils of democracy is more democracy." "Public argument never convinces the other side," he wrote; its only function was to rally the true believers. The "noise of competing theories" drowned out the voice of the expert. To submit social questions to the "feeble judgment of the common herd" was the height of folly. Democracy consisted of giving the people what they wanted—more of everything, presumably—but not in listening to their advice about how to get it. Their ideas originated, as Lippmann had demonstrated, in the "emotional reaction" to the "underlying little pictures" in their heads. They attached more importance to "moral gestures"—antitrust laws, vice crusades, periodic campaigns against corruption—than to efficiency.

The moralistic individualism that dominated public debate drove organizations concerned with efficiency underground. Corporations had to violate the antitrust laws in order to carry on their business. Political machines, which performed a "charitable function" for their constituents, had to operate sub rosa, since the public refused to acknowledge their legitimacy. The foolish attempt to stop people from drinking created an illicit traffic in liquor and a new class of criminals. The puritanical suppression of sex had the same effect, as Lippmann and other critics of "reform" had pointed out a long time ago. "These crusades are not remedies for the evil," Arnold said, "but a part of the total complex which creates it." They grew out of the "curious" concept of sin and the equally curious idea that government should seek to instill strength of character in its citizens. Such attitudes inhibited the growth of a "competent governing class" of "cheerful, practical technicians." The "disinterested type of men we would like to see in government" made the mistake of adopting the "role of missionaries to the heathen, instead of playing the part of anthropologists."

Arnold cited the American occupation of the Philippines as an encouraging example of what administrators could accomplish when they were not inhibited by obsolete notions of sin, guilt, and moral "character." The "heroism and self sacrifice" of American officials, "unselfish in their interests," had produced an "amazing" record of "improvement." "Disease was reduced, social work carried on, living conditions made better"—all because the usual objections to paternalism did not apply to the government of "our little brown brothers." The "imperialistic ideal," together with "our natural humanitarian impulses," made it possible "to treat these primitive people better than our own." "We were not afraid of ruining their character because we did not think of them as equals who had characters to ruin."

Not content with this affront to liberal prejudices against imperialism, Arnold held up the government of insane asylums as another model of enlightened administration. "From a humanitarian point of view the best government is that which we find in an insane asylum," where the presiding physicians tried to make the inmates "as comfortable as possible, regardless of their respected moral deserts." Doctors understood that it was a waste of time to "argue with the insane as to the soundness or unsoundness of their ideas." They considered those ideas "only in the light of their effect on conduct," just as the "government which civilized nations impose on savage tribes" sought to make use of taboos instead of trying to stamp them out. With a studied provocation worthy of Mencken, Arnold added that "the advantage of such a theory of government"—one that treated the governed as inmates or "little brown brothers"—lay in its escape from the "troublesome assumption that the human race is rational." Humanitarian imperialism, as he called it, enabled administrators to pursue vigorous measures without having to answer moral objections. "We need not delay such social undertakings as public relief because we are worried about their effect on the character of the recipients." A dispassionate observer, as distinguished from an "orator," "preacher," or "theologian," could easily see that practical results, especially in an economic emergency, were preferable to arguments about abstract principles or the warfare that so often grew out of those arguments. Thus "a man from Mars might be of the opinion that an orderly government should not permit pitched battles over wages, to the loss and suffering of entire communities." Unfortunately those closer to the ground seldom attained the view from Mars, and "the notion of compulsory arbitration was as uncongenial to labor as it was to capital."

The Soviet Union provided Arnold with a third example of the subordination of ethical disputation to practical results. The Bolsheviks, he noted, "were able to look at the distribution of goods as a purely mechanical problem of production and transportation, without connecting with it the moral problem of the preservation of national character." The Soviet Union offered a "spectacle of internal cooperation" normally seen only in wartime. Such tributes were commonplace in the 1930s. American admirers of the "Soviet experiment," however, usually tried to deny the undemocratic features of the Bolshevik regime or else excused them as a temporary expedient forced on Stalin by economic adversity and Western hostility. Arnold did not have to engage in this kind of self-deception, since he held no brief for democracy in the first place. Insofar as the idea of democracy had any substance, it was simply another name for "humanitarian imperialism," in his view. It meant the universalization of material well-being, engineered by "fact-minded persons" and "competent diagnosticians." A democratic regime, to be sure, had to "carry its people along with it emotionally"; but that did not imply that the people should take an active part in governing themselves. As long as the governing classes grasped the nature and importance of political symbolism, they could satisfy the public demand for inspiring slogans and "ceremonials" without allowing public "ritual" to interfere with production and distribution.

The "Machiavelli" of the Managerial Revolution

· ■ ·

The ideal administrator, in Arnold's view, combined the diagnostic skills of a psychiatrist with the arts of persuasion perfected by the advertising industry. Advertisers relied on "slogans rather than descriptions of their products." They would have ridiculed the "suggestion that the best way to sell goods is by making a rational appeal." Moralists might reject the application of advertising techniques to government as "Machiavellian," but their misguided scruples deprived them of any constructive influence on public affairs. They needed to learn that men are moved by myths and symbols, not by moral arguments, and that if responsible leaders did not provide compelling "faiths and dreams," irresponsible demagogues would gladly leap into the breach. The importance Arnold attached to mythology, together with his recognition of the need for moral equivalents of war, might seem at first to align him with James, Sorel, and Niebuhr. For those writers, however, mythology was suprascientific as well as prescientific, in Niebuhr's words. Arnold understood it in the latter sense alone. Mythology could not shed any light on the nature of things. Only science could do that; but most people, alas, could not live up to the austere demands of science. Unable to look facts in the face, they needed comforting illusions.

Arnold regarded mythology in the same way that Voltaire regarded religion. Men of a scientific turn of mind could live on lean meat and water, but the masses craved sweets. The masses, Arnold observed, foolishly wanted "to believe that government is moral, rational, and symmetrical." They shared this weakness with the priestly classes, including members of his own profession. Practical experience did not seem to disabuse intellectuals—lawyers least of all—of their ingrained belief that "governmental theory is the product of ages of careful scholarly thought." Intellectuals, like most of their fellow men, remained "incurable moralists." For that reason, a "Machiavellian" approach to government would never command widespread acceptance. The "concept of government as an insane asylum," though it was based on the "indestructible" proposition that "it is a good thing to make people comfortable if the means exist by which it can be done," would "never work" as a "general political theory." "Its realism is too apparent, as also is its implied scorn for the human race." It could not serve as a political theory either for the intellectuals or for the masses. "Machiavellianism" had "never been a source of group morale."

In *The Symbols of Government,* Arnold tried to work out a "public philosophy" better adapted to modern conditions than the old competitive individualism but more acceptable to the masses than a theory that treated them simply as inmates of an insane asylum. If ideals had no bearing on conduct, a public philosophy was a contradiction in terms; public discourse could never rise above the level of meaningless babble. But Arnold took it seriously enough, after all, to recommend a new "creed for the future," thereby "deserting" his position as an "objective observer" and taking up the stance of "a preacher and an advocate, rather than an anthropologist." The "new social philosophy," he argued, would have to rest on the "fundamental axiom that man works only for his fellow man." It would "replace the notion of the great man who lived and died for moral and rational purposes" with "tolerance and common sense." Popular acceptance of the "notion of a tolerant adult personality" would promote a "scientific attitude toward government" and put an end to the political ascendancy of the "high-class psychopath and fanatic." The decline of "fanatical devotion to principle on the part of the public" would free "intelligent leaders" from the need to "commit themselves, for political reasons, to all sorts of disorderly nonsense." When the public came to value "practical results" more highly than "preconceived principles," a "competent, practical, opportunistic governing class" would find it possible to get on with the serious work of making people comfortable, without having to inspire and amuse them as well.

As a bold new social myth, this left a good deal to be desired. It was simply a broader statement of the efficiency expert's point of view, which by Arnold's own admission could not command general enthusiasm. It was the creed of the "new class," as he called it in *The Folklore of Capitalism*. The "engineers, salesmen, minor executives, and social workers," because they ran the "country's temporal affairs" behind the scenes, represented the ruling class of the future. In the universities, the new class consisted of a "group of younger economists, political scientists, and lawyers." All these professions shared a "humanitarian" belief in the need for "efficiency in the distribution of goods" and a skeptical attitude toward the "worship of the American businessman." They had not yet developed a fully articulated political theory, but neither had the capitalists developed such a theory before they came to power in the eighteenth century. Adam Smith gave them one after the fact; and the new class would find its own theorist once it found itself securely entrenched in the halls of government.

After explaining at length that the masses needed romance, glamour, and the excitement, Arnold had nothing to give them but tolerance and maturity. It may well have been a sense of the inadequacy of his "new social philosophy" that caused Arnold to cast about for more compelling symbols of the managerial revolution. He found them in an unlikely place. In 1938, he began to discover unsuspected possibilities in the antitrust tradition, which he had previously ridiculed. Those who followed his career were puzzled by the seeming contradiction between his vigorous enforcement of the Sherman Act as assistant attorney general and the contemptuous treatment of antitrust laws in his earlier writings. As head of the Antitrust Division of the Justice Department from 1938 to 1943, he launched almost as many prosecutions as all his predecessors put together. In 1937, however, he had argued that antitrust laws perpetuated the illusion that a "highly organized and centralized industrial organization" was really "composed of individuals." When he entered the Justice Department, Arnold himself wondered "just how" he "was going to explain" his "present enthusiasm for the antitrust laws in the light of what" he "had written just a year before."

The explanation, if there was one, lay in his contention that in order to gain acceptance for a new idea, it was necessary to disguise it as an old one. "A new idea must appear to be an old idea before it will work at all," he wrote in *The Bottlenecks of Business* (1940), and the Sherman Act, as a "symbol of our traditional ideals," might help to dramatize the need for a more comprehensive industrial policy. Perhaps he also hoped that the symbolism of the Sherman Act would clothe the new ideal of industrial efficiency with "the mystery, the romance and magic" formerly associated with competition and free trade. If efficiency itself was a little drab, a crusade against "conspiracies in restraint of trade" might supply some of the missing excitement. Enforcement of the Sherman Act seems to have commended itself to Arnold, in 1938, as a way of resolving the "troubling paradox" he had examined in *The Symbols of Government.* "Social institutions require faiths and dreams to give them morale. They need to escape from these faiths and dreams in order to progress." A carefully orchestrated campaign against monopolies, conducted by a skeptic who nevertheless appreciated the public's longing to believe in something, would serve both needs at once.

Those who had been advocating a return to small-scale production welcomed Arnold's revival of trust-busting, but he failed to galvanize the general public.* Labor remained dubious about the antitrust laws, which could easily be turned against unions. Small businessmen hated anything connected with the New Deal, even when it served their interests. Consumers might have supported a policy that held out the hope of lower prices, but they had no way of expressing themselves politically. No organized and powerful constituency, as Ellis Hawley has pointed out, had a stake in the enforcement of the antitrust laws. It is also possible that people sensed the satirical overtones in Arnold's antitrust crusade. "Disillusioned men," as he himself had written, "do not make effective leaders." No matter how much he dwelled on their symbolic importance, he did not believe in what the antitrust laws symbolized. He did not believe that

---

*G. D. H. Cole and Bertrand Russell, as we have seen, objected to Sorel's myth of the general strike on the grounds that workers would never rally to syndicalism if it was presented to them merely as a "myth." As Sorel thought of it, however, mythology embodied truths that could not be expressed in any other way. Arnold, on the other hand, saw myths as useful untruths, to be circulated among the credulous by leaders who knew better. This contrast helps to explain why syndicalism evoked so much enthusiasm among workers, in spite of the misgivings expressed by Cole and Russell, while Arnold's antitrust campaign fell flat.

small property holders were the hope of democracy. Insofar as he cared about democracy at all, he believed that its future lay with the "new class." After experimenting with a tepid philosophy of altruism and efficiency, he had come to the conclusion that the new class needed a more appealing ideology for mass consumption. In effect, he decided that the new class might have to speak in the idiom of nineteenth-century producerism.

His political instinct told him, quite correctly, that this was the only idiom capable of sustaining general "enthusiasm for action," at least in the United States, but neither he nor any of his fellow New Dealers could speak it with any conviction. In spite of his early years in Wyoming, the spectacle of Thurman Arnold as a champion of the small producer was inherently unconvincing. His accent—the characteristic accent of the New Deal, of genial contempt, sophisticated raillery, and hard-boiled humanitarianism—gave him away as a charter member of the civilized minority.

From Satire to Social Pathology: Gunnar Myrdal on the "American Dilemma"

· ■ ·

Poor Arnold! If the public could not take him seriously as a populist and trustbuster, the new class could not take him seriously as a social scientist. His books were far too lively, his manner too breezy and irreverent, his footnotes too few and far between. Satire, it turned out, was not to be the approved form of managerial speech. It implied the existence of a public, however attenuated, whereas the new class, in its effort to make government scientific, preferred to talk only to itself. The only community it recognized was the community of scientific inquiry, in which satire had no place. Arnold himself recognized this and apologized for writing in a humorous vein. Only in scientifically underdeveloped fields like economics and law, he said, was it necessary to resort to ridicule. Satire was a sure sign of cultural lag.

By the 1940s, most social scientists were ready to put this primitive form of social criticism behind them. Scintillating wit and bold, surprising insights, they agreed, were no substitute for painstaking research. More and more, social scientists emphasized the importance of teamwork. They pursued their studies in close collaboration with each other, not in cantankerous isolation. They felt an overwhelming need to collect masses of "data" beyond the powers of a single individual, to submit their "findings" to co-workers at conferences and symposia, to revise them in the light of "constructive criticism," and to formulate their conclusions as "policy recommendations" accompanied by appropriate suggestions for "implementation." Organized on an elaborate scale, research in the social sciences now required financial support from government and philanthropic foundations, institutions that also constituted the primary audience for reports based on this research. Even the most explosive and controversial issues, accordingly, had to be discussed in a forbidding, inaccessible style designed to repel outsiders as well as to establish the investigators' status as impartial experts unmoved by "oratory."

Gunnar Myrdal's massive study of the race problem—an explosive issue if there ever was one—became a classic example of the new genre. Published in 1944, *An American Dilemma* proclaimed its authoritative status in every detail, most loudly in its sheer bulk—fifteen hundred closely packed and largely unreadable pages, a third of which consisted of appendixes, reference notes, and other impedimenta. Fifty-six tables and graphs contributed to the unmistakable impression of weightiness, as did an introductory list of Myrdal's collaborators, research assistants, and consultants: six members of the working staff; thirty-one scholars who contributed memoranda based on fresh research; thirty-six research assistants; and fifty-two scholars who read parts of the manuscript and made "criticisms and suggestions." Commissioned and funded by the Carnegie Corporation, *An American Dilemma* exuded the atmosphere of the boardroom, the conference table, and the academic seminar. It was judicious, exhaustive, dispassionate, and unremittingly dull. The choice of a Swedish scholar to supervise the study and write up the findings provided the final proof of objectivity. Speaking for the Carnegie Corporation, Frederick Keppel explained that the trustees had chosen a foreigner because "the whole question had been for nearly a hundred years so charged with emotion that it appeared wise to seek . . . someone who could approach his task with a fresh mind, uninfluenced by traditional attitudes or by earlier conclusions."

Beneath this imposing facade of scholarly expertise, Myrdal advanced a simple thesis: race was a moral issue, inherent in the contradiction between the "American creed" of equal opportunity and the reality of racial discrimination. It was this line of argument, which implied the possibility of an appeal to the uneasy conscience of Americans, that made the book a central document in the history of the civil rights movement. Leaders of the movement could cite Myrdal in support of their belief that American society was not irredeemably racist, that a deep though subterranean reservoir of good will remained, and that the movement should seek to evoke whites' better nature by bringing the conflict between their principles and their practice into the open. Not that Myrdal foresaw or advocated any such strategy. He counted on the courts, an enlightened federal bureaucracy, and the general process of economic and cultural development to resolve the "American dilemma." It never occurred to him that black people might take the leading role in their own liberation. The race problem could be solved only by whites. But his emphasis on its moral dimension at least kept open the possibility of a strategy that appealed to the public conscience; and it is saddening to discover, therefore, that it was precisely this moral emphasis that Myrdal's critics on the left singled out as the most objectionable feature of his book. Americans did not really believe in equal opportunity at all, according to these critics. Their commitment to equality was "primarily verbal," as Kenneth Clark put it in a 1964 symposium commemorating the publication of Myrdal's book on its twentieth anniversary. American society was "essentially *not* ethical," James Baldwin argued on the same occasion. Even liberals had never managed to "divest themselves of the whole concept of white supremacy." Their refusal to acknowledge their own racism prevented them from seeing that black people would never win a place in American society, as Myrdal allegedly imagined, by appealing to the moral sympathies of their oppressors.

In fact, however, Myrdal devoted more of his attention to social pathology than to moral appeals. Unlike Martin Luther King, he did not ask Americans to repent; he asked them simply to grow up. When he said that race was "primarily a moral issue," he meant that a "lag of public morals" had perpetuated the "anachronism" of racial discrimination. He was a social scientist, not a moralist, much less a "prophet," as one of his detractors inappropriately referred to him. He saw the race problem as a function of Southern backwardness, one that could be overcome through modernization. He recognized that "America is continuously struggling for its soul," but he tended to think of the struggle as one between enlightenment and popular ignorance, cosmopolitanism and provincialism. His conceptualizaiton of the issue as a "dilemma" seemed to imply that Americans experienced a conflict between theory and practice as individuals, but closer examination reveals that he used phrases like "America's uneasy conscience" as metaphorical abstractions, not as literal descriptions of the divided soul of particular American individuals. The struggle for this abstract American "soul" turned out to be a struggle between white liberals, who believed in racial justice, and Southerners, poor white Southerners especially, who did not. The forces of light and darkness, as Myrdal saw them, instead of coexisting in the same individuals were conveniently arranged on opposite sides of the Mason-Dixon line.

"The Negro problem has nowhere in the North the importance it has in the South," Myrdal declared. Race riots had occasionally broken out in Northern cities, to be sure, but, on the whole, it did not seem likely that there would be "further riots, of any significant degree of violence, in the North."* The North was industrial, prosperous, and cosmopolitan; the South backward, its agriculture "primitive," its labor system "antiquated" and "paternalistic." Its judicial and penal system, "overripe for fundamental reforms," represented a "tremendous cultural lag in progressive twentieth-century America." Modern reform movements—"woman suffrage and economic equality, collective bargaining, labor legislation, progressive education, child welfare, civil service reform, police and court reform, prison reform"—had left the South untouched.†

---

*Myrdal attributed the 1942 riot in Detroit to the large number of white Southern migrants in the city; but "Detroit is almost unique among Northern cities," he noted, "for its large Southern-born population." To give him his due, he added that future riots might take the form of "sporadic and unorganized outbreaks on the part of the Negroes with little opposition from whites," instead of the "two-way conflicts which we are calling riots."

†Myrdal's list of reform movements recalls the one drawn up by Theodore Parker a hundred years earlier. As always, the absence of the spirit of "improvement" provided liberals with conclusive evidence of the South's backwardness—evidence even more

Southern "ideology" remained "static" and "precapitalist"; as in other "pre-competitive" and "traditional" societies, "tradition was in itself a value." A large part of the race problem could be solved simply by "getting the Negro out of the stagnating rural South."

Myrdal drew heavily on W. J. Cash's recent book, *The Mind of the South*, which argued that the South was a "stubbornly lagging frontier society," in Myrdal's words, "with a strong paternalistic tinge inherited from the old plantation and slavery system." Cash, a protégé of Mencken, adopted a tone of cynical contempt in writing about his native region. Like Mencken, he tried to explode the South's aristocratic pretensions, and Myrdal took over much of his analysis, tracing the race problem to the frontier legacy of lawless individualism and to the "puritanical morality" that gave rise to an "obsession with sex" and sexual purity among the "frustrated lower strata of Southern whites." Drawing also on the work of John Dollard and other social psychologists, Myrdal attributed aggression to frustration (sexual frustration in particular), to the "narrow-minded and intolerant, 'fundamentalist' type of Protestant evangelical religion," and to the "dullness of everyday life and the general boredom of rural and small town life in the South." The "inertia and puritanical morality of the masses" stood in the way of needed reforms, including an "extreme birth control program" that could help to alleviate the region's poverty.

Noting that black people were no more receptive to birth control than poor whites, Myrdal painted a picture of black culture in the South almost as unflattering as his picture of the Southern redneck. Blacks were too much absorbed in religion, he thought. Their churches encouraged an "other-worldly outlook," a helpless "fatalism" in the face of oppression. Fortunately "shouting and noisy religious hysteria in old-time Negro churches" were on the decline. The influence of black fundamentalism lingered, however, retarding the development of a secular point of view. Southern blacks were liberal only on the race question; in other respects they remained unenlightened.

---

impressive, in their eyes, than its economic underdevelopment or its lack of art galleries and concert halls.

> In general, poor people are not radical and not even liberal,
> though to have such political opinions would often be in their
> interest. Liberalism is not characteristic of Negroes either.
> ... A liberal outlook is much more likely to emerge among
> people in a somewhat secure social and economic situation and
> with a background of education. The problem for political
> liberalism ... appears to be first to lift the masses to security
> and education and then to work to make them liberal.

The march "toward social democracy and law observance" had to be led
by liberals, and there were "relatively few liberals in the South," white or
black. Progress would come as a result of the "general trend toward social
amelioration and secularization." "More education, better housing, and
increased economic security" would gradually dissipate the remnants of
racial superstition and intolerance. Meritocracy would make education
"more and more important as a vehicle of social mobility," and a well-
planned campaign of popular education," the key to effective "social engineering," would enable the blacks to climb out of poverty. The growth of
a professional civil service would replace vigilante justice with the rule of
law. Even the "common people," Myrdal observed, were beginning to
understand that a "capable and uncorrupted bureaucracy" was "as important for the efficient working of a modern democracy as ... the voter's
final word on the general direction of this administration."

Myrdal invited his readers to count themselves among the "handful of
rational intellectual liberals" who did not object even to racial intermar-
raige, the great American bugaboo. He did not write with the intention
of changing his readers' minds. It was the "mind of the South" that
needed to be changed—not by any direct appeal but by the mobilization
of economic, educational, and governmental resources that would drag
the South into the twentieth century. Yet Myrdal inadvertently changed
the mind of at least one of his readers—probably a greater achievement
than any of the purposes he intended to accomplish. "As a child of
eleven," writes E. D. Hirsch in support of his case for the importance of
cultural literacy, "I turned against the conservative views of my family
and the Southern community in which I grew up, precisely because I had
been given a traditional education and was therefore literate enough to
read Gunnar Myrdal's *An American Dilemma*, an epoch-making book in

my life." It would be hard to prove that *An American Dilemma* had any comparable effect on its primary audience, the policy-making establishment. The policymakers swung into action only at the last minute, when the civil rights movement left them with no other choice. The support of Southern liberals like Hirsch, on the other hand, contributed to the movement's success—in part, because they took quite literally and personally (since Hirsch was presumably not alone in his heartfelt response to Myrdal) an appeal to "America's guilty conscience" that Myrdal himself seems to have intended merely as a figure of speech.

The Discovery of the Authoritarian Personality
· ■ ·

Six years after the appearance of *An American Dilemma*, Theodor W. Adorno, Else Frenkel-Brunswick, Daniel J. Levinson, and R. Nevitt Sanford brought out their monumental volume, *The Authoritarian Personality* (1950). One of five books in a series of sociological studies of prejudice sponsored by the American Jewish Committee, this collaborative, philanthropically funded investigation resembled Myrdal's both in its form and in the concerns that prompted it: the enormously destructive power of racial, ethnic, and religious hatreds, as evidenced not only by the race problem in America but even more terrifyingly in Hitler's war of extermination against the Jews; the persistence of these atavistic hatreds in the most advanced, enlightened civilization known to history; and the urgent need to control them in order to prevent the destruction of what remained of that civilization. In their general introduction to the series, Max Horkheimer and Samuel B. Flowerman formulated the question of the hour, in words that could easily have been written by Myrdal: "How could it be . . . that in a culture of law, order and reason, there should have survived the irrational remnants of ancient racial and religious hatreds?"

The question carried a heavy load of implications. To ask what explained the "survival" of anachronistic racial attitudes ruled out in advance the possibility that racism, as distinguished from tribal parochialism, represented something new in history.* Horkheimer's formulation of the issue left no room for such a distinction. It assimilated modern racism to "ancient" tribalism and implicitly endorsed a theory of cultural lag quite inconsistent with the dialectical way of thinking advanced in other works by Horkheimer and Adorno, including works composed in the very same decade that gave birth to *The Authoritarian Personality* and the other *Studies in Prejudice*. In Horkheimer's *Eclipse of Reason* (1944) and their collaborative *Dialectic of Enlightenment* (1947), Horkheimer and Adorno argued that "enlightenment" was part of the problem, not its solution. Although the Enlightenment liberated mankind from superstition and subservience to authority, it dissolved any awareness of the natural limits on human powers. It gave rise to the dangerous fantasy that man could remodel both the natural world and human nature itself. Enlightenment transformed moral philosophy into social engineering, thus making it impossible for critical thought to serve as "mankind's memory and conscience," in Horkheimer's telling phrase.

The Eclipse of Reason disclaimed any intention to provide a "program of action." Moral philosophy, Horkheimer argued, "must not be turned into

---

*Compare the more compelling interpretation of modern racism offered by Hannah Arendt in her *Origins of Totalitarianism* (1951). According to Arendt, racism took shape in the context of imperialism and the "atmosphere of rootlessness" it generated. The myth of imperial grandeur and racial destiny appealed to "superfluous men" who "had not the slightest idea of the meaning of *patria* and patriotism, nor the vaguest notion of responsibility for a common, limited community." The rise of racism and imperialism coincided with the abandonment of a political conception of equality that grounded civil rights not in nature but in an "equality of human purpose." Whereas an older political theory took the position that citizenship conferred equality on individuals otherwise unequal by birth and circumstances, modern nationalism made equality a precondition rather than a product of citizenship. "Nineteenth-century positivism and progressivism perverted [the] purpose of human equality when they set out to demonstrate what cannot be demonstrated, namely, that men are equal by nature and different only by history and circumstances, so that they can be equalized not by rights, but by circumstances and education." When education and social reform failed to produce homogeneous communities, the more drastic policy of racial purity commended itself, to rootless men and women who "could discover no higher value than themselves," as the only alternative to cultural "decadence." Instead of basing her interpretation on psychological speculation, Arendt tried to put the phenomenon of racism in its historical context.

propaganda, even for the best possible purpose." Even an "outstanding" sociologist like Robert Lynd confused "thinking with planning" and took the position that social science would "stand or fall on the basis of its serviceability to men as they struggle to live." "Shocked by social injustice," such scholars attempted, "in the spirit of Auguste Comte," to "establish a new social catechism." Their application of the "wisdom of engineering to religion" would prove self-defeating, Horkheimer predicted. "The language of the recommendation disavows what it means to recommend."

This could have been a description of *The Authoritarian Personality* itself. The only way to account for the disparity between the critical theory Adorno and Horkheimer propounded in other works and the "new social catechism" that emerged from the *Studies in Prejudice* is that the form of the latter undertaking predetermined its content. Investigations funded by a philanthropic foundation could hardly fail to issue in policy recommendations, in this case recommendations for an ambitious program of popular "re-education, scientifically planned on the basis of understanding scientifically arrived at." What was the point of such investigations if not to provide a "program of action"? Studies designed to enlist social science in the diagnosis and treatment of social maladies did not provide an appropriate forum in which to express reservations about social science. Such studies had to observe rigorous standards of measurement, to lay out the evidence in the form of charts and tables, to remind the reader at every opportunity that the problem was fearfully complex (though by no means insoluble), and thus to justify the claim that experts alone knew how to solve it.

The purpose and design of *Studies in Prejudice* dictated the conclusion that prejudice, a psychological disorder rooted in the "authoritarian" personality structure, could be eradicated only by subjecting the American people to what amounted to collective psychotherapy—by treating them as inmates of an insane asylum, as Thurman Arnold would have put it. This conclusion grew directly out of Horkheimer's premise that "the sincere and systematic scientific elucidation of [anti-Semitism] can contribute directly to an amelioration of the cultural atmosphere in which hatred breeds." As examples of the power of science to correct popular superstition, Horkheimer cited the dissipation of the witchcraft craze by Cartesian rationalism and the "revolution in the relation between parents and children" brought about by the work of Freud. In his introduction to *The Authoritarian Personality*, he compared anti-Semitism to a "social disease," which the "social scientist, like the biologist or the physician," could study in "periods of quiescence" so as to find "more effective ways to prevent or reduce the virulence of the next outbreak." In their general introduction to the five *Studies in Prejudice*, Horkheimer and Flowerman warned that an "aroused conscience is not enough if it does not stimulate a systematic search for an answer." So much for moral philosophy, mankind's memory and conscience! Neither conscience nor the common sense of the community, it appeared, would lead to the "eradication" of prejudice. Indeed the "progress of science" could "perhaps be charted by the advances that scientists have made over commonsense notions of phenomena."

Research for *The Authoritarian Personality*, conducted for the most part in the closing months of the war, proceeded in two stages. Questionnaires designed to elicit prejudiced, "pseudodemocratic," or downright "antidemocratic" attitudes were submitted to a variety of subjects. Of the two thousand individuals who completed these questionnaires, a hundred and fifty were selected for what was rather grandly referred to as "intensive clinical study"—that is, for a two- or three-hour interview. Those selected for interviews had scored either very high or very low on a variety of questionnaires, and the interviews were intended "to determine the factors which most clearly distinguished one extreme from the other." Eighty subjects submitted to a thematic apperception test. The subjects included students at the University of California and other colleges, students at the Alameda School for Merchant Marine officers, inmates at San Quentin, patients at a psychiatric clinic, members of men's service organizations like the Lions and Rotary clubs, a group of professional women, and members of various other groups.

The study made no claim to rest on a representative cross-section of the population. It aimed to discover not "what per cent of the general population would agree that 'labor unions have grown too powerful' and 'that there are too many Jews in government agencies' [but] whether or not there was a general relationship between these two opinions." A pattern of contradictory answers—for example, ones that simultaneously described Jews as seclusive and intrusive, capitalists and revolutionaries—was held to be especially significant, since internal contradictions revealed the irrationality of racial and ethnic prejudice.

Four separate questionnaires measured anti-Semitism, ethnocentrism in general, political and economic conservatism, and "authoritarianism." The last of these questionnaires, the famous F (fascism) scale, attempted to overcome certain difficulties that arose in the earlier stages of research. From the beginning, the investigators had introduced their questionnaires to subjects as a "public opinion inventory—not as a study of prejudice." Hoping to "prevent undue alarm," especially among conservative respondents, they included instructions that misrepresented the purpose of their research. "There are no 'right' or 'wrong' answers. The best answer is *your personal opinion.*"* This deception, however, did not altogether succeed in penetrating the "pseudodemocratic facade" that concealed "potentially antidemocratic" personality traits. Nor was it always possible, on the scales measuring anti-Semitism and ethnocentrism, to construct questions that would be "appealing and 'easy to fall for' "—that would "express subtle hostility without seeming to offend the democratic values which most prejudiced people feel they must maintain." Even the conservatism scale, designed to reveal the "psychological affinity between conservatism and ethnocentrism," produced correlations that "did not approach being high enough." The conservatism scale, moreover, was "too explicitly ideological," consisting of items that "might be too readily associated with prejudice in some logical or automatic way." The F scale, a measure of psychological "tendencies" that reflected "deeper, often unconscious forces," allegedly confirmed the hypothesis that "prefascist tendencies" had their roots in a personality structure characterized by aggressiveness, destructive cynicism, moral rigidity, intolerance of ambiguity, punitiveness, ego weakness, "failure in superego internalization," sadomasochism, and a "preoccupation with the more primitive aspects of

---

*Adorno et al. approached their subjects in the same spirit in which Thurman Arnold thought enlightened administrators should approach the general public—with every intention to deceive. The backwardness of American political culture, as liberals and radicals saw it, required such a strategy. Those who sought to "educate" the public could never avow their real intentions. Thus C. L. R. James saw Martin Luther King as a "Marxist-Leninist" forced to preach a milder message, a sentimental Christian message of brotherly love, from his pulpit.

sex." Individuals who fit this description, according to Adorno and his colleagues, suffered from repressed hostility to authority, which led them to attribute their own forbidden impulses to outsiders and to demand that these outsiders be severely punished. "In other words the individual's own unacceptable impulses are *projected* onto other individuals and groups who are then rejected."

Politics as Therapy

The most obvious objection to all this is that the investigators had arrived at most of their conclusions in advance. Instead of supporting those conclusions, the research consisted of a set of self-validating procedures that could lead only to the expected results. Curiously enough, this objection did not figure very prominently in the voluminous commentary on *The Authoritarian Personality*. A more common objection—one the authors anticipated and answered—was that the study substituted a psychological for a sociological analysis of prejudice. This criticism misconstrued the nature of the work. The authors concentrated on the analysis of personality only because they took the sociological background for granted. They never doubted the importance of social inequalities in the generation of right-wing movements, but they wanted to examine the "reverberations of social patterns within the most intimate realms of individual life," as Else Frenkel-Brunswick put it. None of the contributors, she said, regarded "psychological factors as the major or exclusive determinants of political or social movements." In their introduction, they acknowledged that "broad changes in social conditions and institutions" would have a "direct bearing upon the kinds of personalities that develop within a society." Horkheimer and Flowerman, in their general introduction to *Studies in Prejudice,* noted that the "cause of irrational hostility is in the last analysis to be found in social frustration and injustice."

An almost equally misconceived line of criticism linked *The Authoritarian Personality* to the antifamilial ideologies of the extreme left. According to Brigitte and Peter Berger, the book advanced the thesis argued "even more strongly" by Wilhelm Reich, R. D. Laing, and David Cooper, that "authoritarianism has its roots in the type of family produced by bourgeois-capitalist society." It was only "one small step," the Bergers thought, from *The Authoritarian Personality* to the wholesale condemnation of the family and to the "type of thinking" typified by the "commune movement in America and Western Europe." Whereas the first line of criticism overlooked the Marxist elements that went into the study, the Bergers' reading made too much of them. The general conclusions reached by Adorno and his collaborators fitted comfortably into a liberal consensus that condemned the allegedly repressive family patterns typical of working-class and lower-middle-class milieux and advocated as an alternative not "communes" but the enlightened family patterns already adopted by the professional and managerial classes. It was because *The Authoritarian Personality* appeared to support the prevailing liberal attitudes that it was absorbed so quickly into the mainstream of American social science. Its real importance lay in its contribution to the redefinition of liberalism as a cultural as well as a political impulse. It helped to move public discourse from the political to the psychosocial realm and to substitute medical and therapeutic categories for ethical and philosophical ones.

A third line of criticism rested, like the Bergers', on an overestimation of the importance of Adorno's Marxism. Edward Shils, in an analysis widely regarded as definitive, accused Adorno of confining his attention to right-wing authoritarianism and ignoring authoritarianism on the left. Adorno invited this type of criticism with obiter dicta that made his political opinions unmistakable, as when he denounced the "complete irrationality, not to say idiocy," of the "spurious identification of communism and fascism." Such outbursts enabled Shils to accuse him of treating left and right as opposite poles of the political spectrum and of ignoring the convergence of political extremes in a common antipathy to democratic values. But Shils had no objection to the translation of political categories into psychiatric categories. He did not quarrel with the psychoanalytic reductionism according to which a repressed revolt against parental authority leads to the displacement of aggressive impulses against outsiders. Indeed he regarded this explanation of the psychodynamics of authoritarianism as "one of the Berkeley group's most valuable hypotheses." He objected not to their psychologizing but merely to their politics.

The disagreement between Adorno and the most influential among his critics revealed a deeper level of agreement among Marxists, liberals, and even many American conservatives. This agreement took shape in the political climate generated by the profound shock of National Socialism, growing disenchantment with the transformative potential of working-class movements in the West, and a growing belief in scientific human-ism—more specifically in psychotherapeutic insights and practice—as the best defense against authoritarianism. Attentive readers of *The Authoritarian Personality*, undistracted by occasional expressions of left-wing political orthodoxy, would have been more impressed by its unflattering view of the working class. Adorno and his colleagues found no support in their research for the proposition that the working class could be regarded as the "main carrier of liberal ideas." They qualified this statement with the conventional reminder that "the crucial role in the struggle against increasing concentration of economic power will have to be played by the working people, acting in accordance with their self-interest"; but it was "foolhardy," they thought, "to underestimate the susceptibility to fascist propaganda within these masses." True, working-class respondents scored low on the ethnocentrism scale (and presumably on the conservatism scale as well); but their high scores on the F scale showed that although liberal unions had indoctrinated their members in ideologies opposed to overt racial discrimination, "this indoctrination did not go so far as to modify those attitudes centering around authoritarian-ism, which are more pronounced in this group than in most others."

It is when we turn to the question of how these "attitudes centering around authoritarianism" were actually identified that we can best grasp the way in which *The Authoritarian Personality*, by defining prejudice as a "social disease," substituted a medical for a political idiom and relegated a broad range of controversial issues to the clinic—to "scientific" study as opposed to philosophical and political debate. This procedure had the effect of making it unnecessary to discuss moral and political questions on their merits. Thus "resistance to social change," "traditionalism," and the absence of the ability or disposition "actively to criticize existing author-ity" became pathological by definition. The tendency to see political is-sues "in moral rather than sociological terms" fell under the same suspi-cion. A perception of the world as a jungle, a belief in strict sex roles, a "rigid" sexual morality, a "punitive" and "moralistic" style of child rear-ing, and a "rigid adherence to existing cultural norms" identified the authoritarian "syndrome" and could therefore be dismissed without arguing the pros and cons of these positions or considering the possibility that many people, for example, may have had good reason to hold a "conception of a threatening and dangerous environment" or to reject a middle-class conception of easygoing parental discipline.

The mode of summary judgment and dismissal came too easily to the authors of *The Authoritarian Personality*. Without bothering to present any evidence for their view, they assumed that a woman with a "self-image of conventional femininity" developed an "underlying bitterness" ("since the home does not provide her with satisfactory forms of expression"), which often took "deviously destructive forms." *The Authoritarian Personality* revealed more about the enlightened prejudices of the professional classes than about authoritarian prejudices among the common people. The authors found evidence of "authoritarian submission" in an affirmative answer to the proposition that "science has its place, but there are many important things that can never possibly be understood by the human mind." They saw "authoritarian aggression" in the belief that "an insult to our honor must always be punished" or that "if people would talk less and work more, everybody would be better off." They detected "anti-intraception" in the view that "nowadays more and more people are prying into matters that should remain personal and private." By identifying the "liberal personality" as the antithesis of the authoritarian personality, they equated mental health with an approved political position. They defended liberalism not on the grounds that liberal policies served the ends of justice and freedom but on the grounds that other positions had their roots in personal pathology. They enlarged the definition of liberalism to include a critical attitude toward all forms of authority, faith in science, relaxed and nonpunitive child-rearing practices, and flexible conceptions of sex roles. This expansive, largely cultural definition of liberalism made it easy to interpret adherence to liberalism as a "psychological matter."

The replacement of moral and political argument by reckless psychologizing not only enabled Adorno and his collaborators to dismiss unacceptable opinions on medical grounds; it led them to set up an impossible standard of political health—one that only members of a self-constituted cultural vanguard could consistently meet. In order to establish their emotional "autonomy," the subjects of their research had to hold the right opinions and also to hold them deeply and spontaneously. They had to show a professorial capacity for "critical analysis." It was not enough to have liberal ideas; one had to have a liberal personality. In a country officially committed to a democratic ideology but not yet fully emancipated from its provincial beginnings, as they saw it, the authors of *The Authoritarian Personality* thought it important to distinguish between "surface ideology and real opinion," between automatic adherence to democratic principles and deep-seated psychological commitment to a democratic way of life.

For this reason, they devoted a great deal of attention to the difference between the "genuine liberal" and the "pseudo-progressive," who repeated liberal slogans derived from "continuous newspaper reading" instead of arriving at the right opinions independently. Especially in the chapters contributed by Adorno, the test of spontaneous liberalism, in spite of the claim that liberal attitudes reflected an underlying psychological predisposition, became blatantly political. The pseudo-progressive gave lip-service support to the socialist "experiment" in the Soviet Union but replaced the "traditional socialist concept of class struggle with the image of a kind of joint, unanimous venture—as if society as a whole, as it is today, were ready to try socialism regardless of the influence of existing property relations." The pseudo-progressive clung to individualism and other "traditional values of American democratism" without understanding that "in an era in which 'rugged individualism' actually has resulted in far-reaching social control, . . . an uncritical individualistic concept of liberty may simply serve to play into the hands of the most powerful groups." Pseudo-progressives advocated "education" as a substitute for social change; this "education complex" enabled the "anti-utopian" to oppose change and "yet appear progressive." At one point, Adorno spoke of a "taxation complex," an equally exotic ailment. He found that pseudo-progressives held liberal opinions on a variety of topics but were "so deeply imbued with traditional economic concepts" that they could not follow their opinions to their proper conclusion. These subjects denounced monopoly without understanding just how pervasive it really was. "One cannot escape the impression that monopolism is used as a vague negative formula [by pseudo-progressives] but that very few subjects are actually aware of the impact of monopolization on their lives." The test of "genuine liberalism" had become so rigorous that only a civilized minority could pass it—a minority of one, if Adorno was taken as the final arbiter.

The Liberal Critique of Populism

· ■ ·

The Authoritarian Personality was only one of many postwar studies to argue, at least implicitly, that the people as a whole had little understanding of liberal democracy and that important questions of public policy should be decided by educated elites, not submitted to a popular vote. A widely cited study by Samuel Stouffer, *Communism, Conformity, and Civil Liberties* (1955), found elites to be far more tolerant of political nonconformity than the general public. Edward Shils reached the same conclusion in *The Torment of Secrecy* (1956), which claimed that "both the love of public liberty and the preference for the common good dominate the action of only a minority." In *The Politics of Mass Society* (1959), William Kornhauser argued that the working class and the lower middle class were "less committed to democratic parties and civil liberties" than the educated classes.

Postwar students of foreign policy, notably Walter Lippmann and George F. Kennan, blamed the democratization of diplomacy under Woodrow Wilson and Franklin Roosevelt for the intrusion of moral and ideological passions into policy-making. Their plea for a diplomacy conducted by trained professionals and based on the realistic calculation of national advantage reflected a belief, born of the long struggle against isolationism in the thirties and early forties, that foreign policy had to be removed from the arena of partisan debate and entrusted to a bipartisan administrative apparatus that would not cave in to political pressures. It was a "disconcerting" fact of recent history, Lippmann thought, that the "enfranchised masses have not, surprisingly enough, been those who have most staunchly defended the institutions of freedom." The confrontation with totalitarianism—first with Nazi Germany and then with Soviet Russia—had exposed grave weaknesses in democracy: inertia, indecisiveness, a preference for quick and painless solutions, a readiness to avoid difficult decisions by submitting them to public opinion. A "Jacobin conception of the emancipated and sovereign people" had brought about a "devitalization of the governing power" and a general "decline of the West."

McCarthyism confirmed liberals in their fear of mass movements and "direct democracy," and they turned to Adorno's concept of pseudo-conservatism in order to uncover the social and psychological roots of its "profound if largely unconscious hatred of our society and its ways," in the words of Richard Hofstadter. With a few exceptions, they ignored the international tensions exploited by McCarthy. Most of them refused to admit that Truman's containment policy and his domestic loyalty program had helped to generate the anticommunist hysteria now directed against Truman himself and his principal advisers. Instead they traced McCarthy's "pseudo-conservatism" to the populist tradition in American politics. "This outburst of direct democracy," wrote Peter Viereck in *The New American Right* (1955), a collection of essays on McCarthyism edited by Daniel Bell, "comes straight from the leftist rhetoric of the old Populists and Progressives, a rhetoric forever urging the People to take back 'their' government from the conspiring Powers That Be." According to Leslie Fiedler, the populist "distrust of authority, institutions, and expert knowledge" had found a new champion in McCarthy. Seymour Martin Lipset argued that McCarthy played on the "key symbols" that appealed to populists and compaigned "against the same groups midwest Populism always opposed, the Eastern conservative financial aristocracy."

This interpretation of McCarthyism as a revival of populism drew heavily on Adorno's concept of status politics. McCarthy's obsession with domestic subversion, according to Hofstadter, revealed a "dense and massive irrationality" that distinguished pseudo-conservatism from "practical conservatism." Like Adorno, Hofstadter saw every departure from orthodox liberalism as an expression of a "paranoid" style. Having come to recognize a "wide range of behavior for which the economic interpretation of politics seems to be inadequate," he found status anxiety in everything that could not be accounted for by an economic interpretation.* This approach, though ostensibly designed to replace economic

---

*"My generation," Hofstadter wrote in 1962, "was raised in the conviction that the basic motive power in political behavior is the economic interest of groups." Having

determinism, nevertheless made the pursuit of clearly defined economic interests appear to be the only rational and legitimate form of political activity. Whatever could not be reduced to an economic motive became "paranoid" by default. Thus American farmers began to achieve tangible gains, according to Hofstadter, only when they abandoned the sentimental agrarian myth and learned to define themselves as an interest group. He dismissed populism as a movement driven by the small property holder's typically conspiratorial view of politics, befuddled by soft-money ideologies and other panaceas, given to nativist and anti-Semitic outbursts, and longing for the vanished rural simplicities celebrated by the myth of the yeoman. He dismissed progressivism as another type of petty-bourgeois movement led by representatives of an older middle class experiencing an abrupt decline in status and fearful of the big organizations—trusts and unions—that were coming to dominate industrial society. Hofstadter's interpretation of American history incorporated cultural prejudices so familiar to a broad spectrum of intellectual opinion that its widespread acceptance, in retrospect, seems almost a foregone conclusion.

Probably the most important of these prejudices was an abiding contempt for the petty bourgeoisie. A curious convergence of Mencken and

---

come to understand the shortcomings of this view, he might have asked himself whether the root of the trouble did not lie in a misguided effort to reduce political action to "behavior." In *The Human Condition*, published in the same year as *The New American Right*, Hannah Arendt pointed out that an overly "selective" view of politics had "excluded from articulate conceptualization a great variety of authentic political experiences," the most important of which—the deliberate rejection of revenge, for example, the rejection of the "natural, automatic reaction to transgression"—are precisely those that are least expected and therefore least reducible to anything as predictable as "behavior." The need for a broader conception of the political, however, was the last thing on the mind of American historians in the forties and fifties. They were not interested in Arendt's suggestion that political life represents the institutionalization of the capacity for action—the capacity to initiate something, to make a new beginning (by foregoing revenge). Instead of reconsidering the implications of "behavior," they simply supplemented economic reductionism with sociological and psychological reductionism, adding to an economic interpretation of political behavior a social-psychological interpretation designed to cover cases where no intelligible economic motive seemed to be at work.

Marx informed the liberal critique of populism. Marx admired capitalism because of its dynamism, its destruction of traditional ways of life, and the technical progress it made possible; but neither he nor his followers admired the heterogeneous class of small proprietors, shopkeepers, artisans, and farmers—a class happily destined to "disappear in the face of modern industry," according to the *Communist Manifesto.* In the Marxian scheme of things, many features of which liberals like Hofstadter retained long after they ceased to be Marxists in their politics, the lower middle class shared the capitalists's love of money without his daring. It clung to outworn folkways—conventional religiosity, hearth and home, the sentimental cult of motherhood—and obsolete modes of production. It looked back to a mythical golden age in the past. It resented social classes more highly placed but internalized their standards, lording it over the poor instead of joining them in a common struggle against oppression. It was haunted by the fear of slipping farther down the social scale and clutched the shreds of respectability that distinguished it from the class of manual workers. Fiercely committed to the work ethic, it believed that anyone who wanted a job could find one and that those who refused to work should starve. Lacking liberal culture, it fell easy prey to all sorts of nostrums and political fads—paper money, vague schemes for sharing the wealth, anarchism, utopian (as opposed to scientific) socialism.*

An essay by Victor Ferkiss, "Populist Influences on American Fascism" (1957), illustrated the liberal critique of petty-bourgeois populism in its crudest form. Ferkiss understood populism as a "generic" configuration embracing the People's party of the 1890s and "such closely allied movements as the Greenback party, the Bryan free silver crusades, LaFollette Progressivism," the Non-Partisan League, distributism, and other expressions of "agrarian revolt against domination by Eastern financial and industrial interests." It represented the "American equiva-

---

*According to Lenin, the petty bourgeoisie "suffers constant oppression" under capitalism and "easily becomes revolutionary, but is incapable of displaying perseverance, ability to organize, discipline, and firmness." It is above all its resistance to revolutionary discipline that has made the lower middle class the despair of Marxists. Together with its stubborn refusal to disappear, this political unreliability makes the lower middle class a "historical problem," in the words of the historian Arno Mayer.

lent of European fascism and national socialism." Isolationist, racist, and anti-Semitic, populism was at odds with "democratic socialism in the humanist tradition." It contained no "broad ideas about human freedom or the fuller human life" and hence "aroused no interest in serious American intellectual circles." It did not criticize "private property or the wage system." Instead it attacked symbolic and largely imaginary evils, usually conceived as the product of conspiracies led by Jewish financiers, agents of the Roman Catholic church, or communists. Populists shared a belief in "plebiscitary democracy" and a "despair of liberal democratic institutions." They wanted to "sweep away intervening institutions"— legislatures, courts, parties—and to set up a tyranny of the majority. They hated labor unions as much as they hated big business. Their program appealed to a "middle class composed largely of farmers and small merchants," which feared that it would be "crushed between big business . . . and an industrial working class which tends to question the necessity of the wage system and even of private property itself."

Ignoring evidence that criticism of the wage system was far more closely identified with the populist tradition than with the twentieth-century labor movement, Ferkiss rested his case on inflammatory quotations from Huey Long, Father Charles Coughlin, Gerald L. K. Smith, Ezra Pound, Lawrence Dennis, and Charles Lindbergh. Their pronouncements exposed a "common core of doctrine" and thus relieved the historian of populism of the need to trace their ideas to a specific tradition of thought or to a particular history of political agitation. Torn out of its historical context—the struggle to preserve the moral virtues conferred by property ownership against the combined threat of wage labor and the collectivization of property—"populism" became a makeshift category that included everything that fell outside a liberal or social democratic consensus. Ferkiss made no attempt to prove that his "populists" referred to themselves as such or claimed to stand in the populist succession. The passive subject of his central contention—"the claim is openly made that the fascists are the inheritors of the Populist mantle"—remained unspecified. Since "no figure in this article ever applied the label 'fascist' to himself," as Ferkiss admitted in a footnote to this same sentence, it is hard to see how any of them could have made such a claim. Perhaps this singularly uninformative summary of his thesis referred to the thesis itself— the "claim" that Ferkiss was "openly" making in his own essay!

Populism as Working-Class
Authoritarianism

· ■ ·

For Marxists, criticism of petty-bourgeois populism served as a counterpoint to their praise of the industrial workers, the real revolutionaries. According to Marx and Engels, industrialism uprooted the working class, dragged it out of the "idiocy of rural life" into the factory, divested it of the false consolations of religion and respectability, turned its domestic life upside down by forcing the worker's wife and even his children into the marketplace, and thus transformed former artisans and peasants into a class of revolutionary outlaws. By the 1950s, however, it was plain to all but a few diehards that industrial workers had failed to grasp their revolutionary opportunity. Disclosures of corruption in the unions, the decline of labor militancy, and the advent of "big labor" tore away the romantic aura of the underdog that surrounded the labor movement in the thirties. One study after another depicted a working class newly suburbanized, economically secure for the first time but socially at sea, resentful of blacks and other minorities pressing up from below, beset by status anxiety, and ripe for radical demagogues. These images of working-class "embourgeoisement" made it possible for liberals to assign the classic traits of the petty bourgeoisie even to industrial workers, formerly the hope of the left but now part of the "historical problem" of the lower middle class.

Mounting evidence of "working-class authoritarianism," according to Lipset, "posed a tragic dilemma for those intellectuals of the democratic left who once believed the proletariat necessarily to be a force for liberty, racial equality, and social progress." Personality research, investigations of working-class family patterns, and studies of public opinion all showed that workers viewed political choices as "black and white, good and evil." Their intolerance of ambiguity—the hallmark of the authoritarian personality, according to Adorno—predisposed them to "extremist movements which suggest easy and quick solutions to social problems and have a rigid outlook." Like many other liberals, Lipset had come to the "gradual realization that extremist and intolerant movements in modern society are more likely to be based on the lower classes than on the middle and upper class." Formerly liberals had worried about the decline of popular participation in politics. Now they began to wonder whether "apathy" might not be a blessing in disguise, if it reduced the danger that "status-ridden" people desperately seeking "social approval," as Adorno called them, would find political outlets for their "pent-up social fury."

The voluminous literature on the authoritarian family registered the shift in liberals' opinion of the American worker. Sociologists had argued for some time that a new ethic of sexual and generational egalitarianism was destroying the "traditional concept of the family," according to which the "father is head of the house, the mother is entrusted with the care . . . of the children, and . . . children owe their parents honor" and obedience. After the Second World War, they began to politicize the family by arguing that an "autocratic form of family organization," in the words of the president of the National Conference on Family Relations, "can never prepare children for the new democratic social order." Not until the 1950s, however, did it occur to liberal sociologists to identify the "traditional" family as a working-class institution. Earlier studies had noted with approval that working-class parents were more casual about child rearing than their upper-middle-class counterparts. Upper-middle-class discipline was often criticized as rigid and repressive. Allison Davis and Robert Havighurst noted in 1946 that it produced "orderly, conscientious, responsible, and tame" adults. In 1954, Eleanor Maccoby and Patricia Gibbs challenged this older view with evidence that middle-class parents were permissive about many things and "somewhat warmer and more demonstrative" in their relations with their children. Four years later, Urie Bronfenbrenner could describe as the "most consistent finding" of child-rearing studies that working-class parents typically resorted to physical punishment, whereas middle-class parents relied on "reasoning, isolation, and . . . 'love-oriented' techniques of discipline." By 1971, another review of research indicated that these contrasts now dominated the sociological literature on child rearing. "Middle-class parents tend to be more controlling and supportive of their children than lower-class parents and . . . are less likely to use physical punishment."

In a remarkably short period of time, the middle-class family, once repressively puritanical, had become warm and loving, while the image of working-class domesticity shifted from carefree spontaneity to rigidly authoritarian discipline. As Talcott Parsons noted in 1964, recent research, which indicated that the "discipline imposed on lower-class children tends to be significantly more severe" than middle-class discipline, supported "Lipset's now well-known material on working-class authoritarianism." Subsequent studies added to the charge of punitive discipline a steadily lengthening list of offenses against enlightened practice: rigid sexual stereotypes, an exaggerated sense of personal honor, emotional inexpressiveness, lack of sophistication in interpersonal relations, ignorance of psychology, and a "trained incapacity to share," in Mirra Komarovsky's phrase. In her standard monograph, *Blue-Collar Marriage* (1962), Komarovsky said that her visits to working-class households "transported" her, "as if by a Wellsian time machine, into an older era, one of pre-Freudian innocence about human nature," in which such concepts as "emotional security" and the "capacity to relate to others" were unknown. Komarovsky considered this "paucity of ideas," this "ignorance of psychological dynamics," a source of emotional maladjustment. A similar point of view informed Donald McKinley's observation that working-class parents did not think of the child "as a product." Once this might have been taken as a tribute to working-class spontaneity. To McKinley, however, it suggested an insufficiency of "emotional capital," which led to "severe socialization of the child, hostility to whatever is human and emotional, . . . and general alienation from prevailing social norms."

The shift from a sympathetic to a censorious view of working-class culture reflected a growing enthusiasm for medical and psychiatric expertise as well as a change in the political climate. Working-class resistance to therapeutic intervention provided one more indication of cultural backwardness. A revealing essay, "Underutilization of Medical-Care Services by Blue-Collarites," located the source of the trouble in a fatalistic attitude toward the body.

> It is as though the white-collar class thinks of the body as a machine to be preserved and kept in perfect functioning condition, whether through prosthetic devices, rehabilitation, cosmetic surgery, or perpetual treatment, whereas blue-collar groups think of the body as having a limited span of utility: to be enjoyed in youth and then to suffer with and to endure stoically with age and decrepitude.

Once liberals might have favored working-class realism over the middle-class conception of the body as a machine requiring "perpetual treatment." The authors, however, drew the opposite conclusion. A stoic acceptance of bodily decline, they argued, reflected a "damaged self-image."

Generalizations about the "role of personality in the formation of social beliefs," in the words of Herbert McClosky, served to put objectionable beliefs beyond the pale of political debate and to justify the contention that educated elites were the best guardians of democracy. Drawing on Eric Hoffer's study of the "true believer" as well as on *The Authoritarian Personality*, McClosky traced political conservatism to "psychological rigidity." A belief in man's wickedness, in the need for strong social controls, and in the stabilizing influence of the family and the church derived from unhealthy "psychological impulses," "projections of aggressive personality tendencies." As "doctrinal expressions of a personality pattern," such ideas did not have to be discussed on their merits. They appealed to the wrong sort of people, suspect on socioeconomic as well as on psychological grounds: "the uninformed, the poorly educated, . . . the less intelligent, . . . the more backward and frightened elements of the population." The "articulate and informed classes," on the other hand, were "preponderantly liberal in their outlook" and accordingly constituted the "major repositories of the public conscience." They alone, it appeared, were capable of "reasoning out and forming attitudes on complex social questions" in a "purely disinterested way" and of rising above the "ideological babble of poorly informed and discordant opinions."

Once the symptoms of working-class authoritarianism had been identified and traced to their familial roots, political sociologists had no trouble in explaining their influence on illiberal, "undemocratic" ideologies. "Working-class authoritarianism goes far to explain the rigid and intolerant approach many blue-collarites take to American political affairs," wrote Arthur B. Shostak in one of the standard works on working-class culture. "Unable to understand how politics works, and contemptuous of conciliation and compromise, working-class authoritarians seek to impose on society some sort of 'fundamental truth' that will liberate America from its soft-headed illusions." Students of "political alienation" discovered that contempt for politicians, resentment of big business, and a general sense of powerlessness appeared more often among workers than among upper-middle-class populations. According to William Simon and

John Gagnon, workers were driven by a "mythic sense of the past" and by a desire to restore an older order. William Kornblum traced blue-collar populism, with its irrational "distrust of big business," its sense of alienation from a "government insulated from the popular will," and its "fear of foreign ideologies," to the competition for "rectitude and status" in communities marked by "general provincialism," "parochial neighborhood solidarity," and "cultural isolation."

Workers believed that "big business is running this country," Robert Lane noted. Instead of asking himself whether there was any truth in this perception, Lane explained it as the product of a "cabalistic" mentality or "usurpation complex." Subject to "whim and impulse," workers adopted conspiracy theories as a "counterweight to the chaotic forces of drift and change welling up in anarchic fashion within themselves." Lane's *Political Ideology*, widely regarded as the leading study of political alienation, reduced working-class discontent to personal pathology. Lane wondered why workers did not "see the President or Congress as running things," instead of attributing so much power to big business. The explanation, he decided, was that people with an underdeveloped "ego or self" demanded an image of "absolute power" that was "clearly hard to find in Congress or the President." Only a handful of Lane's subjects, "free of cabalist thinking," realistically perceived power as "generally shared and limited" and respected "legitimate power as superior to and containing . . . the power of private groups." As in *The Authoritarian Personality*, liberal ideology—in this case, the dogma that political power in the United States was distributed so evenly among a plurality of interest groups that none achieved overweening influence—furnished the standard of mental health.

Lane had little patience with the theory of "mass society" advanced by William Kornhauser and others. According to Kornhauser, anomie and political alienation reflected the breakdown of "community." Lane argued, on the contrary, that it was the "very absence of community that makes democracy possible." Democratic institutions were the product of modernization: "industrialization, increased wealth, increased urbanization, increased education, increased communication." The "professional class," more fully exposed to modernizing influences than other classes, was the most liberal in its outlook, the "staunchest defender of democracy's two greatest ideals," freedom and equality. "Neither the commercial classes nor the working classes" had much "affection" for those ideals. "It is not to 'The People,' not to the business class, not to the working class, that we must look for the consistent and relatively unqualified defense of freedom and equality." Lane's attack on working-class pathology served as an apology for his own class, the educated, salaried elite.

James D. Wright came to similar conclusions in *The Dissent of the Governed*, in which he took issue with the commonsensical proposition that democracy required popular trust in government. By means of the usual questionnaires, Wright discovered widespread "alienation" in the form of support for statements to the effect that "people like me don't have any say about what the government does" or that "public officials don't care much about what people like me think." He went on to argue, however, that alienated Americans were too passive and apathetic to threaten the body politic. "Aging, poorly educated, and working-class," they were "unlikely to attend church, inattentive to the mass media," and seldom inclined even to vote. "The evidence . . . suggests that democracies function reasonably well with the consent of no more than half their population." McClosky made much the same point, reassuring his readers that those who were "most confused about democratic ideals" were also "apathetic and without significant influence." "Their role in the nation's decision process is so small," McClosky wrote, "that their 'misguided' opinions or non-opinions have little practical consequence for stability." The only people who really mattered, it appeared, were the members of the professional and managerial class. "The consent of this group," Wright observed, "is critical for the persistence of the regime. . . . The system could quite easily grind to a halt if their consent was withheld."

Educated Insularity

The theory of working-class authoritarianism did not escape criticism, but the broader assumptions behind it proved highly resistant to attack. A few sociologists objected to its emphasis on the pathological roots of unenlightened attitudes, preferring to blame them on a lack of education, not on deep-seated character flaws. "The greater authoritarianism of the working class," Lewis Lipsitz wrote, ". . . appears to be largely a product of lower education. With education controlled, middle-class individuals . . . are not consistently less authoritarian than working-class individuals." The general impression of working-class backwardness remained, however, whether it was attributed to authoritarian family patterns or simply to insufficient education. The worker's "meager education," in the words of Albert Cohen and Harold Hodges, cut him off from "encounters with other, contrasting worlds." An effective challenge to the ruling assumptions about "modernization" and cultural backwardness would have had to question the equation of democracy with social mobility, secularization, educational opportunity, and the abandonment of traditional folkways. It would have had to question the image of working-class insularity popularized even by those who tried, like Mirra Komarovsky, to describe working-class culture with some sympathy but almost invariably spoke of a "narrowly circumscribed" existence unrelieved by contact with the great society beyond the neighborhood horizon. Beyond the neighborhood, Komarovsky said, "extends a vast darkness."

Blind to their own prejudices, the children of light could not see that their own world was in many ways just as narrowly circumscribed as the worker's. If the worker spent his days in the company of "people very like himself," so did the educated classes. Their travels took them around the globe, but the internationalization of the professional and managerial mode of life meant that they encountered the same kind of people and the same living conditions everywhere they went: the same hotels, the same three-star restaurants, the same conference rooms and lecture halls. Education gave them vicarious access to the world's culture, but their acquaintance with that culture was increasingly selective and fragmentary, and it did not seem to have strengthened the capacity for imaginative identification with experience alien to their own. Their educated jargon had lost touch with everyday spoken language and no longer served as a repository of the community's common sense. Academic discourse had achieved a certain analytical precision, in law and medicine and the hard sciences, at the expense of vividness and evocative power; while in fields like psychiatry, sociology, and social work, it merely distinguished insiders from outsiders and gave an air of scientific prestige to practices embarrassed by their homely origins. Academic English—the abstract, uninflected, colorless medium not only of the classroom but of the board-room, the clinic, the court of law, and the governmental bureau—had discarded most of the earthy idioms that betrayed its provincial Anglo-Saxon past, and the spoken form of this English no longer betrayed any hint of regional accent or dialect. The bureaucratization of language indi-cated what was happening to intellectual culture as a whole: its transfor-mation into a universal medium in a curious way seemed to weaken its capacity to promote public communication. The people who stood at the forefront of the "communications age" had lost the ability to communi-cate with anyone but themselves. Their technical jargons were unintelli-gible to outsiders but immediately recognizable, as the badge of profes-sional status, to fellow specialists all over the world. The cosmopolitanism of educated specialists overcame the old barriers of local, regional, and even national identity but insulated them from ordi-nary people and ordinary human experience.

Priding themselves on the global reach of their culture, the educated classes led what was in many ways a constricted, insular life. Modern conveniences sheltered them from everyday discomforts. Air-condition-ing and central heating protected them from the elements but cut them off from the vivid knowledge of nature that comes only to those who expose themselves to her harsher moods. Exemption from manual labor deprived them of any appreciation of the practical skills it requires or the kind of knowledge that grows directly out of firsthand experience. Just as their acquaintance with nature was limited to a vacation in some national park, so their awareness of the sensual, physical side of life was largely recreational, restricted to activities designed to keep the bodily "ma-chine" in working order. Jogging, tennis, and safe sex did not make up for the loss of more vigorous exercise. Nor did open-mindedness make up for the absence of strongly held convictions. The educated classes overcame fanaticism at the price of desiccation.

Having come to regard the scientific community of free and open in-quiry as the "prototype of the free society," as Shils put it, they had redefined democracy in their own image. "Democracy" came to refer to the "thoughtways of a knowledgeable society," in Lane's words—a capac-ity for abstraction, tolerance of ambiguity, rejection of "philosophical idealism" and "theological and metaphysical modes of thought," accept-ance of "mathematical modes of expression." These habits of thought defined an intellectual ideal of open-mindedness and an ethical ideal of tolerance, mutual respect, and suspended judgment. If the "moral perspectives" typical of authoritarianism rested on "crude and mechanical assumptions about human behavior," as Robert Endleman argued in a "composite portrait" of blue-collar workers, then a more enlightened morality had to rest on the academic and therapeutic virtues. It had to rest on a respect for human potential, an aversion to pain and suffering, a critical attitude toward authority, a refusal to be governed by traditional precepts, and a belief that most conflicts could be resolved by submitting them to the arbitration of knowledgeable experts. By reformulating these values as psychological norms, the professional-managerial class made it possible to dismiss dissent from the educated consensus as evidence of emotional and cultural backwardness. Members of the educated elite upheld open-mindedness as the supreme political virtue but refused to debate their own idea of the good life, perhaps because they suspected that it could not withstand exposure to more vigorous ideas.

Camelot after Kennedy: Oswald as Everyman

· ■ ·

"Civilized" liberalism reached its high point in the administration of John F. Kennedy and in the retrospective idealization of Kennedy as its quintessential embodiment. In liberal mythology, Kennedy's assassination became a symbol of thwarted promise, of "excellence" overthrown, of the American dream in decline. The political turmoil that followed his death, even more than McCarthyism, convinced liberals that governmental authority represents a delicate and vulnerable structure of civilizing constraints superimposed on seething popular emotions—racism, violence, vindictiveness, envy of distinction and success. The legend of "Camelot" sheltered the New Frontier and the political tradition behind it from reappraisal. Since the towering stature assigned (both in life and in death) to Kennedy as the symbol of liberalism's finest hour rested on images rather than substance—Arthur Schlesinger's case for Kennedy over Nixon in 1960 having consisted largely of the claim that "Nixon lacks taste"—the illusion of his greatness could be sustained, in the face of his inconclusive, often disappointing record in office, only by retrospective commentary that dwelled on the unfulfilled promise of a career brought prematurely to a tragic close.

Two themes emerged in the flood of commentary following Kennedy's assassination: celebration of his "style" and speculation about the dark undercurrents in American life, the unsuspected flaws in the national character, that had led to his murder. According to *Newsweek*, Kennedy "infused [the presidential] office with a youthful, direct and vigorous style unmatched since the days of Theodore Roosevelt." "The key was style," wrote Ben Bradlee. "His style captured the nation's imagination. The country, reflecting its new leader, had a new look. . . . With his gifts of intellect, purpose, and charm, and his high hopes of winning a second term, what great and lasting accomplishments might he have forged?" Theodore H. White praised Kennedy's "remarkable, astringent candor," his "gaiety, elegance, grace." While historians would argue about the "seminal legislation and proposals of the Kennedy administration," no one could have any doubts about his matchless "style." Schlesinger's eulogy in the *Saturday Evening Post* celebrated Kennedy's "vitality of personality," his "quick intelligence, easy charm, and laconic wit," his "historical imagination," his "vision of America . . . as a noble nation, rising above mean and ugly motives." Kennedy gave the nation a "new sense of itself," Schlesinger wrote, "a new spirit, a new style, a new conception of its role and destiny." Not to be outdone, White published an interview with Jacqueline Kennedy, two weeks after the assassination, that closed with the words from the Broadway musical, as quoted by Mrs. Kennedy: "For one brief shining moment there was Camelot."*

---

*Kennedy's admirers were not wrong to stress the need for a leader who would speak to and represent the "real subterranean life of America," as Norman Mailer put it in his account of the 1960 Democratic convention. There was much to be said for Mailer's contention that "the life of politics and the life of myth had diverged too far" in the postwar years and that the times demanded a leader who could "engage" once again the "myth of the nation" and thus bring a new "impetus . . . to the arts, to the practices, to the lives and to the imaginations of the American." Mailer's mistake lay in identifying Kennedy as such a leader. Those who believe that "history is full of heroes"—a

A hero defined so largely by his style required an appropriate antithesis, and Kennedy's eulogists found one made to order in the person of Lee Harvey Oswald. A misfit, a nobody, a pathetic mouse of a man, Oswald had exactly the right qualities for the role history had evidently assigned him. A kind of aesthetic satisfaction crept into accounts of his role as Kennedy's nemesis. "So hate triumphed," wrote Ralph McGill with a suggestion of its inevitability, at the end of an article deploring political "extremism." Schlesinger closed his post-assassination tribute to Kennedy on a similar cadence. Kennedy had been the "most civilized President we have had since Jefferson," Schlesinger wrote. "And so a crazed political fanatic shot him down." Kennedy's admirers, themselves fascinated by the "majesty and burdens of the Presidency," as *Newsweek* put it, attributed the same fascination to Kennedy's alleged assassin. Like the assassins of Garfield, Lincoln, and McKinley, Oswald was a "lonely psychopath," in the words of a report in *Time*, seeking an "hour of mad glory." The prototype of the little man in his loser's envy of the Kennedy glamour, Oswald reinforced doubts about the common man's ability to rise to the challenge of the modern world. Those who admired Kennedy's patrician disdain for conventional political gestures found in Oswald a perfect outlet for their fear of the mass mind. He represented the worst in American life, just as Kennedy represented the best and brightest.

Speculation about the assassination thus came to hinge not on the question of whether Oswald could have murdered Kennedy unassisted but on the seemingly much larger, momentous question of what his action revealed about the national psyche. The question so often raised in the hours following the assassination—"What have we come to?"—prompted

---

view Mrs. Kennedy attributed to Kennedy himself—need to cultivate the ability to distinguish heroism from imposture, the prophet from the false prophet, the "speaker" from the "babbler," in Carlyle's terms. Those who idolized Kennedy, deceived by the glamour of the White House, confused heroism with celebrity. Their infatuation with Kennedy blinded them to the presence of an authentic hero in their midst. It was not until many years later (as Garry Wills notes in a review of Taylor Branch's history of the civil rights movement) that Americans began to recognize the fifties and sixties not as the age of John F. Kennedy or Lyndon B. Johnson but as the age of Martin Luther King.

an orgy of national soul-searching. Conducted for the most part in the sociological and psychiatric mode, this pseudo-introspection did not address the questions left unanswered by the Warren Report: the number and location of the shots that killed Kennedy, the nature of his wounds, and the specific circumstances that might have led to the shooting. Doubts about the Warren Report were dismissed as evidence of a "conspiracy mentality," part of the same climate of hatred that bred psychopaths like Oswald. The assassinations of Malcolm X, Martin Luther King, and Robert Kennedy, a wave of urban riots, and the increasingly violent clashes between radical students and police gave extra urgency to the demand for socio-psychiatric explanations of the American malaise. In 1969, the National Commission on the Causes and Prevention of Violence reported that all these events could be traced to the country's tradition of random, apolitical violence.* Cross-cultural comparisons indicated that "traditional" and "modern" societies had low rates of violence, whereas violence flourished in "transitional" societies "awakened to a desire for a new way of life but only beginning to achieve it." Since the United States did not conform to expectations about the civilizing effects of modernization, the commission searched for conditions peculiar to American society and found them (as Gunnar Myrdal had found them) in the nation's history of racial conflict, in the vigilante tradition, and in the misguided notions of individualism and popular sovereignty that helped to sustain it. "The vigilante tradition lives on. It has become a permanent part of the American heritage." It received cultural support from such well-established democratic doctrines as freedom of conscience, the right to bear arms, and the right of revolution. Nervous about democracy, the commission stressed the "critical importance" of maintaining an "over-

---

*Like the Warren Report, *Assassination and Political Violence* began by assuming Oswald's guilt and went on to build an elaborate structure of speculation on this shaky premise. In a section on the "psychology of presidential assassins," the authors (James F. Kirkham, Sheldon G. Levy, and William J. Crotty) found a common pattern of familial disruption and alienation, to which Oswald closely conformed: "absence or disruption of the normal family relationship between parent and child," "hostility towards their mother redirected against authority symbols," "difficulty [in] making friends of either sex, especially in establishing lasting relationships with women."

whelming sense of the legitimacy of our government and institutions."
Like the Warren Commission, it attached far more importance to legitimacy than to democracy.

The Commission on Violence recognized the need to remove the "root
causes of social unrest and perceived injustice" and disavowed any "short
cut to political tranquillity"; but it also disavowed the possibility that
social injustices could be corrected through popular action. It deplored
social tensions and "perceived injustice," not injustice itself. It deplored
the rise of "two warring camps of white racists and black militants,"
without examining the issues that had brought those camps into being. It
denounced the "extremism" of left and right, claiming that the "tactics of
the New Left are virtually identical with those used at an early stage by
the Nazis." By innuendo and implication, it defined popular agitation as
the principal threat to "political tranquillity."

The authors of *Assassination and Political Violence* were puzzled by the
popularity of conspiratorial explanations of assassinations. They argued
that presidential assassinations, because of their overtones of patricide,
exposed the vulnerability of cherished symbols of permanence and continuity. Conspiracy theories, however preposterous, cushioned the shock
by providing a "more intelligible explanation" than random violence. "It
seems incredible that the man who commands the largest power in the
world can be destroyed in seconds by the attack of a nonentity." Instead
of admitting that a single "isolated, unstable individual" can threaten the
fragile structure of governmental authority, people took refuge in far-
fetched fantasies of conspiracy. Here again, the commission emphasized
the contrast between the vulnerability of legitimate authority and the
violence of popular irrationality and emotionalism, which threatened to
undermine the imposing but fragile structure of representative institutions. Popular hatred and irrationality came to the surface not only in the
action of the deranged assassin himself but in the hardly less deranged
response to it: the "psychic need" for conspiracy theories, the refusal to
listen to the "seemingly overwhelming evidence" against them, and the
vindictive demand for the assassin's head, even among those who doubted
his sole responsibility for the crime. Polls showing that only a third of
those interviewed thought Oswald should have a fair trial disturbed
right-thinking people almost as much as the polls showing a widespread
belief in conspiracy. "The American public in these circumstances is

more concerned with retribution than with . . . the rule of law," wrote the authors of *Assassination and Political Violence*. The confusion of justice with vengeance—which diminished, they noted, among the more affluent and highly educated classes—provided another indication of the immaturity and emotionalism of the popular mind.

The assumptions underlying the report of the Commission on Violence reappeared even in the writings of observers farther removed from the official view of things. Garry Wills and Ovid Demaris offered a similar explanation of the popular need for conspiracy theories. The bullet that killed Kennedy, they argued, evoked a fear of "dangers more disintegrative than any conspiracy." It evoked a "panicky feeling that chaos had broken loose." Drawing on a study of popular reactions to the assassination conducted by the National Opinion Research Center, Wills and Demaris attributed the need for conspiracy theories to the fear of the unknown and the desire to deny the existential horror of Kennedy's death by reducing it to a plot. Horrified by the radical evil embodied in Oswald, the American people had to get rid of Oswald, "to 'shoot' him with words, talk, theory, proof." Jack Ruby's murder of Oswald vicariously satisfied not only the public's primitive need for retribution but the need to remove the assassin altogether and thus to deny the "obliterative irresponsibility of death."

Even some of those who questioned the Warren Report decried the popular need for conspiracy theories and the psychological needs behind them. In 1968, Edward Jay Epstein, one of the earliest critics of the Warren Commission, published an attack on Jim Garrison, the New Orleans district attorney who claimed to have unraveled a right-wing plot leading to Kennedy's murder. According to Epstein, Garrison exemplified "what Richard Hofstadter has classified as 'the paranoid style in American politics,' to which 'the feeling of persecution is central,' and which is 'systematized in grandiose theories of conspiracy.'" Admitting that Garrison's "paranoid style" did not "of itself rule out the possibility that there is substance to his claims," Epstein nevertheless shifted the burden of proof, in effect, from the government to its critics.*

---

*It was easy, of course, even before Garrison's case collapsed in court, to ridicule his rhetorical attacks on the "Eastern establishment" and his irresponsible, unsubstan-

The most remarkable feature of the controversy surrounding the assassination is not the abundance of conspiracy theories but the rejection, by the "best and brightest," of any possibility of a conspiracy. To this day, they remain convinced that the "search for conspiracy," as Anthony Lewis has written, "only increases the elements of morbidity and paranoia and fantasy in this country. . . . It obscures our necessary understanding, all of us, that in this life there is often tragedy without reason."

---

tiated charges against President Johnson, whose suppression of the truth about Kennedy's murder, according to Garrison, indicated that he too had participated in the plot to kill Kennedy, since he "gained more than any other human from the assassination." The anti-Johnson version of the conspiracy thesis was the ugliest of the many wild and wishful solutions propounded by the left in an attempt not merely to explain events unexplained by the Warren Report but to clear Oswald.

The conspiracy theories advanced by the left, inspired by a search for right-wing villains and venomous hatred of Johnson, helped to discredit the case for conspiracy among people who had doubts about the Warren Report but found the ideas of its critics repellent. The popularity of conspiracy theories on the right, which blamed Moscow or Havana, helped to identify them even more closely with political extremism. Still, the gaps in the official explanation could not be concealed by the government or lost in the ideological counterattack mounted by its opponents. Defenders of the Warren Report could never explain, without invoking even more implausible explanations, how Oswald managed to shoot twice in less than a second with a rifle that could not fire two shots in less than 2.25 seconds. Neither the Warren Commission nor subsequent investigations by a panel of pathologists appointed in 1968 by Attorney General Ramsey Clark, by another medical panel appointed in 1975 by Vice-President Nelson Rockefeller, or by the House Select Committee on Assassinations in 1979 explained how Oswald's rifle could have inflicted the massive wounds on Kennedy's head, which seemed to have been caused by exploding bullets fired from a different type of gun. None of these investigations explained how Kennedy's head wounds could have been inflicted by shots fired from behind him.

Over the years, the case for a single assassin has grown even weaker than it seemed in the sixties. Important evidence has disappeared under suspicious circumstances, notably the president's brain, while on the other hand, a fresh piece of positive evidence, an acoustical tape of the gunshots made by the Dallas police, proves conclusively, if it is genuine, that shots were fired from the front of the president as well as the rear. It was largely on the strength of this tape that the Select Committee on Assassinations, even though it reaffirmed many of the more dubious suppositions of the Warren Commission, concluded in its final report, in 1979, that Kennedy had probably been murdered by a conspiracy.

By ignoring evidence that called into question the official explanation of the assassination, Kennedy's admirers made it unnecessary to ask themselves whether the unfulfilled "promise" of Kennedy's presidency was misconceived to begin with. What is now known about Kennedy's life and death prompts the conclusion that imperial grandeur and cosmopolitan "style" were poor substitutes for the original promise of American life: the hope that a self-governing republic could serve as a source of moral and political inspiration to the rest of the world, not as the center of a new world empire. Kennedy and his friends dismissed this earlier vision of America, in effect, as a vision suited only for a small, backward, provincial nation. If Lawrence Goodwyn is correct in his assertion that "progress" and the "people" symbolize conflicting rather than complementary versions of the American dream, the New Frontier—as the image implied—came down squarely on the side of progress, a rather tawdry conception of progress at that. The New Frontier stood for the precarious ascendancy of a civilized, forward-looking minority over popular backwardness, and the legend of Camelot, as it took shape in retrospect, enabled liberals to blame popular bigotry and "paranoia" for Kennedy's death and for all the troubles that followed, including the disastrous decline of their own influence.

It is time we found a better explanation of those troubles, one less flattering to the vanity of the educated classes but more consistent with the historical evidence.

11

RIGHT-WING POPULISM AND THE
REVOLT AGAINST LIBERALISM

■

The "White Backlash"

It is no secret that liberalism has fallen on hard times. The usual explanation of this development—the explanation offered by liberals themselves—attributes it to a violent "backlash" against the civil rights movement, the student radicalism of the sixties, and the policies of the New Frontier and the Great Society. This explanation simply updates the critique of "working-class authoritarianism" advanced by liberals in the fifties and sixties. White ethnics have allegedly deserted the Democrats, their former benefactors, because they are now prosperous enough to resent high taxes and welfare programs but still insecure in their middle-class status. Status anxiety reinforces their racism and makes them irrationally jealous of the racial minorities currently favored by liberal policy. In 1980, the *New York Times* explained that liberalism once meant "helping the Irish and Italian families who were still mired in the lower working class" but that it now meant "helping poor blacks and other racial minorities"—something the "more prosperous" beneficiaries of an earlier liberalism could not seem to understand. The "deepest issue" in the controversies over busing and affirmative action, which had split the liberal coalition, was "racial." White ethnics simply could not see that dark-skinned people needed the same kind of help they themselves had received from the New Deal.

"White backlash" was already a lively topic in the late sixties. In a study of the student movement, *The Radical Probe* (1971), Michael Miles argued that the student revolt had generated a "counter-revolt," the object of which was "to suppress a radical movement which by its nature poses a threat to the *status quo.*" Ethnic minorities loathed the new youth culture because it offended "their petit-bourgeois sensibilities." Blue-collar workers recently promoted to middle-class status, resentful of the advantages enjoyed as their birthright by upper-middle-class students—advantages for which they themselves had to struggle and save—took out their frustration in an ill-tempered "politics of morality." They had "learned property values from the suburban life," but even though "their social integration [was] ensured for the immediate future by economic growth and general prosperity," they remained culturally "insecure" and therefore full of envy and racial hatred.

These explanations of the revolt against liberalism exaggerate the economic security enjoyed by the working class and lower middle class. These classes have always had to "struggle to keep even," in the words of an antibusing activist, and they have begun to lose ground in recent years. Much of their discontent with liberalism has nothing to do with racial issues. Some of it represents a reaction against the kind of unthinking paternalism that makes liberals see themselves as "helpers" of the needy. Some of it grows out of a determination to defend "family values," which many liberals treat with contempt. Some of it rests on the perception that although liberals often flaunt their cultural superiority, they have not shown that it leads to moral understanding or political insight. To people who have become the objects of liberal contempt, these cultural pretensions look more like social snobbery.

Racial issues themselves, finally, are far more complex than the formula of "white racism" would suggest. They look simple only to those who view them from a distance—to people in the suburbs, for example, who do not have to worry about the safety of their streets or the impact of desegregation on their schools. In city neighborhoods where anxiety about these things has become a way of life, the attempt to achieve racial justice through busing and affirmative action presents itself as a contest between "rich people in the suburbs," as Louise Day Hicks put it at the height of the Boston school wars, and the plain people of the city—"the workingman and woman, the rent payer, the home owner, the law-abiding, tax-paying, decent-living, hard-working, forgotten American." Antibusing activists point out, with good reason, that "limousine liberals" in the suburbs expect the cities to carry the whole burden of desegregation. "The burden is being put unfairly on the poor blacks and the working-class whites." The fact that many black people themselves reject busing and affirmative action further weakens "white racism" as an explanation for the racial crisis and the decline of liberalism.*

These things ought to be obvious to people who keep their eyes open, but political commentary seldom takes any account of them. Nor is it liberal commentary alone that ignores them. The right has made itself the voice of "middle America," but it too perpetuates the commonplace of the "affluent worker"—the source of so much misunderstanding about the decline of liberalism. In order to clear up this misunderstanding, we need to review each of the three objections to the "backlash" theory in some detail: the declining position of the middle class, so called; the cultural conflict between the educated classes and "middle America"; and the complexity of racial politics.

---

*A Gallup poll conducted in 1977 revealed that a bare majority of blacks as well as whites opposed the principle of "preferential treatment in getting jobs and places in college." A survey of New York City residents, carried out in the same year by Louis Henri Bolce III and Susan H. Gray, found that 53 percent of blacks and 85 percent of whites opposed preferential treatment. Opinion about busing was divided in the same proportions. A Harris poll (1976) reported the same alignment on busing: 51 percent of blacks and 81 percent of whites opposed it.

A Growing Middle Class?

· ■ ·

Liberals and conservatives alike have assumed that the middle class is growing and that its standard of living is steadily rising. In fact it is shrinking, and its standard of living is deteriorating. The impression that the United States has become an overwhelmingly middle-class society rests largely on the expansion of the service sector of the economy and on the growth of white-collar jobs in relation to blue-collar jobs. Over the course of the twentieth century, however, the expansion of the white-collar work force has derived for the most part from increases in the number of clerical, sales, and service workers, who usually receive even lower pay than most blue-collar workers. The clerical category consists largely of working-class women, and "the existence of two giant categories of labor—operatives and clerical workers—as the two largest major occupational classifications and the composition by sex of each of these categories leads to the supposition," as Harry Braverman noted in 1974, "that the most common occupational combination within the family is one in which the husband is an operative and the wife a clerk." This supposition in turn suggests not only that blue-collar and white-collar jobs have become for many purposes indistinguishable but also that working-class families, like the rest of the population, find it more and more difficult to get along on one income alone. "More than anything else, it is working wives," writes Andrew Levison, "who have made possible even the modest standard of living workers enjoy."

Levison points out that the Census Bureau omits clerical, sales, and service workers from the category of blue-collar occupations. Most of the jobs thus excluded are repetitive and poorly paid. The service category, for example, includes janitors, watchmen, policemen, firemen, waiters, waitresses, cooks, busboys, dishwashers, maids, and porters. If these three categories—clerical, sales, and service—are reclassified as manual labor, the percentage of workers in the population rises dramatically. It has risen over time as well, from 50 percent in 1900 to 70 percent in 1970. This evidence indicates that workers can be considered a middle class only in the sense that they occupy an intermediate position between the professional and business classes on the one hand and the "underclass," largely black and Hispanic in composition, on the other.

Those who insist that America has become a middle-class society point not only to the proportional decline of the old work force employed in manufacturing but to the rise of a new middle class of salaried employees, which has allegedly absorbed the old middle class of small property holders and will eventually absorb the working class as well. According to these optimists, "every vocation has grown more complicated" in our postindustrial society, and the growing need for technical expertise, at every level of employment, can be expected to reduce the distance between social classes, to equalize educational opportunity, and eventually to make access to steady salaried employment—with all its attendant advantages in the form of job security, benefits, and retirement annuities—almost universal. But this comforting picture of a classless, prosperous society bears little resemblance to the emerging reality. The idea that an "information society" demands a highly skilled work force is untenable. It may still be true, in the words of a recent report on education, that "the demand for highly skilled workers in new fields is accelerating rapidly," but it is also true—as this report characteristically fails to point out—that the demand for unskilled workers is accelerating even faster.

In the mid-eighties, the Bureau of Labor Statistics issued a set of employment projections for the next ten years. Of the twenty-five occupations expected to rank as the most heavily populated in 1995, not one derived in any direct way from the "information explosion."* The first

---

*In order of their projected numbers, on a conservative estimate, these occupations were listed by the Bureau of Labor Statistics as building custodians, sales clerks, secretaries, general office clerks, cashiers, elementary and preschool teachers, waiters and waitresses, truck drivers, nurses, engineers of all kinds, metalworking operatives, sales representatives (technical), cooks and chefs, supervisors of blue-collar workers, nurses' aides and orderlies, farm owners and tenants, store managers, accountants, kitchen helpers, typists, auto mechanics, second teachers, stock handlers, carpenters, and "food preparation and service workers, fast food restaurants." On the other hand, the five fastest-growing lines of work, as distinguished from those expected to be most numerous, owed their existence, at least indirectly, to the high-tech economy: legal assistants, computer service technicians, systems analysts, computer programmers, and computer operators. It is by no means clear, however, that all of these should be considered highly skilled occupations.

five occupations on this list—janitors, sales clerks, secretaries, general office clerks, and cashiers—were expected to account for more than 10 percent of total employment in 1995 and almost 14 percent of all new employment. Only six of the twenty-five occupations in question required education beyond the secondary level, and only three—teaching, engineering, and nursing—required a college degree. Jobs for computer systems analysts would increase by 90 percent (already a drop from the 100 percent increase estimated in the mid-seventies for the years between 1978 and 1990), but only 225,000 new jobs, at most, would result. On the other hand, there might be as many as 850,000 new jobs for janitors—considerably more than the total number of new jobs (660,000) opened up by the five occupations with the highest rate of relative growth. There might be as many as 750,000 new jobs for sales clerks; 580,000 for waiters and waitresses; 470,000 for nurses' aides and orderlies; 460,000 for truck drivers: and 350,000 for auto mechanics. It was expected that 165,000 new positions for computer programmers would open up during the late eighties and early nineties, whereas the demand for fast-food workers and kitchen helpers would produce 525,000 new positions.

A recent study by Barry Bluestone and Bennett Harrison strengthens the impression of persisting unemployment, declining wages and salaries, and a rapid growth of low-wage employment. Forty-four percent of the new jobs created between 1979 and 1985, according to these authors, paid poverty-level wages, while the creation of high-wage professional, technical, and managerial jobs slowed to a mere 10 percent, a third of the pace maintained in the years from 1963 to 1979.* Part-time jobs, moreover, grew twice as fast as full-time jobs, accounting for 30 percent of new positions. The increase in poorly paid employment was not confined to minorities, women, or the young. Indeed the partial elimination of the disparity in wages paid to men and to women—at first glance the only bright spot in an otherwise darkening picture—is accounted for by a

---

*Taking the high wages of 1973 as their standard, Bluestone and Harrison defined high-wage jobs as those paying more than the 1973 average. "Stated in terms of 1986 purchasing power, a low-wage job pays $7,400 or less. A high-wage job pays in excess of $29,000."

decline in the level of wages earned by white males.

According to a University of Michigan study, 39 percent of the population, in the years from 1968 to 1972, earned incomes that fell behind inflation. During the next four-year period, the proportion rose to 43 percent; in the period 1978–1982, it rose all the way to 56 percent. A study by Eli Ginzberg reports that the middle-income share of new jobs fell by nearly 20 percent between 1979 and 1984, while the low-income share (jobs paying less than $7,000 a year, according to Ginzberg's definition) rose to more than 50 percent.

All this evidence undermines the claim that the middle class is growing, if the term refers to a class of nonmanual workers whose jobs require a good deal of education and assure a comfortable income. "As some of its members fall into poverty and others acquire wealth, it has been shrinking," according to a recent report in *Time*. Median family income, adjusted for inflation, remains where it was in the early seventies. But the percentage of middle-income households (those earning between $20,000 and $60,000 a year, in 1985 dollars) declined from 53 percent in 1973 to 49 percent in 1985. These figures may even "overstate the fortunes of the middle class," *Time* admits, since its standard of living has declined along with its numbers. Middle-class incomes have fallen far behind the steep inflation of housing prices and college tuitions, thereby endangering two of the cherished indications of middle-class status. Only by going into debt and by sending their wives into the work force can middle-income groups keep up even a semblance of that status. More than half of American households now owe more than they are worth. In 1985, household debt relative to disposable income rose to almost 90 percent, a postwar high.

Even in the early seventies, at the height of postwar prosperity, an "intermediate" income, as defined by the Bureau of Labor Statistics, hardly conferred a lavish or even a comfortable standard of living. A study conducted by the United Auto Workers found that an "intermediate" income would allow a family to buy a two-year-old car and keep it for four years, to buy a vacuum cleaner that would have to last for fourteen years and a toaster good for thirty-three, to go to the movies once every three months, and to save nothing at all. In 1970, some 35 percent of American families and 60 percent of working-class families lived on less than $10,000 a year—that is, below the "intermediate" level. The average family earned only $9,500 in 1973, the year in which family income reached its postwar peak.

Working-Class and Lower-Middle-Class Convergence

The decline of its standard of living makes it harder than ever to figure out just what Americans mean when they speak of a middle class. In Europe, where the bourgeoisie stood between the remnants of the feudal nobility and a class-conscious proletariat, the term had a sociological precision it never achieved in the United States. American workers never came to see themselves unambiguously as a proletariat. The American dream of equal opportunity encouraged them to hope that their children would move up the social scale. Very few of those children climbed into the salaried class, as it turned out, but they achieved a precarious level of security, in the years of the great postwar expansion, that made it seem reasonable enough for them to think of themselves as a middle class, if only because they were doing better than their parents and better, certainly, than blacks and Hispanics who lived in the "culture of poverty."

The boundary between the middle class and the working class was further blurred by a long-term decline in the position of the old proprietary class of shopkeepers, small businessmen, and independent professionals. In 1900, the middle class could not possibly have been confused with the working class. It was self-employed and not a little self-satisfied. It employed wage labor and domestic servants. Wives did not work—a point of considerable pride. Middle-class professional men were engaged for the most part in private practice, and even when they worked for salaries it was usually in organizations—colleges, hospitals, small firms of various kinds—over which they retained a good deal of responsibility. By the sixties and seventies, however, it was impossible to find a large category of people who shared all these characteristics. Small businessmen had lost out to the big corporations, tradesmen to the retail chains. Salaried professionals now worked mostly in gigantic bureaucracies, in which some of them earned princely incomes and wielded considerable influence while others earned very little money and wielded no influence at all.

The enormous range of wealth and power among professionals makes it difficult to use the concept of a professional-managerial class with precision, but that designation describes the upper levels of the salaried class much better than the usual designation of them as a middle class. Except as a rough description of relative income levels, the middle class, for all practical purposes, has ceased to exist. At the upper levels, it has dissolved into a "new class" with interests and an outlook on life that cannot be called "middle-class" in any conventional sense of the term. At the lower levels, the middle class has become increasingly indistinguishable from a working class whose climb out of poverty stopped well short of affluence.

Time's report on the declining middle class, published at the height of the presidential campaign of 1988, includes a revealing vignette that illustrates the difficulty of distinguishing between the lower reaches of the middle class and the working class, especially in a period when both are faced with straitened circumstances. Bob Forrester, now sixty years old, settled on the west coast in 1953, having grown up in a blue-collar family in East St. Louis. His wife, Carol, was the daughter of a longshoreman on Staten Island. Neither went to college. In 1957, Forrester took a unionized job as a tankerman in Los Angeles harbor, at an annual wage of $5,512, while his wife stayed home to raise their three children. Today he makes $40,000 a year and owns three houses worth a total of $600,000. *Time* refers to him as a member of the middle class, and most Americans—including Forrester himself, perhaps—would probably agree with this classification, even though he clearly owes his material security to the labor movement and continues to serve it as a union official. But *Time* itself acknowledges the ambiguity of middle-class status when it describes Forrester's story as part of a "fundamental shift in the social and economic structure of old working-class neighborhoods."

"I'm definitely better off than my father was," Forrester says. None of his children, however, can make the same claim. The eldest, Billy, went to work on the boats when he graduated from high school. He was making $27,000 a year by the mid-eighties, when the company he worked for began to lay off unionized workers and to replace them with scabs. Having lost his job, Billy moved up the coast to Washington and went into business for himself as a gardener. His income fluctuated between $10,000 and $20,000. In 1987 he bought a house for $43,000, thanks to his father's ability to make the down payment of $11,000. His income barely supports his four children, but he has been unable to find a harbor job in Washington. "You've got to stand in line three days just to get your name on a list," he says. "It's a rat race."

Forrester's youngest child, Bob, is also looking for work in the harbor, but the Longshoremen's Union in Los Angeles has kept his application for three years without offering him a position. "They pass out 50,000 or 60,000 applications," he says, ". . . for about three hundred jobs." Meanwhile he drives a delivery truck at $8.25 an hour. Until 1987, he lived with his parents, as did his sister, Peggy. Now he and his wife live in a one-bedroom apartment. "What I'm afraid of," his wife says, "is to be living like this forever." As for Peggy herself, she earns $25,000 as the manager of a retail clothing store but pays out two-thirds of her income in rent, household expenses, and car payments. Saving is out of the question, and she has no hope of owning a house—the last vestige of proprietary status.* Her car, a Ford Tempo purchased for $8,500, cost her almost as much as the house her father bought in 1957. The down payment came to 6 percent of her salary, whereas her father paid only 14 percent of his annual income as a down payment on his first house, which he sold in 1973 for nearly five times what he paid for it. Peggy's car, on the other hand, is now worth less than half its original price.†

The convergence of the working class and the lower middle class, in an era of downward mobility, reveals itself not only in their standard of living but in a common outlook. If the middle class is a state of mind, as so

---

*Home ownership is a poor substitute for the kind of property that formerly supported a family and relieved people of the need to work for wages. It is not a source of material sustenance, let alone a source of the "virtue" formerly associated with property ownership. It remains an important symbol of independence and responsibility, however, and the decline of home ownership, more vividly than any other development, dramatizes for many people the collapse of the American dream.

†While Bob Forrester and his wife, still loyal to the party that had done so much for the labor movement, planned to vote for Dukakis in 1988, all of his children planned to vote for Bush—a choice that obviously cannot be attributed to upward mobility or "embourgeoisement."

many observers insist, it is a petty-bourgeois state of mind that holds it together. The petty bourgeoisie has no socioeconomic importance now that artisans, farmers, and other small proprietors no longer make up a large part of the population; but its time-honored habits and its character-istic code of ethics linger on, nowhere more vigorously than in the heart of the American worker. The worker's culture and political outlook bear little resemblance to those of his European counterparts. In many ways, however, they bear a close resemblance to the outlook of the old Euro-pean peasantry and petty bourgeoisie—from which the American work-ing class was recruited in the first place.

It is not just that American workers, unlike European workers, fail to support socialist or communist parties (Seymour Martin Lipset to the contrary notwithstanding) or that they have never shown much interest in remodeling the Democratic party along the lines of the British Labour party. The differences go deeper. American workers are more religious than workers in Europe: they declare an affiliation with some church, profess a belief in God, and even attend services occasionally. They have a stronger sense of ethnic and racial identity. They have a heavier invest-ment in the ethic of personal accountability and neighborly self-help, which tempers their enthusiasm for the welfare state. They carry the code of manly independence to extremes—as in the assertion of their sacred right to bear arms—that would be considered ridiculous in Europe. Above all, they define themselves as a "middle class." They also define themselves as "workers," of course, but the meaning of that term, in America, is still closer to "producers" than to "proletarians." In his study of Canarsie, a beleaguered ethnic community in Brooklyn, Jona-than Rieder notes that the residents "showed their hostility to people on welfare"—and also to corporate wealth—"by contrasting parasites and producers." A spokesman for one civic group wrote in its newspaper, "For years, we have witnessed the appeasement of nonproductive and counter-productive 'leeches' at the expense of New York's middle-class work force." This populist language, together with the reference to a "middle-class work force," captures the ambiguity of working-class iden-tity in America.

The Lower-Middle-Class Ethic of Limits and the Abortion Debate

· ■ ·

Lower-middle-class culture, now as in the past, is organized around the family, church, and neighborhood. It values the community's continuity more highly than individual advancement, solidarity more highly than social mobility. Conventional ideals of success play a less important part in lower-middle-class life than the maintenance of existing ways. Parents want their children to get ahead, but they also want them to respect their elders, resist the temptation to lie and cheat, willingly shoulder the responsibilities that fall to them, and bear adversity with fortitude. More concerned with honor than with worldly ambition, they have less interest in the future than do upper-middle-class parents, who try to equip their children with the qualities required for competitive achievement. They do not subscribe to the notion that parents ought to provide children with every possible advantage. The desire "to preserve their way of life," as E. E. LeMasters writes in a study of construction workers, takes precedence over the desire to climb the social ladder. "If my boy wants to wear a goddamn necktie all his life and bow and scrape to some boss, that's his right, but by God he should also have the right to earn an honest living with his hands if that is what he likes."

In his historical studies of nineteenth-century Massachusetts, Stephan Thernstrom found that neither the Irish nor the Italians thought of schooling primarily as a means for their children to climb into a higher social class and to leave their old neighborhoods behind. In Newburyport, Irish parents sometimes sacrificed their children to their passion for home ownership, forcing them into the workplace instead of sending them to school. Irrational by upper-middle-class standards, this choice made sense to people bent on holding their communities together and on assuring the continuation of their own way of life in the next generation. Social workers and educators, however, condemned child labor and sought to create a system of universal education, which would make it possible for children to surpass their parents, break the old ties, and make their own way in the larger world beyond the ethnic ghetto. In the same way, civil service reformers tried to replace the tribal politics of the Irish-American machine with a system more consistent with the principles of meritocracy and administrative efficiency.

Sociologists observed, usually with a suggestion of disapproval, that working people seemed to have no ambition. According to Lloyd Warner, who studied Newburyport in the 1930s, working-class housewives set the dominant tone of cultural conservatism. They adhered to a "rigid" and "conventional" code of morality and seldom dared to "attempt anything new." They took no interest in long-range goals. "Their hopes are basically centered around carrying on [and] take the form of not wanting their present routine disturbed—they want to continue as they are, but, while doing so, better their circumstances and gain more freedom." Anthony Lukas, a journalist, made the same point in his account of the Boston school conflicts of the mid-seventies. Lukas contrasted the "Charlestown ethic of getting by" with the "American imperative to get ahead." The people of Charlestown, deserted by the migration of more ambitious neighbors to the suburbs, had renounced "opportunity, advancement, adventure" for the "reassurance of community, solidarity, and camaraderie."*

Conflicting attitudes about the future, much more than abstract speculation about the immortality of the embryonic soul, underlay the controversy about abortion touched off by the Supreme Court's 1973 decision in *Roe v. Wade.* No other issue more clearly revealed the chasm between "middle-class" values and those of the educated elite. "I think people are foolish to worry about things in the future," an anti-abortion activist declared. "The future takes care of itself." Another woman active in the pro-life movement said, "You can't plan everything in life." For the prochoice forces, however, the "quality of life" depended on planned parenthood and other forms of rational planning for the future. From their point of view, it was irresponsible to bring children into the world when

---

*They regarded Boston's "urban renaissance" across the river without enthusiasm, just as the working-class residents of Oakland, as Lillian Rubin portrayed them in her 1976 study of family patterns, resented the highly publicized development of new "life styles" in Berkeley and San Francisco. As far as Oakland workers were concerned, Berkeley and San Francisco "might just as well be on another planet," according to Rubin.

they could not be provided with the full range of material and cultural assets essential to successful competition. It was unfair to saddle children with handicaps in the race for success: congenital defects, poverty, or a deficiency of parental love. A pro-choice activist argued that "raising a child is a contract of twenty years at least, . . . so if you're not in a life situation where you can [make] the commitment to raising a child, you should have the option of not doing so at that time." Teenage pregnancy was objectionable to advocates of legalized abortion not because they objected to premarital sex but because adolescents, in their view, had no means of giving their offspring the advantages they deserved.

For opponents of abortion, however, this solicitude for the "quality of life" looked like a decision to subordinate ethical and emotional interests to economic interests. They believed that children needed ethical guidance more than they needed economic advantages. Motherhood was a "huge job," in their eyes, not because it implied long-range financial planning but because "you're responsible, as far as you possibly can be, for educating and teaching them . . . what you believe is right—moral values and responsibilities and rights." Women opposed to abortion believed that their adversaries regarded financial security as an indispensable precondition of motherhood. One such woman dismissed "these figures that it takes $65,000 from birth" to raise a child as "ridiculous." "That's a new bike every year. That's private colleges. That's a complete new outfit when school opens. . . . Those figures are inflated to give those children everything, and I think that's not good for them."

The debate about abortion illustrates the difference between the enlightened ethic of competitive achievement and the petty-bourgeois or working-class ethic of limits. "The values and beliefs of pro-choice [people] diametrically oppose those of pro-life people," Kristin Luker writes in her study of the politics of abortion in California. Pro-life activists resented feminist disparagement of housework and motherhood. They agreed that women ought to get equal pay for equal work in the marketplace, but they did not agree that unpaid work in the home was degrading and oppressive. What they found "disturbing [in] the whole abortion mentality," as one of them put it, "is the idea that family duties—rearing children, managing a home, loving and caring for a husband—are somehow degrading to women." They found the pretense that "there are no important differences between men and women" unconvincing. They believed that men and women "were created differently and . . . meant to complement each other." Upper-middle-class feminists, on the other hand, saw the belief in biologically determined gender differences as the ideological basis of women's oppression.

Their opposition to a biological view of human nature went beyond the contention that it served to deprive women of their rights. Their insistence that women ought to assume "control over their bodies" evinced an impatience with biological constraints of any kind, together with a belief that modern technology had liberated humanity from those constraints and made it possible for the first time to engineer a better life for the human race as a whole. Pro-choice people welcomed the medical technologies that made it possible to detect birth defects in the womb, and they could not understand why anyone would knowingly wish to bring a "damaged" child, or for that matter an "unwanted" child, into the world. In their eyes, an unwillingness to grant such children's "right not to be born" might itself be considered evidence of unfitness for parenthood. "I think if I had my druthers," one of them told Luker, "I'd probably advocate the need for licensing pregnancies."

For people in the right-to-life movement, this kind of thinking led logically to full-scale genetic engineering, to an arrogant assumption of the power to make summary judgments about the "quality of life," and to a willingness to consign not only a "defective" fetus but whole categories of defective or superfluous individuals to the status of nonpersons.* A

---

*These fears are by no means fanciful or exaggerated. A 1970 article in the journal of the California Medical Association welcomed the growing acceptance of abortion as a "prototype of what is to occur," the harbinger of a "new ethic" that would substitute the quality of life, in effect, for the sanctity of life. The article predicted that "problems of birth control and birth selection [would be] extended inevitably to death selection and death control" and would lead to an acceptance of the need for "public and professional determination of when and when not to use scarce resources." The courts have tended to transform the right to prevent birth defects by means of abortion into a duty to prevent birth defects and then to apply this kind of thinking to all those whose lives have "no meaning," in the words of a recent decision authorizing a "life-shortening course of action" in the case of an elderly patient—to all those unfortunate human beings, in other words, who can be said "for all practical purposes" to be "merely existing."

pro-life activist whose infant daughter died of a lung disease objected to the idea that her "baby's life, in a lot of people's eyes, wouldn't have been very meaningful. . . . She only lived twenty-seven days, and that's not a very long time, but whether we live ninety-nine years or two hours or twenty-seven days, being human is being human, and what it involves, we really don't understand."

Perhaps it was the suggestion that "we really don't understand" what it means to be human that most deeply divided the two parties to the abortion debate. For liberals, such an admission amounted to a betrayal not only of the rights of women but of the whole modern project: the conquest of necessity and the substitution of human choice for the blind workings of nature. An unquestioning faith in the capacity of the rational intelligence to solve the mysteries of human existence, ultimately the secret of creation itself, linked the seemingly contradictory positions held by liberals—that abortion is an "ethical private decision" and sex a transaction between "consenting adults" but that the state might well reserve the right to license pregnancy or even to embark on far-reaching programs of eugenic engineering. The uneasy coexistence of ethical individualism and medical collectivism grew out of the separation of sex from procreation, which made sex a matter of private choice while leaving open the possibility that procreation and child rearing might be subjected to stringent public controls. The objection that sex and procreation cannot be severed without losing sight of the mystery surrounding both struck liberals as the worst kind of theological obscurantism. For opponents of abortion, on the other hand, "God is the creator of life, and . . . sexual activity should be open to that. . . . The contraceptive mentality denies his will, 'It's my will, not your will.' "

If the abortion debate confined itself to the question of just when an embryo becomes a person, it would be hard to understand why it elicits such passionate emotions or why it has become the object of political attention seemingly disproportionate to its intrinsic importance. But abortion is not just a medical issue or even a woman's issue that has become the focus of a larger controversy about feminism. It is first and foremost a class issue. Kristin Luker's study of activists on both sides of the question leaves no doubt about that. The pro-choice women in her survey were better educated and made more money than their counterparts in the anti-abortion movement. They worked in the professional, managerial, and entrepreneurial sector of the economy. Many were unmarried, many were divorced, and the married women among them had small families. More than 60 percent of Luker's sample of pro-choice women said they had no religion, while most of the rest described themselves as vaguely Protestant. Anti-abortion activists, on the other hand, were housewives with large families. Eighty percent of them were Catholics. These differences defined the difference between two social classes, each with its own view of the world—the one eager to press its recent gains and to complete the modern revolution of rising expectations, the other devoted to a last-ditch defense of the "forgotten American."

The Cultural Class War

· ■ ·

"Two hundred years after the inception of our 'Great American Dream,' " wrote Alan Erlichman, a spokesman for the antibusing forces in the Canarsie section of Brooklyn, in the mid-seventies, "the middle class now finds itself in the midst of a 'Great American Nightmare.' " It was not merely a threat to its standard of living that defined this middle-class nightmare but a threat to its way of life—its beliefs and ideals, its sense of propriety, its distinctive conceptions of justice. Communities like Canarsie were painfully aware that they had become objects of educated contempt. The student radicals of the sixties mocked their patriotism. "Here were these kids, rich kids who could go to college, who didn't have to fight, . . . telling you your son died in vain. It makes you feel your whole life is shit, just nothing." Liberals dismissed their demand for law and order as "proto-fascism," their opposition to busing as "white racism." Feminists told women who wanted to stay at home with their children that full-time motherhood turned a housewife into a domestic drudge, the lowest order of humanity. When social planners tried to determine the racial composition of schools, they assigned blacks and Hispanics to separate statistical categories but lumped whites indiscriminately together as "others," ignoring the way in which white workers, according to Rieder, "viewed themselves not as abstract whites but as members of specific ethnic groups."

Television programs depicted middle-class blacks, career women, and the very rich but paid no attention to working people, except to make Archie Bunker a symbol of lower-middle-class ignorance and bigotry. It is no wonder that working people became increasingly "angry," as Lillian Rubin noted in her study of Oakland, "at the university students and their supporters—a privileged minority who cavalierly dismiss and devalue a way of life these working-class people have struggled so hard to achieve." Nor should it have been surprising that the construction workers interviewed by LeMasters felt "isolated and forgotten." It was a measure of the distance between social classes, papered over by the myth of working-class affluence and "embourgeoisement," that LeMasters found himself "surprised at the depth and extent of the suspicion and distrust the blue-collar workers have of the white-collar middle and upper classes." Ignored by the mass media, condescended to by opinion makers and social critics, deserted by the politicians who once represented their interests, these men believed that the "people who got the money" ran things and that they themselves had nothing to say about the course of public events.

From the wrong side of the tracks, the dominant culture looked quite different from the way it looked from the inside. Its concern for creativity and self-expression looked self-indulgent. Its concern for the quality of human life seemed to imply a belief that life has to be carefully hoarded and preserved, protected from danger and risk, prolonged as long as possible. Its permissive style of child rearing and marital negotiation conveyed weakness more than sympathetic understanding, a desire to avoid confrontations that might release angry emotions. Its eagerness to criticize everything seemed to bespeak a refusal to accept any constraints on human freedom, an attitude doubly objectionable in those who enjoyed so much freedom to begin with. The habit of criticism, from a lower-middle-class point of view, appeared to invite people to be endlessly demanding of life, to expect more of life than anyone had a right to expect.

A white Catholic housekeeper from Somerville, Massachusetts, interviewed by Robert Coles in the mid-seventies, took an unflattering but highly revealing view of Cambridge, where she cleaned for a professional family. The woman she worked for was "crazy," she thought, to enter the job market when she had no visible need of extra income. She reported that her employers spent much of the day weighing themselves, worrying about being "depressed," trying on new clothes, and "looking in one mirror and then another mirror." When the wife had arguments with her husband, she cried or withheld her sexual favors. "I'd never do that!" the maid said indignantly. "I'd rather scream and shout and throw dishes than hold out on my husband that way."

> The house is full of talk [she went on] even early in the morning. He's read something that's bothered him, and she's read something that's bothered her. They're both ready to phone their friends. The kids hear all that and they start complaining about what's bothering *them*—about school, usually. They're all so *critical*. I tell my kids to obey the teacher and listen to the priest; and their father gives them a whack if they cross him. But it's different when I come to fancy Cambridge. In that house, the kids speak back to their parents, act as fresh and snotty as can be. I want to scream sometimes when I hear those brats talking as if they know everything.

It is not hard to see why so much of this kind of indignation came to be vented on the figure of Benjamin Spock, a symbol of everything "middle Americans" distrusted. As the author of *Baby and Child Care,* Spock was identified in the popular mind not only with permissive child rearing but with intrusive medical and psychiatric expertise, so often invoked by those who condemned "working-class authoritarianism." As a leader in the antiwar movement, he symbolized the danger that a remissive morality would undermine civic order and patriotism. Workers had little enthusiasm for the war, but they resented the anti-Americanism so often expressed by the student movement. Their "reverence for the flag," according to Rieder, "embodied a style of patriotism sustained less by abstract ideals than by primordial sentiments of belonging to a particular place." The antiwar movement, on the other hand, denounced "Amerika" as a totalitarian society. "Suddenly, America was the enemy," Julius Lester has written in retrospect. ". . . Common sense should have told us that it is impossible to transform a nation if you hate it." But common sense played little part in the radical wing of the antiwar movement, which hoped to whip up opposition to the war by desecrating the flag, exposing national heroes like Jefferson and Lincoln as racists, imperialists, and male chauvinist pigs, and proclaiming its solidarity with the oppressed millions in Africa, Asia, and Latin America. The result was to strengthen support for the government's policy among people who might otherwise have condemned it. These tactics also heightened popular resentment of men like Dr. Spock—the "strutting pseudo-intellectuals" denounced by Spiro Agnew and George Wallace.

The experts who set themselves up as guardians of children's rights appeared to workers to encourage a spirit of insubordination and to weaken parental confidence. "These days you're afraid to punish the kid or you'll 'alienate' him. . . . Complexes! Complexes!" The jargon of therapeutic understanding and "compassion" seemed to absolve young people, lawbreakers, and other "victims" of an allegedly repressive society from any responsibility for their actions. Violations of social conventions went unpunished, while those who demanded their enforcement were criticized for "blaming the victim." The growing tolerance of profanity, sexual display, pornography, drugs, and homosexuality seemed to indicate a general collapse of common decency. American workers did not regard themselves as models of rectitude, nor did they adhere to a rigid morality that condemned every form of sexual self-expression. What they condemned was the public display of sex and pornography, especially in their deviant forms—the repeal of reticence. "If [people] want to live together and not be married, that's fine. If they want to read pornographic books and see pornographic movies, that's okay, . . . as long as they don't broadcast it . . . on television or in the newspapers." Right-wing criticism of the media struck a sympathetic chord in workers troubled by the publicity accorded to socially disruptive conduct. Their attack on "permissiveness," however, grew out of a sense of decorum, not out of an inflexible moral standard that left no room for tolerance or free speech. Organizations like the American Civil Liberties Union came under fire because they appeared to invoke the constitutional doctrine of free speech for purposes it was never intended to cover.

In an atmosphere inflamed by demands for an apparently unlimited right of personal freedom, on the one hand, and for the restoration of public order, on the other, even graffiti could become a political issue. Liberals saw the graffiti scrawled on subway cars as a vibrant new form of folk art, while ethnic workers saw them as part of the crisis of civility. In their eyes, the city's public facilities no longer belonged to decent, law-abiding citizens. The streets, parks, and subways had been taken over by drug pushers, pornographers, prostitutes, and gangs of noisy black youths, who strutted their contempt for middle-class respectability. "These maniacs, the way they walk the streets and the language they use, forget it!" An air of menace hung over the city. "I don't really hate the blacks," said a Jewish woman in Canarsie. "I hate that they make me look over my shoulder." "When the blacks robbed me," said another Canarsie resident, "I left all that black-and-white together stuff." Instead of writing off "law and order" as a code word for racism, liberals would have been well advised to address themselves to the breakdown of public order. Even if their culture of self-expression and self-advancement made it impossible for them to see any value in lower-middle-class culture, they might at least have acknowledged the problem of public safety. Liberalism itself, after all, was historically dependent on the rise of the modern state, which put an end to feudal and religious warfare, monopolized the means of violence, and took away the right of private vengeance. The erosion of the state's capacity to assure public order forced city residents to improvise solutions of their own, ranging from neighborhood patrols and block associations to gang warfare. Liberals wanted to restrict the sale of handguns, with good reason, but they refused to understand the fears that led people to arm themselves as a last resort against the rising tide of violence and crime. They deplored the campaign for more vigorous law enforcement as a threat to liberties guaranteed by the Bill of Rights, but they did not explain how the Bill of Rights would assure the safety of the streets.

The Politics of Race: Antibusing Agitation in Boston

· ■ ·

From the point of view of those who lived in deteriorating urban neighborhoods, liberals were not only indifferent to their needs but actively hostile, bent on destroying those neighborhoods if they stood in the way of racial integration. The principle of preferential treatment for disadvantaged minorities offended ethnic groups that had never enjoyed any such favoritism, as far as they could see, in their own struggles against poverty and ethnic prejudice. "These bilingual signs drive me crazy," said a resident of Canarsie. "The old Jews and Italians didn't have their language on signs." Even those who supported the civil rights movement rejected the double standard of racial justice summed up by McGeorge Bundy, head of the Ford Foundation, in 1977: "To get past racism, we must . . . take account of race." Nor were they impressed with Justice Thurgood Marshall's argument in the Bakke case, two years later, to the effect that American racism had been "so pervasive" that nobody, "regardless of wealth or position," had escaped its impact. This statement implied that everyone would have to share the burden of its eradication, but the burden fell in fact on those who could least afford to bear it. The case for "race-conscious programs," as Justice William Brennan approvingly called them, might have carried moral weight if the chief proponents of compensatory programs had not so easily escaped their consequences. If the effects of racial discrimination pervaded American society, the effects of reverse discrimination turned out to be highly selective.

Liberals' claim to stand on high moral ground, in the bitter controversies over busing and affirmative action that exploded in the late sixties and early seventies, was suspect from the start. It was not just a question of principle, however, that divided liberals from their former supporters. Workers experienced liberal policies as an invasion of their neighborhoods. In Brooklyn, Jews had retreated from Brownsville, East New York, and Flatbush in the face of successive waves of black migration, only to find themselves confronted in 1972 with a court order designed to achieve racial balance in the Canarsie schools. High mortgage costs and loyalty to Canarsie precluded a further retreat to the suburbs. "The white middle class in Canarsie is up against the . . . wall," one man said: "there's no place to retreat." "They've ruined Brownsville," said another, "but I won't let them ruin Canarsie. . . . The liberals and the press look down on hardhats like me, but we've invested everything we have in this house and neighborhood." The president of the Jewish Community Council, defending a boycott of schools integrated under court order, cried, "We have built the swamps of Canarsie into a beautiful community, and no one is going to take it away from us."

In Charlestown, Massachusetts, the conflict over busing was preceded by protracted conflicts over urban renewal. Here the immediate threat came not from black people pressing into the neighborhood but from advocates of redevelopment, who dreamed of Boston as a model of the "information economy" destined to grow up on the ruins of heavy industry. With a sense of self-importance reminiscent of the city's seventeenth-century founders, but with little of their moral vision, promoters of redevelopment envisioned the "new Boston" as a city on a hill, a showplace of advanced technology, cosmopolitan sophistication, high finance, and architectural splendor. They had big ambitions for Charlestown, a run-down neighborhood long since forsaken by Protestants, more recently by the more prosperous members of its predominantly Irish population, and finally by the Charlestown navy yard, once the basis of the local economy. Planners saw renewal as a matter of "getting a better grade of person" to live in Charlestown. "Charlestown has a dream," exclaimed a columnist in the *Boston Globe*, "a developing dream—to be to Boston what carefully restored, stylish Georgetown has been to Washington." This was not Charlestown's own dream, of course, which was typically small-minded in the eyes of the outside world. "We wanted to help people rehabilitate their houses," said one resident. "We tried to show we could do without the federal government." For old inhabitants, renewal meant the restoration of the community as it had been in its better days, when "Townies" were self-supporting and respectable and the neighborhood known as one of the safest in the whole city, even after dark.

A tumultuous session of the Charlestown city council in 1965 approved a plan calling for demolition of 10 percent of private housing, replacement of the state prison with the Bunker Hill Community College, and other dubious improvements. Subsequent plans called for the construction of luxury housing on the site of the old navy yard, complete with swimming pool, tennis courts, and two marinas. "I am concerned with the destruction of families," said an opponent of gentrification. "We want people back, not a professional man, his secretary, and a dog." Professional planners, however, cared more about real estate values and a "better sort of person." The *Charlestown Patriot* accurately assessed the effect of their efforts when it warned that "Townies" would soon lose the "Charlestown they now know," if indeed they found themselves "able to live here at all," in the "backyard of all this luxury."

The same coalition that designed and built the "New Boston"—banking and real estate interests, university presidents, foundation heads, and civic leaders, including representatives of the small black elite—welcomed the Racial Imbalance Act passed by the state legislature in 1965 as an opportunity to modernize the city's school system. Businessmen and their allies dominated the Citywide Coordinating Council, appointed by Judge Arthur Garrity in 1975 as the "eyes and ears of the court," when his ambitious plan for desegregation began to run into fierce popular opposition.* The *Globe* described the Coordinating Council as a "mixture of community people, clergy, educators and businessmen," which promised to provide the kind of "positive, representative, credible" leadership the city had lacked in the recent past. A prominent member of the Coordinating Council, President Kenneth Ryder of Northeastern University, said that it stood for "intelligence, professionalism, absence of political considerations."

From the beginning, the civic elite took the position that good schools would bring professionals back into the city, generate tax revenues, and train the skilled work force required by the new high-tech economy. According to a report issued by the Ford Foundation in 1965, improvement of public education was a "prerequisite for holding the middle class in the city." James M. Howell, a senior vice-president of the First National Bank, spelled out the familiar rationale for school reform: a new emphasis on "marketable skills"; "innovative pilot projects" designed to link "education to job markets"; increased attention to "skills that reflect the technical orientation of area business firms." Robert Wood, president of the University of Massachusetts and chairman of the Coordinating Council, endorsed the goal of "programs that fit the market place." When he became superintendent of schools in 1978, he made "career-occupation education" his "first priority." In practice, this boiled down to the introduction of programs in "computer literacy" and the purchase of expensive equipment from the electronics industry.

---

*The members of the council included Arthur Gartland of Scituate, an insurance and real estate man and vice-president of the chamber of commerce; Vernon Alden of Brookline, a high-ranking officer of the Boston Safe Deposit and Trust Company; Ted Phillips of Weston, president of the New England Mutual Life Insurance Company; Thomas A. Sampson of Needham, president of the chamber of commerce; John Silber of Brookline, president of Boston University; and Robert Wood of Lincoln, president of the University of Massachusetts. Note that every one of these men lived in the suburbs.

For the business and professional classes, self-interest appeared to coincide with moral idealism—a happy conjunction. Racially integrated and otherwise "innovative" schools would break the hereditary cycle of poverty and make it possible (when accompanied by aggressive programs of affirmative action) for qualified members of the "underclass" to achieve professional status. The only thing that stood in the way of racial justice and civic renewal was the obstinate resistance of "self-enclosed" ethnic "enclaves," as they were invariably referred to by reformers, which clung to their "small-world insularity and intransigence." Neighborhoods like Charlestown and South Boston—"peninsulas ethnically rigid and ingrown," inhabited by "hooligans," "bigots," and "hysterical racist mobs"—automatically opposed any kind of innovation, especially if it promised to benefit black people.

The party of civic improvement could see nothing but racism in their opposition to busing. Mrs. Hicks might denounce Garrity's order as a solution foisted on the city by "rich people in the suburbs," the "outside power structure," the "forces who attempt to invade us"; but "racism" was the "real issue," in the words of Elaine Noble, a liberal in the state legislature. Jon Hillson, a black liberal, attributed opposition to busing to the "extreme insularity" and "backwardness" of the Irish, "fostered and preyed upon by racist politicians" who knew how to exploit "rude, primitive fear." Hillson dismissed the claim that "gains won by the civil rights . . . struggle come out of the pockets of white workers" as an outright "lie" propagated by the "racist alliance that runs America." Jonathan Kozol, well known for his book *Death at an Early Age,* an account of his experiences as a teacher in Boston, traced the antibusing movement to "mob terror and decades of miseducation, stirred by demagogues, preplanned by those who feed on hate." All the violence surrounding the busing controversy, Kozol insisted, derived in the last analysis from the violent resistance initiated by whites. When Michael Faith, a senior at South Boston High School, was stabbed by a black classmate from Roxbury, Kozol managed to convince himself that "it was . . . Louise Day Hicks . . . who put the knife in Michael Faith."

In fact, Mrs. Hicks had lost most of her supporters in South Boston by this time, precisely because of her condemnation of violence. The stabbing incident directly contributed to the decline of her influence. As word of the assault spread through South Boston, a mob gathered outside the high school and refused to let the black students, trapped inside the building, return to Roxbury. Mrs. Hicks pleaded with the crowd to disperse. Paying no attention to her, the crowd took up one of the least attractive chants of the sixties: "Hell, no, we won't go!" "She looked scared," according to a teacher who watched the scene from a window. In the end, the black students were led from the building by a side door while the state police restrained the mob in front.

The wrongs suffered by black people in America were so glaring and their demand for reparation seemingly so compelling that advocates of busing found it impossible to admit that white workers had important grievances of their own, especially when those grievances were couched in the idiom of racial abuse and championed by leaders who exercised no control over their own followers. Liberals were predisposed to see nothing but racial prejudice in the antibusing movement, but the movement itself did very little to correct this misunderstanding. Antibusing agitators sometimes appealed to the example of the civil rights movement, but they had no understanding of its moral self-discipline. They deplored violence but subtly encouraged it by dwelling on the duty to repel the outside "invasion" of their communities. They protested that "although we're opposed to forced busing, we're not racists," in the words of Dennis Kearney, a South Boston politician; but antibusing mobs undermined such claims with their favorite slogan, "Bus the niggers back to Africa!" "We *are* racists," said a white senior at South Boston High School. "Let's face it. That's how we feel about it." Ione Malloy, the English teacher who recorded this defiance in her diary of the busing conflict, tried to persuade her students that South Boston's position was more complicated than that. When students complained that "blacks get everything," she challenged them to change places. When they threatened to "start trouble so the plan won't work," she predicted, quite accurately, that the authorities would close the school. She urged them to avoid violence and provocation, to no avail. As the situation deteriorated, she confessed to a feeling of "futility." "We seem to be going to a dead end."

The best argument against busing was that an "ethnically or racially homogeneous neighborhood respected another community's integrity more easily than a weak, threatened neighborhood did." According to this way of thinking, "strong neighborhoods were the solid building blocks of a healthily diverse city." The "preservation of community," accordingly, should have been recognized as a "value competitive with— yet ironically essential to—equality." But these were the words of a sympathetic observer from outside, Anthony Lukas, not an indigenous analysis of the issue. Leaders of the antibusing movement never resorted to this argument. They seldom rose above the level of resentment, self-righteousness, and self-pity. "We are poor people locked into an economically miserable situation," said Pixie Palladino of ROAR (Restore Our Alienated Rights). "All we want is to be mothers to the children God gave us. We are not opposed to anyone's skin. We are opposed to forced busing."

In default of indigenous leadership, it was left to an occasional outsider or to an ambivalent insider like Ione Malloy to grapple with the difficult question of how to reconcile ethnic solidarity with racial equality. Like other moderates in South Boston—the few who remained by the mid-seventies—Malloy supported integration but shared the local resentment of Garrity's judge-made law. "A great injustice has been done to the people of South Boston by forcing on them a desegregation plan that didn't consider the needs of the students or the working-class background of the community." She admired the community pride she discovered when she attended a meeting of ROAR, but she regretted the community's effort to make the high school a political battleground. She agreed with a statement passed by the faculty senate that if the black and white communities stayed out, refraining from "agitation in the communities with the students," the atmosphere in the school would improve.

An Irish Catholic who grew up in Boston and longed for an "Irish cultural renaissance in South Boston," Malloy nevertheless understood that the Southie's creed, "We take care of our own," represented an "inadequate ideal." She hoped to "change the self-image of the South Boston youth by giving him a sense of his cultural roots so he could stand strong." She did not expect to accomplish this, however, by concealing Irish shortcomings or failures, still less by appealing to a precarious sense of racial superiority. Nor did she propose to strengthen Irish solidarity by sealing off South Boston from the outside world. "I would hear, over and over, 'We just want to be left alone.' " She rejected this simpleminded solution, just as she rejected simpleminded solutions proposed by the other side.* As a teacher, she could not accept either of the competing

---

*She listened with some amusement to a wistful appeal broadcast over WGBH—"not exactly the workingman's station"—in which Elma Lewis, founder of the School of

conceptions of education implicit in the battle over busing and more explicit in controversies over school prayers, in broader discussions about the place of religious instruction in the public schools, and in the general conflict between the demand for schools responsive chiefly to parental pressure and the demand for schools governed by an abstract ideal of "excellence." Malloy took the position, in effect, that the first of these conceptions would simply enforce uncritical adherence to local dogma, while the second would allow a few gifted individuals to escape from their culture into the business and professional class, leaving the rest behind.

Advocates of busing argued that racially integrated schools would destroy racial stereotypes and promote tolerance. Their more ambiguous effect is illustrated by the case of Vinnie, the only student in Charlestown willing to submit to busing into Roxbury during the first year of the desegregation program. Held up as a model of racial enlightenment in an account of the busing crisis by Pamela Bullard and Judith Stoia, Boston television reporters, Vinnie might better have been seen as a model of social mobility and cultural expatriation. As Martha Bayles noted in a perceptive review, Vinnie was a hero for Bullard and Stoia because he was "just like us."

> Unlike his backward and ignorant neighbors, he wants to go to Harvard. Unlike his insular neighbors, he intends to leave Charlestown and never come back. . . . Unlike his sexually repressed neighbors, he sees no harm in unmarried girls having babies. . . . The point is that Bullard and Stoia, in their zeal to show how busing has cured Vinnie of racial prejudice, show also how it has cured him of numerous other beliefs and values. Instead of describing a Charlestown boy who has overcome racism, they describe a Charlestown boy who has overcome Charlestown.

Unfortunately for Judge Garrity's experiment in racial balance, most of Vinnie's neighbors did not share his ambition to "overcome Charles-

---

Fine Arts in Roxbury, said that "all we want is a chance for black students to sit with white students . . . and learn." "It sounds so simple," Malloy noted without conviction.

town," let alone the means to carry it out; but even if they had, they would not necessarily have been the better for it. If racial enlightenment could be achieved only at the price of exile, perhaps it was time to reconsider the whole project of enlightenment.*

"Populism" and the New Right

· ■ ·

The battle over busing, whatever its effect on young people caught up in it, clearly had a devastating effect on the old liberal coalition. Of all the "social issues," as they came to be called, that divided the New Deal coalition down the middle—abortion, the Equal Rights Amendment, the death penalty, gun control, gay rights, school prayers, the pledge of allegiance, judicial lawmaking—busing was the most fiercely contested and the most dramatic in its exposure of the growing distance between

---

*Daniel Monti's study of school reform in St. Louis contains a similarly ambiguous example of successful integration. Monti reports a conversation with a white student in his sociology class at the University of Missouri. The desegregation plan in St. Louis, unlike the one in Boston, required suburban schools to accept black pupils from the city. Monti's student drove a school bus: "I take white county kids into the city and black kids back out to the county schools." Having explained the nature of his job, the bus driver proceeded to describe his black passengers.

> "God, you oughta hear the way those black kids talk! They're unbelievable."
> "That bad, huh?" But I did not really want to know.
> "No, no!" he snapped back. "They're that good."
> "What do you mean 'that good'?" I asked.
> "Just that. I mean they sit there talkin' algebra and poetry for the whole bus ride. It's wild." He paused, then added, "I don't know where they get those kids, but it ain't from no ghetto family."

The bus driver, Monti adds, "knew from his daily experience what many observers of the desegregation order had been complaining about. The black youngsters who 'volunteered' for long bus rides to county schools were not like their peers left back in the city." On the contrary, they were carefully selected as likely prospects for social mobility, gifted with the ambition to overcome the ghetto in the same way that Vinnie overcame Charlestown.

wealthy liberals and workers, formerly united in support of Franklin Roosevelt and his heirs in the liberal succession. When Edward Kennedy tried to address an antibusing rally in 1974, an angry Irish crowd shouted him down and pursued him with eggs and tomatoes when he retreated to the Federal Building, named for his brother. So much for Camelot.

In his study of the Boston school wars, Anthony Lukas describes a confrontation in 1975—International Women's Year in Massachusetts, by gubernatorial proclamation—between the Governor's Commission on the Status of Women and a delegation of women from the antibusing movement. The antibusing agitators claimed that their responsibility for their children's education had been expropriated by the state. "You are supposed to defend women's rights. Why don't you defend ours?" The commission ruled that busing had "nothing to do" with the rights of women. Suburban feminists, "dressed in their Town and Country tweeds, Pierre Cardin silk scarves, and eighty-five-dollar alligator shoes," had nothing to say to a group of dowdy women in tam-o'-shanters, windbreakers, and "Stop Forced Busing" T-shirts.

As "social issues" came to define the difference between the right and the left, a new breed of "populists" began to build a political coalition around lower-middle-class resentment. Like the populists of old, they saw themselves as the enemies of wealth and privilege, champions of the "average man on the street," in the words of George Wallace: the "man in the textile mill," the "man in the steel mill," the "barber" and "beautician," the "policeman on the beat," the "little businessman." The architects of the new right were by no means unanimously committed to free-market economics. Some of them remained New Dealers on economic issues. In 1968, Wallace's American Independent party called for Social Security increases, promised better health care, and reaffirmed the right of collective bargaining. The *National Review* denounced Wallace's "Country and Western Marxism," and his conservative opponents in Alabama judged him "downright pink." Paul Weyrich, a leading ideologist of the new right, was a man of the people, like Wallace—the product of a blue-collar, German Catholic background in Racine, Wisconsin. He felt "closer to William Jennings Bryan," he said, "than to the Tories." The "essence of the new right," as he saw it, was a "morally based conservatism," not free-market economics. "Big corporations are as bad as big government," said Weyrich. "They're in bed together." Insisting that "laissez-faire is not enough," he stressed the need for "some higher value" than the pursuit of wealth. In taking the position that "there can be no such thing as an entirely free market," he acknowledged agreement "with some liberals." What he resented, he said, was liberal "compassion," which was "condescending" and "patronizing."

The new right's constituency included many people who believed that "oil, steel, insurance, and the banks run this country," in the words of a member of the Italian-American Civil Rights League in Brooklyn. "I'd go for public ownership of the oil companies," this man said, "if I didn't think the national politicians were a bunch of thieves." A self-designated conservative Democrat told Jonathan Rieder, "It's not only welfare but the multinational corporations who are ripping us off, taking our jobs away and sending employment to the South and West. The middle classes are the lost people." Kevin Phillips reported in 1982 that the middle-class tax revolt, an important element in the crystallization of the new right, was directed against regressive property taxes, not against the federal income tax. It was "more populist than conservative," according to Phillips. Rising property taxes fell most heavily on blue-collar workers and on members of the lower middle class, and it was they, not the rich, who voted in 1978 for California's famous Proposition 13, which failed to carry a number of upper-income precincts that later went for Reagan in 1980. Both in California and in Oklahoma, voters who favored a reduction of property taxes rejected income tax reduction. The tax revolt, according to Phillips, should not be seen as a mandate for supply-side economics. Few of those who favored cuts in the welfare budget had massive reductions in mind. Phillips found considerable public support, in fact, for a general redistribution of income.

Public opinion polls conducted by Patrick Caddell in the mid-seventies found that a growing number of people simultaneously favored a redistribution of income and tough positions on "social issues." Donald Warren, a Michigan sociologist, reported similar findings in 1973. Thirty percent of his sample said that blacks had too much political power and received more than their share of federal aid, but 60 percent said the same thing about the rich. Eighteen percent said that blacks had a better chance than whites to get fair treatment in the courts, but 42 percent said that rich people had an even better chance. According to recent polls conducted by the National Opinion Research Center, well over half the respondents believed that government is run by the "big interests" and favored federal action designed to reduce the gap between rich and poor, preferably by "raising the taxes of wealthy families." The same people, however, rejected the values liberalism had come to stand for and voted for right-wing candidates who denounced the liberal media, liberal bureaucrats and social planners, liberal do-gooders, and liberal exponents of cultural relativism and sexual permissiveness.

The rise of "neoliberalism" in the mid-seventies made it easier than ever for the right to appropriate the rhetoric and symbolism of populism. In 1974, two years after George McGovern's disastrous campaign for the presidency, the Democrats rebounded from defeat by gaining four governorships, four new seats in the Senate, and forty-nine congressional seats. Most of those elected in this Democratic resurgence at the state and congressional level—politicians like Gary Hart, John Culver, Dale Bumpers, Jerry Brown, Ella Grasso, Richard Lamm, Tom Downey, Christopher Dodd, Toby Moffett, Paul Simon, Paul Tsongas, Les AuCoin, James Blanchard, and Tim Wirth—came out of the "new politics" of the sixties and early seventies. They were graduates of the Peace Corps, the War on Poverty, the antiwar movement, and the McGovern campaign. Their opposition to the war in Vietnam, their commitment to feminism and civil rights, their impatience with the "special interests" that allegedly controlled the party (including labor), their enthusiasm for advanced technology, and their emphasis on professional competence as opposed to ideology distinguished them from older liberals like Edward Kennedy and Hubert Humphrey. Toby Moffett of Connecticut characterized the congressional class of '74, without irony or disapproval, as "very suburban." Economic growth and education impressed neoliberals as the nation's prime concerns. "If the U.S. economy does well," Tsongas explained, "a rising tide lifts all boats." On the other hand, the "class-warfare context" of old-fashioned party politics, in the words of Les AuCoin of Oregon, divided the nation and diverted attention from the technical problems that had to be solved if the United States was to regain its economic leadership of the world. Attacks on business were counterproductive. "The American people do not buy ... a class warfare political argument," AuCoin declared. "The American people, at this point of our history, are looking for leadership that argues for economic growth strategies."

Tsongas, who described himself as a "liberal on social issues," found a "lot of liberal doctrine on economics" offensive to his "pro-business" sensibilities. If any given policy "generates wealth and helps the economy and makes us more competitive, we're for it." When Michael Dukakis announced in 1988, "This election is not about ideology, it's about competence," he expressed the essence of neoliberalism. It was typical of this group that they wanted to make the federal deficit the overriding issue of the eighties, ignoring issues that "middle Americans" considered more important (the distribution of wealth and privilege, the declining prospects of the middle class, the loss of moral purpose), and that they proposed to reduce the deficit not only by cuts in the defense budget but by heavy taxes on tobacco, beer, and hard liquor—the traditional consolations of the working class.

At a time when liberal support for abortion, affirmative action, and busing had already driven masses of Democrats out of the party, nothing could have been less likely to win them back than this managerial, technocratic, "suburban" school of liberalism. Neoliberals like Hart called for "new ideas," but their economic ideas, on which they placed most of their emphasis, seemed indistinguishable except in detail from those of the right. "The important thing," said Jerry Brown, "was to avoid taxes and not spend too much money." The emergence of a bipartisan consensus concerning the importance of low taxes and governmental thrift, together with an unspoken agreement not to raise questions about the distribution of wealth, meant that "social issues" would dominate national campaigns. More precisely, it meant that symbols vaguely evoked by those issues—"family values," the flag, the pledge of allegiance, the "American dream"—would dominate national campaigns and that the Republicans, having solidified their claim to the populist tradition, would continue to win presidential elections with monotonous regularity.

The Theory of the New Class
and Its Historical Antecedents

· ■ ·

The ideological appeal of the new right depended on its ability not only to emphasize social issues at the expense of economic issues but to deflect "middle-class" resentment from the rich to a parasitic "new class" of professional problem solvers and moral relativists. In 1975, William Rusher of the *National Review* referred to the emergence of a " 'verbalist' elite," "neither businessmen nor manufacturers, blue-collar workers or farmers," as the "great central fact" of recent American history. "The producers of America," Rusher said, ". . . have a common economic interest in limiting the growth of this rapacious new non-producing class." The idea of a new class enabled the right to invoke social classifications steeped in populist tradition—producers and parasites—and to press them into the service of social and political programs directly opposed to everything populism had ever stood for.

Speculation about a "new class" had a long history. Three distinct traditions contributed to right-wing theorizing, and it was the right's inability to disentangle them, in part, that explained why its version of the new class turned out to be such a "muddled concept," in the words of Daniel Bell. A progressive tradition, which could be traced all the way back to Saint-Simon, considered the technical intelligentsia a class destined to play an increasingly important role in modern society by virtue of its indispensability. In the United States, Thorstein Veblen was probably the most influential exponent of this view. Veblen distinguished between the "pecuniary" culture of the leisure class and the scientific, critical, and "iconoclastic" culture of the engineers. He ridiculed the idea that the workers, reduced to automata by the modern division of labor, knew enough to expropriate and operate the industrial plant, but he had more faith in professional and managerial personnel, who valued efficiency for its own sake and cared more about industrial growth and productivity than about profits. The engineers already exercised de facto control of the corporation, according to Veblen, but they were hobbled by the constraints imposed by a wasteful system of capitalist production. Once they came to understand their real interests, they would throw out the capitalists and operate the industrial system for the benefit of society as a whole.

In one form or another, this encouraging view of the "knowledge class" influenced the progressive movement, the New Deal, and the New Frontier. The early Walter Lippmann, New Dealers like Stuart Chase and Thurman Arnold, and Keynesian liberals like John Kenneth Galbraith argued that capitalism could be transformed from within by a corporate "technostructure," as Galbraith called it, whose interest in economic growth collided with the profit motive. The well-known study by Adolph Berle and Gardiner Means, *The Modern Corporation and Private Property* (1932), seemed to provide empirical underpinning for the idea of an autonomous category of industrial managers and experts by calling attention to the growing divergence between ownership of the corporation, now dispersed among a multitude of stockholders, and those who actually controlled and operated it. After World War II, the rise of the "multiversity," as Clark Kerr called it, dramatized industry's dependence on scientific and technical knowledge and thus gave further encouragement to speculation about the "knowledge industry."

Socialists as well as liberals often found these ideas attractive. The new left, casting about for a revolutionary "agent" to replace the proletariat, saw the producers of knowledge as a "new working class," in the words of Greg Calvert. When these brain workers came to understand that capitalism prevented them from exercising the full range of their skills, they would side with other dispossessed groups in overthrowing it.

A second, less flattering picture of the new class took shape in the forties and fifties, in the context of angry debates about the failure of socialism in the Soviet Union and eastern Europe. In opposition to Trotsky's characterization of the Stalinist regime as a "degenerated workers' state," Max Schachtman and his followers argued that the Soviet Union was not a workers' state at all but a form of "bureaucratic collectivism" dominated by party hacks. In *The Managerial Revolution* (1941), James Burnham took the position that although capitalism was declining, socialism was not taking its place. State ownership of the means of production transferred power from the capitalists not to the workers but to a new ruling class of professional managers, who proceeded to abolish collective bargaining, to replace the market with central planning, and to suppress every trace of political freedom. Dissident intellectuals in eastern Europe elaborated this thesis in their impassioned critique of Stalinism. Books like *The New Class*, by Milovan Djilas (1957), and *The Intellectuals on the Road to Class Power*, by George Konrad and Ivan Szelenyi (1979), appealed to ex-Marxists, in the United States as in Europe, who had turned against Stalinism but retained the intellectual habits of Marxism and therefore took it for granted that a new form of society implied the existence of a new ruling class. Occasionally someone pointed out that the rise of the monolithic Soviet state called for a reconsideration of the whole concept of a ruling class, not for attempts to stretch it to fit a new situation. Those who had been raised on the Marxian theory of history, however—and this category included a number of intellectuals who later became neoconservatives—did not pay much attention to such objections. They needed a ruling class, if only to sustain their own self-image as a lonely band of truth tellers who dared to question the reigning orthodoxy, and they found it in the makers of the "managerial revolution."

The third source of new-class theory had the longest lineage of all, originating in Burke's attack on the French revolution. As early as 1856, Tocqueville provided a definitive statement of the case against the revolutionary intelligentsia, which informed all subsequent criticism of the revolutionary tradition. In *The Old Regime and the Revolution*, Tocqueville depicted the revolutionary intellectuals as irresponsible dreamers and fanatics, "quite out of touch with practical politics" and therefore lacking the "experience which might have tempered their enthusiasms." Their "fondness for broad generalizations" and for "cut-and-dried legislative systems," their "contempt for hard facts," their "taste for reshaping institutions on novel, ingenious, original lines," and their "desire to reconstruct the entire constitution according to the rules of logic and a preconceived system" were the product of rootless alienation, in Tocqueville's view. Later commentators added to this indictment the accusation that intellectuals were consumed by envy of the rich and powerful and by a desire for revenge; we have seen how Georges Sorel developed this theme in his attack on the Dreyfusard, socialistic intelligentsia of the Third Republic. Julien Benda turned the same kind of argument against Sorel himself in his *Trahison des clercs* (1927), and Raymond Aron turned it against Marxism in *The Opium of the Intellectuals* (1955). French history is full of complaints against visionary, power-mad intellectuals, no doubt because the legacy of the revolution has proved so divisive; but the same tradition informed the work of George Orwell and other English writers and passed into American political discourse in the sixties and seventies, when Lionel Trilling, Daniel Bell, Lewis Feuer, and Norman Podhoretz, among others, began to attack the new left as the latest expression of the "adversary culture" of intellectuals.

Neoconservatives on the New Class

Neoconservative intellectuals' restatement of these well-established traditions of speculation—in which the new class was described variously as practical and efficient, domineering and repressive, alienated and adversarial—represented these intellectuals' most important contribution to the rise of the new right. New-class theory enabled the right to attack "elites" without attacking big business. Businessmen, it appeared, were responsible and public-spirited: they were accountable to the consumers to whom they sold their products, just as practical politicians were accountable to the voters; and the market thus limited any power they could hope to exercise. The new class, on the other hand, was accountable to no one, and its control of higher education and the mass media gave it almost unlimited power over the public mind. Yet the members of this class still felt marginal and isolated: the more power they achieved, the more they resented their lack of power.

Some descriptions of the new class simply transferred the old "authoritarian syndrome" from the workers, now welcomed as allies in the struggle against the adversary culture, to the intellectuals. Feuer spoke of the "intellectuals' acute authoritarianism, arising from frustrated desire for power." *Commentary* caricatured the "radicalized professor" as a "man who has wandered through life, never testing himself outside the university," "envious, resentful," unable to bear his exclusion from the "magic circle where power, glory, and virtue reside." Like the "working-class authoritarians" and the populist "pseudo-conservatives" of the fifties, the new-class intellectuals of the sixties and seventies displayed all the classic symptoms of status anxiety. Analysis of the authoritarian personality, it turned out, could be applied indiscriminately to any group that came under political suspicion—one more indication of its intellectual bankruptcy.

It was never altogether clear, for that matter, just what social grouping the notion of a new class was supposed to refer to. Sometimes it was played off not against business but against the technical intelligentsia, itself a candidate for new-class status in the first of the three traditions on which neoconservatives drew more or less at random. In *The End of Ideology* (1960), Daniel Bell contrasted the "intellectual" with the "scholar," evidently to the advantage of the latter. The scholar had to assume responsibility for a "bounded field of knowledge," but the free-floating intellectual acknowledged no responsibility except to himself. The scholar was "less involved with his 'self,'" whereas the intellectual seldom transcended "*his* experience, *his* individual perceptions." In *The Cultural Contradictions of Capitalism* (1976), Bell argued that the nihilistic hedonism celebrated by adversarial intellectuals undermined the work discipline required by capitalism (though he also argued, well beyond the limits of the neoconservative consensus, that capitalism itself encouraged hedonism and was thus at war with itself). In *The Coming of Post-Industrial Society* (1973), however, "new men" referred to the "technical and professional intelligentsia," whose skills had become essential to the maintenance of an "information society."* In general, neoconservatives took a kindlier view of the new class when they identified it with scientific and technical expertise than when they identified it with cultural radicalism. In *Between Two Ages: America's Role in the Technetronic Era*, Zbigniew Brze-

---

*"While these technologists are not bound by a sufficient common interest to make them a political class, they do have common characteristics. . . . The norms of the new intelligentsia—the norms of professionalism—are a departure from the hitherto prevailing norms of economic self-interest which have guided a business civilization. In the upper reaches of this new elite—that is, in the scientific community—men hold significantly different values [from] those authorizing economic self-aggrandizement, which could become the foundation of the new ethos for such a class." Unfortunately the ethic of professionalism had to compete for the allegiance of the "knowledge class" with the "apocalyptic, hedonistic, and nihilistic" ethic promoted by literary modernism and popularized by the counterculture. In the closing pages of *The Coming of Post-Industrial Society*, Bell argued that "these anti-bourgeois values . . . go hand in hand with the expansion of a new intellectual class huge enough to sustain itself economically as a class. . . . This new class, which dominates the media and the culture, thinks of itself less as radical than 'liberal,' yet its values, centered on 'personal freedom,' are anti-bourgeois."

zinski, later Jimmy Carter's national security adviser, praised the technical elite while condemning literary intellectuals and political militants in the usual terms. Since the latter came "from those branches of learning which are most sensitive to the threat of social irrelevance," their "political activism" could be explained as a "reaction to the . . . fear . . . that a new world is emerging without either their assistance or their leadership." Peter Berger made a similar distinction between responsible specialists and discontented intellectuals, who suffered from a nagging fear of impotence, among other ailments. "Intellectuals," Berger wrote, "have always had the propensity to endow their libidinal emotions with philosophical significance. . . . One suspects that the need for philosophy arises from an unfortunate combination of strong ambitions and weakened capabilities."

Although the "new class" often seemed to refer only to literary intellectuals and their "adversary culture," it could easily expand, when the need arose, to embrace bureaucrats, professional reformers, social workers, and social engineers as well as literary types. In this version, which derived from the theory of the managerial revolution, the "new class" seemed to refer to anyone working in the public sector. According to Irving Kristol, it consisted of "scientists, teachers, and educational administrators, journalists and others in the communications industries, psychologists, social workers, those lawyers and doctors who make their careers in the expanding public sector, city planners, the staffs of the larger foundations, the upper levels of government bureaucracy, and so on." Charles Murray's description was even more expansive: "the upper echelons of . . . academia, journalism, publishing, and the vast network of foundations, institutes, and research centers that has been woven into partnership with government during the last thirty years." Murray included even politicians, judges, bankers, businessmen, lawyers, and doctors—at least those who were liberals. From this point of view, the new class could be recognized not so much by its culture of hedonism as by its relentless pressure for an "activist federal government committed to 'change,'" as Michael Novak put it. Professionals in the public sector wanted massive federal programs, according to Novak, because such programs created "hundreds of thousands of jobs and opportunities" for "those whose hearts itch to do good and who long for a 'meaningful' use of their talents, skills, and years." As Novak, Murray, and Kristol saw it, the culture of the new class was not just antibourgeois but antibusiness. It aimed to replace private enterprise with a vast bureaucracy that would undermine initiative, destroy the free market, and subject everything to central control.

These wildly divergent descriptions of the new class made it clear that the term referred to a set of politically objectionable attitudes, not to an identifiable social grouping, much less a class. Why, then, was it necessary to speak of a new class at all, when it served simply as a vague synonym for "liberalism"? No doubt the term made it possible to introduce attacks on the liberal "intelligentsia" with the disclaimer that it carried "no pejorative connotations," in Murray's words. But the real beauty of the concept lay in the way it obscured the difference between opposition to "middle-class values" and opposition to business. "Liberalism," as a description of what ailed America, did not have the advantage of this ambiguity. The political alignments of the seventies and eighties indicated that a defense of values loosely identified with the counterculture was quite compatible with a defense of business and the free market. Neoliberals declared themselves probusiness at the same time that they endorsed the sexual revolution, championed gay rights and women's rights, opposed the death penalty, and applauded the Supreme Court's decision in *Roe v. Wade.* The free-market element in the Reagan coalition displayed much the same pattern of economic conservatism and cultural liberalism. Quite apart from the libertarian movement—the clearest example of this configuration—public opinion polls consistently showed that a great many of the people attracted to Reagan's economic program either had no particular interest in the "social issues" or held views commonly described as liberal. Even in the heart of the Reagan administration, the White House itself, the right-wing position on social issues elicited little enthusiasm. Nancy Reagan deleted a discussion of abortion from the State of the Union Message in 1987, saying, "I don't give a damn about the right-to-lifers." Reagan made himself the champion of "traditional values," but there is no evidence that he regarded their restoration as a high priority. What he really cared about was the revival of the unregulated capitalism of the twenties: the repeal of the New Deal. As governor of California, he condemned the "wave of hedonism" that had rolled over America and pleaded for a "spiritual rebirth, a rededication to the moral precepts which guided us for so much of our past." In the campaign of 1980, however, he ridiculed Carter for saying very much the same thing. The theme of "spiritual rebirth" gave way to a strategy of evasion and denial. There was nothing wrong with America after all. "Don't let anyone tell you that America's best days are behind her, that the American spirit has been vanquished." Moral regeneration, it appeared, could be achieved painlessly through the power of positive thinking.

Reagan's rhetorical defense of "family and neighborhood" could not be reconciled with his championship of unregulated business enterprise, which has replaced neighborhoods with shopping malls and superhighways. A society dominated by the free market, in which the American dream degenerated into pure acquisitiveness and self-seeking, had no place for "family values."* This was the fundamental contradiction not merely of the Reagan administration but of the new right in general. If the right was to attract support from workers troubled by moral decay, alienated from neoliberalism, but indifferent or hostile to free-market economics, it needed to stir up resentment of elites without stirring up the old populist resentment of capitalists. The notion of a "new class," though not designed with this purpose in mind, enabled people on the right to depict "permissive" social morality, which might otherwise have been seen as the cultural expression of consumer capitalism itself, as part of a "concerted attack on business," in the words of the *Wall Street Jour-*

---

*The ties of kinship and marriage create obligations that override considerations of personal advantage and cannot be discharged simply by a prearranged schedule of payments. By contrast, the market—no respecter of persons—reduces individuals to abstractions, anonymous buyers and sellers whose claims on each other are determined solely by their capacity to pay. The family depends on an active community life, whereas the market disrupts communities by draining off their best talent. Under Reagan, the inner logic of the market became fully explicit: idealization of the man on the make; a pursuit of quick profits; feverish competition leading (as a means of stabilizing it) to the creation of far-flung economic empires impervious to local, state, and finally even national control; a widening chasm between rich and poor; hostility to labor unions; urban redevelopment designed to raise real estate values and to force lower- and middle-income families out of the city; impoverishment of public facilities, public transportation in particular—all in the name of "family, work, neighborhood, peace, and freedom."

nal's Robert Bartley. Thus Rita Kramer, in her contribution to the heated debate about the family, *In Defense of the Family* (1983), blamed the plight of the family on the social service professions, on liberal intellectuals proclaiming their permissive morality as scientific truth, on the mass media, and on the bureaucratic welfare state. Capitalism, she argued—"which gets a bum rap on this issue"—had nothing to do with the growing instability of the family.

In *The War over the Family* (1983), Brigitte Berger and Peter Berger presented a more elaborate version of this analysis. The family debate, the Bergers argued, grew out of the "class struggle" between the business class and the knowledge class, the "new class" of bureaucrats, administrators, and professional experts. The new class attempted to extend its control over marriage, sex, and child rearing in the same way that it had extended its control over private enterprise. In its struggle against the bourgeoisie (a class that now included the workers as well), it spoke a new language of its own, characterized by the "obscurantist use of allegedly scientific terms." By setting up a barrier between professionals and laymen, this impenetrable jargon of expertise reinforced the "claims of the professional to superior wisdom and therefore to status, high income, and possibly even political power." The Bergers advocated a state that would respect "private preferences" instead of attempting to remodel the family according to preconceived theories of child psychology and moral development. The state's responsibility for children ended with adequate nutrition, health care, and education; and even these were more likely to be assured by the market than by an elaborate welfare state. A system of educational vouchers, for example, would provide families with a range of institutional alternatives and thereby introduce market forces into the "monopolistic situation" created by a uniform system of public schools. The best way to assure moral order and economic progress, in short, was to curb the power of the new class.

New-Class *"Permissiveness"* or Capitalist Consumerism?

·■·

The idea of a new class, articulated by neoconservative intellectuals who were themselves members of the new class (as their critics on the left never failed to point out), was more useful for polemical than for analytical purposes. Even as an explanation of contemporary "permissiveness"—itself a shallow description of our moral and cultural disorder—it overlooked a more obvious explanation. Capitalism itself, thanks to its growing dependence on consumerism, promotes an ethic of hedonism and health and thus undermines the "traditional values" of thrift and self-denial. The therapeutic sensibility does not serve the "class interest" of professionals alone, as Daniel Moynihan and other critics of the new class have claimed; it serves the needs of advanced capitalism as a whole. In the late sixties and early seventies, Moynihan argued that by emphasizing impulse rather than calculation as the determinant of human conduct and by holding society responsible for the problems confronting individuals, a "government-oriented" professional class attempted to create a demand for its own services. Professionals had a vested interest in discontent, because discontented people turn to professionally prescribed remedies for relief. But the same principle underlies modern capitalism in general, which continually tries to create new demands and new discontents that can be assuaged only by the consumption of commodities. Professional self-aggrandizement grew up side by side with the advertising industry and the machinery of demand creation. The same historical development that turned the citizen into a client transformed the worker from a producer into a consumer. Thus the medical and psychiatric assault on the family as a technologically backward sector of society went hand in hand with the advertising industry's drive to convince people that store-bought goods are superior to homemade goods.

Neoclassical or post-Keynesian economics—the right's dubious contribution to economic theory—takes no account of the importance of advertising. It extols the "sovereign consumer" and insists that advertising cannot force consumers to buy anything they do not want already. The importance of advertising, however, does not lie in its manipulation of the consumer or its direct influence on consumer choices. The point is that it makes the consumer an addict, unable to live without increasingly sizable doses of externally provided stimulation. Neoconservatives argue that television erodes the capacity for sustained attention in children. They complain that young people now expect education, for example, to be easy and exciting. This argument is sound as far as it goes. Here again, however, neoconservatives incorrectly attribute these artificially excited expectations to liberal propaganda—in this case, to theories of permissive child rearing and "creative pedagogy." They ignore the deeper source of the expectations that undermine education, destroy the child's curiosity, and encourage passivity. Ideologies, no matter how appealing and powerful, cannot shape the structure of perceptions and conduct unless they are embedded in daily experiences that appear to confirm them. In our society, those experiences teach people to want a never-ending supply of new toys and drugs. A defense of free enterprise hardly supplies a corrective to such expectations.

Right-wing economics conceives of the capitalist economy as it was in the time of Adam Smith, when property was still distributed fairly widely, businesses were individually owned, and commodities still retained something of the character of useful objects. The right's notion of free enterprise takes no account of the forces that have transformed capitalism from within: the rise of the corporation, the bureaucratization of business, the increasing insignificance of private property, and the shift from a work ethic to a consumption ethic. When the right takes any note of these developments at all, it is only to attribute them to professional and governmental interference. People on the right decry bureaucracy but see only its public face, missing the spread of bureaucracy in the misnamed private sector. They show no acquaintance with the rich body of historical scholarship that shows how the expansion of the public sector itself came about, in large part, in response to pressure from the corporations themselves.

The right holds that the new class controls the mass media and uses this control to wage a "class struggle" against business. Since the mass media are financed by advertising revenues, however, it is hard to take this contention seriously. It is advertising and the logic of consumerism, not anticapitalist ideology, that govern the depiction of reality in the mass media. The right complains that television mocks "free enterprise" and presents businessmen as "greedy, malevolent, and corrupt," like J. R. Ewing. To see anticapitalist propaganda in a series like *Dallas,* however, requires a suspension not merely of critical judgment but of ordinary faculties of observation. Images of luxury, romance, and excitement dominate such programs, as they dominate the advertisements that surround and engulf them. *Dallas* is itself an advertisement of the good life, like almost everything that comes over the media—for the good life, that is, conceived as endless novelty, change, and excitement, as the titillation of the senses by every available stimulant, as unlimited possibility. "Make it new" is the message not just of modern art (the "adversary culture" deplored by neoconservatives) but of modern consumerism. The modern capitalist economy rests on the techniques of mass production pioneered by Henry Ford but also, no less solidly, on the principle of planned obsolescence introduced by Alfred Sloane when he instituted the annual model change. Relentless "improvement" of the product and upgrading of consumer tastes are the heart of mass merchandising, and these imperatives are built into the mass media at every level.

Even the reporting of news has to be understood not as propaganda for any particular ideology, liberal or conservative, but as propaganda for commodities—for the replacement of things by commodities, use values by exchange values, and events by images. The very concept of news celebrates newness. The value of news, like that of any other commodity, consists primarily of its novelty, only secondarily of its informational value. As Waldo Frank pointed out many years ago, the news appeals to the same jaded appetite that makes a spoiled child tire of a toy as soon as it becomes familiar and demand a new one in its place. As Frank also pointed out (in *The Rediscovery of America,* 1930), the social expectations that stimulate a child's appetite for new toys appeal to the desire for appropriation: the appeal of toys comes to lie not in their use but in their status as possessions. "A fresh plaything renews the child's opportunity to say: this is mine." A child who seldom gets a new toy, Frank noted, "prizes it as part of himself." But if "toys become more frequent, value is gradually transferred from the toy to the toy's novelty. . . . The arrival of the toy, not the toy itself, becomes the event." The news, accordingly, has to be seen as the "plaything of a child whose hunger for toys has been stimulated shrewdly." We can carry this analysis one step further by pointing out that the model of possession, in a society organized around mass consumption, is addiction. The need for novelty and fresh stimulation becomes more and more intense, intervening interludes of boredom increasingly intolerable.

Neoconservatives sense a link between drugs and television, but they do not grasp the nature of this connection any more than they grasp the important fact about news: that it represents another form of advertising, not liberal propaganda. Propaganda in the usual sense of the word plays a less and less important part in a consumer society, where people greet all official pronouncements with suspicion. Mass media themselves contribute to the prevailing skepticism; one of their main effects is to undermine heroism and charismatic leadership, to reduce everything to the same dimensions. The effect of the media is not to elicit belief but to maintain the apparatus of addiction. Drugs are merely the most obvious form of addiction. It is true that drug addiction is one of the things that undermine "traditional values," but the need for drugs—that is, for commodities that alleviate boredom and satisfy the socially stimulated desire for novelty and excitement—grows out of the very nature of a consumerist economy.

It is only in their capacity as quintessential consumers that young professionals dominate the airwaves and set the tone of American life. Their distinctive manner of living embodies the restless ambition, the nagging dissatisfaction with things as they are, that are fostered by a consumer economy. Their careers require them to spend much of their time on the road and to accept transfers as the price of advancement. Though they complain about having to move so often, their willingness to travel long distances even in pursuit of pleasure suggests that they would find a more settled life unendurable. "Leisure," for them, closely resembles work, since much of it consists of strenuous and for the most part solitary exercise. Even shopping, their ruling passion, takes on the character of a grueling ordeal: "Shop till you drop." Like exercise, it often seems to present itself as a form of therapy, designed to restore a sense of wholeness and well-being after long hours of unrewarding work. "I feel like hell and I go out for a run, and before I know it, everything's O.K." Shopping serves the same purpose: "It hardly matters what I buy, I just get a kick out of buying. It's like that first whiff of cocaine. It's euphoric and I just get higher and higher as I buy." Sociological profiles of the "compulsive shopper" report that 40 percent are "most likely to buy something when 'feeling bad' about themselves." According to a summary of these studies in the *Wall Street Journal,* shopping serves as a means of "alleviating loneliness," "dispelling boredom," and "relieving depression." "They don't really need what they are shopping for. Often they don't even know what they're after." A survey of shoppers in malls indicates that only 25 percent come to buy a particular item.

Such evidence suggests that consumerism is a more serious threat to "traditional values" than the allegedly anticapitalist ideology of the new class. It suggests that the threat to those values, moreover, is not very fully or clearly described as a spirit of hedonism and self-indulgence that undermines the work ethic. The new class is just as addicted to work as to exercise and consumption. The intrinsic satisfactions in this work, to be sure, are usually overshadowed by external rewards—high salaries, social status, the expectation of promotion, frequent changes of scene. But there is no lack of willing, not to say compulsive, workers. What is missing is the kind of work that might evoke a sense of calling.

A calling, as opposed to a career, implies a belief in the intrinsic value of a given line of work. When goods are produced merely to satisfy the taste for novelty, it is difficult even for professionals to convince themselves that their work serves some pressing social need. When "people look at products as if they were mood-altering drugs," in the words of James Ogilvy, a market researcher, those who design and produce those products—or merely contribute indirectly to their manufacture and distribution—cannot help wondering whether their efforts really matter in the larger scheme of things. Even the computer industry has lost the sense of mission that animated it in the seventies, according to Dennis Hayes. Technological innovation is no longer "linked to the public good." Computer products are increasingly "ephemeral." "Volatile markets beckon, are saturated, overrun, made obsolescent, and forgotten as quickly as new product releases, or new markets, are created. . . . Computer work has become more and more detached from social contexts. A culture of product indifference and ignorance has engulfed the computer sophisticates."

The New Class as Seen from the Left

· ■ ·

Even if we could agree with the superficial diagnosis of "permissiveness" as the chief threat to the old values, we would find it hard to resist the conclusion, then, that "if there is one clear and ubiquitous source of permissiveness," in the words of Barbara Ehrenreich, ". . . it lies, as it always has, in the consumer culture." Modern capitalism, Ehrenreich points out, is itself "at odds" with the "traditional values" of "hard-work, self-denial, and family loyalty." The attack on the new class, she argues, is therefore misplaced. The corporate elite, not the professional elite, is the only "genuine elite, relative to which the [professional] middle class is only another 'lower class.'" It is the "corporate-financial elite," moreover—especially in its frenzied search for short-term profits through mergers, acquisitions, and speculation—that "most clearly exhibits" the moral defects associated with permissiveness: "present-time orientation and the incapacity to defer gratification."

Ehrenreich's recent book on the "inner life" of the professional class, though it contains many valuable observations, shows why it is so difficult for the left to mount a convincing reply to right-wing populism and more specifically to the theory of the new class. Ehrenreich stands on firm ground as long as she argues that new-class theory deflects resentment of "permissiveness" from its proper target, the corporations and their culture of consumption. Her decision to join the debate at this level, however, precludes a deeper analysis of the issues that trouble "middle Americans" and of the failure of right-wing ideology to address those issues. The right's inability to get beyond clichés about hedonism, permissiveness, and moral relativism ought to invite people on the left to give a more penetrating account of contemporary culture. Careful attention to popular complaints about the media, for example, would suggest that people are troubled by something more elusive than "liberal bias" or sexual license. What people find disturbing about the media, it would seem, is their obsession with the young and affluent, with glamour, celebrity, money, and power; their indifference to working people and the poor, except as objects of satire or "compassion"; the prurient quality of their fascination with violence and sex; their inflated sense of their own importance; their insatiable appetite for scandal; their eagerness to uncover unworthy motives behind every worthy act; the encouragement they give to disrespect and cynicism. A number of studies have indicated that television promotes cynicism in children, and this evidence probably sums up popular uneasiness more effectively than "liberal permissiveness." People object to television because it encourages children to be too demanding, to expect too much, to equate the good life with enormous wealth, and to admire those who get something for nothing, but above all because it destroys the capacity for respect. Behind the popular attack on the media, one can sense the same kind of concerns that make the citizens of Canarsie so anxious about threats to the integrity of their neighborhood. Just as the streets have been taken over by junkies, dope peddlers, pimps, and streetwalkers, so the public airwaves appear to have been taken over by hustlers promoting something of the same vision of the good life, one that mocks decent people with the promise of sudden wealth and glamour.

None of this gets into Ehrenreich's account of the cultural class war. Indeed she denies the existence of such a conflict, preferring to interpret the debate about "values" as a debate confined to the new class. To admit that working people are concerned about such issues and are therefore attracted to right-wing explanations (even if those explanations prove unsatisfactory in the end) would shatter her image of militant workers steadfast in their devotion to social democracy. She therefore tries to exonerate the working class of any responsibility for the "backlash" against liberalism. This backlash, she believes, is a fantasy conjured up by neoconservative intellectuals. Their talk of cultural breakdown and moral anarchy finds an audience not among workers but among upper-middle-class professionals, because it plays insidiously on their "fear of falling" into self-indulgence. In the sixties, neoconservatives led the media campaign against the flower children and student radicals by depicting them as traitors to their class, which is built on discipline and self-denial. They further unnerved the new class by "discovering" working-class opposition to liberalism—another fantasy, according to Ehrenreich, but one that shook liberals' confidence in their ability to speak for Americans as a whole and thus had a deeply demoralizing effect. A "wave of contrition" swept through the new class. The "forgotten" workers came to stand "for what the [professional] class itself had lost, or always seemed to be on the verge of losing: the capacity for self-denial and deferred gratification."

The stereotype of the hard hat blinded the media to the true nature of working-class revolt, according to Ehrenreich. "For all the talk of racial backlash, black and white workers were marching, picketing, and organizing together in a spirit of class solidarity that had not been seen since the thirties." They were "wearing their hair shoulder length, smoking pot, and beginning to question the totalitarian regimen of factory life." Indeed "there was even the possibility, in the late sixties, of an explosive convergence of working-class insurgency and the student movement." The inspirational rhetoric packed into these sentences—"black and white together," "class solidarity," "the thirties," "working-class insurgency," "explosive convergence"—indicates that Ehrenreich has left the land of the living for a visit to the Marxist mortuary, where old revolutionary slogans lie beautifully embalmed. She counters one stereotype of the worker with another, the image of Archie Bunker with the image of revolutionary solidarity enshrined in the annals of the left. The second image bears no closer relation to reality than the first.

New-class theorists attribute the worker's cultural conservatism to his *embourgeoisement,* ignoring his resentment of the rich. Radicals and social democrats accurately perceive the decline in his socioeconomic status but ignore his lower-middle-class values. They also ignore his opposition to busing, affirmative action, abortion, abolition of the death penalty, and other liberal causes. In support of her untenable contention that workers never moved to the right, Ehrenreich feebly argues that workers who voted for Wallace in 1964, 1968, and 1972 were attracted only to his economic "liberalism." But if they wanted economic liberalism, they could just as easily have voted for Johnson, Humphrey, or McGovern. What they wanted, it would seem, was populism, with its petty-bourgeois morality as well as its economic radicalism; and Wallace provided them with the closest available approximation to the real thing.

Ehrenreich's account of "yuppie guilt" is just as fanciful as her account of working-class "insurgency." The title of her book, *Fear of Falling,* refers not to the fear of falling down the social ladder but to the fear of falling away from the upper-middle-class ethic of self-denial. The professional class feels guilty about its increasing affluence. It has an irrational horror of "softness," which it tries to "expiate" by means of exercise and overwork. This residual puritanism makes the new class curiously receptive to ideological denunciations of itself. "The right's attack on the new class . . . rang true because it touched on the perennial fear within the professional middle class of growing soft, of failing to strive, of falling into the snares of affluence."

The left's reply to the neoconservative version of new-class theory turns out to be its mirror image. For neoconservatives, the new class is the source of the attack on "traditional values." For Ehrenreich, its misguided fear of self-indulgence has made it, for the moment, the main bastion of those values. Once it overcomes its irrational need for "expiation," however, the new class can be expected to side with "insurgent" workers in their quest for social justice. The struggle for the "soul" of the new class is still in its early stages. The new class has not yet decided what it wants to be, "generous or selfish, overindulged or aggrieved." If it makes the proper choices, it will become the hope of the future. Ehrenreich concludes that it has the makings of a universal class and that its "program," accordingly, should seek "to expand the class, welcoming everyone, until there remains no other class."

Neither left- nor right-wing intellectuals, strangely united in their determination to rescue the new class from itself, seem to have much interest in the rest of American society. Their view of the United States begins and ends with the knowledge industry. Other classes enter the picture only as images and stereotypes projected on the consciousness of the new class. It does not occur to these intellectuals that the rest of the country may have only a limited interest in the "soul" of the new class. Nor does it occur to them that universal access to professional status may not describe the ambitions of most Americans, much less an ideal of the good society. Ehrenreich herself acknowledges the limits of her perspective at one point. "Left and right, we are still locked in a [professional] culture that is almost wholly insular, self-referential, and, in its own way, parochial." Her book shows, however, just how difficult it is for intellectuals to break out of this comfortable confinement.

A Universal Class?

· ■ ·

The truth about the new class, if we try to see it from the outside, is that its members, in spite of the diversity of their occupations and their political beliefs, have a common outlook, best described as a "culture of critical discourse," in the words of Alvin Gouldner. They share an inordinate respect for educational credentials, a refusal to accept anything on faith, a commitment to free inquiry, a tendency to question authority, a belief in tolerance as the supreme political virtue. At their best, these qualities describe the scientific habit of mind—the willingness to submit every idea, no matter how distasteful or attractive, to critical scrutiny and to suspend judgment until all the relevant evidence can be assessed. "Nothing is sacred to them," Gouldner wrote; "nothing is exempt from reexamination."*

As this observation may suggest, however, the critical temper can easily degenerate into cynicism. It can degenerate into a snobbish disdain for people who lack formal education and work with their hands, an unfounded confidence in the moral wisdom of experts, an equally unfounded prejudice against untutored common sense, a distrust of any expression of good intentions, a distrust of everything but science, an ingrained irreverence, a disposition (the natural outgrowth of irreverence and distrust) to see the world as something that exists only to gratify human desires. The positive and negative features of this worldly, skepti-

---

*Gouldner's last work, *The Future of Intellectuals and the Rise of the New Class* (1979), remains one of the best explorations of the subject. The concept of critical discourse, unlike "hedonism," "nihilism," "permissiveness," or just plain "liberalism," is broad enough to apply to the new class as a whole, the scientists and technicians as well as the literary intellectuals. But Gouldner too was afflicted with new-class myopia. He had no understanding of the terrible limitations of "critical discourse." Like Ehrenreich, he saw the new class as "both emancipatory and elitist" and hoped that the emancipatory impulse would win out over the elitist. Like Ehrenreich—who may well have been influenced by Gouldner in her own conclusions—he regarded the new class as "the universal class in embryo, but badly flawed." With all its faults, it was the "most progressive force in modern society," in his view—the "center of whatever human emancipation is possible in the foreseeable future."

cal, and critical mentality are so closely intertwined that it is impossible to assign them, as Daniel Bell and others have tried to do, to sociologically distinct sectors of the new class—the good qualities to the scientists and technicians, the bad ones to literary intellectuals. Both the virtues and the defects of the professional class spring from the habit of criticism, which, unleavened by a sense of its own limits, soon reduces the world to ashes.

For the same reason—because the enlightened virtues carry with them a long list of enlightened vices—it is impossible to refute the core of truth in the notion of a new class by claiming that all the evils attributed to it can be blamed on capitalist consumerism instead. Capitalism cannot be absolved, but neither can it be made to carry the whole indictment of modern culture. Capitalism was itself the product, in part, of the seventeenth-century scientific revolution. Its material achievements rested on the technology made possible by modern science. The "spirit of capitalism," mistakenly traced by Max Weber to the Protestant ethic, derived far more directly from the sense of unlimited power conferred by science—the intoxicating prospect of man's conquest of the natural world. Scientific inquiry also served, as we have seen, as a model for the distinctive conception of history associated with the promise of universal abundance. Just as each advance accomplished by the critical intelligence was destined to be superseded by the next, so the definition of human needs and wants was thought to expand as those needs and wants were progressively satisfied. The insatiability of curiosity and desire appeared to give the idea of progress a solid foundation in psychological and historical observation.

As the heir to the critical traditions of the scientific revolution and the Enlightenment, the new class pins its hopes on the eventual triumph of critical intelligence over superstition, cosmopolitanism over provincialism, man over nature, abundance over scarcity. Its belief in progress, chastened by twentieth-century events but not yet relinquished by any means, transcends commitment to any particular system of production. We can readily agree with Gouldner's description of the professional class as the "most progressive force in modern society"; the question is whether that can still be regarded as a virtue.

Even if we ignore the unattractive features of "critical discourse" and consider it in the most genial light, we cannot escape the mounting evidence that calls its underlying premise—the limitless possibilities generated by modern science and modern production—into question. The promise of universal abundance has always contained egalitarian implications without which it would have carried very little moral authority. Those implications were open to conflicting interpretations. Some people argued that it was enough to increase the general pool of goods and services, in the expectation that everyone's standard of living would rise as a result. Others demanded more radical measures designed not merely to increase the total wealth but to distribute it more equitably. But no one who believed in progress conceived of a limit on productive capacity as a whole. No one envisioned a return to a more frugal existence; such views fell outside the progressive consensus.

The belated discovery that the earth's ecology will no longer sustain an indefinite expansion of productive forces deals the final blow to the belief in progress. A more equitable distribution of wealth, it is now clear, requires at the same time a drastic reduction in the standard of living enjoyed by the rich nations and the privileged classes. Western nations can no longer hold up their standard of living and the enlightened, critical, and progressive culture that is entangled with it as an example for the rest of the world. Nor can the privileged classes within the West—and these include the professional class as well as the very rich—except to solve the problem of poverty by taking everyone into their own ranks. Even if this were a morally desirable solution, it is no longer feasible, since the resources required to sustain a new-class style of life, hitherto imagined to be inexhaustible, are already approaching their outer limit. Under these conditions, the universalistic pretensions of the new class cannot be taken seriously. Indeed they are deeply offensive, not only because they embody a very narrow ideal of the good life but because the material prerequisites for this particular form of the good life cannot be made universally available.

Populism against Progress

The same developments that make it impossible for those who believe in progress to speak with confidence and moral authority compel us to give a more attentive hearing to those who rejected it all along. If progressive ideologies have dwindled down to a wistful hope against hope that things will somehow work out for the best, we need to recover a more vigorous form of hope, which trusts life without denying its tragic character or attempting to explain away tragedy as "cultural lag." We can fully appreciate this kind of hope only now that the other kind, better described as optimism, has fully revealed itself as a higher form of wishful thinking. Progressive optimism rests, at bottom, on a denial of the natural limits on human power and freedom, and it cannot survive for very long in a world in which an awareness of those limits has become inescapable. The disposition properly described as hope, trust, or wonder, on the other hand—three names for the same state of heart and mind—asserts the goodness of life in the face of its limits. It cannot be defeated by adversity. In the troubled times to come, we will need it even more than we needed it in the past.

Limits and hope: these words sum up the two lines of argument I have tried to weave together. One line of argument seeks to distinguish between hope and optimism and to explore the implications of that distinction. The other explores some of the political and ideological expressions of the sense of limits. It is their recognition of limits alone that justifies consideration of such a great variety of political movements and schools of thought as in any sense part of a single tradition or sensibility. This sensibility—call it populist or petty-bourgeois, for lack of a better term—was defined, in the first place, by deep reservations about the progressive scheme of history. The idea that history, like science, records a cumulative unfolding of human capacities and that modern civilization is heir to all the achievements of the past ran counter to common sense—that is, to the experience of loss and defeat that makes up so much of the texture of daily life. "Are there no calamities in history?" Orestes Brownson demanded. "Nothing tragic?" Brownson and other opponents of "improvement" found little evidence of cumulative enlightenment. Officially discredited concepts like nemesis, fate, fortune, or providence seemed to speak more directly to human experience, in their view, than the concept of progress.

Their political sensibility, in the second place, was formed by a more modest assessment of the economic aspirations appropriate to human beings than the progressive assessment. Those who believed in progress were impressed by the technological conquest of scarcity and the collective control over nature that seemed to be inherent in the productive machinery of modern societies. Abundance, they believed, would eventually give everyone access to leisure, cultivation, refinement—advantages formerly restricted to the wealthy. Luxury for all: such was the noble dream of progress. Populists, on the other hand, regarded a competence, as they would have called it—a piece of earth, a small shop, a useful calling—as a more reasonable as well as a more worthy ambition. "Competence" had rich moral overtones; it referred to the livelihood conferred by property but also to the skills required to maintain it. The ideal of universal proprietorship embodied a humbler set of expectations than the ideal of universal consumption, universal access to a proliferating supply of goods. At the same time, it embodied a more strenuous and morally demanding definition of the good life. The progressive conception of history implied a society of supremely cultivated consumers; the populist conception, a whole world of heroes.

By progressive standards, the ideal of a society composed of small producers was narrow, provincial, and reactionary. It bore the stigma of its petty-bourgeois origins—a refusal to face the future. Contempt for petty-bourgeois backwardness, respectability, and religiosity became the hallmark of the progressive mind. The enlightened caricature of lower-middle-class culture contained undeniable elements of truth; otherwise it would have been unrecognizable even as a caricature. As time went on and large-scale enterprise crowded out small producers, petty-bourgeois movements became increasingly defensive and allied themselves with some of the worst impulses in modern life—anti-intellectualism, xenophobia, racism. But the same tradition of plebeian radicalism gave rise to the only serious attempt to answer the great question of twentieth-century politics: what was to replace proprietorship as the material foundation of civic virtue?

It also gave rise to the most impressive attempts to organize a mode of political action that would overcome resentment and thus break the "endless cycle" of coercion and injustice, as Reinhold Niebuhr called it. If the lower middle class was often attracted to a politics of envy and resentment, for that very reason it grasped the importance of a "spiritual discipline" against it. The progressive tradition, on the other hand, never grappled either with the question of proprietorship and virtue or with the question formulated by Niebuhr in 1932: "If social cohesion is impossible without coercion, and coercion is impossible without the creation of social injustice, and the destruction of injustice is impossible without the use of further coercion, are we not in an endless cycle of social conflict?"

The exhaustion of the progressive tradition—and this tradition, broadly defined, includes not only the left but the Reaganite right as well, which is no less beguiled by the vision of endless economic expansion—betrays itself in its inability to confront these fundamental questions of modern politics or the equally urgent question of how the living standards of the rich can be extended to the poor, on a global scale, without putting an unbearable burden on the earth's natural resources. The need for a more equitable distribution of wealth ought to be obvious, both on moral and on economic grounds, and it ought to be equally obvious that economic equality cannot be achieved under an advanced system of capitalist production. What is not so obvious is that equality now implies a more modest standard of living for all, not an extension of the lavish standards enjoyed by the favored classes in the industrial nations to the rest of the world. In the twenty-first century, equality implies a recognition of limits, both moral and material, that finds little support in the progressive tradition.

The populist tradition offers no panacea for all the ills that afflict the modern world. It asks the right questions, but it does not provide a ready-made set of answers. It has generated very little in the way of an economic or political theory—its most conspicuous weakness. Its advocates call for small-scale production and political decentralization, but they do not explain how those objectives can be achieved in a modern economy. Lacking a clearly developed theory of production, populists have always fallen easy prey to paper money fads and other nostrums, just as they fall prey to the kind of social resentments exploited so effectively by the new right. A populism for the twenty-first century would bear little resemblance to the new right or to populist movements in the past, for that matter. But it would find much of its moral inspiration in the popular radicalism of the past and more generally in the wide-ranging critique of progress, enlightenment, and unlimited ambition that was drawn up by moralists whose perceptions were shaped by the producers' view of the world. The problem of "unearned increment" gave rise both to a distinctive kind of politics and to a distinctive tradition of moral speculation drawn from everyday experience (as well as from the heightened experience of spiritual fervor) and unlikely, therefore, to go out of fashion.

BIBLIOGRAPHICAL ESSAY

T his book was written at the Center for Advanced Study in the Behavioral Sciences, on a grant partially funded by the National Endowment for the Humanities. Over the years, those who staff the Center have perfected a happy combination of solicitude and benign neglect, and I find myself deeply in their debt. In particular, I am indebted to Virginia Heaton for her invaluable services as typist and proofreader. My research assistants at the University of Rochester—Everett Akam, Ken Hawkins, Chris Lehmann, and Colin Morris—have given me many reasons to be thankful. Ian Shapiro, Nell Lasch, and Chris Lehmann read the entire manuscript, proving, if nothing else, that such a thing was possible; they also offered advice, most of which I have reluctantly had to follow. Dan Borus, David Chappell, Dale Vree, Stewart Weaver, Robb Westbrook, and Suzanne Wolk read portions of the manuscript, and I am grateful to them as well, for advice and especially for encouragement. At a time when I was groping for a title, Jim Campbell suggested a rereading of "The Celestial Railroad." Jeanette Hopkins edited the manuscript very thoroughly, not to say aggressively; her innumerable recommendations, even when I turned them down, often had the effect of calling attention to some difficulty that required revision.

I INTRODUCTION: THE OBSOLESCENCE OF LEFT AND RIGHT

Assessments of the conservative "malaise" appear in "The State of Conservatism," *Intercollegiate Review* 21 (spring 1986): 5–25, and in Paul Gottfried and Thomas Fleming, *The Conservative Movement* (1988). Bernard Avishai's plea for a redefinition of liberalism, "The Pursuit of Happiness and Other 'Preferences,' " can be found in *Dissent* 3 (fall 1984): 482–84. Rudolf Bahro explains the environmental implications of extending Western standards of living to the rest of the world in an essay, "Elements of a New Politics," first published in 1980 and reprinted in his *Socialism and Survival* (1982), 98–121; see also his book *From Red to Green* (1984) and, for a similar change in coloration, André Gorz, *Ecology as Politics* (1980). My own view of ecological issues owes a great deal to David Ehrenfeld, *The Arrogance of Humanism* (1978), and to Wendell Berry, *The Unsettling of America: Culture and Agriculture* (1977), as well as to the many works on this subject cited in my earlier book *The Minimal Self* (1984). Bill McKibben, *The End of Nature* (1989), is useful in spite of its commitment to "deep ecology"—for trenchant criticism of which, see Tim Luke, "The Dreams of Deep Ecology," *Telos*, no. 76 (summer 1988): 65–92.

Dwight Macdonald's article on the 1960 election, "The Candidates and I," appeared in *Commentary* 29 (April 1960): 287–94; his attack on *Kulturbolschewismus*, in *Partisan Review* 8 (Nov.–Dec. 1941): 442–51. The call for a "national policy on families" was issued by Nan Fink, "Profamily Hoopla," *Tikkun* 3 (July–Aug. 1988): 61–62. The feminist quoted on "narrow views of men and women" and the importance of "human similarities" is Carol Ziese, in a letter to the editors of *Chronicles*, Sept. 1986. George Wallace's tirade against "strutting pseudo-intellectuals" is quoted in John Kenneth White, *The New Politics of Old Values* (1988), which is also the source of Reagan's statements about "nay-sayers" and "prophets of doom." On "free enterprisers," see Burton Yale Pines, *Back to Basics* (1982).

2 THE IDEA OF PROGRESS RECONSIDERED

On the idea of progress as a secular religion, see Carl Becker, "Progress," *Encyclopedia of the Social Sciences* (1934) 12:495–99; Ernest Lee Tuveson, *Millennium and Utopia* (1949); Christopher Dawson, *Progress and Religion* (1929); and Norman Cohn, *The Pursuit of the Millennium* (1961).

My discussion of the idea of progress as an antidote to despair draws on Karl Mannheim, *Ideology and Utopia* (1936); Sidney Pollard, *The Idea of Progress* (1968); Edward Hallett Carr, *What Is History?* (1963); Clarke A. Chambers, "The Belief in Progress in Twentieth-Century America," *Journal of the History of Ideas* 19 (1958): 197–224; Morris Ginsberg, *The Idea of Progress* (1953), "A Humanist View of Progress," in Julian Huxley, ed., *The Humanist Frame* (1961), and "Moral Progress: a Reappraisal," in A. J. Ayer, ed., *The Humanist Outlook* (1968); W. Warren Wagar, *Good Tidings: The Belief in Progress from Darwin to Marcuse* (1972); Charles Frankel, *The Case for Modern Man* (1956), and *The Faith of Reason: The Idea of Progress in the*

French Enlightenment (1948); Robert Nisbet, *History of the Idea of Progress* (1980); and J. H. Plumb, *Crisis in the Humanities* (1964). Barry Commoner's argument against the " 'limits of growth' approach" comes from the *New Yorker*, 15 June 1987, 46–71.

Hans Blumenberg advances a modified version of the "secularization thesis" in *The Legitimacy of the Modern Age* (1983). See also John Baillie, *The Belief in Progress* (1950); Karl Löwith, *Meaning in History* (1949); Reinhold Niebuhr, *The Nature and Destiny of Man* (1943); and H. Richard Niebuhr, *The Kingdom of God in America* (1937).

My discussion of providence and fortune, grace and virtue, begins—as any such discussion must now begin—with J. G. A. Pocock's seminal work, *The Machiavellian Moment: Florentine Political Thought and the Atlantic Republican Tradition* (1975), which has given rise to a vast literature of commentary, imitation, denunciation, and rebuttal. It is impossible to write about the republican tradition without weighing the issues raised in this controversy, but I will cite specific items, as the need arises, only insofar as they have entered directly into my own argument. On Machiavelli, see also Hanna Fenichel Pitkin, *Fortune Is a Woman: Gender and Politics in the Thought of Niccolò Machiavelli* (1984). On the historical imagination, see J. H. Plumb, *The Death of the Past* (1970). On the common element in the Christian and classical views of history, see Löwith, *Meaning in History*. On Rousseau, see Michael Ignatieff, *The Needs of Strangers* (1984).

Ignatieff's book also contributed to my analysis of the rehabilitation of desire in eighteenth-century political economy and, together with Thomas A. Horne's helpful little study *The Social Thought of Bernard Mandeville* (1978), sent me to Adam Smith's *Wealth of Nations* (1776) and, even more important, to his *Theory of Moral Sentiments* (1759). The most useful recent study of Smith is Donald Winch, *Adam Smith's Politics* (1978). Thomas Macaulay's observations about the march of progress are quoted in Horace Kallen, *The Decline and Rise of the Consumer* (1936). David Hume's misgivings about immediate gratification appear in *An Inquiry concerning the Principles of Morals* (1751); see also David Miller, "Hume and Possessive Individualism," *History of Political Thought* 1 (1980): 261–78.

Along with more familiar sources like Tocqueville's *Democracy in America* (1835, 1840), the following are quoted in my analysis of the domestication of desire: Horace Mann's speech to the Friends of Education, 1850, quoted in Fredrika Bremer, *Homes of the New World* (1853); Theodore Parker, "A Letter on Slavery" (1847), in James K. Hosmer's collection of Parker's antislavery writings, *The Slave Power* (1916); Thomas Hopkins Gallaudet, "Family and School Discipline," *American Annals of Education* 7 (1837): 451–54, 510–14, 550–54; Massachusetts Bureau of Labor Statistics, *Report* (1870); Elizabeth Cady Stanton, Susan B. Anthony, and Matilda Joslyn Gage, eds., *History of Woman Suffrage* (1887) 1:277–82 (Parker's rationale for woman suffrage, Howe's view of woman as "mother of the race"); and William A. Alcott, *The Young Woman's Guide to Excellence* (1840). This part of my argument distills thirty years' work on nineteenth-century ideas of domestic life, the history of feminism, and related subjects.

Shaw's tribute to Henry George appears in John L. Thomas, *Alternative Amer-*

ica: Henry George, Edward Bellamy, Henry Demarest Lloyd and the Adversary Tradition (1983), along with Thomas's own strictures on George's "ahistorical obsession with cataclysm." My disagreement with Thomas's position on this point should not obscure my indebtedness to this useful book. Roosevelt's review of Brooks Adams's *Law of Civilization and Decay* was published in *Forum* 22 (1896): 575–89. The opposition to America's war against Spain and to the acquisition of the Philippines was the subject of my bachelor's thesis, "Imperialism and the Independents" (Harvard, 1954). The quotations are taken from George S. Boutwell, *Republic or Empire?* (1900), and Moorfield Storey, *"Is It Right?"* (1900)—ephemeral writings preserved in Widener Library's splendid collection of anti-imperialist speeches and pamphlets. Robert L. Beisner, *Twelve against Empire: The Anti-Imperialists, 1898–1900* (1968), should be consulted for further details, along with William B. Hixson, *Moorfield Storey and the Abolitionist Tradition* (1972).

In addition to the works mentioned in the text, these inform my interpretation of "inconspicuous consumption": Albion B. Small, *Adam Smith and Modern Sociology* (1907); Rexford G. Tugwell, *The Industrial Discipline and the Governmental Arts* (1933); and Kallen, *Decline and Rise of the Consumer.* For Henry George's understanding of the "prevailing belief" in progress, see *Progress and Poverty* (1879); and for the statement about "managed capitalism," Guy Alchon, *The Invisible Hand of Planning: Capitalism, Social Science, and the State in the 1920s* (1985). My discussion of Keynes rests on the biographies by Roy Harrod (1951), Charles H. Hession (1984), and Robert Skidelsky (1983), and on Robert L. Heilbroner, *The Worldly Philosophers: The Lives, Times, and Ideas of the Great Economic Thinkers* (1953). On Earnest Elmo Calkins and the advertising industry, see Jeffrey L. Meikle, *Twentieth-Century Limited: Industrial Design in America* (1979), and Roland Marchand, *Advertising the American Dream* (1985).

George Orwell's analysis of fascism's emotional appeal comes from a 1940 essay on *Mein Kampf,* reprinted in the second volume of *The Collected Essays, Journalism and Letters of George Orwell,* ed. Sonia Orwell and Ian Angus (1968). Mumford's attack on the "sleek progressive mind" appears in his *Faith for Living* (1940); see also his vigorous polemic in the *New Republic,* 29 April 1940, 568–73, "The Corruption of Liberalism." On the importance of Christianity for slaves in the South, see Eugene D. Genovese, *Roll, Jordan, Roll: The World the Slaves Made* (1974). In *The Warriors: Reflections on Men in Battle* (1959), J. Glenn Gray has a brief passage that distinguishes between optimism and hope: "If optimism and pessimism have become increasingly irrelevant in our terrible dilemma [brought about by the ever-growing destructiveness of human technology], there is great reason nonetheless to practice the ancient virtue of hope. Though generally neglected in recent centuries, when optimism about progress was the rule, hope is that quality of character and virtue of mind which is directed toward the future in trust rather than in confidence."

3 NOSTALGIA: THE ABDICATION OF MEMORY

C. S. Lewis's defense of pastoralism is quoted in Laurence Lerner, *The Uses of Nostalgia: Studies in Pastoral Poetry* (1972). I have consulted a number of other studies that deal in whole or in part with pastoralism: Roger Sales, *English Literature in History: Pastoral and Politics* (1983) and *Closer to Home: Writers and Places in England* (1986); Jean-Paul Hulin and Pierre Coustillas, eds., *Victorian Writers and the City* (1979); Raymond Williams, *The Country and the City* (1973); reviews of Williams's book by Allan Goldfein (*Commentary*, Nov. 1973) and Marshall Berman (*New York Times*, 15 July 1973); Raymond Chapman, *The Sense of the Past in Victorian Literature* (1986); William Empson, *Some Versions of Pastoral* (1935); and Peter Coveney, *Poor Monkey: The Child in Literature* (1957). Coleridge's remark about Wordsworth is quoted in the Norton edition of *The Prelude;* Philip Davis's, in his *Memory and Writing: From Wordsworth to Lawrence* (1983).

Bentham's disparagement of the "wisdom of our ancestors" is quoted in Chapman, *Sense of the Past.* Emerson's plea for an "original relation to the universe" introduces *Nature* (1836). On the mythology of the American West, see Henry Nash Smith, *Virgin Land* (1950), and two books by Richard Slotkin, *Regeneration through Violence: The Mythology of the American Frontier* (1973) and *The Fatal Environment: The Myth of the Frontier in the Age of Industrialization* (1985). Melville's description of the rhetoric of *Moby Dick* as a "nervous lofty language" is mentioned in F. O. Matthiessen, *American Renaissance* (1941). His list of civilized "discomforts" comes from *Typee* (1845). Owen Wister's popular novel *The Virginian* (1902) immortalized the expression "when you call me that, smile."

Richard Lingeman, *Small Town America* (1980), and Anthony Channel Hilfer, *The Revolt from the Village* (1969), furnished material for my exploration of the village idyll. On the medical background of the concept of nostalgia, see Willis H. McCann, "Nostalgia: A Descriptive and Comparative Study" (Ph.D. thesis, Indiana, 1940). The material on Fitzgerald comes from *The Basil and Josephine Stories,* written in the twenties but collected only in 1973. The discussion of Mumford is based on *The Brown Decades* (1931). *Life*'s mid-century issue bears the date of 2 January 1950. George W. S. Trow's observations on the "older, more distant world" invoked by the media appear in *Within the Context of No Context* (1981), one of the few studies of mass media to get beyond clichés.

The material in the last two sections of this chapter, "Nostalgia Politicized" and "The Frozen Past," comes from "The Monotony of the Machine," *Nation,* 23 April 1914, 452–53; C. E. Ayres, "A People's Houses" (review of Mumford's *Sticks and Stones*), *New Republic,* 10 Dec. 1924, 7–8; reviews by Mumford and John Dewey in the same journal, 5 Aug. 1931, 321–22, and 13 April 1932, 242–44; Richard Hofstadter, *The American Political Tradition* (1948); Arthur P. Dudden, "Nostalgia and the American," *Journal of the History of Ideas* 32 (1961): 515–30; Fred Davis, "Nostalgia, Identity, and the Current Nostalgia Wave," *Journal of Popular Culture* 11 (1977): 414–24; "The Great Nostalgia Kick," *U.S. News & World Report,* 22 March 1982, 57;

Gerald Clarke, "The Meaning of Nostalgia," *Time*, 3 May 1971, 77; Michael Wood, "Nostalgia or Never," *New Society* 30 (7 Nov. 1974): 343–47; Alvin Toffler, *Future Shock* (1970); Peter Clecak, *America's Search for the Ideal Self* (1983); "Nostalgia," *Newsweek*, 28 Dec. 1970, 34–38; Frank Heath, "Nostalgia Shock," *Saturday Review*, 29 May 1971, 18; "Why the Craze for the 'Good Old Days'?" *U.S. News & World Report*, 12 Nov. 1973, 72; Howard F. Stein, "American Nostalgia," *Columbia Forum*, n.s. 3 (summer 1974): 20–23; Richard Hasbany, "Irene: Considering the Nostalgic Sensibility," *Journal of Popular Culture* 9 (spring 1976): 816–26; Roy McMullen, "That Rose-Colored Rearview Mirror," *Saturday Review*, 2 Oct. 1976, 22–23; "There's Gold in That Nostalgia," *Newsweek*, 11 Oct. 1976, 49–50; "Packing Up the Past," *Good Housekeeping*, Nov. 1979, 94ff.; Robert Rubens, "The Backward Glance: A Contemporary Taste for Nostalgia," *Contemporary Review* (London) 239 (Sept. 1981): 149–50; Robert L. Tyler, "High Noon in Memory Lane," *Humanist* 41 (May–June 1981): 44–45; Thomas Powers, "Yesterday's Talismans," *Commonweal*, 19 June 1981, 361–62; Jeff Greenfield, "Nostalgia on TV," *Vogue*, March 1982, 200; and Richard Louv, *America II* (1983). More substantial investigations of contemporary nostalgia include Fred Davis, *Yearning for Yesterday: A Sociology of Nostalgia* (1979); Anthony Brand, "A Short Natural History of Nostalgia," *Atlantic*, Dec. 1978, 58–63; Edward Shils, "Mass Society and Its Culture," in Norman Jacobs, ed., *Culture for the Millions* (1961); and David Lowenthal, *The Past Is a Foreign County* (1985). Macaulay's injunction to study "ordinary men as they appear in their ordinary business" is quoted in Chapman, *Sense of the Past*.

4 THE SOCIOLOGICAL TRADITION AND THE IDEA OF COMMUNITY

My discussion of the Enlightenment draws heavily on Thomas J. Schlereth, *The Cosmopolitan Ideal in Enlightenment Thought* (1977); see also Wilson Carey McWilliams, *The Idea of Fraternity in America* (1973). The section on Burke rests largely on his *Reflections on the Revolution in France* (1790), as well as his *Letter to William Smith* (1795) and his *Thoughts on the Prospect of a Regicide Peace* (1796). For commentary on Burke, see Francis P. Canavan, *The Political Reason of Edmund Burke* (1960); Alfred Cobban, *Edmund Burke and the Revolt against the Eighteenth Century* (2d ed., 1960); David Cameron, *The Social Thought of Rousseau and Burke* (1973); and especially the rich and suggestive study by Bruce James Smith, *Politics and Remembrance* (1985).

Hannah Arendt, *The Human Condition* (1958), is the starting point for an understanding of the difference between action and behavior and of the concept of society, which depends so heavily on a behavioral view of human conduct. On the contrast between republican and sociological criticism of modern life, see John T. Miller, *Ideology and Enlightenment: The Political and Social Thought of Samuel Taylor Coleridge* (1987). Lewis Henry Morgan's glowing account of the ancient *gentes* can be found in *Ancient Society* (1877); William Morris's reference to "railers against progress," in Raymond Williams, *Culture and Society, 1780–1950* (1958), which also offers a penetrating examination of the way nineteenth-century writers played off "culture" against "civilization." My remarks about Ruskin derive from Williams, as well as from a reading of *The Two Paths* (1859), *Unto this Last* (1862), and *Sesame and Lilies* (1871). On French intellectuals' contempt for provincial life, see César Graña, *Modernity and Its Discontents* (1964). The brief references to Marx and Engels, at this point in my argument, are to *The Communist Manifesto* (1848), Engels's *Condition of the Working Class in England in 1844* (1845), and Marx's essay "The British Rule in India" (1853). For Maine, see George Feaver, *From Status to Contract: A Biography of Sir Henry Maine* (1969). For the origins of sociology in the conservative reaction against the Enlightenment, see Robert Nisbet, *The Sociological Tradition* (1966); Sheldon Wolin, *Politics and Vision* (1960); and Mack Walker, *German Home Towns* (1971), the last of which explains, among other things, how the concept of society developed, in Germany, in opposition to that of the state.

My analysis of Ferdinand Tönnies rests on *Gemeinschaft und Gesellschaft* (1887), translated by Charles Loomis as *Community and Society* (1957), and on the useful collection of his other writings edited by Werner J. Cahnman and Rudolf Heberle, *Ferdinand Toennies on Sociology* (1971). On the moral ambivalence of the sociological tradition and the structure of historical necessity, the relevant texts are Durkheim's *Professional Ethics and Civic Morals* (1957), Weber's more familiar pair of essays "Science as a Vocation" and "Politics as a Vocation" (both published in 1919); Freud's *Civilization and Its Discontents* (1930) and *The Future of an Illusion* (1928); Robert Redfield's *The Primitive World and Its Transformations* (1953); George Simmel's essay "The Metropolis and Mental Life" (1903); Louis Wirth's imitation "Urbanism as a Way of Life," *American Journal of Sociology* 44 (1938): 1–24; and various works by Marx, including a couple of minor pieces quoted in Jon Elster's admirable study *Making Sense of Marx* (1985). For interpretations of economic development contrary to that of Marx (who insists on the inevitable supersession of small-scale production), see Kins Collins, "Marx on the English Agricultural Revolution," *History and Theory* 6 (1967): 351–81; J. D. Chambers and G. E. Mingay, *The Agricultural Revolution* (1966); and Charles Sabel and Jonathan Zeitlin, "Historical Alternatives to Mass Production," *Past and Present*, no. 108 (Aug. 1985): 133–76. This last contains a more general attack on historical determinism, as does Roberto Mangabeira Unger, *Social Theory: Its Situation and Its Task* (1987). On Simmel, see Thomas Bender, *Community and Social Change* (1978). On "conservative modernization," see Barrington Moore, Jr., *Social Origins of Dictatorship and Democracy* (1966). On the inverse relation between industrialization and democracy, see Lawrence Goodwyn, "Organizing Democracy," *Democracy* 1 (Jan. 1981): 41–60.

The literature on modernization is enormous; my selection includes Edward Shils, "Political Developments in New States," *Comparative Studies in Society and History* 2 (1960): 265–92, 379–411; S. N. Eisenstadt, *Modernization: Protest and Change* (1966) and "Modernization: Growth and Diversity," *India Quarterly* 20 (1964): 17–42; C. E. Black, *The Dynamics of Modernization* (1966); Alex Inkeles, "Making Men Modern," *American Journal of Sociology* 75 (1969): 208–25; Reinhard Bendix, "Tradition and Modernity Reconsidered," *Comparative Studies in Society and History* 9

(1967): 292–346; E. I. Eisenstadt, "Studies of Modernization and Sociological Theory," *History and Theory* 13 (1974): 235–41; Dean Tipps, "Modernization Theory and the Comparative Study of Societies," *Comparative Studies in Society and History* 9 (1967): 199–226; Samuel P. Huntington, *Political Order in Changing Societies* (1968); Neil J. Smelser, "The Modernization of Social Relations," in Myron Weiner, ed., *Modernization: The Dynamics of Growth* (1966); Marion J. Levy, Jr., *Modernization and the Structure of Societies* (1966); Richard D. Brown, "Modernization and the Modern Personality in Early America," *Journal of Interdisciplinary History* 2 (1972): 201–28; Ernest Gellner, *Thought and Change* (1965); Joseph R. Gusfield, "Tradition and Modernity: Misplaced Polarities in the Study of Social Change," *American Journal of Sociology* 72 (1967): 351–62; and Alexander Gerschenkron, *Economic Backwardness in Historical Perspective* (1962).

5 THE POPULIST CAMPAIGN AGAINST "IMPROVEMENT"

Susan Sontag's gloomy reflections on the circulation of everything appear in "AIDS and Its Metaphors," *New York Review,* 27 Oct. 1988, 89–99; see also her essay "The Imagination of Disaster," in *Against Interpretation* (1969). On the discovery of civic humanism, see Michael Sandel, "Democrats and Community," *New Republic,* 22 Feb. 1988, 20–23, and *Liberalism and the Limits of Justice* (1982); an anonymous editorial on Margaret Thatcher, "Society Lady," in *Economist,* 8 Oct. 1988, 13–14; and Benno Schmidt, "A Revival of the Republic of Virtue?" *Yale* (summer 1988): 61–63.

Although the recent interest in republicanism grows, in part, out of a search for communitarian alternatives to liberalism, the republican tradition figures only peripherally, if at all, in Sandel's *Liberalism* or in other works commonly associated with communitarianism: Alasdair MacIntyre, *After Virtue* (1981) and *Whose Justice? Which Rationality?* (1988); Michael Walzer, *Spheres of Justice* (1983); and Charles Taylor, *Sources of the Self: The Making of the Modern Identity* (1989). Attacks on communitarianism include Stephen Holmes, "The Permanent Structure of Antiliberal Thought," in Nancy L. Rosenblum, ed., *Liberalism and the Moral Life* (1989), 227–53; Stephen Holmes, "The Polis State" (review of MacIntyre's *Whose Justice?*), *New Republic,* 6 June 1988, 32–39; H. N. Hirsch, "The Threnody of Liberalism: Constitutional Liberty and the Renewal of Community," *Political Theory* 14 (1986): 423–49; and Amy Gutmann, "Communitarian Critics of Liberalism," *Philosophy and Public Affairs* 14 (1985): 308–22. See also the exchange between MacIntyre and Richard J. Bernstein in *Soundings* 67 (spring 1984): 6–41.

Of the growing number of historical studies of the republican tradition, I have considered only a small sample. In addition to the works of J. G. A. Pocock and Hanna Pitkin already cited, I have consulted Pocock's *Politics, Language, and Time* (1971); his *Virtue, Commerce, and History* (1985); his reply to critics, "A Reconsideration Impartially Considered," *History of Political Thought* 1 (1980): 541–45; and a more recent reply, "Between Gog and Magog: The Republican Thesis and the

Ideologia Americana," *Journal of the History of Ideas* 48 (1987): 325–46; Zera S. Fink, *The Classical Republicans* (1945); Charles Blitzer, *An Immortal Commonwealth: The Political Thought of James Harrington* (1960); Thomas L. Pangle, *Montesquieu's Philosophy of Liberalism* (1973) and *The Spirit of Modern Republicanism* (1988); Edwin G. Burrows, *Albert Gallatin and the Political Economy of Republicanism* (1986); Jeff Weintraub, *Freedom and Community: The Republican Virtue Tradition and the Sociology of Liberty* (1990); John Diggins, *The Lost Soul of American Politics: Virtue, Self-Interest, and the Foundations of Liberalism* (1984) and "Comrades and Citizens," *American Historical Review* 90 (1985): 614–38; Joyce Appleby, "Republicanism and Ideology," *American Quarterly* 37 (1985): 461–73, "Republicanism in Old and New Contexts," *William and Mary Quarterly* 43 (1986): 20–34, and *Economic Thought and Ideology in Seventeenth-Century England* (1978); Bernard Bailyn, *The Ideological Origins of the American Revolution* (1967); Lance Banning, *The Jeffersonian Persuasion* (1978) and "Some Second Thoughts on 'Virtue'" (paper read at the Folger Shakespeare Library, 1987); Jesse R. Goodale, "J. G. A. Pocock's New-Harringtonians: A Reconsideration," *History of Political Thought* 1 (1980): 237–59; J. H. Hexter, review of Pocock's *Machiavellian Moment*, *History and Theory* 16 (1977): 306–37; Istvan Hont and Michael Ignatieff, eds., *Wealth and Virtue: The Shaping of Political Economy in the Scottish Enlightenment* (1983); Allen Kaufman, *Capitalism, Slavery, and Republican Values: American Political Economists, 1819–1848* (1982); Isaac Kramnick, "Republican Revisionism Revisited," *American Historical Review* 87 (1982): 629–64, and "The 'Great National Discussion': The Discourse of Politics in 1787," *William and Mary Quarterly* 45 (1988): 3–32; Drew R. McCoy, "Republicanism and American Foreign Policy," *William and Mary Quarterly* 31 (1974): 633–46; Marvin Meyers, *The Jacksonian Persuasion* (1960); Daniel Walker Howe, *The Political Culture of the American Whigs* (1979); Robert E. Shalhope, "Toward a Republican Synthesis," *William and Mary Quarterly* 29 (1972): 49–80, and "Republicanism and Early American Historiography," *William and Mary Quarterly* 39 (1982): 334–56; and Gordon S. Wood, *The Creation of the American Republic* (1969). Warner Berthoff, *Literature and the Continuances of Virtue* (1986), chap. 2 ("Virtue: A Short History"), is a useful introduction to some of the broader associations of this term.

Interpretations of American political ideas that stress the dominance of liberalism include, in addition to those by Appleby and Diggins, such prerepublican syntheses as Richard Hofstadter, *The American Political Tradition* (1948), Louis Hartz, *The Liberal Tradition in America* (1955), and Carl Degler, *Out of Our Past* (1959). For the opposition between the public realm and the household, see Hannah Arendt, *The Human Condition* (1958).

The *Thomas Paine Reader*, ed. Michael Foot and Isaac Kramnick (1987), is a serviceable compendium. Kramnick's introduction first appeared, in a slightly different version, as an article in *Democracy* 1 (Jan. 1981): 127–38. See also Eric Foner, *Tom Paine and Revolutionary America* (1976). Studies of Cobbett include G. D. H. Cole, *The Life of William Cobbett* (1924); G. K. Chesterton, *William Cobbett* (1925); William B. Pemberton, *William Cobbett* (1949); John W. Osborne, *William Cobbett:*

His Thought and His Times (1966); Marjorie Bowen, *Peter Porcupine* (1971); James Sambrook, *William Cobbett* (1973); Raymond Williams, *Cobbett* (1983); and George Spater, *William Cobbett: The Poor Man's Friend* (1982), now the definitive biography. My analysis of Orestes Brownson rests on the multivolume edition of his works edited by his son and published in Detroit in 1883, together with his uncollected polemic against Horace Mann in the *Boston Quarterly Review* 2 (1839): 393–434. The biography by Thomas R. Ryan (1976) is not "definitive," as its subtitle immodestly asserts. Arthur M. Schlesinger, Jr., *A Pilgrim's Progress* (1939), makes no such claim but offers livelier reading. See also Americo D. Lopati's short biography in Twayne's series on American authors (1965).

Harold Laski, *The Rise of Liberalism: The Philosophy of a Business Civilization* (1936), and C. B. Macpherson, *The Political Theory of Possessive Individualism* (1962), exemplify the kind of interpretations of Locke challenged and largely displaced by recent scholarship, notably by John Dunn, *The Political Theory of John Locke* (1969); Richard Ashcraft, *Revolutionary Politics and Locke's Two Treatises of Government* (1986); Neal Wood, *John Locke and Agrarian Capitalism* (1984); James Tully, *A Discourse on Property: John Locke and His Adversaries* (1980); and John William Marshall, "John Locke in Context" (Ph.D. diss., Johns Hopkins, 1989). My own interpretation of the early opposition to wage labor draws on material found in J. E. Crowley, *This Sheba, Self: The Conceptualization of Economic Life in Eighteenth-Century America* (1974); Meyers, *Jacksonian Persuasion*; Kaufman, *Capitalism, Slavery, and Republican Values*; Howe, *American Whigs*; Sean Wilentz, *Chants Democratic: New York City and the Rise of the American Working Class* (1984); Eric Foner, *Free Soil, Free Labor, Free Men: The Ideology of the Republican Party before the Civil War* (1970); and the published reports of the New York constitutional convention of 1821. Herbert Croly's misgivings about wage labor can be found in *Progressive Democracy* (1914).

My discussion of labor history rests on E. P. Thompson, *The Making of the English Working Class* (1964); Herbert G. Gutman, *Work, Culture, and Society in Industrializing America* (1976); Eric Hobsbawm, *Primitive Rebels* (1959); Craig Calhoun, *The Question of Class Struggle: Social Foundations of Popular Radicalism during the Industrial Revolution* (1982); William H. Sewell, Jr., *Work and Revolution in France* (1980); Robert J. Bezucha, *The Lyon Uprising of 1834* (1974); Joan Wallach Scott, *The Glassworkers of Carmaux* (1974); Edward Berenson, *Populist Religion and Left-Wing Politics in France, 1830–1852* (1984); Alan Dawley, *Class and Community: The Industrial Revolution in Lynn* (1976); Bruce Laurie, *Working People of Philadelphia* (1980); Steven J. Ross, *Workers on the Edge: Work, Leisure, and Politics in Industrializing Cincinnati* (1985); Harry Braverman, *Labor and Monopoly Capital* (1974); David Brody, *Workers in Industrial America* (1980); Daniel Nelson, *Managers and Workers: Origins of the New Factory System* (1975); Richard Edwards, *Contested Terrain: The Transformation of the Workplace* (1979); David Montgomery, *Beyond Equality: Labor and the Radical Republicans* (1967), *Workers' Control in America* (1979), and *The Fall of the House of Labor* (1987); Nick Salvatore, *Eugene V. Debs* (1982); Leon Fink, *Workingmen's Democracy: The Knights of Labor and American Politics* (1983); and Gregory S. Kealey, *Toronto*

Workers Respond to Industrial Capitalism (1980). On class oppression conceived as invasion from outside, see Alan Brinkley, *Voices of Protest: Huey Long, Father Coughlin, and the Great Depression* (1982). On the "transitional" character of producerist ideology, see Alan Trachtenberg, *The Incorporation of America* (1982).

The works of Richard Hofstadter—in particular, *The Age of Reform* (1955) and *The Paranoid Style in American Politics* (1965), which contains his essay on Coin Harvey—helped to identify nineteenth-century agrarian populism with nostalgia and the sentimental "yeoman myth." Hofstadter's interpretation continues to find favor, at least with the general public, because it is superior to those that treat Populism merely as an early version of the New Deal—for example, John D. Hicks, *The Populist Revolt* (1931), or John Chamberlain, *Farewell to Reform* (1932)—or, even more improbably, as a rudimentary form of socialism, as in Norman Pollock, *The Populist Response to Industrial America* (1962). For Marxist historians, on the other hand, the untenability of this latter interpretation leads to an interpretation that is almost as unfair to the Populists as Hofstadter's more openly satirical and dismissive treatment. It is because Populism fell so far short of a socialist program that it is found wanting by James Green, "Populism, Socialism, and the Promise of Democracy," *Radical History Review* 24 (fall 1980): 7–40; by David Montgomery, "On Goodwin's Populists," *Marxist Perspectives* 1 (spring 1978): 166–73; and by Bruce Palmer, *"Man over Money": The Southern Populist Critique of American Capitalism* (1980). Palmer tries harder than most Marxists to judge Populism in its own terms, but he too finds it hard to resist a superior tone. "Being landowners or aspiring landowners and having little experience of industrial America, the Southern Populists overlooked the growth of huge manufacturing complexes like Standard Oil and Carnegie Steel as well as the new classes created by them." Palmer reminds us that "no single worker could hope to own a steel mill," as Populists allegedly believed. He gives the Populists credit for opposing "this maddening rush for money," as Tom Watson called it, but he finds it regrettable that they "stopped short of an attack on the market system" and failed to "follow through on the implications of their demand that American society replace economic competition with . . . the 'cooperative commonwealth.' " Because Populists failed to condemn the institution of private property, Palmer assumes that they "accepted" industrial capitalism and a "profit-oriented market economy." He can then accuse them of inconsistency: they wanted the benefits of capitalism without recognizing their source. In particular, they had "little notion of the role credit played in . . . building the very economic system they accepted."

Steven Hahn's valuable study *The Roots of Southern Populism: Yeoman Farmers and the Transformation of the Georgia Upcountry, 1850–1890* (1983) makes it clear that the Populists and their immediate predecessors, the agrarian radicals of the seventies and eighties, did not "accept" a market economy at all. On the contrary, their defense of customary grazing rights, their opposition to the new fencing laws that nullified these rights, and their refusal to regard land simply as a commodity indicate that their political ideas had a "decidedly nonmarket character," according to Hahn. Similar conclusions can be drawn from Worth Robert Miller, *Oklahoma Populism* (1987). But it is Lawrence Goodwyn's work that most decisively repudiates the usual misunderstandings about Populism. *Democratic Promise* (1976) is a historiographical landmark for that reason; see also Goodwyn's abridged version of that book, *The Populist Moment* (1978), and his essay "The Cooperative Commonwealth and Other Abstractions," *Marxist Perspectives* 3 (summer 1980): 8–42.

6 "NO ANSWER BUT AN ECHO"

CARLYLE. It is the early Carlyle—the author of "Signs of the Times" (1829), "Characteristics" (1831), and *Sartor Resartus* (1833–34), not the author of *Latter-Day Pamphlets* (1850) or "Shooting Niagara" (1867)—who tells us what it is like to live in a world without wonder. *On Heroes and Hero-Worship* (1841) should be read as a further exploration of this theme—an argument to the effect that there is "no knowledge without worship"—and not primarily as a plea for strong political leadership. Only two statesmen, Cromwell and Napoleon, appear in Carlyle's cast of characters. The first commended himself to Carlyle more as a "prophet" than as a statesman, and the second, with his "charlatanism" and his "blamable ambition" to bring all of Europe under his will ("the heavier this Napoleon trampled on the world, holding it tyrannously down, the fiercer would the world's recoil against him be, one day"), was no hero at all, in Carlyle's eyes, but a "great implement too soon wasted." *The French Revolution* (1837) is important, for my purposes, chiefly because it strengthens the case against interpretations that place Carlyle in the tradition of Burkean conservatism. Carlyle did not share Burke's horror of the revolution or his respect for established regimes. His account emphasized the promise as well as the horror of the revolution and repeatedly invoked the "sacred right of Insurrection." *Past and Present* (1843) is easier than Carlyle's other works to reconcile with the tradition of organic conservatism, since it used the Middle Ages as a standard by which to condemn modern capitalism; but even here, Carlyle was interested not so much in medieval organicism as in the heroism he found in Abbot Samson, whose courage, hope, and cheerful industry embodied the moral qualities Carlyle most admired.

Ian Campbell, *Thomas Carlyle* (1974), is the best short life, valuable also for its concluding discussion of Carlyle's reputation over the years. The most authoritative modern biography, Fred Kaplan's *Thomas Carlyle* (1983), shows unfailingly good judgment. A convenient collection of Carlyle's writings, G. B. Tennyson's *Carlyle Reader* (1983), contains the whole of *Sartor Resartus*, most of the important essays, and excerpts from other works. Tennyson's exhaustive study *Sartor Called Resartus: The Genesis, Structure, and Style of Thomas Carlyle's First Major Work* (1965) contains a great deal of useful information, though I am not persuaded by Tennyson's claim that *Sartor Resartus* is best read as a "novel." In general, earlier studies of Carlyle tend to see him chiefly as a man of ideas; later studies, as a literary figure whose ideas do not have to be taken very seriously except as part of a "literary vision." Works in the first category include Bliss Perry, *Thomas Carlyle: How to Know Him* (1915); Emery Neff, *Carlyle* (1932); Charles Frederick Harrold, *Carlyle and German Thought* (1934) and "The Nature of Carlyle's Calvinism," *Studies in Philology* 33 (1936): 475–86; Eric Bentley, *The Cult of the Superman* (1944); and Holbrook Jackson, *Dreamers of Dreams: The Rise and Fall of Nineteenth-Century Idealism* (1948). Literary treatments include Albert J. LaValley, *Carlyle and the Idea of the Modern* (1968); A. Abbott Ikeler, *Puritan Temper and Transcendental Faith: Carlyle's Literary Vision* (1972); and Brian John, *Supreme Fictions: Studies in the Work of William Blake, Thomas Carlyle, W. B. Yeats, and D. H. Lawrence* (1974). Harold Bloom's general introduction to his Chelsea House series, *Prophets of Sensibility: Precursors of Modern Cultural Thought,* is one of the clearest and certainly the shortest statement in favor of a literary reading of Victorian "prophecy." Bloom's anthology *Thomas Carlyle: Modern Critical Views* (1986) contains Philip Rosenberg's interesting essay "A Whole World of Heroes." Useful essays can also be found in K. J. Fielding and Rodger L. Tarr, *Carlyle Past and Present* (1976). See also Carlisle Moore, "The Persistence of Carlyle's 'Everlasting Yea,' " *Modern Philology* 54 (1957): 187–96, and "*Sartor Resartus* and the Problem of Carlyle's 'Conversion,' " *PMLA* 70 (1957): 662–81. On Carlyle's relations with Emerson, see Kenneth Marc Harris, *Carlyle and Emerson: Their Long Debate* (1978).

My initial interest in Carlyle derived from Raymond Williams, *Culture and Society.* Williams's exchange with the editors of *New Left Review* appears in his *Politics and Letters* (1979). Kierkegaard's distinction between the aesthetic and ethical views of life comes from *Either/Or* (1843).

EDWARDS. For my purposes, Jonathan Edwards's most important works are *The Nature of True Virtue* (1755), *The Great Christian Doctrine of Original Sin Defended* (1757), *The Personal Narrative of His Conversion* (ca. 1739), "Christian Charity" (1758), and various sermons, especially "The Justice of God in the Damnation of Sinners" (1734). Jerrold E. Seigel's article on virtue can be found in the *Dictionary of the History of Ideas,* 4:476–86. In the hope of gaining a better understanding of Edwards, I have read (not always with complete agreement) Perry Miller's *Jonathan Edwards* (1949); Miller's essay comparing Edwards and Emerson in his *Errand into the Wilderness* (1964); Patricia J. Tracy's rather unsympathetic account of Edwards's ministry in Northampton, *Jonathan Edwards, Pastor* (1980); Sang Hyun Lee, *The Philosophical Theology of Jonathan Edwards* (1988); Robert W. Jenson, *America's Theologian: A Recommendation of Jonathan Edwards* (1988); and more generally, on the Puritan background of Edwards's thought, Robert Pope, *The Half-Way Covenant* (1969); David Leverenz, *The Structure of Puritan Feeling* (1980); John King, *The Iron of Melancholy* (1983); and Andrew Delbanco, *The Puritan Ordeal* (1989). Two older studies, Herbert W. Schneider, *The Puritan Mind* (1930), and Joseph Haroutunian, *Piety versus Moralism: The Passing of the New England Theology* (1932), analyze the misunderstanding of Edwards's ideas by his opponents and followers alike. Haroutunian's book remains unsurpassed; but it should be supplemented with Allen C. Guelzo, *Edwards on the Will: A Century of American Theological Debate* (1989), which gives a less harshly critical account of the "new divinity" preached by those who tried to carry on Edwards's legacy. Joseph A. Conforti, *Samuel Hopkins and the New Divinity Movement* (1981), sheds additional light on this subject.

Bruce Kuklick, *Churchmen and Philosophers: From Jonathan Edwards to John Dewey* (1985), shows that opposition to the "new divinity" did not come from liberals alone. See also Joseph W. Phillips, *Jedidiah Morse and New England Congregationalism* (1983). Edmund S. Morgan discusses Puritan "tribalism" in *The Puritan Family* (1944). On liberal opposition to the new divinity, see Conrad Wright, *The Beginnings of Unitarianism in America* (1955); Edward M. Griffin, *Old Brick: Charles Chauncy of Boston* (1980); Sydney E. Ahlstrom and Jonathan S. Carey, eds., *An American Reformation: A Documentary History of Unitarian Christianity* (1985); and Conrad Edick Wright, ed., *American Unitarianism* (1989). Daniel Walker Howe, "The Decline of Calvinism," *Comparative Studies in Society and History* 14 (1972): 306–27, and *The Unitarian Conscience* (1970); Henry F. May, *The Enlightenment in America* (1976); and Alan Heimert, *Religion and the American Mind* (1966), bring out the social dimensions of the conflict between liberals and Edwardsians. Channing's essay "The Moral Argument against Calvinism" (1820), appears in the 1849 edition of his *Works* 1:217–41.

EMERSON. Emerson's emergence as the central figure in this book and the mainstay of my argument was unpremeditated. Like many others, I used to think of Emerson as a foolish optimist. My rereading of his works began with "Fate," an essay that revealed my mistake. The Machiavellian overtones in the title drew me to this particular essay, but it was the growing realization that Emerson and Carlyle, together with their Puritan forebears, had more important things to say about "virtue" and "fortune" than writers in the republican tradition that largely determined the final substance and shape of this book. Although my argument has been developed in opposition to much of the recent speculation about "civic virtue" and "community"—one objection to which is precisely that it reinforces the usual view of Emerson as a writer whose work authorized an "isolating preoccupation with the self," as Robert Bellah and his collaborators put it in *Habits of the Heart* (1985)—at the same time it is deeply indebted to the interpretations it takes issue with. Without the recent attempt to revive a discourse of "virtue," I would have lacked the inclination to read Emerson's essay on fate or to reexamine the rest of his major writings: *Nature* (1836); "The American Scholar" (1837); the Divinity School Address (1838); "The Transcendentalist" (1841); *Essays: First Series* (1841), a book that includes "Self-Reliance," "Compensation," "Spiritual Laws," "Heroism," "The Over-Soul," "Man the Reformer," "Friendship," "Prudence," "Circles," "Intellect," and "Art"; *Essays: Second Series* (1844), especially "Nature," "Politics," "Character," and "New England Reformers"; the essays on Montaigne and Napoleon in *Representative Men* (1850); *English Traits* (1856); *The Conduct of Life* (1860), which includes, along with "Fate," the important essays "Wealth" and "Culture"; "Society and Solitude" (1870); and "Historic Notes of Life and

Letters in New England" (1880). As a result of this journey, so full of surprises—not the least gratifying of which was the discovery, at the very end of it, long after the first draft of my book was completed, of Stanley Cavell's moving essay "Hope against Hope," *American Poetry Review* 15 (Jan.–Feb. 1986): 9–13—I have come to share Cavell's belief that Emerson is our most important writer and that the prevailing "condescension" towards him "helps to keep our culture, unlike any other in the West, from possessing any founding thinker as a common basis for its considerations." Condescension, it should be noted, also defines the prevailing attitude towards our most important political tradition, populism.

Part of the trouble, in Emerson's case, is that his early admirers admired him for the wrong reasons. They confused his affirmations with moral uplift, his hopefulness with a belief in progress. Emerson's assimilation to the genteel tradition, as Santayana called it, can be traced in Kenneth Cameron, *Emerson among His Contemporaries* (1967), although this enormous compendium also contains earlier assessments in quite a different vein, which show how deeply some of Emerson's contemporaries were troubled by what they took to be his fatalism. A more manageable compilation, Milton R. Konvitz, ed., *The Recognition of Ralph Waldo Emerson* (1972), ranges from the earliest commentaries to the latest critical opinion at the time of its publication. For the genteel view of Emerson, see also Edwin D. Mead, *The Influence of Emerson* (1903).

When the genteel tradition came under critical fire, so did Emerson's reputation. Van Wyck Brooks set the tone of dismissal in *America's Coming-of-Age* (1915), and his subsequent efforts to make up for his youthful "impudence" in "bearding the prophets" only made matters worse. His *Life of Emerson* (1932) tried to evoke the freshness and innocence of a bygone age, when the country was new and everything seemed possible. But Brooks's revised portrait of Emerson, as sentimental as his earlier portrait was carping and sophomoric, left it unclear why a more sophisticated and disillusioned generation of Americans should take any but a nostalgic interest in the "Orpheus" of the nation's infancy. The same question was left unanswered by Lewis Mumford's more discriminating version of nineteenth-century literary history, *The Golden Day* (1926); by F. O. Matthiessen's *American Renaissance* (1941); and by the many studies guided by the fascination with innocence as a persistent theme in early American culture: R. W. B. Lewis, *The American Adam* (1955); Quentin Anderson, *The Imperial Self* (1971); Larzer Ziff, *Literary Democracy: The Declaration of Cultural Independence in America* (1981); Alfred Kazin, *An American Procession* (1984); and Irving Howe, *The American Newness: Culture and Politics in the Age of Emerson* (1986), among others. In varying degrees, all these critics admired Emerson's vigor of expression and recognized it as the product of reverence and wonder, but by identifying these emotions so closely with the "American newness," they made it impossible to explain why Emerson should have had any continuing appeal except to those who remained intellectually and emotionally retarded. Although it pains me to disagree with Alfred Kazin, a literary historian whose work (usually informed by such a nice balance of appreciation and critical insight) has left us all immeasurably in his debt, his assertion that we can still share Emerson's "thrill" in the "primacy that he shared with Nature and America itself" does not strike me as terribly helpful, especially when it is accompanied by disparagement of Emerson as a "sage-at-large"; a believer in "self-actualization" and "rapturous self-affirmation"; a closet elitist whose "underlying contempt for those who could not live up to his revelation" offends us as deeply as his conviction that " 'life' . . . was indeed nothing but what the 'great man' is thinking of"; an "apostle of perfect personal power" whose "trust in the spiritual life" took no account of hard material realities; and, worst of all, an abstracted, "unctuous" ex-preacher who gave the dominant classes their "favorite image of the literary man as someone removed from 'real' life while remaining an embodiment of the idealism professed as the essence of America."

Communitarians have added to this familiar indictment the charge that Emerson's "expressive individualism," "limited to a language of radical individual autonomy," in Bellah's words, provides an inadequate counterweight to the acquisitive or "utilitarian" individualism that governs America culture. It "promises an inner refuge," according to David Marr, *American Worlds since Emerson* (1988), and thus encourages an "ideological assault upon politics and the political." More recently, in a review of David Van Leer's *Emerson's Epistemology* (1986) in *Clio* 18 (1989): 196–99, Marr has qualified this judgment to the extent of admitting that "the issues with which Emerson was preoccupied were more subtle and his treatment of them more precise than he has been given credit for."

It is not clear whether this remark is intended as an endorsement of Van Leer's contention that Emerson was a Kantian chiefly preoccupied with epistemological issues—a view of Emerson that also plays some part in Evan Carton, *The Rhetoric of American Romance: Dialectic and Identity in Emerson, Dickinson, Poe, and Hawthorne* (1985). John Michael, *Emerson and Skepticism: The Cipher of the World* (1988), argues persuasively that Emerson was more deeply influenced by Hume than by Kant. Like a number of other recent critics, Michael objects to the picture of Emerson as the "triumphant spokesman of self-reliance," stressing instead his "skepticism concerning the coherence and persistence of his own identity." The problematical standing of the concept of selfhood, the "volatility" and "unrelenting doubleness" of Emerson's language, and the self-referential quality of language in general figure prominently in Eric Cheyfitz, *The Trans-Parent: Sexual Politics in the Language of Emerson* (1981). Julie Ellison, *Emerson's Romantic Style* (1984), also assigns central importance to the "problem of language" and its "reflexivity." If these studies make Emerson sound too postmodern, too much like a nineteenth-century Derridean, they do help to correct the impression left by the scholarship of the fifties and sixties, that Emerson's work declined in force and visionary eloquence as he moved from the optimism of *Nature* to the pessimism of "Fate." The most recent assault on this tradition of scholarship is Leonard Neufeldt, *The House of Emerson* (1982), which also challenges another aspect of the conventional wisdom— that Emerson's abandonment of the ministry and his rejection of "all institutionalized allegiances," as Richard Poirier puts it in *A World Elsewhere* (1966), made it necessary for Emerson "to claim a place and function for himself almost wholly through his style," by inventing the "ideal type of self-expressive man." Neufeldt calls for a recognition of the "rigorously descriptive, systematic, analytical, and philosophical" side of Emerson's work, as opposed to the "moral, appreciative, and privately aesthetic" side.

All these studies, helpful as they are in many respects, pay too little attention to the religious background of Emerson's thought. The same objection applies to Carolyn Porter, *Seeing and Being: The Plight of the Participant Observer in Emerson, James, Adams, and Faulkner* (1981), which has the virtue, however, of reminding us that Emerson was interested in social as well as philosophical questions. But Emerson was interested first of all in religion. His ideas emerged out of an engagement with Hume and Kant and with the "ruling order of Boston," in Porter's words; but they emerged much more directly out of an engagement with his Puritan ancestors, with the religious traditions of his own region. If those influences are left out of the story, listening to Emerson will always be like overhearing snatches of a conversation carried on behind closed doors. The scholars of the 1950s and early 1960s understood this much at least, even if their work—notably Stephen E. Whicher, *Freedom and Fate: An Inner Life of Ralph Waldo Emerson* (1953), and Jonathan Bishop, *Emerson on the Soul* (1964)—misleadingly described the direction of Emerson's career as a falling away from affirmation to resignation and compromise. The best corrective to this particular misconception is Newton Arvin's admirable essay "The House of Pain" (in his *American Pantheon*, 1986). According to Arvin, Emerson's rejection of a tragic view of life should be seen as a hard-won advance beyond tragedy, not as the product of a mind unacquainted with tragedy or unable to conceive it even as a hypothetical possibility. "We are in the habit of assuming," Arvin writes, "that the most serious and profound apprehension of reality is the sense of tragedy; but . . . it may be that the tragic sense must be seen as . . . limited and imperfectly philosophical. . . . The best of Emerson lies on the other side."

Stanley Cavell makes a somewhat similar point in three essays that assert Emerson's importance not as a poet or "seer" but as a moral philosopher who, like Nietzsche, Wittgenstein, and Heidegger, attempted to replace both philosophy and theology with a discourse that construed "thinking as the receiving or letting be of something" and thus to refute philosophical skepticism and moral nihilism alike. See, in addition to "Hope against Hope," already cited, "Thinking of Emerson" and "An Emerson Mood," both of which appear in *The Senses of Walden* (1981). These works are of special interest to me because Cavell's appreciation of Emerson, like my own, was preceded by a long period of indifference. "Why did it take me [so long]," Cavell asks, ". . . to begin to look actively at his work, to demand explicitly my inheritance of him?" Many others could ask themselves the same question, the answers to which might add up to an important chapter in the cultural history of our times.

The difficulty of doing justice to a thinker as complex and many-sided as Emerson, even for those who agree on his central importance in American letters, is illustrated by the diametrically divergent interpretations advanced by Harold Bloom and Sacvan Bercovitch. Bloom has written about Emerson in many places, most provocatively in *Agon: Towards a Theory of Revisionism* (1982). Emerson is important to Bloom because he and other modern writers can be seen as heirs of the gnostic tradition Bloom is so eager to revive. Gnosticism, as Bloom observes, is the "knowledge of what in the self . . . is Godlike." It is a "timeless knowing, as available now as it was [in the second century], and available alike to those Christians, to those Jews and to those secular intellectuals who are not persuaded by orthodox or normative accounts or versions of religion, . . . but who know themselves as questers for God." It is easy to see how Emerson, who urged his readers and listeners to be faithful to themselves, condemned institutional religion, and often spoke of the divine spark in human nature, lends himself to such readings (or creative "misreadings," as Bloom would say). But Bloom's and other gnosticizing interpretations of Emerson—including those presented in Barbara Packer, *Emerson's Fall* (1982)—rest largely on highly selective quotation, rarely on careful analysis of the arguments conducted in Emerson's writings. The presupposition that Emerson traffics not in arguments at all but in metaphors, "orphic" wisdom, and sibylline hints of the sublime serves to absolve commentators of any responsibility for following the course of his thought. An attentive reading, however, should make us wonder how anyone who set so much store by common experience (as opposed to the experience shared only by a self-selected spiritual elite), who was so little disposed to regard religious knowledge as a closely guarded body of secrets, and in any case who regarded faith, not knowledge, as the heart of religious experience can be very clearly understood as a gnostic or even as an antinomian. My own explorations of the gnostic tradition, preliminary reports of which appear in "Notes on Gnosticism," *New Oxford Review* 53 (Oct. 1986): 14–18, and "Soul of a New Age," *Omni*, Oct. 1987, 78ff., lead me to the conclusion that the gnostic cult of mysteries accessible only to a few initiates was deeply at odds with the general tendency of Emersonian spirituality.

Bercovitch's interpretation of Emerson in *The Puritan Origins of the American Self* (1975) and *The American Jeremiad* (1978) plays up the very qualities played down by Bloom. Far from articulating a "vision whose fulfillment, by definition, must be always *beyond* the cosmos," as Bloom puts it, Bercovitch's Emerson identified himself all too closely with America and with Americans' image of themselves as a chosen people. "The self he sought was not only his but America's, or rather his *as* America's, and therefore America's as his." Like Bloom—but for opposite reasons—Bercovitch exaggerates the difference between Emerson and Carlyle, finding "fundamentally opposed concepts of greatness in Emerson and Carlyle." Whereas the latter's hero "gathers strength precisely in proportion to his alienation" and thus "stands sufficient in himself" in a "latter-day Antinomian brotherhood," Emersonian heroism is distinguished by its "reliance on a national mission." Emerson warned himself against antinomianism, as Bercovitch points out, and celebrated what he referred to as "common virtue standing on common principles." But these common principles, according to Bercovitch, turn out to be the self-congratulatory illusions that have enabled Americans to identify the Kingdom of God with the future of their own country, to proclaim their moral superiority to the Old World, and to appoint themselves saviors of mankind. In Bloom's view, Emerson's religion (or his literary substitute for religion), was timeless and universal; but in Bercovitch's view it was highly parochial, so completely bound up with the American sense of mission that it lost sight of any larger truths. Emerson was the heir not of the second-century Gnostics but of the seventeenth-century founders of Massachusetts Bay, in whose worldview "the migration to America displaces conversion as the crucial event."

Bercovitch's view of Emerson is just as one-sided as Bloom's, but he is surely right to place Emerson in the Puritan succession. (Bloom, on the other hand, dissents from the "distinguished tradition in scholarship . . . that finds Emerson to have been the heir . . . of the line that goes from the Mathers to Jonathan Edwards.") The Puritan tradition, however, was never monolithic: from the beginning, it was torn between works and grace, tribalism and spiritual individualism—between the Puritans' understanding of themselves as a corporate community and their understanding that the relations between man and God finally take precedence over communal and civic obligations. The point is not simply that Puritanism was always pulled in both directions; the point is that these tensions themselves *constituted* the Puritan tradition, which has to be understood as a continuing attempt to negotiate the treacherous ground between Arminianism and antinomianism. It is the ambiguity of the Puritan legacy, I believe, that enables critics and commentators to come to opposite conclusions about Emerson, to see him simultaneously as an antinomian and as a religious liberal, a gnostic and a poet of American national identity. This ambiguity, incidentally, extends to American impressions of Europe, which were far more complicated than Bercovitch makes them out to be. A deep strain of Anglophilia—often associated with Arminianism—early appeared alongside the ritual denunciation of old-world corruption. Both Edwards and Emerson set themselves against the cultural subservience to Europe that has so often afflicted Americans, especially the "better class" of Americans; and their celebration of America needs to be read in that context—as a corrective to the fashionable demand for imported models of cultural sophistication, not as the assertion of a messianic spirit of national chauvinism.

JAMES. On the eclipse of idealism in the Gilded Age, see "Literature Truly American," *Nation,* 2 Jan. 1868, 7–8; "The Great American Novel," *Nation,* Jan. 1868, 27–29; "The Organization of Culture," *Nation,* 18 June 1868, 486–88; [Henry James], "Mr. Walt Whitman," *Nation,* 16 Nov. 1865, 625–26; Justin Kaplan, *Walt Whitman* (1980); and William T. Stafford, "Emerson and the James Family" (1953), in Edwin Cady and Louis J. Budd, *On Emerson* (1988).

William James's views of Emerson are considered in Stafford's essay and in another essay in the Cady-Budd collection, Frederic I. Carpenter's "William James and Emerson" (1939). See also F. O. Matthiessen, *The James Family* (1947). My reading of James rests on the Gifford Lectures of 1901–2, *Varieties of Religious Experience* (1902); *The Principles of Psychology* (1890); *Pragmatism* (1907); *A Pluralistic Universe* (1909); and the following essays, all of which are reprinted in John J. McDermott's collection *The Writings of William James* (1977): a review of Renan's *Dialogues* (1876); "The Dilemma of Determinism" (1884); "The Moral Philosopher and the Moral Life" (1891); "Is Life Worth Living?" (1895); "The Will to Believe" (1896); "On a Certain Blindness in Human Beings" (1899); and "What Makes a Life Significant" (1899). Ralph Barton Perry, *The Thought and Character of William James* (1935), is indispensable; it contains, along with other material quoted in the text, James's important exchange with Hobhouse. Clarence Karier's ham-handed interpretation of James appears in *Scientists of the Mind: Intellectual Founders of Modern Psychology* (1986). For Henry James, Sr., and the idea of the "fortunate fall," see Lewis, *American Adam*. Horace Bushnell criticized the "piety of conquest" in *Christian Nurture* (1847, 1861).

7 THE SYNDICALIST MOMENT: CLASS STRUGGLE AND WORKERS' CONTROL

AS THE MORAL EQUIVALENT OF PROPRIETORSHIP AND WAR

It would be impossible to list all the works that have sustained my long-standing interest in the turn-of-the-century cult of the "strenuous life." Those referred to or drawn on here include Oliver Wendell Holmes, "The Soldier's Faith" (1896), in Max Lerner's collection, *The Mind and Faith of Justice Holmes* (1943); James's criticism of Holmes's "set speech" in Perry, *Thought and Character of William James;* Theodore Roosevelt, "The Strenuous Life" (1899), in the National Edition of his *Works*, vol. 13 (1926), 319–31; Homer Lea, *The Valor of Ignorance* (1909); Hannah Arendt, *The Origins of Totalitarianism* (1958); Allen J. Greenberger, *The British Image of India: A Study in the Literature of Imperialism* (1969); Susanne Howe, *Novels of Empire* (1949); A. James Gregor, *The Ideology of Fascism* (1969); and George L. Mosse, "Fascism and the Intellectuals," in S. J. Woolf, ed., *The Nature of Fascism* (1968). James's essay "The Moral Equivalent of War" (1910) is reprinted in John J. McDermott, ed., *The Writings of William James* (1977). For Sorel's comments on James, see James H. Meisel, *The Genesis of Georges Sorel* (1951).

Studies of Sorel include, in addition to the one by Meisel, Irving Louis Horowitz, *Radicalism and the Revolt against Reason: The Social Theories of Georges Sorel* (1961); Jack J. Roth, *The Cult of Violence: Sorel and the Sorelians* (1980); Richard Humphrey, *Georges Sorel: Prophet without Honor* (1951); and Arthur L. Greil, *Georges Sorel and the Sociology of Virtue* (1981). None of these explore Sorel's debt either to the republican or to the prophetic traditions. See also the chapter on Sorel in H. Stuart Hughes, *Consciousness and Society: The Reorientation of European Social Thought, 1890–1930* (1958); T. E. Hulme's essay "Reflections on Violence" (1916), in his *Speculations* (1924); Edward Shils's introduction to the translation of *Reflections on Violence* by Hulme

(1950); John Stanley's introduction to the translation of *The Illusions of Progress* by him and Charlotte Stanley (1969); and Stanley's introduction to his collection *From Georges Sorel: Essays in Socialism and Philosophy* (1987). This last contains excerpts from some of Sorel's less familiar works, including *The Trial of Socrates* (1889), "The Socialist Future of the Syndicates" (1898), and "Critical Essays on Marxism" (1898). Horowitz's *Radicalism and the Revolt against Reason* contains a translation of *The Decomposition of Marxism* (1908), the third of Sorel's three major works, along with *The Illusions of Progress* (1906) and *Reflections on Violence* (1908).

My analysis of guild socialism rests principally on several works by G. D. H. Cole: *The World of Labour* (1913); *Guild Socialism Re-stated* (1920); *The Next Ten Years in British Social and Economic Policy* (1929); *Socialist Control of Industry* (1933); *Europe, Russia, and the Future* (1942); and *The History of Socialist Thought* (1953–60). A. W. Wright, *G. D. H. Cole and Socialist Democracy* (1979), is far more helpful than Luther P. Carpenter, *G. D. H. Cole: An Intellectual Biography* (1973). Works by other guild socialists include S. G. Hobson, *National Guilds: An Inquiry into the Wage System and the Way Out* (1919); A. R. Orage, *Political and Economic Writings* (1936); Arthur Penty, *Guilds, Trade, and Agriculture* (1921); and G. R. S. Taylor, *The Guild State* (1919). See also Bertrand Russell, *Proposed Roads to Freedom: Socialism, Anarchism, and Syndicalism* (1919). On British socialism and social democracy, see, among other works, E. P. Thompson, *William Morris* (1955); Willard Wolfe, *From Radicalism to Socialism: Men and Ideas in the Formation of Fabian Socialist Doctrines* (1975); Norman and Jeanne MacKenzie, *The Fabians* (1977) and *H. G. Wells* (1973).

8 WORK AND LOYALTY

In comparing syndicalism in France with the American version, I have relied on the sources already cited in chapter 7 and on Val R. Lorwin, *The French Labor Movement* (1954); F. F. Ridley, *Revolutionary Syndicalism in France* (1970); and Peter N. Stearns, *Revolutionary Syndicalism and French Labor* (1971). The critique of syndicalism formulated by American progressives, social democrats, and revolutionary socialists can be reconstructed from John Graham Brooks, *American Syndicalism: The IWW* (1913); John Spargo, *Syndicalism, Industrial Unionism and Socialism* (1913); William English Walling, *Socialism as It Is* (1912) and *Progressivism—and After* (1914); and Bertram Benedict, *The Larger Socialism* (1921). Brisbane's statement about the distribution of wealth is quoted in Walling, *Socialism*. On this issue, see also Mary Kingsbury Simkhovitch, *The City Worker's World* (1917). For an analysis of the IWW that distinguishes its program from syndicalism, see Earl C. Ford and William Z. Foster, *Syndicalism* (1913). There is no good study of Foster, least of all one that deals in any depth with his syndicalist phase. Arthur Zipser, *Workingclass Giant: The Life of William Z. Foster* (1981), does not fill the bill. Foster's later career can be followed in Theodore Draper, *The Roots of American Communism* (1957), and Maurice Isserman, *Which Side Were You On? The American Communist Party during the Second World War* (1982).

Joseph R. Conlin, *Big Bill Haywood and the Radical Union Movement* (1969), and

Melvyn Dubofsky, *We Shall Be All: A History of the IWW* (1969), contain useful information about the Wobblies. On the romance between the IWW and the intellectuals, see Martin Green, *New York 1913: The Armory Show and the Paterson Strike Pageant* (1988); see also Christopher Lasch, *The New Radicalism in America* (1965), and Robert Humphrey, *Children of Fantasy: The First Rebels of Bohemia* (1978). Hutchins Hapgood's autobiography, *A Victorian in the Modern World* (1939), best conveys the flavor of this bohemian radicalism. Emma Goldman's magazine, *Mother Earth,* especially the various articles on syndicalism in vol. 7 (1913), should be supplemented by her *Syndicalism: The Modern Menace to Capitalism* (1913); by Martha Solomon, *Emma Goldman* (1987); and by the standard works on anarchism by George Woodcock, *Anarchism* (1962), and James Joll, *The Anarchists* (1964).

Mary Parker Follett's thought is best represented by *The New State: Group Organization the Solution of Popular Government* (1918). Croly's interest in the wage question, reflected in *Progressive Democracy* (1914), has been missed by David W. Levy, *Herbert Croly of the New Republic* (1985); by R. Jeffrey Lustig, *Corporate Liberalism* (1982); and by James T. Kloppenberg in his otherwise impressive study, *Uncertain Victory: Social Democracy and Progressivism in European and American Thought* (1986). Kloppenberg recognizes that *Progressive Democracy* is a more radical and interesting book than *The Promise of America Life* (1909), but he does not seem to grasp the reasons for this. His own book seems to have originated, at least in part, in a desire to present turn-of-the-century progressives and social democrats as heirs to the "civic humanist ideal," as he puts it at one point; but the remnants of that tradition survived far more vigorously in guild socialism and syndicalism—movements Kloppenberg passes over in silence—than in the mainstream social democracy he emphasizes instead. Progressives and social democrats were the founders of the modern welfare state—the negation of everything the old republican tradition stood for. How little progressivism resembled republicanism can easily be seen by reading Walter Weyl's manifesto, *The New Democracy* (1912).

A whole book could be written about the debates concerning the democratization of culture that took place during the progressive era. My account draws mainly on Douglas L. Wilson, ed., *The Genteel Tradition: Nine Essays by George Santayana* (1967), which includes the 1911 essay "The Genteel Tradition in American Philosophy," on which Van Wyck Brooks drew so heavily in *America's Coming-of-Age* (1915); on Brooks's earlier book, *The Wine of the Puritans* (1909), and his well-known essay, "On Creating a Usable Past," *Dial* 64 (11 April 1918): 337–41; on Randolph Bourne's *Gary Schools* (1916) and the collections of his essays edited by Olaf Hansen, *The Radical Will* (1977), Lillian Schlissel, *The World of Randolph Bourne* (1965), and Carl Resek, *War and the Intellectuals* (1964); on various works by Lewis Mumford, notably *The Golden Day* (1926), *Findings and Keepings* (1975), and *Interpretations and Forecasts* (1973); and on Waldo Frank's *Our America* (1919).

Like the debate about the democratization of culture, the immigration debate deserves more extensive treatment than I have given it here. The central documents, in addition to ones already cited, are Israel Zangwill, *The Melting Pot* (1909);

Franz Boas, *Race and Democratic Society* (1945), a collection of essays ranging over many years, and his uncollected essay "The Real Race Problem," *Crisis* 1 (Nov. 1910): 22–25; Randolph Bourne, "Americanism," *New Republic*, 23 Sept. 1916, 197, and "Americans in the Making," *New Republic*, 2 Feb. 1918, 30–32; Horace M. Kallen, *Culture and Democracy in the United States* (1924); and Isaac Berkson, *Theories of Americanization* (1920). This last, which I have decided not to consider here, is probably the most elaborate statement of the pluralist position.

At least two works by Josiah Royce bear directly on the questions discussed in this chapter: the essays collected under the title *Race Questions, Provincialism, and Other American Problems* (1908) and *The Philosophy of Loyalty* (1908). Both these books originated as lectures to lay audiences. Royce, like William James, gave many such lectures; their refusal to speak exclusively on technical subjects to an audience composed exclusively of professional colleagues—their insistence that philosophy had something to say about the conduct of daily life—was one of the most admirable and characteristic aspects of their work.

On Mencken, see Robert Morss Lovett, "An Interpretation of American Life," *Dial* 9 (June 1925): 515–18; Edmund Wilson, "H. L. Mencken," *New Republic*, 1 June 1921, 10–13; Walter Lippmann, "H. L. Mencken," *Saturday Review of Literature*, 11 Dec. 1926, 413–14, and "The Near Machiavelli," *New Republic*, 31 May 1922, 12–14; André LeVot, *F. Scott Fitzgerald* (1983); writings by Mencken himself, including "Katzenjammer," *American Mercury* 7 (1926): 125–26; "Mencken on Mencken" (1923), in Henry M. Christman, ed., *One Hundred Years of the Nation: A Centennial Anthology* (1965), 136–39; "On Living in the United States," *Nation*, 7 Dec. 1921, 655–56; and *Notes on Democracy* (1926); and the following secondary works: Edgar Kemler, *The Irreverent Mr. Mencken* (1950); Carl Bode, *Mencken* (1969); Fred C. Hobson, Jr., *Serpent in Eden: H. L. Mencken and the South* (1974); and Edward A. Martin, *H. L. Mencken and the Debunkers* (1984). Other works mentioned in connection with the postwar reaction against progressivism include "Confessions of an Educator," *New Republic*, 18 Aug. 1926, 356–58; Frederick Tupper, "Parables of the Democratic Mob," *Unpopular Review* 3 (1915): 43–60; "Progressivism vs. Democracy," *New Republic*, 27 May 1925, 5–7; "What To Do with the Doughtys?" *Nation*, 9 Jan. 1924, 26; "Coolidge," *Nation*, 18 June 1924, 696; and Matthew Josephson, "On Liberty," *New Republic*, 10 Sept. 1930, 104–5.

Walter Lippmann wrote about public opinion, with increasing skepticism, in "A Test of the News" (with Charles Merz), *New Republic*, Aug. 1920 (special supplement); *Liberty and the News* (1920); *Public Opinion* (1922); and *The Phantom Public* (1925). Ronald Steel's biography, *Walter Lippmann and the American Century* (1980), is exhaustive. John Dewey reviewed the last two books in Lippmann's series in "Public Opinion," *New Republic*, 3 May 1922, 286–88, and "Practical Democracy," *New Republic*, 2 Dec. 1925, 52–54. He advanced a counterargument in *The Public and Its Problems* (1927). See also his *Individualism, Old and New* (1930); *Liberalism and Social Action* (1935); and several articles: "Progress" (1916), in *Characters and Events* 2 (1929): 820–30; "The American Intellectual Frontier," *New Republic*, 10 May 1922, 303–5;

"Who Might Make a New Party?" *New Republic,* 1 April 1931, 177–79; "Social Science and Social Control," *New Republic,* 29 July 1931, 276–77; and "Intelligence and Power," *New Republic,* 25 April 1934, 306–7. James W. Carey, *Communication as Culture: Essays on Media and Society* (1989), finds Dewey's *Public and Its Problems* "maddeningly obscure"—a judgment few readers are likely to question—but extracts from it a more powerful reply to Lippmann than my own account of this exchange would indicate. The heart of Dewey's argument, Carey maintains, is his "espousal of the metaphor of hearing over that of seeing." Dewey believes that "language is not a system of representations but a form of activity" and that "speech captures this action better than the more static images of the printed page." The trouble with the press, accordingly, is not "its failure to represent" events objectively and impartially, as Lippmann thought, but its failure to see itself "as an agency for carrying on the conversation of our culture." Lippmann's "spectator theory of knowledge" misses the point that "we lack not only an effective press but certain vital habits: the ability to follow an argument, grasp the point of view of another, expand the boundaries of understanding, debate the alternative purposes that might be pursued." If this is what Dewey meant—and Carey's gloss is quite consistent with the general direction of Dewey's philosophy—it is too bad he did not say so, in this particular book, more clearly and emphatically. On his exchange with Lippmann, see also Robert Westbrook, *John Dewey and American Democracy* (1991).

9 THE SPIRITUAL DISCIPLINE AGAINST RESENTMENT

Of the voluminous writings of Reinhold Niebuhr, the ones most directly relevant to my purposes are "The Twilight of Liberalism," *New Republic,* 14 June 1919, 218; "War and Christian Ethics," *New Republic,* 22 Feb. 1922, 372; *Does Civilization Need Religion?* (1926); *Moral Man and Immoral Society* (1932); "A Footnote on Religion," *Nation,* 26 Sept. 1934, 358–59 (a review of Dewey's *A Common Faith*); *An Interpretation of Christian Ethics* (1935); *The Nature and Destiny of Man* (1941, 1943); and *The Irony of American History* (1952). Important works on Niebuhr include Donald B. Meyer, *The Protestant Search for Political Realism* (1960); June Bingham, *Courage to Change: An Introduction to the Life and Thought of Reinhold Niebuhr* (1975); and Richard Wightman Fox, *Reinhold Niebuhr* (1985); see also Fox's article, "The Niebuhr Brothers and the Liberal Protestant Heritage," in Michael Lacey, ed., *Religion and Twentieth-Century American Intellectual Life* (1989).

The controversies between Niebuhr and Christian pacifists and the highly selective absorption of his thought by liberal Protestants can be followed in his articles "Must We Do Nothing?" *Christian Century* 49 (23 March 1932): 415–17; "Is Peace or Justice the Goal?" *World Tomorrow* 15 (21 Sept. 1932): 395–97; "The Blindness of Liberalism," *Radical Religion* (fall 1936): 4–5; "The Return to Primitive Religion," *Christendom* 3 (winter 1938): 1–8; and in the following responses provoked either directly or indirectly by his attack on liberal religion: "The Political

Confusion of Liberals," *World Tomorrow* 15 (28 Dec. 1932): 47–51; John C. Bennett, "After Liberalism, What?" *Christian Century* 50 (8 Nov. 1933): 1403–6, and *Social Salvation* (1935); Buell G. Gallagher, "Christians and Radical Social Change," *World Tomorrow* 15 (June 1932): 170–75; S. Ralph Harlow, "Jesus Is Coming!" *Christian Century* 49 (13 Jan. 1932): 56–58; E. G. Homrighausen, "Modern Apocalypticism," *World Tomorrow* 15 (12 Oct. 1932): 354–55; Norman Thomas, "Moral Man and Immoral Society," *World Tomorrow* 15 (14 Dec. 1932): 565–67; Shailer Mathews, *Christianity and Social Process* (1934); Henry J. Cadbury, *The Peril of Modernizing Jesus* (1937); F. Ernest Johnson, *The Social Gospel Re-examined* (1940); Chester Carlton McCown, *The Search for the Real Jesus* (1940); Arthur M. Schlesinger, Jr., *The Vital Center* (1948) and "Reinhold Niebuhr's Role in American Political Thought and Life" (1956), in *The Politics of Hope* (1962); Harvey Cox, *The Secular City* (1965); and Daniel Callahan, ed., *The Secular City Debate* (1966). Niebuhr's failure to come to grips with Rauschenbusch is discussed in my essay "Religious Contributions to Social Movements: Walter Rauschenbusch, the Social Gospel, and Its Critics," *Journal of Religious Ethics* 18 (Spring 1990): 7–25.

My analysis of Martin Luther King rests on his own writings—*Stride toward Freedom: The Montgomery Story* (1958); *Strength to Love* (1963); *Why We Can't Wait* (1964); *Where Do We Go from Here: Chaos or Community?* (1967); and *The Trumpet of Conscience* (1967)—and on the following accounts of his career and of the civil rights movement: David L. Lewis, *King* (1970, 2d ed., 1978); Harvard Sitkoff, *The Struggle for Racial Equality* (1981); Clayborne Carson, *In Struggle: SNCC and the Black Awakening of the 1960s* (1981); Stephen B. Oates, *Let the Trumpet Sound: The Life of Martin Luther King, Jr.* (1982); John J. Ansbro, *Martin Luther King, Jr.: The Making of a Mind* (1982); David J. Garrow, *Bearing the Cross: Martin Luther King, Jr., and the Southern Christian Leadership Conference* (1986); and Taylor Branch, *Parting the Waters: America in the King Years, 1954–63* (1988). Garry Wills's remark about the Age of Martin Luther King appears in the *New York Review*, 10 Nov. 1988, 10–15. Leslie W. Dunbar, *A Republic of Equals* (1966), offers an uncommonly astute analysis of liberal legalism and of the difficulties facing the civil rights movement in the North.

The Ocean Hill–Brownsville experiment with "community control" of the public schools is discussed in Diane Ravitch, *The Great School Wars* (1974), chaps. 29–33, and in Maurice R. Berube and Marilyn Gittell, eds., *Confrontation at Ocean Hill–Brownsville: The New York School Strikes of 1968* (1969). See also Marilyn Gittell et al., *School Boards and School Policy: An Evaluation of Decentralization in New York City* (1973), and David Rogers and Norman H. Chung, *110 Livingston Street Revisited: Decentralization in Action* (1983).

10 THE POLITICS OF THE CIVILIZED MINORITY

My assertions about the vicissitudes of political nomenclature in the progressive era derive for the most part from contemporary periodicals, for example, Whidden Graham, "An Indictment of Liberalism," *Nation*, 26 July 1919, 113; "Explaining the Alleged Breakdown of Liberalism in America," *Current Opinion* 68 (April 1920): 520–22; "The Eclipse of Progressivism," *New Republic*, 27 Oct. 1920, 210–16; "Organizing the Intellectuals," a pamphlet bound into the *Nation*, 28 Feb. 1920; "Programs and Periodicals," *New Republic*, 22 Oct. 1924, 191–93; "Liberalism Today," *New Republic*, 25 Nov. 1925, 3–6; and "Obstreperous Liberalism," *New Republic*, 23 Dec. 1925, 122–24. Many of these articles also document the *New Republic*'s cogent analysis of liberals' failure to create a public consensus in favor of their policies; see also Herbert Croly, "The Outlook for Progressivism in Politics," *New Republic*, 10 Dec. 1924, 60–64. Harold Stearns, *Liberalism in America* (1919), provides perhaps the most vivid evidence of liberals' growing sense of themselves as an endangered species.

Mencken's statement about the artist's "active revolt" against his society appeared in the *Baltimore Sun* (1921) and is quoted in Fred C. Hobson, Jr., *Serpent in Eden: H. L. Mencken and the South* (1974). His description of the artist as a "public enemy" comes from his famous attack on the South, "The Sahara of the Bozart," in *Prejudices, Second Series* (1920). The type of social criticism inspired by this point of view is exemplified by Harold Stearns's collection, *Civilization in the United States* (1922), and by most of the contributors to the *Nation*'s series, "These United States," which ran from 1922 to 1925. The *Nation* was not the only journal to undertake such a survey in the twenties. The *New Republic* ran a similar series on cities, while Mencken's *American Mercury* published a large number of articles on various cities and states, vastly inferior, for the most part, in their undiluted contempt, to the more nuanced articles that ran in the *Nation*. The tone of the *American Mercury*'s commentary on America was unmistakably established by Charles Angoff's contribution, "Boston Twilight," *American Mercury* 6 (1925): 439–44: "What is most depressing about the town is its complete lack of what might be called a civilized minority."

Michael Walzer first explored the difference between "disembodied" and "connected" social criticism in an essay contrasting Sartre and Camus, "Commitment and Social Criticism," *Dissent* 31 (autumn 1984): 424–32. He pursued this contrast in *Interpretation and Social Criticism* (1987) and *The Company of Critics: Social Criticism and Political Commitment in the Twentieth Century* (1988). *Middletown*, by Robert and Helen Lynd (1929), wavered between these two kinds of criticism, while *Middletown in Transition* (1937) fell more clearly into the "disembodied" category. For Lynd's background in the social gospel and his ambivalent feelings about the Middle West, see Richard Fox, "Epitaph for Middletown," in the collection of essays edited by Fox and Jackson Lears, *The Culture of Consumption* (1983). Mencken's review of *Middletown*, "A City in Moronia," appeared in *American Mercury* 16 (March 1929): 379–81; Dewey's "The House Divided against Itself," in *New Republic*, 24 April 1929, 270–71. Robert Lynd's *Knowledge for What?* (1939) shows how easily "anthropological" criticism of society, even when it was launched from a left-wing point of view, led to a cult of the expert.

Thurman Arnold's two major works, *The Symbols of Government* (1935) and *The*

Folklore of Capitalism (1937), can be supplemented by later works, including *The Bottlenecks of Business* (1940) and *Democracy and Free Enterprise* (1942); by Edward N. Kearny's rather humdrum study, *Thurman Arnold, Social Critic* (1970); and by Ellis Hawley, *The New Deal and the Problem of Monopoly* (1966), which describes Arnold's antitrust campaign and some of the reasons for its failure.

The extensive body of commentary on Gunnar Myrdal, *An American Dilemma* (1944), attests to the book's status both as a sociological classic and as a reference point in the civil rights movement. David Southern, *Gunnar Myrdal and Black-White Relations* (1987), provides a useful introduction to this commentary. Among the early reviews that helped to establish Myrdal's study as definitive, see, in particular, the ones by Robert S. Lynd, *Saturday Review of Literature*, 22 April 1944, 5ff.; E. Franklin Frazier, *American Journal of Sociology* 50 (1945): 555–57, and *Crisis* 51 (April 1944): 105ff.; Frank Tannenbaum, *Political Science Quarterly* 59 (1944): 321–40; Henry Steele Commager, *American Mercury* 60 (1945): 751–56; Charles E. Wyzanski, Jr., *Harvard Law Review* 58 (Dec. 1944): 285–91; Harold F. Gosnell, *American Political Science Review* 38 (1944): 995–96; Frances Gaither, *New York Times Book Review*, 2 April 1944; Harold Fey, *Christian Century* 61 (1944): 433–34; and Buell Gallagher, *Christendom* 60 (1944): 476–88. Reinhold Niebuhr argued, in *Christianity and Society* 10 (spring 1945): 21–24, that racial bigotry sprang from "something darker and more terrible than mere stupidity" and that its eradication would therefore depend more on contrition than on enlightenment. Ralph Ellison, in a piece written for *Antioch Review* in the mid-forties but published only twenty years later in *Shadow and Act* (1964), pointed out that Myrdal overlooked the role black people would have to play in their own liberation. Most of the criticism of Myrdal, however, came not from people like Niebuhr and Ellison but from those who refused to consider race a moral issue at all or denied, at any rate, that white people felt uneasy about racial discrimination or perceived any contradiction between racism and American values. For the first type of criticism, see Herbert Aptheker, "A Liberal Dilemma," *New Masses* 59 (14 May 1946): 3–6; Oliver C. Cox, "An American Dilemma: A Mystical Approach to the Study of Race Relations," *Journal of Negro Education* 14 (1945): 132–48; and Ernest Kaiser, "Racial Dialectics: The Aptheker-Myrdal Controversy," *Phylon* 9 (1948): 295–302. Variations on the second position appeared in Mordecai Grossman, "Caste or Democracy?" *Contemporary Jewish Record* 7 (Oct. 1944): 475–86; Oliver Golightly, "Race, Values, and Guilt," *Social Forces* 26 (Dec. 1947): 125–39; Sophia Fagin McDowell, "The Myrdal Concept of 'An American Dilemma,' " *Social Forces* 30 (Oct. 1951): 87–91; Ernest Q. Campbell, "Moral Discomfort and Racial Segregation," *Social Forces* 39 (March 1961): 228–34; and Nahum Z. Medalia, "Myrdal's Assumptions on Race Relations," *Social Forces* 40 (March 1962): 223–37. A twentieth-anniversary round-table discussion by James Baldwin, Nathan Glazer, Sidney Hook, and Myrdal himself, in *Commentary* 37 (March 1964): 25–42, turned largely on the question of whether Americans cared enough about the principle of racial equality to feel uneasy about the practice of racial inequality. Orlando Patterson, "The Moral Crisis of the Black American,"

Public Interest 32 (summer 1973): 43–69, thought not directed specifically against Myrdal, challenged his thesis—that the race problem was a problem for whites alone to resolve—from a quite different point of view. Patterson argued that all types of "sociological determinism"—of which *An American Dilemma*, presumably, was a prime example—encouraged black people to exploit the "status of being a victim," to explain their plight away "as the result of white racism and all the other familiar social and economic determinants," and thus to prolong dependency and to discourage them from assuming responsibility for themselves.

E. D. Hirsch, Jr., refers to the "epoch-making" effect of Myrdal's book on his moral and intellectual development in *Cultural Literacy: What Every American Needs to Know* (1987).

The *Studies in Prejudice* sponsored by the American Jewish Committee included, in addition to *The Authoritarian Personality* (1950), Nathan W. Ackerman and Marie Jahoda, *Anti-Semitism and Emotional Disorder* (1950); Bruno Bettelheim and Morris Janowitz, *Dynamics of Prejudice* (1950); Paul W. Massing, *Rehearsal for Destruction: A Study of Political Anti-Semitism in Imperial Germany* (1949); and Leo Lowenthal and Norbert Guterman, *Prophets of Deceit: A Study of the Techniques of the American Agitator* (1949). Both the methodological crudity of these studies and the ideological presuppositions underlying them, evident enough to anyone who approaches them without too many preconceptions, appear even more clearly when they are set beside Max Horkheimer's *Eclipse of Reason* (1944) and *The Dialectic of Enlightenment* (1947)—works that criticize this very type of social science—or Hannah Arendt's brilliant analysis (cast in the historical rather than the psychologizing mode) of *The Origins of Totalitarianism* (1951). The Bergers' misdirected attack on *The Authoritarian Personality* can be found in Brigitte Berger and Peter L. Berger, *The War over the Family: Capturing the Middle Ground* (1983). Edward Shils's critique, "Authoritarianism: 'Right' and 'Left,' " appeared, along with several others, in Richard Christie and Marie Jahoda, eds., *Studies in the Scope and Method of the Authoritarian Personality* (1954). See also Richard Christie and Peggy Cook, "A Guide to the Published Literature on the Authoritarian Personality," *Journal of Psychology* 45 (1958): 171–99; John P. Kirscht and Ronald C. Dillehay, *Dimensions of Authoritarianism: A Review of Research and Theory* (1967); and David W. McKinney, Jr., *The Authoritarian Personality Studies* (1973). In addition to these collections, I have consulted innumerable reviews of *The Authoritarian Personality;* for the charge of psychological determinism, see, in particular, the ones by Tamotsu Shibutani, *American Journal of Sociology* 57 (1952): 527–29, and Joseph H. Bunzel, *American Sociological Review* 15 (1950): 571–73.

To list all the works inspired either directly or indirectly by *The Authoritarian Personality* would be impossible. Probably the most striking example is *The New American Right* (1955), revised and reissued in 1965 as *The Radical Right*—an enormously influential volume in its own right. This collection contains Richard Hofstadter's essay "The Pseudo-Conservative Revolt." Other works in this tradition include Milton Rokeach, *The Open and Closed Mind* (1960); Gertrude J. Selznick and

Stephen Steinberg, *The Tenacity of Prejudice: Anti-Semitism in Contemporary America* (1969), which attributes right-wing movements to a "syndrome of unenlightenment" that includes anti-Semitism, xenophobia, authoritarianism, etc.; and perhaps also Robert Jay Lifton, *The Broken Connection* (1979). Lifton advances his theory of victimization (according to which injustice against outcast groups originates in a psychological "need to divest others of symbolic immortality in order to reaffirm one's own") as a "unifying principle for the various psychological factors stressed in the vast literature on prejudice," including *The Authoritarian Personality*.

Among the writings that contributed to the identification of populism with right-wing movements, the most important were those by Hofstadter, already cited in chapter 5; by Edward Shils (*The Torment of Secrecy*, 1956; see also "Populism and the Rule of Law," *University of Chicago Law School Conference on Jurisprudence and Politics*, 1954); and by Samuel A. Stouffer, *Communism, Confirmity, and Civil Liberties* (1955). The egregious essay by Victor Ferkiss, "Populist Influences on American Fascism," was published in *Western Political Quarterly* 10 (1957): 350–73. Michael Rogin, *The Intellectuals and McCarthy* (1967), discusses many other works in this vein. Lenin's disparaging remarks about the petty bourgeoisie, from *"Left-Wing" Communism: An Infantile Disorder* (1920), are quoted in Arno J. Mayer, "The Lower Middle Class as a Historical Problem," *Journal of Modern History* 47 (1975): 409–36.

The well-known analysis of "working-class authoritarianism" by Seymour Martin Lipset, originally presented to a conference sponsored by the Congress for Cultural Freedom in 1955, was published in the *American Sociological Review* 24 (1959): 482–501, and in its final version in *Political Man: The Sociological Bases of Politics* (1960). A representative sample of the writing on this subject includes Morris Janowitz and Dwaine Marvick, "Authoritarianism and Political Behavior," *Public Opinion Quarterly* 17 (1953): 185–201; Saul M. Siegel, "Relationship of Hostility to Authoritarianism," *Journal of Abnormal and Social Psychology* 52 (1956): 368–72; William J. MacKinnon and Richard Centers, "Authoritarianism and Social Stratification," *American Journal of Sociology* 61 (1956): 610–20; Albert K. Cohen and Harold M. Hodges, "Characteristics of the Lower-Blue-Collar Class," *Social Problems* 10 (1963): 303–34; James J. Martin and Frank R. Westie, "The Tolerant Personality," *American Sociological Review* 24 (1959): 521–28; Arthur B. Shostak, *Blue-Collar Life* (1969); Patricia Cayo Sexton and Brenda Sexton, *Blue Collars and Hard Hats: The Working Class and the Future of American Politics* (1971); Sar Levitan, ed., *Blue-Collar Workers: A Symposium on Middle America* (1971); and William Kornblum, *Blue Collar Community* (1974). On suburbanization and working-class *embourgeoisement*, see Bennett Berger, *Working-Class Suburb* (1960); William M. Dobriner, *Class in Suburbia* (1963); Harold Wilensky, "Class, Class Consciousness and American Workers," in William Haber, ed., *Labor in a Changing America* (1966); John H. Goldthorpe et al., *The Affluent Worker* (1968) and *The Affluent Worker in the Class Structure* (1969); and James W. Rinehart, "Affluence and the Embourgeoisement of the Working Class: A Critical Look," *Social Problems* 19 (1971): 149–62. For criticism and review of the literature on working-class authoritarianism, see S. M. Miller and Frank Riessman, " 'Working-Class Authoritarianism': A Critique of Lipset," *British Journal of Sociology* 12 (1961): 263–76; Sidney M. Peck, "Ideology and 'Political Sociology': The Conservative Bias of Lipset's 'Political Man,' " *American Catholic Sociological Review* 23 (1962): 128–55; Lewis Lipsitz, "Working-Class Authoritarianism: A Reevaluation," *American Sociological Review* 30 (1965): 103–9; Michael Lerner, "Respectable Bigotry," *American Scholar* 38 (1969): 606–17; and Edward G. Grabb, "Working-Class Authoritarianism and Tolerance of Outgroups: A Reassessment," *Public Opinion Quarterly* 43 (1979): 36–47.

The relationship between family patterns, child-rearing practices, social class, and authoritarianism is discussed in Ray H. Abrams, "The Contribution of Sociology to a Course on Marriage and the Family," *Marriage and Family Living* 2 (1940): 82–84; Sidney E. Goldstein, "Aims and Objectives of the National Conference," *Marriage and Family Living* 8 (1946): 57–58; Martha C. Ericson, "Child-Rearing and Social Status," *American Journal of Sociology* 52 (1946): 190–92; Allison Davis and Robert J. Havighurst, "Social Class and Color Differences in Child-Rearing," *American Sociological Review* 11 (1946): 698–710; Evelyn Mills Duvall, "Conceptions of Parenthood," *American Journal of Sociology* 52 (1946): 193–203; Rachel Ann Elder, "Traditional and Developmental Conceptions of Fatherhood," *Marriage and Family Living* 11 (1949): 98–100; Eleanor Maccoby and Patricia Gibbs, "Methods of Child-Rearing in Two Social Classes," in William E. Martin and Celia Burns Stendler, eds., *Readings in Child Development* (1954); Robert Sears, Eleanor Maccoby, and Harry Levin, *Patterns of Child Rearing* (1957); Urie Bronfenbrenner, "Socialization and Social Class through Time and Space," in Eleanor Maccoby et al., eds., *Readings in Social Psychology* (1958); Melvin L. Kohn, "Social Class and Parental Values," *American Journal of Sociology* 64 (1959): 337–51, and "Social Class and Parent-Child Relationships," *American Journal of Sociology* 68 (1963): 471–80; Mirra Komarovsky, *Blue-Collar Marriage* (1962); Donald G. McKinley, *Social Class and Family Life* (1964), foreword by Talcott Parsons; Daniel Rosenblatt and Edward A. Suchman, "The Underutilization of Medical-Care Services by Blue-Collarites," in Arthur B. Shostak and William Gomberg, eds., *Blue-Collar World: Studies of the American Worker* (1964); Lee Rainwater, "Making the Good Life Good: Working-Class Family and Lifestyles," in Levitan, ed., *Blue-Collar Workers;* James Walters and Nick Stinnett, "Parent-Child Relationships: A Decade Review of Research," *Journal of Marriage and the Family* 33 (1971): 70–111; Alan Kerckhoff, *Socialization and Social Class* (1972); Arlie Hochschild, ed., "A Review of Sex Role Research," *American Journal of Sociology* 78 (1973): 1011–30; and David M. Schneider and Raymond T. Smith, *Class Differences and Sex Roles in American Kinship and Family Structure* (1973).

Studies of political alienation include Franz Neumann, "Anxiety and Politics," published in *Dissent* in 1955 and reprinted in *The Democratic and the Authoritarian State* (1957), 270–300; Alan Westin, "Deadly Parallels: Radical Right and Radical

Left," *Harper's,* April 1962, 25–32; Robert E. Lane, *Political Ideology* (1962) and "The Decline of Politics and Ideology in a Knowledgeable Society," *American Sociological Review* 31 (1966): 649–62; Herbert McClosky, "Conservatism and Personality," *American Political Science Review* 52 (1958): 27–45, and "Consensus and Ideology in American Politics," *American Political Science Review* 58 (1964): 361–82; Gilbert Abcarian and Sherman M. Stanage, "Alienation and the Radical Right," *Journal of Politics* 27 (1965): 776–96; Joel Aberbach, "Alienation and Political Behavior," *American Political Science Review* 62 (1969): 86–99; William Simon and John H. Gagnon, "Working-Class Youth: Alienation without an Image," in Louise Kapp Howe, ed., *The White Majority: Between Poverty and Affluence* (1970); James S. House and William M. Mason, "Political Alienation in America, 1952–1968," *American Sociological Review* 40 (1975): 123–47; and James D. Wright, *The Dissent of the Governed: Alienation and Democracy* (1976).

The emergence of the "Camelot" legend can be traced in Arthur M. Schlesinger, Jr., "The Decline of Greatness" (1958) and "Heroic Leadership and the Dilemma of Strong Men and Weak Peoples" (1960), in *The Politics of Hope* (1962); in the same author's *Kennedy or Nixon: Does It Make Any Difference?* (1960); in Norman Mailer, *The Presidential Papers* (1963); and in the journalistic commentary on Kennedy's assassination and its social significance: *Newsweek,* 2 Dec. 1963, 36; *Saturday Evening Post,* 14 Dec. 1963, 22; *Life,* 29 Nov. 1963, 22; *Time,* 29 Nov. 1963, 84; *U.S. News & World Report,* 16 Dec. 1963, 84; Ben Bradlee, "He Had That Special Grace," *Newsweek,* 2 Dec. 1963, 38–48; Theodore H. White, "One Wished for a Cry, a Sob," *Life,* 29 Nov. 1963, 32D–32E, and "For President Kennedy: An Epilogue," *Life,* 6 Dec. 1963, 158–59; Arthur M. Schlesinger, Jr., "A Eulogy," *Saturday Evening Post,* 14 Dec. 1963, 32–32A; Ralph McGill, "Hate Knows No Direction," *Saturday Evening Post,* 14 Dec. 1963, 8–10; Richard Gilman, "The Fact of Mortality," *Commonweal* 79 (13 Dec. 1963): 337–38; and Ben H. Bagdikian, "The Assassin," *Saturday Evening Post,* 14 Dec. 1963, 22ff. For the persistence and proliferation of conspiracy theories, see "A Primer of Assassination Theories," *Esquire,* Dec. 1966, 205ff.; William Turner, "Some Disturbing Parallels," *Ramparts,* Jan. 1969, 127ff.; Fred J. Cook, "The Irregulars Take the Field," *Nation,* 19 July 1971, 40–46; Peter Dale Scott, "From Dallas to Watergate: The Longest Cover-up," *Ramparts,* Nov. 1973, 10ff.; and "A Decade of Unanswered Questions," *Ramparts,* Dec. 1973, 40ff. Criticism of the public's refusal to accept the Warren Report and its continuing belief in the existence of a conspiracy, often attributed to psychopathological needs of one sort or another, can be found in William V. Shannon, "Enough Is Enough," *Commonweal* 85 (18 Nov. 1966): 191–92; in the report of the National Commission on the Causes and Prevention of Violence, *Assassination and Political Violence* (1969), by James F. Kirkham, Sheldon G. Levy, and William J. Crotty; in Garry Wills and Ovid Demaris, *Jack Ruby* (1968); and in Edward Jay Epstein, "Garrison," *New Yorker,* 13 July 1968, 35–81. Anthony Lewis's disapproval of the search for conspiracy is quoted in Harris Wofford, *Of Kennedys and Kings* (1980).

Of the innumerable books attempting to reconstruct the events surrounding the assassination, beginning with the first challenges to the Warren Report—Mark Lane, *Rush to Judgment* (1966); Richard H. Popkin, *The Second Oswald* (1966); Edward Jay Epstein, *Inquest* (1966)— and continuing through Jean Davison, *Oswald's Game* (1983), the most reliable, I think, is Michael L. Kurtz, *Crime of the Century: The Kennedy Assassination from a Historian's Perspective* (1982).

II RIGHT-WING POPULISM AND THE REVOLT AGAINST LIBERALISM

Steven Roberts argued that the "deepest issue" in the so-called white backlash was "racial"; his report (*New York Times*, 2 March 1980) is quoted in Robert A. Dentler and Marvin B. Scott, *Schools on Trial: An Inside Account of the Boston Desegregation Case* (1981). The idea that "racism" explains all that anyone needs to know about the rise of the new right is so pervasive that it would be pointless to accumulate citations to this effect. It is more important to understand how loose talk of racism blunts our sensibility and deforms our understanding. As Mark Crispin Miller notes, "The word 'racism' ought to be as complex as the tangled thing which it denotes," instead of which it is increasingly "used as a blunt instrument, cutting conversations short and making people circumspect." Thus an NBC documentary, produced in 1981, "America: Black and White," left the impression, in Miller's words, that "if it weren't for 'racism,' . . . our way of life could contain all differences, by painlessly erasing them." NBC rendered white resistance to open housing and affirmative action incomprehensible by depicting blacks exclusively as upper-middle-class, soft-spoken people well launched on the path of upward mobility and thwarted only by irrational white prejudice. Its report paid no attention (except as manifestations of "racism") to the fear of drugs, crime, and violence evoked by the relentless spread of the ghetto. It left the impression that black people are "incapable of the sort of resentment that can turn violent." According to Miller, this stereotype of black innocence and victimization is almost as dehumanizing as the racist stereotypes it tries to correct. His perceptive examination of these matters originally appeared in the *New Republic*, 28 Oct. 1981, 27–31, and is reprinted in his *Boxed In: The Culture of TV* (1988). For evidence that blacks are themselves divided on busing and affirmative action, see Louis Henri Bolce III and Susan H. Gray, "Blacks, Whites, and 'Race Politics,' " *Public Interest* 54 (winter 1979): 61–75.

Michael Miles attributed the white backlash not only to racism but to fear of the "cultural revolution" in *The Radical Probe* (1971). For other interpretations of this kind, see Loren Baritz, *The Good Life: The Meaning of Success for the American Middle Class* (1989); Peter Clecak, *America's Search for the Ideal Self: Dissent and Fulfillment in the Sixties and Seventies* (1983); and Alan Crawford, *Thunder on the Right: The "New Right" and the Politics of Resentment* (1980).

The impression of a growing middle class is called into question by Harry Braverman, *Labor and Monopoly Capital* (1974); Andrew Levison, *The Working-Class Majority* (1974); Richard Parker, *The Myth of the Middle Class* (1972); Henry M. Levin and Russell W. Rumberger, *The Educational Implications of High Technology* (1983); George T. Silvestri et al., "Occupational Employment Projections through 1995," and Valerie A. Personick, "The Job Outlook through 1995," in Bureau of Labor Statistics Bulletin No. 2197, *Employment Projections for 1995* (March 1984); Barry Bluestone and Bennett Harrison, "The Grim Truth about the Job 'Miracle,' " *New York Times*, 1 Feb. 1987; *Time*, 10 Oct. 1988, 28–32; and Katherine S. Newman, *Falling from Grace: The Experience of Downward Mobility in the American Middle Class* (1988).

My analysis of the lower-middle-class ethic of limits draws on E. E. LeMasters, *Blue-Collar Aristocrats: Life-styles at a Working-Class Tavern* (1975); Stephan Thernstrom, *Poverty and Progress: Social Mobility in a Nineteenth-Century City* (1964); Lloyd Warner, *American Life: Dream and Reality* (1953); Lillian Rubin, *Worlds of Pain: Life in the Working-Class Family* (1976); Lee Rainwater, Richard P. Coleman, and Gerald Handel, *Workingman's Wife* (1959); Robert Coles, "The Maid and the Missus," *Radcliffe Quarterly* 65 (March 1979): 77ff.; Jonathan Rieder, *Canarsie: The Jews and Italians of Brooklyn against Liberalism* (1985); Ira Shar, *Culture Wars: Schools and Society in the Conservative Restoration* (1986); Julius Lester, "Beyond Ideology: Transcending the Sixties," *Tikkun* 3 (Jan.–Feb. 1988): 53–56; and Herbert J. Gans, *Middle-American Individualism* (1988). Though Gans persists in misreading my own work as one more example of the highbrow critique of middle America, his book provides a good deal of support for the interpretations I have advanced here. He notes, for example, that "middle America is a combination of working-class and lower-middle-class families," which fall below the "upper middle class of affluent professionals, managers and executives, as well as the upper class of top executives and coupon clippers." He also notes that "their political thinking does not follow conventional Left-Right positions."

Kristin Luker, *Abortion and the Politics of Motherhood* (1984), is the best study of the abortion controversy. E. Patricia McCormick, *Attitudes toward Abortion: Experiences of Selected Black and White Women* (1975); Frederick S. Jaffe et al., *Abortion Politics* (1981); Marilyn Falik, *Ideology and Abortion Policy Politics* (1983); and Hyman Rodman et al., *The Abortion Question* (1987), are not terribly helpful. For the courts' growing attention to questions concerning the "quality of life," see "A New Ethic for Medicine and Society," *California Medicine* 113 (Sept. 1970): 67–68; Robert A. Destro, "Guaranteeing the 'Quality' of Life through Law: The Emerging 'Right' to a Good Life," in Richard John Neuhaus, ed., *Guaranteeing the Good Life* (1990); and Richard John Neuhaus, "The Return of Eugenics," *Commentary* 85 (April 1988): 15–26, reprinted in *Guaranteeing the Good Life*.

The most evenhanded account of the school wars in Boston is J. Anthony Lukas, *Common Ground* (1985). Brian Sheehan, *The Boston School Integration Dispute: Social Change and Legal Maneuvers* (1984), presents a good analysis of the political alignments growing out of earlier battles over urban renewal. Martha Bayles criticizes the single-minded preoccupation with "racism" in her article "On Busing in Boston," *Harper's*, July 1980, 77–79. Ione Malloy's diary of the South Boston conflict was published under the title *Southie Won't Go: A Teacher's Diary of the Desegregation of South Boston High School* (1986). Additional information can be found in J. Michael Ross and William M. Berg, *"I Respectfully Disagree with the Judge's Order": The Boston School Desegregation Controversy* (1981); Thomas J. Cottle, *Busing* (1976); and the book by Dentler and Scott, cited at the beginning of this chapter. Jon Hillson, *The Battle of Boston* (1977), sees nothing but "racism." On desegregation in St. Louis, see Daniel J. Monti, *A Semblance of Justice: St. Louis School Desegregation and Order in Urban America* (1985). On desegregation in general, see George R. Metcalf, *From Little Rock to Boston: The History of School Desegregation* (1983); and Jennifer L. Hochschild, *The New American Dilemma: Liberal Democracy and School Desegregation* (1984). Hochschild's book is a puzzle. The author supports desegregation but introduces a good deal of evidence damaging to the belief that desegregation is the best way to improve black education. Contrary to the assumption underlying the *Brown* decision and the whole struggle for desegregation—"that white institutions are superior to black ones," in Hochschild's words—"evidence seldom shows that racially isolated blacks have impaired self-esteem, and it all too often shows that blacks in desegregated schools do." One study cited by Hochschild concludes that desegregation leads to "bitter rejection, isolation, and intellectual incompetence." Desegregation often means, moreover, that black teachers lose their jobs and that black principals are demoted. The legally sanctioned belief in the inferiority of black institutions endangers black colleges and businesses. The most damning testimony comes from black professionals who contrast their own experience in segregated schools, where teachers "made very strong demands" on them, with their children's experience in desegregated schools. "Lower expectations on the part of the teachers," these parents complain, undermine their children's "drive for educational achievement."

In view of all this discouraging evidence, it is not surprising that black support for desegregation dropped from 78 percent in 1964 to 55 percent in 1978; that a former civil rights lawyer, Derrick Bell, now pronounces desegregation "wasteful, dangerous, and demeaning"; that a number of black scholars have begun to argue that attempts to achieve racial balance may "prove disastrous for black children and their communities"; that the Atlanta NAACP "gave up its fight for mandatory desegregation in favor of black control of the city's public school system"; and that Hochschild herself concedes that opposition to desegregation is no longer "synonymous" with racism. Yet Hochschild, like most liberals, still comes down on the side of desegregation—the only solution, in her view, that assures equal protection under the laws. "After all, we inhabit, not a majoritarian democracy, but a liberal democracy—which means that preferences or consequences cannot override basic rights." She does not seem entirely comfortable with this conclusion, however, since it is by no means clear that racially balanced schools fall into the category of basic rights, even if we could agree to overlook "preferences or consequences"; and her support for desegregation therefore appears doubly arbitrary: not only is the weight of empirical evidence against it, but the argument from abstract rights fails her too.

Amy Gutmann, *Democratic Education* (1987), makes a similarly unconvincing and halfhearted case for desegregation. Gutmann believes that desegregation is the only means of reducing "racial prejudice among whites," but the most generous reading of her own evidence leads to the conclusion that integrated schools reduce prejudice only under optimal conditions and only when every other goal has been systematically subordinated to this one. These conditions are precisely the ones most destructive of local control, which Gutmann rightly considers one of the most important prerequisites of participatory democracy. How to reconcile integration and local control, she concedes, is an unresolved dilemma—the "greatest dilemma of democratic education in our time." But that does not prevent her from advocating a more aggressive program of desegregation. In effect, she chooses liberalism over democracy, while clinging to the hope that it is unnecessary to make such a choice.

When democratic liberalism carries so little conviction, those who once supported liberal policies begin to look to the right for clarity and direction. Legalism is a poor substitute for moral passion and a sense of purpose. As Fred Siegel has shown, liberals' growing inclination to give every question a legalistic answer has contributed to the right-wing reaction against liberalism; see his book *Troubled Journey: From Pearl Harbor to Ronald Reagan* (1984) and his penetrating articles on the 1968 campaign, "Campaign across Cultural Divides," *Commonweal* 115 (11 March 1988): 137–41; "Competing Elites," *Commonweal* 115 (7 Oct. 1988): 523–25; and "What Liberals Haven't Learned and Why," *Commonweal* 116 (13 Jan. 1989): 16–20. Liberalism has been further weakened by its increasingly explicit identification with elitism. "Elitism," Hochschild writes in defense of court-ordered busing, " . . . is perfectly compatible with liberal democracy," which "has always relied on elites to save it from itself." Such opinions have the effect of driving people away from liberalism and of making it possible for the right to claim the populist tradition as its own. The best analysis of right-wing populism is Kevin Phillips, *Post-Conservative America* (1982). See also his earlier book, *The Emerging Republican Majority* (1969); Michael Novak, *The Rise of the Unmeltable Ethnics* (1971); William A. Rusher, *The Making of the New Majority Party* (1975); Richard A. Vigueri, *The New Right: We're Ready to Lead* (1981) and "A Populist and Proud of It," *National Review*, 19 Oct. 1984, 42–44; Samuel S. Hill and Dennis E. Owen, *The New Religious and Political Right in America* (1982); Robert W. Whitaker, ed., *The New Right Papers* (1982); and John Kenneth White, *The New Politics of Old Values* (1988). John B. Judis, *William F. Buckley, Jr.* (1988), sheds light on the tense relationship between the populism of the new right and Buckley's patrician conservatism. Donald T. Regan's memoir, *For the Record: From Wall Street to Washington* (1988), show how little the moral program of the new right influenced the policy of the Reagan administration.

William Schneider, "JFK's Children: The Class of '74," *Atlantic*, March 1989,

35–58, is the source of most of my information about neoliberalism, along with Paul Tsongas's uninspiring book, *The Road from Here* (1981), which was intended to serve as the movement's manifesto.

The idea of the "new class" can be traced, in its progressive version, in the writings of exponents like Walter Lippmann, *Preface to Politics* (1914) and *Drift and Mastery* (1914); Thorstein Veblen, *The Engineers and the Price System* (1921); Adolph A. Berle and Gardiner C. Means, *The Modern Corporation and Private Property* (1932); George Soule, *The Coming American Revolution* (1934); John Kenneth Galbraith, *The New Industrial State* (1967); and David Bazelon, *Power in America: The Politics of the New Class* (1967). Historical accounts of this tradition include Robert Westbrook, "Tribune of the Technostructure: The Popular Economics of Stuart Chase," *American Quarterly* 32 (1980): 387–408; Jean-Christophe Agnew, "A Touch of Class," *Democracy* 3 (spring 1983): 59–72; and Barbara Ehrenreich and John Ehrenreich, "The Professional-Managerial Class," in Pat Walker, ed., *Between Labor and Capital* (1979). Emile Durkheim, *Socialism and Saint-Simon* (1928), remains the best exploration of the antecedents of this tradition; see also Frank Manuel, *The New World of Henri Saint-Simon* (1956).

A more critical view of the technical and managerial elite appears in James Burnham, *The Managerial Revolution* (1941); Peter Mayer, "The Soviet Union: A Class Society," *Politics* (March–April 1944): 48–55, 81–85; Milovan Djilas, *The New Class* (1957); Radovan Richta, *Civilization at the Crossroads: Social and Human Implications of the Scientific and Technological Revolution* (1967); Serge Mallet, "Bureaucracy and Technocracy in Socialist Countries," *Socialist Revolution* (May–June 1970): 44–75; Anthony Giddens, *The Class Structure of Advanced Societies* (1973); and George Konrad and Ivan Szelenyi, *The Intellectuals on the Road to Class Power* (1979).

Criticism of the revolutionary intelligentsia and its dream of power, and more recently of the "adversary culture"—the third tradition of speculation about the new class—begins with Burke and Tocqueville and continues with Julien Benda, *The Betrayal of the Intellectuals* (1927); Joseph Schumpeter, *Capitalism, Socialism, and Democracy* (1942); Raymond Aron, *The Opium of the Intellectuals* (1955); Lewis Feuer, *The Conflict of Generations: The Character and Significance of Student Movements* (1969); and Lionel Trilling, *Beyond Culture* (1965). George B. deHuszar, ed., *The Intellectuals: A Controversial Portrait* (1960), contains many examples of this kind of criticism. Peter Steinfels offers a brief analysis of the "counter-intellectual tradition," as he calls it, in *The Neoconservatives* (1979), as does Richard Gillam, "Intellectuals and Power," *Center Magazine* 10 (May–June 1977): 15–29.

On the new class in conservative and neoconservative thought, see William F. Buckley, Jr., "The Colossal Flunk: How Our Professors Have Betrayed the American People," *American Mercury* 74 (March 1952): 29–37; Will Herberg, "Alienation, 'Dissent,' and the Intellectual," *National Review*, 30 July 1968, 738–39; Gerhart Niemeyer, "The Homesickness of the New Left," *National Review*, 28 July 1970, 779–800; Jeffrey Hart, "Secession of the Intellectuals," *National Review*, 1 Dec. 1970, 1278–82; William A. Rusher, "The New Elite Must Be Curbed," *Conservative*

Digest (Sept. 1975): Irving Kristol, "The Troublesome Intellectuals," *Public Interest* 2 (winter 1966): 3–6, *On the Democratic Idea in America* (1972), and *Two Cheers for Capitalism* (1978); Dorothy Rabinowitz, "The Radicalized Professor: A Portrait," *Commentary* 50 (July 1970): 62–64; Seymour Martin Lipset and Richard B. Dobson, "The Intellectual as Critic and Rebel," *Daedalus* 101 (summer 1972): 138–98; Norman Podhoretz, "The Intellectuals and the Pursuit of Happiness," *Commentary* 55 (Feb. 1973): 7–8, and "The Adversary Culture," in B. Bruce-Briggs, ed., *The New Class* (1979); James Hitchcock, "The Intellectuals and the People," *Commentary* 55 (March 1973): 64–69; and David Lebedoff, *The New Elite: The Death of Democracy* (1981). Speculation about the new class also figures in Daniel Bell, *The End of Ideology* (1960); *The Coming of Post-Industrial Society* (1973); *The Cultural Contradictions of Capitalism* (1976); and "The New Class: A Muddled Concept," *Society* 16 (Jan.–Feb. 1979): 15–23; Zbigniew Brzezinski, *Between Two Ages: America's Role in the Technetronic Era* (1969); Michael Novak, "Needing Niebuhr Again," *Commentary* 54 (Sept. 1972): 52–62; Daniel Patrick Moynihan, "Social Policy: From the Utilitarian Ethic to the Therapeutic Ethic," in Irving Kristol and Paul H. Weaver, eds., *The Americans, 1976* (1976); Charles Murray, *Losing Ground* (1984); Peter L. Berger, *Pyramids of Sacrifice* (1976); and Brigitte Berger and Peter L. Berger, *The War over the Family* (1983).

Waldo Frank, *The Rediscovery of America* (1930), and Dennis Hayes, *Behind the Silicon Curtain* (1989), contain material illustrating the addictive character of consumption. So does Barbara Ehrenreich, *Fear of Falling: The Inner Life of the Middle Class* (1989)—the latest and in many ways the most plausible (but still seriously flawed) account of the new class to emerge from the left. See also Alvin Gouldner, *The Future of Intellectuals and The Rise of the New Class* (1979). For earlier views from the left, see André Gorz, *Strategy for Labor* (1967); Alain Touraine, *Post-Industrial Society* (1971); Claus Offe, "Political Authority and Class Structures: An Analysis of Late Capitalist Societies," *International Journal of Sociology* 2 (1972): 73–108; Claude Lefort, "What Is Bureaucracy?" *Telos*, no. 22 (winter 1975–76): 31–65; and Serge Mallet, *Essays on the New Working Class* (1975). Regis Debray, *Teachers, Writers, Celebrities* (1981), defies classification. Though written by a socialist, it offers pointed criticism of the intelligentsia, instead of the self-celebration usually found in work emanating from the left, the academic left in particular.

INDEX

·■·